Harcourt
Health and Fitness

Harcourt

SCHOOL PUBLISHERS

Orlando • Austin • New York • San Diego • Toronto • London

Visit *The Learning Site!*
www.harcourtschool.com

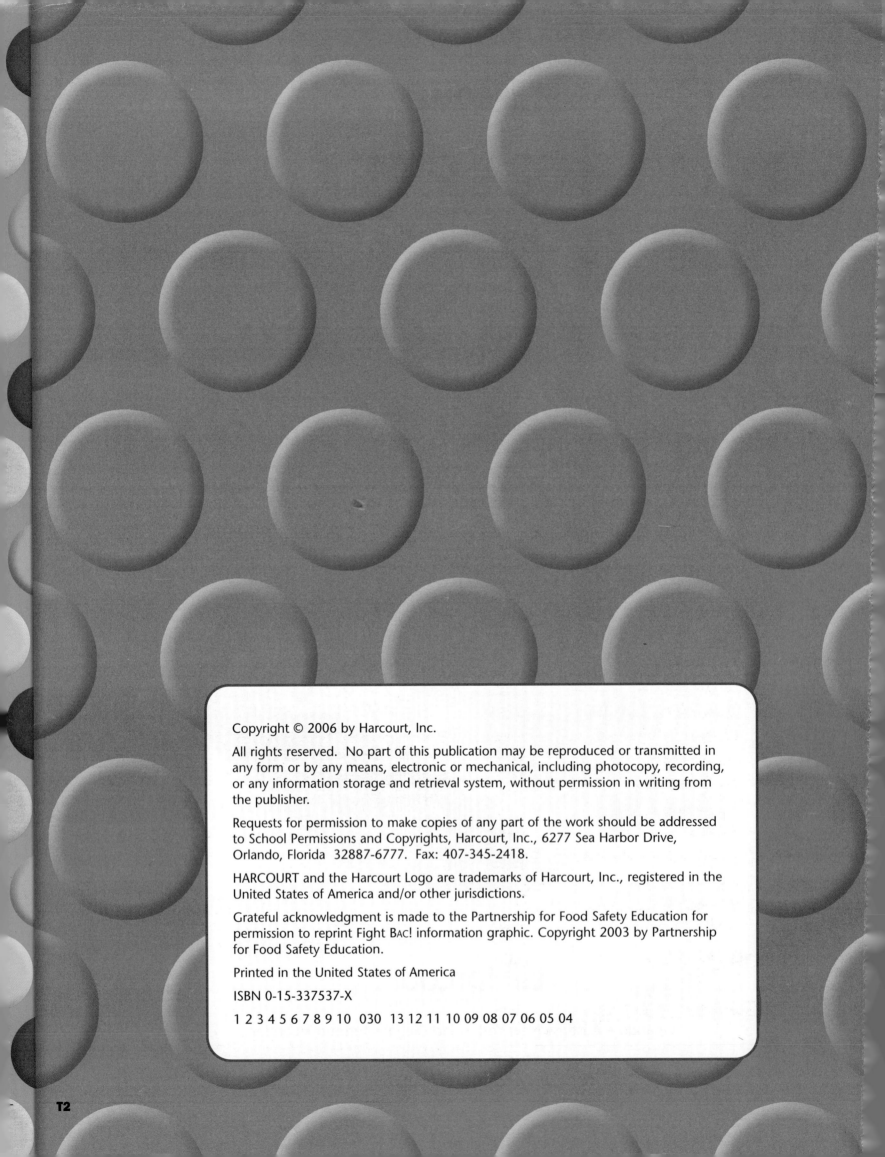

Requests for permission to make copies of any part of the work should be addressed to School Permissions and Copyrights, Harcourt, Inc., 6277 Sea Harbor Drive, Orlando, Florida 32887-6777. Fax: 407-345-2418.

HARCOURT and the Harcourt Logo are trademarks of Harcourt, Inc., registered in the United States of America and/or other jurisdictions.

Grateful acknowledgment is made to the Partnership for Food Safety Education for permission to reprint Fight BAC! information graphic. Copyright 2003 by Partnership for Food Safety Education.

Printed in the United States of America

ISBN 0-15-337537-X

1 2 3 4 5 6 7 8 9 10 030 13 12 11 10 09 08 07 06 05 04

Teacher Edition Contents

CONSULTING AUTHORS

Lisa Bunting, M.Ed., has over 25 years of experience as a coach and physical education teacher in middle and elementary schools in the Houston, Texas area. Her broad-based experience and background in athletics, health, and physical education is evidenced by her extensive professional involvement at the local, state, and national levels. A member of both the American and Texas Associations for Health, Physical Education, Recreation, and Dance (AAHPERD and TAHPERD) and the Texas Classroom Teachers Association, Ms Bunting has served on many TAHPERD committees and state initiatives. Ms Bunting is currently teaching elementary physical education in the Katy Independent School District and is involved with writing and implementing curriculum and training teachers in many aspects of coordinated school health.

Thomas M. Fleming, Ph.D., recently retired as Director of Health and Physical Education at the Texas Education Agency (TEA) in Austin, Texas. As Director, Dr. Fleming oversaw many state initiatives and served on many committees such as the Governor's Council for Physical Fitness, The Texas Diabetes Council, and the Texas School Health Advisory Council. Prior to his work at the TEA, Dr. Fleming was an instructor in the Department of Health and Kinesiology at Stephen F. Austin State University in Nacogdoches, Texas and at the University of Montevallo in Montevallo, Alabama where he was also the university baseball coach. Dr. Fleming recently received a Distinguished Service Citation Award from TAHPERD in recognition of his years of leadership and contributions to the education and health of Texas children.

Charlie Gibbons, Ed.D., recently retired after 30 years of university teaching experience at Alabama State University, Auburn University at Montgomery, and Georgia Southern College. He is presently Director of Youth and School Age Programs at Maxwell Air Force Base, Montgomery, Alabama and serving as an adjunct professor at Alabama State University Department of Health, Physical Education and Dance. Dr. Gibbons is a past president of the Alabama AHPERD and a past vice-president of the Health Division of Southern District AAHPERD. He continues to serve his professional organizations on state and district committees. He has served on numerous public service committees providing inservice workshops and presentations on various areas of school health curricula including such topics as HIV/AIDS prevention, physical fitness for children, and weight control. Dr. Gibbons was presented with the Alabama State and Southern District Honor Awards.

Jan Ozias, Ph.D., R.N., has extensive experience in school health services and health education from a nursing perspective. She worked as Nursing Supervisor and Administrator of Health Services in the Austin Independent School District, Austin, Texas. Dr. Ozias holds adjunct faculty appointments in both the School of Nursing and the College of Education at the University of Texas at Austin from which she also earned an M.A. in Special Education and a Ph.D. in Health Education. Dr. Ozias has worked as Director of Medical Underwriting, Texas Healthy Kids Corporation and presently serves as Director, Texas Diabetes Council/Program at the Texas Department of Health. She is co-chief editor of School Health Alert, a national newsletter for school nurses and educators.

Carl Anthony Stockton, Ph.D., is Dean of the School of Education at the University of Texas at Brownsville and Texas Southmost College. Previously, he served as Department Chair and Professor of Health Education in the Department of Health and Applied Human Sciences at the University of North Carolina in Wilmington. Throughout his professional career, Dr. Stockton has taught health education classes focusing on a wide variety of health topics. His curricula have included such diverse health topics as health programs in the elementary schools, nutrition, national and international health, accident and safety education, public health administration, and the use of technology in health promotion.

Dear Educator,

Harcourt Health and Fitness is a comprehensive program designed to help your students develop positive behaviors and attitudes that will lead to a lifetime of good health. In order to achieve that goal, students need knowledge, life skills, good character, and consumer skills.

Knowledge includes current information, facts, and concepts in the following content areas:

▶ Human Body, Growth and Development
▶ Consumer/Personal Health
▶ Nutrition
▶ Physical Activity and Fitness
▶ Injury Prevention
▶ Disease Prevention and Control
▶ Drug Use Prevention
▶ Emotional, Intellectual, and Social Health
▶ Family Life
▶ Community and Environmental Health

Life Skills are health-enhancing behaviors that help children reduce risks to their health. *Harcourt Health and Fitness* provides opportunities for children to learn and practice life skills through lessons that use real-life situations. These important skills are:

▶ Make responsible decisions
▶ Manage stress
▶ Set goals
▶ Resolve conflicts
▶ Communicate
▶ Refuse risky behaviors

Building Good Character is also an important part of having good health. When students develop good character traits, they have positive relationships with others and can make responsible decisions about their health and fitness. The character traits emphasized in *Harcourt Health and Fitness* include:

▶ Caring
▶ Citizenship
▶ Fairness
▶ Respect
▶ Responsibility
▶ Honesty (Trustworthiness)

Consumer Skills are important for helping students evaluate the enormous amount of information that is transmitted to them via print, electronic, and broadcast media. These skills include:

▶ Analyze advertisements and media messages
▶ Make buying decisions
▶ Access valid health information

We are confident that **Harcourt Health and Fitness** provides you with the tools you need to motivate your students to take an active role in maintaining and improving their health.

Sincerely,
The Authors

CONSULTING HEALTH SPECIALISTS

Sharon A. Braun, M.S., R.D., C.D.E.
Clinical Dietitian
Childrens Hospital Los Angeles
Los Angeles, California

Martha Gwendolyn Roberts Camp, Ph.D.
Educational Consultant
Asheville, North Carolina

Barry Conrad, M.P.H., R.D., C.D.E.
Clinical Dietitian
Childrens Hospital Los Angeles
Los Angeles, California

Elisabeth K. Constandy, M.S., C.H.E.S.
Health Promotion Coordinator
New Hanover County Health Department
Adjunct Faculty
Department of Health and Applied Human
    Sciences
University of North Carolina, Wilmington
Wilmington, North Carolina

Brian O. Coleman, D.D.S.
President, Omega Dental Group
Orlando, Florida

Jim DeLine, M.Ed.
CATCH Program Physical Education
    Coordinator
University of Texas Houston Health Science
    Center
Austin, Texas

Pam Ernest, M.S.
Department Chair, Girl's Athletics
Physical Education Coordinator
Belton Independent School District
Belton, Texas

Michael Hammes, Ph.D.
Associate Professor
University of New Mexico
Program of Health Education
Albuquerque, New Mexico

Francine R, Kaufman, M.D.
Division of Endocrinology and Metabolism
Childrens Hospital Los Angeles
Los Angeles, California

Mark J. Kittleson, Ph.D., F.A.A.H.B.
Professor, Health Education
Southern Illinois University
Carbondale, Illinois

Mary Kathleen Klier, R.D.
Clinical Dietitian
Childrens Hospital Los Angeles
Los Angeles, California

Melody Kyzer, Ph.D., R.D., L.D.N.
Assistant Professor
Department of Health & Applied Human
    Sciences
University of North Carolina, Wilmington
Wilmington, North Carolina

Jaime Orejan, Ph.D.
Assistant Professor
Leisure and Sport Management
Elon University
Elon, North Carolina

Howard Taras, M.D.
Department of Pediatrics
University of California, San Diego
La Jolla, California

Pam Tollefsen, R.N.
Med Program Supervisor
Health/Fitness Education and HIV/STD
    Prevention
Office of Superintendent of Public
    Instruction
Olympia, Washington

KEY	
C.D.E.	Certified Diabetes Educator
C.H.E.S.	Certified Health Education Specialist
D.D.S.	Doctor of Dental Surgery
F.A.A.H.B.	Fellow, American Academy of Health Behavior
L.D.N.	Licensed Dietitian/Nutritionist
M.Ed.	Master of Education
M.D.	Medical Doctor
M.P.H.	Master of Public Health
M.S.	Master of Science
Ph.D.	Doctor of Philosophy
R.D.	Registered Dietician
R.N.	Registered Nurse

REVIEWERS AND FIELD TEST TEACHERS

Janet Ahmed
Grand Oaks Elementary
Citrus Heights, California

Teresa Battle
Orangeburg Consolidated District 5
Orangeburg, South Carolina

Susan J. Bergman
Tarkington Intermediate School
Cleveland, Texas

Jodi Booher
Harrison Elementary
Hamilton, Ohio

Betsy Bowles
DeZavala Elementary
Fort Worth, Texas

Dee Carter
Holmes Elementary
Wilmington, Ohio

Diana Cassels
Charlestown Elementary
Malvern, Pennsylvania

Dr. Bob Cockburn
Syracuse Elementary
Syracuse, Indiana

Terry Condrasky
Great Oaks Elementary
Round Rock, Texas

Emiko Davis
Campbell Elementary
Austin, Texas

Birdia DeShazer
Woods Academy
Chicago, Illinois

Dora Fernandez
Palm Lakes Elementary
Hialeah, Florida

Ana M. Gallo
Bent Tree Elementary
Miami, Florida

Nancy Garman
Jefferson Elementary
Charleston, Illinois

Susan Harkabus
Ready Elementary
Griffin, Indiana

Debra Horton
Alice Drive Elementary
Sumter, South Carolina

Scott Hudson
Covedale Elementary
Cincinnati, Ohio

Julie Huff
Jefferson Elementary
South Bend, Indiana

Roz Husband
Greene Elementary
South Bend, Indiana

Jan Kirk
Needmore Elementary
Bedford, Indiana

Sherry Knickerbocker
Shugart Elementary
Garland, Texas

Lisa Krienke
Mission CISD
Mission, Texas

Kathy Kruthoff
Washington Elementary
Stevens Point, Wisconsin

Theresa Lunsford
Rocklin Academy
Rocklin, California

Daniel Manseau
Boland Elementary
Springfield, Massachusetts

Dana Moore
Cypress Elementary
Leander ISD
Cedar Park, Texas

Christine Moyer
West Pottsgrove Elementary
Stowe, Pennsylvania

Karla Cacho Negrete
Bowen Elementary
Bryan, Texas

Cindy Noyes
Carmichael Elementary
Carmichael, California

Vicki J. Peters
Flower Mound Elementary
Flower Mound, Texas

Clementine Pitts
Van E. Blanton Elementary
Miami, Florida

Danny Poarch
Woodridge Elementary
San Antonio, Texas

Cindy Rau
Burton Hill Elementary
Ft. Worth, Texas

Stayci Roznovak
Johnson Elementary
Irving, Texas

Kathy Seidel
Sam Houston Elementary
Corpus Christi, Texas

Marilyn Spiegel
Greer Elementary
Sacramento, California

Sally Stricklin
PS 182
Bronx, New York

Cindy Terry
Chapel Lakes Elementary
Lee Summit, Missouri

Brenda Thomas
Kyger Elementary
Frankfort, Indiana

Victoria Thompson
Anderson Mill Elementary
Moore, South Carolina

Wendy Wear
Gray Elementary
Balch Springs, Texas

Patti Weid
DeLeon Elementary
Victoria, Texas

Tricia Wong
Commodore Sloat School
San Francisco, California

THE NATIONAL HEALTH EDUCATION STANDARDS

The National Health Education Standards were developed by representatives of various health organizations, including the American School Health Association, the Association for the Advancement of Health Education, and the American Cancer Society. The standards describe what students should know and be able to do in order to be health literate. A health-literate person obtains, interprets, and understands basic health information and services and uses that information and those services in ways that are health-enhancing.

Harcourt Health and Fitness promotes health literacy in the following ways:

- provides all students with the **knowledge** and **behaviors** they need to make informed decisions about their health.
- provides students with opportunities to learn and practice **life skills** and develop **character traits** for positive health behaviors.
- encourages students to **solve problems** and **think critically**.

Every lesson in *Harcourt Health and Fitness* was developed to help students meet the Standards. A correlation to the Standards and their performance indicators is provided beginning on page TR-50 in this Teacher Edition.

National Health Education Standards

1. Students will comprehend concepts related to health promotion and disease prevention.

2. Students will demonstrate the ability to access valid health information and health-promoting products and services.

3. Students will demonstrate the ability to practice health-enhancing behaviors and reduce health risks.

4. Students will analyze the influence of culture, media, technology, and other factors on health.

5. Students will demonstrate the ability to use interpersonal communication skills to enhance health.

6. Students will demonstrate the ability to use goal-setting and decision-making skills to enhance health.

7. Students will demonstrate the ability to advocate for personal, family, and community health.

COORDINATED SCHOOL HEALTH

The development of knowledge and skills alone is not enough to ensure that children achieve health literacy. A collaborative approach that coordinates the efforts of the families, schools, and the community is the most effective way to promote health literacy for all children.

A Coordinated School Health Program involves eight components that work together to develop and reinforce health knowledge, skills, attitudes, and behaviors. Each of these eight components is vital to the overall goal of promoting health literacy. The components are most effective when they are planned and implemented in a consistent and supportive manner.

How Harcourt Health and Fitness Supports Coordinated School Health

- The program provides a comprehensive approach to teaching health, with content that addresses all the major strands of health.

- Where appropriate, the program suggests resources that teachers and other school personnel may consult for making the links to all components of CSH. See the Resources page for each chapter in the Teacher Editions. See also the References for Coordinated School Health in the *Teaching Resources* book.

- The content and teaching strategies address the physical, emotional, and social needs of children.

- *Harcourt Health and Fitness* goes beyond the teaching of health content by focusing on healthful skills and behaviors. For example, the Life Skills and Building Good Character features teach life-enhancing behaviors that will contribute to a lifetime of good health.

- Together with *Be Active! Resources for Physical Education*, the program provides a comprehensive and coordinated approach to teaching physical education.

- Specific features of the *Harcourt Health and Fitness Teacher Editions* that support CSH include the following:

 School-Home Connection

 Daily Physical Activity

 Daily Fitness Tip

Activities for Home and Community

Health Background: Webliography

For more information about Coordinated School Health, please see pages TR18–21.

PROGRAM ASSESSMENT

Harcourt Health and Fitness provides a variety of assessment strategies and tools for assessing student health literacy. The assessment is based on the following model:

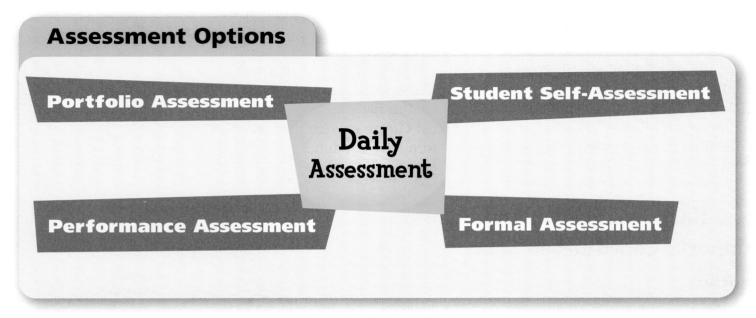

For more information about Program Assessment, please refer to pages 2–3 in the *Assessment Guide*.

CURRICULUM INTEGRATION

Harcourt Health and Fitness is designed to allow you to integrate health into your daily planning through the use of connections to all curriculum areas. Look for Curriculum Integration in the teacher planning section at the beginning of each chapter.

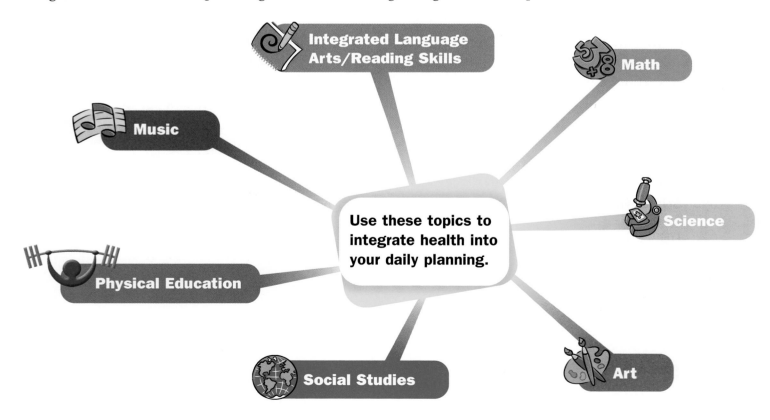

Focus Skill — Reading in Health

Reading underlies everything students do in school, and many of the skills taught in reading programs can be reinforced during health instruction. A Reading Focus Skill is introduced at the beginning of each chapter in *Harcourt Health and Fitness*. Throughout the chapter, the Focus Skill logo alerts the student to each opportunity for practicing and applying the skill.

Grades 1-2	Grades 3-6
1. Find Cause and Effect	**1.** Compare and Contrast
2. Find the Main Idea	**2.** Draw Conclusions
3. Make Predictions	**3.** Identify Cause and Effect
4. Recall and Retell	**4.** Identify Main Idea and Details
5. Sequence	**5.** Sequence
6. Use Context Clues	**6.** Summarize

Reading is also reinforced in *Harcourt Health and Fitness* in the following ways:

▶ A reading comprehension question appears after every "chunk" of text in the student edition. The question helps students check their comprehension of the text and also reinforces the Focus Skills, which are listed above.

▶ In the Teacher Edition, a Reading Mini-lesson appears with the first lesson in every chapter and can be used to provide focused instruction on each skill.

▶ The Reading in Health Handbook in the back of each Student Edition provides detailed, student-friendly information about each skill.

▶ Teaching Transparencies with Graphic Organizers provide visual support and can be used to record student's answers to Focus Skill questions. The Teaching Transparencies are also provided on CD-ROM in interactive format.

▶ Strategies for Content-Area Reading Support appear throughout the Teacher Edition and include skills such as Using Respellings, Using Signal Words, Using Text Patterns, and Using Charts and Graphics.

TEACHING ALL LEARNERS

Harcourt Health and Fitness also provides point-of-use strategies for helping all students be successful as they learn new concepts and skills.

ESL/ELL Support

These features address language issues in three critical areas:

▶ Comprehensible Input
▶ Language and Vocabulary
▶ Background and Experience

They also provide language strategies for students at varied levels of proficiency: Beginning, Intermediate, and Advanced.

Meeting Individual Needs — Leveled Activities

These strategies reinforce key lesson concepts via activities at three instructional levels:

▶ Below-level
▶ On-level
▶ Challenge

They promote hands-on learning in every lesson.

PROGRAM COMPONENTS

Harcourt Health and Fitness provides components that meet a variety of instructional needs.

For Pre K

- Teacher's Guide
- Big Books, Little Books, and Fold-Out Books
- Posters
- Activity Book
- Hand Puppet

For Kindergarten

- Big Book
- Teacher Edition
- Activity Book
- Teaching Resources (includes School-Home Connection letters, Take-Home Booklets, Assessment Options, and Patterns)
- Teaching Transparencies with Accompanying Copying Masters

For Grades 1 through 2

- Student Editions
- Big Book version of the Student Edition
- Teacher Edition
- Activity Book
- Assessment Guide
- Teaching Resources (includes School-Home Connection letters, Take-Home Booklets, and reproducible copies of the Health and Safety Handbook)
- Posters
- Teaching Transparencies with Accompanying Copying Masters
- Teaching Transparencies in Interactive Format (CD-ROM)
- Be Active! Music for Daily Physical Activity

For Grades 3 through 6

- Student Editions
- Teacher Edition
- Activity Book
- Assessment Guide
- Teaching Resources (includes School-Home Connection letters, Take-Home Booklets, and reproducible copies of the Health and Safety Handbook)
- Posters
- Teaching Transparencies with Accompanying Copying Masters
- Teaching Transparencies in Interactive Format (CD-ROM)
- Be Active! Music for Daily Physical Activity
- Growth, Development, and Reproduction (an optional resource)

The Learning Site

Visit Harcourt's growing Learning Site for a variety of teacher resources and student activities, including:

- The Health Webliography for Teachers (carefully chosen links to health background and teaching resources)
- Student games and activities

www.harcourtschool.com/health

For Physical Education

Be Active! Resources for Physical Education

Primary and Intermediate Levels

This program provides a wealth of lessons, activities, games, and ideas for health-related fitness. Promotes a lifetime of physical activity for all students.

Chapters

Contents

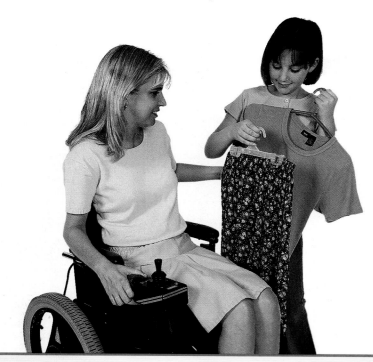

Why should you learn about health?

You can do many things to help yourself stay healthy and fit. Just as importantly, you can avoid things that will harm you. If you know ways to stay safe and healthy and do these things, you can help yourself have good health throughout your life.

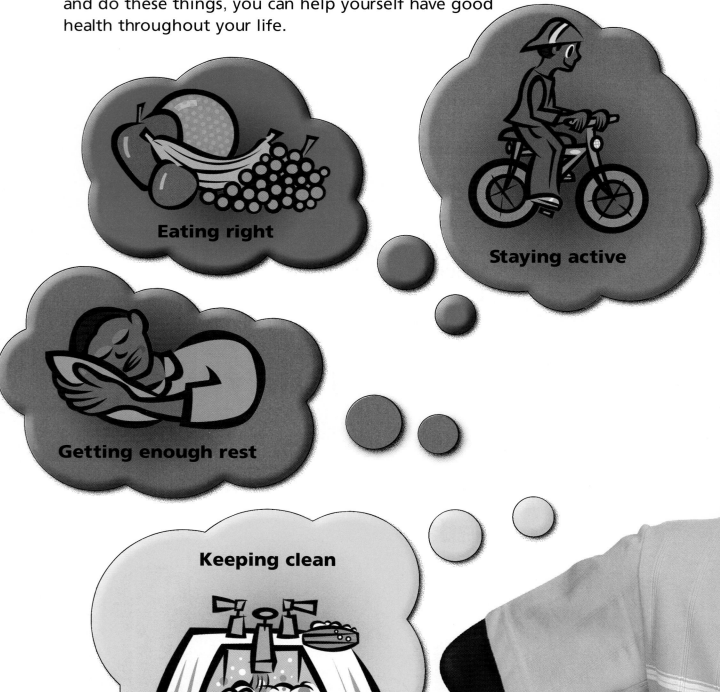

Eating right

Staying active

Getting enough rest

Keeping clean

Why should you learn about life skills?

Being healthy and fit doesn't come from just knowing facts. You also have to think about these facts and know how to use them every day.

These are some important life skills for you to have:

Managing Stress
Finding ways to avoid and relieve negative feeling and

Communicating
Sharing ideas, needs, and feelings with others

Making Responsible Decisions
Deciding the most responsible thing to do to avoid taking risks

Refusing
Saying *no* to doing things that are risky and dangerous

Setting Goals
Deciding on specific ways to make improvements to your health and fitness

Resolving Conflicts
Finding solutions to problems in ways that let both sides win

Whenever you see LIFE SKILLS in this book, you can learn more about using life skills.

Why should you learn about good character?

Having good character is also an important part of having good health. When you have good character, you have good relationships with others and can make responsible decisions about your health and fitness. These are some important character traits:

Caring

Showing kindness and concern for friends, family, and others

Citizenship

Having pride in your school and community and obeying rules and laws

Fairness

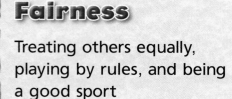

Treating others equally, playing by rules, and being a good sport

Respect

Showing consideration for yourself and others

Responsibility

Doing what you are supposed to do, practicing self-control, and completing tasks

Trustworthiness

Being honest, dependable, and loyal

Whenever you see **Building Good Character** in this book, you can learn more about building good character.

What are ways to be a successful reader?

You need good reading skills to do well in school. Here are some tips to help you understand, remember, and use information you read.

Reading Tip

These sections can help you know what to look for as you read.

Reading Tip

Vocabulary words are listed at the beginning of the lesson so you can preview them. They are also highlighted and defined when they are first used.

LESSON 1

Body Transport Systems

Lesson Focus
Four systems transport materials throughout the body.

Why Learn This?
Understanding how transport systems work together can help you keep them healthy.

Vocabulary
cell
tissue
organ
system
capillaries
alveoli
nephrons

From Cells to Systems

The basic unit of structure of all living things is the **cell**. Your body is made up of trillions of cells, but they aren't all the same. Different types of cells do different jobs in your body. For example, red blood cells, which are disc-shaped, carry oxygen that other cells need. Muscle cells, which are long and slender, can *contract*, or get shorter. The contracting and relaxing of muscle cells makes your body move.

Cells that look alike and work together make up a **tissue** (TISH•oo). Each kind of tissue works to carry out the jobs of the cells that form it. For example, muscle cells that make up heart tissue don't tire as easily as other muscle cells. This kind of muscle tissue is found only in the heart. Another type of muscle tissue lines the walls of the stomach. This tissue helps digestion.

  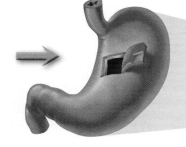

▲ Cells have different sizes and shapes. This cell is from the lining of the stomach.

▲ One tissue that lines the stomach helps protect the stomach from the strong acid it produces.

▲ Several kinds of tissues make up an organ. The stomach is one of the organs that breaks down the food you eat.

4

Reading Tip

Check your understanding by answering these questions at the end of each section. These questions also help you practice reading skills. You will see six reading focus skills:

► Compare and Contrast

► Draw Conclusions

► Identify Cause and Effect

► Identify Main Idea and Details

► Sequence

► Summarize

Whenever you see 🟊 in this book, you can learn more about using reading skills.

Reading Tip

Use this section to summarize what you have read, review vocabulary and concepts, and practice writing skills.

Excretory System

The kidneys and bladder are the major organs of the excretory system. This system takes certain wastes from the blood and removes them from the body as *urine*. Urine is collected wastes and water. This job is important because it keeps the right amount of water in the body at all times. It also helps keep wastes from building up in the body. These wastes, in large amounts, are harmful.

As blood passes through the kidneys, **nephrons** (NEF•rahnz) filter out wastes and excess water. Cleaned blood leaves the kidneys and continues through the body. The urine, which contains the wastes, is stored in the bladder until it passes out of the body.

kidneys

ureter

bladder

CAUSE AND EFFECT What are the effects of the kidneys' removing wastes and excess water?
keeps amount of water in body the same; keeps wastes from building up

In the kidneys, capillaries pass through microscopic filters called nephrons. Materials the body needs are returned to the blood. ►

nephron

Lesson 1 Summary and Review

❶ Summarize with Vocabulary

Use vocabulary from this lesson to complete these statements.

Groups of cells make up _____, which make up _____. Groups of these body parts then make up _____. Tiny blood vessels that enable materials and wastes to pass between the blood and body cells are called _____. Gases pass into and out of the blood in the _____ of the lungs. The _____ remove wastes from blood as the blood passes through the kidneys.

❷ Critical Thinking Why do you think the air tubes in the lungs branch again and again until they are very small?

❸ Why is the removal of wastes by the kidneys important to the body?

❹ 🟊 **SEQUENCE** Draw and complete this graphic organizer to show the order in which organs work to digest food.

1.

2. *Esophagus*

3.

4. *Large intestine*

5.

❺ Write to Inform—Explanation

Write a paragraph that explains why the circulatory, respiratory, digestive, and excretory systems are considered transport systems for the body.

9

Throughout **Harcourt Health and Fitness**, you will have many opportunities to learn new ideas and skills that will lead to good health.

Lesson	Pacing	Objectives	Reading Skills
Introduce the Chapter pp. 2–3		• Preview chapter concepts.	**Sequence** p. 3; pp. 372–383
1 Body Transport Systems pp. 4–9	1 class period	• Identify the basic structure of the human body. • Explain the functions of the body transport organs and systems. • Recognize how personal habits affect the health of body systems.	**Sequence** pp. 5, 7, 9 • Compare and Contrast, p. 6 • Summarize, p. 8 • Cause and Effect, p. 9
2 Body Coordination Systems pp. 10–13	1 class period	• Identify the three body systems that coordinate body movements. • Explain ways to keep body coordination systems healthy.	**Sequence** p. 13 • Summarize, p. 10 • Cause and Effect, pp. 11, 13
3 Growth, Heredity, and the Endocrine System pp. 14–19	1 class period	• Learn about heredity and environmental influences on growth. • Identify major hormones of the endocrine system. • Examine some functions of hormones. • Describe how growth occurs.	**Sequence** p. 19 • Summarize, p. 15 • Cause and Effect, p. 17 • Compare and Contrast, p. 19
4 Growth Comes in Stages pp. 20–24	1 class period	• Describe the growth stages from the prenatal stage to older adulthood. • Learn about changes that occur during puberty.	**Sequence** p. 24 • Main Idea and Details, pp. 21, 23 • Cause and Effect, p. 24
Building Good Character p. 25		• Identify ways to build a good reputation by showing trustworthiness.	
5 Dealing with Adolescence pp. 26–29	1 class period	• Learn about the physical, mental, and emotional changes accompanying the growth spurt during puberty. • Compare and contrast concrete thinking and abstract thinking. • Explain problem-solving choices to handle problems of adolescence.	**Sequence** p. 29 • Compare and Contrast, p. 27 • Draw Conclusions, p. 29
Life Skills pp. 30–31	1 class period	• Identify the steps for conflict resolution. • Use the steps to resolve a conflict.	
6 Choices You Make Affect Your Growth pp. 32–34	1 class period	• Explain how exercise and good nutrition help growing bodies. • Describe how sleep, rest, and hygiene can affect growth.	• Cause and Effect, p. 33 • Main Idea and Details, p. 34
Activities p. 35		• Extend chapter concepts.	
Chapter Review pp. 36–37	1 class period	• Assess chapter objectives.	

Vocabulary	Program Resources
	 Music CD Teaching Resources, p. 21
cell tissue organ system capillaries alveoli nephrons	Transparencies 5, 7–10 Activity Book, pp. 1–2, 3
joint ligaments tendons neurons reflex action	Transparencies 5, 11–13 Activity Book, pp. 1–2
heredity environment hormones	Transparencies 5, 14 Activity Book, pp. 1–2
prenatal growth spurt puberty body image	Transparency 5 Activity Book, pp. 1–2
	Poster 6
concrete thinking abstract thinking	Transparency 5 Activity Book, pp. 1–2
	Activity Book, p. 9 Poster 11
hygiene	Transparency 5 Activity Book, pp. 1–2, 5
	The Learning Site www. harcourtschool.com/health
	Assessment Guide, pp. 20–22

 **Interactive Transparencies** available on CD-ROM.

 Reading Skill

These reading skills are reinforced throughout this chapter and one skill is emphasized as the Focus Skill.

Sequence
- Draw Conclusions
- Identify Cause and Effect
- Identify Main Idea and Details
- Compare and Contrast
- Summarize

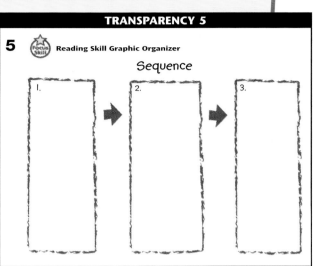

TRANSPARENCY 5

5 Reading Skill Graphic Organizer

Sequence

1. 2. 3.

Life Skills

Life Skills are health-enhancing behaviors that can help students reduce risks to their health and safety.

Six Life Skills are reinforced throughout *Harcourt Health and Fitness.* The skill emphasized in this chapter is Resolve Conflicts.

POSTER 11

Resolve Conflicts

The girls are resolving a conflict by negotiating politely.

Steps to Resolve Conflicts

1. Use I-messages to tell how you feel.
2. Listen to each other. Consider the other person's view.
3. Negotiate.
4. Find a way for both sides to win.

How do **YOU RESOLVE CONFLICTS**?
POSTER 11

 Building Good Character

Character education is an important aspect of health education. When students behave in ways that show good character, they promote the health and safety of themselves and others.

Six character traits are reinforced throughout *Harcourt Health and Fitness.* The trait emphasized in this chapter is Trustworthiness.

POSTER 6

Trustworthiness

The older girl is showing trustworthiness by taking good care of the children.

DO
- Be honest. Tell the truth.
- Do the right thing.
- Report dangerous situations.
- Be dependable.
- Be loyal to your family, friends, and country.
- Take care of things you borrow, and return them promptly.

DON'T
- Don't tell lies.
- Don't cheat.
- Don't steal.
- Don't break promises.
- Don't borrow without asking first.

How have **YOU** shown **TRUSTWORTHINESS** today?
POSTER 6

Resources

Coordinated School Health Program

A Coordinated School Health Program endeavors to improve children's health and, therefore, their capacity to learn through the support of families, schools, and communities working together. The following information is provided to help classroom teachers be more aware of these resources.

The National Center for Chronic Disease and Health Promotion, part of the **CDC**, funds the Coordinated School Health Program. Visit its website for information about the eight components that make up this program. **www.cdc.gov/nccdphp/dash/**

Thirteen percent of children and adolescents are now overweight or obese, which represents more than a doubling in the last thirty years. The National Governors' Association **(NGA)** Center for Best Practices endorses the Coordinated School Health Program and offers information on the obesity epidemic. **www.nga.org/center/divisions/**

A Coordinated School Health Program makes a significant contribution, not only to individual students but also to entire communities. The National Center for Health Education **(NCHE)**, in cooperation with the CDC, endorses this program to improve and maintain children's health to allow them to attain their learning potential. **www.nche.org/**

Other resources that support a Coordinated School Health Program:
- School-Home Connection
- Daily Physical Activity
- Daily Fitness Tips
- Activities: Home & Community
- Health Background: Webliography
- *Be Active! Resources for Physical Education*

Media Resources

Books for Students

Wiese, Jim. ***Head to Toe Science.*** John Wiley and Sons, 2000. Has human body health activities. **EASY**

Day, Trevor. ***The Random House Book of 1001 Questions and Answers About the Human Body.*** Random House, 1994. Explains body systems. **AVERAGE**

McClafferty, Carla. ***The Head Bone's Connected to the Neck Bone: The Weird, Wacky, and Wonderful X-Ray.*** Farrar, Straus & Giroux, 2001. Looks at Roentgen's experiments including X rays. **ADVANCED**

Books for Teachers and Families

Good Housekeeping, Ed. ***The Good Housekeeping Book of Child Care Including Parenting Advice, Health Care, and Child Development for Newborns to Preteens.*** Hearst Publications, 2000. Provides tips through all ages of child development.

Schmitt, Barton D. ***Your Child's Health.*** Bantam, 1999. A guide from birth through adolescence.

Free and Inexpensive Materials

Federal Citizen Information Center
Will send a booklet, *Kids and Their Bones: A Parents' Guide,* which looks at the health of children's bones.

Social Studies School Service
Will send a copy of their publication, *Health Education,* containing topics such as The Human Body.

National Institute of Child Health
Has pamphlets, posters, and stickers on growth and development topics such as "Exercise to Build Healthy Bones."

To access free and inexpensive resources on the Web, visit **www.harcourtschool.com/health/free**

Videos

Circulatory System. Educational Video Network, 1999.

Looking from the Inside/Out. AIT Productions, 1996.

Introducing the Cell. Rainbow Educational Media, 1995.

These resources have been selected to meet a variety of individual needs. Please review all materials and websites prior to sharing them with students to ensure the content is appropriate for your class. Note that information, while correct at time of publication, is subject to change.

Visit **The Learning Site** for related links, activities, resources, and the health **Webliography.**

www.harcourtschool.com/health

Meeting Individual Needs

ESL/ELL

Below-Level

Recalling facts is easier when students have visual aids. Have students take turns telling one fact they learned from reading the selection. Write that fact on an index card, and have the student hang the card on a classroom clothesline.

Activities
- Making Flash Cards, p. 6
- Inherited Traits, p. 15
- Make Time Lines, p. 22
- Make Art, p. 27

On-Level

Using graphic aids can help students understand information given in text. Tell students that maps, graphs, diagrams, time lines, and pictures help convey the meaning of text. Have them look for graphic aids and tell what information is given and how it is helpful.

Activities
- Circulatory Problems, p. 6
- Cartilage Query, p. 15
- Puberty Rites, p. 22
- Plan a Trip, p. 27

Challenge

Using chapter content as a springboard, work with students to brainstorm topics and people they would like to know more about. Organize their responses in a web. Students may use reference books and the Internet to begin inquiry projects related to the completed web.

Activities
- Heart Rate, p. 6
- Glands, p. 15
- Prodigies, p. 22
- Write a Book, p. 27

Learning Log

Oral language can be developed through rhythmic activities. Have students repeat words and phrases rhythmically. Chants help students remember phrases and practice language skills. Have students slap knees or clap hands while saying words related to the chapter.

Activities
- Language and Vocabulary, p. 8
- Comprehensible Input, pp. 11, 18, 33

Curriculum Integration

Integrated Language Arts/Reading Skills
- Fight or Flight, p. 13
- Childhood Poems, p. 23
- Reading About Adolescence, p. 24
- Teen Problems, p. 29

Math
- Boning Up on Bones, p. 10
- Calculate Calories, p. 32

Physical Education
- Daily Fitness Tip, pp. 4, 10, 14, 20, 26, 32
- Daily Physical Activity, p. 3
- Take a Hike, p. 7

Use these topics to integrate health into your daily planning.

Science
- Elements in Your Diet, p. 12
- Test Senses, p. 13
- Fetal Development, p. 20
- Studying the Teen Brain, p. 26
- Sleep, p. 34

Social Studies
- Baby Firsts, p. 21

Art
- Family Resemblances, p. 14
- Comic Relief, p. 28
- Greeting Cards, p. 29

CHAPTER SUMMARY

In this chapter students
► learn about the structure, function, and interdependence of body systems.
► find out about stages of growth and how growth is affected by heredity and environment.
► examine changes that accompany puberty and learn how healthful choices can make puberty a positive experience.

 Life Skills
Students use *steps for resolving conflicts* to help them work out disagreements.

 Building Good Character
Students earn *trust* by building a good reputation.

 Consumer Health
Students access valid health information to find alternatives to expensive sports equipment.

📖 Literature Springboard

Use the article "Stand Up and Be a Winner" to spark interest in the chapter topic. See the Read-Aloud Anthology on page RA-2 of this *Teacher Edition*.

Prereading Strategies

SCAN THE CHAPTER Have students preview the chapter content by scanning the titles, headings, pictures, and tables. Ask volunteers to predict what they will learn. Use their predictions to determine their prior knowledge.
PREVIEW VOCABULARY Invite students to sort vocabulary into three groups.

Words I Know	Words I've Seen or Heard	New Words

CHAPTER
1 **A Growing and Changing Body**

2

⭐ (Focus Skill) Reading Skill

SEQUENCE To introduce or review this skill, have students use the Reading in Health Handbook, pp. 372–383. Teaching strategies and additional activities are also provided.

Students will have opportunities to practice and apply this skill throughout this chapter.

• Focus Skill Reading Mini-Lesson, p. 4
• Reading comprehension questions identified with the
• *Activity Book* p. 3 (shown on p. 9)
• Lesson Summary and Review, pp. 9, 13, 19, 24, 29, 34
• Chapter Review and Test Preparation, pp. 36–37

Focus Skill: Reading Skill

SEQUENCE When you sequence events, you place them in the order in which they happen. Use the Reading in Health Handbook on pages 372–383 and this graphic organizer to help you read the health facts in this chapter.

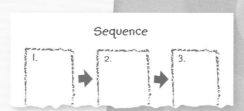

Sequence

1. → 2. → 3.

Health Graph

INTERPRET DATA Sleep patterns change as people grow older. Infants spend most of their time asleep, sometimes as much as sixteen hours each day. Adults, on the other hand, sleep eight hours or less each day. About how long does a ten-year-old child sleep each day?

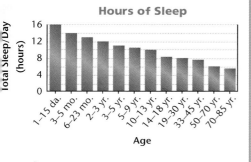

Hours of Sleep

Total Sleep/Day (hours)

16, 12, 8, 4, 0

Age: 1–15 da., 3–5 mo., 6–23 mo., 2–3 yr., 3–5 yr., 5–9 yr., 10–13 yr., 14–18 yr., 19–30 yr., 33–45 yr., 50–70 yr., 70–85 yr.

Daily Physical Activity

Regular physical activity helps keep all your body systems working and growing the way they should.

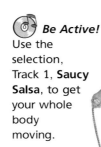

Be Active!
Use the selection, Track 1, **Saucy Salsa**, to get your whole body moving.

3

School-Home Connection

Distribute copies of the School-Home Connection (in English or Spanish). Have students take the page home to share with their families as you begin this chapter.

Follow Up Have volunteers share the results of their activities.

 Supports the Coordinated School Health Program

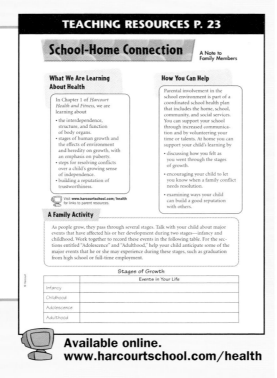

TEACHING RESOURCES P. 23

School-Home Connection   A Note to Family Members

What We Are Learning About Health

In Chapter 1 of *Harcourt Health and Fitness*, we are learning about

- the interdependence, structure, and function of body organs.
- stages of human growth and the effects of environment and heredity on growth, with an emphasis on puberty.
- steps for resolving conflicts over a child's growing sense of independence.
- building a reputation of trustworthiness.

Visit www.harcourtschool.com/health for links to parent resources.

A Family Activity

As people grow, they pass through several stages. Talk with your child about major events that have affected his or her development during two stages—infancy and childhood. Work together to record these events in the following table. For the sections entitled "Adolescence" and "Adulthood," help your child anticipate some of the major events that he or she may experience during these stages, such as graduation from high school or full-time employment.

How You Can Help

Parental involvement in the school environment is part of a coordinated school health plan that includes the home, school, community, and social services. You can support your school through increased communication and by volunteering your time or talents. At home you can support your child's learning by

- discussing how you felt as you went through the stages of growth.
- encouraging your child to let you know when a family conflict needs resolution.
- examining ways your child can build a good reputation with others.

Stages of Growth

Events in Your Life
Infancy
Childhood
Adolescence
Adulthood

**Available online.
www.harcourtschool.com/health**

INTRODUCE THE CHAPTER

Health Graph

Interpret Data

Have a volunteer read the title of the graph and then explain what the graph is showing.

What trend do you see in the amount of sleep people get as they age? The older a person is, the less sleep he or she gets.

How much sleep do those in your age group get each day? about 10 hours

Daily Physical Activity

Use *Be Active! Music for Daily Physical Activity* with the Instant Activity Cards to provide students with movement activities that can be done in limited space. Options for using these components are provided beginning on page TR2 in this *Teacher Edition*.

Chapter Project

Theater of Life (*Assessment Guide* p. 56)

ASSESS PRIOR KNOWLEDGE Use students' initial ideas for the project as a baseline assessment of their understanding of chapter concepts. Have students complete the project as they work through the chapter.

PERFORMANCE ASSESSMENT The project can be used for performance assessment. Use the Project Evaluation Sheet (rubric), *Assessment Guide* p. 62.

LESSON 1

Pages 4–9

Objectives

► Identify the basic structures of the human body.

► Explain the functions of the body transport organs and systems.

► Recognize how personal habits affect the health of body systems.

 When Minutes Count . . .

Assign the Quick Study, Lesson 1, Activity Book pp. 1–2 (shown on p. 5).

Program Resources

► Activity Book pp. 1–2, 3

► Transparencies 5, 7–10

Vocabulary

cell p. 4, **tissue** p. 4, **organ** p. 5, **system** p. 5, **capillaries** p. 6, **alveoli** p. 7, **nephrons** p. 9

Daily Fitness Tip

Regular, vigorous exercise can help keep your heart and lungs healthy. Remind students that regular exercise helps increase blood circulation, reduces cholesterol in the blood, and helps one maintain a healthful weight.

 For more guidelines about exercise and the heart, see *Be Active! Resources for Physical Education,* p. 139.

1. MOTIVATE

Have students examine the diagrams on page 4 and read the captions.

Does a cell in the lining of the stomach look like a cell in a muscle? no

Let students know that the size and shape of a cell depend on the tissue and the organ it is in and what job the cell performs in the body. Because a stomach-lining cell and a muscle cell are from different tissues and have different functions, they do not look alike.

 LESSON 1

Body Transport Systems

From Cells to Systems

The basic unit of structure of all living things is the **cell**. Your body is made up of trillions of cells, but they aren't all the same. Different types of cells do different jobs in your body. For example, red blood cells, which are disc-shaped, carry oxygen that other cells need. Muscle cells, which are long and slender, can *contract*, or get shorter. The contracting and relaxing of muscle cells makes your body move.

Cells that look alike and work together make up a **tissue** (TISH•oo). Each kind of tissue works to carry out the jobs of the cells that form it. For example, muscle cells that make up heart tissue don't tire as easily as other muscle cells. This kind of muscle tissue is found only in the heart. Another type of muscle tissue lines the walls of the stomach. This tissue helps digestion.

Lesson Focus

Four systems transport materials throughout the body.

Why Learn This?

Understanding how transport systems work together can help you keep them healthy.

Vocabulary

cell
tissue
organ
system
capillaries
alveoli
nephrons

  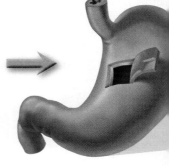

▲ Cells have different sizes and shapes. This cell is from the lining of the stomach.

▲ One tissue that lines the stomach helps protect the stomach from the strong acid it produces.

▲ Several kinds of tissues make up an organ. The stomach is one of the organs that breaks down the food you eat.

4

Focus Skill Reading Skill

Mini-Lesson

SEQUENCE Remind students that sequence is the order of events or things. Have them practice this skill by responding to the Focus Skill question on page 5. Have students draw and complete the graphic organizer as you model it on the transparency.

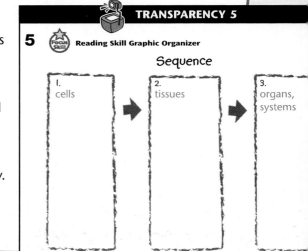

TRANSPARENCY 5

5 Reading Skill Graphic Organizer

Sequence

1. cells

2. tissues

3. organs, systems

Interactive Transparencies available on CD-ROM.

Many body parts are made up of several tissues. A group of tissues that work together to do a job is called an **organ**. The heart is an organ. It is made up of muscle and other tissues. The heart's job is to pump blood to all parts of your body.

Each organ in your body is part of a body system. A **system** is a group of organs that work together to do a job. The heart, for example, can't *transport*, or carry, blood to all parts of the body on its own. To transport blood to all parts of the body, the heart depends on blood vessels, which are also organs. The heart, blood vessels, and blood make up the *circulatory system*.

Other body transport systems include the *respiratory system*, the *digestive system*, and the *excretory system*. You will learn about each of these systems in this lesson.

SEQUENCE Beginning with cells, in which order are body systems built?

cells, tissues, organs, systems

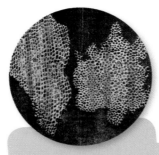

Did You Know?

In the mid-seventeenth century, Robert Hooke, a scientist and inventor, coined the term *cell* after he viewed thin slices of cork through a microscope. The boxlike structure of the cork cells reminded Hooke of the cells, or rooms, of a monastery. The photograph above shows cork cells like the ones Hooke observed.

◀ The stomach is part of a body system that digests food, transfers digested food into the blood, and stores wastes.

5

2. TEACH

Interpret Visuals—Pictures

Have students examine the diagrams on these pages as you explain that many cells working together form a tissue, tissues form organs, and so on.

What is formed by many systems working together? a whole organism

Content-Area Reading Support

Using Typographic Clues Direct attention to the following sentence in the first paragraph on this page: *A group of tissues that work together to do a job is called an* **organ.** Point out that words in boldface type are the most important in a sentence. In this case, the sentence is a definition of the boldface word.

Urge students to pay special attention to words or phrases in boldface type, as they usually express the most important ideas in a sentence or paragraph.

Discuss

Critical Thinking What are at least two kinds of tissue that make up your arm? Possible answers: muscle, skin, blood, fat, nails, hair

When Minutes Count ...

Transparency 7: The Circulatory System can be used to present material in this lesson. *Interactive Transparencies available on CD-ROM.*

QUICK STUDY, ACTIVITY BOOK PP. 1–2

CHAPTER 1 A Growing and Changing Body

Directions
• Use lesson vocabulary in the Word Bank to complete each **Summary.**
• Read the directions provided to complete each **Lesson Details.**

Word Bank

abstract thinking	environment	hormones	neurons	system
cell	growth spurt	joint	organs	tendons
concrete thinking	heredity	ligaments	prenatal	tissues

Lesson 1 pp. 4–9

Summary The basic unit of structure of all living things is the ___cell___.
Cells that look alike and work together make up the ___tissues___ that form body parts. A group of ___organs___ form a body ___system___.

Lesson Details Use pages 4–9 to complete the graphic organizer.

Cells → Organs
Tissues → Transport systems → Circulatory system, Respiratory system, Digestive system, Excretory system

Lesson 2 pp. 10–13

Summary Two or more bones fit together at a ___joint___. There, ___ligaments___, which are strong bands of tissue, attach bones together. Muscles are attached to bones by ___tendons___. ___Neurons___ send and receive messages to all parts of the body.

Lesson Details Use page 13 to explain what happens during a reflex action. Possible answer: Nerves send messages directly to the spinal cord, which tells muscles to react. The message does not go through the brain.

Quick Study (continued)

Lesson 3 pp. 14–19

Summary The passing of traits from parents to children is called ___heredity___. Some traits and the way you grow are influenced by your ___environment___. Chemicals called ___hormones___, produced by your endocrine system, also influence growth.

Lesson Details Look at pages 18–19. Use another sheet of paper to explain why physical activity and proper nutrition are important as you grow. See p. 128 in *Teaching Resources* for possible answers.

Lesson 4 pp. 20–24

Summary The time before birth is called the ___prenatal___ stage. During this stage you experienced your first period of rapid growth, called a ___growth spurt___.

Lesson Details Use the chart on page 21 to match the phrases to the stage of life. Each stage has two phrases that match.

___c___ and ___d___ **1.** prenatal
___b___ and ___f___ **2.** infancy
___a___ and ___e___ **3.** childhood

a. slow, constant growth
b. birth until two years
c. nine months before birth until birth
d. develop the systems needed to support life
e. two years until about ten years
f. learn to sit up, crawl, walk, and talk

Lesson 5 pp. 26–29

Summary Solving problems involving real objects that you can see and touch is called ___concrete thinking___. Being able to imagine different solutions to problems is called ___abstract thinking___.

Lesson Details Use the "Problem Solving Steps" on page 27 to put the list in its proper order.

___3___ Choose the best solution.
___2___ Brainstorm many possible solutions.
___4___ Test the solution. Think about what might happen if you try it.
___1___ Identify the problem. State it to yourself.

Available online.
www.harcourtschool.com/health

Discuss

How are veins and arteries the same?
Both are blood vessels that move blood through the body.

How do arteries and veins differ?
Arteries carry blood away from the heart; veins carry blood to the heart. Most arteries carry oxygen and other nutrients; most veins carry wastes, such as carbon dioxide.

Critical Thinking What is the role of capillaries?
Capillaries are tiny blood vessels that connect arteries and veins. Nutrients pass through capillary walls into cells. Wastes pass from cells through capillary walls into the blood.

Discuss

Have students explain how to maintain the healthy status of body systems, such as avoiding smoking to protect the lungs. Tell students that cigarette smoke damages lungs, narrows blood vessels, and restricts blood flow.

Problem Solving What are some ways to keep your circulatory system healthy?
Never smoke a cigarette; eat foods that are low in fat.

Health Background

Components of Blood The average adult has about 5 liters of blood in his or her body. Of this volume, about 2.75 to 3 liters is plasma, a straw-colored liquid that contains proteins, hormones, and food nutrients. About 40 to 45 percent of blood consists of red blood cells. Red blood cells contain a protein called hemoglobin. Hemoglobin picks up oxygen in the lungs and then transports it to the rest of the body's cells. Blood also contains white cells, which fight infection, and platelets, which cause blood to clot.

Source: *HowStuffWorks, Inc.*

For more background, visit the **Webliography** in Teacher Resources at **www.harcourtschool.com/health Keyword** human body

---

Circulatory System

Your body depends on your circulatory system to deliver important materials throughout your body. These materials are carried by blood, which circulates through your body in blood vessels. The circulatory system also helps remove wastes. In other systems, organs such as the lungs and kidneys help the blood get rid of the wastes.

Blood is carried throughout your body by three kinds of blood vessels—arteries, veins, and capillaries. Most arteries carry needed materials, such as oxygen, to body tissues. Most veins carry wastes, such as carbon dioxide, away from body tissues. **Capillaries** (KAP•uh•lair•eez) are tiny blood vessels that connect arteries and veins. Capillaries enable nutrients and oxygen to reach every body cell. They also pick up wastes from body cells.

The foods you eat and the physical activities you do are important in keeping your circulatory system healthy. In Chapters 3 and 4 you'll learn about foods and physical activities that help your circulatory system stay healthy.

Blood circulates throughout your body in one direction. Your heart provides the force to push the blood. Arteries carry blood away from the heart and to all parts of the body. Veins carry blood from all parts of the body back to the heart. ▼

heart

vein

artery

Alike: Both are blood vessels. Different: Most arteries carry oxygen and other nutrients away from the heart and to the body's cells. Most veins carry blood containing wastes from cells back toward the heart.

6

COMPARE AND CONTRAST How are arteries and veins alike? How are they different?

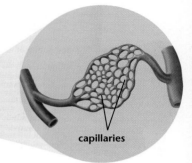

capillaries

▲ Oxygen and nutrients pass from the blood, through capillary walls, and into the cells. Cell wastes pass through capillary walls and into the blood.

Meeting Individual Needs
Leveled Activities

BELOW-LEVEL Ask students to make flash cards with the name of a circulatory organ (heart, arteries, veins, capillaries) on one side and the organ's function on the other. Have them work in pairs to test each other with the flash cards.

ON-LEVEL Have students use resource material or the Internet to find out about at least one health problem associated with each part of the circulatory system. Examples: heart (valve defects), arteries (cholesterol), veins (varicosity), capillaries (smoking). Have students report their findings to the class.

CHALLENGE Have students cirount their pulses at the wrist for ten seconds and multiply the number by six to find the number of heartbeats per minute. Then have students keep a log of how their heart rates change with various activity levels in one day. Ask them to write a hypothesis about why the rate changes.

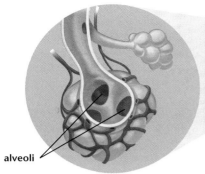

▼ Oxygen in the air enters the blood through capillaries that surround the alveoli. Carbon dioxide leaves the blood through these capillaries and enters the alveoli.

alveoli

nasal passages

trachea

lungs

To keep your respiratory system healthy, don't smoke, and avoid other people's tobacco smoke. Also, avoid air pollutants and get plenty of exercise. ▶

Respiratory System

The respiratory system's job is to take in oxygen, which body cells need, and to get rid of carbon dioxide, a waste gas. Muscles help your respiratory system move gasses into and out of your body.

When you breathe in, air enters through your nose, where it is cleaned and warmed. The air then passes through the windpipe, or *trachea* (TRAY•kee•uh). A branch of the trachea enters each lung.

The lungs are the major organs of the respiratory system. They are filled with air tubes, air sacs, and blood vessels. In each lung the air tubes branch again and again. At the ends of the smallest branches are the air sacs, called **alveoli** (al•VEE•uh•ly).

In the alveoli oxygen from the air enters the blood and carbon dioxide leaves the blood. When you breathe out, carbon dioxide is forced out of your body.

 SEQUENCE **What happens to air right after it enters through your nose or mouth?**
It is cleaned and warmed.

Quick Activity

Write an Explanation Write a paragraph that explains how the circulatory and respiratory systems work together.

7

Content-Area Reading Support

Using Respellings Direct attention to the phonetic respelling (TRAY•kee•uh) in the second paragraph on this page. Explain that respellings show how words are pronounced. Point out that the dots within the respelling divide the word into syllables and that small capital letters indicate the stressed, or accented, syllable. Urge students to look at respellings for help in pronouncing unfamiliar words and in recognizing words with unfamiliar spellings.

Discuss

Many organs belong to more than one system. For example, the lungs, the major organs of the respiratory system, are also organs of the excretory system because they rid the body of waste.

Critical Thinking Describe the interdependence of the circulatory system and the respiratory system.
The heart pumps oxygen-poor blood through the lungs, where the blood picks up oxygen and leaves carbon dioxide to be exhaled. Then the heart pumps oxygenated blood through the circulatory system to the entire body.

 When Minutes Count ...

Transparency 8: The Respiratory System can be used to present material in this lesson. *Interactive Transparencies available on CD-ROM.*

Discuss

Vigorous activities such as running and swimming benefit the respiratory system.

Problem Solving Which sport would be more beneficial to the respiratory system—speed skating or golf? Why?
Speed skating involves more vigorous movement than golf and would be of more benefit to the respiratory system.

Quick Activity

The circulatory system picks up oxygen in the lungs and leaves carbon dioxide.

Discuss

Explain that digestion involves both chemical and mechanical processes. Mechanical processes break the food into smaller pieces but do not change the chemical nature of the foods. Chemical processes involve reactions that change food into usable nutrients. For example, starches are changed to sugars.

Critical Thinking **What is the first mechanical process involved in digestion?** chewing food

What does the first mechanical process accomplish in the process of digestion? breaks food into smaller pieces and mixes it with saliva

Interpret Visuals—Pictures

Have students study the picture of the digestive system, noting that the intestines are folded many times to fit into the abdominal cavity.

What is the length of the human digestive tract? Most students will probably be surprised that an adult digestive tract is about 10 yards long.

When Minutes Count ...

Transparency 9: The Digestive System can be used to present material in this lesson. *Interactive Transparencies available on CD-ROM.*

Health Background

Eating Disorders Eating disorders affect millions of people in the United States, most of them female. An estimated 0.5 to 3.7 percent of females suffer from anorexia nervosa in their lifetime. Anorexia nervosa is a disorder in which a person eats as little food as possible for fear of gaining weight. Bulimia is another eating disorder. A person with bulimia eats large amounts of food in a short time, only to eliminate it immediately by self-induced vomiting or excessive laxative use.

Source: *National Institutes of Health*

Digestive System

The food you eat cannot be used by your body until it is *digested*, or broken down. This is the job of the digestive system. This process begins in your mouth, where food mixes with saliva. Saliva begins breaking down carbohydrates. When you swallow, muscles push the food through the *esophagus* (ih•SAHF•uh•guhs), a long tube that leads to your stomach. The stomach contains acid and other chemicals that begin to break down proteins.

After a few hours in the stomach, partly digested food moves into the small intestine. The gallbladder, the pancreas, and the small intestine itself release chemicals to finish the job. In the small intestine, materials from digested food move into the blood. Undigested food passes into the large intestine. There, minerals and water move into the blood, and solid wastes are stored temporarily.

You can help keep your digestive system healthy by eating a variety of low-fat foods, including fruits, vegetables, and foods made with whole grains. You should also drink plenty of water. ▼

salivary glands

esophagus

liver

pancreas

stomach

small intestine

large intestine

SUMMARIZE **List the organs of the digestive system, and tell the role of each.** Students should identify and describe the roles of organs shown in the diagram on this page.

villi

▲ Materials from digested food enter the blood through projections called *villi* in the walls of the small intestine.

8

ESL/ELL Support

LANGUAGE AND VOCABULARY Help students learn the parts of the digestive system and their functions.

Beginning Have students work in pairs to make posters describing the structure of the digestive system.

Intermediate Give students markers to write the names of the parts of the digestive system on the posters. Have them draw a line from the name to the part.

Advanced Help student groups choose one organ and write on a card as many functions of that organ as they can think of. They should include the organ's functions within other systems, if applicable.

Excretory System

The kidneys and bladder are the major organs of the excretory system. This system takes certain wastes from the blood and removes them from the body as *urine*. Urine is collected wastes and water. This job is important because it keeps the right amount of water in the body at all times. It also helps keep wastes from building up in the body. These wastes, in large amounts, are harmful.

As blood passes through the kidneys, **nephrons** (NEF•rahnz) filter out wastes and excess water. Cleaned blood leaves the kidneys and continues through the body. The urine, which contains the wastes, is stored in the bladder until it passes out of the body.

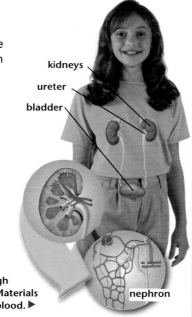
kidneys
ureter
bladder

CAUSE AND EFFECT What are the effects of the kidneys' removing wastes and excess water?
keeps amount of water in body the same; keeps wastes from building up

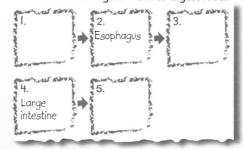
In the kidneys, capillaries pass through microscopic filters called nephrons. Materials the body needs are returned to the blood. ▶
nephron

Lesson 1 Summary and Review

❶ Summarize with Vocabulary

Use vocabulary from this lesson to complete these statements.

Groups of cells make up _____, which make up _____. Groups of these body parts then make up _____. Tiny blood vessels that enable materials and wastes to pass between the blood and body cells are called _____. Gases pass into and out of the blood in the _____ of the lungs. The _____ remove wastes from blood as the blood passes through the kidneys.

❷ Critical Thinking Why do you think the air tubes in the lungs branch again and again until they are very small?

❸ Why is the removal of wastes by the kidneys important to the body?

❹ (Focus Skill) **SEQUENCE** Draw and complete this graphic organizer to show the order in which organs work to digest food.

1.
2. Esophagus
3.
4. Large intestine
5.

❺ Write to Inform—Explanation

Write a paragraph that explains why the circulatory, respiratory, digestive, and excretory systems are considered transport systems for the body.

9

 When Minutes Count ...

Transparency 10: The Excretory System can be used to present material in this lesson. *Interactive Transparencies available on CD-ROM.*

3. WRAP UP

Lesson 1 Summary and Review

1. tissues, organs, systems, capillaries, alveoli, nephrons

2. The air tubes branch repeatedly so that they can reach all parts of the lungs.

3. It keeps harmful wastes from building up in the body.

4. Possible answers are shown.

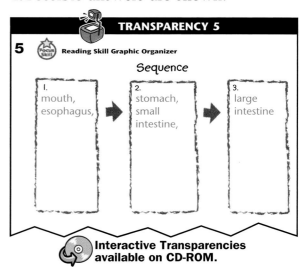
TRANSPARENCY 5

5 (Focus Skill) **Reading Skill Graphic Organizer**

Sequence

1. mouth, esophagus,
2. stomach, small intestine,
3. large intestine

 Interactive Transparencies available on CD-ROM.

5. A transport system moves needed materials or waste materials from one place to another in the body. The circulatory system moves blood, the respiratory system moves oxygen and carbon dioxide, the digestive system moves food and nutrients, and the excretory system moves waste from the blood and out of the body.

For **writing models** with examples, see *Teaching Resources* pp. 47–61. Rubrics are also provided.

 When Minutes Count ...

Quick Study Students can use *Activity Book* pp. 1–2 (shown on p. 5) as they complete each lesson in this chapter.

LESSON 2

Pages 10–13

Objectives

▶ Identify the three body systems that coordinate body movements.

▶ Explain ways to keep body coordination systems healthy.

 When Minutes Count . . .

Assign the Quick Study, Lesson 2, Activity Book pp. 1–2 (shown on p. 5).

Program Resources

▶ Activity Book pp. 1–2

▶ Transparencies 5, 11–13

Vocabulary

joint p. 10, **ligaments** p. 10, **tendons** p. 11, **neurons** p. 12, **reflex action** p. 13

Daily Fitness Tip

Tell students calcium is necessary for healthy bones. Milk, dairy products like yogurt and cheese, and some dark green, leafy vegetables are good sources of calcium. Remind students to move and flex their joints regularly through exercise. If they don't, they might get injured or become stiff and sore.

CSHP For more guidelines about your muscles and movement, see *Be Active! Resources for Physical Education,* p. 151.

1. MOTIVATE

Ask students to stand and try running in place without bending their knees. Then ask them to sit and to try writing their names as they normally would but without bending their fingers.

Why is having bones and joints important? Without bones, it would be impossible to stand because there would be nothing to support the body. Without joints, we could not move our bones in ways that allow us to run or write or move as we normally do.

Body Coordination Systems

Lesson Focus

Three body systems coordinate your body movements.

Why Learn This?

Knowing what the coordination systems do helps you understand how to protect them.

Vocabulary

joint
ligaments
tendons
neurons
reflex action

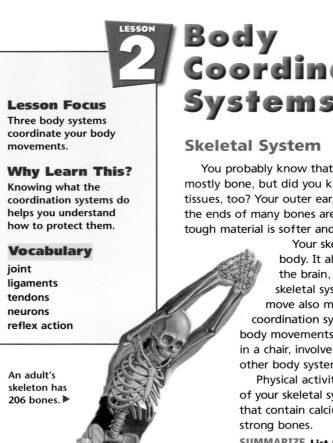

An adult's skeleton has 206 bones. ▶

Skeletal System

You probably know that your skeletal system is mostly bone, but did you know it is made of other tissues, too? Your outer ear, the tip of your nose, and the ends of many bones are made of *cartilage*. This tough material is softer and more flexible than bone.

Your skeletal system supports your body. It also protects organs, such as the brain, heart, and lungs. The skeletal system's role in helping you move also makes it one of the body's coordination systems. Even the simplest body movements, such as changing positions in a chair, involve the skeletal system and other body systems.

Physical activity is important to the health of your skeletal system. So is eating foods that contain calcium—which helps build strong bones.

SUMMARIZE List three jobs of the skeletal system.
support, protection, and movement

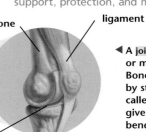

bone   ligament

joint

◀ A **joint** is a place where two or more bones fit together. Bones are attached at joints by strong bands of tissue called **ligaments**. Ligaments give joints flexibility for bending and stretching. Muscles also attach to bones near joints.

10

Teacher Tip

Joints The body has five types of joints. Hinge joints, such as those in the elbows and fingers, allow back-and-forth movements. Gliding joints allow bones to slide against each other, as in the wrists and ankles. Ball-and-socket joints, found in the hips and shoulders, permit rotational movement. Pivot joints, such as the one between the first two vertebrae in the neck, allow bones to twist against each other. Immovable joints allow little or no movement. The skull and pelvis contain immovable joints.

Math

Boning Up on Bones Ask same-gender pairs of students to use tape measures to determine the lengths of the following bones: humerus, ulna/radius, phalanges in the fingers, sternum, spinal column, femur, and tibia/fibula. The class can then tabulate the data by age (in months) and by gender and can note any trends in the values.

Muscular System

Your skeletal system wouldn't be able to move without your muscular system. The muscles that make your body move are attached to bones. For this reason they are called skeletal muscles. A skeletal muscle has a bulging middle and narrow tendons near each end. **Tendons** are strong, flexible bands of tissue that attach muscles to bones near the joints.

Skeletal muscles work in pairs. When one muscle contracts, it pulls on the bone it's connected to. The bone moves. To move the bone back again, a muscle on the other side of the bone must contract.

You can protect your muscles by warming up and stretching before doing strong physical activity. Be sure to ease out of activity, too, so muscles won't get sore.

CAUSE AND EFFECT What causes a bone to move? the contraction of one or more muscles attached to it

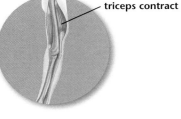
triceps contract

Muscles can pull bones but can't push them. Arm movement requires a pair of muscles—the triceps and the biceps.

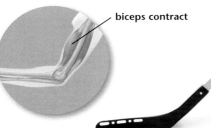
biceps contract

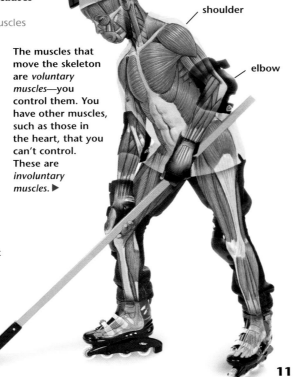
shoulder

elbow

The muscles that move the skeleton are *voluntary muscles*—you control them. You have other muscles, such as those in the heart, that you can't control. These are *involuntary muscles.* ▶

11

ESL/ELL Support

COMPREHENSIBLE INPUT Help students understand how muscles move bones when they contract. Have each student straighten one arm in front of the body and put the other hand on the biceps (upper arm muscle) of the straightened arm. Tell students to bend their arms and feel the muscle contract.

Beginning Have students say the word *contract* as they do this.

Intermediate Help students use the words *contract* and *pull* in a sentence that explains what is happening.

Advanced Ask students to write a short paragraph explaining, in their own words, the interdependence of the muscular and skeletal systems.

2. TEACH

Interpret Visuals—Pictures

Ask students to use the diagrams on this page to identify the muscle on the front of the upper arm as the biceps and the one on the back as the triceps. Make sure students understand that when the arm is flexed, the triceps relaxes while the biceps contracts and gets thicker. When the arm is extended, the opposite is true.

Have students read the picture captions. Tell them that all the muscles shown on this page are voluntary muscles.

When Minutes Count ...

Transparencies 11 and 12: The Skeletal System and **The Muscular System** can be used to present material in this lesson. *Interactive Transparencies are available on CD-ROM.*

Critical Thinking What are some involuntary muscles? Possible answers: muscles in the eyelids, heart, and stomach

Consumer Activity

Make Buying Decisions Divide the class in half. Have one group think of active games for which they could use homemade equipment. They may even wish to invent a game. Have the other group look for ads for sports equipment on sale. They can choose a sport and try to find all the equipment needed for it at the best prices.

Health Background

Types of Muscles There are three types of muscles. *Smooth* muscles are found in the walls of internal organs and blood vessels. They strengthen the organs they line. *Skeletal* muscles are striated and are attached to bones. They are responsible for most body movements. *Cardiac* muscle makes up the heart.

Source: *HowStuffWorks, Inc.*

TEACH continued

Interpret Visuals—Pictures

Ask students to look at the diagram of the nerve cell as you review its parts. A neuron has three major parts: dendrites, cell body, and axon. Dendrites are the small extensions of the neuron that receive signals and carry them toward the cell body. The axon is a single projection that carries signals away from the cell body. You may also want to use Transparency 13 here.

Where are the dendrites, the axon, and the cell body on the diagram? The cell body is the large central area of the neuron. The dendrites are the thin, wispy projections above the sides of the cell body. The axon is the thick extension below the cell body.

Discuss

Nicotine is a poison to the body. Nicotine, caffeine, and alcohol are drugs. Nicotine and caffeine are stimulants, which means they speed up the nervous system. Alcohol is a depressant. Depressants slow down the nervous system.

When Minutes Count ...

Transparency 13: The Nervous System can be used to present material in this lesson. *Interactive Transparencies available on CD-ROM.*

Critical Thinking **What are some sources of caffeine?** caffeinated colas, coffees and teas, chocolate, cocoa

What is a source of nicotine? cigarettes

Health Background

Divisions of the Nervous System The brain and the spinal cord make up the central nervous system, or CNS. All the other nerves in the body form the peripheral nervous system.

Source: *"Neuroscience for Kids," University of Washington*

For more background, visit the **Webliography** in Teacher Resources at **www.harcourtschool.com/health** **Keyword** human body

---

Studying the Brain Brain research used to be done on diseased brains. Now, the use of brain imaging has enabled scientists to study healthy brains. As a result, scientists have made many discoveries about the brains of adolescents. For example, scientists have suggested that teenagers may be more emotional than adults because they use a different part of the brain to interpret emotions than adults do.

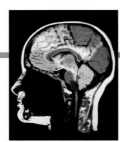

Nervous System

Your nervous system is responsible for your thoughts and your body's movements. It keeps your heart beating and makes sure your lungs take in oxygen. It enables you to see, smell, hear, taste, and touch. Your nervous system lets you learn, remember, and feel emotions. It is important as a system because it controls most of the activities of your body.

Your brain is your body's command center. Different parts of the brain control different body actions. Your spinal cord is a thick bundle of nerve tissue located inside the column of bones along your back. The job of the spinal cord is to transfer messages between your brain and different parts of your body. Nerves that branch from the brain and spinal cord receive information from the environment and send signals to muscles.

Sense organs in your body have nerves that gather information about conditions around you. Your skin, for example, has nerves that sense heat, cold, and pressure. Your eyes detect light, and your

neurons

brain

spinal cord

nerves

The nervous system includes the brain, spinal cord, and nerves. Nerves are bundles of cells, or neurons, which send messages to and receive messages from other neurons. ▶

12

Science

Elements in Your Diet The elements potassium (K) and sodium (Na) must be present for an impulse to move along a nerve. Have students find out what foods are high in these two elements. (Kiwis, bananas, potatoes, nuts, and meat are high in potassium. Meats, milk, cheeses, beets, celery, and carrots are among foods high in sodium.)

Teacher Tip

Caring for Your Nervous System Share these tips for keeping a healthy nervous system.

- Don't take any drug unless it is given by a parent, a doctor, or another trusted adult. Many drugs circulate throughout the body and affect all cells, including the cells of the brain and nervous system.

- Eat a well-balanced diet. The nervous system cannot work well without certain nutrients.

- Practice new skills. Learning new skills builds new nerve connections in the brain.

ears pick up sound waves. Your sense organs provide information to prepare you for most situations.

Most of the time, information from sense organs travels to the brain. The brain receives and analyzes the information. If a response is needed, the brain sends out signals to muscles to take the necessary action.

In some situations, such as the one shown at the right, a response is needed right away. In a case like this, a **reflex action**, or automatic response, involving the spinal cord, but not the brain, may occur.

You can protect your nervous system in several ways. Don't take illegal drugs, and don't take any medicines unless they are given by your doctor or a parent. Eat a variety of healthful foods. Use safety gear when participating in sports.

CAUSE AND EFFECT **What causes a muscle to respond?**

The nervous system receives a message from a sense organ. The message is sent to the brain. The brain responds by sending a message to a muscle.

▲ This girl reacts to the hot pan before she even feels the pain. Nerves in her hand, sensing heat, send a message directly to nerves in her spinal cord that control muscles in her arm and hand.

Lesson 2 Summary and Review

❶ Summarize with Vocabulary

Use vocabulary from this lesson to complete these statements.

Bones fit together at _____. Bones are attached to one another by _____. Muscles are attached to bones by _____. Messages from the brain travel to muscles through nerves, which are made up of _____. In an emergency, a _____ may occur to prevent injury.

❷ How can you keep your skeletal, muscular, and nervous systems healthy?

❸ Critical Thinking Besides the heart, where might involuntary muscle be found?

❹ **SEQUENCE** Draw and complete this graphic organizer to show the order of events in a reflex action that occurs when someone touches a hot pan.

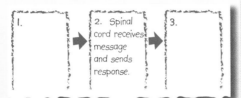

I. |→| 2. Spinal cord receives message and sends response. |→| 3.

❺ Write to Inform—Description

Write a paragraph that describes how the coordination systems work together when you bend your arm.

13

---

3. WRAP UP

Lesson 2 Summary and Review

1. joints, ligaments, tendons, neurons, reflex action

2. Skeletal system—Eat foods that have calcium; be physically active. Muscular system—Warm up and stretch before doing hard physical activity; ease out of exercise. Nervous system—Eat a well-balanced diet; use safety gear; don't take illegal drugs.

3. eyelids, digestive system, diaphragm, most internal organs

4. Possible answers are shown.

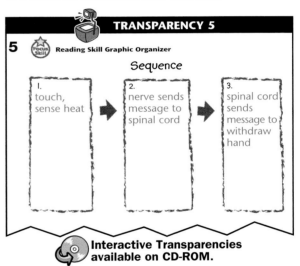

TRANSPARENCY 5

5 Reading Skill Graphic Organizer

Sequence

| I. touch, sense heat | → | 2. nerve sends message to spinal cord | → | 3. spinal cord sends message to withdraw hand |

Interactive Transparencies available on CD-ROM.

5. The nervous system sends a message to the nerves in the biceps muscle to contract and to the nerves in the triceps muscle to relax. The biceps muscle responds by contracting and pulling on the bones in the forearm, causing the elbow to bend.

 For **writing models** with examples, see *Teaching Resources* pp. 47–61. Rubrics are also provided.

⏱ When Minutes Count ...

Quick Study Students can use *Activity Book* pp. 1–2 (shown on p. 5) as they complete each lesson in this chapter.

LESSON 3

Pages 14–19

Objectives

► Learn about hereditary and environmental influences on growth.
► Identify major hormones of the endocrine system.
► Examine some functions of hormones.
► Describe how growth occurs.

When Minutes Count . . .

Assign the Quick Study, Lesson 3, Activity Book pp. 1–2 (shown on p. 5).

Program Resources

► Activity Book pp. 1–2
► Transparencies 5, 14

Vocabulary

heredity p. 14, **environment** p. 15, **hormones** p. 16

Daily Fitness Tip

Students will learn in this lesson that heredity and environment combine to affect each person's growth and development. Although hereditary factors are predetermined, the choices students make regarding their diets, activity level, and safety can have a great impact on overall health.

 For more guidelines about activity, inactivity, and your health, see *Be Active! Resources for Physical Education,* p. 155.

1. MOTIVATE

Ask students to brainstorm ways that people differ physically while you write their contributions on the board. Possible responses: height, weight, eye color, hair color, skin color, face shape, and handedness Then ask them to separate this list into two groups: traits that will change over a person's lifetime and traits that will change little over a lifetime.

Why will some of these traits, such as eye color, never change? They are traits passed on to people by their parents.

Growth, Heredity, and the Endocrine System

Lesson Focus

Both heredity and environment affect your growth.

Why Learn This?

If you know what affects your body's growth, you can make choices to help your body grow.

Vocabulary

heredity
environment
hormones

Heredity and Environment

Is your hair light or dark? Do you play a musical instrument? Are you good at math? Whatever your traits may be, where did they come from?

Heredity and environment combine to affect who you are and the way you grow. **Heredity** (huh·RED·ih·tee) is the passing of traits from parents to children.

You inherited a set of traits, such as your eye color, hair color, and the shape of your nose. Instructions for these traits are carried in your cells. The combination of traits you inherited from your parents affects the way you look and act.

Your parents give you guidance to help you make good choices. Close ties with family and friends enable you develop your abilities. This helps you grow as a person.

14

Teacher Tip

Sensitive Issues Some children do not live with their biological families because they are adopted or live with foster parents. Some, in fact, may never have known their biological families and may bear no physical resemblance to their adoptive or foster parents. For this reason, when teaching this lesson, select activities that utilize relationships other than the child's own. In your focus on heredity, select television families, famous personalities, or animals.

Art

Family Resemblances Have students search magazines for pictures that display family resemblances. Have them cut the pictures out to create collages, adding arrows and text to identify the physical traits the family members have in common. Good magazines for this activity are those that focus on families, parenting, and the home.

Some inherited traits aren't easily noticed. One of these is the rate at which you grow. No two people grow at exactly the same rate or in the same way.

Your body and some of your talents were determined by your heredity before you were born. However, as you grow, the way your body, talents, and other traits develop also depends on your environment (en•vy•ruhn•muhnt). The **environment** is all the things that surround you every day.

An environment that is good for growth includes clean air to breathe, clean water to drink, nutritious food to eat, and a safe neighborhood to live in. As you get older, you become more responsible for your environment. Healthful choices, such as avoiding the use of drugs, alcohol, and tobacco, encourage growth and help you stay well.

Your parents gave you your inherited traits. They also do their best to provide you with a healthful environment. You will take on more and more responsibility for your development as you grow. Your parents, other trusted adults, and friends will continue, however, to be an influence.

SUMMARIZE **Explain how environment and heredity influence growth.**
Possible answer: Heredity determines the traits you were born with, and environment affects how you develop.

Quick
Activity

Take a Survey Take a survey to determine how many of your classmates can roll their tongues. This trait is passed from parents to their children.

◀ Has anyone ever said you look like someone else in your family? Inherited traits can make family members look very much alike.

15

Interpret Visuals—Pictures

Have students look at the photograph on this page. Explain that the glands in the picture are actually drawings superimposed on the photograph. The text boxes and arrows have been added to help students see the locations and functions of the six major glands of the body. As students read the text boxes, ask them to locate each gland on their own bodies.

When Minutes Count . . .

Transparency 14: The Endocrine System can be used to present material in this lesson. *Interactive Transparencies available on CD-ROM.*

Discuss

Have students describe the function of the endocrine system.

Critical Thinking What "messages" do you pick up from your body when you are frightened or very nervous?
Possible answers: heart racing, goose bumps, palms sweating, muscles tight, upset stomach, hands shaking

Health Background

Hormones The term *hormone* comes from the Greek word *horman*, which means "to stimulate, excite, or set in motion." More than fifty hormones are made by the body's endocrine glands. These glands are the pineal and pituitary, located in the head; the thyroid and parathyroid, in the neck; the thymus, high in the chest; the adrenals, at the top of the kidneys; the pancreas, between the kidneys; and the ovaries and testes of the reproductive system. Some hormones, such as growth hormone, are released only at certain times. Other hormones are produced continually in the body and help it function properly.

Source: *National Cancer Institute*

For more background, visit the **Webliography** in Teacher Resources at **www.harcourtschool.com/health** **Keyword** human body

---

Did You Know?
About one in ten young people experience "growing pains" in their legs. The pains usually happen at night, and the aching can wake you up. Fortunately, growing pains normally do not last long and can be helped by massage, heat, or medication.

Endocrine System

Heredity and environment affect your growth, but your body's systems actually make growth happen. One system, the *endocrine system*, is especially important in determining how your body grows. The endocrine system sends messages in the form of chemicals throughout your body. The chemicals, called **hormones** (HAWR•mohnz), travel in your blood to the organs and tissues of your body systems.

Hormones are produced by *glands*. Each gland has certain organs, or target organs, that its hormones act on. The whole endocrine system has many glands. The diagram below shows the locations and roles of several of the body's endocrine glands.

1 The pituitary gland (pih•TOO•uh•tair•ee) controls growth. The pituitary is sometimes called the master gland because it makes hormones that control other glands.

2 The thyroid gland controls the rate at which the body produces and uses energy.

3 The parathyroid glands help regulate the body's use of calcium and vitamin D.

4 The thymus gland helps the body fight disease.

5 The pancreas produces a hormone that helps body cells use sugar.

6 The adrenal glands produce a hormone that prepares the body to react quickly.

16

Teacher Tip

The Endocrine Game Have groups of students play this game. Write the name of one gland (thyroid, pancreas, parathyroid, thymus, adrenal, pituitary) on each of six index cards. Next, write the functions of the glands on six other cards. Place the cards, face down. Play by turning over one card and then another. If the cards do not match—gland and function— turn both face down and try again. When a match is found, both cards are removed. The object is to clear all the cards.

Teacher Tip

Discuss the term *trusted adult* with students. Explain that sometimes their parents or guardians may not be nearby when they need help. Students should be encouraged to identify other adults they can trust in the absence of their parents or legal guardians. Such "trusted adults" should be individuals well known to the child and MAY include grandparents, teachers, counselors, nurses, doctors, firefighters, police officers, and neighbors.

Hormones cause you to feel thirsty if your body fluids are low. ▼

Most glands make and release several different hormones. Every body function controlled by the endocrine system is controlled by more than one hormone. Hormones work together. If the level of one hormone is too high or too low, the level of another hormone changes to fix the problem.

Several hormones affect body growth. Growth hormone, which is produced by the pituitary gland, controls how much and how fast you grow. It affects the growth of your bones and skeletal muscles. Growth hormone causes the rapid growth that many teenagers experience. Other hormones aid in growth, too.

CAUSE AND EFFECT **What effects do the pituitary, parathyroid, thymus, and thyroid glands have on the body?**
pituitary—controls growth and other glands; parathyroid—regulates body's use of calcium and vitamin D; thymus—helps body fight disease; thyroid—controls rate at which body produces and uses energy

Hormones

1 prepare you to react quickly for your own safety when you are frightened.

2 keep your body working steadily while you rest.

3 help your body use nutrients.

4 determine your body's rate of growth.

Myth and Fact

Myth: Sports drinks are better than water if you are really thirsty.
Fact: Water is just as good as sports drinks for people who are really thirsty. Sports drinks may be better, however, for people who exercise for long periods, such as long-distance runners.

17

Content-Area Reading Support

Using Text Format Have students read the text on the clipboard.

How does the information connect to the lesson? Both the text and the lesson are about the functions of hormones.

Point out that textbooks may use text boxes to give high-interest facts that are related to the topic of a lesson. This bulleted list summarizes important facts. Comment that students may want to read the primary text through first before reading a text box, so as not to interrupt the flow of ideas.

Discuss

Have students review the interdependence of major body systems.

Critical Thinking Using what you already know about the nervous system, compare the ways the endocrine system and the nervous system communicate. The endocrine system is much slower. Through the release of hormones, it can communicate for long periods of time. The nervous system is much faster and enables a person to respond quickly.

The process by which one hormone controls the level of another is called a feedback mechanism. Compare this mechanism to the following situation: A room is full of students listening to music. Someone slowly turns down the volume until students complain, "Turn it up!" Then the volume is slowly turned up until others protest, "Turn it down!" When a hormone level is high, the pituitary or another controlling gland senses this and stops or slows its signal to produce the hormone. When levels get too low, the controlling gland signals for increased production of the hormone.

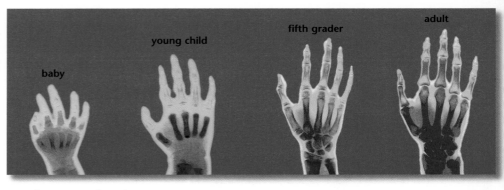

▲ These X rays show the hands of a baby, a young child, a fifth grader, and an adult. Notice how the bones of the hand change from one period of life to the next.

TEACH *continued*

Interpret Visuals—Pictures

Explain to students that the X rays at the top of the page are a type of photograph taken with a special camera. A form of energy called an X ray is directed at an object. It passes through soft (less dense) material but is reflected back by hard (dense) material. Bone is the densest material in the hand, so the greater detail in the X rays from the older people shows that they have more bone and less cartilage.

Tell students that when Wilhelm Roentgen discovered X rays, he called them X rays because he didn't know what they were!

Discuss

Talk about the role of cartilage during bone development and its function after bone growth has stopped.

Critical Thinking What are the functions of cartilage at different stages of life? Cartilage protects toddlers as they learn to walk. Because it is flexible, it does not break easily when they fall. In adults, cartilage remains in places such as the knees, elbows, and ankles to help bones slide smoothly past each other.

Discuss

The strength of your bones as an adult is determined both by heredity and by the amounts of calcium and vitamin D in your diet while you are growing.

Problem Solving What can you do to make sure you have strong bones when you are grown up? You cannot change your heredity, but you can include in your diet foods rich in calcium and vitamin D, such as milk and other dairy products.

Discuss

Have students describe the interdependence of the endocrine system and the skeletal system.

How Growth Occurs

You may think of your bones as hard, dry, dead body parts, but less than half of a bone contains hard material. About one-fourth is water. The rest is living tissue.

When you were a baby, your bones contained a lot of soft, rubbery cartilage. Cartilage bends instead of breaking. It helped protect you when you fell as you learned to walk. As you grew older, much of the cartilage hardened into bone. By the time you are twenty-five years old, your bones will be fully developed. Cartilage will remain only in places such as your knees and elbows. In these places cartilage works like a cushion so your bones can easily move against one another.

growth plate

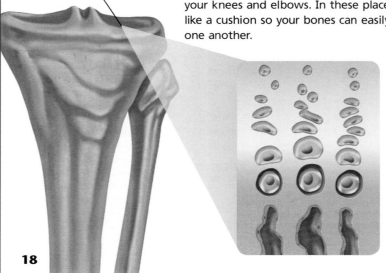

◀ Growth occurs at a bone's growth plates. In adults, growth plates are replaced with ordinary bone tissue. This change causes bone growth to stop.

18

Until you become an adult, your bones grow by making new cells. New cells increase the length and thickness of your bones. When you are a teenager, your bones will grow rapidly. They may grow several inches in a year's time.

Your muscles, too, grow in length and thickness. Like bones, your muscles stop getting longer after you become an adult. However, physical activity can make your muscles grow thicker and stronger. Physical activity will remain important for your muscles and bones even after you have finished growing. Throughout adulthood you will need to stay active to keep your muscles strong. The changes in your bones and muscles as they grow over the next few years will enable you to do more physical activities.

COMPARE AND CONTRAST Compare the growth of bones to the growth of muscles.
Both stop getting longer at adulthood; however, muscles can keep getting stronger with exercise.

▲ The exercise this firefighter gets will tire his muscles. When he rests, his muscles will use materials from food for repair.

Lesson 3 Summary and Review

❶ Summarize with Vocabulary

Use vocabulary and other terms from this lesson to complete these statements.

Both _____ and _____ affect the way you grow. The body system most responsible for your growth, however, is the _____. In this system, _____, or groups of specialized cells, produce _____ that cause changes in the tissues of the body. During growth, _____ changes to bone.

❷ What substances should you stay away from to help keep your body healthy?

❸ Critical Thinking How does the function of cartilage in a baby differ from its function in an adult?

❹ (Focus Skill) SEQUENCE Draw and complete this graphic organizer to show how the endocrine system sends a message to a target organ.

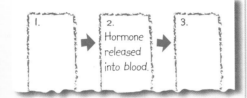

❺ Write to Inform—Explanation
Write a paragraph that explains why it is important to continue exercising throughout life.

19

3. WRAP UP

Lesson 3 Summary and Review

1. heredity, environment, endocrine system, glands, hormones, cartilage

2. drugs, alcohol, tobacco

3. Cartilage in a baby bends instead of breaking. It protects a baby when he or she falls. In an adult, cartilage cushions joints in the knees, elbows, and ankles so the bones can move easily against each other.

4. Possible answers are shown.

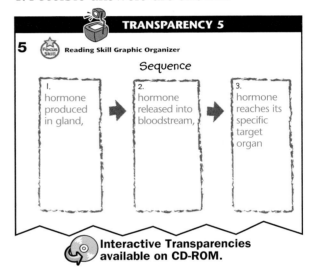

TRANSPARENCY 5

5 (Focus Skill) Reading Skill Graphic Organizer

Sequence

1. hormone produced in gland,

2. hormone released into bloodstream,

3. hormone reaches its specific target organ

Interactive Transparencies available on CD-ROM.

5. Physical activity helps strengthen bones as they grow. Even after growth is complete, physical activity can make bones stronger and muscles thicker and stronger.

 For **writing models** with examples, see *Teaching Resources* pp. 47–61. Rubrics are also provided.

 **When Minutes Count . . .**

Quick Study Students can use *Activity Book* pp. 1–2 (shown on p. 5) as they complete each lesson in this chapter.

Objectives

► Describe the growth stages from the prenatal stage to older adulthood.

► Learn about changes that occur during puberty.

 When Minutes Count . . .

Assign the Quick Study, Lesson 4, Activity Book pp. 1–2 (shown on p. 5).

Program Resources

► Activity Book pp. 1–2

► Transparency 5

Vocabulary

prenatal p. 20, **growth spurt** p. 20, **puberty** p. 22, **body image** p. 23

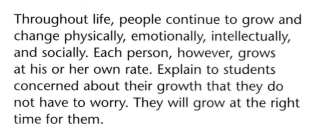

Daily Fitness Tip

Throughout life, people continue to grow and change physically, emotionally, intellectually, and socially. Each person, however, grows at his or her own rate. Explain to students concerned about their growth that they do not have to worry. They will grow at the right time for them.

 For more guidelines about fitness, see *Be Active! Resources for Physical Education.*

1. MOTIVATE

Have students write three sentences that describe a ten-year-old. Then have them write three sentences describing a six-year-old and three describing someone who is thirteen.

In general, how does a person who is ten differ from a six-year-old? Possible answer: A six-year-old is smaller and can't do as many mental activities.

How does someone who is thirteen years old differ from a ten-year-old? Possible answer: The thirteen-year-old is taller and has developed some adult characteristics, such as facial or body hair.

 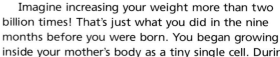

Growth Comes in Stages

Growth Changes You

Lesson Focus

You go through several stages of growth during your lifetime.

Why Learn This?

Learning about the stages of growth will help you prepare for changes ahead.

Vocabulary

prenatal
growth spurt
puberty
body image

Imagine increasing your weight more than two billion times! That's just what you did in the nine months before you were born. You began growing inside your mother's body as a tiny single cell. During the **prenatal** (pree·NAYT·uhl) stage, or the time before birth, the single fertilized cell divided rapidly to form many new cells. These cells developed into different types of cells with different purposes. Your major body organs formed. By the time of your birth, your heart, lungs, stomach, and other organs were working together in systems. You could now live outside your mother's body.

In the prenatal stage, you went through a period of rapid growth, called a **growth spurt**. You went through a similar period during *infancy*, or babyhood. That growth spurt began the day you were born. Throughout infancy, your appearance changed and so did the things you were able to do. At first, you depended on your parents for survival. During your first year, your brain, muscles, and bones grew quickly. Your increased strength made sitting, crawling, and walking possible. You also learned new ways to communicate.

 During the prenatal stage, new kinds of cells form and divide over and over again. From a tiny cell no bigger than the period at the end of this sentence, you grew into a baby. ►

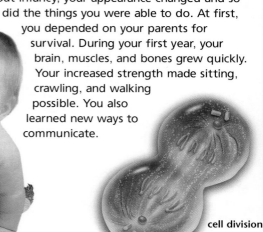

cell division

20

 **Science**

Fetal Development Invite students to investigate the growth and development that occurs during the nine months of pregnancy. Ask students to sketch and label important developmental stages. Ask them to draw a time line that indicates significant developmental events.

 Cultural Connection

Name Origins Parents-to-be typically spend a lot of time thinking about what to name their baby. Have students find out, if possible, how they were named and whether they were named in honor of someone. Then have them investigate the history and meaning of their names. After students complete their research, have them create colorful banners illustrating their names and the interesting information they discovered.

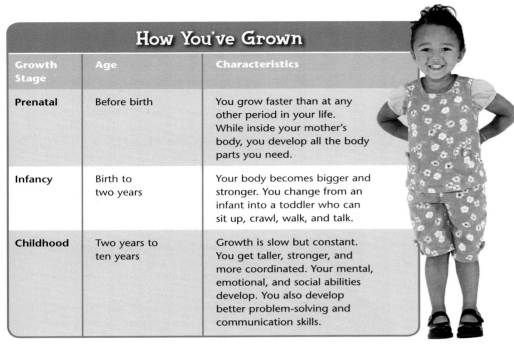

How You've Grown

Growth Stage	Age	Characteristics
Prenatal	Before birth	You grow faster than at any other period in your life. While inside your mother's body, you develop all the body parts you need.
Infancy	Birth to two years	Your body becomes bigger and stronger. You change from an infant into a toddler who can sit up, crawl, walk, and talk.
Childhood	Two years to ten years	Growth is slow but constant. You get taller, stronger, and more coordinated. Your mental, emotional, and social abilities develop. You also develop better problem-solving and communication skills.

▲ Every child grows at his or her own rate.

In time you began to think problems through and do things that you couldn't do before. Infancy prepared you for the next growth stage—childhood. During childhood, your body and mind developed even more. As you grew taller, stronger, and more coordinated, you were able to do things such as dance and twirl, play games and sports, and type on a computer keyboard.

Mental, emotional, and social changes also occurred during childhood. You learned to read. You discovered new interests and skills in a variety of areas. You learned to write and do math. These skills help you communicate with other people. Also during childhood, you began to develop friendships, and you became involved in many kinds of social activities.

MAIN IDEA AND DETAILS The growth stages on the chart above are three main ideas. List two details for each main idea.
Students should list appropriate characteristics of the prenatal stage, infancy, and childhood.

Information Alert!

Research on Human Growth As scientists develop new techniques for studying the human body, they learn more about changes that happen during each stage of growth.

GO ONLINE For the most up-to-date information, visit The Learning Site. www.harcourtschool.com/health

21

Cultural Connection

First Words Some of the first words that babies of English-speaking parents say are *Mama, Dada, no,* and other simple words. Have each student with a first language other than English write a list of common first words in that language. Have students share their lists with the class and then write the English equivalent of each word.

Social Studies

Baby Firsts Ask students to make a list of firsts in a baby's growth and development. For example, they might mention babies' speaking their first words, sitting up for the first time, smiling for the first time, beginning to crawl, taking their first steps, and getting their first teeth. Ask students to find out when they accomplished these exciting firsts. Have students compile the information in illustrated tables or time lines that reflect their growth and development.

2. TEACH

Content-Area Reading Support

Using Tables and Graphs Show students that a table like the one on this page is an easy way to organize information. Ask students what the next growth stage would be if they were to develop this table further. adolescence Encourage students to copy the table in their notebooks and add information to it as they read.

Interpret Visuals—Tables

Explain to students that a table contains data organized to help them find information quickly. Ask students to find the following information in the table:

In what growth stage does the body experience the most rapid growth? prenatal

What is the age span of infancy? birth to two years

Which growth stage is characterized by slow, constant growth? childhood

Discuss

Each of the first three stages of growth and development is marked by unique characteristics.

Problem Solving If you could use only one or two words to describe each of these stages of growth, what words would you use? Possible answers: prenatal—organ development; infancy—body growth; childhood—skill development

Growth, Development, and Reproduction Optional lessons about changes during puberty are provided in this supplement on pp. 16–25. Use this component in compliance with state and local guidelines.

TEACH *continued*

Discuss

Discuss some of the changes that occur during adolescence in addition to a physical growth spurt.

Critical Thinking **In what ways do you become more mature as you move through adolescence?** Answers will vary but should reflect specific skills and abilities.

Point out that as students go through adolescence, they will assume more responsibilities and will be given more privileges.

Critical Thinking **Why do parents link responsibilities with privileges?** When children demonstrate that they can handle greater responsibilities, they show that they can manage greater independence safely and responsibly. Parents are protective until they feel confidence in their children's decision-making abilities.

 Activity

Caring Student responses may include comments about reassuring the person that he or she is doing just fine in the activity, never teasing or making fun of the person's lack of coordination, remembering to include the person in activities, showing the person that you are glad to have him or her in your group, and treating the person normally.

ACTIVITY

Building Good Character

Caring A person who feels that he or she is too far ahead or too far behind in growth may feel awkward and shy in group activities. Name at least two things you could do to help such a person feel at ease in your group.

You Continue to Grow

Like the boy in the picture, you may have noticed that some of your clothes are suddenly too small. Your body is getting ready to enter the next and final growth spurt of your life. The period of rapid growth and development from about age ten to age nineteen is called *adolescence* (ad•uh•LES•uhnts). You enter this period as a child and leave it as an adult.

The physical changing a person experiences during adolescence is called **puberty** (PYOO•ber•tee). Puberty can begin in girls as young as eight years of age and in boys as young as ten years of age. However, everyone enters puberty at his or her own time. During puberty, hormones affect the body not only by increasing growth but also by causing the development of adult characteristics. Some of the changes in your body may seem unfamiliar and odd.

As a teenager, you will also experience mental, emotional, and social growth. Your ability to think and solve problems will increase. You will be better able to use logic and reasoning. Your feelings may become stronger than they were before. Relationships with other people will become more important.

Adolescence is not without its problems, though. You may experience many different *moods*, or general feelings. Your moods may change quickly from great excitement and happiness to anger and sadness.

◀ Physical changes aren't the only changes during adolescence. You'll develop skills to help you deal with the consequences of your actions. You'll also learn to make better decisions about what is right and wrong.

22

 **Meeting Individual Needs
Leveled Activities**

BELOW-LEVEL **Make Time Lines** Have each student make a time line of the growth stages he or she has gone through and will go through. Ask students to include three things that they did or hope to do during each stage.

ON-LEVEL **Puberty Rites** Have students choose a region of the world and research the puberty rites that are or were practiced there.

CHALLENGE **Prodigies** Provide students with a list of famous people who developed special abilities at a very young age, such as Wolfgang Mozart and Niels Bohr. Have each student research one of those prodigies and present a report to the class.

Sometimes, feelings during adolescence are affected by physical changes. When people change physically, they may compare themselves with others. They may think of themselves as too tall, too short, too thin, or too heavy—even if they aren't. Such people have an unrealistic body image of themselves. **Body image** is how you think your body looks. People who develop an unrealistic body image may also feel low in self-esteem. They may become shy or try to change their looks by dieting or changing their hair. Most teenagers overcome an unrealistic body image as they get older.

The physical, mental, and emotional changes you experience during adolescence help prepare you to be an adult. During adolescence you will learn to take on more responsibilities, and you will earn more privileges. Adolescence is sometimes called "coming of age." You grow up and become more independent.

MAIN IDEA AND DETAILS **Describe adolescence, and identify the three types of growth people experience during this stage.**
Adolescence is the period of rapid growth and development from about age ten to about age nineteen; physical, mental, and emotional growth.

▲ Some people don't like what they see in a mirror. Their ideals may be based on how movie and TV stars look.

Growth

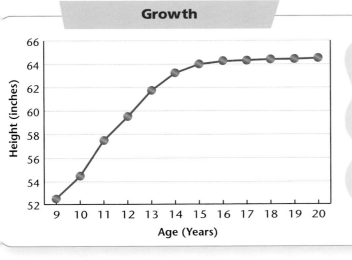

Height (inches) vs *Age (Years)*

23

Quick Activity

Graphing Growth
This graph shows the growth of one person during adolescence. Start a similar growth chart to track changes in your own growth. If you keep track on a monthly basis, you may be amazed at how quickly you grow.

Discuss
Talk about the mood fluctuations that can be expected during adolescence. Explain that the causes of these emotional swings are mostly physical and that emotional changes will be addressed further in the next lesson.

Critical Thinking **Why might a teenager's body image change along with his or her moods during adolescence?** Adolescents don't have a lot of experience to fall back on, and they are taking on challenges in unfamiliar areas, such as rapid changes in their bodies. Their levels of overall confidence may waver at times. When they are excited or happy, they will probably feel confident. If they are emotionally down, they may feel less confident.

Interpreting Visuals—Graphs
Direct attention to the graph on this page. Tell students that parents often keep a graph of a child's growth. By comparing the graph with a graph of averages, a parent can readily see that a child is developing normally.

During which age range do boys and girls begin to differ significantly in height and weight? Accept ranges that are near thirteen to fifteen. Girls' height and weight tend to level off during this period.

During which age range are boys and girls about the same in height? from age two to age eleven

---

Teacher Tip

Puberty Some students may be uncomfortable discussing puberty. Be sensitive to these feelings, and do not pressure those students to participate in class discussions. Be sure to establish an environment in which students feel comfortable discussing the topic without fear of ridicule or embarrassment.

Integrated Language Arts/ Reading Skills

Childhood Poems Select a variety of poems from *Where the Sidewalk Ends* by Shel Silverstein to read to the class. Allow time after each poem for students to jot down brief descriptions of personal experiences the poem brought to mind. After reading the selection of poems, ask volunteers to share their responses to the poetry. Ask students to write their own poems about strong feelings.

3. WRAP UP

Lesson 4 Summary and Review

1. prenatal, growth spurt, adolescence, puberty, body image

2. unfamiliar and odd changes in the body, mood changes, unrealistic body image, low self-esteem, shyness

3. The prenatal stage is a time of preparation for life outside the mother's body. In infancy, a person learns to walk and speak. Childhood is characterized by skill development. Adolescence is marked by mental, intellectual, emotional, and social growth.

4. Possible answers are shown.

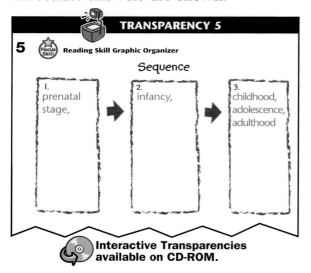

TRANSPARENCY 5

5 Reading Skill Graphic Organizer

Sequence

1. prenatal stage, → 2. infancy, → 3. childhood, adolescence, adulthood

Interactive Transparencies available on CD-ROM.

5. Both the prenatal stage and infancy are characterized by rapid growth. In both stages, the individual depends on its parents for survival. The main difference is that an infant lives outside its mother's body, begins to learn about the world, and develops physical abilities.

 For **writing models** with examples, see *Teaching Resources* pp. 47–61. Rubrics are also provided.

 When Minutes Count . . .

Quick Study Students can use *Activity Book* pp. 1–2 (shown on p. 5) as they complete each lesson in this chapter.

Becoming an Adult

Although you won't experience physical growth spurts after puberty, you will continue to grow emotionally, mentally, and socially. Entering adulthood, you'll probably continue your education, choose a career, and begin to support yourself financially. You'll develop close personal relationships. You may marry, have children, and take the responsibility of providing a healthful family environment.

As an older adult, you will change physically again. Some of your physical abilities will decline. However, you can help yourself stay healthy and active as an older adult by practicing good habits during all stages of your life. These habits include being physically active; eating healthful foods; getting plenty of rest; and avoiding alcohol, tobacco, and illegal drugs.

CAUSE AND EFFECT **What is the effect of practicing healthful habits during all stages of your life?**
It will help me remain healthy as I age.

▲ As you approach adulthood, you'll change less physically, but you'll "grow" in other ways.

Lesson 4 Summary and Review

❶ Summarize with Vocabulary

Use vocabulary and other terms from this lesson to complete these statements.

During the _____ stage, before birth, there is a(n) _____, or time of rapid growth. The stage after childhood is _____. You experience _____, the physical changing that makes you develop into an adult. Some people have a problem with changes in their appearance and develop an unrealistic _____.

❷ What kinds of problems do adolescents sometimes experience?

❸ Critical Thinking What are some ways a person becomes more independent at each life stage?

❹ SEQUENCE Draw and complete this graphic organizer to show the order of growth stages.

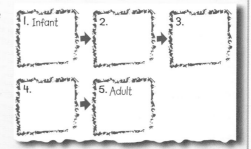

| 1. Infant | 2. | 3. |
| 4. | 5. Adult | |

❺ Write to Inform—Explanation

Write a paragraph that explains the similarities and differences between the prenatal stage and infancy.

24

Integrated Language Arts/ Reading Skills

Reading About Adolescence
Ask your school media specialist to share a sampling of the best children's books whose characters are entering adolescence. Many excellent nonfiction books provide valuable information and insights into this period. Fiction books paint a picture of adolescence through realistic, humorous, or serious stories that carry truths about this stage of life.

Trustworthiness

Building a Good Reputation

On the road to becoming an adult, there will be times when your character may be tested. For example, a test of your trustworthiness could be having the honesty to return something valuable that you have found. Making choices that show that you have good character can help you build a good reputation. Here are some tips for building a reputation of trustworthiness.

- **Have the courage to do what is right.**
- **Be honorable.**
- **Live by your principles, no matter what others say.**
- **Follow your conscience.**
- **Always tell the truth.**
- **Be sincere.**
- **Keep your promises.**
- **Be dependable.**
- **Return what you borrow.**
- **Be on time.**
- **Don't repeat gossip or say bad things about others.**

Activity

Make a character map about trust. Write the word *trust* in a circle at the center of a sheet of paper. In each corner of the paper, draw a large box connected to the circle by a line. During one day, take note of all the things you do that show that you can be trusted. Select four of those things, and describe them in the boxes of your map.

25

Using the Poster

Activity Divide the class into small groups. Have each group select one of the tips for building a reputation of trustworthiness and make a poster about that tip. Display the posters around the classroom.

Display Poster 6 to remind students of ways to show respect. The poster can be displayed in the classroom, the school cafeteria, the library, or another common area.

POSTER 6

Trustworthiness

The older girl is showing trustworthiness by taking good care of the children.

DO
- Be honest. Tell the truth.
- Do the right thing.
- Report dangerous situations.
- Be dependable.
- Be loyal to your family, friends, and country.
- Take care of things you borrow, and return them promptly.

DON'T
- Don't tell lies.
- Don't cheat.
- Don't steal.
- Don't break promises.
- Don't borrow without asking first.

How have **YOU** shown **TRUSTWORTHINESS** today?

POSTER 6

Building Good Character

Caring
Citizenship
Fairness
Respect
Responsibility
Trustworthiness

Objective
► Identify ways to build a good reputation by showing trustworthiness.

Program Resource
► Poster 6

BEFORE READING
Ask students to think about someone they trust. Ask what it is about that person that causes the student to trust him or her. What are the characteristics of someone who can be trusted? Write the characteristics students identify.

DISCUSS
After students have read the page, have them review the list on the board. Ask if they would add or delete any characteristics. Ask students to explain why each characteristic is important in building a good reputation for trustworthiness.

ACTIVITY
Some students may not wish to share their completed maps. Respect the privacy of those students.

Objectives
► Learn about the physical, mental, and emotional changes accompanying the growth spurt during puberty.
► Compare and contrast concrete thinking and abstract thinking.
► Explain problem-solving choices to handle problems of adolescence.

When Minutes Count . . .
Assign the Quick Study, Lesson 5, Activity Book pp. 1–2 (shown on p. 5).

Program Resources
► Activity Book pp. 1–2
► Transparency 5

Vocabulary
concrete thinking p. 27,
abstract thinking p. 27

Daily Fitness Tip

Suggest that students practice healthful ways to express their feelings. Have them talk with a parent or another trusted adult about how they are feeling. Then have them go out and get some exercise. Exercise is a great way to reduce stress.

 For more guidelines about exercise for stress relief, see *Be Active! Resources for Physical Education,* p. 157.

1. MOTIVATE

Ask students if they have ever had disagreements with younger brothers or sisters and whether it seemed there was just no way to reason with them. Allow one or two volunteers to relate stories. Inform students that young children can't see much beyond their own experiences and can't reason like adolescents.

When and how do we develop the ability to reason and solve problems? As a result of hormonal changes, brain development, and experiences, the ability to think and reason increases during adolescence.

Dealing with Adolescence

Lesson Focus
Physical, mental, and emotional changes accompany the growth spurt during puberty.

Why Learn This?
Knowing about the different kinds of changes during puberty will help you appreciate your own growth and development.

Vocabulary
concrete thinking
abstract thinking

Learning New Skills

It's easy to see how your growth spurt during puberty affects you physically. What isn't as easy to see is how it affects you mentally and emotionally.

During adolescence, new cells that are produced and the actions of hormones increase your ability to reason, solve problems, imagine, and invent. You add new thoughts, dreams, and opinions to what you already know. You may find that your interests change often. For the first time, you may become interested in different kinds of music, a team sport, or new hobbies.

Your new interests open doors to new friends, new activities, and new ideas. By following your interests, you add further to your abilities and knowledge. At this stage you are able to understand the value of practice in sports, schoolwork, and music. As your skills increase through practice, so does your self-confidence.

Quick Activity

Listing Interests Make a list of all the things you did for the first time this year. Include new hobbies, skills, and interests. Then list three new things you might like to try in the next year.

As you enter puberty, you'll notice your mental growth as you discover new ways to accomplish tasks.

26

Science

Studying the Teen Brain
Recent studies have found new evidence about how the teen brain differs from the brains of younger children and adults. Have students research this information and make a labeled drawing of the brain to summarize. A summary of the information can be found at the website of the Public Broadcasting System.

Teacher Tip

Practice Makes Perfect As students read this lesson about some of the problems they might encounter as they move through puberty, they may express worry. Tell them that often what happens to a person is less important in determining his or her sense of happiness than the person's attitude about what happens. Explain to students that practicing thinking positively can help them develop a healthful perspective and maintain greater emotional stability.

When you were younger, you were able to solve problems only by using things around you. For example, you could fit shapes together in a jigsaw puzzle, and you enjoyed sorting blocks by color and size. Solving problems involving real objects that you can see and touch is called **concrete thinking**.

Over the years, your thinking abilities have changed. You've learned ways to analyze and solve more complicated problems. Now you are able to use a more complex kind of thinking, called **abstract thinking**. With abstract thinking, you are able to imagine different solutions to problems.

Your thinking abilities will continue to develop as you enter puberty. You will become even better at identifying problems, thinking about possible solutions, and testing those solutions in your own mind. Using this abstract-thinking process, you will be able to handle even harder problems and learn to share your opinions and ideas with others.

COMPARE AND CONTRAST **How are your present thinking abilities similar to and different from those of a young child?**
Similar: Both of us are growing in our ability to think. Different: A young child uses only concrete thinking, but I can use both concrete and abstract thinking.

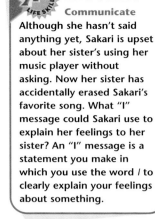

ACTIVITY

Life Skills

Communicate

Although she hasn't said anything yet, Sakari is upset about her sister's using her music player without asking. Now her sister has accidentally erased Sakari's favorite song. What "I" message could Sakari use to explain her feelings to her sister? An "I" message is a statement you make in which you use the word *I* to clearly explain your feelings about something.

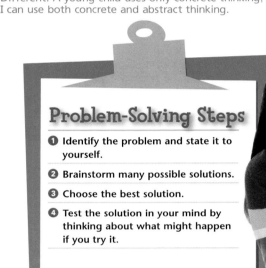

Problem-Solving Steps

❶ Identify the problem and state it to yourself.

❷ Brainstorm many possible solutions.

❸ Choose the best solution.

❹ Test the solution in your mind by thinking about what might happen if you try it.

◀ When you are faced with a problem, you may discover that it has more than one solution and that a solution can be reached in more than one way.

27

Meeting Individual Needs
Leveled Activities

BELOW-LEVEL **Make Art** Have students work in pairs to make posters entitled "Decisions for Life." Have students use pairs of photos found in newspapers, magazines, or other print media. Each pair of pictures should depict alternatives, such as an alcoholic beverage and a glass of milk. Display the posters in class.

ON-LEVEL **Plan a Trip** Have students plan an imaginary one-month vacation to a place of their choice. Have them make a packing list that includes everything they need but will keep the total weight of their baggage under 20 pounds.

CHALLENGE **Write a Book** Have students write books geared to parents of fifth graders about what it is like to be their age. Ask them to address issues all fifth graders face. Encourage them to show their books to their families.

---

2. TEACH

Interpret Visuals—Pictures
Direct attention to the illustration of the student thinking about a problem.

Might the student have more than one idea about how to solve the problem? yes **What makes you think so?** The thought bubbles indicate two different ideas. Perhaps the student is thinking about calculating an answer or going to the lab and experimenting.

Discuss
Have students assess the role of assertiveness on problem solving. Certain skills or concepts require different kinds of thinking—concrete or abstract. Write the following words on the board: *classification, love, ordering, justice, sequencing, prejudice.*

Critical Thinking **Which of these concepts require concrete thinking, and which require abstract thinking?** concrete: classification, ordering, sequencing; abstract: love, justice, prejudice

Quick Activity
Listing Interests To help students who seem stuck for ideas, make this a class brainstorming activity. Write students' contributions on the board or an overhead in two columns, headed *New Skills* and *Next Year*. Children at this age often develop at different rates, and the whole-class participation prevents singling out a child who has less to contribute.

Activity
Make Decisions As students test the long-term effects of Sakari's decision, encourage them to include such concerns as how long it takes Sakari to save $20.00, how often she thinks she would skate if she had skates, and how much she would wear the shirt. Then have them assess the role of assertiveness on decision making.

TEACH *continued*

Discuss

Talk with students about the types of decisions they may have to make as they move toward adulthood. Have them brainstorm decisions that vary in complexity, such as how to dress or wear their hair (minor), whether to smoke (critical), or whether to marry (major). List their responses on the board. Students should be able to sort the list into three categories: minor, major, and critical.

Critical Thinking **Who or what could help you make these decisions?** Possible answers include parents, teachers, clergy, trusted adults, or books that are recommended by parents or other trusted adults. (The Internet should not be a trusted source for advice on major or critical issues without parental guidance.)

For each idea listed on the board, discuss possible outcomes or consequences. For example, clothing choices could invite critical comments about appearance or could bring compliments. The decision to marry is a choice that could bring a life of happiness or could be troublesome. Smoking is a choice that would be devastating to health, even if it seems "cool" at the moment.

Can consequences of decisions always be predicted? no Remind students that even when they make the best decisions they can, the consequences can be different from what they expect. For example, they may think smoking is "cool" now, but they will painfully regret the decision as an adult.

Personal Health Plan ▶

Students' plans should use the problem-solving steps to envision a better outcome for decisions that have had unsatisfactory results in the past.

Personal Health Plan ▶

Real-Life Situation
Think of some decisions you made in the past year. Consider how you made each one and if you were satisfied with the results.
Real-Life Plan
Choose one decision that didn't turn out well. Identify some ways to improve the way you make similar decisions in the future.

Handling Feelings and Problems

The road to maturity is exciting, but at times it can be scary. As you grow up, you will have feelings and experiences you've never had before. You will also have important decisions to make and new problems to solve.

At this time of your life, you may be dealing with some personal problems. You may question who your friends are and what kinds of friends you want to have. You may want more independence from your family. New responsibilities may challenge you. Solving personal problems can require a great deal of effort and attention.

During adolescence you will learn how to reason through problems. You will learn that you have many options and that your choices bring both responsibilities and consequences. You will learn to make decisions after carefully weighing several possible outcomes.

As you travel toward adulthood, you will come across many challenges. Some will be like obstacles to get over or around. Other challenges will be rewarding and will be proof of your progress.

Teacher Tip

Setting Goals Help students set and work toward goals. Work with them to make a list of new things they want to try. Write this list on the board and label it *Goals*. As a class, choose one goal from the list and develop a plan to reach it. Then divide the class into pairs, and assign each pair one or two ideas from the list. Have each pair come up with a plan for reaching its goals. Ask students to use a separate sheet of paper for each plan.

Art

Comic Relief Invite students to make short comic strips depicting the complex emotions or moods experienced by adolescents. Each comic strip could reflect one emotion or an entire range of emotions. It could show an internal struggle or a struggle with another person. Although the comic strips can be created with or without words, the emotions depicted should be evident. Have students compile their comic strips to resemble a comics section of a newspaper.

Adolescence is also a time when many people develop strong emotions and opinions. You may have mood swings, in which your mood changes often and quickly. You may feel happy one moment and sad the next, and your feelings may be stronger than ever before. As you learn to manage your emotional changes, you will need time to be alone with your thoughts. Talking about your feelings and problems with a parent or other trusted adult can also be helpful.

DRAW CONCLUSIONS Which events will likely be problems to overcome on your way to adulthood?
Possible answers: mood swings, body changes, strong opinions.

Lesson 5 Summary and Review

❶ Summarize with Vocabulary

Use vocabulary and other terms from this lesson to complete the statements.

When you were younger, you used _____ thinking to solve problems involving real objects you could see and touch. Now you also can use _____ thinking, which helps you see many options during decision making. During adolescence you may experience _____, in which your moods change often and quickly.

❷ Critical Thinking Do you use concrete thinking or abstract thinking when you decide whether to wear a coat to school?

❸ How can the road to adulthood be both difficult and rewarding?

❹ SEQUENCE Draw and complete this graphic organizer to show how to apply the steps for solving a problem.

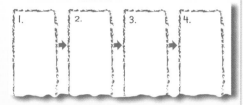

❺ Write to Entertain—Short Story

Write a short story titled "A Day in the Life of a Teenager." In your story, describe how your main character learns to handle a problem.

29

Integrated Language Arts/ Reading Skills

Teen Problems Have students look through magazines and newspapers for articles about adolescents' problems or their solutions. Some topics they might consider are teen crime, teen pregnancies, teen drug use, teens helping the community, or teen clubs. Ask each student to write a brief summary of an article and to share the information with the class.

Art

Greeting Cards Have students design and write greeting cards for friends who are experiencing adolescence. Cards can be humorous or serious but should address at least two of the common feelings and problems of adolescence.

3. WRAP UP

Lesson 5 Summary and Review

1. concrete thinking, abstract thinking, puberty

2. abstract

3. The results of decisions made along the way are sometimes unpredictable, and decisions must be reevaluated. Growth into adulthood is often accompanied by new situations, feelings, and choices. But growth is also accompanied by new ways of thinking, maturity, and skills for making good decisions.

4. Possible answers are shown.

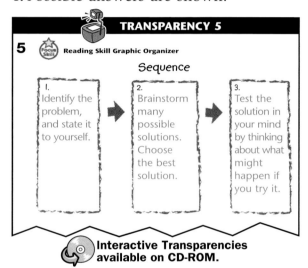

5. These stories will vary, but each of them should present a problem, show how the problem-solving steps were used to handle it, and conclude with the results of the decision.

 For **writing models** with examples, see *Teaching Resources* pp. 47–61. Rubrics are also provided.

 When Minutes Count ...

Quick Study Students can use *Activity Book* pp. 1–2 (shown on p. 5) as they complete each lesson in this chapter.

Life Skills

Communicate
Make Responsible Decisions
Manage Stress
Refuse
Resolve Conflicts
Set Goals

Objectives
► Identify the steps for conflict resolution.
► Use the steps to resolve a conflict.

Program Resources
► Activity Book p. 9
► Poster 11

1. MOTIVATE

Ask students to recall silently a recent time when they wanted more independence than adults would give them. Have volunteers relate in general terms how their conflicts were resolved. (Keep the discussion away from personal family information.) Was the resolution a compromise?

2. TEACH

Direct attention to the photos of Cody and his mother talking. Have students analyze respectful ways to communicate with family.

Step 1
How can Cody express how he feels so his mother will listen? Cody should state his feelings in "I" messages.

Step 2
Have students utilize critical thinking in problem solving.
How can Cody understand why his mother made the school-night rule? by listening to what his mother says

Critical Thinking Why is listening to another person's point of view important? Besides understanding his or her point of view, it is fair to listen if you expect to be heard.

Resolve Conflicts
with Your Family About Becoming Independent

During adolescence you will start to make decisions for yourself. Some of your decisions may cause conflicts with parents because they are still responsible for your well-being. Using the steps for **Resolving Conflicts** can help you work out disagreements.

Cody's friends plan to go to a movie on a school night. Cody wants to go, too. His mother reminds him that school nights are for homework. What should Cody do?

1 Use "I" messages to tell how you feel.

> Mom, I want to go out to a movie tonight.

> Not tonight, Cody. It's a school night.

Cody knows that school nights are supposed to be for studying, but he wants to join his friends.

2 Listen to the other person. Consider that person's point of view.

> But Mom, all of my friends are going!

> You need to do your homework.

Cody and his mom listen to each other. Cody considers his mother's view and understands her rules.

30

Teacher Tip

Privacy It is important to remember that some students may come from environments in which conflicts are not negotiated. In some students' homes negotiation is not allowed. Offer examples of situations in which the steps for resolving conflicts can be applied safely in students' daily lives. Use a sensitive approach when asking the class to relate examples of conflict. Avoid asking students to provide private family information or information that makes them uncomfortable.

ACTIVITY BOOK P. 9

Name _____

🔍 Problem Solving

Life Skill
Communicate

Steps for Communicating
1. Understand your audience.
2. Give a clear message. Use a respectful tone of voice.
3. Listen carefully and answer any questions.
4. Gather feedback.

Help Denzel and Marta use the steps for communicating.

A. The boys in Denzel's class have volunteered to make 100 sandwiches for a local shelter. Denzel's job is to see that the sandwiches are made and wrapped for delivery. Before work begins, Denzel must make sure the boys' hands and fingernails are clean.
• How can Denzel get his classmates to cooperate about washing their hands?
  Possible answer: Denzel can explain that germs can be passed from
  one person to another by unwashed hands. He can make sure there are
  soap, nail brushes, and towels and a proper place for everyone to
  wash up.

B. Marta and her friends Ellen and Callen are shopping for sunscreen, and they are having a difficult time making a choice. Ellen wants to buy the brand her favorite TV actress advertises. Callen wants the cheapest brand, and Marta wants a sunscreen with an SPF of at least 30.
• How can Marta help her friends make a responsible selection?
  Possible answer: First, she should explain that the most important
  thing the product must do is protect the girls' skin from ultraviolet rays.
  Marta can suggest that they compare prices and ingredients of three
  brands. Then they can add other criteria to use as they make their
  comparisons.

Available online.
www.harcourtschool.com/health

3 Negotiate.

Let's see how well you do it.

If I do my homework, may I go?

Cody offers a solution to satisfy both of them. His mother agrees but has a condition that must be met.

4 Find a way for both sides to win.

You did a nice job! You may go to the movie.

Cody does his homework—he knows his grades depend on it. His mother knows she has done what is best for Cody. And Cody gets to go to the movie.

💡 Problem Solving

A. Rashawn's father has told Rashawn to mow the lawn on Friday afternoon. At school on Friday, Rashawn learns that all his friends are getting together that afternoon for a basketball game. He wants to play, too, but he knows his father expects the lawn to be mowed.
   • Use the steps for **Resolving Conflicts** to help Rashawn handle the situation.

B. Courtney has promised friends they can come to her house on Saturday to watch a movie. However, she knows her sister wants to watch her favorite TV program at the same time.
   • How could Courtney handle the conflict in a caring way?

31

Using the Poster

Activity Have students role-play situations in which they can practice conflict resolution.

Display the poster to remind students of the steps for resolving conflicts.

POSTER 11

🏃 **Resolve Conflicts**

The girls are resolving a conflict by negotiating politely.

Steps to Resolve Conflicts

1. Use I-messages to tell how you feel.
2. Listen to each other. Consider the other person's view.
3. Negotiate.
4. Find a way for both sides to win.

How do YOU RESOLVE CONFLICTS?
POSTER 11

Step 3

What important step in conflict resolution has Cody taken? He has made an offer that might satisfy both of them. He is negotiating.

What other response could Cody's mother have made? She could have stood by the family rule and refused to negotiate. However, Cody's willingness to negotiate influenced her to trust Cody to do what he said he would do.

Step 4

What is the final outcome of Cody's applying the steps of conflict resolution in this case? Everyone is satisfied. Cody gets to go to the movie, he has done his homework, and Cody's mother is pleased that Cody listened to her and understands the rule.

 Building Good Character
Remind students that when making any decision, they should consider how the decision shows good character. Cody could ask himself, "Am I being trustworthy and responsible? Am I showing consideration for others? Am I being respectful?"

3. WRAP UP

Problem Solving

A Rashawn should tell how he feels, using "I" messages, and then listen to his father. Rashawn could offer to do the mowing on Saturday morning and include trimming along the sidewalks.

B Courtney should have checked with her sister before she made the promise to her friends. Now she must listen while her sister tells her how she feels about Courtney's plans. Courtney could offer to do one or more of her sister's chores if she will let her and her friends watch a movie. She could also invite her sister to join them.

Objectives
► Explain how exercise and good nutrition help growing bodies.
► Describe how sleep, rest, and hygiene can affect growth.

When Minutes Count . . .
Assign the Quick Study, Lesson 6, Activity Book pp. 1–2 (shown on p. 5).

Program Resources
► Activity Book pp. 1–2, 5
► Transparency 5

Vocabulary
hygiene p. 34

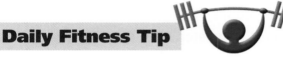

Daily Fitness Tip

Tell students that when participating in organized sports or playing with friends, they should take time to warm up properly. Warming up can improve performance and help prevent injury.

 For more guidelines about reducing exercise hazards, see *Be Active! Resources for Physical Education,* p. 191.

1. MOTIVATE

Write the following on the board:

"Everything's a circle. We're each responsible for our own actions. It will come back."

—Betty Laverdure (Ojibway), *Wisdom's Daughters* by Steve Wall, Harper Collins, 1993

Why do you think a circle was used by this Native American author to describe the course of our actions? A circle is formed by beginning at one point and returning to that same point. Everything we do comes back to affect us in some way. Knowing this, we have to assume responsibility for what we do.

How might this apply to health? Any habits we form, good or bad, affect our health.

Lesson Focus
Healthful choices about physical activity, diet, rest, and hygiene can make puberty a positive time of growth and development.

Why Learn This?
Information about healthful choices can help you develop a program for taking care of your body.

Vocabulary
hygiene

Personal Health Plan ►

Real-Life Situation
You're having trouble sleeping because you're worried about a test.
Real-Life Plan
Make a list of things you can do to stop your worrying about the test.

Exercise and Proper Diet Help Your Body Grow

Your body needs special care as it goes through the changes of puberty. Being physically active and eating properly are two important ways to support your growing body.

You probably know that exercise is good for you physically. People who exercise regularly increase their endurance, strength, and flexibility, and they are likely to sleep better. However, you may not know that physical activity is also good for you mentally and emotionally. Exercise helps you feel more confident and enables you to focus better, such as when doing schoolwork. Exercise also reduces emotional stress so

Physical activity is more fun when you work out with a friend and vary the kinds of activities you do. ►

32

Teacher Tip

Physical Activity Students often think that the only way to get the physical activity they need is to participate in organized sports. Help students prepare a list of as many physical activities as possible that contribute to overall health. Be sure to include activities such as riding a bike, mowing the lawn, dancing, snow shoveling, and similar activities. Help students recognize that they can get the physical activity they need through a variety of activities.

Math

Calculate Calories If playing tennis burns 0.049 calories per pound for each minute played, how many calories would a person who weighs 100 pounds burn while playing tennis for one hour? (0.049 C $\times$ 100 lbs $\times$ 60 min = 294 calories)

▲ Eating different types of foods, such as grains, fruits, meats, and vegetables, is the best way to get the nutrients you need. You will learn more about foods in Chapter 3.

that you are better able to solve any problems you might have. You will learn more about the benefits of exercise in Chapter 4.

Eating a healthful diet will supply you with energy and provide you with nutrients to help you grow. The food you eat affects how you look and feel, how well you resist diseases, and how well you perform mentally and physically. Since foods differ in the nutrients they provide, it's important to have variety in your diet. The photograph above shows many healthful food choices.

The amount of food you eat should match your body's needs. Eating too much food and getting too little exercise can make you gain weight. Eating too little food will make you become tired and too thin. Both extremes put your growth and health at risk. By choosing to eat healthfully and to exercise, you show that you are growing up and taking responsibility for yourself.

CAUSE AND EFFECT **What can cause a person to gain weight?**
eating too much food and getting too little exercise

Consumer Activity

Access Valid Health Information Packaged foods have labels that tell you what the foods are made of and what nutrients they provide. Read the labels of any packaged foods that make up your next few meals. Compare the nutrients they offer.

33

2. TEACH

Discuss
Recall with students the benefits of exercise. Explain that when they decide to make an exercise plan, they should select activities that best fit their needs and interests.

Problem Solving **What questions might you ask yourself when considering an exercise plan?** Students should consider what they enjoy doing, what their interests are, how much time they have to exercise, how much time a particular activity requires, how convenient the activity is, whether equipment or participation by others is required, and what setting and amount of space are required. They also should differentiate between health-related and skill-related activities.

Personal Health Plan ▶

Have students analyze the components of a personal health plan for individuals, such as stress management. Students should write this as number one on the list: The best way to prevent worrying about a test is to be prepared for the test—that is, to pay attention in class, do the assignments, and study. Students' lists should also include getting plenty of rest and sleep, eating nutritious food, and getting lots of exercise.

Consumer Activity
Access Valid Health Information
Ask students to examine the nutrition label instead of the ingredients list, which would probably be confusing because of difficult chemical names. Ask them to compare calories with total grams of fat. Grams of fiber are important, as is vitamin and mineral content.

3. WRAP UP

Lesson 6 Summary and Review

1. choices, exercise, diet, rest, hygiene
2. Exercise helps you feel more confident, enables you to focus better, reduces emotional stress, increases strength and flexibility, and helps you sleep better.
3. have a healthful snack and take a nap, or rest
4. Possible answers are shown.

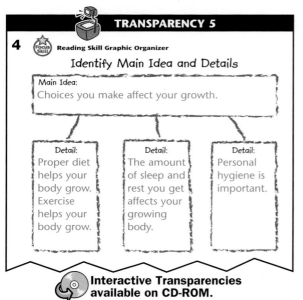

TRANSPARENCY 5

4 Reading Skill Graphic Organizer

Identify Main Idea and Details

Main Idea:
Choices you make affect your growth.

Detail:
Proper diet helps your body grow. Exercise helps your body grow.

Detail:
The amount of sleep and rest you get affects your growing body.

Detail:
Personal hygiene is important.

Interactive Transparencies available on CD-ROM.

5. Sleep is important to your growth and health. When you sleep, your body has time to recover from its daytime activities. It repairs tissues and releases built-up stress. Much of your body's growth takes place while you sleep.

For **writing models** with examples, see *Teaching Resources* pp. 47–61. Rubrics are also provided.

When Minutes Count . . .

Quick Study Students can use *Activity Book* pp. 1–2 (shown on p. 5) as they complete each lesson in this chapter.

Myth and Fact

Myth: If you eat a spicy food, such as pizza, at bedtime, you will have nightmares.

Fact: The only thing spicy foods may do when you eat them at bedtime is to keep you awake. That's because you will feel too full to fall asleep.

Other Choices Affect Your Growing Body

Sleep, too, is important to your growth and health. When you sleep, your body has time to recover from its daytime activities. It repairs tissues and releases built-up stress. Much of your body's growth takes place while you sleep.

Taking care of your body also includes making choices about personal <u>hygiene</u> (HY•jeen), or cleanliness. As your body changes, perspiration odors and skin problems can make hygiene important. Develop a daily routine you can follow before leaving for school in the morning or before going to bed. You will learn more about the importance of good hygiene in Chapter 2.

MAIN IDEA AND DETAILS Give details to support this statement: Exercise, diet, rest, and sleep affect your growing body.

Answers should include at least one detail for each factor.

Resting during the day has many of the same benefits as sleeping at night. Find various ways to rest during the day. ▶

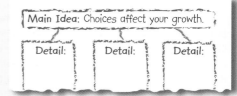

Lesson 6 Summary and Review

❶ Summarize with Vocabulary
Use vocabulary and other terms from this lesson to complete the statements.

Many _____ you make can affect your growth. _____ reduces stress. Eating a healthful _____ supplies you with energy. Sleep and other kinds of _____ allow your body to recover. Practicing good _____ helps prevent body odor.

❷ What are five benefits of exercise?

❸ Critical Thinking If you feel tired after school and have only half an hour before soccer practice, what two things might you do to help restore your energy?

❹ MAIN IDEA AND DETAILS
Draw and complete this graphic organizer to show the supporting details in this lesson.

Main Idea: Choices affect your growth.

Detail: Detail: Detail:

❺ Write to Inform—Explanation
Write a paragraph that explains the importance of sleep for a teenager.

34

ACTIVITY BOOK P. 5

Name _____

Vocabulary Reinforcement

Use Word Meanings

A. Underline the word in parentheses that will make the statement correct.
1. The basic unit of structure of all living things is the (organ, <u>cell</u>).
2. Cells that look alike and work together make up a (<u>tissue</u>, system).
3. At the ends of the smallest air tube branches in the lungs are (capillaries, <u>alveoli</u>).
4. As blood passes through the kidneys, (<u>nephrons</u>, neurons) filter wastes from it.
5. Two or more bones fit together at a (<u>joint</u>, ligament).

B. Complete the puzzle.

Clues

Across
1. Passing of traits from parents to children
3. Personal cleanliness
5. Chemical messengers
6. The way you think you look
7. Before birth
8. A kind of thinking based on real things
9. Period of rapid development
10. Bands that attach muscles to bones

Down
2. Everything around you
4. An automatic nerve response
7. The period of change to adolescence

Available online.
www.harcourtschool.com/health

Science

Sleep Some parts of the body are more active when a person is asleep than when he or she is awake. Have students research what happens in the body during sleep. Tell them to find out why sleep is necessary and what happens in the body when a person doesn't get enough sleep. Ask students to share what they learn with the class.

ACTIVITIES

Physical Education

Perform a Song Select a song you like that has a strong beat. You can use the song's tune, but write your own lyrics about any or all of the body systems. Or, make up lyrics to go with your own tune. Perform your song as you exercise, skip rope, or bounce a basketball in time with the song's beat.

Science

Research Heredity Do research on heredity. What are some physical characteristics that children inherit from their parents? Can a child have characteristics that grandparents have but parents do not have? Describe your findings in a booklet, and place it in the class library.

Technology Project

With a computer, make a slide presentation about the main parts and the jobs of each body transport system. Present your slides to your family or classmates.

 For more activities, visit The Learning Site.
www.harcourtschool.com/health

Home & Community

Communicating Make a poster encouraging teenagers who are having problems to talk with a parent or another trusted adult. Display your poster in your classroom or cafeteria.

Career Link

Endocrinologist Endocrinologists are doctors who specialize in the endocrine system. Suppose you are an endocrinologist. What might you say to an eleven-year-old boy who complains that he has not yet gone through puberty? Write your response in a paragraph.

Career Link

Endocrinologist Student answers will vary but should mention that everyone enters puberty in his or her own time. They should assure the eleven-year-old that he has plenty of time to reach puberty. Tell students to back up their response with information that they learned in this lesson.

 For more information on health careers, visit the **Webliography** in Teacher Resources at **www.harcourtschool.com/health Keyword** health careers

Activities

Physical Education

Perform a Song Encourage students to begin by clapping a rhythm while they chant the words they have made up. Then they can add a simple tune of their own if they have difficulty selecting a tune they have heard before.

Science

Research Heredity Students will probably list common characteristics, such as eye color and hair color, and some may cite examples from their own families. However, reinforce the idea that this research is not personal family genealogy. Students should find out that a person can have his or her grandparents' characteristics even if the parents do not.

Home & Community

Communicating Students should incorporate the steps for resolving conflicts in their posters and use drawings or pictures they cut from magazines. When the study of this topic is complete, have students take their posters home to show their families.

 Supports the Coordinated School Health Program

Technology Project

Students can use presentation software for this project. If students do not have access to a computer, you might suggest using colored markers and construction paper or poster board to make "slides."

Chapter Review and Test Preparation

Pages 36–37

 Reading Focus 5 pts. each

1. heart
2. capillaries

 Use Vocabulary 3 pts. each

3. F, systems
4. H, tissues
5. G, tendons
6. D, ligaments
7. C, heredity
8. E, puberty
9. B, concrete thinking
10. A, abstract thinking

 Check Understanding 3 pts. each

11. A, alveoli
12. G, nephrons
13. C, joints
14. J, neurons
15. B, environment
16. F, (picture of gland)
17. A, adolescence
18. H, body image
19. C, rest
20. G, hygiene

 Think Critically 5 pts. each

21. Food nutrition labels contain information about the nutrients, fiber, and fat in the food.
22. digestion

 Reading Skill

SEQUENCE
Draw and then use this graphic organizer to answer questions 1 and 2.

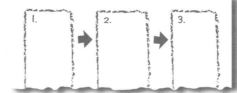

1 Which organ of the circulatory system pumps blood to the rest of the body?
2 Which blood vessels allow oxygen and nutrients to pass through their walls?

 Use Vocabulary

Match each term in Column B with its meaning in Column A.

Column A	Column B
3 Groups of organs	**A** abstract thinking
4 Groups of similar cells	**B** concrete thinking
5 Bands that connect bones at joints	**C** heredity
6 Bands that attach muscles to bones	**D** ligaments
7 Passing of traits from parents to children	**E** puberty
8 The physical changes during adolescence	**F** systems
9 Solving problems by using real objects	**G** tendons
10 Solving problems by imagining solutions	**H** tissues

36

Check Understanding

Choose the letter of the correct answer.

11 What are tiny air sacs in the lungs called? (p. 7)
   A alveoli   C nephrons
   B capillaries   D blood vessels

12 Blood passes through tiny filters in the kidneys, called _____. (p. 9)
   F neurons   H capillaries
   G nephrons   J glands

13 Places where two or more bones meet are called _____. (p. 10)
   A ligaments
   B tendons
   C joints
   D cartilage

14 What is another name for nerve cells? (p. 12)
   F nephrons   H alveoli
   G systems   J neurons

15 All the things that surround you every day make up your _____. (p. 15)
   A systems   C hormones
   B environment   D heredity

16 Hormones are produced by _____ in the endocrine system. (p. 16)

F   H

G   J

Formal Assessment

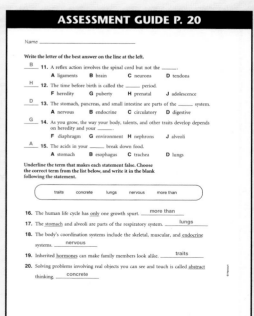

Growth Spurts
- prenatal stage
- infancy

17 Which growth stage is missing from the graphic organizer? (p. 21)
  A adolescence
  B puberty
  C independence
  D adulthood

18 Your _____ is the way you think your body looks. (p. 23)
  F puberty   **H** body image
  G adolescence **J** privilege

19 Sleep and other kinds of _____ allow your body to recover from the day's activities. (p. 34)
  A nutrition
  B exercise
  C rest
  D hygiene

20 Cleanliness, or _____, involves cleaning your whole body. (p. 34)
  F puberty   **H** perspiration
  G hygiene   **J** relaxation

Think Critically

21 How could the food label below be helpful in choosing healthful foods?

22 If you had a problem with your esophagus, which body function would likely be affected?

Apply Skills

23 **BUILDING GOOD CHARACTER**
Trustworthiness You promised to meet a friend to go jogging after school. When you get home, you become interested in a TV show that won't end until after you are supposed to meet your friend. Use what you know about being trustworthy to make a decision about what you should do.

24 **LIFE SKILLS**
Resolve Conflicts You and your father disagree about whether you should get an expensive pair of basketball shoes for the upcoming season. He thinks you will grow out of the shoes too quickly. Use what you know about resolving conflicts to work out a fair agreement with your father.

Write About Health

25 Write to Inform—Explanation Explain why you might expect to face new problems during adolescence.

37

Apply Skills 8 pts. each

23. Student answers will vary but should include meeting the friend on time and should be justified by these elements of trustworthiness: being dependable, keeping promises, and being on time. Possible answers: Videotape the TV show and meet the friend on time. Meet the friend on time, and ask someone who watched the show how it came out. Telephone the friend if possible, and ask if it would be all right to meet a little later, but if the friend can't be reached, meet the friend on time.

24. Student answers will vary but should contain the elements of conflict resolution, as in the following: Use "I" messages to tell your father how you feel. Listen to your father and consider his point of view. He knows you will be growing. Ask him if he will negotiate with you. Offer to pay for part of the cost with your allowance or offer to do extra chores. This is a solution that might work for both of you.

Write About Health 10 pts.

25. Student answers will vary but should contain elements of the following: Adolescence is a time of rapid growth and change. The changes and growth involve the body and the mind. There will be mood swings, strange new circumstances to face, and decisions to be made. New circumstances, new abilities, and new responsibilities can all present conflict and confusion.

Performance Assessment

Use the Chapter Project and the rubric provided on the Project Evaluation Sheet. See *Assessment Guide,* pp. 18, 56, 62.

Portfolio Assessment

Have students select their best work from the following suggestions:
- Leveled Activities, p. 15
- Quick Activity, p. 27
- Write to Inform, p. 24
- Activities, p. 35

See *Assessment Guide* pp. 12–16.

Lesson	Pacing	Objectives	Reading Skills
Introduce the Chapter pp. 38–39		• Preview chapter concepts.	**Draw Conclusions** p. 39; pp. 372–383
1 Healthy Skin, Hair, and Nails pp. 40–46	1 class period	• Explain why it's important to keep your skin, hair, and nails healthy. • Explain how changes in hormone levels can affect personal health habits.	**Draw Conclusions** pp. 40, 46 • Cause and Effect, p. 41, 45 • Summarize, p. 42 • Main Idea and Details, p. 43 • Sequence, p. 46
★ **Building Good Character** p. 47		• Identify ways to develop self-confidence.	
2 Healthy Teeth and Gums pp. 48–51	1 class period	• Identify the structure and function of teeth. • Explain how to keep teeth and gums healthy. • Identify dental problems.	**Draw Conclusions** pp. 48, 51 • Sequence, p. 49 • Cause and Effect, p. 50 • Compare and Contrast, p. 51
3 Care of Your Eyes and Ears pp. 52–57	1 class period	• Identify parts of the eye and the ear and explain how the parts of each function. • Describe how to take good care of your eyes and ears.	**Draw Conclusions** pp. 52, 57 • Cause and Effect, p. 53 • Summarize, p. 54 • Sequence, p. 55
Life Skills pp. 58–59	1 class period	• Identify steps to communicate. • Use the communicating steps to solve problems.	
4 Being a Health Consumer pp. 60–66	1 class period	• Explain the importance of choosing health-care products wisely. • Identify and evaluate sources of health information. • Demonstrate how to use labels to make wise product choices.	**Draw Conclusions** pp. 61, 66 • Summarize, pp. 63, 66 • Main Idea and Details, p. 65
Activities p. 67		• Extend chapter concepts.	
Chapter Review pp. 68–69	1 class period	• Assess chapter objectives.	

Vocabulary	Program Resources
	Music CD Teaching Resources, p. 25
ultraviolet rays SPF hair follicle oil gland	Transparencies 2, 15 Activity Book, pp. 6–7, 8
	Poster 4
plaque gingivitis orthodontia	Transparencies 2, 16 Activity Book, pp. 6–7
farsighted nearsighted astigmatism decibels	Transparencies 2, 17, 18 Activity Book, pp. 6–7
	Activity Book, p. 9 Poster 7
health consumer ingredients	Transparency 2 Activity Book, pp. 6–7
	The Learning Site www. harcourtschool.com/health
	Assessment Guide, pp. 22–24

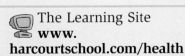 **Interactive Transparencies** available on CD-ROM.

 Focus Skill

Reading Skill

These reading skills are reinforced throughout this chapter and one skill is emphasized as the Focus Skill.

Draw Conclusions

- Compare and Contrast
- Identify Cause and Effect
- Identify Main Idea and Details
- Sequence
- Summarize

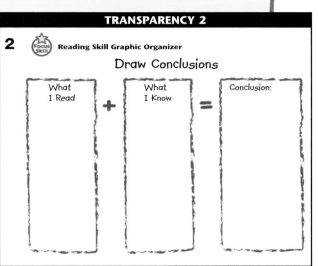

TRANSPARENCY 2

2 Focus Skill **Reading Skill Graphic Organizer**

Draw Conclusions

What I Read + What I Know = Conclusion:

Life Skills

Life Skills are health-enhancing behaviors that can help students reduce risks to their health and safety.

Six Life Skills are reinforced throughout *Harcourt Health and Fitness*. The skill emphasized in this chapter is Communicate.

POSTER 7

Communicate

The boy is communicating with his parents.

Steps for Communicating

1 Understand your audience.
2 Express your message in a clear, organized way.
3 Listen carefully, and answer any questions.
4 Gather feedback.

How well have **YOU COMMUNICATED** today?

POSTER 7

Building Good Character

Character education is an important aspect of health education. When students behave in ways that show good character, they promote the health and safety of themselves and others.

Six character traits are reinforced throughout *Harcourt Health and Fitness*. The trait emphasized in this chapter is Respect.

POSTER 4

Respect

The children are showing respect by sharing their different interests.

DO

- Treat others the way you want to be treated.
- Accept people who are different from you.
- Be polite and use good manners.
- Be considerate of the feelings of others.
- Stay calm when you are angry.
- Develop self-respect and self-confidence.

DON'T

- Don't use bad language.
- Don't insult or embarrass anyone.
- Don't threaten or bully anyone.
- Don't hit or hurt anyone.

How have **YOU** shown **RESPECT** today?

POSTER 4

Resources

Coordinated School Health Program

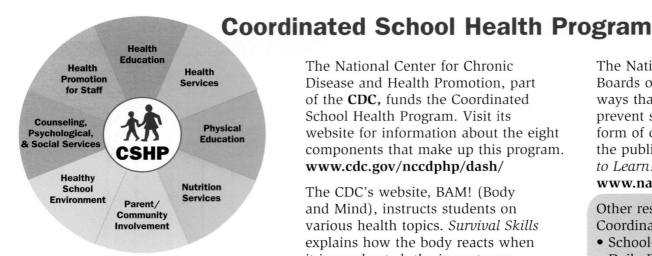

A Coordinated School Health Program endeavors to improve children's health and, therefore, their capacity to learn through the support of families, schools, and communities working together. The following information is provided to help classroom teachers be more aware of these resources.

The National Center for Chronic Disease and Health Promotion, part of the **CDC,** funds the Coordinated School Health Program. Visit its website for information about the eight components that make up this program. **www.cdc.gov/nccdphp/dash/**

The CDC's website, BAM! (Body and Mind), instructs students on various health topics. *Survival Skills* explains how the body reacts when it is overheated; the importance of sunscreen, sunglasses, and skin protection; and similar topics. **www.bam.gov/**

The National Association of State Boards of Education (**NASBE**) explains ways that schools can help children prevent skin cancer, the most common form of cancer in the United States, in the publication, *Fit, Healthy, and Ready to Learn! A School Health Policy Guide.* **www.nasbe.org/**

Other resources that support a Coordinated School Health Program:
- School-Home Connection
- Daily Physical Activity
- Daily Fitness Tips
- Activities: Home & Community
- Health Background: Webliography
- *Be Active! Resources for Physical Education*

Media Resources

Books for Students

Parsons, Alexandra. *Fit for Life.* Watts Publishing Group, 1996. Looks at fitness and drug use. **EASY**

Silverstein, Alvin. *Can You See the Chalkboard? (My Health).* Franklin Watts, 2001. Looks at the function and care of the human eye. **AVERAGE**

Silverstein, Alvin. *Earaches (My Health).* Franklin Watts, 2002. Explains the workings of the ear and children's earaches. **ADVANCED**

Books for Teachers and Families

Schissel, Marvin J. *Healthy Teeth: A User's Manual.* Griffin Trade, 1999. Debunks many myths about teeth.

Forness, Larry M. *Don't Get Duped! A Consumer's Guide to Health and Fitness.* Prometheus Books, 2002. Helps evaluate health-care and fitness products and services.

Free and Inexpensive Materials

American Academy of Pediatric Dentistry
Will send brochures on fluoride, X-ray use, and calming the anxious child.

Purell
Download "Healthy Hands. Healthy Kids™," free curriculum lesson plans.

P&G Companies
Will send hygiene product samples.

American Dental Association
Download word games and puzzles.

Colgate-Palmolive Kids World
Has a free chart to print out.

To access free and inexpensive resources on the Web, visit **www.harcourtschool.com/health/free**

Videos

Skeletal and Muscular Systems. Schlessinger Media, 2001.

Human Body: The Inside Scoop (Bill Nye, the Science Guy Series). Walt Disney Home Video, 1995.

Come See About Nutrition and Exercise. ETR Associates, 1996.

These resources have been selected to meet a variety of individual needs. Please review all materials and websites prior to sharing them with students to ensure the content is appropriate for your class. Note that information, while correct at time of publication, is subject to change.

Visit **The Learning Site** for related links, activities, resources, and the health **Webliography.**

www.harcourtschool.com/health

Meeting Individual Needs

ESL/ELL

Below-Level
Display a copy of a paragraph from the text. Help students identify the main idea and the important details that tell *who, where, when,* and *what happens.* Have students draw a picture of the main idea and tell how the details of the paragraph are important for understanding the main idea.

Activities
- Mime Hand Washing, p. 42
- Make a Bulletin Board, p. 48
- Explain Sound, p. 55
- Compare Ingredients, p. 60

On-Level
Understanding nonfiction is easier when students picture in their minds what they are reading about. After students read a descriptive passage, for example, on ways to stay safe at home, have them draw a cartoon strip depicting those ways. Combine the strips into a class book.

Activities
- Design Sunhats, p. 42
- Functions of Teeth, p. 48
- Explore Sound, p. 55
- Write an Ad, p. 60

Challenge
Have small groups of students choose a topic related to a healthful life-style. Have each group make a visual advertisement persuading others of the benefits of that healthful choice. Students may use computers or video cameras, if available, to present their ads.

Activities
- Investigate Sunscreens, p. 42
- Research Fluoride, p. 48
- Demonstrate Sound, p. 55
- Explore Myths, p. 60

Learning Log
After students have read the text, have them present the information in another form. Encourage students to share their new knowledge in pictures, diagrams, charts, posters, dramatizations, songs, or stories in oral or written form.

Activities
- Comprehensible Input, pp. 44, 52, 62
- Language and Vocabulary, p. 50

Curriculum Integration

Integrated Language Arts/Reading Skills
- Word Family, p. 51
- Sign Language, p. 56
- Helen Keller, p. 57
- Advertisements vs. Labels, p. 61
- Cold Medicines, p. 63

Math
- Calculate Hair Growth, p. 45
- Converting Units, p. 64

Music
- Product Jingles, p. 65

Physical Education
- Daily Fitness Tip, pp. 40, 48, 52, 60
- Daily Physical Activity, p. 39

Use these topics to integrate health into your daily planning.

Science
- Lenses, p. 53
- Vision in Animals, p. 54

Drama
- Talking to Health-Care Professionals, p. 61

Art
- Cartoons, p. 57

CHAPTER 2

Pages 38–69

CHAPTER SUMMARY

In this chapter students

► learn the importance of personal hygiene and how it is related to good health.

► find out about the structure and function of the eyes and ears and how to keep them healthy.

► learn how to analyze health information from a variety of sources.

 Life Skills
Students practice *communicating* about protecting their hearing.

 Building Good Character
Students show *respect* for themselves by developing self-confidence.

 Consumer Health
Students *make buying decisions* about health-care products.

 Literature Springboard

Use the article "Health and Beauty—Then and Now" to spark interest in the chapter topic. See the Read-Aloud Anthology on page RA-3 of this *Teacher Edition*.

Prereading Strategies

SCAN THE CHAPTER Have students preview the chapter by scanning the titles, headings, pictures, graphs, and tables. Ask volunteers to predict what they will learn. Use their predictions to determine their prior knowledge.

PREVIEW VOCABULARY As students scan the chapter, have them write the vocabulary words listed at the beginning of each lesson. Tell them to cross out words they know, make a box around words they think they know, and circle words they don't know. Have them cross out words they have boxed or circled as they confirm or learn them.

CHAPTER 2 Being a **Wise Consumer**

 Reading Skill

DRAW CONCLUSIONS To introduce or review this skill, have students use the Reading in Health Handbook, pp. 372–383. Teaching strategies and additional activities are also provided.

Students will have opportunities to practice and apply this skill throughout this chapter.

• Focus Skill Reading Mini-Lesson, p. 40

• Reading comprehension questions identified with the

• *Activity Book* p. 8 (shown on p. 46)

• Lesson Summary and Review, pp. 46, 51, 57, 66

• Chapter Review and Test Preparation, pp. 68–69

Reading Skill

DRAW CONCLUSIONS When you draw conclusions, you use what you know and what you read. Use the Reading in Health Handbook on pages 372–383 and this graphic organizer to help you read the health facts in this chapter.

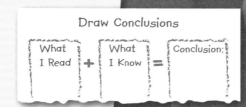

Draw Conclusions

| What I Read | + | What I Know | = | Conclusion: |

Health Graph

INTERPRET DATA Although most dental cavities can be prevented, the graph shows that as children grow older, the number of cavities increases. How does the average number of cavities for twelve-year-olds compare with the number for seventeen-year-olds? What do you think could reduce the difference?

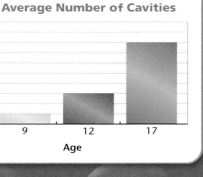

Average Number of Cavities

Number of Cavities (y-axis: 0–10)
Age (x-axis: 9, 12, 17)

Daily Physical Activity

One of the easiest ways to take care of your body is to be sure to include some physical activity every day.

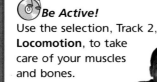**Be Active!**
Use the selection, Track 2, **Locomotion**, to take care of your muscles and bones.

39

School-Home Connection

Distribute copies of the School-Home Connection (in English or Spanish). Have students take the page home to share with their families as you begin this chapter.

Follow Up Have volunteers share the results of their activities.

 Supports the Coordinated School Health Program
CSHP

INTRODUCE THE CHAPTER

Health Graph

Interpret Data

Ask volunteers to explain what information the graph is presenting. **How does the average number of cavities of a twelve-year-old compare with that of a seventeen-year-old?** The seventeen-year-old has more than double the cavities of the twelve-year-old. **What do you think could help prevent this difference?** better dental health habits, brushing and flossing every day, getting regular dental checkups

Why is it important to keep teeth healthy? Teeth are used to chew food and help pronounce words correctly. Healthy teeth give you a nice smile.

Daily Physical Activity

Use *Be Active! Music for Daily Physical Activity* with the Instant Activity Cards to provide students with movement activities that can be done in limited space. Options for using these components are provided beginning on page TR2 in this *Teacher Edition*.

Chapter Project

Puzzling Words (*Assessment Guide* p. 56)

ASSESS PRIOR KNOWLEDGE Use students' initial ideas for the project as a baseline assessment of their understanding of chapter concepts. Have students complete the project as they work through the chapter.

PERFORMANCE ASSESSMENT The project can be used for performance assessment. Use the Project Evaluation Sheet (rubric), *Assessment Guide* p. 63.

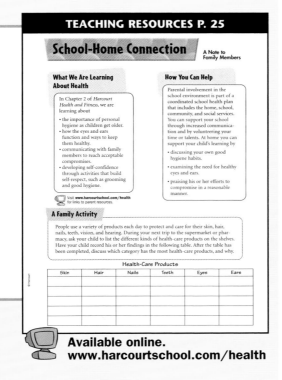

TEACHING RESOURCES P. 25

School-Home Connection A Note to Family Members

What We Are Learning About Health

In Chapter 2 of *Harcourt Health and Fitness*, we are learning about
- the importance of personal hygiene as children get older.
- how the eyes and ears function and ways to keep them healthy.
- communicating with family members to reach acceptable compromises.
- developing self-confidence through activities that build self-respect, such as grooming and good hygiene.

How You Can Help

Parental involvement in the school environment is part of a coordinated school health plan that includes the home, school, community, and social services. You can support your school through increased communication and by volunteering your time or talents. At home you can support your child's learning by
- discussing your own good hygiene habits.
- examining the need for healthy eyes and ears.
- praising his or her efforts to compromise in a reasonable manner.

Visit www.harcourtschool.com/health for links to parent resources.

A Family Activity

People use a variety of products each day to protect and care for their skin, hair, nails, teeth, vision, and hearing. During your next trip to the supermarket or pharmacy, ask your child to list the different kinds of health-care products on the shelves. Have your child record his or her findings in the following table. After the table has been completed, discuss which category has the most health-care products, and why.

Health-Care Products

Skin	Hair	Nails	Teeth	Eyes	Ears

Available online.
www.harcourtschool.com/health

Objectives

► Explain why it's important to keep your skin, hair, and nails healthy.

► Explain how changes in hormone levels can affect personal health habits.

When Minutes Count . . .

Assign the Quick Study, Lesson 1, Activity Book pp. 6–7 (shown on p. 41).

Program Resources

► Activity Book pp. 6–7, 8

► Transparencies 2, 15

Vocabulary

ultraviolet rays p. 41, **SPF** p. 42, **hair follicle** p. 44, **oil gland** p. 44

Daily Fitness Tip

The Food and Drug Administration estimates that up to 40 percent of food poisoning outbreaks result from poor hand-washing and subsequent contamination. Encourage students to wash their hands often throughout the day, particularly after the situations listed in the text.

 For more guidelines on fitness, see *Be Active! Resources for Physical Education.*

1. MOTIVATE

Optional Activity Materials bowl of flour or corn starch

Have a student volunteer immerse a hand in the flour or corn starch. The material represents dirt and germs that collect on an unwashed hand throughout the day. Have the student with the "dirty" hand shake hands with another volunteer.

What happens? The second student's hand should have powder on it. Then have the second student shake hands with other students. Tell students that germs are spread in a similar way.

LESSON 1 — Healthy Skin, Hair, and Nails

Lesson Focus

Taking care of your skin, hair, and nails can help you stay healthy and look and feel your best.

Why Learn This?

Learning about skin, hair, and nails can help you make wise choices about caring for them.

Vocabulary

ultraviolet rays
SPF
hair follicle
oil gland

Caring for Your Skin

You may think of your skin as just a covering for your body. But it's much more than that. Your skin is an organ that protects you from diseases and helps keep body tissues from drying out. Keeping your skin healthy is important. Showering or bathing regularly with soap and water helps remove dirt, germs, dead skin cells, and excess oil from your skin. Use a mild soap to help keep your skin from drying out. You may want to use lotion if you have dry skin.

Wash your hands often to stop the spread of germs that cause illness. Always wash your hands before you prepare food or eat and after you use the bathroom. Wash your hands after you touch items that may have germs on them, such as trash or an animal. If you cough or sneeze into your hands, wash them before you touch anything.

DRAW CONCLUSIONS Why should you wash your hands after sneezing into them?
When you sneeze, germs from inside your body can land on your hands.

◄ Wash your hands carefully. Using soap and warm water, rub your hands together for about twenty seconds. Then rinse your hands well and dry them with a clean cloth or towel.

40

Focus Skill — Reading Skill

Mini-Lesson

DRAW CONCLUSIONS
Remind students that they use facts from their reading plus what they already know to draw conclusions. Have them practice this skill by responding to the Focus Skill question on page 40. Have students draw and complete the graphic organizer as you model it on the transparency.

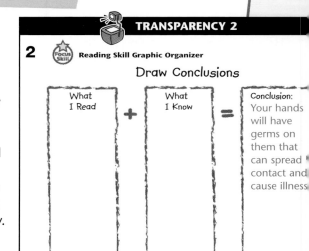

TRANSPARENCY 2

2 Reading Skill Graphic Organizer

Draw Conclusions

| What I Read | + | What I Know | = | Conclusion: Your hands will have germs on them that can spread contact and cause illness |

Interactive Transparencies available on CD-ROM.

Sun Dangers

The sun can be more dangerous for your skin than dirt and germs are. The sun gives off invisible waves of energy called **ultraviolet rays** (uhl·truh·vy·uh·lit), or UV rays. These rays cause sunburn and tanning, which are signs that the skin has been harmed. Years of being in the sun can damage your skin, causing wrinkles, loss of stretchiness, and dark spots. Over time, skin damage may lead to skin cancer. If some skin cancers aren't treated early, they can cause death.

It is important to find skin cancer in its early stages. A change in the appearance of a mole or birthmark may be an early indication of skin cancer. Know the simple ABCD rules for possible signs of skin cancer. If you find any of these signs, see a health-care professional.

CAUSE AND EFFECT What is the effect if the cause is "I spend hours in the sun"?
Possible answer: damage to the skin and possibly skin cancer

Did You Know?

If you are like most kids, you'll spend more time in the sun before you're eighteen years old than you will for the rest of your life. By protecting your skin now, you can greatly reduce your chances of developing skin cancer as an adult.

ABCD Rules for Signs of Skin Cancer

- **Asymmetry** One-half of a mole doesn't match the other half.

- **Border** The edges of a mole are irregular, ragged, uneven, or blurred.

- **Color** The color of the mole isn't the same all over but may have differing shades of brown or black. Sometimes the spot will have patches of red, white, or blue.

- **Diameter** The diameter of the mole is larger than $\frac{1}{4}$ inch or is growing larger.

People with fair skin sunburn especially easily. ▶

41

2. TEACH

Interpret Visuals—Pictures

Direct attention to the picture of the girl washing her hands.

How is the girl helping keep her body healthy? Hand-washing helps get rid of germs that can cause illness. Cold viruses can live for several hours on objects such as doorknobs, towels, and hands. Most people catch colds by touching contaminated objects and then touching their eyes, noses, or mouths. **What have you touched since the last time you washed your hands?** Answers will vary.

Discuss

Critical Thinking **Why is it important to see a health-care professional as soon as possible if you have a suspicious-looking mole or sore on your skin?** The mole could be cancerous. The sooner cancer is diagnosed and can be treated, the better the chance of a full recovery.

Health Background

Tanning Becoming tan is the skin's way of protecting itself from ultraviolet (UV) rays. Melanin, the pigment that gives skin its color, absorbs UV light. When the skin is exposed to UV rays, granules of melanin gather over the nuclei of skin cells and produce a shield that protects important genetic information in the nucleus from damage by UV light. Students may have the misconception that tanning in a tanning bed or under a sun lamp may be safer for skin than being out in the sun. The American Academy of Dermatology states that these alternative ways of tanning are just as damaging to skin as natural sunlight is.

Source: *American Academy of Dermatology*

For more background, visit the **Webliography** in Teacher Resources at **www.harcourtschool.com/health Keyword** personal care

---

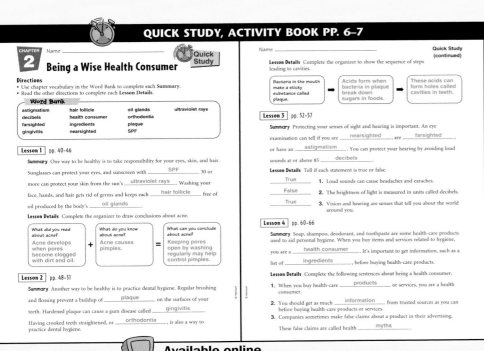

QUICK STUDY, ACTIVITY BOOK PP. 6–7

CHAPTER 2 Name _____ Quick Study

Being a Wise Health Consumer

Directions
- Use chapter vocabulary in the Word Bank to complete each **Summary**.
- Read the other directions to complete each **Lesson Details**.

Word Bank

astigmatism	hair follicle	oil glands	ultraviolet rays
decibels	health consumer	orthodontia	
farsighted	ingredients	plaque	
gingivitis	nearsighted	SPF	

Lesson 1 pp. 40–46

Summary One way to be healthy is to take responsibility for your eyes, skin, and hair. Sunglasses can protect your eyes, and sunscreen with ___SPF___ 30 or more can protect your skin from the sun's ___ultraviolet rays___. Washing your face, hands, and hair gets rid of germs and keeps each ___hair follicle___ free of oil produced by the body's ___oil glands___.

Lesson Details Complete the organizer to draw conclusions about acne.

What did you read about acne?		What do you know about acne?		What can you conclude about acne?
Acne develops when pores become clogged with dirt and oil.	+	Acne causes pimples.	=	Keeping pores open by washing regularly may help control pimples.

Lesson 2 pp. 48–51

Summary Another way to be healthy is to practice dental hygiene. Regular brushing and flossing prevents a buildup of ___plaque___ on the surfaces of your teeth. Hardened plaque can cause a gum disease called ___gingivitis___. Having crooked teeth straightened, or ___orthodontia___, is also a way to practice dental hygiene.

Name _____ Quick Study (continued)

Lesson Details Complete the organizer to show the sequence of steps leading to cavities.

Bacteria in the mouth make a sticky substance called plaque.	→	Acids form when bacteria in plaque break down sugars in foods.	→	These acids can form holes called cavities in teeth.

Lesson 3 pp. 52–57

Summary Protecting your senses of sight and hearing is important. An eye examination can tell if you are ___nearsighted___, are ___farsighted___, or have an ___astigmatism___. You can protect your hearing by avoiding loud sounds at or above 85 ___decibels___.

Lesson Details Tell if each statement is true or false.

___True___ 1. Loud sounds can cause headaches and earaches.

___False___ 2. The brightness of light is measured in units called decibels.

___True___ 3. Vision and hearing are senses that tell you about the world around you.

Lesson 4 pp. 60–66

Summary Soap, shampoo, deodorant, and toothpaste are some health-care products used to aid personal hygiene. When you buy items and services related to hygiene, you are a ___health consumer___. It's important to get information, such as a list of ___ingredients___, before buying health-care products.

Lesson Details Complete the following sentences about being a health consumer.

1. When you buy health-care ___products___ or services, you are a health consumer.

2. You should get as much ___information___ from trusted sources as you can before buying health-care products or services.

3. Companies sometimes make false claims about a product in their advertising. These false claims are called health ___myths___.

Available online.
www.harcourtschool.com/health

Content-Area Reading Support

Using Text Patterns Direct attention to the bulleted list. Point out the sentence preceding the list: *Following these precautions will help you stay safe in the sun.* Explain that this sentence tells what information will be presented in the list. Information shown in a bulleted list is easier to read and remember than it would be if written as a paragraph. This format also gives the list greater importance. Urge students to pay attention to changes in text format because they often signal important information.

Quick Activity

Choose Sun Protection For both activities students should choose a sunscreen with an SPF of 30 or higher. Sunscreen should be reapplied after sweating and after swimming. Other protective items include light-colored, tightly woven clothes that cover as much of the skin as possible, a hat, sunglasses, and lip balm with sunscreen. Also, try to stay out of the sun as much as possible when it is the strongest—between the hours of 10 A.M. and 4 P.M.

Consumer Activity

Make Buying Decisions Jana should select a sunscreen with an SPF of 30 or higher. She should read the label to find information about the product and then make sure the product meets her needs. Jana should use the steps to Make Responsible Decisions as she makes her choice.

When Minutes Count ...

Transparency 15: The Skin can be used to present material in this lesson. *Interactive Transparencies available on CD-ROM.*

Consumer Activity

Make Buying Decisions Jana is standing in front of the sunscreens at the store. Write what Jana should look for on the labels when making a buying decision.

Sunscreen Protection

When you go outside, it's important that you protect yourself from the sun. Following these precautions will help you stay safe in the sun.

- Cover up. Wear shirts and pants that cover and protect as much of your skin as possible.
- Use a sunscreen with **SPF**, sun protection factor, of at least 30. Apply the sunscreen 30 minutes before going outside. Be generous when applying the sunscreen to your body. Reapply sunscreen every two hours if you are swimming or sweating. Use lip balm with sunscreen to protect your lips.
- Wear a hat to protect your face, neck, and ears.
- Wear sunglasses to protect your eyes from harmful UV rays.
- Limit your sun exposure. Stay out of the sun between 10 A.M. and 4 P.M., when UV rays are strongest.

Quick Activity

Choose Sun Protection Do you need a different sunscreen for an afternoon at the beach than you do for bike riding? Write down other items you need for sun protection for both activities.

Sunscreen Protection

SPF	Amount of Protection
0–14	Offers little or no protection from the sun. Not recommended for UV-ray protection.
15–30	Provides some UV-ray protection. The higher the SPF, the more protection. An SPF of at least 30 is recommended.
30+	Recommended for high UV-ray exposure, as in high altitudes and on or near water, sand, or snow.

SUMMARIZE Tell what you should do to protect your body from UV rays when you're outdoors.

Cover up; use sunscreen with an SPF of at least 30; wear a hat and sunglasses; limit your exposure to the sun.

42

Meeting Individual Needs
Leveled Activities

BELOW-LEVEL Mime Hand-Washing Ask each student to choose a partner. One partner should mime washing his or her hands while the other times the action. The washer estimates how long the washing took, and then partners switch roles. Students should compare the estimated and actual times.

ON-LEVEL Design Sun Hats Have students draw designs for effective sun hats. The designs can be practical or imaginative. Encourage students to use commonly available materials to make models of their hats.

CHALLENGE Investigate Sunscreens Suggest that students choose one brand of sunscreen and make charts to compare the relationships between the prices and the SPF numbers. Direct students to find the best value for each SPF and present their findings to the class.

Caring for Your Nails

Your nails protect the tips of your fingers and toes. Like hair, nails grow from your skin. Keeping your nails trimmed is important for their appearance and health.

Long nails can break or tear easily, exposing living skin. Dirt and germs can get under your nails even when they are neatly trimmed. To prevent the spread of germs, clean your nails at least once a day. Use warm, soapy water and a nail brush to remove the dirt and germs. Watch for changes in your nails. A change can be a sign of illness.

Don't bite your nails. Doing so can spread germs from your nails to your mouth. Use nail clippers or manicure scissors to cut your toenails and fingernails. Don't cut your nails too short. Making them too short can expose living skin or cause the nail to grow into the skin. Exposing the living skin around a nail can lead to infection. Cut each toenail straight across, just beyond the tip of your toe.

▲ Biting your nails can lead to infection. Toenails should be cut straight across, not rounded like fingernails.

MAIN IDEA AND DETAILS **Give two details to support this statement: Keeping your nails trimmed to the right length is important.**

Long nails can break, exposing living skin; nails cut too short can grow into the skin.

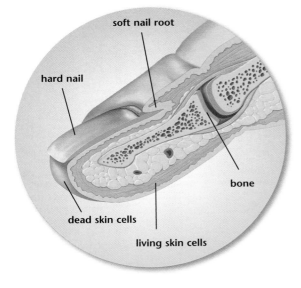

soft nail root

hard nail

dead skin cells

living skin cells

bone

◀ The fingernails you can see are dead cells that grow from living skin cells in the soft nail root.

43

Interpret Visuals—Illustrations

Have students study the illustration of a nail. Have them locate the hard nail.

Why doesn't clipping your nails hurt? The nail itself is composed of dead skin cells. **If a nail is made of dead skin cells, why does it bleed if cut too low or if it is injured?** Nails are attached to the living skin cells beneath them. If a nail is cut or ripped away from the skin, the living cells can be damaged and bleed.

Health Background

SPF Effectiveness Using a sunscreen with SPF 30 means that a person can stay in the sun about thirty times longer without burning than if not using sunscreen. The actual length of time is different for each individual. To calculate the length of time you can stay in the sun without burning, multiply the SPF of the sunscreen by the amount of time it takes for your skin to start to turn red when exposed to the sun. For example, if you correctly apply SPF 30 sunscreen onto skin that ordinarily begins to burn after ten minutes, you will have about 300 minutes of protection.

Nail Health Common nail disorders include ingrown nails and fungal infections. Ingrown nails can result from improper clipping or wearing tight shoes. Fungal infections, which account for almost 50 percent of all nail disorders, can be treated with oral antifungal medication. Bacterial infections can occur as a result of injury to the nail or to the skin surrounding the nail. Unexplained changes in the appearance of the nails can indicate serious changes in health. Pale nail beds can be an indication of anemia, red nail beds can signal a heart condition, and yellowish nails can be a sign of diabetes. Liver diseases, kidney diseases, and lung diseases can also cause changes in nail appearance.

Source: *American Academy of Dermatology*

For more background, visit the **Webliography** in Teacher Resources at **www.harcourtschool.com/health** **Keyword** personal care

Teacher Tip

Sun-Protection Clothing
Explain to students that clothing for covering up needs to be tightly woven and light colored. Ask students to watch as you hold up different samples of clothing in front of a light bulb. If lots of light shows through, the clothing will not offer strong protection against UV light. Remind students that sheer shirts and bathing-suit cover-ups do not provide much sun protection. In tests, some of the best sun-protecting clothing included blue jeans and polyester.

Cultural Connection

Skin Color Melanin is a pigment that gives skin its color. The amount of melanin produced varies among individuals and ethnic groups. For example, the cells of individuals who live in sunny climates have more melanin than those who live in less-sunny locations. Likewise, those who are descendents of individuals from Africa, Asia, or Central and South America produce more melanin than people of northern European descent.

Personal Health Plan

Students should respond that they wouldn't share combs or brushes with others because doing so can pass on head lice or scalp infections.

Discuss

Like skin, hair is colored mostly by the pigment melanin. (Other pigments can also be present, such as a red pigment in red hair.) Hair color, texture, and shape are determined by genes, which are inherited from one's parents. People with large hair follicles usually have thick hair. Small hair follicles yield fine hair. The shape of your hair—straight, curly, or wavy—is determined by the structure of your hair follicles.

Problem Solving **You have straight hair but want curly hair. Can you do anything to change your hair permanently? Why or why not?** No; the shape of your hair depends on the structure of the hair follicle, which is an inherited trait.

Health Background

Head Lice Head lice are small parasitic insects that infect scalp hair, feeding on blood. Itching and the appearance of lice or eggs on the scalp, in hair, or on clothing are indications of an infection. Treatment of head lice includes the removal of lice and eggs, the use of a shampoo that will kill lice and eggs, and washing the bedding, clothing, combs, and brushes of the infected person in hot water. Medical treatment may be needed if intense scratching leads to a secondary skin infection or if over-the-counter shampoos are not effective.

Source: *National Institutes of Health*

For more background, visit the **Webliography** in Teacher Resources at **www.harcourtschool.com/health** **Keyword** personal care

---

Personal Health Plan

Real-Life Situation
Combing or brushing your hair is important for looking your best. Suppose a person in your gym class asks to borrow your comb or brush.

Real-Life Plan
Write down what you would say to politely refuse to lend your comb or brush.

Caring for Your Hair

Much of your body is covered with hair. Each hair grows from a pitlike area called a **hair follicle** (FAHL·ih·kuhl). Special cells in the follicle grow to form hair. These cells grow, die, and then harden. The dead cells are forced out of the hair follicle as new cells form. The dead cells stack up, one on top of another, in a long column that makes up the hair shaft. An **oil gland** in each follicle makes oil that coats the hair and spreads over the surface of your skin. The oil makes your hair and skin soft and smooth and keeps it from drying out.

There are about 200,000 hairs on your head. They help protect your scalp from the sun. They also keep you warm in cold weather. Each hair grows from four to seven years and then falls out.

To keep hair looking neat, brush or comb it each day. Brushing gets rid of tangles and spreads oil over the hair shafts. Brushing once a day is usually enough to keep your hair healthy. Comb your hair often throughout the day to keep it looking neat.

Grooming is important, but don't share combs or

Although it may appear healthy, the part of the hair that you can see is actually dead. Only the hair follicle is alive. ▼

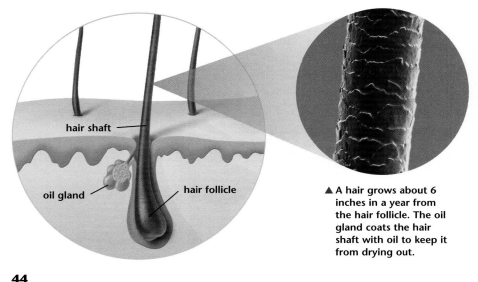

hair shaft

oil gland

hair follicle

▲ A hair grows about 6 inches in a year from the hair follicle. The oil gland coats the hair shaft with oil to keep it from drying out.

44

ESL/ELL Support

COMPREHENSIBLE INPUT Help students understand the structure of hair.

Beginning Provide students with unlabeled diagrams of hair along with corresponding lists of labels. Have them copy each label onto the correct structure on the diagram.

Intermediate Have students do the same activity as Beginning students, but have them also write a sentence about each label.

Advanced Have students write the names of the structures of hair on individual index cards. On the opposite side of each card, have students write a description of the structure. Have pairs of students use the cards to review.

brushes with friends. Head lice can be passed from person to person by sharing items that are used on the head.

Shampooing your hair keeps it clean. Talk with a parent about how often to wash your hair. If your hair is naturally oily, you may need to wash it every day. If your hair is dry, you can wash it less often. A parent can help you find a shampoo that works well with your hair type.

Comb your hair gently after shampooing. Gentle combing helps keep wet hair from being damaged. Unless your hair is very curly, let it dry a little before combing. To make your hair easier to comb, use a small amount of conditioner to coat the hair shafts.

Letting your hair dry naturally is best. Electric dryers can make your hair brittle, causing it to break. Curling irons, hot rollers, and hot combs damage hair, too. If you want to dry and style your hair, use a blow-dryer on a warm setting. Brush your hair gently as you blow-dry it.

CAUSE AND EFFECT
What might happen if you blow-dry your hair every day?

Your hair might dry out, become brittle, and break.

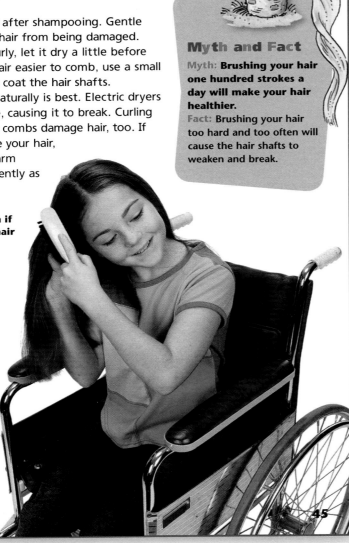

About 200,000 hairs grow on your head. They protect your scalp from the sun and cold weather. ▶

Myth and Fact

Myth: Brushing your hair one hundred strokes a day will make your hair healthier.
Fact: Brushing your hair too hard and too often will cause the hair shafts to weaken and break.

---

3. WRAP UP

Lesson 1 Summary and Review

1. ultraviolet rays; SPF; hair follicle; oil glands; Deodorant, antiperspirant

2. It protects your body from diseases and keeps it from drying out.

3. Go to a health-care professional to have it checked.

4. Possible answers are shown below.

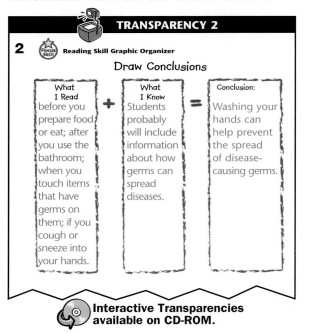

TRANSPARENCY 2

2 Reading Skill Graphic Organizer

Draw Conclusions

What I Read		What I Know		Conclusion:
before you prepare food or eat; after you use the bathroom; when you touch items that have germs on them; if you cough or sneeze into your hands.	+	Students probably will include information about how germs can spread diseases.	=	Washing your hands can help prevent the spread of disease-causing germs.

Interactive Transparencies available on CD-ROM.

5. Accept answers that correctly explain that acne results from hormone changes that cause an increase in oil production.

For **writing models** with examples, see *Teaching Resources* pp. 47–61. Rubrics are also provided.

When Minutes Count ...

Quick Study Students can use *Activity Book* pp. 6–7 (shown on p. 41) as they complete each lesson in this chapter.

Personal Hygiene

Before and during puberty, hormones will cause changes in your body. For example, your oil glands will release more oil, which may cause pimples called *acne*.

Acne forms when a pore becomes clogged with oil, dead skin cells, and bacteria. The bacteria grow in the blocked pore. The pore may swell and become red, forming a pimple. To remove excess oil and control acne, wash your face often with soap and water. If you do get acne, it's not your fault. Acne develops because of changes caused by hormones.

You may also notice that you sweat more than you did when you were younger and that the sweat has an odor. These changes are normal and are also caused by hormones. Daily bathing and using a deodorant or an antiperspirant can help control body odor and excess sweating.

▲ Hormone changes may cause coarse hair to grow on your body during puberty. Ask a parent before using a razor to remove unwanted hair.

SEQUENCE Tell how a pimple forms.
Glands release oil; pore becomes clogged; bacteria grow; pore swells and becomes red.

Lesson 1 Summary and Review

❶ **Summarize with Vocabulary**

Use vocabulary and other terms from this lesson to complete these statements.

The sun gives off _____, which can damage your skin. Sunscreen with a(n) _____ of 30 is recommended for all skin types. Hair grows from a pit in the skin called a(n) _____. Your skin and hair are protected from water loss by oil from _____. _____ and _____ control body odor and excess sweating.

❷ Why do you need your skin?

❸ **Critical Thinking** What should you do if a mole on your body is growing larger and its border is irregular?

❹ **DRAW CONCLUSIONS** Complete this graphic organizer to draw a conclusion about the importance of washing your hands.

What I Read	+	What I Know	=	Conclusion:

❺ **Write to Inform—Explanation**
Some classmates are making fun of a boy who has acne. Write a paragraph to explain why the acne isn't the boy's fault.

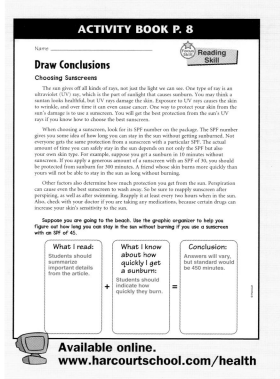

ACTIVITY BOOK P. 8

Name _____

Reading Skill

Draw Conclusions

Choosing Sunscreens

The sun gives off all kinds of rays, not just the light we can see. One type of ray is an ultraviolet (UV) ray, which is the part of sunlight that causes sunburn. You may think a suntan looks healthful, but UV rays damage the skin. Exposure to UV rays causes the skin to wrinkle, and over time it can even cause cancer. One way to protect your skin from the sun's damage is to use a sunscreen. You will get the best protection from the sun's UV rays if you know how to choose the best sunscreen.

When choosing a sunscreen, look for its SPF number on the package. The SPF number gives you some idea of how long you can stay in the sun without getting sunburned. Not everyone gets the same protection from a sunscreen with a particular SPF. The actual amount of time you can safely stay in the sun depends on not only the SPF but also your own skin type. For example, suppose you get a sunburn in 10 minutes without sunscreen. If you apply a generous amount of a sunscreen with an SPF of 30, you should be protected from sunburn for 300 minutes. A friend whose skin burns more quickly than yours will not be able to stay in the sun as long without burning.

Other factors also determine how much protection you get from the sun. Perspiration can cause even the best sunscreen to wash away. So be sure to reapply sunscreen after perspiring, as well as after swimming. Reapply it at least every two hours when in the sun. Also, check with your doctor if you are taking any medications, because certain drugs can increase your skin's sensitivity to the sun.

Suppose you are going to the beach. Use the graphic organizer to help you figure out how long you can stay in the sun without burning if you use a sunscreen with an SPF of 45.

What I read:		What I know about how quickly I get a sunburn:		Conclusion:
Students should summarize important details from the article.	+	Students should indicate how quickly they burn.	=	Answers will vary, but standard would be 450 minutes.

Available online.
www.harcourtschool.com/health

Respect

Develop Self-Confidence

Almost everyone would like to have the same self-confidence that many of their favorite celebrities have. But for some people, being confident isn't easy, especially when they're in front of others. To be confident, you must respect yourself. Here are some tips to help you respect yourself and develop self-confidence:

- **Always look your best. The extra time you spend on grooming will boost your confidence.**
- **Use antiperspirant or deodorant to control sweating and body odor.**
- **Keep your hair clean and neatly combed.**
- **Take care of your teeth and gums to prevent cavities, gum disease, and tooth loss.**
- **Wash your face with soap and water to control acne. See your doctor for acne cleansers and creams, if necessary.**
- **If you are asked to speak in front of an audience, prepare notes about what you're going to say. Practice giving your presentation in front of a mirror, making eye contact with a pretend audience. Avoid reading to the audience from your notes.**

Activity

Speaking in front of an audience can be frightening. Ask your teacher if you may read your favorite short story aloud to the class. Practice the tips above to help yourself gain confidence.

47

Using the Poster

Activity Suggest that students design and display their own posters about self-confidence.

Display Poster 4 to remind students of ways to develop self-confidence. The posters can be displayed in the classroom, school cafeteria, or another common area.

POSTER 4

Respect

The children are showing respect by sharing their different interests.

DO
- Treat others the way you want to be treated.
- Accept people who are different from you.
- Be polite and use good manners.
- Be considerate of the feelings of others.
- Stay calm when you are angry.
- Develop self-respect and self-confidence.

DON'T
- Don't use bad language.
- Don't insult or embarrass anyone.
- Don't threaten or bully anyone.
- Don't hit or hurt anyone.

How have YOU shown RESPECT today?

POSTER 4

Building Good Character

Caring
Citizenship
Fairness
Respect
Responsibility
Trustworthiness

Objective
▶ Identify ways to develop self-confidence.

Program Resources
▶ Poster 4

BEFORE READING
Ask students what they think it means to be or feel self-confident. **How is self-confidence related to the subject of respect?** You can be self-confident only if you respect yourself. Have students think of times when they felt self-confident and times when they did not feel self-confident.

DISCUSS
After students have read the page, ask them what most of the suggestions presented on the page have in common. Most of the suggestions have to do with personal hygiene. Ask them what other things a person could do to increase his or her self-confidence. Record their answers on the board.

ACTIVITY
Students can choose something they enjoy reading and share it with the class. They can practice at home in front of the mirror or with a parent or guardian. Have students rate their level of self-confidence before they begin and then again after they finish. Encourage the audience members to be good listeners, and positively reinforce the courage of the presenter.

Objectives
► Identify the structure and function of teeth.
► Explain how to keep teeth and gums healthy.
► Identify dental problems.

 When Minutes Count . . .
Assign the Quick Study, Lesson 2, Activity Book pp. 6–7 (shown on p. 41).

Program Resources
► Activity Book pp. 6–7
► Transparencies 2, 16

Vocabulary
plaque p. 50, **gingivitis** p. 50, **orthodontia** p. 51

Daily Fitness Tip

Brushing and flossing your teeth every day are important parts of maintaining good oral health. They are the best ways to remove plaque from teeth and stop the progression of gingivitis. The American Dental Association also recommends limiting between-meal snacks and avoiding foods high in sugar.

 For more guidelines on fitness, see *Be Active! Resources for Physical Education.*

1. MOTIVATE

Optional Activity Materials string, scissors, ruler

Have each student cut an 18-inch piece of string. Tell students that 18 inches is the length of floss they should use when they floss their teeth. Direct students to stretch the piece of string out between their fingers to see how long the floss should be. As an alternative, have students hold their hands 18 inches apart, with partners measuring the exact length.

 LESSON 2

Healthy Teeth and Gums

Lesson Focus
To stay healthy, you need to take care of your teeth and gums.

Why Learn This?
Learning about teeth and gums can help you make wise choices about their care.

Vocabulary
plaque
gingivitis
orthodontia

Kinds of Teeth

Taking care of your teeth is important to your smile and to your health. Your first teeth started coming in when you were a baby. These teeth, called primary teeth, continued to come in during childhood. As you lost your primary teeth, they were replaced by permanent teeth. Permanent teeth have to last the rest of your life. If one is lost, no tooth will replace it.

By your late teens, you will have thirty-two teeth. This includes four "extra" molars in the back of your mouth. These molars are sometimes called wisdom teeth. Your wisdom teeth may not appear until you are an adult, or maybe not at all.

 DRAW CONCLUSIONS **Why is taking care of your permanent teeth important?**
If one is lost, no tooth will grow to replace it.

The shape of each tooth is well suited to its function. *Incisors* have sharp edges for cutting food. The pointed *cuspids* are good for tearing food. *Molars* and *bicuspids* have flat surfaces for grinding food. ▶

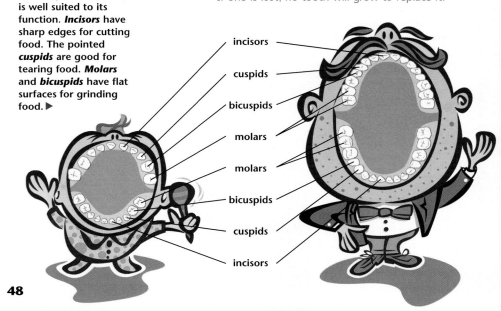

incisors
cuspids
bicuspids
molars
molars
bicuspids
cuspids
incisors

48

 Meeting Individual Needs
Leveled Activities

BELOW-LEVEL **Make a Bulletin Board** Have students make a bulletin board showing the instruments used to keep teeth clean and how to use them correctly.

ON-LEVEL **Functions of Teeth** Have students find out the function of each type of tooth and write the function next to the name of the tooth.

CHALLENGE **Research Fluoride** Tell students that many localities add fluoride to the water to help prevent tooth decay. Have students check with their local water authority to find out if fluoride is being added to the water and, if so, how much fluoride is added. As an extension, you may wish to have them find out the amount of fluoride in bottled water, well water, or the water in surrounding communities.

Caring for Your Teeth and Gums

Teeth are made up of three layers. Each tooth has a hard, protective *crown* made of *enamel*. Under the crown is a softer material called *dentin*. Dentin makes up most of the tooth. The *pulp* contains blood vessels that nourish the tooth. It also contains nerves that sense pain and temperature. The *root* anchors the tooth in the jaw. The teeth are surrounded by soft tissue—the gums.

Brushing and flossing remove food and bacteria from teeth and gums. Floss your teeth at least once a day before brushing. Brush your teeth at least twice a day after eating. Use a soft-bristled toothbrush and toothpaste that contains fluoride. *Fluoride* is a mineral that helps protect teeth. Your toothbrush and toothpaste should have the American Dental Association (ADA) seal.

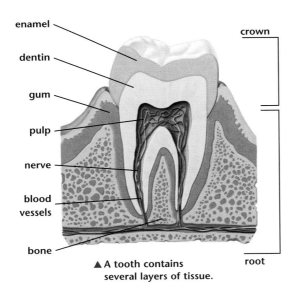

enamel
crown
dentin
gum
pulp
nerve
blood vessels
bone
root

▲ A tooth contains several layers of tissue.

SEQUENCE Name the layers of a tooth in order, starting with the outermost layer.
enamel, dentin, pulp

Brushing and Flossing

Brush using short, back-and-forth strokes. To brush along the gumline and the inner surfaces of your back teeth, angle the toothbrush. To clean the inner surfaces of your front teeth, use the tip of the toothbrush. Also brush your tongue.

Cut a piece of floss about 18 inches long. Wrap it around your middle fingers. Insert the floss between two teeth. Gently rub the side of each tooth, moving away from the gumline, with up-and-down motions. Unwind a clean piece of floss, and repeat to clean between all teeth.

49

---

2. TEACH

Interpret Visuals—Diagrams

Have students look at the diagram on page 48 and read the caption. Have students identify each type of tooth as you read its name. Ask students to look at the shape of each type of tooth as you review its function.

Direct attention to the diagram of the tooth. Ask a volunteer to read the labels aloud. Explain that enamel, the hard outer covering, is the hardest material in the human body. Tell them that the dentin is a bonelike layer and that the pulp is a soft core. Point out that the enamel is not living tissue but that the dentin and pulp are.

When Minutes Count . . .

Transparency 16: The Teeth can be used to present material in this lesson. *Interactive Transparencies available on CD-ROM.*

Health Background

Tooth Structure Enamel is composed of calcium phosphate and calcium carbonate. It is the hardest substance in the body and contains the highest amount of calcium salts. Enamel protects the teeth from wear and the underlying dentin from decay. Dentin consists of hardened connective tissue that contains a high amount of calcium salts. Dentin is harder than bone and gives teeth their basic shape and strength. The pulp, with the nerves and blood vessels, brings nutrients and oxygen to cells. Cementum, which holds teeth in place, is made up of fibers that surround the dentin in the root and run into the jawbone.

Source: *Principles of Anatomy and Physiology*

For more background, visit the **Webliography** in Teacher Resources at **www.harcourtschool.com/health Keyword** personal care

---

Teacher Tip

Tooth Care at Home Be aware that some students may come from families who do not practice healthful dental habits. They may not be in the habit of brushing and flossing on a daily basis. Other students may be uncomfortable discussing the lesson content because they themselves are self-conscious about wearing dental appliances. Do not call attention to these students during the lesson or encourage other students to ask them questions.

Teacher Tip

Oral Problems Students are often more concerned about developing cavities than gingivitis, an early stage of periodontal disease. In the United States more teeth are lost to periodontal disease than to cavities. Oral cancer is also possible with certain risk factors, such as smoking, chewing tobacco, using snuff, and drinking alcohol. Oral piercings are another factor, causing infections at the piercing site and broken teeth from accidently chewing on the jewelry.

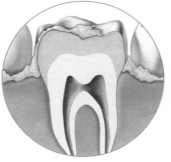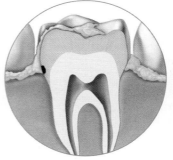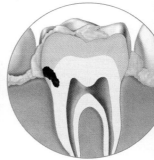

▲ Regular visits to the dentist can catch dental problems. The tooth at left is covered with plaque. The center tooth shows the beginning of a small cavity. The tooth at the right has a large cavity. See page 390 for what to do in a dental

Interpret Visuals—Pictures

As you discuss the formation of a cavity, have students refer to the diagram. You may also want to use Transparency 16.

What parts of the tooth in the second diagram are affected by decay? the enamel **What parts in the third diagram are affected?** the enamel and dentin

Why is it possible for a cavity to develop without a person being aware of it? The person does not feel pain during the beginning stages of cavity formation because the enamel and dentin do not contain nervous tissue.

At what point will a person begin to feel pain from a cavity? when the decay reaches the pulp, which contains nervous tissue

Health Background

Halitosis Halitosis, or bad breath, can result from certain foods being ingested. Foods such as garlic and onions can cause temporary odors to occur. Onions and garlic contain sulfur compounds which move into the bloodstream and then the lungs, affecting the breath each time a person exhales. Plaque build-up in the mouth can decay and smell bad if a person does not floss once and brush twice a day.

Halitosis can also be an indicator of periodontal disease. Persistent bad breath can be a warning sign of gum disease. Bacteria feeding in the gums can give off hydrogen sulfide, which smells like rotten eggs.

Bad breath may also be a sign of a medical disorder such as an infection in the respiratory tract, a sinus infection, diabetes, gastrointestinal diseases, and kidney or liver diseases. Persistent halitosis should be discussed with a doctor or dentist.

Source: *American Dental Association*

For more background, visit the **Webliography** in Teacher Resources at **www.harcourtschool.com/health Keyword** personal care

Health & Technology

Computer-Enhanced X Rays Dentists use computer-enhanced X rays to find cavities that are just beginning to form. When a cavity is found early, there is little tooth damage. A small cavity can be repaired without removing a large portion of the tooth.

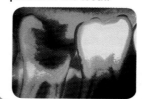

Dental Problems

Everyone—including you—has bacteria in his or her mouth. These bacteria make a sticky substance called **plaque** (PLAK), which coats your teeth. When the bacteria in plaque break down sugars in the foods you eat, acids form. These acids make holes, called cavities, in your tooth enamel. If a cavity isn't treated, the hole spreads through the dentin to the pulp and then to the root. A dentist treats a cavity by removing the damaged portion of the tooth. The dentist then fills the hole with a hard material, and the tooth is saved.

Plaque can cause other problems, too. If plaque is allowed to remain on the teeth, it forms a hardened material. This material can cause **gingivitis** (jin·juh·VYT·is), a gum disease in which the gums become red and swollen. Untreated gingivitis can develop into a more severe form of gum disease, in which the gums weaken and pull back from the teeth. Teeth may then fall out. Brushing and flossing can stop gingivitis in its early stages.

CAUSE AND EFFECT Tell how plaque can affect your teeth. Plaque can lead to cavities and gum disease, which can result in tooth loss.

50

ESL/ELL Support

LANGUAGE AND VOCABULARY Help students understand the multiple-meaning words *crown* and *root*. Provide students with an outline of a tooth.

Beginning Have students label the crown and the root. Have them draw a crown on the top of the tooth and roots extending from the bottom of the tooth. Help them relate the common meanings of the words to the names of the tooth parts.

Intermediate Have students label the crown and the root. Tell them to write the common and tooth-related meanings of each word.

Advanced Have students label the drawing with sentences that tell how the crown and root of a tooth are related to the more common meanings of *crown* and *root*.

Orthodontia

You may know someone who wears a *dental appliance*—a device that straightens crooked teeth. Some people wear braces, usually for several years, to straighten teeth. After the braces are removed, a person may wear another dental appliance, called a retainer, at night. The retainer keeps the teeth from moving out of place.

The straightening of crooked teeth is called **orthodontia** (awr•thuh•DAHN•shuh). Straightening teeth makes them easier to clean and helps prevent cavities and gum diseases. Straightening can also prevent uneven wear of the teeth. Orthodontia helps ensure that your teeth will last a lifetime.

COMPARE AND CONTRAST
Tell how braces and a retainer are alike and different.

◀ Cleaning the teeth carefully while wearing braces is very important.

Lesson 2 Summary and Review

❶ Summarize with Vocabulary

Use vocabulary and other terms from this lesson to complete the statements.

Babies have _____ teeth. Older children and adults have _____ teeth. Bacteria cause a sticky substance called _____ to form on your teeth. When acids attack the teeth, _____ form. Crooked teeth can be corrected by_____.

❷ Why is taking care of your teeth and gums important?

❸ Critical Thinking Why should you floss before you brush?

❹ DRAW CONCLUSIONS Complete this graphic organizer to draw a conclusion about taking care of your teeth.

| What I Read | + | What I Know | = | Conclusion: |

❺ Write to Inform—How-To
In your own words, tell how to floss and brush your teeth.

Alike—Both are dental appliances. Different—Braces are worn to straighten teeth; retainers are worn to keep teeth straight.

51

Cultural Connection

Teeth and Culture Many children in the United States expect a visit from the "tooth fairy" when they lose teeth, but children on the Omaha Indian Reservation bury their lost teeth in the ground as a sacred duty to give back to the earth. Have students research this and other cultural practices involving teeth.

Integrated Language Arts/ Reading Skills

Word Family Have students look up the derivation of the word *orthodontia* to learn the meanings of its two word parts. Have students list other related words that use the same word parts and provide a meaning for each. Be sure they mention *orthodontist*, a dental specialist who treats crooked, crowded, or otherwise improperly positioned teeth.

Activity

Make Decisions The best choice for Anna is an apple because it does not contain as much sugar as the other foods and will not stick to her teeth.

3. WRAP UP

Lesson 2 Summary and Review

1. primary; permanent; plaque; gingivitis; orthodontia

2. Cavities and gum diseases can form. You only get one set of permanent teeth, so you must take care of them.

3. Flossing loosens particles of food, which brushing then removes.

4. Possible answers are shown below.

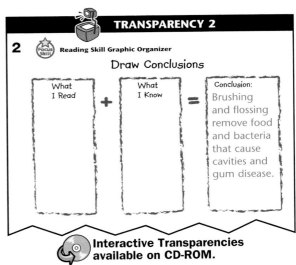

5. Accept responses that include the important steps of brushing and flossing.

For **writing models** with examples, see *Teaching Resources* pp. 47–61. Rubrics are also provided.

When Minutes Count ...

Quick Study Students can use *Activity Book* pp. 6–7 (shown on p. 41) as they complete each lesson in this chapter.

Objectives

► Identify parts of the eye and the ear and explain how the parts of each function together.

► Describe how to take good care of your eyes and ears.

 When Minutes Count . . .

Assign the Quick Study, Lesson 3, Activity Book pp. 6–7 (shown on p. 41).

Program Resources

► Activity Book pp. 6–7

► Transparencies 2, 17, 18

Vocabulary

farsighted p. 53, **nearsighted** p. 53, **astigmatism** p. 53, **decibels** p. 57

 **Daily Fitness Tip**

Remind students to avoid touching or rubbing their eyes. Unwashed hands have dirt and bacteria on them that can be transferred to the eyes and cause infections. Rubbing your eye when it has sand or another foreign object in it can scratch the cornea. Advise students to seek help from an adult if they have something in an eye that is not being washed away naturally by tears.

 For more guidelines on fitness, see *Be Active! Resources for Physical Education.*

1. MOTIVATE

Optional Activity Materials about ten marbles per group

Have each group of students put the marbles in a straight line, with each one touching the next. Tell each group to tap the end marble with a finger or pencil and observe what happens. Explain that sound travels in a similar manner. Sound causes air molecules to vibrate, or move back and forth. These vibrations cause waves of sound to travel through the air or other medium.

Care of Your Eyes and Ears

Lesson Focus

Vision and hearing are important senses that tell you about the world.

Why Learn This?

Knowing how your eyes and ears work can help you protect your vision and hearing.

Vocabulary

farsighted
nearsighted
astigmatism
decibels

How You See

When you wake up in the morning, the first thing you probably do is open your eyes and look around. Your eyes are organs that sense light and let you see the world around you.

When you look in a mirror, you can see several parts of your eye. The *cornea* (KAWR•nee•uh), is a clear covering that protects the eye. The black-looking *pupil* in the center of your eye is surrounded by the colored *iris* (EYE•ris). Muscles in the iris control the size of the pupil. This determines how much light enters your eye. Using the diagram below, trace the path of light through your eye.

Your body has several built-in ways to protect your eyes. The bones of your skull protect the eyes from injury. Eyelashes keep out dust and other particles. Your eyelids close if anything comes near your eyes. And tears flush away particles that enter the eye.

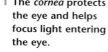 **DRAW CONCLUSIONS** How does the iris control the amount of light that enters the eye?
Muscles in the iris control the size of the pupil.

1 The *cornea* protects the eye and helps focus light entering the eye.

2 Light enters the eye through the *pupil.*

3 The *iris* adjusts the amount of light entering the eye.

4 The *lens* bends light rays so that images focus on the *retina.*

5 Light-sensing cells in the retina change light into nerve signals.

6 The *optic nerve* carries messages from the eye to the brain.

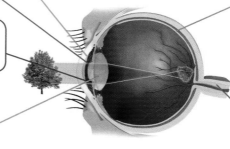

52

 ESL/ELL Support

COMPREHENSIBLE INPUT Help students understand the meanings of the words *farsighted* and *nearsighted* on page 53.

Beginning Help students see that each word is made up of two smaller words. Ask volunteers to demonstrate the meanings of *far* and *near*. Then have them draw pictures to illustrate the meanings of *farsighted* and *nearsighted.*

Intermediate Point to an object in the classroom. Ask students to draw it as both a farsighted and a nearsighted person would see it if the people were standing on the other side of the room. Tell students to label their drawings.

Advanced Have students make labeled drawings to explain farsightedness and nearsightedness.

Vision Problems

Many people don't have perfect vision. A **farsighted** person can see things that are far away, but things that are nearby look blurry. For other people the opposite is true. A **nearsighted** person can see things nearby, but objects far away are blurry. For people with **astigmatism** (uh·sᴛɪɢ·muh·tiz·uhm), the cornea or lens of the eye is curved unevenly. Everything looks blurry to people with astigmatism.

Eye exams are important to ensure that your eyes are healthy and working well. Be sure to cooperate with vision checks at school. If you wear glasses, it's important to have your eyes rechecked every two years; more often if there is a family history of eye disease or if you wear contact lenses. Also, have a parent take you to an eye doctor anytime you have a problem seeing.

CAUSE AND EFFECT What may be the cause if everything you see on the chalkboard appears blurry?
astigmatism

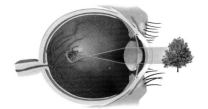
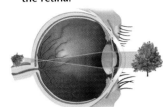

If you are nearsighted (above), the image will focus in front of the retina. If you are farsighted (below), the image will focus behind the retina.

If your eyes feel tired or you get headaches when using a computer, tell a parent. You may need to see an eye doctor. ▶

53

Science

Lenses Corrective lenses work by bending light. Have students do research to find out about concave and convex lenses. Have them make drawings to illustrate how each type of lens works and some instruments that use each type of lens.

Teacher Tip

Vision Problems If you have visually impaired students, be sensitive as you discuss this lesson. Some students may be sensitive or embarrassed about having to wear glasses. Encourage any student who wants to volunteer information. Also, refer students who seem to have problems reading or seeing the board to the school nurse or other appropriate personnel. Remind students that it is important to cooperate in school health screenings, such as vision checks.

---

2. TEACH

Interpret Visuals—Diagrams

Ask volunteers to use the diagram on page 52 to trace the path of light as it travels through the eye. Tell them to use the labels on the diagram as they explain the path. You may also want to use Transparency 17.

How does the iris control the amount of light entering the eye? Muscles in the iris control the size of the pupil, which determines how much light can enter.

Do you have to think about changing the size of the pupil for it to happen? No; the action is automatic and involuntary.

Discuss

Tell students that the shape of the eyeball determines farsightedness or nearsightedness. People who are farsighted have eyeballs that are slightly flattened; people who are nearsighted have eyeballs that are slightly elongated.

Critical Thinking Name some of the things that would be hard to see clearly if you were farsighted. Possible answer: words in a book, an art project, a computer game **Name some things that would be hard to see clearly if you were nearsighted.** Possible answer: a friend standing across the street, football players on a field, signs on streets or buildings

▰ **Pᴇʀsᴏɴᴀʟ Hᴇᴀʟᴛʜ Pʟᴀɴ** ▶

Answers should include the following:
- Tell your parents or another adult that you are having trouble seeing.
- Get your eyes checked by an optometrist or ophthalmologist.
- Follow through on the doctor's recommendation, such as getting glasses and wearing them as directed.

Using Visuals—Pictures

Have students study the picture of the person mowing the lawn. Ask them to identify the equipment he is using to protect his eyes and ears. Ask students to tell how each piece of equipment offers protection.

When Minutes Count ...

Transparency 17: The Eye can be used to present material in this lesson. *Interactive Transparencies available on CD-ROM.*

Activity

Caring Students' responses will vary. Students may suggest that Montel explain to his classmates the importance of wearing goggles or use another method of spreading the word about eye safety.

Health Background

Selecting Sunglasses The following are suggestions for selecting sunglasses.

- Check the American National Standards Institute (ANSI) rating. Sunglasses labeled general-purpose block 60 percent to 90 percent of visible light, 95 percent of ultraviolet B light (UVB) light, and 60 percent of ultraviolet A (UVA) light. Special-purpose sunglasses are rated higher for visible light (about 97 percent) and for UVB light (about 99 percent); these glasses are made for very bright conditions, such as those found on beaches and in the snow. Cosmetic sunglasses rate lower and are more for show than for protection.

- Lenses need to be quite dark, but darkness does not guarantee UV protection. Glasses that are too dark can decrease vision, which can lead to accidents or injuries.

Source: *American National Standards Institute*

For more background, visit the **Webliography** in Teacher Resources at **www.harcourtschool.com/health** **Keyword** personal care

---

ACTIVITY

Building Good Character

Caring During a science experiment, students are using hot liquids, glassware, and chemicals. Montel is surprised that some classmates remove their goggles when the teacher isn't looking. List two things that Montel can do to encourage his classmates to wear their safety goggles.

Protecting Your Vision

Although your body has ways to protect them, your eyes can still be damaged. If you play sports, fast-moving objects can hit your eyes. You should wear safety goggles for protection. You should also wear them when you work with sharp objects, hot liquids, or household cleaners. All of these things can seriously damage your eyes. If you're around someone who is cutting grass, sanding wood, or pounding nails, wear safety goggles to protect your eyes from dust and flying objects.

The UV rays that damage your skin can damage your eyes, too. Even on partly cloudy days, wear sunglasses to protect your eyes. The darkness of the tint is not a good indicator of UV protection. Look for sunglasses with a label stating that they block all UV rays.

SUMMARIZE Name five situations in which you should wear safety goggles.

Possible answer: when playing sports; when working with sharp objects; when using hot liquids; when using household cleaners; when around someone mowing a lawn

People mowing their lawns should protect their eyes, ears, and skin by wearing safety goggles (below), ear plugs, a hat, and sunscreen. ▶

54

Teacher Tip

20/20 Vision A person who has 20/20 vision can see from 20 feet what should normally be seen at that distance. A person who has 20/80 vision must be as close as 20 feet to see what a person with normal vision can see from 80 feet. The term *20/20 vision* refers only to the clarity or sharpness of images seen at a distance. It does not measure other important elements of vision, such as peripheral vision, depth perception, or focusing ability.

Science

Vision in Animals Have students research information about vision in animals such as deer, insects, or fish. Some topics they might consider include these: (1) Do other animals have color vision? (2) How do insects use UV light to help them find nectar? (3) Which animals can see farthest? (4) Why are the eyes of some animals, such as rabbits, placed far apart on the head?

The outer ear directs sound waves into the *ear canal.*

2 Sound waves cause the *eardrum* to vibrate.

3 Vibrations cause the *hammer* to move the *anvil,* which moves the *stirrup.*

4 The moving stirrup causes fluid in the *cochlea* to vibrate. Hairlike cells lining the cochlea move, changing the vibrations into nerve signals.

5 The *auditory nerve* carries the signals to the brain, where they are interpreted as sound.

How You Hear

Your ears collect sound waves, process them, and send nerve messages to your brain. This enables you to hear sounds. The outer ear collects sound waves and directs them into the ear canal. There, sound waves make the eardrum vibrate. The vibrations are passed to three small bones in the middle ear. As the bones move, fluid in the inner ear vibrates. Tiny hairlike cells turn the vibrations into nerve signals. These signals are carried to the brain, where they are interpreted as sound. Trace the path of sound in the diagram above.

Like your eyes, your ears have some built-in protection. Most of the ear is within the skull and so is protected by bone. In the ear canal, glands produce a waxy material that traps dirt before it can reach the internal ear parts.

Tubes lead from your middle ear to your throat. These tubes drain fluid that collects in your ears and helps keep air pressure the same on both sides of the eardrum. This protects the delicate eardrum and keeps your ears working well.

> **SEQUENCE Describe the path, as a series of ordered steps, that sound takes through the ear.**
> outer ear, ear canal, eardrum, hammer, anvil, stirrup, cochlea, auditory nerve

Did You Know?

Did you ever feel your ears "pop" when you were riding in an airplane or in an elevator? This feeling was caused by pressure building up in your ears. The popping occurred when the tubes that run between your ears and your throat opened up to relieve the pressure. This is your body's way to prevent ear damage.

55

Interpret Visuals—Diagrams

Have students use the diagram to trace the path of sound as it travels through the ear canal to the auditory nerve.

Where are sound waves converted into mechanical vibrations? eardrum

Where do vibrations become nerve signals? auditory nerve

Discuss

Tell students that the inner ear contains a structure called the semicircular canal, which is filled with fluid. When a person moves his or her head in any direction, the fluid in the canal sloshes around. This enables the nervous system to constantly track body position. Confusing or rapidly changing movements can cause a person to feel dizzy or sick.

Critical Thinking Why could riding in a car or on a wild carnival ride cause a person to feel sick? because the movements of the car or ride can produce confusing or rapidly changing movements in the semicircular canal

When Minutes Count . . .

Transparency 18: The Ear can be used to present material in this lesson. *Interactive Transparencies available on CD-ROM.*

Health Background

Earwax The outer ear is lined with hair follicles and glands that produce a wax called cerumen. Together, the hairs and wax prevent dust and other foreign materials from entering the ear. Normally the wax moves to the opening of the ear, where it falls out or is removed during washing. Sometimes, however, the wax isn't removed and instead builds up and hardens, which can cause some hearing loss. The buildup may also cause some discomfort. Hardened earwax should be removed only by a health-care professional.

Source: *Washington State University*

For more background, visit the **Webliography** in Teacher Resources at **www.harcourtschool.com/health** **Keyword** personal care

Meeting Individual Needs Leveled Activities

BELOW-LEVEL Explain Sound Have students make a series of drawings to explain how sound is produced, how it is transmitted to the ear, and how it moves through the ear.

ON-LEVEL Explore Sound Have students perform experiments to find out how sound travels through solids, liquids, and gases. Encourage them to use science books to find experiments that they can reproduce.

ADVANCED Demonstrate Sound Have students prepare demonstrations to show the rest of the class that sound is produced from vibrations. Encourage them to use science books and other resources to find demonstrations.

TEACH *continued*

Content-Area Reading Support

Using Text Format Direct students' attention to the text in the Health & Technology box. Have them identify the use of health-related technology in the school. Remind them of the importance of cooperating in school health screenings, such as hearing tests.

How does the information in the box relate to the lesson? Both are about sound waves and hearing. The text in the feature provides information about hearing tests and how they work.

Point out that textbooks often use features to present interesting facts that are related to the topic of a lesson. Comment that students may want to read the primary text through before returning to feature text so as not to interrupt the flow of ideas and information.

Interpret Visuals—Graphs

Have students read the graph on page 57.

How many times louder is a firecracker than a whisper? six times louder **The horn of an automobile produces a sound of 115 decibels. Between which sounds on the graph does this fall?** between a firecracker (120 decibels) and headphones/loud concert (110 decibels) **A sewing machine and some printers both produce sounds at 60 decibels. Are these sounds harmful to the ear? How do you know?** No; both are below the 80-decibel level, the level at which the

When Minutes Count . . .

Transparency 18: The Ear can be used to present material in this lesson. *Interactive Transparencies available on CD-ROM.*

Quick Activity

Students' lists will vary. Preventive measures may include using earplugs and turning down the volume.

▲ Earmuffs and earplugs can reduce the sound level that reaches your ears. You should use ear protection when you're around loud noises.

56

Protecting Your Hearing

Like your eyes, your ears are delicate organs. Follow these guidelines to take care of your ears and protect your hearing.

- Be careful when you wash your ears. Wash only the outside of your ears.
- Never put anything into your ear canals. Small objects, including cotton swabs, can damage your ears.
- Ask a parent if you think your ear canals need to be cleaned. You may need an appointment with a doctor or nurse to clean them.
- If something gets stuck in your ear, don't try to get it out yourself. You may push the object deeper into your ear. A doctor should remove the object.

Loud sounds can harm your ears by damaging the tiny hairlike cells in the cochlea. If these cells are damaged, you could lose part of your hearing. The body can't replace these cells, so the damage may be permanent. The best way to protect your hearing is to avoid loud sounds as much as possible. Keep your television, stereo, and other sources of sound at a reasonable volume. You should also cooperate during hearing tests at school.

Hearing tests can determine if you have a hearing loss. A doctor can prescribe a hearing aid if there is a serious hearing loss.

Teacher Tip

Easing Earache Frequency, Fear, and Pain Pain from an ear infection can be very intense. To avoid ear pain, students should learn to blow their noses in a steady, easy way. Tell students to see a doctor if they have an earache. The doctor will use an otoscope, a tool with a bright light, to look inside the ear canal to check for redness and inflammation and for signs of fluid buildup.

Integrated Language Arts/ Reading Skills

Sign Language Have interested students find out about the different types of communication, such as sign language and lip reading, that are used by people with hearing impairments. Tell them to use diagrams and demonstrations to inform the class about one type of communication.

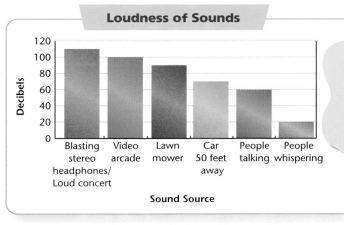

Loudness of Sounds

Decibels / Sound Source

Quick Activity

Based on the graph, list three sounds that could damage your hearing. What can you do to prevent damage in each example you list?

The loudness of sounds is measured in units called **decibels** (DEHS•uh•buhlz). Over time, any continuous sound at or above 85 decibels can damage your ears.

 DRAW CONCLUSIONS Name two things you do for which you should wear ear protection.
Possible answer: ride a snowmobile, use a lawn mower

Lesson 3 Summary and Review

❶ Summarize with Vocabulary

Use vocabulary and other terms from this lesson to complete these statements.

A person who is _____ clearly sees things that are far away, but nearby things look blurry. A person who is _____ clearly sees things that are nearby, but faraway things look blurry. Everything looks blurry to a person who has_____. The loudness of sound is measured in _____. Cells in your eye that sense light are in the _____.

❷ How can you protect your eyes from UV rays?

❸ Critical Thinking Name three things that would appear blurry to you if you were farsighted.

❹ DRAW CONCLUSIONS Complete this graphic organizer to draw a conclusion about taking care of your ears.

❺ Write to Express— Solution to a Problem

Write how you would solve the problem of your brother playing music too loudly.

57

Art

Health Information Have students make posters or brochures about a situation in which a person encounters the loud music of another person, such as when pulling up beside a car that has its radio blaring. Tell students that their posters or brochures should show how to deal with the situation.

Integrated Language Arts/ Reading Skills

Helen Keller Have students read a book about Helen Keller, the American author who was blind, deaf, and mute. Ask students to report to the class about how Keller overcame these life challenges. What personal qualities helped her become successful?

3. WRAP UP

Lesson 3 Summary and Review

1. farsighted; nearsighted; astigmatism; decibels; retina

2. wear sunglasses with UV protection

3. Possible answer: words in a book, images on a computer screen, words on a package label

4. Possible answers are shown below.

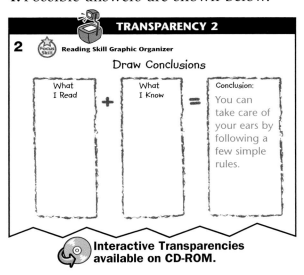

TRANSPARENCY 2

2 **Reading Skill Graphic Organizer**

Draw Conclusions

What I Read + What I Know = Conclusion: You can take care of your ears by following a few simple rules.

Interactive Transparencies available on CD-ROM.

5. Responses will vary but should include information about the harm loud music can cause to the ear.

For **writing models** with examples, see *Teaching Resources* pp. 47–61. Rubrics are also provided.

 When Minutes Count . . .

Quick Study Students can use *Activity Book* pp. 6–7 (shown on p. 41) as they complete each lesson in this chapter.

Life Skills

Communicate
Make Responsible Decisions
Manage Stress
Refuse
Resolve Conflicts
Set Goals

Objectives
▶ Identify the steps to communicate.
▶ Use the communicating steps to solve problems.

Program Resources
▶ Activity Book p. 9
▶ Poster 7

1. MOTIVATE

Have students identify ways to enhance personal communication skills. Have them think of times when they needed to talk to a parent or guardian about a possible health concern or conflict. How did they handle the situation? How can they improve communication with the parent or guardian in the future?

2. TEACH

Direct students' attention to the photos of Kayla thinking about how she will talk to her father about the concert tickets.

Step 1
Why will Kayla's dad be concerned about the front-row tickets? He knows the music may be loud enough to damage their ears.

Step 2
Why is it important that Kayla use respect while talking with her dad? Respectful behavior, such as using a pleasant tone of voice and making eye contact, is part of good communication.

Communicate
with Your Family About Protecting Your Hearing

You communicate every day with family, friends, and strangers. Learning to do this better can improve your relationships with others. You can use the steps for **Communicating** to help you communicate more effectively.

Kayla has won front-row tickets to a rock concert. She knows that the music will be loud and her dad will be concerned about protecting her hearing. How can Kayla communicate with her dad about the concert?

1 **Understand your audience.**

"Wow! Great tickets!" thinks Kayla. But she wonders how she'll tell her dad that they're sitting in the front row. He'll tell her it's bad for her hearing.

2 **Give a clear message. Use a respectful tone of voice.**

I've never had tickets for the front row before. What if we wear earplugs?

Kayla calmly and respectfully explains to her dad why she wants to sit in the front row. Then she makes a suggestion.

58

Teacher Tip

Communication Students may have difficulty discussing certain health issues with a parent or guardian. Encourage students to discuss the Steps to Communicate with family members so that in the future, communicating may be made easier for everyone in the family.

ACTIVITY BOOK P. 9

Name _____

🔍 Problem Solving

Life Skill
Communicate

Steps for Communicating

1. Understand your audience.
2. Give a clear message. Use a respectful tone of voice.
3. Listen carefully and answer any questions.
4. Gather feedback.

Help Denzel and Marta use the steps for communicating.

A. The boys in Denzel's class have volunteered to make 100 sandwiches for a local shelter. Denzel's job is to see that the sandwiches are made and wrapped for delivery. Before work begins, Denzel must make sure the boys' hands and fingernails are clean.
• How can Denzel get his classmates to cooperate about washing their hands?

Possible answer: Denzel can explain that germs can be passed from one person to another by unwashed hands. He can make sure there are soap, nail brushes, and towels and a proper place for everyone to wash up.

B. Marta and her friends Ellen and Callen are shopping for sunscreen, and they are having a difficult time making a choice. Ellen wants to buy the brand her favorite TV actress advertises. Callen wants the cheapest brand, and Marta wants a sunscreen with an SPF of at least 30.
• How can Marta help her friends make a responsible selection?

Possible answer: First, she should explain that the most important thing the product must do is protect the girls' skin from ultraviolet rays. Marta can suggest that they compare prices and ingredients of three brands. Then they can add other criteria to use as they make their comparisons.

 Available online.
www.harcourtschool.com/health

3 Listen carefully, and answer any questions.

That's a good idea, but if it's still too loud, will you agree to leave?

Yes.

Kayla listens to her dad telling her about leaving if the music is still too loud.

4 Gather feedback.

Enjoying the concert, Kayla?

Kayla asks her dad how the earplugs are working for him. "They're working great," he replies. "They make the concert enjoyable."

Problem Solving

A Roberto shares a room with his older brother. His brother likes to play loud music in their room. Roberto's ears ring after he leaves the bedroom when his brother is playing his music.
- Use the steps for **Communicating** to help Roberto work out this problem with his brother.

B When Susie's dad mows the lawn, the noise is very loud. Susie is afraid that the noise will damage her dad's hearing.
- Explain how Susie can respectfully share her concerns with her dad. Describe solutions she might suggest.

59

Using the Poster

Activity Have students design and display their own posters showing how to communicate to solve problems.

Display Poster 7 to remind students of the Steps to Communicate. The poster can be displayed in the classroom, school cafeteria, or another common area.

POSTER 7

Communicate

The boy is communicating with his parents.

Steps for Communicating

1 Understand your audience.
2 Express your message in a clear, organized way.
3 Listen carefully, and answer any questions.
4 Gather feedback.

How well have YOU COMMUNICATED today?

POSTER 7

Critical Thinking How can Kayla use "I" messages to tell her dad her idea? by making statements such as "I know you are concerned about the loudness of music," "I really want to attend the concert," and "I think I have a solution"

Building Good Character
Remind students that showing respect is an important part of good communication. Using good manners when communicating, such as not interrupting and not using foul language, shows that you respect the person with whom you are talking.

Step 3
What are the signs of a good listener? paying attention while the other person is speaking, nodding, not interrupting, and making sure you understand what the other person is saying

Step 4
What if Kayla's father decides later that they should leave the concert because the music is too loud? Kayla should stick to the compromise that she and her father agreed upon.

3. WRAP UP

Problem Solving

A Roberto should use "I" messages to tell his brother how he feels about the noise. He should also give his brother an opportunity to express his feelings. The two brothers should compromise on a solution.

B Susie should respectfully tell her dad about her concerns and the reasons for them.

Objectives
► Explain the importance of choosing health-care products wisely.
► Identify and evaluate sources of health information.
► Demonstrate how to use labels to make wise product choices.

When Minutes Count . . .
Assign the Quick Study, Lesson 4, Activity Book pp. 6–7 (shown on p. 41).

Program Resources
► Activity Book pp. 6–7, 10
► Transparency 2

Vocabulary
health consumer p. 60,
ingredients p. 62

Daily Fitness Tip

Health products may contain chemicals that cause allergic reactions in some people. If students develop a rash, hives, or an area of irritation after using a new product, they should inform an adult.

 For more guidelines on fitness, see *Be Active! Resources for Physical Education.*

1. MOTIVATE

Have students list brand names of health-care products, such as soaps, shampoos, and lotions. List the names on the board. Discuss what each name suggests.

Why do companies name products the way they do? Possible answers: to get a buyer's attention; to make products sound appealing; to be easy to remember **Do these product names tell you anything about the quality of the products?** no **Where do you think you could get information about the product?** Answers will vary but might include the label.

Being a Health Consumer

LESSON 4

Sources of Health Information

Lesson Focus
As a consumer you make choices about products and services that can affect your health.

Why Learn This?
Learning to read labels carefully and to analyze advertisements can help you become a wise health consumer.

Vocabulary
health consumer
ingredients

Do you help choose your own brand of health-care products, such as soap, shampoo, and toothpaste? If you do, you are a **health consumer**, a person who buys and uses health products or services. Getting good information about products is an important step in making good choices as a health consumer. You also need to know how to compare and evaluate products. Having these skills will help you choose the best products for you and avoid wasting money.

When you gather health information, it's important to choose information that is reliable. Some of the information available to you contains myths. Myths are ideas that are thought to be true by some people but are actually false. Advertising can be one source of health myths.

Your library has books and magazines with information about health. To get facts rather than myths, look for books written by health-care professionals. ▼

Books, posters, newsletters, videos, and magazines about health are sources that can contain reliable health information. ►

60

Meeting Individual Needs
Leveled Activities

BELOW-LEVEL Compare Ingredients Have students choose two similar products, such as two shampoos or two sunscreens. One should be a brand-name product and the other a store-brand product. Have students compare the ingredients and discuss the differences.

ON-LEVEL Write an Ad Bring in samples of beauty products, and give them to small groups of students. Have them write ads that are totally honest about the products. Share the ads with the class.

CHALLENGE Explore Myths Have students find, read, and report on a literary myth. Discuss how these myths relate to the meaning of *myth* in the lesson.

Advertisements appear in many places, including on television, in magazines, on the Internet, on the radio, and in newspapers. Their purpose is to make you want to buy a product, whether it's the best one for you or not. The information in advertisements may be true, false, or misleading. It's important to use reliable sources to determine the truth. That way you can make wise buying choices.

In addition to the sources pictured on these pages, your family is a good source of health information. Health-care professionals are also good sources. Your doctor, dentist, pharmacist, and school nurse can give you and your parents reliable information for making wise consumer choices.

Other good sources of consumer information are magazines published by consumer groups. Consumer groups test and rate health products, such as soaps, hand lotions, shampoos, and sunscreens. Newsletters that are produced by health organizations sometimes rate health products, too.

 DRAW CONCLUSIONS Why might an article from a toothpaste company be a poor source of information about which toothpaste to buy? The article will probably tell only the information that makes you want to buy the product; the information might be misleading or untrue.

Information Alert!

Health information changes as new health studies and new medicines are introduced.

 For the most up-to-date information, visit The Learning Site. www.harcourtschool.com/health

Organizations such as the American Heart Association and the American Cancer Society have pamphlets that contain reliable health information. ▼

61

2. TEACH

Interpret Visuals—Pictures

Direct students' attention to the photographs showing different sources of health information. Have students identify each source.

Where might you find each of these sources? All can be found in a library. Health newsletters can also be found on the Internet at the organizations' websites or by visiting, e-mailing, or phoning the organizations' offices.

Discuss

Ask students what myths they have read. Answers will vary. **In what ways are the myths alike?** Lead students to understand that myths contain characters and events that are not real.

Critical Thinking How can advertising and health information be myth? The information may not be true, although some people may think it is.

 Drama

Talking to Health-Care Professionals Many young people are anxious or self-conscious about asking their doctors or other health-care professionals about health concerns. Remind students that health-care professionals are there to help them and will respect them for asking questions about health-care products. Have pairs of students role-play asking a health-care professional about a certain product. Remind students that questions should be valid and that answers should provide reliable information.

 Integrated Language Arts/ Reading Skills

Advertisements vs. Labels Have students compare the wording in an advertisement to that of a label for the same product. How are the two different? What information does the label contain that the advertisement does not? Have students write a few paragraphs that compare and contrast the advertisement and the product label.

TEACH *continued*

Interpret Visuals—Pictures

Have students study the toothpaste labels pictured on this page.

What information can you find on the labels? Possible answers: product name, amount of the product in the package, list of ingredients. directions for use, cautions

How would this information help consumers when buying the product? Consumers will know what ingredients the product contains so they can decide whether the product is right for them.

What other information might you find on product labels? Possible answers: purpose of the product, directions for use, warnings

Discuss

The first major laws for food labeling were passed in 1906. Labeling on cosmetic products such as shampoo, soap, and makeup was not required by law until 1938.

Critical Thinking Why do you think labeling for cosmetics lagged behind food labeling? Possible answers: The government was more concerned about things people ate because it was obvious these could harm or kill people; the government may not have realized the dangers of products used on the outside of the body.

Learning from Product Labels

Most health products have detailed labels. The label on the front of a product usually gives the product name, a brief explanation of what the product does, and the amount of product in the package. Since this front label shows on the store shelves, manufacturers often include advertising there. Remember to carefully evaluate the information presented in advertising. The toothpaste and shampoo labels on these pages show information that usually appears on the front of a product.

The label on the back of a product often includes additional information. That label includes a fuller explanation of what the product does. You should still be careful when reading the label on the back. It may also contain advertising that may or may not be true.

Also shown on labels is the list of **ingredients** (in•GREE•dee•uhnts), or the things that are in the product. Some products, such as toothpastes and dandruff shampoos, provide health benefits. The ingredients that provide the benefits are listed on the labels as active ingredients.

Myth and Fact

Myth: Certain shampoos can revive lifeless hair.
Fact: The only living parts of your hair are the cells in the hair follicles deep in your scalp. The strands of hair that you see are all dead. Nothing can make them "come alive."

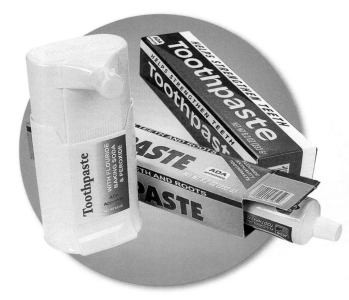

Toothpaste containing fluoride provides a health benefit. The ADA seal tells you the product is approved by the American Dental Association. ▶

62

ESL/ELL Support

COMPREHENSIBLE INPUT Help students understand the meanings of the words *ingredients, directions,* and *warnings.*

Beginning Have students mime the following: adding ingredients to a bowl to make a cake; giving directions to go from the classroom to another school location; and warning someone to stop. Help them relate their mimes to the use of these words in this lesson.

Intermediate Have students write the three words on a sheet of paper and then copy an example of the word from the labels on these pages.

Advanced Tell students to make their own product label that contains a list of ingredients, directions, and a warning label.

Quick Activity

Analyze Labels Make a table with two columns. Label one column *Advertising Claims* and the other *Useful Information*. Analyze the labels on several bottles of shampoo. Then write information from the labels into the table.

Reading the list of ingredients can be important if you have allergies to soaps, perfumes, dyes, flavorings, or other materials. If you read the label, you can avoid using products with ingredients that may harm you.

Most labels give directions for using the products. You may not need directions for some products, such as shampoo. For other health products, such as medicines, it's important to follow the directions very carefully. Failing to follow the directions may be harmful to your health.

Some labels contain product warnings. The warnings contain information that may save your life. It's important to read and follow all product warning information carefully.

SUMMARIZE List the information that is included on health product labels.

ingredients; explanation of what the product does; product warnings; amount of product in container; directions for use; may also include advertising claims

63

Cultural Connection

Health and Cosmetic Products
Have students research health and cosmetic products from around the world, now and at one period in history. They will learn that people have used many natural resources to create efficient health-care products and cosmetics. For example, the ancient Egyptians made eye shadow using black kohl made from the mineral antimony, the lead ore galena, and green malachite, a copper ore. Encourage students to share what they learn by using pictures as well as words.

Integrated Language Arts/ Reading Skills

Cold Medicines Drug companies offer a wide choice of medicines to treat cold symptoms. It is up to consumers to select the right ones for their needs. Although only adults should make decisions about medicines, students should know what they're taking and why. Have students look up the terms *decongestant, antihistamine, analgesic,* and *cough suppressant.* Tell them to summarize what they find out.

Content-Area Reading Support

Using Signal Words Have students read the second paragraph on this page, paying special attention to the words *some* and *other.* Explain that these words signal a comparison—in this case, products that do and do not need directions. Tell students that being aware of words that signal comparisons will help them identify important information as they read. Remind them to stop before they continue reading to make sure they understand what is being compared.

Discuss

Have students demonstrate methods of accessing health information. Help students compare the information from the labels by listing the ingredients from each label on the board. Have volunteers circle any ingredients that are not found in all three products. Then have students identify which ingredient is listed first on each label. Tell students that the first ingredient on a label is the one the product contains the most of.

Critical Thinking What ingredient is the most common in most of these products? water

Quick Activity

Analyze Labels Tell students that one way to decide if information on a label is useful is to ask themselves *Why am I buying this product?* If the information doesn't help meet the purpose of the purchase, then it isn't useful information. Students' answers will vary based on the product label they analyze.

Interpret Visuals—Pictures

Have students read the advertisement on the bus.

What message is the ad presenting? that the product will produce whiter teeth

Why do you think the advertiser chose to place an ad on this bus? because many people will see it as the bus travels around **Where else have you seen advertisements in public places?** Possible answers: on bulletin boards; in store windows; on trains, cars, and trucks

Problem Solving You see an ad on a billboard for a soap that appeals to you. Should you buy the soap? Why or why not? First, you should check the actual product to see if the ingredients and price seem right and if the product meets your particular needs. If so, the product probably is worth buying.

Discuss

Have students research the effects of media on health-promoting behaviors.

Problem Solving A friend says that you can't help being influenced by ads, so you might as well pay attention to them. How would you respond? Not all ads contain reliable information. If you pay attention to ads, especially to ones that are not reliable, you should know how to recognize advertising tricks that are used and know how to get valid

Advertisers try to keep the names of their products in front of you as much as possible. That way, the products will be familiar to you and you might choose them when the time comes to buy. ▶

Consumer
Activity

Make Buying Decisions Which deodorant is the best value? Find out how much three different brands of deodorant cost. Record the number of ounces for each brand. Divide the cost of the deodorant by the number of ounces. This will give you the unit price for each.

Analyzing Advertisements

Ads appear all around you—in magazines and newspapers, on radio and TV, on the Internet and billboards. You even see ads on T-shirts, backpacks, and drinking cups. Advertisers may use easy-to-remember songs to remind you of their products. They might use catchy logos or slogans to grab your attention. Advertising can have a strong influence on you. But if you know the tricks advertisers use to get your attention, you can make good buying choices.

One trick of advertisers is to try to convince you that everyone is using their products. The message is that you should use the products, too, if you want to be popular. Some advertisers use famous people to tell you why you should buy certain products. Advertisers hope that you'll trust the good things the famous people say about the products.

Another trick advertisers use is to make you think that their products are good buys. They may offer free gifts or tell you that buying their products will save you money. Don't be fooled by these tricks. Check what the advertisers are saying to see if the products really are bargains.

64

Social Studies

New Product Development Have students find out how companies develop new health products. You might divide students into groups to research one of the following questions: Who provides the money for the research? How are the products tested? How are they manufactured? Do new products require government approval before they are marketed? How do companies introduce new products to consumers?

Math

Converting Units The amount of a product that is in a container can be identified by using various units, including ounces (oz), fluid ounces (fl oz), grams (g), pounds (lb), liters (l), and milliliters (mL). The differences in labeled units can make it difficult for people to compare prices of different products. Have interested students make charts that show conversions between common metric and customary units as well as equivalent units within each system.

White Toothpaste

Don't be fooled by advertising tricks. Use common sense to evaluate products. Consider a product's cost, features, quality, and safety, and listen to the advice of others. Before you buy something, ask yourself these questions: "Do I really need this product? Will it do what I want it to do? Is the price reasonable?" If you can answer *yes* to all of these questions, you're probably making a wise choice. If you answer *no* to any of the questions, you should think again before buying the product.

Parents and health-care professionals can help you decide whether you really need a product. They may suggest different products. They also may suggest stores that have lower prices for the products you are considering. By listening to the advice of informed consumers, such as your parents, and by using common sense, you can become a wise health consumer.

Advertisers use celebrities to promote their products. People trust celebrities because they feel they know them. This advertiser wants you to believe you can be a celebrity, too, if you visit Dr. Capps. ▼

I got my famous smile from Dr Capps!

MAIN IDEA AND DETAILS Give three details to support this idea: Some advertisers use tricks to get consumers to buy their products.
Answers should include any three tricks from these pages.

65

Consumer Activity

Make Buying Decisions Students' answers will vary based on the different brands they analyze. You might want to have students indicate other factors, such as extra ingredients, they would consider before deciding which product to buy.

Health Background

Evaluating Websites The Internet can be an excellent source of health information. However, not every website contains reliable information. The list below presents tips from the National Institutes of Health about how to evaluate websites that provide health and medical information. Share this information with students and have them describe other methods of accessing health information

- Investigate the source of the website. Read the "About Us" page to find out who is presenting the information.

- Beware of websites that make claims of "miracle" cures or promise quick or effortless results.

- Search for information that is backed by reliable medical or scientific research and not based on opinions or personal testimonials.

- Check the date of the source. When was the website last updated? When was the research completed?

- Consider who may be paying for the website. Does this party have a vested interest in making a product or procedure seem better than it is?

- Check more than one website. Is there conflicting information between different websites? Which is more reliable?

Source: *National Institutes of Health*

For more background, visit the **Webliography** in Teacher Resources at **www.harcourtschool.com/health Keyword** consumer issues

 Music

Product Jingles Have each group of students choose a jingle from a product advertisement and identify any information in the jingle that is not reliable. Tell them to rewrite the words of the jingle so that it tells only true information about the product. Have each group present its new jingle to the class. Allow time for students to evaluate whether each new jingle is as effective at drawing consumers as the original jingle is.

Teacher Tip

Ads Targeting Children Students may not see the subtleties in advertisements that are geared toward people their age. Show students ads from magazines or a video of television ads for products they may use. As a class, evaluate the ads. Help students identify the advertising appeals used in each ad, especially false image and popularity.

3. WRAP UP

Lesson 4 Summary and Review

1. health consumer; ingredients; myths; active ingredients

2. The goal of advertisements is to get you to buy the product, not to give health information.

3. Students' answers will vary but may include books, the Internet, and newsletters from professional organizations.

4. Possible answers are shown below.

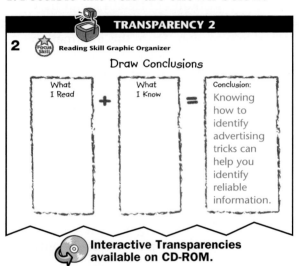

TRANSPARENCY 2

2 **Reading Skill Graphic Organizer**

Draw Conclusions

| What I Read | + | What I Know | = | Conclusion: Knowing how to identify advertising tricks can help you identify reliable information. |

Interactive Transparencies available on CD-ROM.

5. Accept poems that show an understanding of the advertising tricks discussed in this lesson.

For **writing models** with examples, see *Teaching Resources* pp. 47–61. Rubrics are also provided.

When Minutes Count . . .

Quick Study Students can use *Activity Book* pp. 6–7 (shown on p. 41) as they complete each lesson in this chapter.

New Sources of Health Information

The website of the CDC, or Centers for Disease Control and Prevention, has accurate health information. ▼

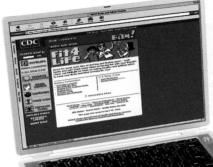

Today you can get reliable health information with the click of a mouse. The Internet enables you to quickly find the answers to many health questions. But anyone can put information on the Internet, so you must make sure that the source you use is reliable. Unreliable sources may give wrong or even dangerous health information. Websites hosted by the government and by hospitals, universities, and professional organizations are the most reliable.

Remember that even reliable sites aren't designed to answer all health questions. They can't replace the advice that you get from a parent, your doctor, or other health-care professional.

SUMMARIZE Tell why evaluating health information on the Internet is important.
Some Internet sites give wrong or dangerous health information.

Lesson 4 Summary and Review

❶ Summarize with Vocabulary

Use vocabulary and other terms from the lesson to complete the statements.

A _____ buys or uses health products or services. A person who is allergic to certain things should check the lists of _____ that are on the health-care products he or she uses. Ideas that are thought to be true by some people but are actually false are known as _____. Ingredients that provide medical benefits are known as _____.

❷ Why do you think some advertisers use misleading information instead of reliable health information?

❸ Critical Thinking What sources could you use to find reliable information about the benefits of adding fluoride to toothpaste?

❹ DRAW CONCLUSIONS Complete this graphic organizer to draw a conclusion about the importance of being a wise consumer.

| What I Read | + | What I Know | = | Conclusion: |

❺ Write to Entertain—Poem

Write a poem that tells about the tricks advertisers use to get consumers to buy their products.

66

Teacher Tip

Search for Answers Have each student write a health question that cannot be answered with information from the textbook. Tell students to research their topics and write answers based on their findings. Explain that they must identify three sources that support their answers. Have students share their questions and answers with the class.

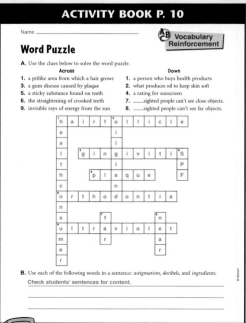

ACTIVITY BOOK P. 10

Name _____

Vocabulary Reinforcement

Word Puzzle

A. Use the clues below to solve the word puzzle.

Across
1. a pitlike area from which a hair grows
3. a gum disease caused by plaque
5. a sticky substance found on teeth
6. the straightening of crooked teeth
9. invisible rays of energy from the sun

Down
1. a person who buys health products
2. what produces oil to keep skin soft
4. a rating for sunscreen
7. _____ sighted people can't see close objects
8. _____ sighted people can't see far objects

B. Use each of the following words in a sentence: *astigmatism, decibels,* and *ingredients*.
Check students' sentences for content.

Available online. www.harcourtschool.com/health

Math

Calculate Savings Your favorite shampoo is on sale in two different sizes. The 12-ounce bottle is $4.49, and the 8-ounce bottle is $3.19. Which size is less expensive per ounce? How much less?

Science

Show How Sound Travels Research sound to find out how sound waves travel. Then make a visual display to show what you learn.

Technology

Tell About Dental Lasers Dental lasers are replacing drills in some dentists' offices. Lasers can be used to treat cavities with less pain and noise than a drill. Lasers are used for gum surgery, too. Find more information about dental lasers. Then make a video, a slide presentation, a poster, or a brochure about this new technology.

GO ONLINE For more activities, visit The Learning Site. www.harcourtschool.com/health

Home & Community

Identify Noise Pollution Make a list of loud noises that you hear in or around your home. Talk with your parents or, with your parent's approval, community leaders about possible ways to reduce any dangerously loud noise. If it can't be reduced, identify ways to protect your hearing from this noise pollution.

Career Link

Orthodontist Orthodontists are dentists who specialize in straightening teeth and correcting other problems of the mouth. Suppose you are an orthodontist. Make a brochure for your patients to explain the importance of orthodontia to good dental health. In the brochure, explain the importance of cleaning your teeth carefully while wearing braces.

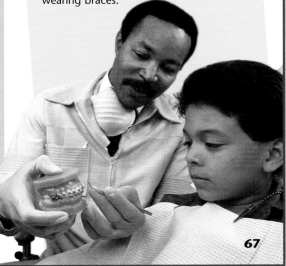

67

Activities

Science

Sound waves are mechanical waves that travel somewhat like water waves. Students might use the Internet to find details about the movement of sound.

Math

The 12-ounce bottle is cheaper per ounce ($0.37 per ounce, compared to $0.40 per ounce for the 8-ounce bottle).

Home & Community

Noises might include music from home stereo or car stereo systems, construction equipment from the street, lawn mowers, jet planes flying overhead, power tools, and automobile horns. Hearing can be protected by wearing earplugs or earmuffs.

Supports the Coordinated School Health Program

Technology Project

Dental lasers can be used to vaporize tooth decay and remove bacteria from the area of decay as well. The laser is set at a precise wavelength so that the healthy part of the tooth is not damaged. Most patients do not need any anesthetic for the procedure. Have students present their finished video, slide presentation, poster, or brochure to the class.

Career Link

Orthodontist Only about 6 percent of dentists are orthodontists. Orthodontists are dentists who have completed an additional two- to three-year residency program in orthodontics.

Students' brochures should include information about why it is important to have a proper bite alignment. In many cases, having braces is not just to make the person look good, but also to preserve the health of the teeth and provide proper alignment of the bite and the jaws.

For more information on health careers, visit the **Webliography** in Teacher Resources at **www.harcourtschool.com/health** **Keyword** health careers

Chapter Review and Test Preparation

Pages 68–69

 Reading Skill 8 pts. each

1. Accept graphic organizers that include the important information about UV rays from pages 41–42.

2. Answers will vary.

3. Possible answer: UV rays can harm the body; therefore, the body should be protected from them.

 Use Vocabulary 3 pts. each

4. gingivitis

5. plaque

6. orthodontia

7. decibels

8. astigmatism

9. farsighted

10. myths

 Check Understanding 3 pts. each

11. A, deodorant

12. J, ultraviolet rays

13. D, oil glands

14. H, hair follicles

15. B, sun protection factor

16. J, bathing suit

17. D, retina

18. J, crown

19. A, optic nerve

20. J, cochlea

 Think Critically 5 pts. each

21. Look at the ingredients list on the label to see if it is listed as an ingredient.

 Reading Skill

DRAW CONCLUSIONS
Draw and then use this graphic organizer to answer questions 1–3.

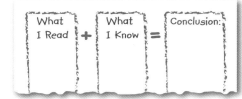

1 Write what you read in this chapter about the sun's effects on your body.
2 Write what you already knew about the sun's effects on your body.
3 Write a conclusion you can draw from this information.

 Use Vocabulary

Use vocabulary and other terms from this lesson to complete the statements.

4 If left untreated, _____ can lead to serious gum disease that may cause tooth loss.

5 A sticky substance called _____ forms naturally on your teeth.

6 The correction of crooked teeth is called _____.

7 The loudness of sound is measured in units called _____.

8 All images are blurry for a person with _____.

9 A(n) _____ person can see things clearly that are far away.

10 Ideas thought to be true but which are actually false are called _____.

68

Check Understanding

Choose the letter of the correct answer.

11 Which of the following would a health consumer purchase? (p. 60)
A deodorant   C candy bar
B compact disc   D ice-cream bar

12 Invisible rays given off by the sun are called _____. (p. 41)
F sonic rays   H tanning rays
G sound waves   J ultraviolet rays

13 The _____ release oil that coats your hair and your skin. (p. 44)
A hair shafts   C hair follicles
B hair surfaces   D oil glands

14 Hair grows from pitlike areas in your skin, called _____. (p. 44)
F hard nails   H hair follicles
G bones   J retinas

15 The term *SPF* means _____. (p. 42)
A sound protection factor
B sun protection factor
C silent protection factor
D saving protection factor

16 Which of the following would **NOT** be used for sun protection? (p. 42)

F   H

G   J

Formal Assessment

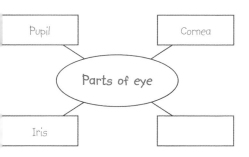

Pupil

Cornea

Parts of eye

Iris

17 Which word or phrase is missing from the graphic organizer? (p. 52)
A follicle   **C** auditory nerve
B shaft   **D** retina

18 The top part of a tooth, as shown in the diagram, is called the _____. (p. 49)

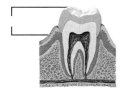

F root   **H** pulp
G dentin   **J** crown

19 Which of the following is **NOT** part of the ear? (p. 55)
A optic nerve
B auditory nerve
C cochlea
D hammer

20 The coiled tube in your inner ear is known as the _____. (p. 55)
F stirrup   **H** Eustachian tube
G anvil   **J** cochlea

Think Critically

21 Suppose your doctor tells you to use a face wash that contains benzoyl peroxide. At the drugstore, you see several face washes. How can you be certain that the one you choose contains benzoyl peroxide?

22 You want to floss your teeth every day, but you keep forgetting. What type of cue could you use to remind you to floss at the same time every day?

Apply Skills

23 **BUILDING GOOD CHARACTER**
Respect You have been asked by a youth group to give a presentation on skin care. Apply what you know about respect and developing self-confidence to tell how you would prepare for your presentation.

24 **LIFE SKILLS**
Communicate Your sister likes to listen to her favorite CDs with her headphones. The music is so loud that you can hear it across the room. How can you communicate a responsible way for her to listen to music?

Write About Health

25 **Write to Inform—Explain** Identify a variety of consumer influences, including advertising methods, that affect the buying habits of you and your classmates. Write a paragraph to explain how these influences affect your buying decisions.

69

---

22. Possible answer: Hang a piece of floss on your toothbrush or around the toothpaste tube.

Apply Skills 5 pts. each

23. Responses should include that a person can respect himself or herself and feel self-confident by looking his or her best and being prepared.

24. Possible answer: You should respectfully tell your sister that you are concerned about the damage that the loud music will cause to her ears. You could support your concerns with facts from this chapter.

Write About Health 5 pts.

25. Students' answers will vary but may include some of the consumer influences described on page 64.

Performance Assessment

Use the Chapter Project and the rubric provided on the Project Evaluation Sheet. See *Assessment Guide* pp. 18, 56, 63.

Portfolio Assessment

Have students select their best work from the following suggestions:
- Leveled Activities, p. 60
- Quick Activity, p. 63
- Write to Inform, p. 51
- Activities, p. 67

See *Assessment Guide* pp. 12–16.

ASSESSMENT GUIDE P. 24

Name _____

Complete the following table by supplying the missing situation, action, or reason for acting or not acting.

Possible answers:

	Situation	Action Taken or Not Taken	Reason
	You have coughed or sneezed into your hands.	Wash your hands thoroughly.	Washing helps stop the spread of germs left on your hands by coughing or sneezing.
21.	You are going to be out in the sun all afternoon.	You apply a sunscreen.	The sunscreen will help prevent sunburn and skin damage.
22.	You are changing clothes after soccer practice.	Do not share combs, hairbrushes, or hair decorations.	Head lice can be passed from person to person by sharing combs, hairbrushes, and hair decorations.
23.	You are near someone who is cutting grass, sawing wood, or heating chemicals.	Wear safety goggles.	Small particles can fly into your eyes and injure them.
24.	You are working near loud noise such as the sound of a jackhammer.	Wear earmuffs or earplugs.	Exposure over time to sounds louder than 85 decibels can damage your hearing.
25.	You are going to purchase a new shampoo.	Read the ingredients lists on product labels.	You may be allergic to certain soaps or perfumes.

24 • Assessment Guide   (page 3 of 3)   Being a Wise Health Consumer • Chapter 2

Lesson	Pacing	Objectives	Reading Skills
Introduce the Chapter pp. 70–71		• Preview chapter concepts.	🔵 **Compare and Contrast** p. 71; pp. 372–383
1 Food—Fuel for the Body pp. 72–77	1 class period	• Identify the six basic nutrients. • Describe how the basic nutrients give the body energy.	🔵 **Compare and Contrast** pp. 72, 76, 77 • Sequence, p. 73 • Draw Conclusions, pp. 74, 75 • Main Idea and Details, p. 77
2 The Food Guide Pyramid pp. 78–83	2 class periods	• Explain how to use the USDA Food Guide Pyramid to help plan a balanced diet. • Identify the food groups used in the USDA Food Guide Pyramid. • Understand the size of a serving.	🔵 **Compare and Contrast** pp. 79, 81 • Summarize, p. 81
3 Eating Healthfully pp. 84–87	1 class period	• Understand the importance of portion control when deciding on the number and size of servings. • Describe the importance between calories and energy balance.	🔵 **Compare and Contrast** pp. 86, 87 • Main Idea and Details, pp. 82, 84 • Summarize, p. 85
4 Influences on Your Food Choices pp. 88–94	1 class period	• Explain how family, friends, and culture affect food choices. • Explain how health, the seasons, emotions, and knowledge about foods may affect food choices.	🔵 **Compare and Contrast** pp. 92, 94 • Main Idea and Details, p. 89 • Summarize, p. 91 • Cause and Effect, p. 94
⭐ **Building Good Character** p. 95		• Learn how practicing self-control helps you choose healthful foods.	
5 Food Labels and Advertising pp. 96–99	1 class period	• Explain how to use food labels to evaluate the nutrition of foods. • Describe the influences of advertising on food choices.	🔵 **Compare and Contrast** p. 99 • Summarize, p. 97 • Main Idea and Details, p. 99
Life Skills pp. 100–101	1 class period	• Identify decision-making steps. • Use decision-making steps to make healthful food choices.	
6 Food Preparation and Safety pp. 102–106	1 class period	• Explain how germs get into food and what they do to it. • Describe how to store and prepare food safely.	🔵 **Compare and Contrast** pp. 103, 106 • Cause and Effect, p. 102
Activities p. 107		• Extend chapter concepts.	
Chapter Review pp. 108–109	1 class period	• Assess chapter objectives.	

Vocabulary	Program Resources
	Music CD Teaching Resources, p. 27
nutrients enzymes carbohydrates fats proteins vitamins minerals	Transparencies 1, 9 Activity Book, pp. 11–13
nutritionist Food Guide Pyramid serving	Transparencies 1, 19 Activity Book, pp. 11–12
portion control anorexia calories energy balance	Transparency 1 Activity Book, pp. 11–12
food allergy	Transparency 1 Activity Book, pp. 11–12
	Poster 4
ingredients additives preservatives	Transparency 1 Activity Book, pp. 11–12
	Activity Book, p. 14 Poster 8
food poisoning	Transparency 1 Activity Book, pp. 11–12, 15
	The Learning Site www. harcourtschool.com/health
	Assessment Guide, pp. 25–27

 Interactive Transparencies available on CD-ROM.

 Focus Skill **Reading Skill**

These reading skills are reinforced throughout this chapter and one skill is emphasized as the Focus Skill.

Compare and Contrast

- Draw Conclusions
- Identify Cause and Effect
- Identify Main Idea and Details
- Sequence
- Summarize

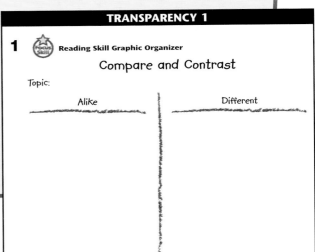

TRANSPARENCY 1

1 Reading Skill Graphic Organizer
Compare and Contrast
Topic:
Alike   Different

POSTER 8

Life Skills

Life Skills are health-enhancing behaviors that can help students reduce risks to their health and safety.

Six Life Skills are reinforced throughout *Harcourt Health and Fitness*. The skill emphasized in this chapter is Make Responsible Decisions.

Make Responsible Decisions

The boy is making a responsible decision about choosing a healthful snack.

Steps for Making Responsible Decisions

1 Find out about the choices you could make.

2 Eliminate choices that are against your family rules.

3 Ask yourself: What could happen with each choice? Does the choice show good character?

4 Make what seems to be the best choice.

What RESPONSIBLE DECISIONS have YOU MADE today?

POSTER 8

Building Good Character

Character education is an important aspect of health education. When students behave in ways that show good character, they promote the health and safety of themselves and others.

Six character traits are reinforced throughout *Harcourt Health and Fitness*. The trait emphasized in this chapter is Responsibility.

POSTER 5

Responsibility Character

The boy is showing responsibility by being a good role model for his sister.

DO
- Practice self-control.
- Express feelings, needs, and wants in appropriate ways.
- Practice good health habits.
- Keep yourself safe.
- Keep trying. Do your best.
- Complete tasks.
- Set goals and work toward them.
- Be a good role model.

DON'T
- Don't smoke. Don't use alcohol or other drugs.
- Don't do things that are unsafe or that destroy property.
- Don't be led by negative peer pressure.
- Don't deny or make excuses for your mistakes.
- Don't leave your work for others to do.
- Don't lose or misuse your belongings.

How have YOU shown RESPONSIBILITY today?

POSTER 5

Coordinated School Health Program

A Coordinated School Health Program endeavors to improve children's health and, therefore, their capacity to learn through the support of families, schools, and communities working together. The following information is provided to help classroom teachers be more aware of these resources.

The National Center for Chronic Disease and Health Promotion, part of the **CDC,** funds the Coordinated School Health Program. Visit its website for information about the eight components that make up this program.
www.cdc.gov/nccdphp/dash/

California Healthy Kids provides reviewed health educational, instructional materials for free loan to California residents. The materials include such topics as nutrition education and food safety.
www.californiahealthykids.org

The U.S. surgeon general has declared childhood obesity an epidemic in the United States. For photocopies of journal articles on this and related topics, visit the **Texas Medical Association** website.
www.texmed.org

The goals of the Coordinated Approach to Child Health **(CATCH)** are to help schools, children, and families adopt positive changes in eating and physical activity to improve long-term health.

CATCH has four components, one of which is *Eat Smart. Play Hard*™.
www.fns.usda.gov/FNS/

Other resources that support a Coordinated School Health Program:
• School-Home Connection
• Daily Physical Activity
• Daily Fitness Tips
• Activities: Home & Community
• Health Background: Webliography
• *Be Active! Resources for Physical Education*

Media Resources

Books for Students

Silverstein, Alvin. *Eat Your Vegetables! Drink Your Milk!* Franklin Watts, 2000. Explains why proper eating habits make for wellness. **EASY**

Peters, Celeste A. *Peppers, Popcorn, and Pizza.* Raintree/Steck-Vaughn, 2000. Explains the scientific aspects of food. **AVERAGE**

Harbison, Elizabeth M. *Loaves of Fun.* Chicago Review Press, 1997. Teaches about bread through illustrations and recipes. **ADVANCED**

Books for Teachers and Families

USDA. *Science in Your Shopping Cart.* United States Department of Agriculture, Agricultural Research Service, 1999. Explains how the ARS improves our lives in the food we eat.

Rickert, Vaughn I., Ed. *Adolescent Nutrition.* Chapman & Hall, 1995. Explains the needs of this age student.

Free and Inexpensive Materials

Get Healthy Shop
Get a free PocketPlan journal to help start a lifestyle fitness program.

Dairy Council of California
Classroom health education materials on nutrition are free of charge to California teachers.

Leafy Greens Council
Will send free book covers, trading cards, brochures, and posters.

Eden Foods
Will send a free T-shirt to students submitting Eden-themed drawings and photos.

To access free and inexpensive resources on the Web, visit
www.harcourtschool.com/health/free

Videos

Nutrition Facts—The New Food Label. Family Experiences Productions, Inc., 1994.

Food into Fuel: Our Digestive System. Rainbow Educational Media, 1992.

Start Shopping for Good Nutrition. Educational Video Network, 1999.

These resources have been selected to meet a variety of individual needs. Please review all materials and websites prior to sharing them with students to ensure the content is appropriate for your class. Note that information, while correct at time of publication, is subject to change.

Visit **The Learning Site** for related links, activities, resources, and the health **Webliography.**

www.harcourtschool.com/health

Meeting Individual Needs

ESL/ELL

Below-Level

Have students write a new word on an index card and cut it into parts based on its syllables or word parts. Have them identify the strategy, such as context clues or spelling patterns, that helped them identify the word. Students can tape the parts back together to make the word.

Activities

- Plastic Bag Digestion, p. 74
- Student Cookbook, p. 88
- Sequencing Nutrients, p. 96
- Draw and Label Bacteria, p. 105

On-Level

Using text structure and format can help students understand new words and information. Have them look at the chapter headings for clues on how the author organized information. If students have trouble, tell them to think about how the words and pictures go together.

Activities

- Balloon Esophagus, p. 74
- Finding "Hidden Sugars," p. 88
- Comparing Labels, p. 96
- Research One Bacterium, p. 105

Challenge

Have students use the Internet or library resources to explore the history of a health-related subject. Have them make a time line on paper strips of facts or events related to the topic. They should write the related facts or events at appropriate points on the time line.

Activities

- Digestion Models, p. 74
- Comparing Sugars, p. 88
- Calculate Recommended Daily Allowances, p. 96
- How to Prevent Illness from One Bacterium, p. 105

Learning Log

After reading about a concept, students can use a Learning Log to think about what they have learned. In it they can reflect on new information, evaluate areas that are unclear to them, and write questions they want to discuss with the class.

Activities

- Comprehensible Input, pp. 76, 78, 98, 102
- Background and Experience, p. 84
- Language and Vocabulary, p. 92

Curriculum Integration

Integrated Language Arts/Reading Skills

- Write a Jingle, p. 99

Math

- Calculate Servings, p. 81
- Calorie Combinations, p. 86
- Unit Pricing Problems
- Storage-Time Graph, p. 103

Physical Education

- Daily Fitness Tip, pp. 72, 78, 84, 88, 96, 102
- Daily Physical Activity, p. 71

Use these topics to integrate health into your daily planning.

Science

- Food Science, p. 79
- Dairy Dilemmas, p. 81
- Food, Climate, and Soil, p. 91

Social Studies

- International Food Pyramids, p. 79
- Mapping Foods, p. 90
- Food Poisoning Outbreaks, p. 103

Art

- Replace the Pyramid, p. 80
- Body Image Collage, p. 85
- How-To Checklist, p. 104

CHAPTER 3

Pages 70–109

CHAPTER SUMMARY

In this chapter students
- ► identify and describe the basic nutrients.
- ► discover how to use the USDA Food Guide Pyramid to get a balanced diet.
- ► recognize the importance of portion size and energy balance.
- ► discuss proper storage and handling of foods to avoid food poisoning.

Life Skills
Students practice *making responsible decisions* about the food they eat.

Building Good Character
Students show they have *respect* for themselves by showing self-control in choosing foods.

Consumer Health
Students *analyze media messages* in food advertisements.

 Literature Springboard

Use the article "Beware of the Vegetables!" to spark interest in the chapter topic. See the Read-Aloud Anthology on page RA-4 of this *Teacher Edition*.

Prereading Strategies

SCAN THE CHAPTER Have students preview the chapter content by scanning the titles, headings, pictures, and tables. Ask volunteers to speculate on what they will learn. Use their predictions to determine their prior knowledge.

PREVIEW VOCABULARY As students scan the chapter, invite them to sort vocabulary into three groups as shown.

Words I Know	Words I've Seen or Heard	New Words

CHAPTER 3 Foods for Good Nutrition

 Reading Skill

COMPARE AND CONTRAST To introduce or review this skill, have students use the Reading in Health Handbook, pp. 372–383. Teaching strategies and additional activities are also provided.

- Students will have opportunities to practice and apply this skill throughout this chapter.
- Focus Skill Reading Mini-Lesson, p. 72
- Reading comprehension questions identified with the
- *Activity Book* p. 13 (shown on p. 77)
- Lesson Summary and Review, pp. 77, 83, 87, 94, 99, 106
- Chapter Review and Test Preparation, pp. 108–109

COMPARE AND CONTRAST When you compare things, you tell how they are alike. When you contrast things, you tell how they are different. Use the Reading in Health Handbook on pages 372–383 and this graphic organizer to help you read the health facts in this chapter.

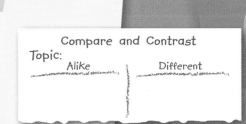

Compare and Contrast
Topic:
Alike   Different

Health Graph

INTERPRET DATA Americans eat a lot of [fru]its and vegetables. At least five serving[s a] [d]ay is recommended for good health. [Wh]at is the difference in the percent of [pe]ople who eat the least amount of fruits [an]d vegetables and the people who eat [th]e greatest amount?

Fruit and Vegetable Consumption

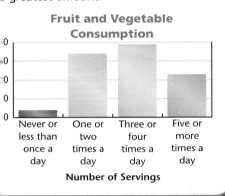

Never or less than once a day | One or two times a day | Three or four times a day | Five or more times a day
Number of Servings

Daily Physical Activity

Eating the right foods in the right amounts is one way to stay healthy. Being physically active is another way.

Be Active!
Use the selection, Track 3, **Late for Supper**, to use some food energy.

71

School-Home Connection

Distribute copies of the School-Home Connection (in English or Spanish). Have students take the page home to share with their families as you begin this chapter.

Follow Up Have volunteers share the results of their activities.

 Supports the Coordinated School Health Program

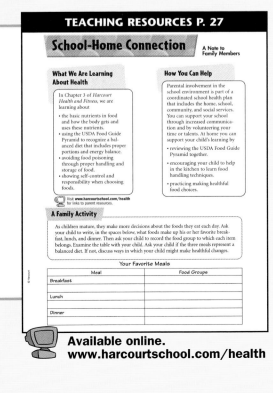

TEACHING RESOURCES P. 27

School-Home Connection   A Note to Family Members

What We Are Learning About Health

In Chapter 3 of *Harcourt Health and Fitness*, we are learning about
• the basic nutrients in food and how the body gets and uses these nutrients.
• using the USDA Food Guide Pyramid to recognize a balanced diet that includes proper portions and energy balance.
• avoiding food poisoning through proper handling and storage of food.
• showing self-control and responsibility when choosing foods.

How You Can Help

Parental involvement in the school environment is part of a coordinated school health plan that includes the home, school, community, and social services. You can support your school through increased communication and by volunteering your time or talents. At home you can support your child's learning by
• reviewing the USDA Food Guide Pyramid together.
• encouraging your child to help in the kitchen to learn food handling techniques.
• practicing making healthful food choices.

Visit www.harcourtschool.com/health for links to parent resources.

A Family Activity

As children mature, they make more decisions about the foods they eat each day. Ask your child to write, in the spaces below, what foods make up his or her favorite breakfast, lunch, and dinner. Then ask your child to record the food group to which each item belongs. Examine the table with your child. Ask your child if the three meals represent a balanced diet. If not, discuss ways in which your child might make healthful changes.

Your Favorite Meals

Meal	Food Groups
Breakfast	
Lunch	
Dinner	

Available online.
www.harcourtschool.com/health

INTRODUCE THE CHAPTER

Health Graph

Interpret Data

Ask for a volunteer to explain what the circle graph shows. how many times per day people eat fruits and vegetables

What answer did the greatest number of people give when they were asked the survey question? 3–4 times per day

What is the difference in the percent of people who eat fruits and vegetables most often and the percent of those who eat them least often? 19 percent

What is the percent of those who eat fruits and vegetables 1 to 4 times per day? 73 percent

How many people were surveyed? The graph does not say. Observant students may notice that since the percents are precise, it is likely that at least 100 people were surveyed.

Daily Physical Activity

Use *Be Active! Music for Daily Physical Activity* with the Instant Activity Cards to provide students with movement activities that can be done in limited space. Options for using these components are provided beginning on page TR2 in this *Teacher Edition*.

Chapter Project

Invitation to a Balanced Meal (*Assessment Guide* p. 57)

ASSESS PRIOR KNOWLEDGE Use students' initial ideas for the project as a baseline assessment of their understanding of chapter concepts. Have students complete the project as they work through the chapter.

PERFORMANCE ASSESSMENT The project can be used for performance assessment. Use the Project Evaluation Sheet (rubric), *Assessment Guide* p. 64.

LESSON 1
Pages 72–77

Objectives
► Identify the six basic nutrients.
► Describe which of the basic nutrients give the body energy.

When Minutes Count . . .
Assign the Quick Study, Lesson 1, Activity Book pp. 11–12 (shown on p. 73).

Program Resources
► Activity Book pp. 11–13
► Transparencies 1, 9

Vocabulary
nutrients p. 72, **enzymes** p. 73, **carbohydrates** p. 74, **fats** p. 74, **proteins** p. 75, **vitamins** p. 76, **minerals** p. 76

Daily Fitness Tip

Drinking enough water each day helps the digestive system do its job. Remind students that the human body is about 60–75 percent water. The water that is lost through all the body's functions must be replenished. Encourage students to drink water throughout the day.

 For more information on how foods affect the body, see *Be Active! Resources for Physical Education,* p. 143.

1. MOTIVATE

Optional Activity Materials several unopened boxes of cereal, paper plates, hand lenses

Ask volunteers to read aloud the lists of nutrients on the cereal boxes. Divide the class into small groups. Have each group examine a few pieces of cereal with a hand lens to try to see the nutrients listed on the box. **Do you think you can see the protein, the fat, or other nutrients in the cereal?** no

Explain that food scientists use chemicals and high-tech equipment to determine the amounts of nutrients in foods.

LESSON 1 Food—Fuel for the Body

Lesson Focus
Your digestive system breaks down food to give your body energy and building materials.

Why Learn This?
Eating the right foods in the right amounts can help keep you healthy.

Vocabulary
nutrients
enzymes
carbohydrates
fats
proteins
vitamins
minerals

Alike: Both need fuel for energy. Different: A car does not need to break down its fuel into a different form, but your body does.

Food As Fuel

Your body is a little like a car. A car needs fuel to run, and so do you. While most cars use gasoline as fuel, the human body uses food. Burning fuel releases energy the car uses to run. A car doesn't need to change gasoline into another form in order to release this energy. Your body is different. It must *digest*, or break down, food before it can use the nutrients food contains.

Nutrients (NOO•tree•uhnts) are substances in food that provide your body with energy. Nutrients also provide building materials the body needs for growth, repair, and daily activities.

Breaking down food is your digestive system's main function. When your digestive system breaks down food, it releases several kinds of nutrients. These include carbohydrates, fats, and proteins.

 COMPARE AND CONTRAST How are your body and a car alike? How are they different?

Your car needs fuel (gasoline) to run. Your body's fuel is food. ►

72

 **Reading Skill**

Mini-Lesson

COMPARE AND CONTRAST Remind students that when they compare, they tell how things are alike. When they contrast, they tell how things are different. Have them practice this skill by responding to the Focus Skill question on this page. Have students draw and complete the graphic organizer as you model it on the transparency.

TRANSPARENCY 1

1 Reading Skill Graphic Organizer
Compare and Contrast
Topic: Human body and a car

Alike	Different
Both need fuel for energy.	A car does not need to b its fuel down into a differ form; the body does.

 Interactive Transparencies available on CD-ROM.

Digestion

Let's follow a bite of a turkey sandwich to discover how your digestive system breaks down the sandwich into nutrients your body needs. Digestion begins in your mouth. Your teeth chew the bite into smaller pieces. Your saliva contains **enzymes** (EN•zymz), chemicals that help break down foods to release nutrients. Different enzymes are needed to digest different foods.

After you swallow, the food mass moves toward your stomach. There, the partly digested food is squeezed and churned. And more nutrients are released from your bite of sandwich.

Next, the food mass moves into the small intestine, where more enzymes finish the job of digestion. Now the nutrients are ready to move into your bloodstream and into your body cells. Anything that cannot be digested passes into your large intestine.

> **SEQUENCE** List the parts of your digestive system in the order that food moves through them.

Did You Know?

The small and large intestines are like long hoses connected to each other. In an adult, the small intestine is about 23 feet long and 1 to 2 inches wide! The large intestine is about 5 feet long. It's called the large intestine because it is wider than the small intestine. It is about $2\frac{1}{2}$ inches across.

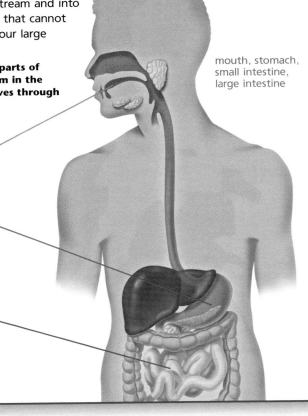

mouth, stomach, small intestine, large intestine

1 Enzymes in your saliva begin to break down starch in the bread.

2 In your stomach, acid begins to break down the meat in the sandwich.

3 Additional enzymes complete digestion in your small intestine. Then nutrients pass into your blood. You can review this process on page 8.

73

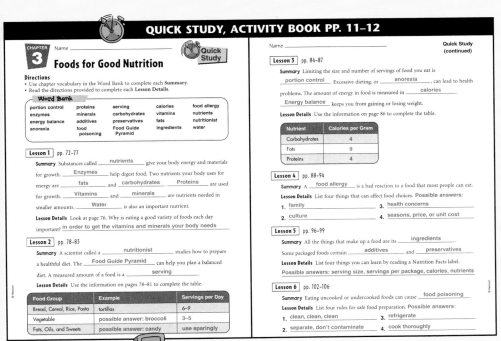

QUICK STUDY, ACTIVITY BOOK PP. 11–12

CHAPTER 3
Foods for Good Nutrition

Quick Study

Directions
• Use chapter vocabulary in the Word Bank to complete each **Summary**.
• Read the directions provided to complete each **Lesson Details**.

Word Bank

portion control	proteins	serving	calories	food allergy
enzymes	minerals	carbohydrates	vitamins	nutrients
energy balance	additives	preservatives	fats	nutritionist
anorexia	food poisoning	Food Guide Pyramid	ingredients	water

Lesson 1 pp. 72–77
Summary Substances called ___nutrients___ give your body energy and materials for growth. ___Enzymes___ help digest food. Two nutrients your body uses for energy are ___fats___ and ___carbohydrates___. ___Proteins___ are used for growth. ___Vitamins___ and ___minerals___ are nutrients needed in smaller amounts. ___Water___ is also an important nutrient.
Lesson Details Look at page 76. Why is eating a good variety of foods each day important? in order to get the vitamins and minerals your body needs

Lesson 2 pp. 78–83
Summary A scientist called a ___nutritionist___ studies how to prepare a healthful diet. The ___Food Guide Pyramid___ can help you plan a balanced diet. A measured amount of a food is a ___serving___.
Lesson Details Use the information on pages 78–81 to complete the table.

Food Group	Example	Servings per Day
Bread, Cereal, Rice, Pasta	tortillas	6–9
Vegetable	possible answer: broccoli	3–5
Fats, Oils, and Sweets	possible answer: candy	use sparingly

Name _____ pp. 11–12 **Quick Study** (continued)

Lesson 3 pp. 84–87
Summary Limiting the size and number of servings of food you eat is ___portion control___. Excessive dieting, or ___anorexia___, can lead to health problems. The amount of energy in food is measured in ___calories___. ___Energy balance___ keeps you from gaining or losing weight.
Lesson Details Use the information on page 86 to complete the table.

Nutrient	Calories per Gram
Carbohydrates	4
Fats	9
Proteins	4

Lesson 4 pp. 88–94
Summary A ___food allergy___ is a bad reaction to a food that most people can eat.
Lesson Details List four things that can affect food choices. Possible answers:
1. family
2. culture
3. health concerns
4. seasons, price, or unit cost

Lesson 5 pp. 96–99
Summary All the things that make up a food are its ___ingredients___. Some packaged foods contain ___additives___ and ___preservatives___.
Lesson Details List four things you can learn by reading a Nutrition Facts label. Possible answers: serving size, servings per package, calories, nutrients

Lesson 6 pp. 102–106
Summary Eating uncooked or undercooked foods can cause ___food poisoning___.
Lesson Details List four rules for safe food preparation. Possible answers:
1. clean, clean, clean
2. separate, don't contaminate
3. refrigerate
4. cook thoroughly

Available online.
www.harcourtschool.com/health

---

2. TEACH

Interpret Visuals—Pictures

Have students look at the diagram of the digestive system on this page. Point out that the illustration leaves out most of the body's other organs to make the organs of the digestive system visible. A photograph might be more accurate, but other organs would block our view of the entire digestive system.

When Minutes Count . . .

Transparency 9: The Digestive System can be used to present material in this lesson. *Interactive Transparencies are available on CD-ROM.*

Discuss

Critical Thinking What would happen if your body stopped producing saliva? How might this affect the digestive process? Food that would normally begin to be broken down in the mouth would not be broken down at all before it reached the stomach and intestines. More or different enzymes would be needed somewhere else in the digestive tract to make up for the digestion that didn't take place in the mouth.

Health Background

Enzymes Almost all enzymes are proteins, although a few are nucleic acids. Enzymes are classified according to structure. *Simple enzymes* are made entirely of protein, whereas *complex enzymes* are made of protein plus another, smaller molecule. Nearly all chemical reactions in the human body involve enzymes. Without enzymes, the reactions would take too long. Here is one example of the effect enzymes have on reactions: One molecule of the enzyme that removes carbon dioxide from the blood causes 1,000,000 carbon dioxide molecules to react in one second!

Source: *Indiana State University website*

For more background, visit the **Webliography** in Teacher Resources at **www.harcourtschool.com/health** **Keyword** nutrition

Carbohydrates and Fats

Most of the energy your body needs comes from nutrients called carbohydrates. The **carbohydrates** (kar•boh•HY•draytzs) we eat most are sugars and starches.

Some foods, such as syrup and hard candy, are nothing but sugar. Many other foods, including fruits, some vegetables, and milk, contain sugars along with other nutrients. Starches are made of many sugars linked together. Beans, breads, and pasta are all rich in starches. During digestion, your body breaks down starches into sugars.

The nutrients that contain the most energy are **fats**. Plants, animals, and people store excess energy as fats. Butter, margarine, and oils are mostly fats. Most *junk-food* snacks, such as chips, cookies, cakes, and chocolate, have lots of fat. Foods such as meats, nuts, and milk products also contain fats. But unlike junk food, these foods also contain other important nutrients.

DRAW CONCLUSIONS Which food would supply more energy—a handful of raisins or a handful of peanuts? Why?
The peanuts; fats are the nutrients that contain the most energy.

◄ What nutrients give these kids the quick energy they need to play basketball?

TEACH *continued*

Discuss

Carbohydrates are broken down more quickly than fats are. But more energy is contained in fats than in carbohydrates.

Problem Solving You are getting ready to leave for soccer practice. You want to choose a snack that will give you energy both now and later. Which would you choose: a snack that is all carbohydrate, a snack that is mostly carbohydrate and some fat, or a snack that is all fat? A snack that is mostly carbohydrate and some fat will give you a quick boost of energy from the carbohydrates and lasting energy from the fat.

Quick Activity

Encourage students to use at least three different kinds of milk cartons. Not only will the number of calories differ, but the number of fat grams per serving will differ as well.

Interpret Visuals—Pictures

Have students look at the picture.

Why do these girls need nutrients and energy? What parts of their bodies need energy? They need nutrients and energy to be able to move, think, see, hear, and react. Their muscles, bones, brains— every system in their bodies needs energy in order to play basketball. Point out that the girls need nutrients even to smell and taste. Zinc deficiencies, for example, are linked to a loss of taste and smell.

Meeting Individual Needs
Leveled Activities

BELOW-LEVEL Plastic-Bag Digestion Have each student put two crackers in about 1/8 cup of water in a zip-top plastic bag. Students should squeeze the mixture, observing its consistency, until the crackers have dissolved. Explain that the water in the bag breaks down the crackers somewhat as saliva in the mouth breaks down food.

ON-LEVEL Balloon Esophagus Have each student blow up a long balloon about three-fourths full. Ask students to squeeze the balloon at the top with one fist. Next, have them squeeze the balloon just below that fist with the other fist. This squeezing should force the air farther down the balloon. Now tell students to remove the fist at the top and place it below the other fist. Explain that this activity demonstrates how food moves down the esophagus toward the stomach.

CHALLENGE Digestion Models Have students create a model of digestion, using a material of their choosing.

▲ Which of these protein-rich foods do you like?

Proteins

You've certainly grown a lot since you were a baby. You can thank nutrients called proteins for most of this growth. **Proteins** (PROH•teenz) are the building blocks of your body. Your body uses proteins to build and repair cells.

Remember that your body can store extra energy in the form of fats. Your body cannot store extra protein. It needs a new supply every day. You get proteins just as you get carbohydrates and fats—from the foods you eat. Some foods have more proteins than others. Meat, fish, eggs, and milk products are all good protein sources. Dried beans and peas, nuts, and grains also contain proteins.

DRAW CONCLUSIONS Why do you think a child needs more protein than an adult?
Children grow more than adults do. A child's body needs protein to build cells.

Quick Activity

Research Fat Find out how the amount of fat in different kinds of milk is indicated on the milk bottle or carton. What do the numbers mean? Make a table comparing the number of fat grams in different kinds of milk.

75

TEACH continued

Interpret Visuals—Pictures

Vitamins and minerals do not work alone in the body. They work with other nutrients, such as proteins and carbohydrates. Vitamins are regulators that often act as coenzymes to help enzymes (made of proteins) function. Minerals are components of cells and enzymes.

Have students look at the picture of foods on this page. Ask volunteers to identify the foods shown and the vitamins and minerals each provides. Poll students to find out which of these foods they like to eat. Remind them that a healthful diet includes many different sources of the needed nutrients.

Discuss

The symptoms of most vitamin deficiencies do not appear right away. Therefore, it is important to take in vitamins and minerals every day.

Critical Thinking **Suppose you stop drinking milk for a week. The next week you fall and suffer a minor fracture in your arm. Could your injury be the result of a calcium deficiency? Why or why not?** Probably not; it would take longer than a week for a calcium deficiency to have an effect. Also, milk is not the only food that is high in calcium, so I was probably still getting some calcium from other foods, such as cheese.

Vitamins and Minerals

In addition to carbohydrates, fats, and proteins, there are other nutrients that your body needs in smaller amounts. **Vitamins** (VYT•uh•minz) are nutrients that help your body perform specific functions. They are essential to life. Some vitamins help your body use other nutrients. Other vitamins help keep parts of your body strong and healthy. Your body cannot make most vitamins. It has to get them from foods you eat.

Minerals (MIN•uhr•uhlz) are another kind of nutrient, helping your body to grow and work. Minerals help keep your bones and teeth strong, help your body release energy from food, and keep your cells working well. The photograph below shows foods that are rich in different vitamins and minerals.

Similar: Both are found in milk and broccoli, and both are nutrients. Different: Calcium is a mineral, and vitamin A is a vitamin; vitamin A keeps eyes and skin healthy, while calcium keeps bones and teeth healthy.

COMPARE AND CONTRAST **Name two ways in which calcium is similar to vitamin A and two ways it is different.**

Vitamin A keeps your skin and eyes healthy. It is found in yellow and orange vegetables, tomatoes, and leafy green vegetables.

Vitamin B₁ is needed to release energy from nutrients. It is found in meats, fish, whole-grain breads, and some beans.

Vitamin C helps keep your blood, gums, and teeth healthy. It is found in citrus fruits, strawberries, and tomatoes.

Iron keeps oxygen moving throughout the body and protects against infection. It is found in meats, leafy green vegetables, beans, dried fruits, and nuts.

Calcium builds strong bones and teeth, helps muscles work, and helps blood clot. It can be found in milk, milk products, and broccoli.

Phosphorus builds strong bones and teeth and helps cells function. It is found in meat, poultry, dried beans, nuts, milk, and milk products.

76

ESL/ELL Support

COMPREHENSIBLE INPUT Familiarize students with the different vitamins and minerals in foods.

Beginning Display drawings or photographs of the food sources listed for each of the vitamins and minerals. Name one of the vitamins or minerals, and ask students to choose or point to the picture of a food in which the vitamin or mineral is found.

Intermediate Ask students to draw pictures of foods that are high in each of the vitamins or minerals listed on this page. Encourage them to make their drawings colorful and to make the name of the vitamin or mineral big and easy to read.

Advanced Have students make a three-column table showing the vitamins and minerals discussed on this page, their benefits, and the foods they are found in.

Water and Fiber

Water is the nutrient your body needs most. You need water to digest food, to transport nutrients to your cells, and to build new cells. Water helps keep your body temperature stable. It also helps remove carbon dioxide, salts, and other wastes from your body.

You get some water from the foods you eat, but you get most of the water you need from drinks like water, milk, and juice. To stay healthy, most people need six to eight glasses of water each day.

Fiber is another part of a healthful diet. Your body needs fiber to help move other foods through the digestive system. Fresh vegetables, fruits, and whole grains are all high in fiber.

MAIN IDEA AND DETAILS **What are two important things water does for your body?**
Possible responses: helps digest food, takes nutrients to cells, builds new cells, keeps body temperature stable, and removes wastes

Whole-grains cereals, like shredded wheat, have more fiber than processed cereals. ▼

Lesson 1 Summary and Review

1 **Summarize with Vocabulary**

Use vocabulary from this lesson to complete the statements.

Nutrients with a lot of energy are _____ and _____. Nutrients called _____ are used to build and repair cells in your body. Your body cannot make most _____. Your blood needs iron, a _____, to carry oxygen throughout your body.

2 What are the main uses of nutrients in your body?

3 **Critical Thinking** Why is water a nutrient, even though most of the water you take in doesn't come from food?

4 (Focus Skill) **COMPARE AND CONTRAST** Draw and complete this graphic organizer to show how carbohydrates and proteins are alike and different.

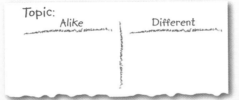

5 **Write to Inform—How-To**
Describe how a person could design a weekly menu that includes all the necessary nutrients every day.

77

3. WRAP UP

Lesson 1 Summary and Review

1. fats, carbohydrates; proteins; vitamins; minerals

2. for energy and as building materials for growth, repair, and daily activities

3. Water is needed to digest food, transport nutrients to the cells, build new cells, keep the body temperature stable, and remove wastes from the body. Even though water is found in many foods, most people also need to drink water so the body has enough to perform its functions.

4. Possible answers shown below.

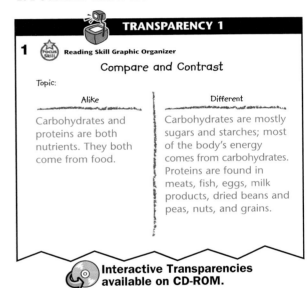

TRANSPARENCY 1

1 (Focus Skill) **Reading Skill Graphic Organizer**

Compare and Contrast

Topic:

Alike	Different
Carbohydrates and proteins are both nutrients. They both come from food.	Carbohydrates are mostly sugars and starches; most of the body's energy comes from carbohydrates. Proteins are found in meats, fish, eggs, milk products, dried beans and peas, nuts, and grains.

Interactive Transparencies available on CD-ROM.

5. Students' menus should supply all of the nutrients, vitamins, and minerals mentioned in the lesson.

For **writing models** with examples, see *Teaching Resources* pp. 47–61. Rubrics are also provided.

When Minutes Count ...

Quick Study Students can use *Activity Book* pp. 11–12 (shown on p. 73) as they complete each lesson in this chapter.

Objectives

► Explain how to use the USDA Food Guide Pyramid to help plan a balanced diet.

► Identify the food groups used in the USDA Food Guide Pyramid.

► Understand the size of a serving.

When Minutes Count . . .

Assign the Quick Study, Lesson 2, Activity Book pp. 11–12 (shown on p. 73).

Program Resources

► Activity Book pp. 11–12

► Transparencies 1, 19

Vocabulary

nutritionist p. 78,

Food Guide Pyramid p. 78,

serving p. 79

Daily Fitness Tip

According to the USDA Food Guide Pyramid, you should eat three to five servings of vegetables each day. Students may find this difficult since for most, vegetables are not favorite foods. Suggest that, whenever possible, students try new vegetables or vegetables prepared in different ways.

For more information on how foods affect the body, see *Be Active! Resources for Physical Education,* p. 143.

1. MOTIVATE

Optional Activity Materials 3 strips of paper per student, measuring about 1" x 4", 1" x 3", and 1" x 2"

Ask students to list the three foods they would most like to eat each day. Have them write each choice on a paper strip, writing the food they'd like to eat most often on the largest and the food they'd like to eat least often on the smallest. Ask them to arrange their three strips in a pyramid shape, with the largest strip on the bottom and the smallest on top. Tell them that in this lesson they will see how their desired diet compares to what nutritionists recommend.

Lesson Focus

The Food Guide Pyramid groups foods with similar nutrients and shows how many servings from each food group the average person should have each day.

Why Learn This?

You can use the Food Guide Pyramid to help you plan a balanced diet.

Vocabulary

nutritionist
Food Guide Pyramid
serving

Milk, Yogurt, and Cheese Group includes foods such as low-fat milk, yogurt, ice cream, cottage cheese, and hard cheese.

Vegetable Group includes foods such as corn, carrots, broccoli, lettuce, and tomatoes.

Bread, Cereal, Rice, and Pasta Group includes foods such as rice, bread, tortillas, pasta, and cereals.

78

ESL/ELL Support

COMPREHENSIBLE INPUT Help students become more familiar with the food groups represented in the Food Guide Pyramid.

Beginning Name each of the food groups shown in the Food Guide Pyramid, and have students point to the group on the pyramid. Suggest that students work in pairs to repeat the activity.

Intermediate Name two or three foods from one of the food groups in the Food Guide Pyramid. Ask students to name the food group to which the foods belong. Repeat for other foods in other groups.

Advanced Have students create a graphic organizer with the names of the food groups used in the Food Guide Pyramid and examples of foods included in each group.

The USDA Food Guide Pyramid

Meat, Poultry, Fish, Dry Beans, Eggs, and Nuts Group includes foods such as salmon, eggs, mixed nuts, chicken, steak, and peanuts.

Fruit Group includes foods such as strawberries, apples, pineapple, cantaloupe, blueberries, and plums.

People who work in supermarkets arrange similar foods together so they are easy to find. Nutritionists do something very similar but for a different reason. A **nutritionist** is a scientist who studies nutrition and healthful diets. Look at the **Food Guide Pyramid**, which is a tool to help you eat a balanced diet. It was prepared by nutritionists at the United States Department of Agriculture (USDA).

If you look carefully, you will see that the nutritionists grouped each food with other foods that have similar nutrients.

They arranged the groups in a pyramid form so that you can quickly see how many servings from each food group you should eat every day. A **serving** is the measured amount of food recommended for a meal or snack. Generally, you should eat more servings per day of foods near the base of the pyramid than foods near the top.

MAIN IDEA AND DETAILS What two kinds of information does the Food Guide Pyramid give you?
It tells which foods have similar nutrients and which groups you should eat the most of each day to stay healthy.

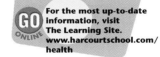

Information Alert!

Nutrition As scientists learn more about nutrition and health, the USDA Food Guide Pyramid may change.

GO ONLINE For the most up-to-date information, visit The Learning Site. www.harcourtschool.com/health

79

---

2. TEACH

Interpret Visuals—Pictures

Direct attention to the USDA Food Guide Pyramid. To help students interpret the information in the caption boxes, ask questions such as the following: **Which foods form the base of the pyramid? Which foods should you eat the least of? Which foods should you eat in approximately equal amounts?**

Explain to students that serving sizes for the Food Guide Pyramid are recommendations for children ages 6–11, not for adults.

Discuss

The USDA Food Guide Pyramid provides flexible guidelines to help people choose healthful, varied diets. All foods that people eat fit into one or more of the food groups. Have students indentify foods that are sources of one or more of the six major nutrients.

Problem Solving You are planning dinner for your family. You would like the meal to include foods from the Meat, Poultry, Fish, Dry Beans, Eggs, and Nuts Group, the Vegetable Group, and the Milk, Yogurt, and Cheese Group, but no foods from the Bread, Cereal, Rice, and Pasta Group. **What foods will your dinner include?** Answers will vary.

Critical Thinking How can people who are allergic to wheat products still get enough servings from the Bread, Cereal, Rice, and Pasta Group? How can they be sure foods contain no wheat?
They can eat foods in the group that do not come from wheat. These could be foods made with corn, rye, or oats. They can make sure by checking the ingredients listed on the product packaging.

 When Minutes Count . . .

Transparency 19: The Food Guide Pyramid can be used to present material for this lesson. *Interactive Transparencies are available on CD-ROM.*

TEACH *continued*

Discuss

Critical Thinking **A girl you know has a 14-year-old brother who plays soccer. Your friend complains that her brother always eats twice as much as she does. What do you think?** Students should recognize that the friend's brother probably needs more food because he is growing quickly and is very active. Also, in general, boys need more food than girls.

Discuss

Inform students that the current USDA Food Guide Pyramid is being evaluated as a response to a growing rate of obesity among Americans.

Critical Thinking **How did the USDA think the Food Guide Pyramid would help with the problem of Americans developing heart disease?** They thought that people were developing heart disease because they didn't eat healthfully, didn't understand the importance of eating well, and didn't know what foods are nutritious.

How do you think the USDA created the Food Guide Pyramid? They probably researched the different foods to see what nutrients they contained. They probably compared the diets of very healthy people with the diets of people who had health problems such as heart disease.

Myth and Fact

Myth: Brown eggs are more nutritious than white eggs.
Fact: The color of an egg's shell has nothing to do with the nutrients it contains.

A Balanced Diet

Your body needs the right amounts of different nutrients each day to stay healthy. You get those nutrients by eating a balanced diet. The foods in each group of the USDA Food Guide Pyramid contain similar nutrients. That means you can substitute one food for another in the same group. For example, instead of meat, you could eat fish or eggs. You get many of the same nutrients in fish and eggs as you do in meat.

The number of servings from each food group are suggested for children ages 7–12.

Bread, Cereal, Rice, and Pasta Group

Foods in this group are made from grains, such as wheat and rice. Grains contain carbohydrates, protein, fiber, minerals, and vitamins. You should eat six to nine servings daily from this group. A serving is one slice of bread, 1 cup of dry cereal, or $\frac{1}{2}$ cup of cooked pasta.

Fruit Group

Fruits contain carbohydrates, including sugar, fiber, vitamins, and minerals. You should eat two to four servings daily from this group. A serving is one apple, one small banana, or fifteen grapes.

Vegetable Group

Vegetables contain many vitamins and minerals. Many vegetables also contain fiber and carbohydrates, such as starch. You should eat three to five servings daily from this group. A serving is $\frac{1}{2}$ cup cooked vegetables or 1 cup of salad or raw vegetables.

80

🎨 Art

Replace the Pyramid Challenge students to think of other ways to illustrate the information given in the USDA Food Guide Pyramid. (They could show the information in the shape of a piece of food or an animal, for example.) Encourage students to be creative. Ask volunteers to present their illustrations and to explain why each illustration is better than, as good as, or not as good as a pyramid for representing the information.

Teacher Tip

Practice Makes Perfect Help students put into practice what they are learning about using the USDA Food Guide Pyramid to begin planning the foods for their next class celebration. Make sure the plans include whole-grain products, fresh fruits and vegetables, and beverages of juice, milk, or water.

Meat, Poultry, Fish, Dry Beans, Eggs, and Nuts Group

These foods contain protein, fats, vitamins, and minerals. You should eat two to three servings daily from this group. A serving is 3 ounces of cooked meat, poultry, or fish (about the size of a deck of cards), one egg, or a handful of nuts.

Milk, Yogurt, and Cheese Group

This group is sometimes called the dairy group because all of these foods are made from milk. Milk products contain a lot of carbohydrates, protein, fats, and minerals. You should eat three servings daily from this group. A serving is 8 ounces of low-fat milk, 8 ounces of yogurt, or $1\frac{1}{2}$ ounces of cheese.

Fats, Oils, and Sweets Group

These foods contain a lot of carbohydrates (sugars) and fats, but not many other nutrients. You should eat only small amounts of foods from this group, and not every day.

By eating a variety of foods from each food group every day, you will be eating a balanced diet. You will be giving yourself the nutrients you need for energy and for your body to grow and repair itself. Just be careful to limit the amount of fats and sweets you eat.

SUMMARIZE Name the six food groups, and give examples of at least two foods from each group.
Possible response: Fats, Oils, and Sweets: doughnuts, sugar, butter. Milk, Yogurt, and Cheese: skim milk, cottage cheese, sour cream. Meat, Poultry, Fish, Dry Beans, Eggs, and Nuts: steak, chicken, tuna. Vegetable: broccoli, spinach, carrots. Fruit: apples, pineapples, strawberries. Bread, Cereal, Rice, and Pasta: whole-wheat bread, oatmeal, pasta.

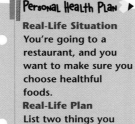

Personal Health Plan

Real-Life Situation
You're going to a restaurant, and you want to make sure you choose healthful foods.

Real-Life Plan
List two things you can do to make sure you choose healthful foods from a menu.

81

Personal Health Plan ▶

Plans might include:
- choosing foods that are low in fats and sugar.
- making sure each meal includes vegetables.
- drinking water or milk with your meal.

Discuss
Assess students' understanding of food groups by asking questions such as these about the USDA Food Guide Pyramid:

Which foods are especially high in protein? meat, poultry, fish, dried beans, eggs, nuts, milk, yogurt, and cheese

From which food groups would you choose if you wanted foods with fiber in them? the Vegetable Group, the Fruit Group, or the Bread, Cereal, Rice, and Pasta Group

Problem Solving What can you do if you have trouble eating more than small servings of fruits and vegetables or drinking more than half a glass of milk at mealtimes? I can add small snacks to my daily eating plan that include fruits, vegetables, and small glasses of milk. This will help me make up for what I miss at mealtimes.

Content-Area Reading Support
Using Headings Direct attention to the subheadings under the heading *A Balanced Diet*. Point out that the heading identifies the overall topic and is in a larger type than the subheadings, which identify subtopics. Explain that type size and color are based on the topics and the organization of information in the text passage.

Science

Dairy Dilemmas Have students research why many people have problems digesting dairy foods. (They lack the enzyme lactase, which breaks down the milk sugar lactose.) Have them find out which ethnic groups this problem most often affects (Asians, Africans, Mediterranean people). Ask them to find out why persons without lactase can comfortably eat most yogurts. (The bacteria in yogurt break down the lactose.)

Teacher Tip

Pyramids and Portions Refer students to the pyramids they made in the Motivate activity. Have them now identify the food group(s) in which their favorite food choices belong. Do their pyramids reflect the healthful diet they now know they should eat? How would they adjust the relative amounts of each of their favorite foods to have more healthful diets? How could they incorporate each of their favorite foods into a balanced diet?

TEACH *continued*

Interpret Visuals—Graphics

Have students examine Keya's mother's weekly menu for nutritional content. Ask them if the menu follows the USDA Food Guide Pyramid recommendations.

When making a weekly or daily menu, why is it a good idea to include foods you like? If I don't include foods I like, I will be less likely to follow the menu.

Discuss

Have students describe other weekly activities that promote the health of a family.

Activity

Make Decisions Review the decision-making model with students. To help students know how to plan a menu, analyze Keya's mother's weekly menu for nutritional content. Help students make a menu for one day based on this weekly menu. Then have students make their own daily menus, referring to the USDA Food Guide Pyramid. Ask volunteers to share their menus and discuss which choices on the menus are healthful.

Health Background

Obesity Fat in the body is a major source of energy when other sources are lacking. It also provides insulation and protection for internal organs. However, when too much fat accumulates in the body, the risk of diabetes mellitus, coronary heart disease, stroke, arthritis, and some forms of cancer increases dramatically. People who are 20 percent or more above their ideal body weight are said to be obese. According to the Centers for Disease Control and Prevention (CDC), approximately 21 percent of the adult population in the United States is obese.

Source: *National Center for Chronic Disease Prevention and Health Promotion*

For more background, visit the **Webliography** in Teacher Resources at **www.harcourtschool.com/health** **Keyword** nutrition

---

ACTIVITY

Life Skills

Make Responsible Decisions
Using the USDA Food Guide Pyramid, review the types and amounts of foods people should eat each day. Use the guidelines to write a menu of meals for yourself for one day. Remember to include foods that you like, and leave out those that you are not allowed to eat.

Planning Meals

You can use the USDA Food Guide Pyramid to plan a healthful snack when you get home from school. A healthful snack would include foods from several of the food groups, except the Fats, Oils, and Sweets Group.

When planning your snack menu, think about what you ate for breakfast and lunch. Think about what you might eat for dinner. Check the number of servings recommended on each level of the pyramid. Design your snack so that it gives you more of the foods you might not get enough of during the rest of the day.

The menu below shows what Keya's mother has planned for dinner each night. Which food groups are represented in the menu? Which food groups are missing?

COMPARE AND CONTRAST Suppose you aren't allowed to eat the same foods for your after-school snack two days in a row. What menu could you make up so that your snack on Tuesday includes the same food groups as your snack on Monday?
Possible response: yogurt and strawberries, crackers, boiled egg, and cheese

Planning meals helps you eat a balanced diet. ▼

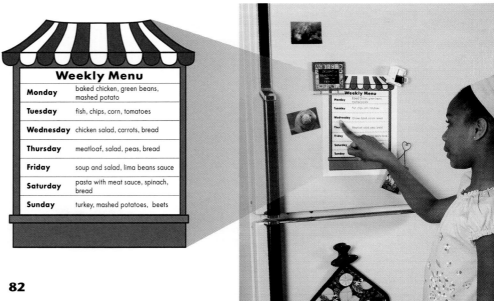

Weekly Menu	
Monday	baked chicken, green beans, mashed potato
Tuesday	fish, chips, corn, tomatoes
Wednesday	chicken salad, carrots, bread
Thursday	meatloaf, salad, peas, bread
Friday	soup and salad, lima beans sauce
Saturday	pasta with meat sauce, spinach, bread
Sunday	turkey, mashed potatoes, beets

82

Teacher Tip

Looking for Signs You may notice some preteens beginning to pay more attention to their body size and shape. To achieve the bodies they think they should have, some preteens might try fad diets or other unhealthful methods for losing or gaining weight. Be aware of comments students make regarding their own body images and dieting.

Math

Calculating Servings Have students calculate the number of servings they would consume from each food group in one week, one month, and one year if they followed the USDA Food Guide Pyramid suggestions.

Jennie's friend is coming for lunch. What if she can't eat what Jennie has chosen? ▶

Lesson 2 Summary and Review

❶ Summarize with Vocabulary

Use vocabulary and other terms from this lesson to complete the statements.

The _____ was prepared by USDA _____ to show how a person might plan a balanced _____. It tells how many _____ from each food group people should eat every day.

❷ Which food group contains foods you should choose least often?

❸ Critical Thinking What foods could you substitute for a friend who doesn't eat meat?

❹ (Focus Skill) **COMPARE AND CONTRAST** Draw and complete this graphic organizer to show how the Vegetable Group and the Bread, Cereal, Rice, and Pasta Group are alike and different in terms of nutrients.

Topic:

Alike	Different

❺ Write to Inform—Explanation

List the foods you like to eat, and explain whether they make a balanced diet or not.

83

Quick Activity

Jennie could substitute an egg, turkey, fish, or meat sandwich. She could also include lettuce and tomato on the sandwich.

3. WRAP UP

Lesson 2 Summary and Review

1. USDA Food Guide Pyramid, nutritionists, diet, servings

2. Fats, Oils, and Sweets

3. eggs, beans, nuts

4. Possible answers are shown below.

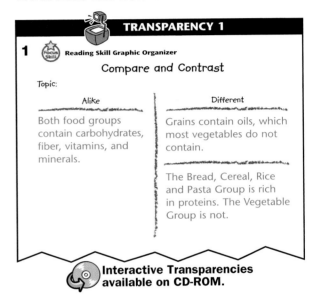

TRANSPARENCY 1

1 (Focus Skill) **Reading Skill Graphic Organizer**

Compare and Contrast

Topic:

Alike	Different
Both food groups contain carbohydrates, fiber, vitamins, and minerals.	Grains contain oils, which most vegetables do not contain.
	The Bread, Cereal, Rice and Pasta Group is rich in proteins. The Vegetable Group is not.

 Interactive Transparencies available on CD-ROM.

5. Students' responses should correspond to the guidelines suggested by the USDA Food Guide Pyramid.

 For **writing models** with examples, see *Teaching Resources* pp. 47–61. Rubrics are also provided.

When Minutes Count ...

Quick Study Students can use *Activity Book* pp. 11–12 (shown on p. 73) as they complete each lesson in this chapter.

Objectives
► Understand the importance of portion control when deciding on the number and size of servings.
► Describe the relationship between calories and energy balance.

When Minutes Count . . .
Assign the Quick Study, Lesson 3, Activity Book pp. 11–12 (shown on p. 73).

Program Resources
► Activity Book pp. 11–12
► Transparency 1

Vocabulary
portion control p. 84,
anorexia p. 85, **calories** p. 86,
energy balance p. 87

Daily Fitness Tip

When people are very hungry, are in a hurry, or feel stressed, they tend to eat more than they should. Overeating can lead to health problems. Ways to avoid overeating at a meal include sitting down to eat, eating slowly, chewing food thoroughly, and waiting 20 minutes before considering a second helping.

 For more information on how foods affect the body, see *Be Active! Resources for Physical Education*, p. 143.

1. MOTIVATE

Optional Activity Materials
containers from regular and supersize servings of fast-food fries and drinks, measuring cup, water, 30 pencils

Display the containers, and ask students to compare the serving sizes with the serving sizes the Nutrition Council of Cincinnati recommends for fried potatoes (10 pieces or 3 ounces) and a soft drink (12 ounces, or $1\frac{1}{2}$ cups). Pencils can represent fries; cups of water can be used to measure drink servings. Ask students to estimate how many actual servings the regular and supersize containers hold.

LESSON 3 — Eating Healthfully

Lesson Focus
To stay healthy, a person needs to eat only as many servings as his or her body needs each day.

Why Learn This?
Eating more or fewer servings than your body needs can be unhealthful.

Vocabulary
portion control
anorexia
calories
energy balance

Portion Control

Almost everyone who eats in a fast-food restaurant has been asked this question: "Do you want to supersize that?" Supersizing means adding more food—sometimes a lot more—for a little extra money. Every time you supersize a meal, you are eating two or three or more additional servings of food. The items that are most often supersized are those that you should be eating less of, such as fries, soft drinks, and shakes. These often lack important nutrients.

You need to eat a variety of foods to get all the nutrients your body needs. But you also need to control the size of the portions you eat. **Portion control** means limiting the number of servings you eat and the sizes of the servings. Without portion control, you may gain more weight than is healthy. In the United States, more than 15 percent of preteens are greatly overweight. Being greatly overweight as an adult is called *obesity*. Obesity can double the chances of getting diseases such as diabetes and heart disease.

Did You Know?
In the United States, about 15 percent of ten-year-olds are overweight. In Italy, about 30 percent are overweight.

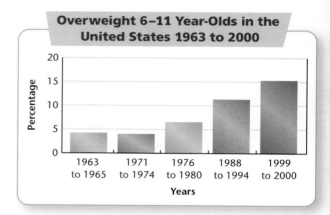

Overweight 6–11 Year-Olds in the United States 1963 to 2000

84

ESL/ELL Support

BACKGROUND AND EXPERIENCE Help students understand what *portion control* means.

Beginning Have students think of ways to model portion control. For example, they might show a serving of meat as being about the size of the palm of their hand.

Intermediate Have students write words that come to mind when they think about portion control.

Advanced Have students write short paragraphs explaining why portion control is important to good health. Tell them to include two reasons for practicing portion control.

▲ Low self esteem sometimes causes young women to "see" themselves as overweight, even when they are not.

Obesity isn't the only problem related to portion control. As they grow, many teenage girls think they are overweight, whether they really are or not. To avoid gaining weight, some eat smaller or fewer servings than their bodies need to stay healthy.

About 5 percent of young women develop a serious eating order called anorexia (an•uh•REKS•ee•uh). **Anorexia** is excessive dieting and, at times, *self-starvation*. Starvation means not eating at all. Anorexia causes poor general health, low blood pressure, heart problems, bone weakness, and even death.

 COMPARE AND CONTRAST How are serving size and portion control alike? How are they different?

Alike: Both have to do with the amount of food eaten. Different: Serving size refers to the amount of food that should be eaten at one time; portion control means limiting the numbers and sizes of servings.

85

---

2. TEACH

Content-Area Reading Support

Using Respellings Direct attention to the phonetic respelling of the word *anorexia*. Explain that respellings show how words are pronounced. Point out that the dots in the respelling divide the word into syllables and that small capital letters indicate the stressed, or accented, syllable.

Discuss

Explain to students that both weighing too much and weighing too little can cause health problems. Lead students in a discussion about the importance of eating, in reasonable amounts, foods that are high in nutrients.

How is portion control related to being overweight? How is it related to being underweight? Eating portions that are too big all the time will lead to being overweight. Eating portions that are too small all the time will lead to being underweight.

Health Background

Binge Eating Disorder One type of eating disorder is binge eating disorder, a condition that includes repeated episodes of eating very large amounts of food in a short period of time. Binge eating disorder is found in about 2 to 5 percent of the population and is more common in women than in men. Many people suffering from binge eating disorder binge to relieve stress and anxiety. Treatment for binge eating disorder includes counseling, working with a dietitian, and sometimes medication.

Source: *National Association of Anorexia Nervosa and Associated Disorders*

 For more background, visit the **Webliography** in Teacher Resources at **www.harcourtschool.com/health Keyword** nutrition

---

 Art

Body Image Collage Have students collect magazine pictures that show healthy, fit, happy people. Encourage them to focus on healthy images, not images that promote being very thin. Students can arrange the images on sheets of poster board to make collages of healthy body images. Suggest to students that they include a few phrases or words in their collages to act as positive messages about having a healthy body image.

Teacher Tip

Supportive Comments Students often make degrading comments about other students' weight, height, and other physical features. Discourage students from making fun of each other. Remind them that even though the target of a joking negative comment may laugh, the comment may still be hurtful. Explain that such comments are never helpful and, in the end, reflect badly on the person who makes them. Encourage students to be supportive of each other.

TEACH continued

Consumer Activity

After students make their tables, discuss how the term *supersize* may be affecting our society's eating habits.

What other marketing tricks might affect people's eating habits? Possible answer: diet foods

Interpret Visuals—Pictures

Ask students to look at the picture on this page. Have them use what they have learned in this chapter to identify each of the foods and the nutrients contained in them.

Which nutrients are most represented in the photo on this page—fats, carbohydrates, or proteins? carbohydrates

Discuss

Have students calculate the relationship between caloric intake and energy expenditure. Make sure students understand the different calorie contents of carbohydrates, proteins, and fats. Explain that even though 200 grams of carbohydrate, 200 grams of protein, and 200 grams of fat weigh the same, your body would get more calories from the fat.

How many calories would your body obtain from 200 grams of protein? 800 calories **From 200 grams of fat?** 1,800 calories

Discuss

In chemistry a calorie is a unit of heat energy. It is the energy needed to raise the temperature of one gram of water one degree Celsius. Food calories are the same except that one food calorie is actually one kilocalorie—1,000 calories. The word comes from the Latin word *calor,* which means "heat." The energy you get from one calorie of food is enough to raise the temperature of a kilogram of water one degree Celsius.

Consumer Activity

Analyze Media Messages
Do advertisements for supersize portions make people want to eat more? Ask ten of your classmates if they supersize meals when eating at fast-food restaurants, and why or why not. Write their responses in a table.

Energy Balance

To keep your body at a healthy weight, you must balance the calories you take in with the calories you use up. Calories are a measure of the amount of energy in a food. All three nutrient groups—carbohydrates, fats, and proteins—contain calories. Your body can use these nutrients for energy. Carbohydrates and proteins have the same number of calories—about 4 per gram of food eaten. Fat has about 9 calories per gram.

When you take in more calories per day than you need, your body changes the excess calories into fat, and you gain weight. If you use more calories per day than you take in, your body uses stored fat for energy, and you lose weight. The ideal, called energy balance, is to take in the same number of calories as you use. Energy balance keeps you from gaining weight or losing weight. The best way to keep your body at a healthy weight is to combine good eating habits with regular exercise. You will learn more about the benefits of exercise in Chapter 4.

All the foods we eat provide calories for daily activities. ▼

Chicken Soup

86

Math

Calorie Combinations Have students create combinations of carbohydrates, proteins, and fats that would provide different calorie totals. For example, ask students what combination would provide 205 calories. Possible answer: 20 g carbohydrates, 20 g protein, 5 g fat

Have students use the table on page 87 to calculate how long they would have to walk to use these calories. about $1\frac{1}{4}$ hours

Calories Used per Hour

Activity	Calories Used
Walking	155
Swimming	345
Basketball	430
Running	455

SUMMARIZE What is the best way to keep your weight the same as it is now?

Athletes can usually eat a lot because they use more calories than the average person. ▶

Quick Activity

Calorie Intake and Energy Use Your body burns calories all the time, but some activities use more calories than others. The table shows how many calories a 100-pound person uses doing a variety of activities. Suppose you eat a 750-calorie dessert. Calculate how long you would have to walk or swim to use up those extra calories.

Lesson 3 Summary and Review

❶ Summarize with Vocabulary

Use vocabulary from this lesson to complete the statements.

The amount of energy in food is measured in _____. Taking in and using the same amount of food energy is called _____. Gaining or losing weight is often the result of poor _____. Supersizing meals can cause weight gain, which can lead to health problems. Excessive dieting, or _____, is also unhealthful.

❷ Why is portion control important?

❸ Critical Thinking What might happen to your muscles if you exercise a lot but don't take in enough calories?

❹ COMPARE AND CONTRAST Draw and complete this graphic organizer to show how obesity and anorexia are alike and different.

Topic:
Alike   Different

❺ Write to Inform—Explanation

Research, then explain why someone shouldn't gain or lose weight too quickly.

Possible response: I can keep eating the same amount of food I now eat and exercise the same amount.

87

Teacher Tip

Muscle and Fat Many people think that muscle, if not used enough, can turn into fat. This myth probably arises from the observation that many athletes get flabby when they retire or quit their sport. In fact, muscle tissue cannot turn into fat. Muscles can, however, atrophy, that is, lose muscle tissue. The main reason athletes get fatter when they quit exercising is that they continue to eat the same amount of food as when they were active. With less exercise, they use fewer calories and store the rest as fat.

Quick Activity

To use 750 calories, a person would have to walk for about 5 hours or swim for about $2\frac{1}{4}$ hours. Pose several other energy balance problems for students to calculate.

3. WRAP UP

Lesson 3 Summary and Review

1. calories; energy balance; portion control; anorexia

2. Portion control helps you get the nutrients your body needs but prevents you from eating too much.

3. Your muscles would not get enough nutrients to stay strong and healthy. Exercise would become more difficult.

4. Possible answers are shown below.

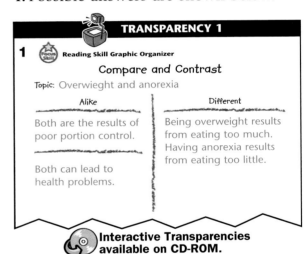

TRANSPARENCY 1

1 **Reading Skill Graphic Organizer**

Compare and Contrast

Topic: Overwieght and anorexia

Alike	Different
Both are the results of poor portion control.	Being overweight results from eating too much. Having anorexia results from eating too little.
Both can lead to health problems.	

Interactive Transparencies available on CD-ROM.

5. Paragraphs should explain that losing weight too quickly can cause health problems. Also, losing weight too quickly does not allow the mind to adjust to the change in eating habits. The lack of adjustment makes it easier to regain the weight.

For **writing models** with examples, see *Teaching Resources* pp. 47–61. Rubrics are also provided.

When Minutes Count ...

Quick Study Students can use *Activity Book* pp. 11–12 (shown on p. 73) as they complete each lesson in this chapter.

Objectives

▶ Explain how family, friends, and culture affect food choices.

▶ Explain how health, the seasons, emotions, and knowledge about foods may affect food choices.

 ## When Minutes Count . . .

Assign the Quick Study, Lesson 4, Activity Book pp. 11–12 (shown on p. 73).

Program Resources

▶ Activity Book pp. 11–12

▶ Transparencies 1, 19

Vocabulary

food allergy p. 93

 ### Daily Fitness Tip

Point out to students that bacteria can thrive in foods that are not cooked properly. In restaurants it is safest to order meat that is fairly well done. Before eating poultry or seafood, make sure it has been cooked all the way through. Food poisoning is often linked to undercooked foods.

 For more guidelines on how food affects the body, see *Be Active! Resources for Physical Education,* p. 143.

1. MOTIVATE

Optional Activity Materials globe or world map

On a globe or a map, have volunteers point out places where they have traveled or countries linked to their cultural backgrounds. Ask students to describe regional foods they have eaten.

What do you notice about the foods students mentioned? Foods from different places vary greatly. People eat a variety of different foods.

Explain that in this lesson students will learn how family, friends, and cultural backgrounds affect people's food choices.

Influences on Food Choices

Lesson Focus

Factors such as family, culture, the seasons, and your health can influence what foods you choose to eat.

Why Learn This?

You can use what you learn to make wise choices about what you eat.

Vocabulary

food allergy

Family, Friends, and Culture Affect Food Choices

The United States is full of people who came here from other countries and brought their foods with them. The cultures of your parents and grandparents influence your food choices the most. How can the country where your family came from influence what you eat?

Family members can influence the foods you eat, too. Suppose you have an older brother whom you admire. You might want to imitate his food choices. Or, if you don't get along with him, you might choose foods that are different from those he chooses. The same is true of your classmates. The way you feel about them might make you go along with or reject their food choices. No matter what kinds of foods you choose, you should make sure they are healthful.

Many restaurants offer foods of different countries. Which kinds of foods do you like? Why? ▶

88

 ### Meeting Individual Needs
Leveled Activities

BELOW-LEVEL Student Cookbook Have students research recipes for their favorite healthful foods. Have them copy the recipes and bind them into a class cookbook. Encourage students to use the recipes to prepare healthful foods at home.

ON-LEVEL Finding "Hidden Sugars" Inform students that different kinds of sugar may be listed as ingredients on the labels of food products. These hidden sugars include *fructose, sucrose, dextrose, corn sweetener, molasses, honey,* and *sorghum.* Have students examine food labels and find the hidden sugars in each product.

CHALLENGE Comparing Sugars Have students research different forms of sugar (such as those listed above) to find out how they are alike and how they are different. Ask students to find out where the sugars come from, how they are made, and what they are used for.

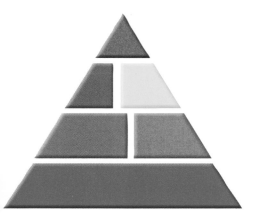

▲ People who don't eat meat can still have a healthful diet. A *vegetarian food pyramid* includes foods such as beans that replace meats, poultry, and fish.

▲ The *Mediterranean food pyramid* reflects foods eaten in countries like Spain, Italy, and Greece. It has more fish than meat.

People's diets are also influenced by their environments. In some places, people eat the wild plants and animals that live in the area. Some people eat the crops they grow and the meat of the animals they raise. People who live in coastal areas tend to eat more seafood than people who live far from the sea. How does the place where you live influence what you eat?

A person's values can also influence what he or she eats. For example, vegetarians choose not to eat meat. Some people don't eat meat because they are against the killing of animals or because of their religious beliefs. How do your personal values affect what you eat?

MAIN IDEA AND DETAILS **Give two reasons why one person's diet might be different from another's.**

Possible responses: They live in different places; they have different values or different religions; they like different foods.

Quick Activity

Compare Pyramids Compare sources of protein and serving sizes in the USDA Food Guide Pyramid and one of the pyramids above. Colors show similar food groupings. Then make a table of any differences.

89

2. TEACH

Interpret Visuals—Pictures

Direct students' attention to the two food guide pyramids. Have them read the name of each pyramid. Then discuss the differences between them. Ask volunteers to point out the general differences and similarities between these two pyramids and the USDA Food Guide Pyramid shown earlier in the chapter.

When Minutes Count . . .

Transparency 19: The Food Guide Pyramid can be used to present material in this lesson. *Interactive Transparencies are available on CD-ROM.*

Quick Activity

Students should identify sources of protein in the vegetarian food guide pyramid, such as dairy products, eggs, beans, nuts, seeds, and legumes. In the USDA Food Guide Pyramid, protein comes mainly from meat, dairy products, nuts, beans, and eggs. Most of the protein in the Mediterranean food guide pyramid comes from beans, nuts, cheese, and yogurt.

Critical Thinking Suppose you are a vegetarian, and you have a friend who lives in Spain who is not a vegetarian. What might be some differences between the two diets? The diet in Spain would have more fish than the vegetarian diet. The vegetarian diet might have more beans and legumes than the Spanish diet.

TEACH *continued*

Content-Area Reading Support

Using Titles and Headings Direct attention to the heading on this page. Call on a volunteer to read the heading aloud and make a prediction about the type of information that follows. Explain that the heading tells what the text that follows is about. Urge students to pay attention to headings as a way to prepare themselves for reading information about a particular topic.

Interpret Visuals—Pictures

Point out the pictures of the foods being eaten. Ask volunteers to identify the foods, and ask whether students eat these foods throughout the year or primarily during a particular season, as the picture caption suggests.

Discuss

Today, food transportation is rapid and reliable. Many foods are transported internationally, and most foods can be obtained year-round. Despite these advances, some foods can lose freshness during transportation.

What are some ways you can tell how fresh a food is? Fresh fruits and vegetables will have a natural color, with no mold or brown spots. Many foods give off a bad odor when they begin to spoil.

How can you be sure the fruits and vegetables you buy are as fresh as possible? Buying from local growers helps ensure that the fruits and vegetables are fresher than those that are transported over long distances before arriving at your grocery store.

Why is it important to have foods that are as fresh as possible? Fresh fruits and vegetables are usually more nutritious; you are less likely to get sick from them; they taste better.

Seasons Affect Food Choices

Do you like a hot bowl of soup or maybe a cup of hot chocolate on a cold winter day? A cool salad and an ice-cold glass of milk might be better if the weather is hot and humid. People often eat different foods depending on the weather. What foods do you like in different kinds of weather?

People used to eat different things during different seasons, too. Your parents and grandparents had to wait for late summer to find fresh corn in the market. They could buy canned or frozen corn in the winter, but not fresh. Some foods, like apples and potatoes, are easy to keep fresh. But strawberries, blueberries, tomatoes, and peppers spoil easily. So why can we find all these fruits and vegetables in most supermarkets all year? Look carefully at the labels on these foods and you will find the answer.

Many of these foods are grown in countries like Mexico, Panama, and Brazil, where it's warm all year.

Fresh foods grown in other countries or regions can be brought to supermarkets in places where the foods are not grown; many foods are available all year in frozen, canned, or irradiated forms.

When the weather is cold, you probably choose hot foods, like soup. ▼

SUMMARIZE Why don't seasons influence a person's choice of foods much anymore?

When the weather is hot, you might eat fresh fruits and vegetables that don't need to be heated. ▶

90

 Social Studies

Mapping Foods Have students find out the sources of the fresh and processed foods they eat. Some fresh foods list the location of the grower on the packaging. Processed foods indicate the location where they are packaged or canned. Have students plot these locations on a map, using different symbols for growing regions and packaging plants.

Teacher Tip

Canned, Frozen, Dried, or Fresh One of the United States government's Dietary Guidelines for Americans is to choose a variety of fruits and vegetables daily. Eating seasonal fruits and vegetables satisfies this guideline. Explain to students that even when their favorite fruits or vegetables are not in season, they can often be found frozen, dried, or in cans.

Freezing, drying, canning, vacuum-packing, smoking, and salting are methods of preserving food. ▼

Cost and Unit Price Affect Food Choices

Foods imported from other parts of the world usually cost more than those produced locally. This may influence what people eat. For example, peaches grown in Chile may be available in February, but they may be too expensive for most families. So, they may buy frozen or canned peaches instead.

Unit price, or the cost of a certain amount of a food, may also influence choice. Suppose a 10-oz can of Brand A peas costs $0.60, while a 12-oz can of Brand B costs $0.66. Which is the better buy? The unit price of Brand A is $0.06/oz, while the unit price of Brand B is $0.55/oz. Brand B is more economical and may be the choice of many shoppers.

Unit pricing also allows shoppers to choose the most economically sized package of the same brand. Buying a half-gallon of juice, for example, is usually less expensive per ounce than buying two quarts.

Unit pricing enables shoppers to choose foods and other products that are more economical. ▼

80¢ per ounce Unit price	Retail Price $2.49
096253	pint of Strawberries
	6 ounces net weight

DRAW CONCLUSIONS Which is more economical—a 6-oz box of cereal for $2.49 or a 12-oz bag of the same cereal for $4.89?
the 12-oz bag

91

Health & Technology

Students might find some controversy over food irradiation. Encourage students to research the pros and cons of this preservation technology.

Discuss

Have students check for unit pricing the next time they go to a supermarket with a parent. Point out that buying larger packages of an item usually results in a lower unit price. However, sometimes a sale price or a two-for-one price actually makes the unit price of the smaller packages a better bargain.

Problem Solving When fresh fruits and vegetables are "out of season," frozen produce will probably be less expensive, provide nearly the same nutrients, and taste as fresh. **Suppose fresh blueberries are $2.00 for a four-ounce container, while frozen blueberries are $7.00 for a 20-ounce bag. Which is the better deal? What is the unit price of each?** The frozen blueberries are the better deal at about $0.35 per ounce, while the fresh blueberries are $0.50 per ounce.

Health Background

Fresh vs. Frozen Fruits and vegetables that are transported long distances are often picked before they are ripe. This means that they are not actually as nutritious as those that come from local farms, or even as nutritious as those that are frozen. Frozen fruits and vegetables are usually allowed to ripen more before they are frozen. After being picked, they are taken to a nearby or on-site processing facility. There they are blanched so that they retain their appearance and flavor. They are then quickly frozen. In the blanching process, vegetables may lose some vitamin C, folic acid, and thiamin, but no more than they would if cooked and served fresh. Frozen vegetables can actually retain more carotene than fresh vegetables.

Source: *United States Department of Agriculture*

For more background, visit the **Webliography** in Teacher Resources at **www.harcourtschool.com/health** **Keyword** nutrition

---

Math

Unit Pricing Problems Be sure students understand that the only way they can be sure they are getting the best price for an item is to determine how much the item costs per unit. Comparing actual costs of two items can often be misleading. Set up this problem for students to solve. Suppose Bill goes to the market to buy two pounds of grapes. When he gets there, he finds that grapes come prepackaged in one-pound bags for $1.59, or loose for $.10 per ounce. Would he be better off buying the prepackaged grapes or the loose grapes? Explain in terms of unit pricing. Set up several additional sets of unit-pricing problems for students to solve.

Personal Health Plan ▶

Students' menus could include these foods:

- soup
- flavored gelatin
- fruit
- whole-grain toast or crackers
- yogurt

Discuss

A food craving, or desire for a particular type of food, is usually emotional. People crave comfort foods even when their bodies don't really need the food. Hunger, on the other hand, is the body's physical need to replace glucose used by the cells for energy.

Critical Thinking **How might a habit or experience affect eating choices?**
Answers will vary but could include the following: When certain foods are eaten at a particular event or occasion, such as a party, a person is likely to want to choose those same foods at similar events or occasions.

Do comfort foods really give people comfort? In the short term, they can make you feel better. But if they are not healthful foods and you eat them too often, they can make you feel worse. For some people, however, their comfort foods are actually healthful and can help in the long term as well.

Interpret Visuals—Pictures

Ask students to look at the picture on this page.

Would you say that the pizza being eaten in the picture is an emotional food choice? Why or why not? It depends; the girls are at a slumber party, and pizza is fun to eat. On the other hand, the girls are probably hungry.

Emotions Affect Food Choices

Often, people who feel stress or who are upset are likely to eat unhealthful foods. Some people eat large amounts of food or they eat junk food, like chips, cookies, and ice cream when they are upset. These kinds of foods are sometimes called *comfort foods*, because people think eating them makes them feel better. Other people stop eating altogether when they are upset or stressed.

Unfortunately, it won't help your feelings to eat lots of food, to eat junk food, or to eat nothing at all. Eating a balanced diet is more likely to make you feel better. The nutrients provided by the right amounts of healthful foods help you deal with stressful situations.

Even when you're feeling fine, you might choose foods because of some emotion. For example, if your grandma always makes pizza when you visit, you might enjoy having pizza with your friends because it reminds you of the fun you have at your grandma's.

Personal Health Plan ▶

Real-Life Situation
Suppose you're feeling upset about something and don't feel like eating.
Real-Life Plan
Make a menu of well-balanced meals for days when you aren't feeling well. Use your plan when you need it.

 COMPARE AND CONTRAST **What two opposite changes in eating habits can occur when a person is upset?**
People might eat lots of food, especially junk food, or eat little or no food.

▼ What foods do you eat when you're having fun?

Hearth Baked to Perfection

92

ESL/ELL Support

LANGUAGE AND VOCABULARY Help students understand the meaning of the term *comfort food* as it is used in the lesson. Remind students that the word *comfort* means "to provide strength, relaxation, warmth, or freedom from stress."

Beginning Have students pantomime how something can provide comfort. Then have them pantomime a way that a particular food can act as a comfort food.

Intermediate Lead students in a discussion about the meaning of the word *comfort*. Ask students to name as many non-food items as they can that provide comfort and to explain why each item seems to do so. Then ask students to name foods that provide the same kind of comfort.

Advanced Ask students to write a paragraph to describe the comfort food of their choice and explain why they consider it a comfort food.

Health Concerns Affect Food Choices

Your food choices can be affected by how your body reacts to certain foods. If you have a food allergy, you probably become ill if you eat the food you are allergic to. A **food allergy** (AL•er•jee) is a bad reaction to a food that most other people can eat. Food allergies can give people rashes, upset stomachs, and headaches. Sometimes food allergies interfere with breathing. People who have severe allergic reactions to certain foods can even die.

Some foods contain chemicals that change the way the body functions. For example, caffeine is a chemical that speeds up body activity. It can make you jittery and keep you awake at night. Caffeine is found in coffee, tea, chocolate, and many soft drinks. You should either avoid foods that have caffeine or limit the amount you eat or drink.

Illnesses can also influence people's food choices. For example, people with diabetes must keep track of the carbohydrates they eat. People with heart disease should limit the amount of fats they eat. And people with high blood pressure should avoid salty foods.

93

Teacher Tip

Be Alert to Food Allergies
Some students might have food allergies of which you are unaware. When planning a class party or other event that involves food, talk to students individually and ask if they are allergic to any foods, or send a note home to parents.

Teacher Tip

Caffeine Content There are significant amounts of caffeine in many food products besides coffee and colas. Most students are unaware of the amount of caffeine found in some of their favorite foods. Many iced-tea products contain as much as 45 mg of caffeine per serving. Some noncola drinks have between 40 and 55 mg of caffeine per serving. Also, a bar of milk chocolate has approximately 10 mg of caffeine.

Discuss

Have students explain how to maintain the healthy status of body systems. To help students understand why caffeine can make a person jittery, explain that caffeine speeds up the nervous system and other body processes, such as heart rate and breathing.

Critical Thinking Should caffeine be a large part of your daily diet? Why or why not? No. It should be limited or left out completely because it can make you jittery and nervous. It can also keep you awake at night.

Explain that many adults drink caffeine to help them wake up in the morning or stay up late at night. The problem with this is that they become addicted. People who are addicted to caffeine can get very bad headaches when they try to quit. Other people use caffeine for medicinal purposes. It is found in some painkillers, and in headache and migraine medicines.

Content-Area Reading Support

Using Signal Words Direct attention to the third paragraph on this page. Point out that the first sentence states the main idea: *Some foods contain chemicals that change the way the body functions.*

Call on a volunteer to read the second sentence aloud: *For example, caffeine is a chemical that speeds up body activity.* Explain that the phrase *For example* signals that the detail sentence contains an example of the main idea. Point out that caffeine is just one example of a chemical that can change the way the body functions. It is not the only such chemical.

3. WRAP UP

Lesson 4 Summary and Review

1. food allergy; caffeine; diabetes

2. Possible answer: A person may decide to buy a large bag of cereal with a unit price of $0.25 per ounce rather than a small box of cereal with a unit price of $0.39 per ounce.

3. Eating large amounts of any kind of food can be harmful and can lead to health problems.

4. Reponses will vary according to the countries chosen.

5. Students might respond that their families help them make more healthful food choices. Some families might have certain preferences or religious restrictions that influence their diets.

 For **writing models** with examples, see *Teaching Resources* pp. 47–61. Rubrics are also provided.

When Minutes Count . . .

Quick Study Students can use *Activity Book* pp. 11–12 (shown on p. 73) as they complete each lesson in this chapter.

A number of different foods, including peanuts, strawberries, shellfish, and milk, may cause allergies. If you discover that you are allergic to certain foods, you should avoid those foods.

If you are already healthy and want to stay that way, you should eat a healthful diet. Eat a wide variety of foods so you get all the nutrients you need. Avoid foods high in sugar, fat, and salt. Be aware of the amounts of food you eat, too. Too much of a good thing can still be bad for you. Follow portion size guidlines. However, don't cut out something altogether unless you are allergic to it. You still need carbohydrates, fats, and proteins—just not in large amounts.

CAUSE AND EFFECT Identify three possible effects of caffeine on a person's body.
Possible response: Caffeine can increase the heart rate, make a person jittery, and keep a person awake at night.

▲ Strawberries and peanuts can cause food allergies.

Lesson 4 Summary and Review

❶ Summarize with Vocabulary

Use vocabulary and other terms from this lesson to complete the statements.

If you break out in a rash after eating a certain food, you may have a _____. _____ is a chemical found in some foods and drinks that can make you jittery. People who have _____ should limit the amount of sugar they eat.

❷ Give an example that shows how unit price can influence a person's choice of foods.

❸ Critical Thinking Why is it a bad idea to eat large amounts of healthful foods?

❹ COMPARE AND CONTRAST
Choose two countries whose foods you eat. Draw and complete this graphic organizer to show how the foods of these countries are alike and different.

Topic:
Alike   Different

❺ Write to Inform—Explanation

Describe how your family influences your food choices.

94

Teacher Tip

Salt and High Blood Pressure
About one in every five Americans has high blood pressure. Approximately 30 percent of those with high blood pressure don't know they have it. Many factors contribute to this condition, such as genetics, age, gender, weight, and salt (sodium) intake. Although people cannot change their genetics or age, they can help prevent high blood pressure. Choosing foods low in salt and preparing foods with less salt are parts of a more healthful lifestyle.

Responsibility

Self-Control

As you grow older, you must take more and more responsibility for your health. This includes choosing healthful foods. It also includes practicing self-control. With self-control you can choose portion sizes that are right for you.

When you look at three popcorn containers at a theater refreshment stand, you might be tempted to get the biggest one. Even if you aren't very hungry, the smell may be tempting you. Or maybe it's the price—the biggest one might cost only a little more than the medium size.

But is the biggest container the most healthful for you? Popcorn is made mostly of carbohydrate. On its own, popcorn is a healthful snack. But at most theaters, popcorn is cooked in fatty oil and covered with butter and salt. Too much carbohydrate, oil, butter, and salt are not good for you.

Activity

Suppose you are the person at the theater refreshment stand. What should you do? You can ask for the popcorn without butter and salt, or you can have just a little of each. You can buy the small container or you can share the larger one with a friend. Write about and explain a healthful choice.

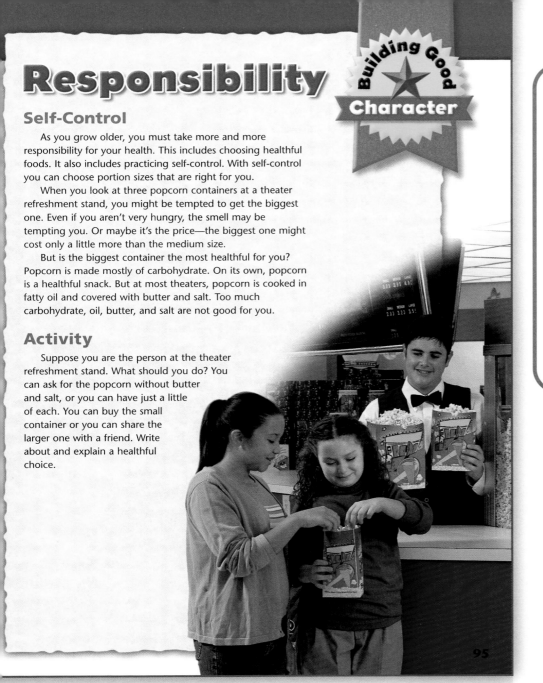

95

Building Good Character

Caring
Citizenship
Fairness
Respect
Responsibility
Trustworthiness

Objective
► Learn how practicing self-control helps you choose healthful foods.

Program Resource
► Poster 4

BEFORE READING
Ask students how showing self-control in making food choices demonstrates responsibility. Help students see that learning to resist temptation and make healthful choices shows taking responsibility for their health.

DISCUSS
Have students apply strategies for self control. Help students name and describe other situations in which self-control would help them choose a healthful food over one that is not as healthful.

Discuss the main character trait in this scenario: responsibility. **In what way is practicing self-control responsible?** By practicing self-control, you are showing responsibility for your health.

ACTIVITY
Have students ask themselves which of the options described in the Activity is the most healthful. **Are there any choices other than the ones given?** yes; not getting any popcorn at all; getting something different **Suppose you buy the large container without thinking about your options. Then what?** Explain that it is not too late to exhibit self-control. There is nothing wrong with leaving some in the container or saving some for later. Have students practice self control.

Using the Poster

Activity Have students write slogans to accompany the poster. The slogans can be written with colored markers on slips of heavy paper, decorated as desired, and then attached to the edge of the poster.

Display Poster 5 to remind students of ways to show responsibility. The poster can be displayed in the classroom, the school cafeteria, or another common area.

POSTER 5

Responsibility

The boy is showing responsibility by being a good role model for his sister.

DO
► Practice self-control.
► Express feelings, needs, and wants in appropriate ways.
► Practice good health habits.
► Keep yourself safe.
► Keep trying. Do your best.
► Complete tasks.
► Set goals and work toward them.
► Be a good role model.

DON'T
► Don't smoke. Don't use alcohol or other drugs.
► Don't do things that are unsafe or that destroy property.
► Don't be led by negative peer pressure.
► Don't deny or make excuses for your mistakes.
► Don't leave your work for others to do.
► Don't lose or misuse your belongings.

How have **YOU** shown **RESPONSIBILITY** today?

POSTER 5

Objectives
► Explain how to use food labels to evaluate the nutrition of foods.
► Describe the influences of advertising on food choices.

When Minutes Count . . .
Assign the Quick Study, Lesson 5, Activity Book pp. 11–12 (shown on p. 73).

Program Resources
► Activity Book pp. 11–12
► Transparency 1

Vocabulary
ingredients p. 96, **additives** p. 97, **preservatives** p. 97

Daily Fitness Tip

Remind students that eating fruits and vegetables every day is a healthful and refreshing way to get valuable nutrients. Students should wash fresh foods to remove pesticides and harmful bacteria. They should also wash eggs and be sure shells are not cracked.

 For more information on how foods affect the body, see *Be Active! Resources for Physical Education*, p. 143.

1. MOTIVATE

Optional Activity Materials small paper bags, sets of crayons or markers, "products" such as pencils or erasers

Divide the class into several groups. Give each group a paper bag, a set of markers, and a "product." Ask students to imagine that they are advertisers trying to sell the product to as many people as possible. They need to design the packaging. Remind them that they are competing for customers against other groups with the same product.

When students are finished, have a volunteer from each group present the group's package. Discuss the influence of packaging on consumers' decisions.

LESSON 5 Food Labels and Advertising

Lesson Focus
Food labels and advertising can influence the choices you make when you are selecting foods.

Why Learn This?
Reading food labels and analyzing advertisements can help you make healthful food choices.

Vocabulary
ingredients
additives
preservatives

Food Labels Provide Information About Nutrition

What's in a box of macaroni and cheese? You might think it's just macaroni and cheese. In fact, even something as simple as macaroni and cheese is made up of many different ingredients. **Ingredients** (in•GREE•dee•uhnts) are all the things that make up a food. What are the ingredients in macaroni and cheese? Look at the label on the following page to find out.

On every box of macaroni and cheese—and on every packaged food—there is a Nutrition Facts label. It tells you how big a serving size is and how many servings are in each package. It also tells you how many calories a serving contains and the nutrients that are in every serving. The label even tells you how much of each day's recommended nutrients one serving provides.

Quick Activity

Analyze Food Labels Study the food labels on the boxes of two different dry cereals. Make a table comparing the nutritional values of the two cereals. Which cereal gives you more fiber? Less sugar? More calories? More protein?

You can learn a lot about what you are eating by reading the Nutrition Facts labels on packaged foods. ►

96

Meeting Individual Needs
Leveled Activities

BELOW-LEVEL **Sequencing Nutrients** Provide students with a food label, and ask them to list the nutrients in order of Percent Daily Value.

ON-LEVEL **Comparing Labels** Provide students with two labels from the same type of food—one "all natural" and the other with additives and preservatives. Have students evaluate the differences between the foods, using the information given on the labels.

CHALLENGE **Calculate Recommended Daily Allowance** Have students use the Percent Daily Values for one of the nutrients listed to determine the total Daily Value for that nutrient. Then ask them to calculate how many servings of the food they would need to eat to get 100 percent of the Daily Value.

Nutrition Facts

Serving Size 2.5 oz
(70g/about 1/3 Box)
(Makes about 1 cup)
Servings Per Container about 3

Amount Per Serving	In Box	Prep*
Calories	260	410
Calories from Fat	25	170

	%Daily Value*	
Total Fat 2.5g**	4%	28%
Saturated Fat 1.5g	8%	23%
Cholesterol 10mg	3%	3%
Sodium 560mg	23%	31%
Total Carbohydrate 48g	16%	16%
Dietary Fiber 1g	4%	4%
Sugars 7g		
Protein 11g		

Vitamin A	0%	15%
Vitamin C	0%	0%
Calcium	10%	15%
Iron	15%	15%

*Prepared with Margarine and 2% Reduced Fat Milk.
**Amount in Box. When prepared, one serving (about 1 cup) contains an additional 1g total fat (3.5g sat. fat), 190mg sodium, and 1g total carbohydrate (1g sugars).
***Percent Daily Values are based on a 2,000 calorie diet. Your daily values may be higher or lower depending on your calorie needs:

	Calories:	2,000	2,500
Total Fat	Less than	65g	80g
Sat Fat	Less than	20g	25g
Cholest	Less than	300mg	300mg
Sodium	Less than	2400mg	2400mg
Total Carb		300g	375g
Dietary Fiber		25g	30g

INGREDIENTS: ENRICHED MACARONI PRODUCT (WHEAT FLOUR, NIACIN, FERROUS SULFATE (IRON), THIAMIN MONONITRATE (VITAMIN B1), RIBOFLAVIN (VITAMIN B2) FOLIC ACID), CHEESE SAUCE MIX (WHEY, WHEY PROTEIN CONCENTRATE, MILKFAT, MILK PROTEIN CONCENTRATE, SALT, SODIUM TRIPOLYPHOSPHATE, CITRIC ACID, SODIUM PHOSPHATE, LACTIC ACID, CALCIUM PHOSPHATE, YELLOW 5, YELLOW 6, ENZYMES, CHEESE CULTURE).

Serving Size tells you how much to eat to get the calories and nutrients listed.

Servings per Container is equal to the total amount of food in the package, divided by the serving size.

Calories tells you how much energy you get from eating one serving.

Lists amounts of protein, fats, carbohydrates, sodium, sugar, cholesterol, and fiber per serving.

Percent Daily Values shows how much of an adult's daily need for a nutrient is met by one serving.

Lists vitamins and minerals in the food, including those in the food naturally and those that are added.

Ingredients includes the main ingredients as well as any additives and preservatives.

The Nutrition Facts label also tells you what nutrients are in the food. Many of the ingredients in the macaroni and cheese, such as wheat and milk, are on the Food Guide Pyramid. Some, like calcium and vitamin D, are also nutrients. Other ingredients are additives and preservatives.

Additives (AD·uh·tivz) are things food manufacturers add to foods. Some additives, such as sugar, are nutrients. Other additives, such as salt and food coloring, change the way a food tastes or looks. Manufacturers sometimes add vitamins and minerals to restore the nutritional value of a processed food.

Preservatives (pree·ZERV·uh·tivz) are chemicals added to foods to keep them from spoiling. By law, additives and preservatives must be listed as ingredients on food labels.

You can use the information on food labels to compare different foods or to compare different brands of the same food. You can also use it to decide how much of a food you should eat at one time. It is important to read the label if you are on a special diet or are allergic to any foods. Nutrition Facts and ingredients lists can help you choose foods that are good for you.

SUMMARIZE What kinds of information are shown on food labels?
ingredients, serving size, servings per package, calories, nutrients

97

2. TEACH

Interpret Visuals—Charts

Direct students' to examine and analyze the Nutrition Facts label. Ask questions like these about the information provided on the label: **What information do you get by reading the calories per serving?** how much energy you get from one serving **How is the amount of sodium expressed?** amount per serving and Percent Daily Value **How is the amount of fiber expressed?** amount per serving and Percent Daily Value

Critical Thinking What information would be important to you in deciding between two similar products with slightly different nutritional information on the labels? Answers will vary. Some students might decide on the product with lower sugar while others might choose a product with higher fiber.

Quick Activity

Make sure the serving size is the same for both cereals. If not, the nutritional values will have to be adjusted.

Health Background

Dietary Fiber Not all the parts of food are digested when we eat them. Insoluble dietary fiber passes through the digestive system without being absorbed into the body. Insoluble dietary fiber consists of complex carbohydrates known as cellulose, lignin, and hemicellulose. Some dietary fiber, like pectin and gum, is soluble in water. Although dietary fiber contains no nutrients, studies suggest that it reduces the risk of colon cancer, decreases the buildup of cholesterol, and helps regulate blood sugar.

Source: *Johns Hopkins Bayview Medical Center*

For more background, visit the **Webliography** in Teacher Resources at **www.harcourtschool.com/health Keyword** nutrition

Teacher Tip

Understanding Food Labels
Some ingredients, such as sugars and fats, come in various forms and can be listed by many names. For example, a corn cereal with an ingredients list that begins with "corn flour, sugar, corn syrup, fructose" may actually contain more sugar (three kinds listed here) than corn flour. Similarly, an ingredients list for wheat crackers that begins with "wheat flour, soybean oil, partially hydrogenated soy oil, lard" may contain more fats or oils than wheat.

Lesson 5 • Food Labels and Advertising **97**

▲ Ads make you more aware of products. However, they may not give you much information about the products.

Interpret Visuals—Pictures

Direct attention to the advertising pictures on this page. Ask students what information is provided by these ads and what information is missing.

Would you buy this product just because of the advertisement for it? Why or why not? Students will probably respond that the ads are designed only to increase sales, not to provide useful information to the consumer.

Discuss

Define some techniques that advertisers use to sell products. The *testimonial* is a device in which a well-known person recommends a product. Advertisers use the *bandwagon technique* to convince people that everyone is buying the product. *Slogans*, or catchy sayings, capture consumers' attention and are easy to remember.

Critical Thinking Ask students to think of specific examples of each of these techniques.

Discuss

Explain that some advertisers use the food label itself as a form of advertising.

Critical Thinking How could advertisers change the serving size to make a food seem more nutritious? They could make the serving size bigger to make the food seem to have more nutrients. They could make it smaller to make the food seem to have fewer calories or less fat.

 Activity

Encourage students to be polite, saying, for example, "I'm really sorry. I would love to eat that, but I can't [or I'm not allowed to]." Students should also know to resist pressure or temptation to eat the foods they know they shouldn't—for whatever reason. If a student is worried that the friend's family will ask questions, he or she might prepare a response in advance.

Consumer Activity

Make Buying Decisions Think back to the last time you asked your parents to buy a certain food because of an ad you saw. What was it about the ad that made you want the food? Write how you could use ads to help you make good decisions about buying foods.

98

Advertisements Influence Food Choices

Do you watch television, read magazines, or look at billboards along the highways? If so, you've probably seen ads for foods. Have you ever seen a food ad and then really wanted that food? If so, the ad did its job.

Many ads appeal to your emotions. They try to make you think that eating certain foods will make you feel good. An ad could show a group of children having fun while eating pizza. A movie star might tell you how good a hamburger tastes. Or a sports star might suggest that drinking a certain juice will make you more like him or her. Some food products have prizes inside the packages. People may buy the product just to get the prize. Advertisers use these "tricks" to get you to buy.

Some ads make claims about the healthfulness of a food. An ad might say the food is low in fat, high in fiber, or sugar-free. While it is against the law to lie in an advertisement, ads can still be misleading. For example, many foods labeled "low-fat" are still high in

ESL/ELL Support

COMPREHENSIBLE INPUT Help students understand that advertisements often provide only the information that will increase sales of the product.

Beginning Show students examples of advertisements that use slogans, the bandwagon technique, and testimonials to sell a product. Ask students to identify each of these advertising techniques by pointing to it in the ad.

Intermediate Have students create an ad designed to sell a food product that has very little nutritional value. Tell students to use a slogan, a testimonial, or the bandwagon technique in the ad.

Advanced Have students write a script for a short commercial about a made-up unhealthful product. Tell students to use either a slogan, a testimonial, or the bandwagon technique in their commercial. Students may perform their commercials for the class.

calories if they contain extra sugar in place of some of the fat. Food packages can also claim to offer health benefits that have not been proved.

If you prefer to eat foods without additives or preservatives, you might choose products labeled "all natural." But be careful. Having no additives or preservatives doesn't mean that a food is good for you. For example, some potato chips are labeled "100 percent natural." But the potatoes are still fried in oil and contain a lot of fat and salt. It's true that salt and oil are natural. But too much salt in your diet can increase your blood pressure, and too much fat can lead to heart disease.

Just remember that food ads and food packages are designed to make you want to buy the foods. If you look carefully at the Nutrition Facts labels, you can decide for yourself what foods are healthful if eaten in the proper amounts.

MAIN IDEA AND DETAILS What is an ad designed to do, and how does it do it?
Ads are designed to get people to buy products. Ads often appeal to people's emotions by linking foods to things people like to do or to people they admire.

Lesson 5 Summary and Review

❶ Summarize with Vocabulary

Use vocabulary and other terms from this lesson to complete the statements.

The _____ in a package of food are written on the _____ label. Sometimes, manufacturers put things in foods to improve how the foods look or taste. These things are called _____. To keep a food from spoiling, a food manufacturer might add one or more _____.

❷ On a Nutrition Facts label, what does the information under Percent Daily Value tell you?

❸ Critical Thinking Why might the label "100 percent natural" on a packaged food be misleading?

❹ **COMPARE AND CONTRAST** Draw and complete this graphic organizer to show how the food labels of two cereals can be alike and different.

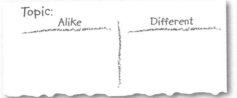

❺ Write to Inform—Description
Describe an ad that might persuade your classmates or friends to buy a particular food product.

99

3. WRAP UP

Lesson 5 Summary and Review

1. ingredients; Nutrition Facts; additives; preservatives

2. how much of one day's recommended nutrients one serving provides

3. Many ingredients can be "100 percent natural" but still be unhealthful.

4. Possible answers are shown below.

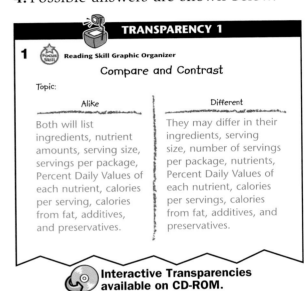

TRANSPARENCY 1

1 **Reading Skill Graphic Organizer**

Compare and Contrast

Topic:

Alike	Different
Both will list ingredients, nutrient amounts, serving size, servings per package, Percent Daily Values of each nutrient, calories per serving, calories from fat, additives, and preservatives.	They may differ in their ingredients, serving size, number of servings per package, nutrients, Percent Daily Values of each nutrient, calories per serving, calories from fat, additives, and preservatives.

Interactive Transparencies available on CD-ROM.

5. Students' descriptions should mention the use of one or more of the techniques described in the lesson.

 For **writing models** with examples, see *Teaching Resources* pp. 47–61. Rubrics are also provided.

 **When Minutes Count . . .**

Quick Study Students can use *Activity Book* pp. 11–12 (shown on p. 73) as they complete each lesson in this chapter.

Life Skills

Communicate
Make Responsible Decisions
Manage Stress
Refuse
Resolve Conflicts
Set Goals

Objectives
► Identify decision-making steps.
► Use decision-making steps to make healthful food choices.

Program Resources
► Activity Book p. 14
► Poster 8

1. MOTIVATE

Lead a discussion of fast-food restaurants. Have students brainstorm the food options at popular fast-food chains. Ask them to group or rank the foods, first according to popularity and then according to the nutritional value they think the foods have.

2. TEACH

Direct students' attention to the photos showing somebody their age deciding what to order for dinner at a fast-food restaurant. Have students assess the role of assertiveness on decision making.

Step 1
What are the dinner choices at the fast-food restaurant? a double cheeseburger, fries, and a large cola; grilled chicken sandwich, a green salad, and a nonfat banana smoothie

Step 2
Which choices can be eliminated? cola and fries

Make Responsible Decisions
About Fast Food

Suppose you're at a fast-food restaurant for dinner. You got up too late to eat breakfast this morning. Then you had pizza and a cola for lunch. Now you want to order the supersized double cheeseburger special. Follow the steps for **Making Responsible Decisions** about eating a more healthful dinner.

1 Find out about the choices you could make.

You could order the special—double cheeseburger, fries, and large cola. Or, you could order a grilled chicken sandwich, a green salad, and a banana smoothie.

2 Eliminate any choices that will make you sick or are against your family rules.

You like cola, but you have already had one today. Fries are your favorite, but your parents allow you to have only one serving per week.

100

Teacher Tip

Dietary Differences Be sensitive to the variety of cultures represented by the students in your classroom and the variety of foods and eating practices common in their homes. You may wish to discuss food practices and food choices of those cultures represented in your classroom or in the larger community—practices and choices such as fasting, vegetarian diets, avoidance of certain foods or beverages, and preferences for corn, wheat, potatoes, or rice as a main carbohydrate source.

ACTIVITY BOOK P. 14

Name _____

Problem Solving

Life Skill
Make Responsible Decisions

Steps for Making Responsible Decisions

1. Find out about the choices you could make.
2. Eliminate any choices that might make you sick or are against your family rules.
3. Imagine the possible results of each choice.
4. Make the decision that is right for you.

Use the steps to help these students make responsible decisions.

A. Miguel ate a bowl of cereal with milk and a granola bar for breakfast. For lunch, he had yogurt, a tortilla with peanut butter, and milk. Miguel wants an after-school snack. He can choose either crackers or an apple.
• Use what you know about the Food Guide Pyramid to explain the most responsible choice for Miguel.

Possible answer: Miguel has not had any servings from the Fruit group today. He has had several servings from the Bread, Rice, Cereal, and Pasta group already, so crackers would not be the best choice. Therefore, Miguel should choose the apple.

B. Leah's baseball team is having a game and a picnic. The chicken salad, made with mayonnaise, looks delicious. By the time Leah finishes playing baseball and gets in line to select her food, the food has been out in the heat for more than two hours. Leah really wants a small helping of chicken salad. There are peanut butter and jelly sandwiches on the table, too.
• What would be the most responsible decision Leah could make?

Possible answer: Leah looks at her choices. She knows that chicken salad that has been out for more than two hours might make her sick. Leah knows that eating the sandwiches would be the safer choice. She decides to pass up the chicken salad.

Available online.
www.harcourtschool.com/health

3 Imagine the possible results of each choice.

The cheeseburger and fries are high in fat and the cola contains sugar. The chicken has less fat, there are vegetables in the salad, and fruit in the smoothie.

4 Make the decision that is right for you.

You order the grilled chicken sandwich, salad, and smoothie.

Problem Solving

A. Joanna needs a lot of energy for track practice, but she isn't sure what she should eat at the coffee shop.
- Use what you know about the steps for **Making Responsible Decisions** to help her choose healthful foods.

B. Jerry's mom prepares three healthful meals every day. She gives him fruits and raw vegetables for snacks. This afternoon Jerry wants to go to the Burger House with his friends.
- What should Jerry order to show that he is trustworthy when eating away from home?

101

Using the Poster

Activity Have students think of other real-life situations in which the decision-making steps can be used to make healthful food choices.

Display Poster 8 to remind students of the decision-making steps. The poster can be displayed in the classroom, the school cafeteria, or another common area.

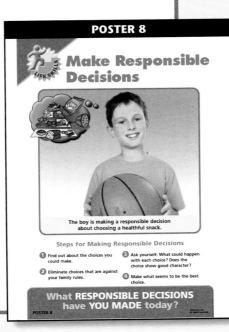

POSTER 8

Make Responsible Decisions

The boy is making a responsible decision about choosing a healthful snack.

Steps for Making Responsible Decisions

1 Find out about the choices you could make.

2 Eliminate choices that are against your family rules.

3 Ask yourself: What could happen with each choice? Does the choice show good character?

4 Make what seems to be the best choice.

What RESPONSIBLE DECISIONS have YOU MADE today?

POSTER 8

Step 3

What would be the results of each choice? The cheeseburger dinner won't provide fresh fruits or vegetables but will provide a lot of fat. The chicken dinner will provide vegetables, fruit, and dairy foods and less fat than the cheeseburger dinner.

Have students utilize critical thinking in decision making.

Critical Thinking Consider what you learned about the nutrients your body needs. How do you think you might feel after dinner if you order the cheeseburger dinner? Remember, you had no breakfast, and your lunch was pizza and a cola. You might feel tired, weak, and irritable and have a headache.

 Building Good Character

Remind students that when they make healthful food choices, they are demonstrating the respect they have for themselves. Any choice that helps the body stay healthy and fit is a choice that shows self-respect.

Step 4

Which is the better choice? grilled chicken sandwich dinner

3. WRAP UP

Problem Solving

A Students should use the four steps of decision making. Their suggestions for Joanna should include foods that contain nutrients her body needs for energy. She should choose foods with simple carbohydrates (such as fruits), foods with complex carbohydrates (such as whole grains), and foods low in fats and sugars.

B Jerry should order foods that are like those his mother chooses for him—foods low in fat, salt, and sugar.

Objectives
▶ Explain how germs get into food and what they do to it.
▶ Describe how to store and prepare food safely.

When Minutes Count . . .
Assign the Quick Study, Lesson 6, Activity Book pp. 11–12 (shown on p. 73).

Program Resources
▶ Activity Book pp. 11–12, 15
▶ Transparency 1

Vocabulary
food poisoning p. 102

Daily Fitness Tip

Tell students that part of staying healthy is avoiding spoiled food. Fruits, breads, and dairy products should be checked for mold growth, which appears as dark spots. Meats and dairy products that look or smell bad should be thrown away. Vegetables should be crisp, not wilted. Cans of food should not be bulging, swollen, rusted, or discolored. Tell students to ask a parent if the quality of a particular food is in doubt.

 For more information on how foods affect the body, see *Be Active! Resources for Physical Education,* p. 143.

1. MOTIVATE

Optional Activity Materials ink pads, paper, other throwaway items

Tell students that the ink represents germs. Have students press their fingers on an ink pad and then touch the paper and other items. Some fingerprints should be transferred. (As an alternative, describe the scenario and have students speculate about what might happen and why.)

Why is it important to wash your hands before handling food? Anything on your hands can get onto food. Germs on your hands could make foods unsafe to eat.

Have students describe other daily activities that promote the health of a family.

LESSON 6

Food Preparation and Safety

Lesson Focus
Foods must be stored and prepared properly in order to be safe.

Why Learn This?
You can use what you learn to safely store and prepare foods in your home and to avoid food poisoning.

Vocabulary
food poisoning

Food Poisoning

You probably wouldn't think of eating uncooked chicken or eggs. They just don't taste good. But there are more important reasons for not eating uncooked foods. Eating certain uncooked or undercooked foods can cause food poisoning. **Food poisoning** is an illness caused by eating foods containing harmful germs.

Germs get into foods from soil, water, air, and people who haven't washed their hands. Germs also spread from one food to another. Suppose you use a knife to cut some uncooked chicken. Then you use the same knife to cut a sandwich. You could transfer germs from the chicken to the sandwich.

Food poisoning can cause stomach cramps, nausea, and diarrhea. Some forms of food poisoning are very dangerous and can even cause death.

CAUSE AND EFFECT How can someone working in a kitchen spread germs to the food?
A person who does not wash his or her hands properly can spread germs. Using the same board or knife for cutting different foods can spread germs from one food to another.

◀ Uncooked chicken should never be cut on the same board or with the same knife as other foods.

102

ESL/ELL Support

COMPREHENSIBLE INPUT Help students understand the importance of proper food preparation by having them act out or otherwise demonstrate different ways to prepare food.

Beginning Draw three pictures, or find magazine pictures, showing a person cutting up uncooked chicken; washing the knife in warm, soapy water; and cutting up some raw vegetables. Ask students to place the pictures in the correct order to represent a safe way to prepare raw vegetables when also handling uncooked chicken.

Intermediate Use the same three-picture sequence as above. Ask students to write sentences that describe what each picture represents.

Advanced Use the same three-picture sequence as above. Ask students to write a paragraph to describe the correct sequence.

Proper Storage Keeps Foods Safe

Germs are everywhere. You can't get rid of them all. The important thing is not to let germs multiply. When germs in food multiply, the food starts to look odd, smell unusual, and taste bad. It has spoiled. The way to keep foods from spoiling is to store them correctly.

Germs multiply rapidly at room temperature but more slowly at low temperature. That's why it's important to store cooked foods and all meats, milk, and eggs in a refrigerator. Covering foods like breads and cereals by wrapping them or putting them in containers can help keep them from spoiling. Although vegetables and fruits don't spoil quickly, storing them in a refrigerator keeps them fresh.

Different foods spoil at different rates. Even in a refrigerator, uncooked meat spoils in a few days. Milk will last for about a week, and cheeses and eggs last for several weeks. Juices, vegetables, and most fruits will last much longer. Freezing foods keeps them safe much longer. See also page 391.

 COMPARE AND CONTRAST What foods spoil the fastest in the refrigerator? The slowest?
fastest: uncooked meat; slowest: juices, vegetables, and most fruits

▼ Different foods need to be stored in different parts of the refrigerator.

Store cooked foods in plastic containers or wrapped in plastic.

Keep meat, poultry, and fish in the coldest part of the refrigerator. Store them wrapped.

Store eggs and milk in their original cartons. Throw away any cracked eggs. Don't keep eggs or milk on the refrigerator door.

Store fruits and vegetables in a vegetable crisper or in unsealed plastic bags.

---

2. TEACH

Interpret Visuals—Pictures
Have students look at the picture and read each of the captions.

Why is it important not to keep milk or eggs in the refrigerator door? The temperature changes often in that area, so food stored there can spoil more quickly.

Why is the temperature of your refrigerator critical to keeping foods from spoiling? A refrigerator that isn't kept cold enough will not slow down the growth of germs in food.

Critical Thinking Why shouldn't you refreeze a frozen food item once it has been thawed? During thawing, the temperature of food increases and the food begins to spoil. When the food is refrozen, the germs stop multiplying but are still present when the food is thawed again.

Health Background

Salmonella bacteria are found most often in raw or undercooked poultry, eggs, meat, fish, and unpasteurized milk. These bacteria are killed by thorough cooking.

Staphylococcus aureus (staph) bacteria are spread to food by people. They can be carried on skin and in the nose and throat. Since ordinary cooking does not kill these bacteria, cleanliness is vital to prevent staph infections.

Escherichia coli (E. coli) bacteria are found in the human digestive tract. They are spread to food by people with unclean hands. These bacteria are especially common in ground meats, such as hamburger. They can be killed by very high temperatures.

Source: United States Food and Drug Administration

 For more background, visit the **Webliography** in Teacher Resources at **www.harcourtschool.com/health** **Keyword** diseases

TEACH *continued*

Interpret Visuals—Pictures
Have students look at the pictures on this page and explain what they show. Discuss the importance of cleanliness in the kitchen—and personal cleanliness—when handling foods.

Discuss
Problem Solving **You have just begun mixing some cookie dough when the telephone rings. Describe what you should do before answering the phone and returning to your mixing.** Put dough in the refrigerator, wash hands, answer the phone, wash hands, return to the mixing. The important thing to remember is to wash your hands before and after handling food.

Content-Area Reading Support
Using Text Format Direct attention to the list of bulleted items on this page.

How is the appearance of this text different from the text above it? Each statement has a dot next to it. Its background is a different color. Explain that the dot is called a bullet. Have students read each of the bulleted statements aloud. **How else might the writers have presented this information?** in a paragraph **Why do you think the writers decided to show this information in a bulleted list rather than in a paragraph?** The information is easier to read as separate bulleted items; the bullets make the text stand out and show that it is important.

Myth and Fact
Myth: Mayonnaise causes food poisoning.
Fact: Mayonnaise doesn't cause food poisoning—germs do. The vinegar and lemon juice in mayonnaise actually slow the growth of germs. However, when mayonnaise is mixed with other foods, like chicken or eggs, the vinegar and lemon juice don't work as well, and the germs multiply.

Prepare a Safe Meal
Think about everything you've touched today. Think about all the other hands that have touched those things. There are hundreds of places you could have picked up germs. To prevent food poisoning when you prepare food, remember these four rules:

- Clean, clean, clean!
- Separate—don't contaminate!
- Refrigerate properly!
- Cook thoroughly!

Clean, clean, clean!
The first and most important thing to do before you prepare a meal is to wash your hands. Do this before you touch anything. Use warm water and plenty of soap, and scrub for twenty seconds. Make sure to clean under your fingernails and between your fingers. After you wash your hands, dry them with a clean towel. Make sure countertops are clean and dry.

Preparing foods carefully makes it less likely that they will have germs that make you or your family ill. ▼

Copyright 2003, Partnership for Food Safety Education

104

Art
How-To Checklist Have students design and create checklists to post in their own kitchens at home. Checklists should list each of the safety precautions learned in this lesson about handling and preparing food safely. Encourage students to make their checklists colorful and eye-catching, so that all members of the family will enjoy them.

Teacher Tip
Washing Hands Students might benefit from knowing that washing their hands thoroughly with warm water and soap for 20 seconds takes only about as long as reciting the alphabet.

Before preparing or eating fresh fruits or vegetables, wash them thoroughly. This will help get rid of germs as well as any chemicals that were used to kill insect pests. After eating, wash dishes and set them out to dry. If you use towels to dry dishes, always use clean ones.

Separate—don't contaminate!

Raw meat, poultry, seafood, and eggs are the foods most likely to carry harmful germs. After you handle these foods, wash your cutting board and utensils thoroughly with hot water and soap. *Never* cut fruits or vegetables on a surface where you have had raw meat, poultry, seafood, or eggs.

Refrigerate properly!

Keep cold foods cold until you use them. If you are going to cook a food that is frozen, thaw the food in a refrigerator or in a microwave, not on a countertop.

Never leave food that needs to be refrigerated sitting at room temperature for more than two hours.

◄ Why is it important to wash your hands and anything used with raw meat?

105

Interpret Visuals—Pictures

Have students look at the picture and name the health precautions they see being followed. Ask students to discuss how each example demonstrates a way to handle food safely.

Content-Area Reading Support

Using Titles and Headings Direct attention to the heading at the top of page 104. Point out that this heading, which identifies the overall topic of the section, is in larger type than the other headings, which identify subtopics shown in the bulleted list. Explain that type size and color are clues to the topic and organization of a text passage.

Discuss

Critical Thinking When Carla stores large amounts of leftovers, she divides them up into small containers before putting them in the freezer. Marcos puts all of his leftovers into a larger container. Which is the safer method for storing leftovers? Explain. Carla's method of dividing her leftovers into smaller amounts and storing them in small containers is safer. Small containers cool faster than large containers, which helps keep food safe. Also, storing food in smaller containers enables Carla to defrost only what she needs. Marcos has to defrost the entire container and will have to throw away the food that he can't use right away.

3. WRAP UP

Lesson 6 Summary and Review

1. nausea, diarrhea, food poisoning; germs

2. A person can die from food poisoning.

3. Germs multiply fastest at room temperature.

4. Possible answers are shown below.

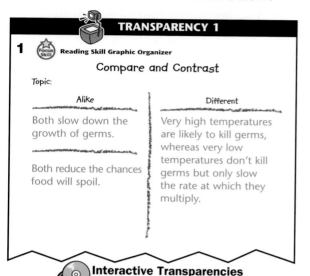

TRANSPARENCY 1

1 Reading Skill Graphic Organizer

Compare and Contrast

Topic:

Alike	Different
Both slow down the growth of germs.	Very high temperatures are likely to kill germs, whereas very low temperatures don't kill germs but only slow the rate at which they multiply.
Both reduce the chances food will spoil.	

Interactive Transparencies available on CD-ROM.

5. Methods could include washing any utensils used to prepare the chicken; washing your hands between handling the cooked and uncooked pieces of chicken; and preparing them on different surfaces.

For **writing models** with examples, see *Teaching Resources* pp. 47–61. Rubrics are also provided.

When Minutes Count ...

Quick Study Students can use *Activity Book* pp. 11–12 (shown on p. 73) as they complete each lesson in this chapter.

Cook thoroughly!

Cooking kills most harmful germs in food. But foods that are not cooked all the way through can still cause food poisoning. To be safe, cook eggs until the yolks are hard. Cook meat and poultry until they are no longer pink inside.

Finally, remember that your eyes, nose, and taste buds are there to protect you. If something looks odd, smells unusual, or tastes bad, throw it out. If you follow these guidelines, you will reduce the chances of getting or causing food poisoning. You can review more tips for kitchen safety in the Health and Safety Handbook, pp. 392–393.

▲ Cooking foods completely will reduce the risk of getting food poisoning. Most germs are killed by heat.

 COMPARE AND CONTRAST How do high and low temperatures fight food poisoning in different ways?
High temperatures kill most germs. Low temperatures slow their growth.

Lesson 6 Summary and Review

❶ Summarize with Vocabulary

Use vocabulary and other terms from this lesson to complete the statements.

Pains in your stomach with cramps, ____, and _____ might be signs that you have _____. Refrigeration and freezing slow the growth of _____ that can make foods spoil, while sitting out at room temperature speeds up their growth.

❷ Critical Thinking What is the worst thing that can happen to a person who gets food poisoning?

❸ At what kind of temperature do germs multiply fastest?

❹ COMPARE AND CONTRAST

Complete this graphic organizer to show how high and low temperatures affect the growth of germs in ways that are alike and different.

Topic:

Alike	Different

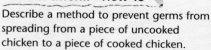

❺ Write to Inform—How-To

Describe a method to prevent germs from spreading from a piece of uncooked chicken to a piece of cooked chicken.

106

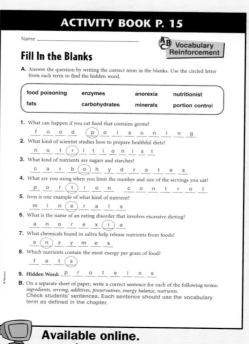

ACTIVITY BOOK P. 15

Name _____

Vocabulary Reinforcement

Fill In the Blanks

A. Answer the question by writing the correct term in the blanks. Use the circled letter from each term to find the hidden word.

food poisoning	enzymes	anorexia	nutritionist
fats	carbohydrates	minerals	portion control

1. What can happen if you eat food that contains germs?
f o o d (p) o i s o n i n g

2. What kind of scientist studies how to prepare healthful diets?
n u t (r) i t i o n i s t

3. What kind of nutrients are sugars and starches?
c a r b (o) h y d r a t e s

4. What are you using when you limit the number and size of the servings you eat?
p o r (t) i o n c o n t r o l

5. Iron is one example of what kind of nutrient?
m i n (e) r a l s

6. What is the name of an eating disorder that involves excessive dieting?
a n o r e x (i) a

7. What chemicals found in saliva help release nutrients from foods?
e n z y m e s

8. Which nutrients contain the most energy per gram of food?
f a t (s)

9. **Hidden Word:** P r o t e i n s

B. On a separate sheet of paper, write a correct sentence for each of the following terms: *ingredients, serving, additives, preservatives, energy balance, nutrients.* Check students' sentences. Each sentence should use the vocabulary term as defined in the chapter.

 Available online. www.harcourtschool.com/health

ACTIVITIES

Physical Education

Carbo-Loading Athletes prepare in many ways for long-distance races called *marathons*. The winner will run for more than two hours without stopping. In addition to training, a marathon runner may do something before a race called carbo-loading. Find out what carbo-loading is, and write a paragraph explaining it.

Science

In the Body Use a sheet of poster board to make an outline of a body. Then cut out photos or drawings from magazines and newspapers of foods that represent the six nutrient groups. Paste these on the poster board, and write a short caption explaining the ways in which each nutrient helps the body.

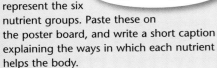

Technology Project

Compare Nutrients Different foods contain different amounts of nutrients. Nutrients and their amounts are listed on the nutrition labels. Using a computer, make a table that compares the nutrients of three similar foods. If a computer is not available, make a poster.

GO ONLINE For more activities, visit The Learning Site. www.harcourtschool.com/health

Home & Community

At School Many school cafeterias provide menus in advance. Study next week's menu for your school cafeteria. If a menu isn't available, keep a journal of what is served each day for one week. Look at the USDA Food Guide Pyramid on pages 78–79. Add up the number of lunch foods that fit into each group. Then describe ways the foods can be used as part of a balanced diet.

Career Link

School Dietitian School dietitians plan meals for school lunches. They prepare nutritious menus for schoolchildren, making sure students get a balance of the nutrients they need. Suppose you are the dietitian for your school. Prepare a series of menus for one week of school lunches. Be sure to use the information you have learned in this chapter as you prepare your menu.

Activities

Physical Education
Remind students that marathon runners use carbo-loading for specific reasons and usually do so with the advice of a personal trainer and doctor.

Science
Encourage students to use large, colorful photos or drawings so that viewers can easily identify the foods and the nutrients they represent. Students may want to make labels for the nutrients represented by each food and attach them to each photo or drawing.

Home & Community
Students might be surprised to find that the school lunches offer an easy way of getting the suggested number of servings from each food group on the USDA Food Guide Pyramid. Suggest to students that they identify any individual lunch combinations that seem to be especially well balanced.

CSHP Supports the Coordinated School Health Program

Technology Project
Remind students to write the name of the food product above or on the back of each nutrition label so they know at a glance which label belongs to which product.

Career Link

School Dietitian Remind students that a school dietitian tries to plan meals that will appeal to many different students. Not only must a school dietitian learn how to prepare meals that are attractive, tasty and healthful, but he or she must also make sure the meals are part of a healthful diet as recommended by the USDA Food Guide Pyramid.

GO ONLINE For more information on health careers, visit the **Webliography** in Teacher Resources at **www.harcourtschool.com/health** **Keyword** health careers

Chapter Review and Test Preparation

Pages 108–109

Reading Skill 8 pts. each

1. Possible answers: Both contain nutrients. Both contain carbohydrates. Both store lots of energy.

2. Possible answers: Most carbohydrates in bread are starches, made up of many sugars; the carbohydrate in a lump of sugar is a simple sugar. Bread contains nutrients other than carbohydrates; sugar contains only a carbohydrate. Bread is at the base of the USDA Food Guide Pyramid; sugar is at the top.

Use Vocabulary 2 pts. each

3. D, mineral

4. A, calorie

5. F, anorexia

6. B, preservative

7. C, additive

8. E, fat

Check Understanding 3 pts. each

9. C, helps release energy from food

10. J, mouth

11. B, have soft bones

12. H, breads, cereals, rice, and pasta

13. B, fresh corn on the cob

14. F, [T-bone steak]

15. A, fats

16. J, water content

17. C, 68°F

18. G, pink

19. A, ground beef

Think Critically 6 pts. each

20. The chicken had germs that were passed to the tomato by the blade of the knife.

Chapter Review and Test Preparation

Reading Skill

COMPARE AND CONTRAST
Draw and then use this graphic organizer to answer questions 1 and 2.

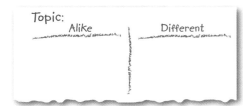

1 Write at least two ways in which a piece of whole-wheat bread and a lump of sugar are alike.
2 Write at least two ways in which a piece of bread and a lump of sugar are different.

Use Vocabulary

Match each term in Column B with its description in Column A.

Column A	Column B
3 A nutrient such as calcium or iron	A calorie
4 A measure of the energy in food	B preservative
	C additive
5 A condition resulting from extreme dieting	D mineral
	E fat
6 Something added to a food to keep it from spoiling	F anorexia
7 Something put in food to make it more nutritious	
8 Nutrient at top of Food Guide Pyramid	

108

Check Understanding

Choose the letter of the correct answer.

9 An enzyme ____. (p. 73)
 A holds energy needed by your body
 B is a carbohydrate
 C helps release energy from food
 D causes food poisoning

10 Digestion begins in the ____. (p. 73)
 F stomach   H small intestine
 G esophagus   J mouth

11 If calcium is missing in a person's diet, the person might ____. (p. 76)
 A have difficulty seeing at night
 B have soft bones
 C have swollen gums
 D have digestion problems

12 The base of the USDA Food Guide Pyramid is made up of ____. (pp. 78–79)
 F fats, oils, and sweets
 G fruits and vegetables
 H bread, cereal, rice, and pasta
 J meat, poultry, and fish

13 Which of these foods would your grandparents **NOT** have found in a supermarket in winter? (p. 90)
 A apples   C steak
 B fresh corn on the cob   D fish

14 If you were trying to add protein to your diet, which of these foods would be the best to eat? (p. 75)

F   H

G   J

Formal Assessment

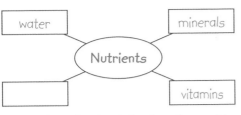

water   minerals

Nutrients

vitamins

15 Which nutrient is missing from the graphic organizer? (pp. 74–77)

A fats   C carbohydrates
B proteins D all of these

16 Which of the following will you **NOT** find on a Nutrition Facts label? (pp. 96–97)

F protein   H carbohydrate
  content   content
G fat content J water content

17 At which of the following temperatures will germs grow fastest? (p. 103)

A 5°F (freezer)   C 68°F (room)
B 40°F (refrigerator) D 150°F (dishwasher)

18 Eat chicken only if it is cooked so thoroughly that the inside is no longer _____. (p. 106)

F red   H white
G pink   J orange

19 In a refrigerator, which of the following foods spoils fastest? (p. 103)

A uncooked meat   C milk
B hard cheese   D pasteurized juice

Think Critically

20 You slice a peach, a piece of chicken, and a tomato, in that order, with the same knife without washing it. Only the people who eat the chicken, the tomato, or both get food poisoning. Explain how this could happen.

21 Your doctor says your bones are too soft. What question about your diet might your doctor ask? Why? What might he or she suggest you do to make your bones stronger?

22 You see a TV commercial advertising a breakfast cereal. Your favorite basketball player is shown in the background dunking the ball into the basket. How would this affect the way you think about the cereal? Would you be more tempted to buy it? Why or why not?

Apply Skills

23 **BUILDING GOOD CHARACTER**
Respect You are invited to dinner at a friend's home. You and your friend have the chore of cleaning up after dinner. You notice that a plate of leftover meat is sitting on the countertop. Your friend suggests you play some games now and leave the meat where it is. How can you show good self-control in this situation?

24 **LIFE SKILLS**
Make Responsible Decisions You learn from some friends about a new diet. It's supposed to make you lose 10 pounds in a week. Do you decide to try it? Why or why not?

Write About Health

25 Write to Inform—Explanation Explain why reading Nutrition Facts labels is important to your health.

109

ASSESSMENT GUIDE P. 27

Name _____

The Food Guide Pyramid is a tool you can use to plan a healthful diet. Complete the pyramid below by writing the number of daily servings from the listed food groups that the government suggests people should have each day to stay healthy.

21. 3 servings per day
22. 2–4 servings per day
23. 6–9 servings per day

Andrea and Hiroko are shopping for a snack to share with their friends. They want to choose a healthful, delicious snack. Describe two things they could learn about foods by reading the Nutrition Facts label.

24. Possible answer: servings per container

25. Possible answer: what percentages of each day's recommended amounts of several nutrients are in one serving of food

Chapter 3 • Foods for Good Nutrition   (page 3 of 3) Assessment Guide • 27

Performance Assessment

Use the Chapter Project and the rubric provided on the Project Evaluation Sheet. See *Assessment Guide,* pp. 18, 57, 64.

Portfolio Assessment

Have students select their best work from the following suggestions:
• Leveled Activities, p. 74
• Quick Activity, p. 91
• Write to Inform, p. 106
• Activities, p. 107
See *Assessment Guide* pp. 12–16.

---

21. The doctor might ask, "How much milk, cheese, and yogurt is in your diet?" These foods contain high amounts of calcium, which you need to build strong bones. The doctor might suggest that you eat more foods that are calcium-rich or take a calcium supplement.

22. Possible answer: Since you admire the basketball player, you might be tempted to buy the cereal. But if you remember what ads are designed to do, you might take time to investigate the cereal before you buy it to see if it is right for you.

Apply Skills 7 pts. each

23. You should postpone playing the games and suggest wrapping up the meat and storing it in the refrigerator right away; if it stays out too long, germs will grow in it. This could give food poisoning to anyone who eats the leftover meat.

24. Friends and other peers are not always reliable sources of health information. Losing 10 pounds in a week is not healthful. You should discuss it with your doctor.

Write About Health 7 pts.

25. Reading these labels tells you what is in the food you eat. It helps you know if you are eating a balanced diet. If you have a food allergy, it helps you identify foods that could be dangerous to your health. It helps you be a more responsible consumer.

Lesson	Pacing	Objectives	Reading Skills
Introduce the Chapter pp. 110–111		• Preview chapter concepts.	**Main Idea and Details** p. 111; pp. 372–383
1 Being Active and Fit pp. 112–116	1 class period	• List three reasons sleep, food choices, and physical activity are important to a healthful lifestyle. • Define *physical activity*, and give examples of its benefits and barriers.	**Main Idea and Details** pp. 113, 116 • Cause and Effect, p. 115 • Draw Conclusions, p. 116
★ Building Good Character p. 117		• Identify ways to demonstrate fairness during a competitive game.	
2 How Exercise Helps Your Body Systems pp. 118–123	1 class period	• List three ways exercise helps the respiratory and circulatory systems. • Apply the Activity Pyramid when planning physical activities.	**Main Idea and Details** p. 123 • Sequence, p. 119 • Compare and Contrast, p. 121 • Draw Conclusions, p. 123
Life Skills pp. 124–125	1 class period	• Identify the four steps in goal setting. • Apply the goal-setting model to set up plans for a healthful lifestyle.	
3 Ways to Exercise pp. 126–132	1 class period	• List the three issues that should be addressed to exercise safely. • List three kinds of exercise and give an example of each.	**Main Idea and Details** p. 132 • Compare and Contrast, p. 127 • Summarize, p. 129 • Draw Conclusions, pp. 130, 132
Activities p. 133		• Extend chapter concepts.	
Chapter Review pp. 134–135	1 class period	• Assess chapter objectives.	

Vocabulary	Program Resources
	Music CD Teaching Resources, p. 29
physical activity	Activity Book, pp. 16–18
	Poster 3
cardiovascular fitness aerobic exercise anaerobic exercise	Transparencies 4, 20 Activity Book, pp. 16–17
	Activity Book, p. 19 Poster 12
muscular strength flexibility muscular endurance	Transparency 4 Activity Book, pp. 16–17, 20
	The Learning Site www. harcourtschool.com/health
	Assessment Guide, pp. 28–30

Focus Skill Reading Skill

These reading skills are reinforced throughout this chapter and one skill is emphasized as the Focus Skill.

Main Idea and Details

- Draw Conclusions
- Identify Cause and Effect
- Compare and Contrast
- Sequence
- Summarize

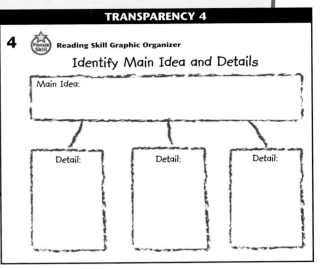

TRANSPARENCY 4

4 Reading Skill Graphic Organizer

Identify Main Idea and Details

Main Idea:

Detail: Detail: Detail:

Life Skills

Life Skills are health-enhancing behaviors that can help students reduce risks to their health and safety.

Six Life Skills are reinforced throughout *Harcourt Health and Fitness*. The skill emphasized in this chapter is Set Goals.

POSTER 12

Set Goals

The girl is setting a goal to get more exercise.

Steps for Setting Goals

1 Choose a goal.
2 Plan steps to reach that goal. Determine whether you will need help.
3 Check your progress as you work toward the goal.
4 Evaluate the results of your work.

What GOALS have YOU SET?

POSTER 12

Building Good Character

Character education is an important aspect of health education. When students behave in ways that show good character, they promote the health and safety of themselves and others.

Six character traits are reinforced throughout *Harcourt Health and Fitness*. The trait emphasized in this chapter is Fairness.

POSTER 3

Fairness

The children are showing fairness by being good sports.

DO	DON'T
▸ Play by the rules. ▸ Be a good sport. ▸ Share. ▸ Take turns. ▸ Listen to the opinions of others.	▸ Don't take more than your share. ▸ Don't be a bad loser or a bad winner. ▸ Don't take advantage of others. ▸ Don't blame others without cause. ▸ Don't cut in front of others in line.

How have YOU shown FAIRNESS today?

POSTER 3

Interactive Transparencies available on CD-ROM.

Coordinated School Health Program

A Coordinated School Health Program endeavors to improve children's health and, therefore, their capacity to learn through the support of families, schools, and communities working together. The following information is provided to help classroom teachers be more aware of these resources.

The National Center for Chronic Disease and Health Promotion, part of the **CDC,** funds the Coordinated School Health Program. Visit its website for information about the eight components that make up this program. **www.cdc.gov/nccdphp/dash/**

The American Alliance for Health, Physical Education, Recreation, and Dance (**AAHPERD**) suggests parents, teachers, and health-care providers emphasize the words *play* and *activities*, rather than *exercise*, when discussing physical activity with children. **www.aahperd.org/**

The **American Heart Association's** website reviews information about the FIT (Frequency, Intensity, and Time) Formula as part of an effective fitness program. **www.americanheart.org/**

The "Walk Texas!" program from the **Texas Department of Health** encourages a united effort to help meet timely societal needs consistent with the Healthy People 2000 Goals and the Surgeon General's Report on Physical Activity. **www.tdh.state.tx.us/diabetes/walktx/index.html**

Other resources that support a Coordinated School Health Program:
- School-Home Connection
- Daily Physical Activity
- Daily Fitness Tips
- Activities: Home & Community
- Health Background: Webliography
- *Be Active! Resources for Physical Education*

Books for Students

Middleton, Haydn. *Ancient Olympic Games.* Heinemann Library, 2000. Explains the origins and end of the ancient games. **EASY**

Silverstein, Alvin. *Physical Fitness (My Health).* Watts Publishing Group, 2002. Explains fitness, sleep, and exercise. **AVERAGE**

Hirschfeld, Robert. *Run for It.* Little, Brown and Company, 2002. Theo raises money for a worthy cause. **ADVANCED**

Books for Teachers and Families

Cooper, Kenneth H., M.D. *Fit Kids! The Complete Shape-Up Program from Birth Through High School.* Broadman and Holman Publishers, 1999. A parental guide to raising healthy and fit children.

Micheli, Lyle J., and Mark Jenkins. *The Sports Medicine Bible: Prevent, Detect, and Treat Your Sports*

Media Resources

Injuries Through the Latest Medical Technologies. HarperCollins, 1995. Tells how to prevent, detect, and treat injuries.

Free and Inexpensive Materials

Magazine City
Offers a free trial subscription to *Bicycling* magazine.

The President's Council on Physical Fitness and Sports
Has exercises that will encourage students to get up and get out.

United Health Foundation
Request their free book *Be Happy, Be Healthy.*

Fitness and Freebies
Will send a newsletter on fitness and other health information.

American Institute for Cancer Research
Request a free copy of their brochure *Getting Active, Staying Alive.*

To access free and inexpensive resources on the Web, visit **www.harcourtschool.com/health/free**

Videos

Yoga Fitness for Kids. Gaiam Publications, 2001.

Come See About Nutrition and Exercise. ETR Associates, 1996.

Fit 4 Kids: Complete Workout Just for Kids. Professional Video, 1998.

These resources have been selected to meet a variety of individual needs. Please review all materials and websites prior to sharing them with students to ensure the content is appropriate for your class. Note that information, while correct at time of publication, is subject to change.

Visit **The Learning Site** for related links, activities, resources, and the health **Webliography.**

www.harcourtschool.com/health

Meeting Individual Needs

ESL/ELL

Below-Level

Ask students to tell where they find answers to questions. If the answer is in the text, they write *Here* on a self-stick note and attach it to the page. If the answer is on more than one page, they write *Think and Search* on that note. They write *On My Own* if they have to answer it themselves.

Activities

- Illustrate SAFE Activities, p. 114
- Exercise Promotion Poster, p. 120
- Exercise Collage, p. 128

On-Level

When students adjust their reading rate, they can often comprehend more facts and details in a nonfiction passage. Explain that a selection that includes a lot of facts and details should be read more slowly than a passage that is intended for entertainment.

Activities

- Dear Diary, p. 114
- Create a Skit, p. 120
- Make an Exercise Plan, p. 128

Challenge

Have students work together to create a class newsletter relating to topics discussed in health class. Have students conduct interviews of school personnel or other students to get opinions, perspectives, and information on health issues discussed in the classroom.

Activities

- Explore the World of Tomorrow Today, p. 114
- Explore Famous Athletes, p. 120
- Graph Your Favorite Exercises, p. 128

Learning Log

Build background with students through frequent use of concrete contextual referents, such as visuals, props, and graphics. Being able to touch a prop or see a picture of a new word makes the experience more meaningful and the concept more understandable.

Activities

- Language and Vocabulary, p. 118
- Comprehensible Input, p. 123
- Background and Experience, pp. 127, 130

Curriculum Integration

Integrated Language Arts/Reading Skills

- Write About It, p. 115
- Letter Campaign, p. 131

 Music

- Activity Song, p. 131

 Science

- Interacting Respiratory and Circulatory Systems, p. 119

Use these topics to integrate health into your daily planning.

 **Physical Education**

- Daily Fitness Tip, pp. 112, 118, 126
- Daily Physical Activity, p. 111
- Unfamiliar Activity, p. 122

 Social Studies

- Cross-Culture Athletes, p. 121
- Foreign Sports, p. 126

 Art

- SAFE Poster, p. 116
- Make an Exercise Mobile, p. 129

CHAPTER SUMMARY

In this chapter, students
► examine how a healthful lifestyle improves health in many ways.
► explore how safe and fun physical activities can improve health.

Life Skills
Students *set goals* to increase physical activity.

Building Good Character
Students show *fairness* by following the rules of soccer.

Consumer Health
Students *explore the various community sites* where they can be physically active.

Literature Springboard

Use the article "Get Ready, Get Fit, Go!" to spark interest in the chapter topic. See the Read-Aloud Anthology on page RA-5 of this *Teacher Edition*.

Prereading Strategies

SCAN THE CHAPTER Have students preview the chapter content by scanning the titles, headings, pictures, graphs, and tables. Ask volunteers to predict what they will learn. Use their predictions to determine what they already know about fitness.

PREVIEW VOCABULARY As students scan the chapter, have them write down the vocabulary terms listed at the beginning of each lesson. Tell them to cross out the terms they know, draw a box around terms they think they know, and circle terms they don't know. Have students cross out terms they have boxed or circled as they confirm or learn them.

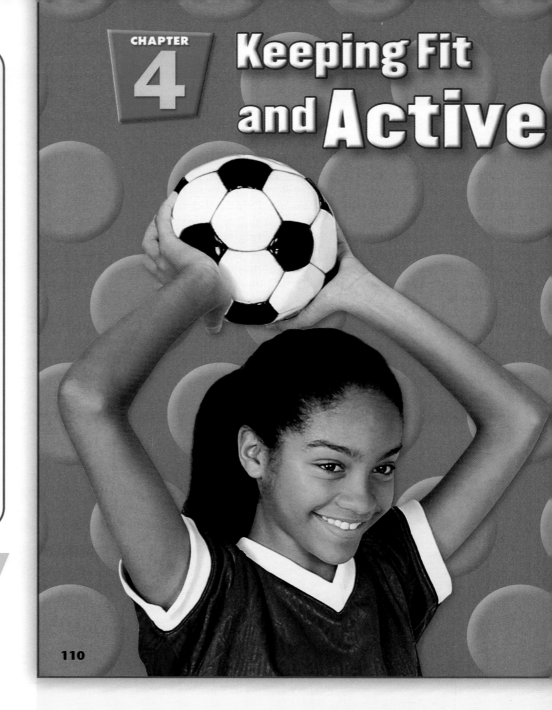

CHAPTER

4

Keeping Fit and Active

110

Reading Skill

IDENTIFY MAIN IDEA AND DETAILS To introduce or review this skill, have students use the Reading in Health Handbook, pp. 372–383. Teaching strategies and additional activities are also provided.

Students will have opportunities to practice and apply this skill throughout this chapter.

• Focus Skill Reading Mini-Lesson, p. 112
• Reading comprehension questions identified with the
• *Activity Book* p. 18 (shown on p. 116)
• Lesson Summary and Review, pp. 116, 123, 132
• Chapter Review and Test Preparation, pp. 134–135

Reading Skill

IDENTIFY MAIN IDEA AND DETAILS
The main idea is the most important thought in a passage. Details tell about the main idea. They tell *who, what, when, where, why,* and *how.* Details help you understand the main idea. Use the Reading in Health Handbook on pages 372–383 to help you read the health facts in this chapter.

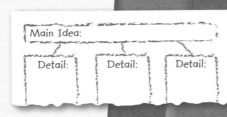

Main Idea:

Detail: | Detail: | Detail:

Health Graph

INTERPRET DATA These are the results of a recent study that looked at the relationship between physical activity and body weight. Based on the graph, list three facts about physical activity, eating, and weight. Do you think the trends shown will change in the near future? Why or why not?

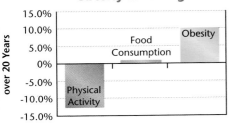

Health Behaviors and Obesity in Teenagers

Percentage Change over 20 Years

15.0%
10.0%
5.0%
0%
-5.0%
-10.0%
-15.0%

Food Consumption
Obesity
Physical Activity

Daily Physical Activity

Along with good food choices, some physical activity every day will help keep your muscles, bones, and heart healthy.

 Be Active!
Use the selection, Track 4, **Jam and Jive**, to give your heart a workout.

111

School-Home Connection

Distribute copies of the School-Home Connection (in English or Spanish). Have students take the page home to share with their families as you begin this chapter.

Follow Up Have volunteers share the results of their activities.

 Supports the Coordinated School Health Program

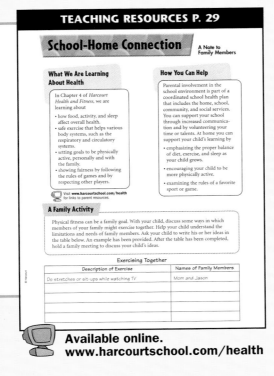

TEACHING RESOURCES P. 29

School-Home Connection — A Note to Family Members

What We Are Learning About Health

In Chapter 4 of *Harcourt Health and Fitness,* we are learning about
• how food, activity, and sleep affect overall health.
• safe exercise that helps various body systems, such as the respiratory and circulatory systems.
• setting goals to be physically active, personally and with the family.
• showing fairness by following the rules of games and by respecting other players.

How You Can Help

Parental involvement in the school environment is part of a coordinated school health plan that includes the home, school, community, and social services. You can support your school through increased communication and by volunteering your time or talents. At home you can support your child's learning by
• emphasizing the proper balance of diet, exercise, and sleep as your child grows.
• encouraging your child to be more physically active.
• examining the rules of a favorite sport or game.

Visit www.harcourtschool.com/health for links to parent resources.

A Family Activity

Physical fitness can be a family goal. With your child, discuss some ways in which members of your family might exercise together. Help your child understand the limitations and needs of family members. Ask your child to write his or her ideas in the table below. An example has been provided. After the table has been completed, hold a family meeting to discuss your child's ideas.

Exercising Together

Description of Exercise	Names of Family Members
Do stretches or sit-ups while watching TV	Mom and Jason

Available online.
www.harcourtschool.com/health

Health Graph

Interpret Data

Ask for volunteers to explain what information the graph is presenting. **What are three facts that you can learn from the graph on exercise, eating, and weight?** more overweight, less exercise, and not much change in energy in foods eaten **In what ways have the eating habits of Americans changed over the last 20 years?** less healthful choices, skipping breakfast, and eating more fast food **In what ways could people today change their lives so that this graph would reflect the way people lived 20 years ago?** increase exercise; make better food choices; eat breakfast; include the family in these changes

Daily Physical Activity

Use *Be Active! Music for Daily Physical Activity* with the Instant Activity Cards to provide students with movement activities that can be done in limited space. Options for using these components are provided beginning on page TR2 in this *Teacher Edition.*

Chapter Project

Blaze a Trail to Physical Fitness (*Assessment Guide* p. 57)

ASSESS PRIOR KNOWLEDGE Use students' initial ideas for the project as a baseline assessment of their understanding of chapter concepts. Have students complete the project as they work through the chapter.

PERFORMANCE ASSESSMENT The project can be used for performance assessment. Use the Project Evaluation Sheet (rubric), *Assessment Guide* p. 65.

Objectives

► List three reasons sleep, food choices, and physical activity are important to a healthful lifestyle.

► Define *physical activity*, and give examples of its benefits and barriers.

 When Minutes Count . . .

Assign the Quick Study, Lesson 1, Activity Book pp. 16–17 (shown on p. 113).

Program Resources

► Activity Book pp. 16–18
► Transparency 4

Vocabulary

physical activity p. 113

 **Daily Fitness Tip**

All three aspects of being fit—adequate sleep, physical activity, and a healthful diet—are necessary for fitness and good health. Ignoring any one of them makes it difficult to have the other two and results in negative effects on overall health.

 For more guidelines on your need for rest and sleep, see *Be Active! Resources for Physical Education,* p. 159.

1. MOTIVATE

Have students name several activities they do in their spare time, and write them on the board. Then ask students to identify those that involve physical activity. Draw an asterisk next to the activities that involve physical activity.

Roughly, what proportion of these activities involve physical activity?
Answers will vary, but guide students to determine whether more or less than half of the activities are physical in nature.

Why are physical activities important?
They improve a person's health.

 LESSON 1

Being Active and Fit

Lesson Focus
Young people who get the proper amount of Sleep, participate in physical Activity, and make healthful Food choices Every day (SAFE) will enjoy good health.

Why Learn This?
You can use what you learn for making healthful choices about sleep, activity, and food.

Vocabulary
physical activity

Sleep, Activity, and Food

Have you ever thought about things that keep you healthy and fit? Tanisha was interested in how sleep, activity, and food help keep people fit. She went to her teacher with an article on healthful lifestyles. The article said that a healthful lifestyle should include a proper amount of sleep, physical activity that is fun and is done most days of the week, and wise food choices. Tanisha asked if her class could form a group she called the SAFE club to promote good health and physical fitness. *S* stands for *Sleep*, *A* stands for *Activity*, *F* stands for *Food choices* that are healthful, and *E* stands for *Every day*. Her teacher thought it was a great idea.

Your body needs all parts of the SAFE routine. The first part, sleep, is important in several ways. When you sleep, body tissues work to build new cells, repair old cells, and help fight infections.

Healthful foods provide energy to help you do activities longer. ▶

112

 Reading Skill

Mini-Lesson

MAIN IDEA AND DETAILS
Tell students that the main idea is the most important statement, and the details explain the main idea. Have students practice this skill by responding to the Focus Skill question on page 113. Have students draw and complete the graphic organizer as you model it on the transparency.

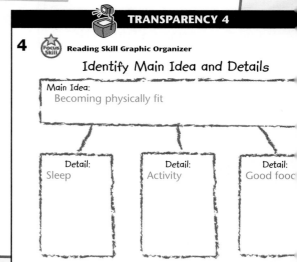

TRANSPARENCY 4

4 Reading Skill Graphic Organizer

Identify Main Idea and Details

Main Idea:
Becoming physically fit

Detail: Sleep

Detail: Activity

Detail: Good food

Interactive Transparencies available on CD-ROM.

▲ These girls and their dogs help one another stay physically active.

Personal Health Plan ▶

Real-Life Situation
Studies show that fifth graders do best in school if they get nine hours of sleep each night. Suppose because of soccer practice, homework, and TV, you sleep only seven hours.
Real-Life Plan
Write a plan for changing your schedule so you can get more sleep.

A lack of sleep can cause you to have trouble thinking clearly. It also can make you feel tired. A wise choice is to get plenty of rest before school, because sleep helps you do your best.

To be healthy and fit, your body needs physical activity. **Physical activity** is using your muscles to move your body. There are many reasons why physical activity can improve health. Activities such as walking, biking, swimming, and running can help keep your bones, muscles, and heart healthy and help you maintain a healthful weight.

Your body also needs good food. Good food choices are important decisions to learn to make. The foods you choose can affect your weight and your energy level.

Remember: To be physically fit and healthy, your body needs these things—sleep, activity, and good food every day. Healthful living should be a habit. It needs to be part of your daily life.

Did You Know?
A person who has trouble sleeping can go to a sleep clinic for help. The person sleeps there for a night or two as part of a test to determine why he or she does not sleep normally.

MAIN IDEA AND DETAILS List the main ways you can become fit. Include three things you can do to maintain your health.
Possible answer: Get plenty of sleep and physical activity, and make wise food choices. Lists will vary.

113

QUICK STUDY, ACTIVITY BOOK PP. 16–17

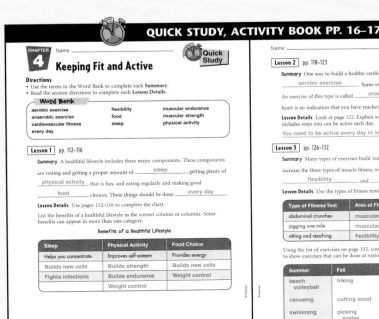

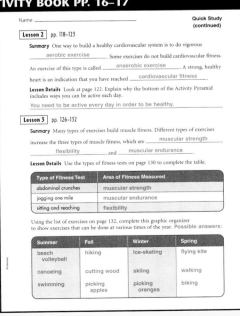

 Available online.
www.harcourtschool.com/health

Do you think you are getting enough physical activity? If not, what can you do to increase the amount? Help students realize that activities such as watching television and playing computer games take up time they could use for physical activities.

2. TEACH

Interpret Visuals—Pictures
Direct students' attention to the picture on this page. Have students discuss their pets and tell how they exercise with them. **Do some pets enjoy exercise? How can this benefit a pet's owner as well?** Ask small groups of students to list some benefits of exercising with their pets.

Discuss
Problem Solving How do you think food choices would change if there were no vending machines in schools? Have students form small groups and brainstorm changes.

Critical Thinking Think about a time when you did not get enough sleep. How did you feel the next day? Have students form small groups and brainstorm the effects of not having enough sleep.

 Personal Health Plan ▶

Plans should include:
• Lists of activities students can spend less time on.
• Lists of activities students can give up.

Building Good Character
Citizenship Greg could congratulate the Mustangs on being challenging opponents. Greg could then gently scold his own teammates for their poor sportsmanship.

TEACH *continued*

Discuss

Point out the benefits of physical activity that are listed on these pages. In addition, physical activity can help students feel better emotionally and get along better with others.

How could it benefit students in your school to have a SAFE club? Possible answer: Many people need the support and participation of others to keep up healthful lifestyles.

Have you ever worked with another person on a fitness program? What are some of the benefits of working together on a physical activity? Possible answers: It's more fun with a partner; partners help each other reach the goal; partners serve as cheerleaders to help each other along the way.

Consumer Activity

Discuss ways sporting goods companies try to get people to buy expensive equipment.

If you used the same fitness plan, could you run a mile in the same amount of time with old running shoes as with new shoes? Yes, it is the training that is most important.

What problems could you have if you wore tight shoes? You could get sore feet or blisters, which could cause pain while training.

Health Background

Overweight Youth Almost every state reports that at least 15 percent of people between ages six and nineteen are overweight. Engaging students in healthful lifestyles is a challenge educators must face.

Source: *Centers for Disease Control and Prevention*

 For more background, visit the **Webliography** in Teacher Resources at **www.harcourtschool.com/health Keyword** physical fitness

▲ Hiking with your family is a fun way to stay physically active.

ACTIVITY

Building Good Character

Citizenship The Mustangs' point guard missed a jump shot as the buzzer sounded. Greg's team won, and some of his teammates started teasing the Mustangs as they left the court. Name two ways both teams could show good citizenship.

The Benefits of Physical Activity

Being physically active has many benefits. Suzanne joined the SAFE club. She thought she was watching too much television and playing too many video games. She made a personal health plan that included biking, inline skating, and keeping a journal to record her TV watching.

For one month, Suzanne exercised and watched less TV. Then she made a list of the benefits to her of being physically active. At the next meeting of the SAFE club, she shared the list.

114

Meeting Individual Needs
Leveled Activities

BELOW-LEVEL Illustrate SAFE Activities Have students write *SAFE* in the middle of a sheet of paper and draw pictures illustrating the benefits of sleep, activity, and good food choices.

ON-LEVEL Dear Diary Have students keep a weeklong chart of one of the three parts of SAFE. At the end of the week, they can evaluate how well they did.

CHALLENGE Explore the World of Tomorrow Today Invite students to imagine they are archaeologists living one hundred years from today. They have dug up five food wrappers from a home. Have students bring these wrappers to class and describe the lives the people led, based on the information on the wrappers.

- Being physically active helped me reach a healthy weight.
- I feel that exercise has helped me build stronger muscles and bones. It's also helped me do physical activities for a longer period of time.
- Exercise has improved my self-esteem because I can do things I couldn't do before.
- I feel more relaxed and can better handle stressful situations at home and at school.

CAUSE AND EFFECT **What changes did Suzanne see in herself after she joined the SAFE club?**
Possible answer: Being physically active helped Suzanne build stronger muscles and bones, attain a healthful weight, increase her self-esteem, and handle stressful situations.

Quick Activity

List Safety Needs Pick an activity you like to do. List the safety equipment you need for it. Also list the rules you need to follow to stay safe.

Consumer Activity

Equipment You don't need to spend a lot of money to be fit or to have fun. Many activities require little more than comfortable shoes and loose-fitting clothes. List the things people actually need for some physical activities.

▼ Boating is a fun activity you can do with friends. Many communities rent small boats and offer instruction on how to use them.

115

Integrated Language Arts/ Reading Skills

Write About It Have students think about how sitting around watching television for hours makes them feel. Then have them write an advertisement encouraging people to do physical activities instead of watching television.

Teacher Tip

Nutrition and Physical Activity Action for Healthy Kids is a nonprofit coalition of public and private organizations working to improve the health and educational performance of students through better nutrition and physical activity in schools. More information on the organization is available on its website.

Discuss
How does exercising with your family have positive benefits? provides time for sharing and enjoyment

How does exercising with your friends have positive benefits? helps build strong relationships

Content-Area Reading Support
Using Text Format Direct attention to Suzanne's list, which begins on page 114, and the sentence that precedes it. Point out that the colon is used to draw attention to what follows it—in this case the benefits of being physically active. Explain that the items could have been put into sentences within the paragraph, but the list format gives the information greater importance.

What would it be like to live without television and video games for a week? Would you exercise more? Challenge students to see how many can go a week without watching television or playing video games. Afterward, ask students to report on the change in their physical activity.

Personal Health Plan ▶

Plans should include:
- Determine how much time is available after meeting important obligations.
- Determine how much time the new activity will take.
- Set realistic goals for the activity.
- Measure progress toward these goals.

Quick Activity
All needed safety equipment and rules should be listed. In the case of a potentially dangerous activity, there should be mention of the presence of an adult as well.

3. WRAP UP

Lesson 1 Summary and Review

1. Physical activity

2. Sleep helps repair the body and mind, builds new cells, and helps fight infections.

3. It gives you energy and affects your weight.

4. Possible answers are shown below.

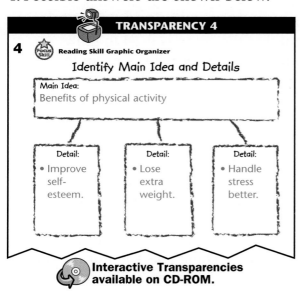

TRANSPARENCY 4

4 Reading Skill Graphic Organizer

Identify Main Idea and Details

Main Idea:
Benefits of physical activity

Detail:	Detail:	Detail:
• Improve self-esteem.	• Lose extra weight.	• Handle stress better.

Interactive Transparencies available on CD-ROM.

5. Possible answer: Phil Fit is an active member of his SAFE team. After sleeping nine hours, Phil eats a breakfast of whole-wheat toast, cereal, and orange juice. He bikes to school every day and plays basketball each lunch hour after having a sandwich, a small salad, and skim milk. After school Phil bikes to his soccer practice. He has spaghetti, salad, and water for supper and eats two cookies before he goes to bed at 9 P.M.

For **writing models** with examples, see *Teaching Resources* pp. 47–61. Rubrics are also provided.

When Minutes Count ...

Quick Study Students can use *Activity Book* pp. 16–17 (shown on p. 113) as they complete each lesson in this chapter.

Overcoming Barriers to Physical Activity

Some people can't do some physical activities because they face physical challenges. But everyone can be active. People just may need to make a change in their activities so they can do them.

For example, Saul couldn't run with his friends because he was in a wheelchair. Saul talked to his physical education teacher. His teacher encouraged him to become more active using his wheelchair. He also suggested that Saul and his friends try swimming together. Saul found several new activities to enjoy with his friends and to help him stay fit.

DRAW CONCLUSIONS Saul stayed fit by using his wheelchair and by swimming. What conclusion can you draw about fitness and physical challenges?

◄ List some of the barriers this person has overcome to do this activity.

Possible answer: You can find a way to make fitness a goal, even if you face physical challenges.

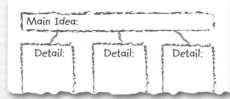

Lesson 1 Summary and Review

❶ Summarize with Vocabulary
Use vocabulary from this lesson to complete the statement.

_____ is using your muscles to move your body.

❷ Why is sleep important to your health? About how many hours of sleep does a person your age need each night?

❸ Critical Thinking How can making good food choices be an important part of your plan for keeping physically fit?

❹ MAIN IDEA AND DETAILS Draw and complete this graphic organizer to show some benefits of physical activity.

Main Idea:

Detail:	Detail:	Detail:

 ❺ Write to Inform—Description
Make up a story about Phil Fit, a boy in the SAFE club at his school. Write about a day in the life of Phil. Include sleep, physical activities, and good food choices.

116

Art

SAFE Poster Have students make a poster that promotes the SAFE idea. The poster should have a positive message for each of the letters in the acronym.

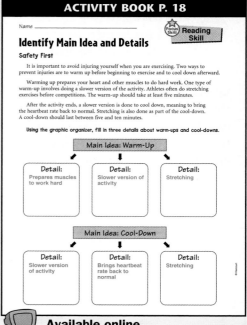

ACTIVITY BOOK P. 18

Name _____

Reading Skill

Identify Main Idea and Details

Safety First

It is important to avoid injuring yourself when you are exercising. Two ways to prevent injuries are to warm up before beginning to exercise and to cool down afterward.

Warming up prepares your heart and other muscles to do hard work. One type of warm-up involves doing a slower version of the activity. Athletes often do stretching exercises before competitions. The warm-up should take at least five minutes.

After the activity ends, a slower version is done to cool down, meaning to bring the heartbeat rate back to normal. Stretching is also done as part of the cool-down. A cool-down should last between five and ten minutes.

Using the graphic organizer, fill in three details about warm-ups and cool-downs.

Main Idea: Warm-Up

Detail: Prepares muscles to work hard	Detail: Slower version of activity	Detail: Stretching

Main Idea: Cool-Down

Detail: Slower version of activity	Detail: Brings heartbeat rate back to normal	Detail: Stretching

Available online. www.harcourtschool.com/health

Fairness

Play by the Rules

Any game or activity is more fun when all the players respect each other and follow all the rules. When players cheat, the game becomes pointless and players lose respect for each other.

Here are some rules to follow when you play any game:

- **Always listen for instructions when you receive the signal to stop. This may be the most important rule to ensure a fun game.**
- **If you're not familiar with the rules of a game, ask questions or ask for an explanation.**
- **Show respect for other players by not fighting or arguing. Players receive penalties for those behaviors.**
- **When someone breaks a rule, politely tell him or her or your coach.**
- **Understand the consequences of breaking a rule.**
- **If a rule is broken, team members should discuss the problem so it won't happen again.**
- **Learn how to properly care for equipment.**

Activity

Make a list of the important rules for your soccer team. Ask your teacher or coach to help you rank the rules in order of importance. Then list the rules in order of how often they are broken. Show the list to the soccer team. At the end of the season, compare your lists.

It's important to be fair and play by the rules at all times. ▶

117

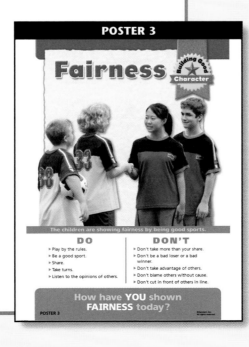
Building Good Character

Caring
Citizenship
Fairness
Respect
Responsibility
Trustworthiness

Objective
► Identify ways to demonstrate fairness during a competitive game.

Program Resources
► Poster 3

BEFORE READING

Have students name some of the people who show fairness when playing or judging sports. After a discussion of showing fairness, lead students to discuss ways players and referees can show fairness during a competitive sport. List some of the ideas on the board.

DISCUSS

After students have read the page, have them close their books. Lead a discussion of situations in which an issue of fairness made a difference in a competition. Examples may include a player or coach arguing with a referee about a call and a player cheating.

ACTIVITY

Have students create a chart of the rules for soccer. Discuss situations in which fairness is critical to the game.

- Parents and participants need to know the offside rule and follow it to prevent arguments.
- Parents and participants need to know the meaning of carding and need to avoid the behaviors that can lead to receiving yellow or red cards.

Objectives

► List three ways physical activity helps the respiratory and circulatory systems.

► Apply the Activity Pyramid when planning physical activities.

When Minutes Count . . .

Assign the Quick Study, Lesson 2, Activity Book pp. 16–17 (shown on p. 113).

Program Resources

► Activity Book pp. 16–17

► Transparencies 4, 20

Vocabulary

cardiovascular fitness p. 120,

aerobic exercise p. 121,

anaerobic exercise p. 121

Daily Fitness Tip

Two skills are needed to measure the benefits of physical activity on body systems: counting breaths—inhalation and exhalation per minute—and the ability to take pulse rates. There are many activities you can do in class to measure the impact of exercise on respiration and pulse.

 For more guidelines on exercise and your heart, see *Be Active! Resources for Physical Education,* p. 139.

1. MOTIVATE

Optional Activity Materials age-appropriate board game, popular book, walking path in the room, telephone, DVD player and monitor

Have students demonstrate the following activities: reading a book, walking around the class, watching a DVD, having a phone conversation, and playing a board game.

Which organ or organs of the body are most used during each activity? the brain for playing a board game, reading, watching a DVD, and talking on the phone; the heart and lungs when walking around the room

---

How Exercise Helps Your Body Systems

Lesson Focus

Being physically active makes you stronger, helps you feel good, and improves your self-image.

Why Learn This?

Learning about the benefits of physical activity can help you exercise regularly.

Vocabulary

cardiovascular fitness
aerobic exercise
anaerobic exercise

Exercise Helps Your Respiratory System

Regular exercise, such as swimming and biking, helps your entire respiratory system. Your respiratory system includes all the parts of your body that work to get oxygen into your blood and carbon dioxide out of it. Look at the diagram of the respiratory system, on page 119. Find the *diaphragm* (DY•uh•fram). It is a large, flat muscle that separates your lungs from the organs in the lower part of your body. When you breathe in, your diaphragm contracts and moves down. This pulls air in through your nose, down your *trachea*, and into your lungs. When you breathe out, your diaphragm relaxes and moves up. This pushes air out of your lungs.

The diaphragm does most of the work of breathing. The rest is done by your ribs and the muscles around them. As you breathe in, muscles move your ribs up and out to the side. Then, as you breathe out, your ribs

Swimming uses a lot of energy, making you need a lot of oxygen. ▶

118

ESL/ELL Support

LANGUAGE AND VOCABULARY The word *cardiovascular* may be difficult for students to understand and remember.

Beginning Explain to students that *cardio* refers to the heart and *vascular* refers to blood vessels. Provide an illustration of the circulatory system, and have students draw a picture of the heart and the blood vessels that are connected to it.

Intermediate Have students draw a picture of the heart and its blood vessels and label the heart, arteries, and veins.

Advanced Help students use a dictionary to find other words with the word part *cardio-*, such as *cardiogram* and *cardiology*, and write them with brief definitions.

move back down and in. Like all muscles, your diaphragm and the muscles around your ribs get stronger with regular exercise.

Recall from Chapter 1 that when air enters your lungs, it goes into *alveoli*. In those tiny sacs oxygen enters your blood. Your blood then carries the oxygen to all the cells of your body. Body cells use oxygen to convert the nutrients from the food you eat into energy. During that process body cells produce carbon dioxide. This waste gas travels to your lungs. Then it is breathed out.

When you exercise, your body needs a lot of energy and produces a lot of waste. Your lungs need to take in more oxygen and get rid of more carbon dioxide, so you breathe more deeply and more often. As you take deep breaths, the alveoli open up. When you exercise regularly, the alveoli stay open most of the time. This makes your lungs take in extra oxygen each time you breathe.

SEQUENCE Write the steps by which oxygen gets into the blood.
Oxygen in the air goes through your nose, down the trachea, into the lungs, and into the alveoli. From the sacs, it enters the blood.

The diaphragm and the muscles around your ribs become stronger with exercise.

ribs

muscles

diaphragm

119

Personal Health Plan ▶

Real-Life Situation
The more you do a physical activity, the easier it becomes. Suppose you sign up to run in a 5-kilometer (5K) race to be held in three months.
Real-Life Plan
After talking with your physical education teacher, write a step-by-step plan for training that would enable you to complete the race.

Do you need to do activities that work all those organs? yes

Why is it important to do activities that work the heart and lungs? The heart and lungs work better with regular physical activity.

2. TEACH

Interpret Visuals—Pictures
Direct students to look at the visuals on these pages. Ask them to describe some of the health problems that could affect the respiratory system.

Discuss
Critical Thinking Why do Presidents make sure they get a lot of physical exercise? The President's demanding schedule and high stress level make it very important to maintain a good level of fitness.

Personal Health Plan ▶

Plans should include:
- Decide on goals.
- Decide how far in advance to start training.
- Determine how much more to do each week.
- Decide how to measure progress.

Discuss
Problem Solving If the majority of fifth graders never exercised, what kind of respiratory problems might they have? Their lungs might not work well, and they might get out of breath easily.

Are there activities that work both the heart and the lungs? Exercises that make the heart beat faster also make the lungs breathe faster.

Science

Interacting Respiratory and Circulatory Systems Have students refer to pages 4–7 to review how the respiratory and circulatory systems work together to carry nourishment to the body's cells and to remove waste materials. Students should draw pictures of the main organs of the two systems, using colored pencils to draw arrows showing the directions of blood and air flow.

Teacher Tip

Web Activities The United States government has a number of websites related to health and science that include educational activities for young people. The FirstGov site provides links to many such sites, including the Centers for Disease Control and Prevention website, where you can find activities, quizzes, and other materials.

TEACH *continued*

Guide students to recognize that exercises that speed up both the heart and the lungs are aerobic exercises.

What is your favorite activity that works both the heart and the lungs, and for how long do you do this activity? Possible answers: Soccer, bike riding, jogging, and hockey; I do these activities for about an hour at a time.

Have students brainstorm the ways their respiratory and circulatory systems are helped through exercise.

If you do these activities a lot, do they become easier to do? Why? Yes; both the heart and the lungs work better as a result of conditioning through repeated extended effort.

Discuss

Write the term *cardiovascular fitness* on the board, and have students find this term on this page. Ask them to think about a time they became very tired while doing a physical activity. Point out that it could have been tiring because their bodies had not been doing that activity on a regular basis.

Health Background

Fitness Campaign The Centers for Disease Control and Prevention sponsors a national campaign called VERB: It's What You Do. This program is designed to increase physical activity among people between the ages of eight and thirteen. VERB offers educational materials to classroom teachers, principals, and parents.

Source: *Centers for Disease Control and Prevention*

For more background, visit the **Webliography** in Teacher Resources at **www.harcourtschool.com/health** **Keyword** physical fitness

Exercise Helps Your Circulatory System

Exercising regularly helps your circulatory system stay healthy. Exercise strengthens your heart, a muscle that pumps blood to all the cells of your body. When you exercise, your heart beats faster. More oxygen and nutrients are carried to your body's cells.

Regular exercise also reduces the amount of fat in your blood. Fat can build up on the inner walls of arteries. This reduces the flow of blood to body organs. It can also cause serious problems in the circulatory system, such as heart attacks and strokes.

Cardiovascular fitness (kar•dee•oh•VAS•kyoo•ler) is the good health of the circulatory system, including a strong heart. When your heart is strong, you can be active for a long time without getting tired. A strong heart pumps more blood with each beat. When you are resting, it beats more slowly, pausing longer between beats.

Notice the differences between a healthy artery (above) and one clogged with fat (below).

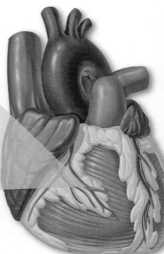

Clogged arteries in the heart can cause chest pains and heart attacks.

120

Meeting Individual Needs
Leveled Activities

BELOW-LEVEL Exercise Promotion Poster Have students create a poster of a positive activity for the heart, using the acronym HEART (Health Education About Activity Reduces Trouble).

ON-LEVEL Create a Skit Have students develop a skit about friends who try to get another friend to join their soccer team. The students should tell the friend how exercise benefits the heart and lungs.

CHALLENGE Explore Famous Athletes Give students a list of famous male and female athletes. Ask students to use library resources to research the amount of exercise these athletes typically need to maintain their high performance levels.

Aerobic exercise (air·oh·bik) increases your heartbeat rate for a period of time. This helps build cardiovascular fitness. Aerobic exercise includes bicycling, jogging, and swimming. As you do this kind of exercise, you also breathe harder and faster. Your muscles receive all the oxygen they need to keep working. You should do aerobic exercise at least three times a week for at least twenty minutes at a time. Aerobic exercise also can reduce stress. If you feel angry, sad, or bored, aerobic exercise can help lift your mood.

Not all types of exercise build cardiovascular fitness. In **anaerobic exercise** (an·er·oh·bik), the muscles work hard for a short time. They use the oxygen they already have faster than it can be replaced. Sprinting and rowing as fast as you can are examples of anaerobic exercise. Anaerobic exercise builds muscle strength.

COMPARE AND CONTRAST **How are aerobic exercise and anaerobic exercise different? What does each help build?**
Possible answers: Aerobic exercise takes place over a longer period of time, increasing your heartbeat rate and improving cardiovascular fitness. Anaerobic exercise takes place in a shorter period of time, increasing your muscle strength.

◀ Working together is important in a relay race. Think of other physical activities in which you work with others as a team.

Myth and Fact

Myth: More children are overweight now than in the past because kids today eat more.
Fact: Over the last twenty years, young people have been eating only 1 percent more food but have become 13 percent less active physically.

Other family members, peers, teachers, and celebrities are the people most likely to influence young people to be physically active. Students who are physically fit often keep exercising because of the influence of others.

What does it mean for a person to have cardiovascular fitness? The person has a strong heart that is able to pump more blood with each beat; the person is able to be active for long periods of time without getting tired.

Point out that aerobic exercise helps build cardiovascular fitness. The body of a person who has cardiovascular fitness takes in enough oxygen to keep working for long periods. Ask students to brainstorm their favorite aerobic activities.

How does aerobic exercise affect your stress level? It helps improve your mood when you are under stress.

Why doesn't anaerobic exercise build cardiovascular fitness? It is done for only a short period of time because the activity takes more oxygen than can be replaced right away.

Interpret Visuals—Pictures
Direct students' attention to the diagram on page 122, and point out that this Activity Pyramid is designed to help people increase their physical activity. Ask students if they have ever developed fitness plans and, if so, whether they would share them with the class. **Why are the bottom four parts of the Activity Pyramid important?** These activities help build cardiovascular fitness.

TEACH *continued*

What are some things you can do to keep active on a rainy day? You can play indoor games in which you keep moving; you can walk up and down steps for 20 minutes; you can do exercises as you are watching a television program or listening to the radio.

Content-Area Reading Support

Using Tables and Graphics Direct students' attention to the various sections of the Activity Pyramid. Point out that the sections are of different sizes to correspond to the amounts of time people should spend doing the activities.

Discuss

Guide students to differentiate between skill-related and health-related physical activities. **How are these two types of activities different?** Health-related activities have to do with overall health, while skill-related activities have to do with sports performance.

Ask students to make lists of activities they do each day. Have them circle the ones that are related to skill building, such as team practice after school. Have them underline those that they think benefit their health. It may be that all of the activities that students underline benefit health and that only one or two activities are related to skills.

Emphasize that everyday activities such as walking a dog, walking to school, keeping the room clean, or playing games with friends can have great health benefits because of the number of times they are done.

When Minutes Count ...

Transparency 20: The Activity Pyramid can be used to present information from this lesson. *Interactive Transparencies available on CD-ROM.*

The Activity Pyramid

The activity pyramid gives guidelines for ways to build fitness. Some activities build skill-related fitness. These help you improve your performance in a sport. Other activities promote health-related fitness. These help you improve your overall health and fitness. You can use the pyramid to plan physical activities based on the goals you want to achieve.

Sitting Still Watching TV; playing computer games **small amounts of time**

Light Exercise Playtime; yardwork; softball **2–3 times a week**

Strength and Flexibility Exercises Weight training, dancing, pullups **2–3 times a week**

Aerobic Exercises Biking; running; soccer; hiking **30 + minutes, 2–3 times a week**

Regular Activities Walking to school; taking te stairs; helping with housework **everyday**

122

🏋️ Physical Education

Unfamiliar Activity Have students use the library or the Internet to identify and learn about a physical activity they are unfamiliar with. Students should present their activities to the class by telling how the activity is performed, what equipment is required, and where it falls on the Activity Pyramid. If possible, they should illustrate their presentations with pictures of people performing the activities.

Teacher Tip

Identifying Activities It's likely that there are many physical activities students are unfamiliar with. Most students are aware of activities they have engaged in at or outside of school as well as those they have viewed, such as professional baseball. However, they may be unfamiliar with activities such as certain kinds of Olympic sports, horseback riding, and ballroom dancing.

If you are just beginning to exercise, you could do the following:

- Increase participation in everyday activities, like walking, whenever you can.
- Decrease the amount of time you spend watching television and playing video and computer games.

If you already exercise, you could use the activity pyramid to do the following:

- In the middle of the pyramid, find activities that you enjoy, and do them more often.
- Set up a plan to do your favorite activities more often.
- Explore new activities.

Did You Know?

One video-arcade game is actually good for your health. Using background music as a guide, you follow lighted arrows with your feet. Young people report they really work up a sweat and it's fun, too!

DRAW CONCLUSIONS Write down the activities you do in a typical day. At which level on the pyramid is most of your activity? What types of activities do you need to add to your routine?

Possible answers: I walk the dog, ride my bike, practice as part of a dance team, and watch three hours of TV. Watching TV is at the top of the pyramid. I should do more exercise.

Lesson 2 Summary and Review

❶ Summarize with Vocabulary

Use vocabulary from this lesson to complete the statements.

Exercise that makes the heart work hard builds _____. Exercise that increases the heartbeat rate is called _____. Exercise that works your muscles hard for a short time, such as sprinting, is called _____.

❷ Critical Thinking How can following the activity pyramid improve physical fitness?

❸ How does exercise benefit the respiratory system?

❹ **MAIN IDEA AND DETAILS** Draw and complete this graphic organizer to show ways that exercise helps your body.

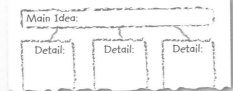

Main Idea:

Detail: Detail: Detail:

❺ Write to Inform—How-To

Write a description of how to use the activity pyramid to begin an exercise program.

123

3. WRAP UP

Lesson 2 Summary and Review

1. cardiovascular fitness; aerobic exercise; anaerobic exercise
2. It suggests many ways to increase physical activity.
3. It makes your respiratory system work better.
4. Possible answers are shown below.

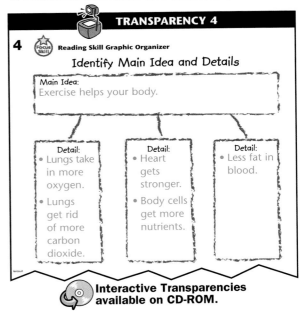

TRANSPARENCY 4

4   Reading Skill Graphic Organizer

Identify Main Idea and Details

Main Idea:
Exercise helps your body.

Detail:
- Lungs take in more oxygen.
- Lungs get rid of more carbon dioxide.

Detail:
- Heart gets stronger.
- Body cells get more nutrients.

Detail:
- Less fat in blood.

Interactive Transparencies available on CD-ROM.

5. Possible response: I would begin by writing down the activities I do and how much time each takes. Then I would see what kinds of activities I need to add. I would make a plan to add those activities.

 For **writing models** with examples, see *Teaching Resources* pp. 47–61. Rubrics are also provided.

 When Minutes Count ...

Quick Study Students can use *Activity Book* pp. 16–17 (shown on p. 113) as they complete each lesson in this chapter.

Life Skills

Communicate
Make Responsible Decisions
Manage Stress
Refuse
Resolve Conflicts
Set Goals

Objectives
► Identify the four steps in goal setting.
► Apply the goal-setting model to set up plans for a healthful lifestyle.

Program Resources
► Activity Book p. 19
► Poster 12

1. MOTIVATE

Optional Activity Materials pictures of famous athletes

Display pictures of famous male and female athletes. Ask students what these athletes did to become famous and whether they set goals to reach.

2. TEACH

Discuss the steps involved in making a family fitness plan. Have students describe the benefits of setting long-term goals. Besides setting goals, choosing activities, and checking progress, the discussion could cover safety equipment, training, pacing, nutrition, and fitness conditioning.

Step 1
What is the goal that Marco's mother chooses for the family? The family is going to exercise together and exercise more than before.

What are the advantages of exercising in a group? The members support and encourage each other.

Critical Thinking You want to go to a camp but do not have enough money to pay for it. What could you do? do chores for your parents or neighbors to earn the money you need

124 Chapter 4 • Keeping Fit and Active

Set Goals
About Family Fitness

To stay healthy and fit, you need to keep active. Because our lives are so busy, it's often hard to find time for physical activities. Using the steps for **Setting Goals** can help you build a successful exercise plan.

At the dinner table one evening, Marco's mother says she thinks the family doesn't get enough physical activity. She feels that if the family members do physical activities together, they'll be more physically fit. What should Marco's family do?

1 Choose a goal.

> We should do things together!

Marco's mother suggests that the family do physical activities together. Marco decides to use goal setting to help his parents plan the activities.

2 Plan steps to meet the goal, and determine whether you need help.

Marco meets with his father to plan some activities. Marco knows that Mom likes biking and the whole family likes to cross-country ski in the winter.

124

Teacher Tip

The VERB Campaign If you have your students create their own activity plans, the VERB: It's What You Do website has many ideas. This program is sponsored by the Centers for Disease Control and Prevention.

ACTIVITY BOOK P. 19

Name _____

 Problem Solving

Life Skill
Set Goals

Steps Used in Setting Goals

1. Choose a goal.
2. Plan steps to meet the goal, and determine whether you need help.
3. Check your progress as you work toward the goal.
4. Reflect on and evaluate your progress toward the goal.

Use the steps to help these students set and reach a goal.

A. Suzanne's friend Lily wants to run in the big five-kilometer (5-K) race on July 4. She talks Suzanne into training with her so they can run the event together.
• What should Suzanne and Lily do, starting eight weeks before the run, to reach their goal?

Possible answer: They should gradually build their endurance over the eight-week training period. At various points, they should check their progress, and after completion of the run they should celebrate success.

_____
_____
_____

B. Tom received in-line skates for his birthday, and he wants to learn how to use them before summer vacation starts in two months. The local fitness center offers lessons. To be allowed to participate, every student must have the proper safety equipment. Tom buys the safety equipment and signs up for the lessons.
• Can Tom reach his goal safely? Why or why not?

Possible answer: Tom should be able to reach his goal. He has purchased the safety equipment he needs to prevent injury and is taking lessons from trained, qualified individuals.

_____
_____

 Available online.
www.harcourtschool.com/health

③ Check your progress as you work toward the goal.

Marco writes the planned activities on a calendar. He checks them off as the family finishes each one.

④ Reflect on and evaluate your progress toward the goal.

Marco is proud that his family is working together to reach a fitness goal.

Problem Solving

A. Serena's goal is to be able to run a mile without stopping.
  • How can she use the steps for **Setting Goals** to help her reach this endurance goal?

B. Juan lives a block away from a park and wants to shoot 300 baskets each day during the summer.
  • How might Juan reach his goal while keeping up his responsibility to help with family chores?

125

Using the Poster

Activity Have students write and perform skits showing situations in which young people use the steps for setting goals in appropriate ways.

Display the poster to remind students of the steps for setting goals.

POSTER 12

Set Goals

The girl is setting a goal to get more exercise.

Steps for Setting Goals

1 Choose a goal.
2 Plan steps to reach that goal. Determine whether you will need help.
3 Check your progress as you work toward the goal.
4 Evaluate the results of your work.

What GOALS have YOU SET?

POSTER 12

Step 2

Why is it important for Marco to plan the family activities with his father? to choose activities that are safe and fun

Step 3

Why does Marco create a calendar of planned activities? so the family can check progress toward the goal

Have students describe weekly activities that promote the health of a family. **Why is it important to make a plan when working toward a goal?** Sometimes, difficult goals need to be accomplished in steps.

★ Building Good Character
Remind students to show respect to family members when they are helping with a family fitness plan. Have them explain the importance of parental guidance in goal setting. Parents' ideas are important because parents think of every family member's safety first.

Step 4

Why is it important to reflect on and evaluate your progress toward the goal? to plan for improvement and be proud of finishing

Have students describe the benefits of implementing long-term goals. **What do you think happened as a result of this family's meeting its goal?** The family is likely to continue this into the future.

3. WRAP UP

Problem Solving

A Serena could start with a quarter mile and add one-fourth of a lap each day. She should be able to complete one mile in about twelve days.

B Juan needs to respect his family by completing his chores. He can make a calendar of his activities and schedule a time each day to shoot baskets.

Objectives
▶ List three issues that should be addressed to exercise safely.
▶ List three kinds of exercise and give an example of each.

When Minutes Count . . .
Assign the Quick Study, Lesson 3, Activity Book pp. 16–17 (shown on p. 113).

Program Resources
▶ Activity Book pp. 16–17, 20
▶ Transparency 4

Vocabulary
muscular strength p. 128,
flexibility p. 128,
muscular endurance p. 129

Daily Fitness Tip

When students take ownership of their activities, they are more likely to participate. Have students pick three activities that improve muscular strength, muscular endurance, and flexibility that can be done in class. Have them set passing scores for each and build an in-class fitness test.

 For more guidelines on choosing activities for fitness, see *Be Active! Resources for Physical Education,* p. 137.

1. MOTIVATE

Optional Activity Materials old gym bag containing old running shoes, thick warm-ups, a bike helmet, hand pads for in-line skating, a pedometer, and a picture of a person stretching

Describe the following scenario to students: It is a hundred years in the future. An archaeologist has unearthed an old gym bag in a dump. **How can we learn something about the person who owned this bag?** Look at what is in it.

Have the students open up the old gym bag and sort the items.

LESSON
3 Ways to Exercise

Lesson Focus
Exercising in the right way helps you improve your physical fitness safely and enjoyably.

Why Learn This?
You can use what you learn to build your own fitness plan.

Vocabulary
muscular strength
flexibility
muscular endurance

Exercise Safely

Is exercise a part of your daily life? Exercising can include skill-related activities, such as basketball, tennis, or dancing. However, ordinary chores can provide health-related activity, too. These include walking the dog, raking the lawn, or vacuuming the carpet. To increase your level of physical fitness, try adding new activities to those you already do.

To help prevent injuries when you exercise, always begin with a *warm-up*. A warm-up is exercise that prepares your muscles—including your heart—to work hard. Always warm up your muscles gradually before harder exercise and before stretching.

Some stretching exercises help upper-body muscles.

Other stretching exercises help lower-body muscles. Always warm up before stretching.

126

Social Studies

Foreign Sports Have the students research sports popular in other countries to learn what kind of safety equipment, if any, is used. Create a bulletin board with the name of the sport, a drawing of a person with the safety equipment, and a list of injuries the equipment prevents.

Teacher Tip

Differentiate Between Health-related and Skill-related Activities Write a list of activities on the board that could be used to improve physical fitness. Include sports, such as soccer, football, and tennis, as well as everyday activities, such as walking, dancing, jumping rope, and bike riding. Then have students divide the list into two groups: those that require some sort of skill or practice and those that do not.

One way to warm up is to do a slower version of your main activity. The warm-up might be easy pedaling if you are cycling, or jogging in place before running. Be sure to warm up for at least five minutes. After a warm-up, your body is prepared to stretch and exercise hard without harming muscles, joints, or your heart.

After exercising, do a *cool-down*. A cool-down includes doing your main exercise at a slower pace. That gives your heartbeat rate time to return to normal. Then stretch the muscles you used during your main exercise. Spend five to ten minutes cooling down.

Wearing the proper clothing for your activity and for the weather can help keep you safe. Wear loose, comfortable clothing that lets air move through. Choose cotton or other fabrics that allow sweat to evaporate. Use layers of clothing to keep warm in cold weather.

To prevent injury, wear shoes that provide support for your ankles and a cushion for your heels. The shoes must fit well and give you the traction you need. Also to prevent injury, always use the right safety gear. This may include a mouth guard, a helmet, shin guards, elbow pads, and kneepads.

MAIN IDEA AND DETAILS To prevent injuries, what should you do before and after exercising?

You should warm up before exercising and cool down after exercising.

▲ Wear the proper safety gear for the sport you're playing. What safety equipment is used in baseball?

Quick **Activity**

Keeping Safe Talk with a parent about the physical activities he or she liked to do at your age. What safety equipment do people use now that was not used in the past for some of those activities?

127

What activities did this person like, and how did he or she prepare for exercise? bicycling, in-line skating, walking or running; warmed up, stretched, and used safety equipment

2. TEACH

Interpret Visuals—Pictures
Have students look at the pictures on these pages and tell what they observe about safety while exercising.

Content-Area Reading Support
Using Signal Words Direct attention to the first complete paragraph on this page. Point out that the fourth sentence begins with the word *Then*. Explain that the word indicates that the steps must be done in a particular order—first the exercise should be done at a slower pace, and after that, stretching should be done.

Discuss
Problem Solving What equipment would you put in a school fitness center, and why? Equipment may include stationary bikes, treadmills, rowing machines, and strength equipment. This mix enables both aerobic and anaerobic exercise.

Critical Thinking Suppose you are the head of the Governor's Council on Physical Fitness. Create a fun name for your state's fitness day. Possible examples with alliteration: Missouri Moves, Active Alaska

Interpret Visuals—Pictures
Direct students' attention to the photographs on pages 128–129, and ask them how the pictures show strength, flexibility, or endurance. Remind them that different types of exercises are used to build strength and flexibility in various muscles.

ESL/ELL Support

BACKGROUND AND EXPERIENCE Have students talk about the safety precautions they take before exercising.

Beginning Have students show warm-ups they do or draw safety gear they wear.

Intermediate Ask students to name safety gear they wear when they exercise.

Advanced Help students write paragraphs about warm-ups they do or safety gear they use.

TEACH *continued*

What other activities help build muscular strength? Walking uphill builds leg muscles; curl-ups improve abdominal strength; pull-ups and push-ups build arm strength; and weight lifting can increase the strength of various muscles.

What other activities increase flexibility? dancing; activities that are done during warm-ups and cool-downs

In what sports do people need flexibility, and why? Possible responses: gymnastics; track and field; swimming and diving; karate; also many positions in team sports, such as a hockey goalie, a baseball catcher, and an end on a football team. Being flexible is vital to every activity in terms of getting ready to do the activity.

Consumer Activity

Many schools also have fitness equipment available for use by students and community members.

Health Background

Fitness Objectives Healthy People 2010 proposes numerous objectives designed to improve the health of Americans. The objectives on physical activity in children and adolescents call for:

- moderate exercise on five out of seven days.
- vigorous exercise three days per week for twenty or more minutes.
- daily physical education, with half of the class time involving movement.
- less than two hours of television a day.
- walking to school if less than 1 mile or biking if less than 2 miles.

Source: *Centers for Disease Control and Prevention*

 For more background, visit the **Webliography** in Teacher Resources at **www.harcourtschool.com/health Keyword** physical fitness

Leg stretches increase your flexibility. ▼

▲ Chin-ups develop muscular strength.

Consumer Activity

To exercise and be fit, you don't need to belong to a gym. You can get lots of physical activity, at no cost, in your school playground, in a neighborhood park, or in your own home.

Kinds of Exercise

Aerobic exercises mostly strengthen your heart and lungs. They build cardiovascular fitness. Anaerobic exercises mostly strengthen your muscles. Many exercises help improve strength, flexibility, and endurance.

Strength: Exercises that build muscular strength make your muscles stronger. Several types of anaerobic exercises build strength. Walking up steps strengthens leg muscles. Crunches strengthen stomach muscles. Pull-ups and push-ups strengthen arm muscles.

Flexibility (flek·suh·BIL·uh·tee): Exercises that increase flexibility help your body bend and move comfortably. Stretching helps you become more flexible. Dancing is also good for flexibility.

128

Meeting Individual Needs
Leveled Activities

BELOW-LEVEL **Exercise Collage** Have students cut out pictures of various kinds of exercises and put them together into a collage with a catchy title like Fitness Feels Fantastic or Exercise Is Excellent.

ON-LEVEL **Make an Exercise Plan** Have each student put together a plan on a large sheet of paper for a particular fitness goal he or she would like to achieve. Students should include short-term and long-term goals and list various things they need to do to exercise safely.

CHALLENGE **Graph Your Favorite Exercises** Have students make a list of fun activities, and ask them which ones they do a lot. Then have them compile the results and make a bar graph of the favorite activities in the class.

Endurance: Exercises that build **muscular endurance** enable you to use your muscles for long periods without getting tired. Aerobic exercises build endurance. Hiking with the family, swimming, and biking are a few examples.

Include endurance exercises in your fitness plans. For these exercises, set both short-term and long-term goals. Suppose you want to be able to run a mile without stopping. Your short-term goal might be to run half a mile. When you can do that, add 100 yards several times until you reach your final goal.

SUMMARIZE What kinds of exercises build strength, flexibility, and endurance?
Anaerobic exercises build strength; stretching and dancing build flexibility; aerobic exercises build endurance.

Did You Know?

A wearable heart monitor gives you immediate feedback about your heartbeat rate as you exercise. You can use a monitor to keep your heartbeat rate within a safe range. Some schools use monitors in physical education classes.

◄ Running builds muscular endurance and cardiovascular fitness.

129

Teacher Tip

Fitness Takes Effort Emphasize that fitness cannot be attained without muscular effort. Physical activities that involve regular increase of the heart rate have a strong impact on improving people's physical fitness levels. It is also important to emphasize that people can lose their gains in fitness within six to eight weeks if they quit exercising. This points out that fitness is a lifetime pursuit.

Art

Make an Exercise Mobile
Review with students the types of exercises that improve strength, endurance, and flexibility. Have them cut out paper shapes in the form of a running shoe, write the name of a type of exercise on one side of each shape, and draw or paste a cutout picture on the other side. Hang the shapes from a coat hanger, and display the mobiles in the classroom, media center, or cafeteria. This could be done to promote a fitness month at your school.

Discuss
Endurance is very important in many sports. Ask students what sports demand the greatest endurance. Possible answers: The Tour de France and cycling, distance swimming, and cross-country skiing
The blend of swimming, bicycling, and running called the triathlon has been called the most demanding endurance challenge. There are triathlons of various lengths. Ask students if they have heard of the Ironman Triathlon, and have them visualize swimming, biking, and running for nearly 140 miles in one day.

Point out the heart rate monitor sidebar as you read the text aloud. **How do aerobic exercises build muscular endurance?** They require you to use your muscles for a long time.

Plans for exercise need to include both short-term and long-term goals. **How could making short-term and long-term plans help the person in the picture on this page?** The runner needs to build up endurance over a period of time. The gradual increase could include small increases in distance in the short-term goal and longer distances in the long-term goal.

Content-Area Reading Support
Using Respellings Direct attention to the respelling flek•suh•BIHL•uh•tee. Explain that respellings show how words are pronounced. Point out that the dots divide the word into syllables and that small capital letters indicate the stressed, or accented, syllable.

Urge students to pay attention to respellings for help in pronouncing unfamiliar words and in recognizing words with unfamiliar spellings.

TEACH *continued*

Interpret Visuals—Pictures

Ask students to look at the picture on this page. **What can happen to a person who does not warm up before fitness testing?** The person can be injured.

Discuss

After students review the three fitness tests on this page, have them name the possible uses of a fitness test. Fitness tests measure students' fitness strengths and weaknesses, compare students to other people of the same age, and measure improvement from an earlier time.

Discuss the steps students can take to improve their results on the fitness tests. A possible class challenge would be to improve the results by 10 percent (or another percentage) by the end of the term.

Quick Activity

Sixty-nine percent of the students in this survey accomplished four or more of the six fitness standards, which means that these students generally have placed the proper priority on fitness in their daily routines.

Health Background

The President's Challenge The President's Council on Physical Fitness and Sports aims to make health and fitness a priority for all Americans. The Council dates to 1956, when President Eisenhower started the first national testing program. The mission of the council today is to promote the benefits of fitness wherever possible.

Source: *The President's Challenge*

For more background, visit the **Webliography** in Teacher Resources at **www.harcourtschool.com/health** **Keyword** physical fitness

Fitness Testing

You can measure your fitness by taking some simple tests. These tests will help you determine your fitness level and decide what you can do to improve. **Caution:** Don't take these tests if your doctor has limited your physical activity for any reason. To take the test for endurance, you need to have been doing aerobic exercises for at least eight weeks.

- Try doing at least 36 abdominal crunches in 2 minutes. This measures muscular strength.
- Try doing the sit-and-reach at 9 inches or farther. Using a box and a ruler, stretch as far as you can with your knees straight, toes up, and one hand over the other. This measures flexibility.
- Try jogging 1 mile on a measured track. If you are a girl, try to jog the mile in 12 minutes or less. If you are a boy, aim for 11 minutes or less. This measures muscular endurance and cardiovascular fitness.

DRAW CONCLUSIONS After practicing, try all three of these fitness tests. What do the results tell you about your level of fitness?

Possible answer: how many of the three tests I could pass and which ones I need to do better on

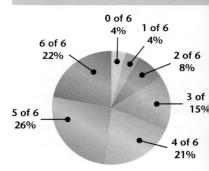

Meeting the Standards: Fifth-Grade Fitness Results

- 0 of 6 — 4%
- 1 of 6 — 4%
- 2 of 6 — 8%
- 3 of — 15%
- 4 of 6 — 21%
- 5 of 6 — 26%
- 6 of 6 — 22%

Quick Activity

Analyze Graphs On tests of six fitness standards, a group of fifth graders scored as shown on the graph. What total percentage of the students met at least four of the standards?

The sit-and-reach is a test of flexibility, while sit-ups test muscular strength.

130

ESL/ELL Support

BACKGROUND AND EXPERIENCE Invite students to discuss times in which they have used physical activity to reduce stress.

Beginning Have students draw pictures showing why they felt stressed and what activity helped them reduce the stress.

Intermediate Help students fill out two cause-and-effect graphic organizers, one with the reason for stress as the cause and stress as the effect, and the other with the type of activity as the cause and the outcome as the effect.

Advanced Help students write a paragraph about the stress they experienced and the activity that helped reduce it.

Jumping rope is fun and a stress reliever. ▶

▲ Playing catch with a flying disk is fun. It also provides you with several different types of physical activity.

Fitness Is Fun

Many of the activities that improve your physical fitness are lots of fun. You can make up games with your friends, go on bike trips or hikes with your family, or swim at a local pool. Physical activities also help reduce stress. If you feel angry, sad, or just bored, exercising can lift your mood. Exercising can even give you a lift if you're feeling tired.

131

ACTIVITY
Life Skills
Make Responsible Decisions
Coach Jones wants you to try out for the soccer team next year. You've already committed to taking piano lessons and playing in the band. Make a list of the pros and the cons of being on the soccer team.

 Music

Activity Song Have the class write a song about a physical activity that can be sung to the tune of "Row, Row, Row Your Boat" or another familiar song. For example: Hit, hit, hit the ball/Hit it hard and far/It will sail to the wall/You will be a star.

 Integrated Language Arts/ Reading Skills

Letter Campaign Have students write a letter to the editor about the need for bicycle lanes and walking paths to connect community schools with surrounding neighborhoods. The letters should include an explanation of how these lanes and paths will improve the health and fitness of people in the community.

Discuss

Ask students to think of times they looked forward to doing a physical activity. The reason students remember these experiences is because they were fun, they built relationships, and they made students feel better.

Ask students if they have ever enjoyed exercise after a rough day at school. Many people use exercise to relieve stress. Others exercise to gain energy for the rest of the day. That is why a lot of fitness centers have early-morning classes for adults to take before they head off to work.

Interpret Visuals—Pictures

Direct students' attention to the photographs on pages 131–132. Ask how students are building strength, flexibility, and endurance as well as having fun. Ask students if they have done any of these activities.

Physical activities are ways to build friendships and connect with other members of the family. **How can you do physical activities throughout the year?** During cold or wet weather, you can do indoor activities, such as basketball. Winter sports like skiing and ice-skating are also possibilities.

Activity

Make Responsible Decisions
It is important to weigh the positives and negatives of each choice. This is a difficult case because you have to decide how much time you wish to spend on the other activities you like and whether you like soccer more than those activities. A list of pros and cons will help you answer this dilemma.

3. WRAP UP

Lesson 3 Summary and Review

1. muscular endurance, flexibility, muscular strength

2. 5 to 10 minutes

3. They must fit well and give you the traction that you need to do the activity.

4. Sample answer: Anaerobic exercises build muscular strength.

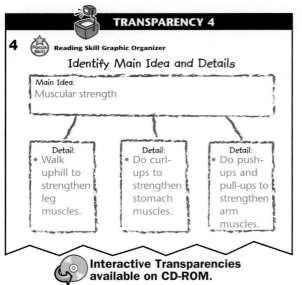

TRANSPARENCY 4

4 Reading Skill Graphic Organizer

Identify Main Idea and Details

Main Idea:
Muscular strength

Detail:
• Walk uphill to strengthen leg muscles.

Detail:
• Do curl-ups to strengthen stomach muscles.

Detail:
• Do push-ups and pull-ups to strengthen arm muscles.

Interactive Transparencies available on CD-ROM.

5. Possible response: I like physical activity for a number of reasons. I have met lots of friends playing basketball in the park. I also think I do better in school after exercising. I look forward to physical education class, and my soccer coach always gives us a good workout.

For **writing models** with examples, see *Teaching Resources* pp. 47–61. Rubrics are also provided.

When Minutes Count ...

Quick Study Students can use *Activity Book* pp. 16–17 (shown on p. 113) as they complete each lesson in this chapter.

Try some physical activities with your family to enjoy different seasons of the year.

- Ice-skate, ski, or build snow sculptures in the winter.
- Fly kites, walk in the woods, or bicycle in the spring.
- Play beach volleyball, go canoeing, or go swimming in the summer.
- Take hikes, chop wood, or pick apples in the fall.

DRAW CONCLUSIONS Survey the members of your family about the activities they like to do. Then draw a conclusion about two activities your family would most enjoy doing together.

Sample answer:

Me	Brother	Mother	Father
Ski	Bike	Swim	Baseball
Bike	Swim	Walk	Bike
Soccer	Skate	Bike	Swim

The family's top choices would be biking and swimming.

Playing ball is an activity that is easy and fun for people of all ages. ▶

Lesson 3 Summary and Review

1 **Summarize with Vocabulary**

Use vocabulary from this lesson to complete the following statements.

Jogging is an example of an activity that builds _____.

The sit-and-reach measures _____.

Weight lifting has become a popular activity because it builds _____.

2 How long should your cool-down last after you have been running for 15 minutes?

3 **Critical Thinking** When buying shoes, what are two important features to look for so you can exercise comfortably?

4 **MAIN IDEA AND DETAILS**

Complete this graphic organizer by starting with muscular strength as the main idea.

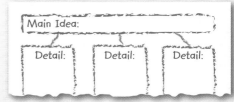

Main Idea:

Detail: | Detail: | Detail:

5 **Write to Inform—Narration**

Write a story about the types of physical activities you like and the benefits you see in them. You might name your favorite activity and tell why you like it.

 Cultural Connection

The World's Sport Point out countries in which the men's and women's World Cup soccer matches have recently been held. The first two women's matches were held in the United States. Men's matches were held in the United States in 1994, France in 1998, and Japan and Korea in 2002. Soccer's popularity has never been greater, as shown by the number of countries competing to join the final teams that make up the World Cup field.

ACTIVITY BOOK P. 20

Name _____

Vocabulary Reinforcement

Use Word Meanings

A. For each of the following sentences, circle the letter of the correct answer.

1. Sammy's mother runs four miles a day. She can use her muscles for long periods of time, which means that she has _____.
   A aerobic exercise C flexibility
   B muscular endurance D anaerobic exercise

2. Amanda likes _____ that increases her heart rate over a long period of time, like biking, swimming, and jogging.
   F aerobic exercise H flexibility
   G muscular endurance J anaerobic exercise

3. Loren set a record for the sit-and-reach. She has great _____, or the ability to bend her body easily.
   A aerobic exercise C flexibility
   B muscular endurance D anaerobic exercise

4. Sprinters do _____, which works muscles hard for a short time.
   F aerobic exercise H flexibility
   G muscular endurance J anaerobic exercise

5. Robert wants to build his _____. He works out every day to try to build a strong, healthy heart.
   A physical activity C cardiovascular fitness
   B flexibility D aerobic exercise

6. Michael enjoys weight lifting, which helps him build his _____.
   F flexibility H cardiovascular fitness
   G muscular strength J aerobic activity

B. Choose two of the following vocabulary terms: *physical activity, muscular endurance, muscular strength, flexibility, cardiovascular fitness, aerobic exercise, anaerobic exercise.* Write a correct sentence using each term. Check students' sentences.

_____
_____
_____

Available online. www.harcourtschool.com/health

ACTIVITIES

Math

Add Up Activity Time Make a table of all the physical activities you do each week. Give yourself a point for each ten-minute period you spend doing each activity. Then make a bar graph that shows four weeks of each activity.

Science

Measure Time Differences Run the 100-meter dash on three trials, and find the differences in your times. First, measure a 100-meter distance, or use the markings on a track. Then run your three trials, with a 2-minute rest between runs. Your teacher or a partner can help you time them. Tell whether your times increased, decreased, or stayed the same. Find the size of each increase or decrease.

Technology Project

Based on the main ideas in this chapter, make a list of reasons to get SAFE—plenty of Sleep, Activity, and healthful Food choices Every day. Make a computer slide show or a poster that shows examples of each of the four parts of SAFE.

GO ONLINE For more activities, visit The Learning Site. www.harcourtschool.com/health

Home & Community

Pro-Fitness Postage Stamp Make a postage stamp that promotes positive physical activity. The stamp should be labeled "Fitness Is Fun" and should show people doing fun activities or exercises.

Career Link

Physical Education Instructor Suppose that you work as a physical education instructor at your school. Write out a lesson plan for one day. It should include aerobic and anaerobic activities. Make sure you indicate the length of time for each class and that you include warm-up and cool-down activities.

133

Activities

Math

An extension of this lesson might include graphing the entire class from week to week and discussing why totals one week might be higher or lower than the previous week.

Science

If pressed for time or facilities for this activity, students can do push-ups in class for one minute and figure out the amount of time to do one push-up in each of three one-minute blocks. Make sure the room is set up properly for doing this activity modification.

Home & Community

Give students paper with fake perforations to simulate stamps and some guidelines about different media they could use. Three-dimensional stamps are also appropriate.

 Supports the Coordinated School Health Program

Technology Project

Computer presentations or posters should show pictures or drawings that represent components of SAFE.

Career Link

Physical Education Instructor Some students may not know what a lesson plan looks like. It has an outline of what the physical education instructor is going to teach the students and how long it will take. For writing a lesson plan, see page 27 in *Teaching Resources*.

Students may wish to study the types of classes a physical education instructor may have to take in their state.

GO ONLINE For more information on health careers visit the **Webliography** in Teacher Resources at **www.harcourtschool.com/health Keyword** health careers

Chapter Review and Test Preparation

Pages 134–135

 Reading Skill 8 pts. each

1. Possible answers: slower version of the main activity, stretch muscles involved in the activity, warm muscles

2. Possible answers: running for 15 minutes, swimming for 10 minutes, biking for 30 minutes, or other activities that get your heart rate up for an extended period of time

 Use Vocabulary 2 pts. each

3. E, muscular strength

4. D, cool-downs

5. A, aerobic exercise

6. F, warm-ups

7. B, anaerobic exercise

8. C, Activity Pyramid

 Check Understanding 3 pts. each

9. C, Sleep

10. H, repair

11. B, playing video games for three hours at a time

12. F, plan

13. A, volunteer

14. H, weight lifting

15. C, heart

16. F, bottom

17. D, top

18. H, fat

19. C, warm-up, exercise, cool-down

 Think Critically 6 pts. each

20. Possible answer: Water; the body loses lots of water in exercise, and water needs to be replaced throughout the exercise.

21. Possible answers: I might be too tired to do as well as I would like on the test; I might be too sleepy to remember what I studied.

 Reading Skill

IDENTIFY MAIN IDEA AND DETAILS
Draw and then use this graphic organizer to answer questions 1 and 2.

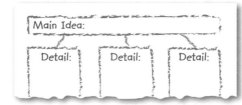

1 Using exercise as the main idea, write down details related to warm-ups.
2 Using physical fitness as the main idea, write down details that show how to measure muscular endurance.

 Use Vocabulary

Match each term in Column B with its meaning in Column A.

Column A	Column B
3 What pull-ups can help build	A aerobic exercises
4 Should be done after hard exercise	B anaerobic exercises
5 Exercise that increases heartbeat rate	C activity pyramid
6 Should be done before exercise	D cool-down
7 Exercises that work your muscles hard for a short time	E muscular strength
8 Diagram that shows guidelines for activity	F warm-up

134

 Check Understanding

Choose the letter of the correct answer.

9 The letter *S* in the acronym SAFE stands for _____. (p. 112)
  A Stretch   C Sleep
  B Stress   D Serving size

10 Sleep has been found to help _____ old cells. (p. 112)
  F destroy   H repair
  G feed   J change

11 Which of these behaviors is a poor health habit? (p. 114)
  A walking to school each day
  B playing video games for three hours
  C eating an apple each day
  D watching no more than one hour of TV

12 When you are starting a new physical activity, it's important to develop a _____ to help you reach your fitness goal. (pp. 122–123)
  F plan   H menu
  G label   J report

13 Being _____ helps you and others have fun and gain respect. (p. 117)
  A fair   C fast
  B strong   D first

14 Which of the following is the **BEST** example of anaerobic exercise? (p. 121)

Formal Assessment

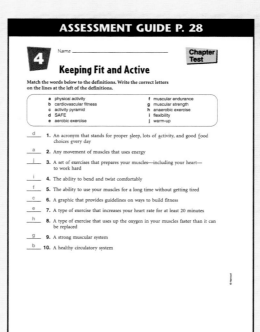

ASSESSMENT GUIDE P. 28

ASSESSMENT GUIDE P. 29

Respiratory system
- trachea
- lungs
- _____

15 Which detail is missing from the list of the parts of the respiratory system? (pp. 118–119)

A leg muscles   C heart
B liver   D alveoli

16 On the activity pyramid, the activities that build flexibility are located at the _____. (pp. 122–123)

F bottom   H center
G middle   J top

17 If you are following the activity pyramid to improve fitness, which section of the pyramid do you use least? (p. 122)

A bottom   C center
B middle   D top

18 Regular exercise reduces the amount of _____ in your blood. (p. 120)

F oxygen   H fat
G protein   J cells

19 Which of the following is the correct order for exercising safely? (pp. 127–128)

A cool down, warm up, exercise
B warm up, cool down, exercise
C warm up, exercise, cool down
D exercise, warm up, cool down

Think Critically

20 You are planning a long-distance hike and want to bring along the best beverage. What would you choose? Why?

21 Suppose you stayed up late studying for your math test and slept only six hours. How might this affect your ability to do well on the test?

22 You are telling others about the health benefits of the SAFE club. What are some of the benefits you would tell about?

Apply Skills

23 **BUILDING GOOD CHARACTER**
Fairness You are asked to fill in on a friend's soccer team. You notice that one of the rules is being broken. Apply what you know about fairness to help correct the problem.

24 **LIFE SKILLS**
Set Goals Your SAFE club is planning a game day for the school. Use what you know about setting goals to plan this activity.

Write About Health

25 **Write to Inform—Explanation** Explain how following a fitness plan can help you meet a goal.

---

22. Possible answer: The major benefit of a SAFE club is that you would be doing these activities with other people. There is strength in numbers when it comes to activity.

Apply Skills 7 pts. each

23. Possible answer: I would calmly tell the person that the rule is being broken. If it continued I would tell the coach.

24. Possible answer: The goal is a successful game day. You create a schedule with all the activities, and have each student sign up for three of them. Then you create a master schedule with people's names and the times they will be doing their activities. At the end of the day, you celebrate your success.

Write About Health 7 pts.

25. Accept all reasonable answers. A plan keeps you on task to accomplish the activity you want to do. It gives you an outline or framework for what you are planning to do over a period of time.

Performance Assessment

Use the Chapter Project and the rubric provided on the Project Evaluation Sheet. See *Assessment Guide*, pp. 18, 57, 65.

Portfolio Assessment

Have students select their best work from the following suggestions:

- Leveled Activities, p. 114
- Quick Activity, p. 130
- Write to Inform, p. 123
- Activities, p. 133

See *Assessment Guide* pp. 12–16.

ASSESSMENT GUIDE P. 30

Name _____

21. Complete the table below by naming two aerobic exercises, two anaerobic exercises, and two warm-up/cool-down exercises.
Answers will vary. Possible answer:

Aerobic Exercises	Anaerobic Exercises	Warm-up/Cool-down Exercises
bicycling	weight lifting	stretching
jogging	100-meter sprint	slower version of activity

22. Ron is getting ready for basketball season and wants to improve his endurance and arm strength. What activities could he do to reach these fitness goals?
Possible response: Ron could build up endurance by jogging a little longer every day. He could lift stacks of books to help build arm strength.

23. Name five activities you could do with your family during the summer that everyone would enjoy.
Possible answers: swimming, biking, hiking, tennis, playing baseball, volleyball, going on a picnic, and going to a park.

24. Sally has set a goal to score high in the stomach crunch event on the school's physical fitness test. Put together a plan she can use to reach this goal. Use the planning steps of the goal-setting skill.
1. Sally can make a plan and determine whether she needs help.
2. She can start with a small number of crunches each day and gradually increase both the number of crunches and the number of times she does crunches each day.
3. To measure improvement, she can record in a chart how many crunches she is able to do.

25. What warm-up activities could you do before going for a long bike ride?
Possible answers: muscle stretches for both the arms and the legs and riding slowly to warm up the muscles, including the heart.

Lesson	Pacing	Objectives	Reading Skills
Introduce the Chapter pp. 136–137		• Preview chapter concepts.	**Sequence** p. 137; pp. 372–383
1 Preparing for the Unexpected pp. 138–145	1 class period	• Recognize and reduce the hazards that lead to unexpected injuries. • Explain how to respond to emergency situations. • Practice first aid for injuries.	**Sequence** pp. 139, 145 • Summarize, p. 141 • Draw Conclusions, p. 143
Life Skills pp. 146–147	1 class period	• Identify steps for making responsible decisions. • Use the decision-making steps to make healthful decisions about safety.	
2 Practicing Safety pp. 148–156	2 class periods	• Practice safety at play and in motor vehicles. • Analyze safety equipment.	**Sequence** pp. 155, 156 • Summarize, p. 149 • Draw Conclusions, p. 151 • Main Idea and Details, p. 153 • Compare and Contrast, p. 156
Building Good Character p. 157		• Identify ways to show compassion for injured persons.	
3 Fire Safety pp. 158–166	2 class periods	• Explain how to prevent home fires. • Recognize fire hazards in the home. • Describe how to survive a home fire.	**Sequence** p. 166 • Draw Conclusions, pp. 158, 162 • Cause and Effect, pp. 161, 163 • Summarize, p. 155 • Main Idea and Details, p. 166
Activities p. 167		• Extend chapter concepts.	
Chapter Review pp. 168–169	1 class period	• Assess chapter objectives.	

Vocabulary	Program Resources
	Music CD Teaching Resources, p. 31
hazard **emergency** **first aid** **concussion** **antiseptic**	Transparency 5 Activity Book, pp. 21–22
	Activity Book, p. 24 Poster 8
pedestrians	Transparency 5 Activity Book, pp. 21–22
	Poster 1
flammable **natural disasters**	Transparency 5 Activity Book, pp. 21–22
	The Learning Site www. harcourtschool.com/health
	Assessment Guide, pp. 31–33

 Interactive Transparencies
available on CD-ROM.

Reading Skill

These reading skills are reinforced throughout this chapter and one skill is emphasized as the Focus Skill.

- **Sequence**
  - Draw Conclusions
  - Identify Cause and Effect
  - Identify Main Idea and Details
  - Compare and Contrast
  - Summarize

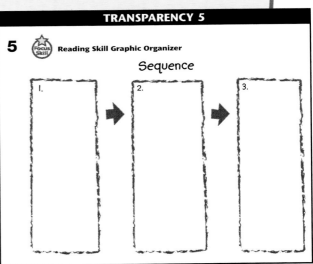

TRANSPARENCY 5

5 Reading Skill Graphic Organizer

Sequence

1. → 2. → 3.

Life Skills

Life Skills are health-enhancing behaviors that can help students reduce risks to their health and safety.

Six Life Skills are reinforced throughout *Harcourt Health and Fitness*. The skill emphasized in this chapter is Make Responsible Decisions.

POSTER 8

Make Responsible Decisions

The boy is making a responsible decision about choosing a healthful snack.

Steps for Making Responsible Decisions

1. Find out about the choices you could make.
2. Eliminate choices that are against your family rules.
3. Ask yourself: What could happen with each choice? Does the choice show good character?
4. Make what seems to be the best choice.

What RESPONSIBLE DECISIONS have YOU MADE today?

POSTER 8

Building Good Character

Character education is an important aspect of health education. When students behave in ways that show good character, they promote the health and safety of themselves and others.

Six character traits are reinforced throughout *Harcourt Health and Fitness*. The trait emphasized in this chapter is Caring.

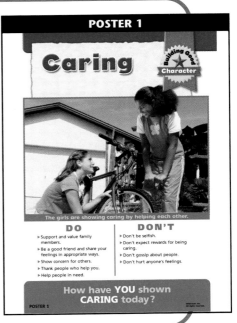

POSTER 1

Caring

The girls are showing caring by helping each other.

DO
- Support and value family members.
- Be a good friend and share your feelings in appropriate ways.
- Show concern for others.
- Thank people who help you.
- Help people in need.

DON'T
- Don't be selfish.
- Don't expect rewards for being caring.
- Don't gossip about people.
- Don't hurt anyone's feelings.

How have YOU shown CARING today?

POSTER 1

Coordinated School Health Program

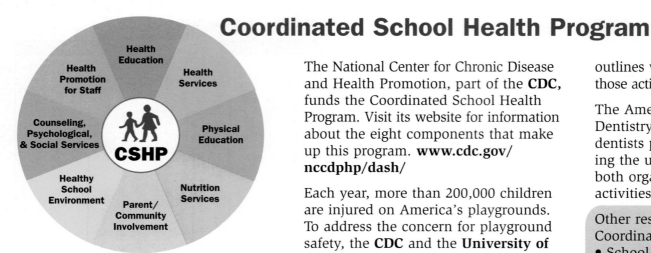

A Coordinated School Health Program endeavors to improve children's health and, therefore, their capacity to learn through the support of families, schools, and communities working together. The following information is provided to help classroom teachers be more aware of these resources.

The National Center for Chronic Disease and Health Promotion, part of the **CDC**, funds the Coordinated School Health Program. Visit its website for information about the eight components that make up this program. **www.cdc.gov/nccdphp/dash/**

Each year, more than 200,000 children are injured on America's playgrounds. To address the concern for playground safety, the **CDC** and the **University of Northern Iowa** established the National Program for Playground Safety (NPPS). **www.uni.edu/playground/**

The best thing anyone can do to stay safe in and around the water is to learn to swim. The **American Red Cross** identifies specialized water activities and outlines ways to stay safe while enjoying those activities. **www.redcross.org**

The American Academy of Pediatric Dentistry (**AAPD**) recommends that dentists play an active role in encouraging the use of protective equipment for both organized and informal sporting activities. **www.aapd.org/**

Other resources that support a Coordinated School Health Program:
- School-Home Connection
- Daily Physical Activity
- Daily Fitness Tips
- Activities: Home & Community
- Health Background: Webliography
- *Be Active! Resources for Physical Education*

Books for Students

Children's Hospital at Yale-New Haven. ***Now I Know Better: Kids Tell Kids About Safety.*** Millbrook Press, 1996. Children describe emergencies. **EASY**

Kasis, Karin. ***Disaster Blaster: A Kid's Guide to Being Home Alone.*** Avon Books, 1996. Offers practical advice on staying home alone. **AVERAGE**

Galiano, Dean. ***Thunderstorms and Lightning.*** Rosen Central, 2003. Explains how storms form and includes a chapter on safety. **ADVANCED**

Books for Teachers and Families

National Safety Council. ***First Aid and CPR.*** Jones & Bartlett Publishers, 2000. This manual outlines the necessary steps to victim resuscitation.

Manoff, David H., and Stephen N. Vogel. ***Mosby's Outdoor Emergency Medical Guide: What to Do in an Outdoor Emergency When Help***

Media Resources

May Take Some Time to Arrive. Mosby Year Book, 1996. This life-saving guide offers pertinent information to the untrained person.

Free and Inexpensive Materials

Character Education
Look for guides and tips on topics such as bullying and working out conflicts.

Federal Emergency Management Agency
Ask for *Are You Ready? A Guide to Citizen Preparedness.*

Underwriter's Laboratories
Ask for their free copy of UL's room-by-room home safety tip guide.

Federal Citizen Information Center
Ask for CPSC #627J, a checklist to ensure a safe, home playground.

U.S. Fire Administration
Has free books, videotapes, and kits on fire prevention on their Kids Page.

To access free and inexpensive resources on the Web, visit **www.harcourtschool.com/health/free**

Videos

On Fire: A Family Guide to Fire Safety. KCET Video, 1990.

Home Alone! A Kid's Guide on Playing Safe When on Your Own. Hi-Tops Video, 1992.

Basic First Aid. Educational Video Network, 1999.

These resources have been selected to meet a variety of individual needs. Please review all materials and websites prior to sharing them with students to ensure the content is appropriate for your class. Note that information, while correct at time of publication, is subject to change.

Visit **The Learning Site** for related links, activities, resources, and the health **Webliography.**

www.harcourtschool.com/health

Meeting Individual Needs

Below-Level

To help students recognize letter patterns in words, have them go through the chapter on a "word hunt." For example, tell them that you are looking for any word that contains *er* as in emergency. Write the words on the board, and circle the *er* in each one.

Activities

- Emergency Action, p. 144
- Product Recalls, p. 148
- Design a Reflective Vest, p. 152
- Disaster Drills, p. 164

On-Level

When students use strategies, they are thinking as a good reader thinks. Have students make predictions about the information that will be given in the selection. Then have them read to find out if they are right.

Activities

- Call 911, p. 144
- Write a Manufacturer, p. 148
- Survey Street Safety, p. 152
- FEMA, p. 164

Challenge

Have students use a minimum number of vocabulary words to make up brief stories or dialogues. Students can write their stories or dialogues on paper and then record them. Have other students listen for the words in context and tell the meanings.

Activities

- Taking CPR, p. 144
- Change Public Policy, p. 148
- Request a Park, p. 152
- Helping Disaster Victims, p. 164

Learning Log

Students can use a Learning Log to record new information gained from text. Have students write a newspaper article about a topic related to the chapter content. Encourage students to include information in their articles that answers the questions *who, what, when, where,* and *why.*

Activities

- Comprehensible Input, pp. 140, 150, 158
- Language and Vocabulary, p. 143

Curriculum Integration

Integrated Language Arts/Reading Skills

- Crash Scene, p. 141
- Public Safety Announcement, p. 151
- Rules for All, p. 154
- Safety Is No Accident, p. 163

Math

- Playground Safety Check, p. 149
- Recent Floods, p. 165

Physical Education

- Daily Fitness Tip, pp. 138, 148, 158
- Daily Physical Activity, p. 137

Use these topics to integrate health into your daily planning.

Science

- Cars, Bicycles, Pedestrians, and the Environment, p. 155
- Fire Extinguishers, p. 159
- Smoke Inhalation, p. 161

Drama

- On the Road, p. 156

Social Studies

- Local Bicycle Trails, p. 155
- Fire Prevention Week, p. 162
- Civic Responsibility, p. 146

Art

- Dangerous Diane and Safe Sam, p. 149
- Bicycle Safety Board Game, p. 156

CHAPTER 5

Pages 136–169

CHAPTER SUMMARY

In this chapter students
► examine situations inside and outside the home that can lead to injuries.
► learn to recognize and respond to emergency situations.
► practice safety at play and during sports.

Life Skills
Students practice *making responsible decisions* that help prevent injury.

Building Good Character
Students show *caring* for others by learning what to do for a person who has been injured.

Consumer Health
Students *make buying decisions* about equipment that can prevent injuries.

 Literature Springboard

Use the article "Protecting Life—A Brief History of Safety Equipment" to spark interest in the chapter topic. See the Read-Aloud Anthology on page RA-6 of this *Teacher Edition*.

Prereading Strategies

SCAN THE CHAPTER Have students preview the chapter content by scanning the titles, headings, pictures, and charts. Ask volunteers to predict what they will learn. Use their predictions to determine their prior knowledge.

PREVIEW VOCABULARY As students preview the vocabulary terms in each lesson, have them select one term to write and illustrate in each square as shown.

pedestrian	

Chapter 5 • Planning for Safety

CHAPTER 5 Planning for Safety

 Focus Skill **Reading Skill**

SEQUENCE To introduce or review this skill, have students use the Reading in Health Handbook, pages 372–383. Teaching strategies and additional activities are also provided.

Students will have opportunities to practice and apply this skill throughout the chapter.

• Focus Skill Reading Mini-Lesson, p. 138
• Reading comprehension questions identified with the
• *Activity Book* p. 23 (shown on p. 145)
• Lesson Summary and Review, pp. 145, 156, 166
• Chapter Review and Test Preparation, pp. 168–169

SEQUENCE Sequence is the order in which events take place. It is also the order of the steps for carrying out a task. Use the Reading in Health Handbook on pages 372–383 and this graphic organizer to help you read the health facts in this chapter.

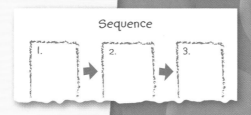

Health Graph

INTERPRET DATA In the United States, an average of 98,000 people die as a result of unintentional, or accidental, injuries. What is the leading cause of death from unintentional injuries?

Leading Causes of Death from Unintentional Injuries

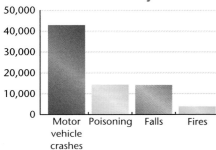

Daily Physical Activity

Staying safe is part of being healthy. So is getting some physical activity every day/

 Be Active!
Use the selection, Track 5, **Flexercise**, to practice safe warm-ups and exercises.

137

School-Home Connection

Distribute copies of the School-Home Connection (in English or Spanish). Have students take the page home to share with their families as you begin this chapter.

Follow Up Have volunteers share the results of their activities.

 Supports the Coordinated School Health Program
CSHP

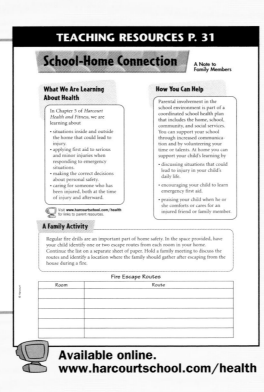

TEACHING RESOURCES P. 31

School-Home Connection — A Note to Family Members

What We Are Learning About Health

In Chapter 5 of *Harcourt Health and Fitness,* we are learning about
· situations inside and outside the home that could lead to injury.
· applying first aid to serious and minor injuries when responding to emergency situations.
· making the correct decisions about personal safety.
· caring for someone who has been injured, both at the time of injury and afterward.

Visit **www.harcourtschool.com/health** for links to parent resources.

How You Can Help

Parental involvement in the school environment is part of a coordinated school health plan that includes the home, school, community, and social services. You can support your school through increased communication and by volunteering your time or talents. At home you can support your child's learning by
· discussing situations that could lead to injury in your child's daily life.
· encouraging your child to learn emergency first aid.
· praising your child when he or she comforts or cares for an injured friend or family member.

A Family Activity

Regular fire drills are an important part of home safety. In the space provided, have your child identify one or two escape routes from each room in your home. Continue the list on a separate sheet of paper. Hold a family meeting to discuss the routes and identify a location where the family should gather after escaping from the house during a fire.

Fire Escape Routes

Room	Route

Available online.
www.harcourtschool.com/health

INTRODUCE THE CHAPTER

Health Graph

Interpret Data

Ask volunteers to explain what information is displayed in the graph. **What is the leading cause of death from unintentional injury?** Students should recognize that the leading cause of death is represented by the longest bar in the graph, the bar representing death from motor vehicle accidents. **Which two causes on the graph are each responsible for about 13 percent of unintentional deaths?** falls and poisoning

Daily Physical Activity

Use *Be Active! Music for Daily Physical Activity* with the Instant Activity Cards to provide students with movement activities that can be done in limited space. Options for using these components are provided beginning on page TR2 in this *Teacher Edition.*

Chapter Project

Take One! Action! (Assessment Guide p. 58)

ASSESS PRIOR KNOWLEDGE Use students' initial ideas for the project as a baseline assessment of their understanding of chapter concepts. Have students complete the project as they work through the chapter.

PERFORMANCE ASSESSMENT The project can be used for performance assessment. Project Evaluation Sheet (rubric), *Assessment Guide* p. 66

Objectives
▶ Recognize and reduce hazards that lead to unexpected injuries.
▶ Explain how to respond to emergency situations.
▶ Practice first aid for injuries.

 When Minutes Count . . .
Assign the Quick Study, Lesson 1, Activity Book pp. 21–22 (shown on p. 139).

Program Resources
▶ Transparency 5
▶ Activity Book pp. 21–22, 23

Vocabulary
hazard p. 138, **emergency** p. 140, **first aid** p. 142, **concussion** p. 143, **antiseptic** p. 144

 **Daily Fitness Tip**

Emphasize that students should avoid wearing certain types of clothing on playgrounds. Children wearing loose clothing or clothing with drawstrings can fall if clothing becomes snagged on playground equipment.

 For more guidelines on choosing proper clothing and shoes, see *Be Active! Resources for Physical Education,* p. 185.

1. MOTIVATE

Optional Activity Materials
several issues of sports periodicals and newspapers; poster board; paste

Ask students to search through the materials for articles that describe accidental injuries. As you discuss the types of injuries described in the articles, ask students to demonstrate strategies for preventing accidental injuries.

Are there any accidental injuries you think could have been avoided? Explain.
Accept any answers that indicate a plan that might have avoided the injury.

Preparing for the Unexpected

Lesson Focus
Being aware of hazards can help reduce the risk of injury. In an emergency certain first-aid steps should be taken.

Why Learn This?
You can use what you learn to help prevent injuries and to deal with emergency situations.

Vocabulary
hazard
emergency
first aid
concussion

Common Hazards

Injuries often occur when people are tired or careless. Sometimes injuries happen when people don't realize that an action is unsafe.

Some injuries occur during everyday activities such as riding in a vehicle, riding a bike, swimming, and playing sports. Other injuries happen in the home. Whatever the setting or situation, you can avoid injuries by thinking through your actions before you act. The list below shows common causes of injuries among young people.

- drowning
- poisoning
- fires
- falls
- motor vehicle crashes
- bicycle crashes
- being shot by firearms

To reduce the risk of injury, always wear the right safety gear.

138

 Focus Skill **Reading Skill**

Mini-Lesson

SEQUENCE Remind students that sequence refers to the order in which actions or events happen. Have students practice this skill by responding to the Focus Skill question on page 139. Have students draw and complete the graphic organizer as you model it on the transparency.

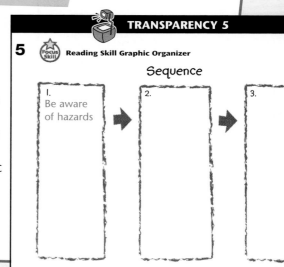

TRANSPARENCY 5

5 **Focus Skill** Reading Skill Graphic Organizer

Sequence

1. Be aware of hazards → 2. → 3.

Interactive Transparencies available on CD-ROM.

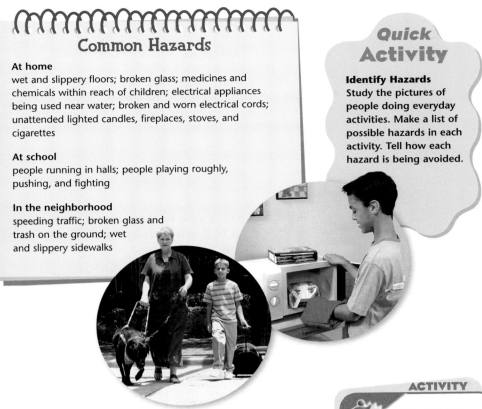

Common Hazards

At home
wet and slippery floors; broken glass; medicines and chemicals within reach of children; electrical appliances being used near water; broken and worn electrical cords; unattended lighted candles, fireplaces, stoves, and cigarettes

At school
people running in halls; people playing roughly, pushing, and fighting

In the neighborhood
speeding traffic; broken glass and trash on the ground; wet and slippery sidewalks

Quick Activity

Identify Hazards
Study the pictures of people doing everyday activities. Make a list of possible hazards in each activity. Tell how each hazard is being avoided.

The first step in preventing injuries is to be aware of hazards. A **hazard** is something in the environment or something about a person's actions that can cause harm or injury.

Sometimes people like to show off or take risks. They might play dangerously in a swimming pool or on the playground. They might give someone a ride on bicycle handlebars or play with matches. These actions are hazards because they place the person doing them and other people at risk. The table above lists common hazards at home, at school, and in the neighborhood.

SEQUENCE **What is the first step in preventing injuries?**
being aware of hazards

ACTIVITY
Life Skills
Communicate
Yvonne is at her neighborhood swimming pool. She wants to use the diving board, but people are not taking turns. Instead, they are jumping off together. Act out how she can communicate to her friends that this behavior is unsafe.

139

---

2. TEACH

Interpret Visuals—Pictures
Direct students' attention to the illustrations on these pages. Ask students to identify any safety gear they see. Have students tell what injuries are possible for the activity in each illustration. Accept all reasonable responses.

Content-Area Reading Support
Using Text Patterns Direct students to read the boxed text. Point out that the box contains three groups of information: common hazards at home, at school, and in the neighborhood. Comment that grouping the hazards according to location can make it easier to recall the information.

Activity
Communicate Have students describe the value of seeking advice from parents and educational personnel about unsafe behaviors. Yvonne could tell her friends that jumping from a diving board together is unsafe because they might bump into each other. She could also point out the sign listing the pool rules, especially if one rule says "One diver at a time." Yvonne could ask an adult, especially the lifeguard or a parent, to remind the swimmers to follow the rules to prevent diving injuries.

Quick Activity
Identify What's Wrong Possible answers: Popcorn could burn the child's fingers—use an oven mitt; the child might walk out into traffic—obey the crosswalk signal.

 QUICK STUDY, ACTIVITY BOOK PP. 21–22

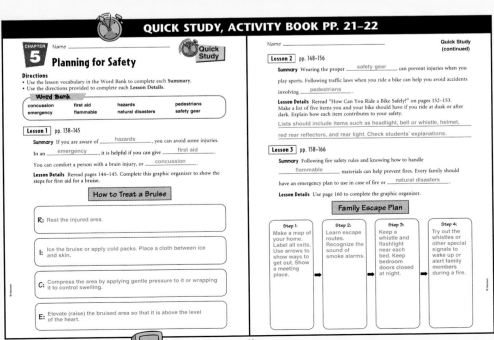

CHAPTER 5 Name _____ **Quick Study**
Planning for Safety

Directions
• Use the lesson vocabulary in the Word Bank to complete each **Summary.**
• Use the directions provided to complete each **Lesson Details.**

Word Bank

concussion	first aid	hazards	pedestrians
emergency	flammable	natural disasters	safety gear

Lesson 1 pp. 138–145

Summary If you are aware of ____hazards____, you can avoid some injuries.
In an ____emergency____, it is helpful if you can give ____first aid____.
You can comfort a person with a brain injury, or ____concussion____.

Lesson Details Reread pages 144–145. Complete this graphic organizer to show the steps for first aid for a bruise.

How to Treat a Bruise

R: Rest the injured area.

I: Ice the bruise or apply cold packs. Place a cloth between ice and skin.

C: Compress the area by applying gentle pressure to it or wrapping it to control swelling.

E: Elevate (raise) the bruised area so that it is above the level of the heart.

Name _____ **Quick Study (continued)**

Lesson 2 pp. 148–156

Summary Wearing the proper ____safety gear____ can prevent injuries when you play sports. Following traffic laws when you ride a bike can help you avoid accidents involving ____pedestrians____.

Lesson Details Reread "How Can You Ride a Bike Safely?" on pages 152–153. Make a list of five items you and your bike should have if you ride at dusk or after dark. Explain how each item contributes to your safety.

Lists should include items such as headlight, bell or whistle, helmet, red rear reflectors, and rear light. Check students' explanations.

Lesson 3 pp. 158–166

Summary Following fire safety rules and knowing how to handle ____flammable____ materials can help prevent fires. Every family should have an emergency plan to use in case of fire or ____natural disasters____.

Lesson Details Use page 160 to complete the graphic organizer.

Family Escape Plan

Step 1: Make a map of your home. Label all exits. Use arrows to show ways to get out. Show a meeting place.

Step 2: Learn escape routes. Recognize the sound of smoke alarms.

Step 3: Keep a whistle and flashlight near each bed. Keep bedroom doors closed at night.

Step 4: Try out the whistles or other special signals to wake up or alert family members during a fire.

Available online.
www.harcourtschool.com/health

TEACH *continued*

Discuss

In any emergency situation, it is important that rescuers and helpers remain calm and focused. People who are calm are able to think clearly and act; they also tend to make sound judgments about what to do. On the other hand, people who become hysterical at the sight of blood or a broken bone add to the crisis situation and often delay or hinder help for an injured person. Have students describe response procedures for emergency situations.

Problem Solving **Knowing that emergency situations can be highly emotional, what methods might you use to stay calm during an emergency?** Possible answers: Take a few deep breaths; review the emergency action steps in my mind.

Quick Activity

Survey the Scene Students' answers should be similar to the following: A child on a bike has collided with a pedestrian. Two people are injured. The bicyclist has fallen off his bike and hurt his leg; the pedestrian fell and hurt his head. If the person surveying the crash rushes across the street to help, he or she may be hit by the oncoming car. The injured persons do not appear to be in immediate danger, but the person who hit his head could have a serious injury.

Content-Area Reading Support

Using Typographic Clues Draw attention to boldface and bulleted text. Point out that the boldface type tells what to do in each step. The bulleted information that follows gives more details about each step. Discuss how organizing the information in this manner makes understanding and remembering what to do easier.

Responding to a Serious Injury

When someone is seriously injured, it is an emergency. An **emergency** (ee·MER·juhn·see) is a situation that calls for quick action. If you come across an emergency, follow these three steps:

   Step 1 Perform a ten-second survey. Quickly look over the scene. Try to answer the following questions. You will need this information when you call for help.

- What happened?
- How many people are injured?
- Is anyone at the scene in danger of further injury?

   Step 2 Call 911 or your local emergency number. When you call for help, listen carefully to the emergency operator's questions and be prepared to

- give the location of the emergency, including the street address, landmarks, and the names of the nearest cross streets.
- give your name and, if asked by the operator, the phone number from which you are calling.

Quick Activity

Survey the Scene Take a ten-second survey of the emergency situation shown here. Answer the questions in Step 1 of the text at the right.

If you witness an accident, your body may react to the stress of the emergency. Remain calm and remember what you learned in this lesson. ▶

140

ESL/ELL Support

COMPREHENSIBLE INPUT Encourage students to relay information about an accident.

Beginning Encourage proficient students to describe the accident in the picture. Have beginning students repeat each sentence, pointing to the appropriate part of the illustration.

Intermediate Ask students questions about the accident. If necessary, allow students to respond with one-word answers.

Advanced Help students describe the accident scene in English only. Emphasize that using perfect grammar and precise words is not as important as getting help to provide needed care.

▲ Call 911 in emergencies such as drowning, severe bleeding, electrocution, choking, poisoning, severe burns, spinal cord injury, difficult or stopped breathing, and unconsciousness.

- Tell what happened and how many people need help.
- Describe the conditions of the injured people and what help they are receiving.
- Remain on the phone until the operator instructs you to hang up.

Step 3 Care for the injured person. If it's safe for you to do so, give the person comfort. Inform the injured person in a calm voice that help is on the way. In cases of broken bones and possible head or spinal injuries, don't move or touch the injured person.

Sometimes it is safer to call for help instead of approaching an emergency scene or an injured person. For example, don't approach a wrecked car surrounded by moving traffic. That would be unsafe.

> **SUMMARIZE Tell what information you should be ready to give an emergency operator.**

location of emergency (street address, landmarks, names of nearest cross streets); name and phone number of caller; description of what happened and how many people need help; the conditions of the injured persons and what help they are receiving

141

Enhanced 911 In the United States, nearly 100 percent of communities have Enhanced 911 (E911) service. With E911, emergency operators can automatically get callback numbers and street addresses for callers using traditional phones. However, operators can seldom locate callers who are using wireless phones.

Discuss

During an emergency, a person may become disoriented and forget his or her own name, telephone number, and address. Have students describe response procedures for emergency situations.

Problem Solving What can you do to make sure this doesn't happen? Before an emergency happens, write down your name, phone number, address, and directions to your home. Place the information in a clearly visible place near the telephone.

Critical Thinking Why do you think it is important to give a 911 operator as much information as possible about an injured person? Possible answers: The operator needs information to decide how important the call is; the operator can advise the caller about first-aid treatment for the victim; so the appropriate equipment and vehicles can be sent (such as whether a fire truck and an ambulance are needed).

How do you know that the steps for responding to a serious injury should be done in a specific sequence? The steps are numbered.

Why should step 1 be completed before step 2? The 911 operator will likely ask some questions; completing step 1 prepares you to answer the questions.

Teacher Tip

Report Hazards Have students describe the value of telling a parent or another adult when something is unsafe or when someone is behaving in an unsafe way. Remind them that it is not tattling; it is looking out for the well-being of others.

Integrated Language Arts/ Reading Skills

Crash Scene Have groups of three students dramatize the scene pictured on page 140 as well as other emergency situations. Students should incorporate the emergency steps described on these pages into their dramatizations. Ask students to rehearse and then perform their scenes for the class. Encourage the class to evaluate the actions of the characters.

TEACH *continued*

Interpret Visuals—Pictures

Direct students to look at the pictures on pages 142 and 143. Ask a volunteer to describe the action shown in each illustration. Point out that although immediate first aid can help save a life in a critical situation, applying the wrong treatment can cause more harm than good. Indicate that if a person is unsure about what first aid to give, he or she should wait for experienced help, such as EMTs, to arrive. Be certain students can demonstrate strategies for responding to injuries.

Problem Solving How can you learn more about first aid? Possible answers: Take a first-aid course; ask a person trained to administer first aid to demonstrate techniques.

Critical Thinking Why is it important to know first aid? Possible answers: You can help yourself or someone else who is injured; by knowing first aid, you might help save someone's life.

Health Background

EMT Careers People's lives often depend on the quick reactions and competent care of emergency medical technicians (EMTs) and paramedics. (EMTs are certified to perform more difficult procedures.) Typically, a 911 operator dispatches EMTs or paramedics to an accident scene, where they may also work with police and fire department personnel. Once EMTs arrive, they determine the nature and extent of the patient's condition and try to learn whether the patient has preexisting medical problems. Following strict rules and guidelines, EMTs give appropriate emergency care and, when necessary, transport the patient. Formal training and certification are needed, but requirements vary from state to state.

Source: *U.S. Department of Labor, Bureau of Labor Statistics*

 For more background, visit the **Webliography** in Teacher Resources at **www.harcourtschool.com/health Keyword** health careers

---

People trained to respond to emergencies include emergency medical technicians (EMTs), paramedics, and some firefighters and police officers. ▶

Did You Know?

One way of being prepared for an emergency or serious injury is to have a first-aid kit. Items that belong in a first-aid kit include sterile bandages, sterile water, disposable gloves, adhesive tape, scissors, tweezers, a cold pack, a blanket, and a small flashlight. Do you know where to find a first-aid kit in your home or school?

Treating Serious Injuries

Suppose you are out playing, and your friend falls and hurts himself badly. Would you know what to do? For the injuries described below, the first things anyone should do are to stay calm and call for help. When help arrives, a paramedic or EMT can give the injured person emergency treatment. Until help arrives, a person who knows first aid can provide help. **First aid** is immediate care given to an injured person.

First Aid for Serious Wounds The paramedic should be wearing disposable gloves. A *sterile bandage*, which is a bandage free of germs, should be placed over the wound. See also page 386.

- If there is bleeding from the wound, pressure should be applied. If gloves aren't available, the victim's hand should be used to apply pressure.
- If no bones seem broken, the wounded part of the body should be raised above the level of the heart. This slows the flow of blood to the wound.

142

Teacher Tip

First-Aid Risk AIDS and hepatitis B and C are life-threatening diseases that can be spread through contact with an infected person's blood. If a person has cuts on his or her hands when treating a wound, the patient's blood could come into contact with the first-aid giver's own blood and could transmit one of these diseases. Emphasize that wearing disposable gloves or using the patient's own hand to apply pressure to a wound reduces the risk of transmitting disease-causing germs.

First Aid for Burns Hot or burned clothing should be removed. However, clothing that is stuck to burned skin should not be removed. See also page 388.

- Less serious burns appear red or blistered and are painful. Cool the burned area by putting it under gently running cool water. Or, cover it with a sterile bandage that has been soaked in cool water. Then cover the burned area with a dry, sterile bandage.

- Severe burns appear whitish or black and are not felt by the victim. These should be treated by a doctor. In the meantime, protect burned areas with clean, dry cloth, like sheets.

First Aid for Concussions A **concussion** (kuhn•KUHSH•uhn) is a brain injury caused by a strong blow to the head. Signs of a concussion include vomiting, headache, unconsciousness, weakness, confusion, and blurred vision.

- If the scalp is bleeding, place a sterile bandage over the wound. The caregiver should wear disposable gloves or use the victim's hand to apply pressure to the wound.
- Remain with the injured person, monitoring breathing rate and heartbeat rate until help arrives.

DRAW CONCLUSIONS Why should a less serious burn be covered with a sterile bandage?
to keep germs from entering the wound

A person who might have a concussion should be observed for at least twenty-four hours. ▼

143

Discuss

What usually happens when a person is injured in or near a crowd? People crowd around the victim. **How might a crowd surrounding an injured person be harmful to the victim?** The crowd might block a person who can give first aid from reaching the victim.

Point out that in such a situation, one person in the crowd should call for help while another person stays with the injured person and gives first aid.

Health Background

Home Safety Each year in the United States, more children die from unintentional injuries than from any other cause. About 5,600 children die each year from unintentional injuries, an average of 15 children each day. In addition, 16 percent of all hospitalizations for unintentional injuries result in permanent disability. Many of these injuries are the result of fire or other incidents in the home. Increased awareness of potential dangers in and around the home can help prevent many of these injuries. Encourage students to discuss home safety with their families and to work with their families to develop home safety plans.

Source: *National Safe Kids Campaign*

GO ONLINE For more background, visit the **Webliography** in Teacher Resources at www.harcourtschool.com/health **Keyword** first aid

ESL/ELL Support

LANGUAGE AND VOCABULARY Alert students to the words *wound* and *burn*, both of which can be used as nouns and as verbs.

Beginning Write the words on the board. Discuss the verb and noun meanings of each. Then ask students to draw pictures to illustrate the noun and verb meanings.

Intermediate Ask students to act out the verb meanings of the words. Then have students use the noun form of the word in a sentence.

Advanced Encourage students to choose one of the words. Direct them to write two complete sentences—one sentence using the word as a verb and the second sentence using the word as a noun.

TEACH *continued*

Interpret Visuals—Pictures

Direct students' attention to the picture of a person cleaning a wound. Invite volunteers who have recently received scrapes to describe what happened to them.

Critical Thinking **Why is cleaning a wound important?** Cleaning helps remove germs that can cause infection.

Problem Solving **What would you say to a child who is afraid that cleaning a scrape will hurt?** Possible answer: It will only hurt a little and may help prevent the wound from becoming infected, which could hurt a lot more.

Discuss

Write the letters *R, I, C,* and *E* vertically on the board. Point out that put together, the letters form an acronym, or a word formed by using the first letters of other words. Explain that *R.I.C.E.* stands for *Rest, Ice, Compress,* and *Elevate.* Tell students that acronyms are used to help readers remember details.

Explain that students can use *R.I.C.E.* to remind them how to treat a bruise. Direct students to read the steps for treating a bruise. Then ask a volunteer to go to the board, indicate what the *R* stands for, and explain the step. Continue for the remaining letters.

First Aid for Common Injuries

Everyone has gotten cuts, scrapes, muscle cramps, and bruises at one time or another. Most common injuries aren't serious. They hurt, but if you take care of them, they heal quickly.

A *cut* is a skin break, usually one that bleeds. Cuts are caused by sharp objects, such as broken glass, scissors, and knives. To treat a cut, first wash your hands with soap and water. Then do the following:

- Wash the cut with mild soap and running water.
- Control the bleeding. Place a sterile bandage or clean cloth directly over the cut, and apply pressure until the bleeding stops.
- Cover the cut with a sterile bandage.

A *scrape* is a wound in which skin has been rubbed or scraped away. It usually oozes blood. The scraped area may have dirt and germs in it. Begin by washing your hands with soap and water. Then do the following:

- Clean the scrape thoroughly, using mild soap and a washcloth under running water. Try to wash out any pieces of dirt and debris.
- Cover the scrape with a sterile bandage.

Myth and Fact

Myth: The most common injuries in skating are head injuries.
Fact: The most common injuries are to the wrists. Always wear a helmet, a mouth guard, wrist guards, elbow pads, and kneepads when skating.

Cleaning a wound reduces the chance of infection. Signs of infection include redness, swelling, heat, and pus around the wound. ▶

144

Meeting Individual Needs
Leveled Activities

Have students demonstrate strategies for responding to deliberate and accidental injuries.

BELOW-LEVEL **Emergency Action** Ask each student to think of an injury scene. Then have each student draw a picture showing the event and write next to it a list of steps that should be taken by someone seeing the event. Allow students to present their work to the class.

ON-LEVEL **Call 911** Have partners role-play several calls to a 911 operator. Ask the operator to explain the purpose of his or her questions during the calls.

CHALLENGE **Take CPR** Have students call the local fire department to ask about first-aid and CPR classes. Request that they sign up for the next class, with the permission of a parent or guardian. (Classes are usually free.) Upon completion, ask students to speak to the class about how it feels to be trained to help save a life.

A *muscle cramp* is a spasm, or an uncontrolled tightening of a muscle. To relieve a muscle cramp, gently and slowly stretch out the cramped muscle. Then relax the muscle by massaging it gently.

A *bruise* is an injury in which blood vessels break under the skin. Treat bruises with **R.I.C.E.**, which means **R**est, **I**ce, **C**ompress, and **E**levate.

1. Protect the bruised area from further injury by *resting* it.
2. Apply *ice* or cold packs to reduce swelling. Keep a cloth between ice and the skin.
3. If possible, *compress* the area, or apply pressure to it, by wrapping it to control swelling. Use an elastic bandage.
4. *Elevate*, or raise, the bruised area above the level of the heart. This helps limit swelling by slowing blood flow to the area.

 SEQUENCE **What should a person do immediately after applying ice or a cold pack to a bruise?**

compress to control swelling

Muscle cramps occur when your muscles are tired, when your body needs water, or when you are overheated. ▶

Lesson 1 Summary and Review

❶ **Summarize with Vocabulary**

Use vocabulary from this lesson to complete the statements.

Something in the environment that can cause harm or injury is a(n) _____. If someone is seriously injured, it is a(n) _____. The immediate care given to an injured person is _____. An injury to the head may result in a(n) _____.

❷ Identify two common hazards in each of these places: at school, at home, and in the neighborhood.

❸ **Critical Thinking** Give an example of how a person's actions can be a hazard or cause an accident.

❹ **SEQUENCE** Draw and complete this graphic organizer to show the steps for handling an emergency.

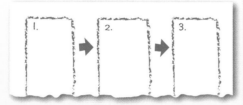

❺ **Write to Inform—How-To**

Write a short paragraph that describes how to treat a common injury, such as a cut or scrape.

145

---

3. WRAP UP

Lesson 1 Summary and Review

1. hazard; emergency; first aid; concussion; antiseptic

2. Possible answers: School—running in hall; pushing; fighting. Home—wet or slippery floors; broken glass; medicines or chemicals within reach of children; electrical appliances used near water; broken or frayed electrical cords; unattended lighted cigarettes, candles, fireplaces, and stoves. Neighborhood—speeding traffic; slippery sidewalks; broken glass; trash on the ground

3. Possible answer: a person running across a street to offer assistance may cause a traffic accident.

4. Answers may include the following:

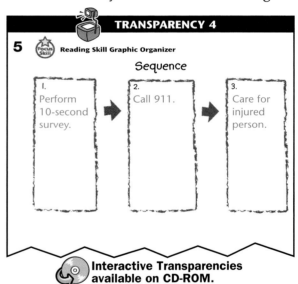

TRANSPARENCY 4

5 Reading Skill Graphic Organizer

Sequence

| 1. Perform 10-second survey. | → | 2. Call 911. | → | 3. Care for injured person. |

 Interactive Transparencies available on CD-ROM.

5. Paragraphs should include the following information: Cuts—Wash the cut with water, control any bleeding, and cover with a sterile bandage. Scrape—Clean the scrape, and cover it with a sterile bandage.

For **writing models** with examples, see *Teaching Resources* pp. 47–61. Rubrics are also provided.

Life Skills

Communicate
Make Responsible Decisions
Manage Stress
Refuse
Resolve Conflicts
Set Goals

Objectives
► Identify steps for making responsible decisions.
► Use the decision-making steps to make healthful decisions about safety.

Program Resources
► Activity Book p. 24
► Poster 8

1. MOTIVATE

Invite volunteers to describe several routes they could use to bike from home to school. For each of the routes they offer, ask them to identify what risks may be involved. Guide the discussion so that students realize there are consequences involved with choosing any route.

2. TEACH

Direct students' attention to the photos of Kelly thinking about his route choices.

Step 1
What are Kelly's choices? the main road or the park path

Step 2
Utilize critical thinking in desision making.

Critical Thinking Why is it important for Kelly to eliminate a choice that is illegal or against family rules?
Knowingly making a wrong choice will get him in trouble. Eliminating bad choices makes the decision-making process easier.

Make Responsible Decisions
That Prevent Injury

Sometimes you need to make choices to protect your health and safety. You can use the steps for **Making Responsible Decisions** to help you make healthful choices.

Kelly is going to ride his bike to soccer practice after school. He can take several different routes. Which one should he choose for getting to practice safely?

1 **Find out about the choices you could make.**

Kelly looks at two possible routes—the main road and the park path.

2 **Eliminate choices that are against your family rules.**

The main road is shorter, but it has traffic. Kelly's parents have told him not to ride his bike where there is traffic.

146

Social Studies

Civic Responsibility Discuss with students the role of civic responsibility as it relates to bicycle helmet laws and riding along bicycle paths.

ACTIVITY BOOK P. 24

Name _____

Problem Solving

Life Skill
Make Responsible Decisions

Steps for Making Responsible Decisions
1. Find out about the choices you could make.
2. Eliminate any choices that are illegal or against your family rules.
3. Ask yourself: What is the possible result of each choice? Which choice would show good character?
4. Make what seems to be the best choice.

Use the steps to help these students make responsible decisions.

A. Amanda is at the pool with her swim team. Before practice, some of the girls start a game of "chicken" at the deep end of the pool. Amanda knows the game is fun but that it can be dangerous. She's not sure if she should join in, sit at poolside, or tell a lifeguard or the swim team coach.
• How can Amanda use the steps for **Making Responsible Decisions** to choose what to do?

Possible answers: If Amanda decides to join in, she is putting her
safety at risk. If she sits quietly at poolside, some other team member
may get hurt. If she tells a lifeguard or a coach, her teammates may get
into trouble, but they will be safe. The last choice is the safest and
shows good character.

B. Mac has invited Duane to his house after school. Mac lives about a mile from school. Today, like most days, Mac rode his bicycle to school. Mac suggests that they take side streets where there is little traffic. That way, Duane could ride on the handlebars, and they would get to Mac's house quickly. Duane points out that Mac could leave his bike at school, and they could both walk or take the city bus to Mac's house.
• How can the boys make a responsible decision about what to do?

Possible answer: If Duane rides on the handlebars, both boys may get
hurt. However, if Mac leaves his bike at school, it might get stolen.
Duane can decide to walk to Mac's, and Mac can walk his bike home as
well. This would be a safe choice and show good character.

Available online.
www.harcourtschool.com/health

3 Ask yourself: What is the possible result of each choice? Which choice would show responsibility?

 4 Make what seems to be the best choice.

Kelly realizes that the path through the park is safer. Choosing the main road would not be a responsible decision.

Kelly takes the park path and gets to practice safely and on time. Riding a little farther helps him warm up, too. He is pleased with his decision.

Problem Solving

A. Jason is in a car pool with some of his basketball teammates. When he gets into the car, he notices that none of the other riders are wearing safety belts. Jason knows that he is supposed to wear a safety belt when he is in a vehicle.

- Use the steps for **Making Responsible Decisions** to help Jason make the best decision.

B. Selena has an early-morning paper route. She rides her bicycle to deliver the papers. Today her bicycle headlight is not working. It is still dark outside.

- How can Selena make a decision that shows responsibility for her safety in this situation?

147

Using the Poster

Activity Have students illustrate comic strips showing situations in which students use the steps for Making Responsible Decisions in appropriate ways.

Display the poster to remind students of the steps for making responsible decisions.

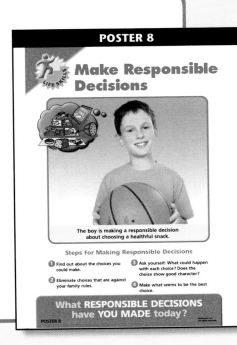

POSTER 8

Make Responsible Decisions

The boy is making a responsible decision about choosing a healthful snack.

Steps for Making Responsible Decisions

❶ Find out about the choices you could make.

❷ Eliminate choices that are against your family's rules.

❸ Ask yourself: What could happen with each choice? Does the choice show good character?

❹ Make what seems to be the best choice.

What RESPONSIBLE DECISIONS have YOU MADE today?

POSTER 8

Step 3

What could happen with each choice? The park path is longer, so it could take more time to ride than the main road. The main road has potholes and a lot of traffic. Kelly's bike could hit a pothole and he could be injured. The traffic makes the road more dangerous than the park path.

Building Good Character

Remind students that when making decisions, they should think about whether their choices show good character. Here are questions they can ask themselves: Am I being responsible? Am I showing consideration for others? Does my decision show that I am being a good citizen? Am I respecting others?

Step 4

What happened as a result of Kelly's choice? He had a safe and uneventful ride to soccer practice, and he used the extra time on his bike to help him warm up for soccer practice.

3. WRAP UP

Problem Solving

Answers should reflect the steps for Making Responsible Decisions. Have students assess the role of assertiveness on problem solving.

A Jason should think about the choices he could make. He should make a decision based on his family's rules and what seems to be the best choice.

B Selena should think about the choices she could make and make a decision based on her family's rules and what seems to be the best choice. Selena would show she is trustworthy if she borrows her brother's bike, which has a working headlight, walks her delivery route rather than rides, or waits until it is light enough to ride her bike safely.

LESSON 2

Pages 148–156

Objectives
► Practice safety at play and in motor vehicles.
► Analyze safety equipment.

When Minutes Count . . .
Assign the Quick Study, Lesson 2, Activity Book pp. 21–22 (shown on p. 139).

Program Resources
► Activity Book pp. 21–22
► Transparency 5

Vocabulary
pedestrians p. 154

Daily Fitness Tip

Tell students that daily physical activity is important for people of all ages and that biking can be a good way to get some of that activity. However, biking can be dangerous if safety rules and tips aren't followed.

 For more guidelines on safe cycling and skating, see *Be Active! Resources for Physical Education,* p. 187.

1. MOTIVATE

Write this sentence on the board: *A playground is always a safe place for children to play.*

Ask students to recall their own experiences on playgrounds. **Do you agree that a playground is always a safe place for children to play? Why or why not?** A playground is usually a safe place to play, but some obvious dangers can make a playground unsafe.

Practicing Safety

Lesson Focus
Using safety gear and following safety rules can help prevent accidents and injuries.

Why Learn This?
You can use what you learn to help reduce the risk of injuries when playing, riding your bike, and taking part in sports.

Vocabulary
pedestrians

You Can Prevent Injuries While Playing

One of the best ways to prevent injuries is to know and follow safety rules. Most safety rules are common sense. Here are some examples: Play in areas that are safe and familiar. Avoid places where people may carry weapons, such as guns and knives. Stay away from areas where you know crimes have taken place. Don't play in areas where there is traffic, such as in streets and parking lots. Never push, shove, or fight while playing with others. Always wait your turn.

Playground Safety

A playground is supposed to be a safe place to play. But every year in the United States, about 200,000 children are taken to emergency rooms because of playground injuries. It's important to be careful and to follow safety rules when using playgrounds.

◄ Always use playground equipment properly. For example, go down the slide feet first, and hold handrails or ropes tightly when climbing.

148

Meeting Individual Needs
Leveled Activities

BELOW-LEVEL **Product Recalls** Have students research information about the Consumer Product Safety Commission (CPSC), including who funds the CPSC, what its goals are, and how it determines whether a product should be recalled.

ON-LEVEL **Write to a Manufacturer** Have students write letters to a manufacturer of safety gear. Tell students to ask how the gear was developed and how it is tested. Students may wish to ask about new equipment being developed.

CHALLENGE **Change Public Policy** Students can call a local consumer advocacy group to learn how the group interacts with the CPSC to set new guidelines for products. After students report on the consumer group, have the class discuss whether consumers have power over public safety.

◀ Be careful when walking around swings. Never walk or play close to a moving swing.

Falls are common causes of injuries on playgrounds. Kids fall when climbing ladders, when running in slippery areas, and when climbing or standing on surfaces that slide or tip.

Some playground equipment is old or unsafe. It can have splinters, sharp corners, loose parts, or bolts and nails that stick out. Before you play, have an adult make sure the equipment is in good condition.

Another important part of playground safety is the surface on which the equipment is placed. Softer materials, such as sand, chipped or shredded bark, and shredded rubber, make good surfaces for playgrounds. These surfaces help break a fall. Hard surfaces, such as pavement and dirt, are not as safe to play on.

The clothes you wear can also help keep you from being injured. Always wear closed shoes when using playground equipment. Broken glass, splinters, and other sharp objects can be hidden in sand or wood chips and injure bare feet. Don't wear loose clothing or clothing with drawstrings. Keep your shoes tied. Remove necklaces or scarves at the playground. Loose fabric, drawstrings, shoelaces, and necklaces can get caught in playground equipment and lead to injury. Also remove bicycle or other helmets before playing.

SUMMARIZE List four things you can do to play safely on a playground.
Any four of these: Use equipment properly; be careful; follow safety rules; check equipment condition; check playground surface; wear proper clothing and shoes; remove helmet; be careful around swings; wait your turn; don't push or fight.

149

Consumer Activity

Make Buying Decisions
Marla's neighborhood is getting a new playground. Marla's mom is a member of the neighborhood purchasing committee. Make a list of features the committee should consider as it chooses equipment for the new playground.

2. TEACH

Interpret Visuals—Pictures
Direct attention to the pictures on these pages of students on playground equipment. Ask what safe and unsafe behaviors students can identify in the pictures. Be sure that students notice the boy with headphones. Point out that he isn't paying attention to where he is walking and could be hit by the child on the swing.

Discuss
Help students demonstrate strategies for preventing accidental injuries.

Critical Thinking What other advice might you give children to help them stay safe and avoid injuries on playgrounds? Possible answers: Hold on to both sides of a swing's chains or ropes; watch out for people walking in front of or behind you when you are on a swing; don't jump from moving swings or from the top of slides; go down a slide feet first.

Consumer Health
Making Buying Decisions Possible answers: playground surface (chips vs. rubber); equipment free of sharp corners; bolts unlikely to loosen; enough room around swings; minimal maintenance

Health Background

Playground Safety About 15 children die each year in the United States from injuries related to playground equipment. As many as 200,000 children receive emergency room treatment for playground injuries. The National Program for Playground Safety, established by the University of Northern Iowa, is working to raise awareness amid growing concerns for the safety of children on playgrounds.

Source: *Consumer Product Safety Commission*

For more background, visit the **Webliography** in Teacher Resources at **www.harcourtschool.com/health Keyword** safety

 **Art**

Dangerous Diane and Safe Sam Encourage students to make comic strips that compare the actions of two young characters— one who practices safety and one who doesn't. Provide the following example to prompt ideas: Dangerous Diane and Safe Sam are at a water park. Dangerous Diane horses around, runs on the slippery pavement, and ignores the lifeguard. Safe Sam walks, pays attention to the other swimmers when in the pool, and listens to the lifeguard.

 Math

Playground Safety Check Have groups of students make playground safety checklists to evaluate the safety level of local playgrounds. Each playground gets 100 points to start. For each major hazard, students deduct 10 points; for each minor hazard, they deduct 5 points. Students can make a bar graph of the information to compare the safety levels of the different playgrounds. Help students find ways to present their results to a parents' group or to a local official so that the information can be used to improve safety.

TEACH *continued*

Interpret Visuals—Pictures

Direct attention to the pictures of the children using the safety belts. Read and discuss the safety tips provided in the caption.

Discuss

Problem Solving What can you do if the shoulder part of the safety belt is too high and crosses your neck or face? Use a booster seat.

Washington, Rhode Island, Delaware, North Carolina, and other states have had laws requiring children age twelve and under to ride in the back seat of any vehicle that has a passenger-side air bag. Tickets and fines can be issued for violations.

Critical Thinking Who should be responsible for making certain that children are sitting in the safest place possible? Students should be able to support their answers. Possible answer: the adult driving the car

Content-Area Reading Support

Using Subheadings Direct students to read the subheadings—the phrases in boldface type at the beginning of certain paragraphs—on pages 150 and 151. Explain that a subhheading tells what the text following it discusses. Call on volunteers to predict what kind of information will follow each of the subheadings.

Health Background

Air Bags Automobile air bags, introduced in the late 1980s, are credited with saving an estimated 8,367 lives from 1987 to 2001. However, these lifesaving devices, which release at speeds of more than 200 miles per hour, pose some risks as well. Air bags can cause serious injuries and even death, especially among young children. Remind students that air bags should never be used without safety belts or as a substitute for them. Emphasize that the safest place to ride in a car is in the back seat, wearing a safety belt.

Source: *National Highway Traffic Safety Administration*

Adjust your safety belt so that it lies across your shoulder. The belt should not cross your neck or face. Adjust the lap part of the belt so that it fits snugly across your hips, not your stomach. Children shorter than 57 inches tall must use a booster so the safety belt fits correctly. ▶

Did You Know?

Although vehicle air bags help protect adults from injury during crashes, children age twelve and under should ride in the back seat of a vehicle to avoid being hurt by an air bag. Some vehicles have a switch that allows the driver to turn off the passenger-side air bag if there is no other place for a child to ride.

150

Safety Equipment Reduces the Risk of Injury

Helmets, mouth guards, kneepads, and safety belts are just some of the kinds of equipment that help prevent injuries. Using the right safety equipment is especially important when you are riding in motor vehicles, bicycling, skating, skateboarding, and playing any active sport.

Vehicle Safety

Following safety rules while riding in motor vehicles can save your life. The leading cause of accidental injury or death of children age five to fourteen is motor vehicle crashes. Wearing a safety belt is the most important thing you can do to prevent injury while riding in a car. In fact, many states have laws that require everyone in a vehicle to wear a safety belt. The best type of safety belt is one that crosses over your shoulder and lap. Never share a safety belt with another person.

Other ways to reduce the risk of injury while riding in a car include staying in your seat and not bothering the driver. Never lean out the car window. Be sure to keep your fingers and hands inside the vehicle.

ESL/ELL Support

COMPREHENSIBLE INPUT Help students identify important safety gear.

Beginning Provide students with pictures of the safety gear described in this lesson. Ask volunteers to pantomime activities mentioned in the lesson. Help students choose pictures of the safety gear that should be used for each activity.

Intermediate Have students draw pictures of people involved in various activities mentioned in this lesson. Tell students to draw and label the appropriate safety gear for each activity.

Advanced Have students make a chart that shows the safety gear and the activities for which each kind should be used.

Helmets

Some places require all children to wear helmets while bicycling, skateboarding, and riding scooters. Even if your area doesn't have this law, you should always wear a helmet.

For the best protection, a helmet should fit snugly but comfortably. It should be level on your head, not tipped forward or backward. People playing sports such as football, hockey, and baseball should wear helmets with face guards to protect the nose and eyes.

Mouth Guards and Goggles

Mouth guards help protect the mouth, teeth, and tongue from painful injuries during sports. Goggles help protect the eyes from impact with elbows, flying objects, and other hazards. Goggles are often worn when playing racquetball and while snowboarding.

Wrist Guards, Elbow Pads, and Kneepads

Skateboarders, skaters, and players of team sports can easily get wrist, elbow, and knee injuries. These injuries can range from minor scratches to broken bones. Wearing wrist guards, elbow pads, and kneepads when playing certain sports can help reduce the risk of injuries to these areas of the body.

DRAW CONCLUSIONS Why should you know the correct safety gear to wear for a particular activity?
Each sport or activity has different safety gear requirements.

Using safety gear that fits you properly is important. Gear that is too big or too small won't protect you as well as gear that fits correctly. ▶

PERSONAL HEALTH PLAN ▶

Real-Life Situation Wearing safety gear is an important part of preventing injuries while being active. Suppose you are going to add a sport to your health plan.
Real-Life Plan Tell what sport you will choose. List the safety gear you will need.

151

Interpret Visuals—Pictures

Ask students to read the label for each piece of equipment pictured and explain how each item can help prevent injuries. For example, helmets protect hockey players, bicyclists, skaters, and skateboarders from serious head injuries such as concussions and skull fractures; reflective vests help make runners and bicyclists visible to motorists and help protect against injuries from motor vehicles.

Critical Thinking What other kinds of safety equipment can help protect you when you ride a bicycle or skateboard, go skating, or play other sports? Possible answers: long pants; padded clothing; athletic shoes with appropriate soles

Problem Solving What would you say to someone who teases you for wearing safety equipment when you ride a bicycle or skateboard, go skating, or play other sports? Encourage students to use facts and humor in their responses. For example, they might say something like "I'd rather have flat hair than a flat head."

PERSONAL HEALTH PLAN ▶

Have students analyze the components of a personal health maintenance plan for individuals, such as personal safety. Plans should include:
- Name and description of sport
- Name of gear and its safety advantage
- If appropriate, check with national association of the sport to learn about recommended safety gear.

Integrated Language Arts/ Reading Skills

Public Safety Announcements
Point out that some adults who always buckle up their children may not always use their own safety belts. Ask students to write and tape-record three 10-second public-safety announcements that urge people of all ages to fasten their safety belts. Students might contact a local radio station to ask the station to play their announcements as part of a public-safety campaign.

Teacher Tip

Sports Injuries Even when sports players wear protective gear, injuries occur. Have students investigate a sport of their choosing to learn the most common injuries for that sport, how and why the injuries usually occur, and the recommended treatment and recovery time for those injuries. Tell them also to find out what players can do to help avoid each type of injury. Encourage students to share with the class what they learn.

Discuss

The Snell Memorial Foundation, a nonprofit group dedicated to establishing helmet safety standards throughout the world through research and development, provides these guidelines for choosing a helmet.

- Size is important. A helmet should be comfortable and snug. Try on a variety of helmets before making a decision.
- Note the comfort and snugness of the chin strap around your ears and under your chin. Be sure that the helmet does not shift on your head.
- Make sure the helmet is worn properly—straight and low on the forehead, a little above the eyebrows.

Critical Thinking Why are the size and fit of a bicycle helmet important? If the helmet doesn't fit right, it could slip or come off during a fall, and then it would not protect you.

Consumer Health
Access Valid Health Information

Retroreflective materials are marketed under the trademarked names of Scotchlite, Reflexite, and JPC Reflex. If possible, have samples of retroreflective tape for students to examine.

Health Background

Helmets Thousands of children and adolescents are seriously injured or killed in bicycle crashes each year. Studies indicate that 75 percent of bicycle-related deaths among children could have been prevented with the use of bicycle helmets. Riders without helmets are fourteen times more likely to be involved in fatal crashes than riders who wear helmets. In fact, between 135 and 155 fewer children ages fourteen and under would be killed each year if all bike riders wore helmets.

Source: *National Safe Kids Campaign*

Consumer Activity

Access Valid Health Information When buying clothing for bike riding, look for *retro-reflective* material. It bounces light back to its source, making it 1,500 times as bright as white clothing. Compare the prices of regular and retro-reflective clothing. Summarize your findings.

How You Can Ride a Bike Safely

Besides always wearing a helmet, you should follow several other safety rules when you ride a bike. Always ride in the same direction as traffic. Wear reflective clothing or bright colors so that drivers can see you. Watch for doors of parked cars being opened and for hazards on the road. Keep your bike in good working condition. Never carry another person on a bike, and never ride by holding onto the back of a moving vehicle.

Riding your bike after dark is not a good idea. It's hard for you to see hazards and hard for drivers to see you. If you must ride your bike after dark, be sure to check with your parents. Make sure they know when you are leaving and what route you are taking. Your bike should have equipment for nighttime riding, such as reflectors on the front and rear, on the wheels, and on the pedals. Your bike should also have bright front and rear lights.

MAIN IDEA AND DETAILS Give details to support this statement: *You can bicycle safely by following safety rules.*
Possible responses: Wear a helmet; ride in the same direction as traffic; wear reflective clothing; watch for doors of parked cars being opened and for road hazards; keep your bike in good condition.

▲ If you must ride your bike at dawn or dusk, be sure to wear a reflective vest. Also, be sure your helmet has reflective tape on it.

For Bike Riders

❶ Learn and practice riding straight, making turns, signaling, braking, stopping, and looking over your shoulder to change lanes.

❷ Obey all traffic signs, signals, and rules.

❸ Wear a bicycle helmet that fits correctly.

152

Meeting Individual Needs
Leveled Activities

BELOW-LEVEL Design a Reflective Vest Have students design a reflective vest that would increase visibility and be lightweight. Display their designs.

ON-LEVEL Survey Street Safety Direct students to survey their community's safety features. Are the traffic signs easy to read? Are bicycle paths and routes clearly marked? What are the safest areas for bicycle riding?

ADVANCED Request a Park Students can write the city council to request a bike path or skating park. Encourage students to tell why they are requesting the facility, what it should include, how it will improve safety for bikers and skaters. If current facilities exist, students can write to thank the council.

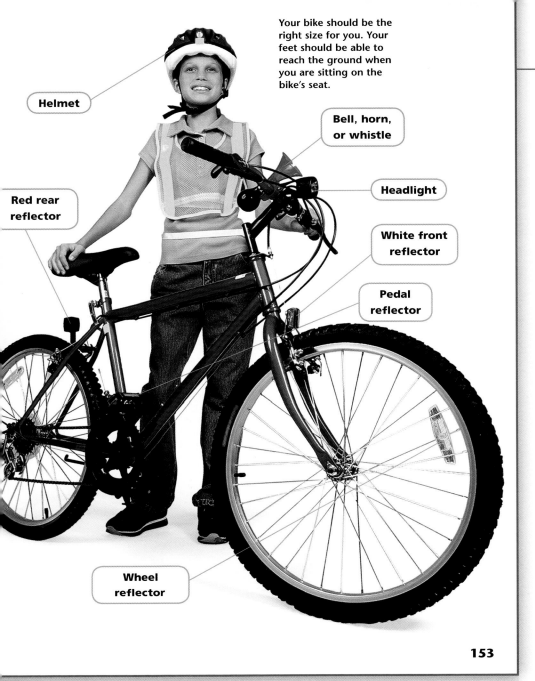

Your bike should be the right size for you. Your feet should be able to reach the ground when you are sitting on the bike's seat.

Helmet

Bell, horn, or whistle

Headlight

Red rear reflector

White front reflector

Pedal reflector

Wheel reflector

Interpret Visuals—Pictures

Draw attention to the picture of the bicyclist and the bicycle. Ask students to explain how each labeled piece of equipment helps prevent injuries. Then have them read the caption.

Critical Thinking Why is it important that your feet touch the ground when you sit on the seat? Possible answer: so that if you must stop suddenly, you will be able to prevent yourself from falling

Content-Area Reading Support

Using Signal Words Have students read the last sentence of the paragraph: *Your bike should also have bright front and rear lights.* Point out that the word *also* signals a list of two or more facts, ideas, or things. Tell students that when they come across this word, they should pause briefly to recall or reread related information that preceded it.

Health Background

Traumatic Brain Injury Traumatic brain injury (TBI) is sudden physical damage to the brain. Damage is usually confined to a small area of the brain. However, there is often diffuse brain injury, or damage to several other areas of the brain. Victims may have difficulty communicating. They may also have difficulty with swallowing, walking, remembering, thinking, and maintaining balance and coordination, and may experience changes in the ability to smell. Approximately 200,000 Americans die each year from TBI injuries. About 10 percent of the surviving individuals have mild to moderate problems that threaten their ability to live independently. Another 200,000 have serious problems that may require institutionalization or some other form of close supervision.

Source: *National Institute on Deafness and Other Communication Disorders, National Institutes of Health*

 For more background, visit the **Webliography** in Teacher Resources at **www.harcourtschool.com/health** **Keyword** safety

Teacher Tip

Night Riding Riding a bicycle at night is dangerous and should be avoided; young children should never ride at night. If students must ride at night, remind them to ride on familiar, well-lit streets with an adult. They should also equip their bicycles with the brightest light possible and wear a reflective vest or light-colored clothing. Additionally, night riders should always assume that they are not visible to drivers and should proceed with extreme caution.

Cultural Connection

Asia and the Bicycle People in China and other Asian countries have long regarded walking and bicycling as their main modes of transportation. Many Asians use their bikes to travel long distances on a daily or regular basis. Encourage students to investigate the historical importance and popularity of the bicycle in Asia; how the growing popularity of the automobile in China has changed its bicycle tradition and its environment; and what rules help ensure the safety of bicycle riders in Chinese cities.

Discuss

Have students read the bicycling rules. After each bulleted item, stop to query students. For example, after reading the first rule, ask students why it is best to bike in the same direction as the cars around you. Allow students to offer several explanations, and have the class determine which is the most important. Continue discussing each rule in turn.

Critical Thinking **Why is it important for bicycle riders and car drivers to obey the same road safety rules?** to set a pattern of behavior in order to avoid confusion and crashes

Bicyclists must stay alert at all times. Common road hazards, such as sand, leaves, potholes, and railroad tracks, can cause bicyclists to fall. Rainy, wet conditions pose additional problems, especially when sidewalks and streets turn icy and slick. An alert bicyclist looks ahead and prepares to maneuver around any unexpected hazards. When a hazard is spotted, the bicyclist should plan what he or she is going to do and then check traffic ahead and behind, looking for a place to safely go around the object. Once the bicyclist determines a course of action, he or she should clearly signal the intended course of action.

Problem Solving **What should you do if you are riding your bike and you are unsure of your ability to handle a difficult road hazard?** Possible answer: Get off the bike and walk it around the hazard.

Activity

Citizenship Discuss with students whether they show good citizenship while riding a bicycle. Make certain that students relate the concept of good citizenship with the activity of obeying the traffic laws of their community.

▲ If there is a pedestrian signal at an intersection, wait for a green light. Then walk your bike across the street.

ACTIVITY

Building Good Character

Citizenship An important part of being a good citizen is obeying the laws of your community. How can you show good citizenship while riding a bike? See page 273 for ideas.

154

Rules Make Bicycling Safer

When you ride a bike on a street, you are expected to know and obey traffic laws. Following the rules below also helps protect you and drivers from hazards and accidents.

- Ride in single file, close to the curb, and in the same direction as traffic. Ride in a straight line to the left of cars parked along the curb. Never ride between parked cars. Whenever possible, ride in bike lanes.
- Never wear headphones while riding your bike. You might not hear approaching traffic.
- Pass parked cars slowly, watching for people who might open doors into the street.
- Be careful around **pedestrians** (pih•DES•tree•uhnz), or people who are walking. If pedestrians are crossing a street, stop to let them cross in front of you.
- If you have to walk your bike in the street, walk facing traffic, on the left side of the street.
- Know and obey all traffic signs and signals.
- When entering the street from a driveway or starting to walk your bike across an intersection, STOP. LOOK left, right, and left again. LISTEN for traffic, and wait for it to pass. Again look left, right, and left. THINK, and decide whether it is safe to go.
- Use signals to alert other traffic before you make a stop or a turn.

Teacher Tip

Consumer Awareness: Types of Helmets Encourage students to investigate and report on the three types of bicycle helmets available: hard-shelled, thin-shelled, and no shell. If possible, provide samples of each helmet type for students to examine. Students may wish to visit the Snell Memorial Foundation website for a list of Snell-certified helmets.

Integrated Language Arts/ Reading Skills

Rules for All Point out that pedestrians also have a responsibility to follow safety rules. Encourage partners to expand the For Bike Riders chart on page 152 to include road rules for automobiles and pedestrians. Students can use their own experiences and can look in reference books and on the Internet for additional information. Have all students combine their information into a single list.

In addition to these safety rules, here are a few other tips to help keep you safe on a bike: Think ahead ten seconds to avoid hazards. This means that you should check the road ahead one block at a time. Keep your eyes moving. Scan the areas around you. Watch for things that are about to happen, such as a car coming up behind you, a ball rolling into the street, or a car backing out of a driveway.

 SEQUENCE Tell the steps you should follow when starting to cross an intersection with your bike. Students should describe the Stop, Look, Listen, and Think steps in the correct order.

Quick Activity

Listing Steps Suppose you are riding a bike in traffic. You come to a busy intersection where you plan to turn left. List the steps you should take, including the hand signals you should use.

Using hand signals is an important part of bike safety. Study the hand signals, shown here from left to right, for a stop, a right turn, and a left turn. Then practice each one.

155

Interpret Visuals—Pictures

Draw attention to the pictures of children using bicycle hand signals. Help students practice these signals by initiating a game of "Simon Says." Have students stand. Tell them they are to make each hand signal if it follows the phrase *Simon says.* Students who give incorrect signals or give signals without the password take their seats.

Discuss

Critical Thinking How important is it for bicycle riders to know the meanings of traffic signs and signals? Why? Possible answer: very important to avoid crashes and injuries

Critical Thinking In your opinion, what is the greatest safety hazard for bicycle riders? Explain why you think as you do. Accept all reasonable answers.

Quick Activity

Listing Steps Steps should include the following: slow down; signal left turn; check traffic behind and in front; check oncoming traffic; and turn into the right lane. Discuss with students what they should do if there are two lanes of traffic in each direction. Point out that in this case, the wise choice would be to get off the bike and walk it across the intersection.

 Science

Cars, Bicycles, Pedestrians, and the Environment Ask students to research the following:

- how automobiles contribute to air pollution
- how pollution endangers the health and safety of people
- how riding a bike and walking can help reduce air pollution and improve a person's health at the same time

Invite students to share what they learn with the class.

 Social Studies

Local Bicycle Trails Communities around the country are responding to increased public support for safe walking and bicycling paths. Groups such as Rails to Trails, the Bicycle Industry Organization, and the League of American Bicyclists promote progress on these bicycle-related issues. Encourage students to identify bicycle trails that are already established in their community and to find out about plans that exist for future bike trails.

3. WRAP UP

Lesson 2 Summary and Review

1. helmet; pedestrians; hand signals; mouth guard; goggles

2. Possible answers: helmet, lamp, horn, front-tire reflectors, chain guard, rear-tire reflectors

3. Look ahead of and behind you, and then think of a plan to avoid the grate. Signal your intentions so others around you know what you plan to do.

4. Answers may include the following:

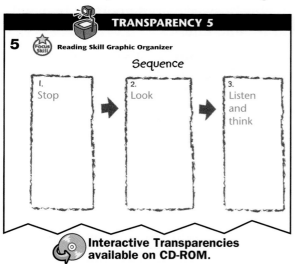

TRANSPARENCY 5

5 Reading Skill Graphic Organizer

Sequence

1. Stop → 2. Look → 3. Listen and think

 Interactive Transparencies available on CD-ROM.

5. Answers will vary but should include safety rules pertaining to riding in traffic; what to do at intersections; and hazards such as parked cars, other bikers, children playing, or potholes.

> For **writing models** with examples, see *Teaching Resources* pp. 47–61. Rubrics are also provided.

 When Minutes Count . . .

Quick Study Students can use *Activity Book* pp. 21–22 (shown on p. 139) as they complete each lesson in this chapter.

Traffic Signs and Signals

When riding a bike, you must obey the same traffic signs and signals that the driver of a vehicle does.

1 You must make a full stop before you enter or cross a street.

2 You must yield, or let other traffic pass, before you proceed. Slow down and be ready to stop.

3 You may not ride your bike on this road.

4 One-way traffic. Traffic may go only in the direction shown by the arrow.

5 Do not enter. If you did enter, you would be going against traffic.

6 Railroad tracks ahead. Before crossing, STOP, LOOK in both directions, and LISTEN.

7 Red means "stop." Yellow means "caution." Because the light will turn red soon, prepare to stop. Green means "go." Be sure traffic has stopped before you go ahead.

COMPARE AND CONTRAST **Compare and contrast the use of stop signs and yield signs.**

4 Both are traffic signs. Stop: Stop fully before entering or crossing the street; proceed when you know it is safe. Yield: Let other traffic pass before you go; slow down; be ready to stop.

Lesson 2 Summary and Review

1 Summarize with Vocabulary

Use vocabulary and other terms from this lesson to complete the statements.

When riding your bike, always wear a(n) _____ to protect yourself from a head injury. Watch for _____, or people who are walking. Using _____ tells drivers what you are planning to do next. When playing sports, wear a _____ to protect your teeth and _____ to protect your eyes.

2 List six items necessary for riding a bike safely.

3 Critical Thinking Suppose you are riding your bike and see a sewer grate in your path ahead. What should you do?

4 SEQUENCE Draw and complete this graphic organizer to show the steps to take when entering the street from a driveway.

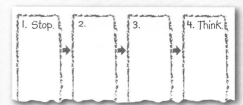

1. Stop. → 2. → 3. → 4. Think.

5 Write to Inform—Description

Draw a map of a route you often take on your bike or when walking. List the safety rules to follow on this route.

 ## Art

Bicycle Safety Board Game
Encourage small groups of students to design and produce bicycle safety board games for two to four players. The games should incorporate the safety tips and rules presented in this lesson, typical road hazards, and the traffic safety signs and signals illustrated. Students might enjoy demonstrating their games for other classes and faculty members.

 ## Drama

On the Road Encourage groups of students to write and perform skits about road safety for pedestrians, bicycle riders, and motor vehicle drivers, including car, truck, and school bus drivers. Invite students to present their skits to the class. Have the class evaluate how well the safety issues discussed in this lesson were covered in the skit.

Caring

Show Compassion for Others

When people have been injured, they need help—not just at the time of the injury, but during recovery as well. Here's what you can do to show that you care about a person who has been injured.

- **At an accident scene, stay with the person who has been injured. Call for help, if needed.**
- **Help the injured person stay calm by telling him or her that help is on the way.**
- **If a classmate has been injured and misses school, collect homework assignments for him or her. Help the classmate, if needed, with the work.**
- **Phone the injured person regularly to offer support. Ask what you can do for him or her.**
- **Visit the injured person. Take along games or funny videos to help cheer the person.**

Even when someone isn't injured, you can show you care by pointing out safety hazards. Offer to help reduce hazards at home, at school, or in your neighborhood.

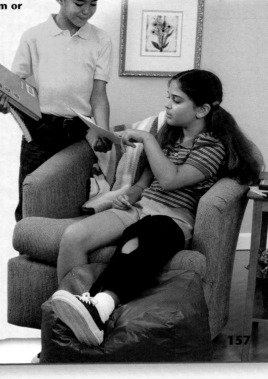

Activity

Role-play with a partner situations in which someone is injured. Practice showing compassion by applying the tips on this page. Include other things you might do to help the person feel better.

Using the Poster

Activity Suggest that students design and display their posters about caring.

Display Poster 1 to remind students of ways to show caring. The posters can be displayed in the classroom, school cafeteria, or other common areas.

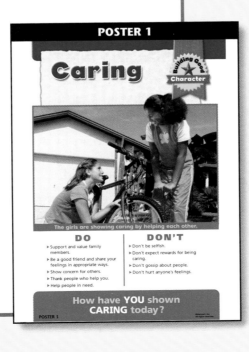

POSTER 1

Caring

The girls are showing caring by helping each other.

DO
- Support and value family members.
- Be a good friend and share your feelings in appropriate ways.
- Show concern for others.
- Thank people who help you.
- Help people in need.

DON'T
- Don't be selfish.
- Don't expect rewards for being caring.
- Don't gossip about people.
- Don't hurt anyone's feelings.

How have **YOU** shown **CARING** today?

POSTER 1

Building Good Character

Building Good Character

Caring
Citizenship
Fairness
Respect
Responsibility
Trustworthiness

Objective
► Identify ways to show compassion for injured persons.

Program Resource
► Poster 1

BEFORE READING
Work with students as they generate a list of ways they can show compassion for injured persons. Then lead a discussion of ways to show caring for injured or ill persons.

DISCUSS
After students have read the page, ask volunteers to restate the points of caring and compassion. Ask students to add examples not listed in the text.

ACTIVITY
Have students work in groups of three—an injured person, a spectator, and a compassionate person. Allow enough time for students to exchange roles so that each student has an opportunity to play each role. Encourage students to personalize the situation by including actions they would be likely to take if the injured person was a family member, a close friend, or a stranger.

Objectives
► Explain how to prevent home fires.
► Recognize fire hazards in the home.
► Describe how to survive a home fire.

When Minutes Count . . .
Assign the Quick Study, Lesson 3, Activity Book pp. 21–22 (shown on p. 139).

Program Resources
► Activity Book pp. 21–22, 25
► Transparency 5

Vocabulary
flammable p. 158,
natural disasters p. 164

Daily Fitness Tip

Building strong lungs and strong, flexible muscles not only aids health but also can be important during emergencies, such as when escaping a fire. Remind students that they should engage in physical activity every day.

 For more guidelines on choosing activities for fitness, see *Be Active! Resources for Physical Education,* p. 137.

1. MOTIVATE

Provide students with local newspapers, or have them look at the news section of a website for a local television station, radio station, or newspaper. Ask students to count how many home fires occurred in one month in your city or town.

Critical Thinking Do you think home fires are a problem in our city? Explain. Accept all reasonable answers supported by the data.

Problem Solving What is the first thing you would do if you found that your house or school had any hazards? Allow a variety of answers, and list them on the board. Have students review their responses at the end of the lesson. All responses should involve seeking advice from parents or educational personnel first.

What You Can Do to Prevent Fires

Each year in the United States, almost 40,000 children under the age of fourteen are injured in fires. You can help prevent a fire in your home by acting responsibly with heat and flame, by eliminating fire hazards, and by practicing fire safety. The list on the next page tells how to prevent some fires.

Lesson Focus
You can do many things to prevent fires. You can take steps to safely escape a fire.

Why Learn This?
Knowing fire safety rules and how to escape a fire can save your life and the lives of others.

Vocabulary
flammable
natural disasters

Almost 25 percent of all fires are home fires. Having smoke alarms and knowing how to use a fire extinguisher can save lives. But the most important thing is to reduce the hazards that cause many home fires. Make a list of the fire hazards you find in this home. ►

158

 ESL/ELL Support

COMPREHENSIBLE INPUT Reinforce identification of flammable items.

Beginning Ask volunteers to point to a hazard in the picture on this page that they think might cause a fire. Help them pronounce the name of each hazard.

Intermediate Ask pairs of students to list the fire hazards shown on this page. Tell students to group hazards according to the rooms where they are likely to be found.

Advanced Help students write a sentence or two about three of the hazards they find in the illustration. For each hazard, students should explain why the hazard could cause a fire and what should be done to avoid the hazard.

- Materials that will burn if they are exposed to enough heat are **flammable** (FLAM•uh•buhl). Things such as newspapers are flammable. Curtains and blankets may be flammable. They should be kept away from heat sources such as space heaters, lamps, and candles.
- Store flammable liquids, such as gasoline, outside your home in a well-ventilated area.
- Matches, lighters, and other sources of flame should be kept out of the reach of children.
- Electrical fires can start from overloaded electrical outlets. Avoid plugging several appliances, such as a microwave, a blender, and a toaster, into one outlet.

DRAW CONCLUSIONS Why should flammable liquids be stored outside the home?
They could easily start a fire if they are spilled.

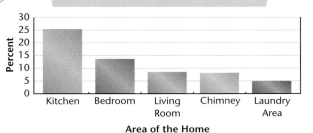
Where Home Fires Start

Percent (y-axis: 0, 5, 10, 15, 20, 25, 30)
Areas (x-axis): Kitchen, Bedroom, Living Room, Chimney, Laundry Area
Area of the Home

Quick Activity

Analyze Data Study the graph. In which of the areas shown do the most home fires start? Infer what the causes of fires in each area might be. How can each cause be eliminated?

159

Teacher Tip

Dangerous Water Water is the most familiar extinguishing material, and it is one of the most effective. A water extinguisher can put out fires in wood, paper, and cardboard. However, a water extinguisher can be dangerous in the wrong situation. Water does not work well on electrical fires, in which it may conduct the current and possibly electrocute a person. For fires involving flammable liquids, water will dilute and spread the liquid, making the fire larger in scope.

Science

Fire Extinguishers Have students gather information about fire extinguishers, such as what materials they contain and their ratings (that is, what kinds of fires they can extinguish). Students can present their findings in 60-second public-service announcements for TV. Students can support their presentation with visuals showing extinguisher ratings. (Class A: wood, plastic, and paper; Class B: burning liquids, such as gasoline and grease; Class C: electrical fires; Class D: burning metal)

2. TEACH

Interpret Visuals—Pictures
Have students examine the picture of the home and read the labels. Have students describe the value of seeking advice from parents about unsafe behaviors.

Problem Solving How can the owners of this home correct the hazards to prevent fires? Students can use the fire prevention tips on page 158 to answer the question.

Problem Solving What else might the homeowners do to make this home safe in case of fire? Possible answers: install smoke detectors; keep a fire extinguisher on hand; have fire drills

Content-Area Reading Support
Using Text Format Direct attention to the text below the heading on page 158. Point out that the text following the paragraph is arranged in four sections, each beginning with a bullet. Have students reread the heading and the text following the bullets. Help students see that the information in the four bulleted items taken together explains and responds to the heading. Point out to students that recognizing this relationship will help them better understand the text.

Interpret Visuals—Graphs
Draw student's attention to the graph.

What does the horizontal line (*x*-axis) of the graph show? the area of the home

What does the vertical line (*y*-axis) show? the percent of fires in increments of 5 percent

How do the bars in the graph tell which area has the most fires? Taller bars stand for greater quantities.

Quick Activity
Analyze Data Most home fires start in the kitchen. Encourage students to answer the second question by making a chart with the headings *Place*, *Cause*, and *Eliminate Cause*.

Upstairs bedrooms should have an escape ladder next to each window. ▶

TEACH *continued*

Interpret Visuals—Diagrams

Point out the floor plan for the family escape plan. Have students trace the escape routes from each room. Ask students if they can suggest alternative escape routes.

Discuss

Have students analyze the components of a personal health maintenance plan for families, such as personal safety. Invite volunteers to read the bulleted steps for a family escape plan. Point out that an escape ladder should be fire resistant. Remind students who live in apartment buildings to use stairwells and not elevators if they need to escape. Emphasize the importance of crawling low, under smoke and heat, to escape fire.

Problem Solving What should you do if you are crawling along your escape route and find yourself surrounded by smoke? Use the second escape route.

Point out to students that if it becomes impossible to avoid crawling through smoke, they should bend over and keep their heads as close to the floor as possible.

Quick Activity

Plan Your Escape Tell students that one of the escape routes should be the most direct route from the home. Emphasize that agreeing on a meeting place ensures that everyone who gets out safely will be accounted for. Students might suggest a neighbor's home, a certain tree, the end of the driveway, or another easily located spot.

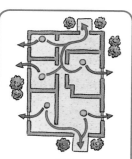

Quick Activity

Plan Your Escape
Make a floor plan of your own home, showing at least two ways to escape from each room. Then suggest some places the family could meet after a fire.

Escaping a Fire

When fires occur, people don't have time to plan. In less than one minute, a small flame can turn into a large, out-of-control fire. An important part of fire safety is to have a family escape plan. Include the steps below in your plan.

- Draw a floor plan, or a map of your home. Label all exits, the location of each smoke alarm, and an outside meeting place. Use arrows to show two ways to escape from each room.
- Make sure that everyone knows the escape routes and the sound of the smoke alarms. Be sure that all windows and doors open easily.
- Keep a whistle and a flashlight next to each bed. Make sure bedroom and hall doors are closed while you sleep. Closed doors slow the spread of a fire.
- Try out the whistles or other special signals to awaken and alert family members during a fire.

Practice the escape plan at least two times a year with your entire family. With your eyes closed, practice feeling your way out of your home. Practice crawling fast, and try to increase your crawling speed. Practice pounding on the walls, yelling, and using the whistles to alert family members during a fire.

160

Teacher Tip

Special-Needs Students
Students with a loss of hearing should plan with family members how they will be alerted in case of fire if they cannot hear smoke detector alarms, shouted alerts, or banging on their door. Families should also arrange for family members who are physically disabled to sleep on the ground floor of a multilevel house, if possible. It is also advisable for people with physical disabilities to have telephones in their rooms.

Teacher Tip

Fire Drill Safety If you recently have had a school fire drill, ask volunteers to describe what they observed during the practice. Did everyone cooperate? Did everyone leave the building quickly, carefully, and according to plan? Did anyone act in a way that could put others in harm's way? If there haven't been any recent school fire drills, discuss what will be expected of students during the next one.

Make sure windows open easily. You should be able to remove screens or security bars quickly.

▲ Make sure all family members know how to use the escape ladders.

Suppose it's the middle of the night. You wake up to the sound of a smoke alarm! You smell smoke and realize your home is on fire. What do you do?

- Quickly roll out of bed and onto the floor. Smoke and other harmful gases from a fire rise toward the ceiling. The air is better near the floor.
- Crawl toward the door. If the smoke has made seeing difficult, reach out for a wall so you can feel your way. If possible, hold a damp cloth over your nose and mouth. Breathe through the cloth to screen out smoke.
- If you have a whistle, blow it loudly. Bang on the walls and yell "Fire" as loudly as you can.
- When you reach the door, feel it with the back of your hand. If it is cool, you may open it and crawl out as quickly as possible. If it is hot, do not open it. Use another exit, such as a window, to escape.
- Keep crawling until you are outside. Continue yelling to warn other family members.

CAUSE AND EFFECT What is the cause if a closed door feels hot during a fire?
fire on the other side of the door

Personal Health Plan ▶

Real-Life Situation
It is important to know the locations of fire-safety equipment, such as window ladders, fire extinguishers, and flashlights.
Real-Life Plan
Identify where fire-safety equipment is located in your home. Tell how to use it in case of a fire.

161

Science

Smoke Inhalation Have students research what happens to the body when it is overcome by smoke and why it is important to get out of a smoke-filled house as quickly as possible. Students can refer to pages 6 and 7 of this text to review the respiratory system.

Interpret Visuals—Pictures

Draw students' attention to the pictures on these pages, showing the use of a safety ladder. Explain that each family member should have time to practice releasing the window security locks and using the ladder.

Discuss

Invite volunteers to read aloud the bulleted steps of the family escape plan.

Critical Thinking Why is it important to know and practice the steps for escaping a fire? It is easier to remain calm and do the right thing during a fire if you are prepared. Knowing and practicing the steps will help you be prepared.

Personal Health Plan ▶

Plans should include a list of where fire-safety equipment is located. Students should be able to describe how to use each piece of equipment.

Health Background

Smoke Detectors More than 50 percent of the deaths that occur in home fires happen late at night when people are sleeping. The risk of dying in a home fire, however, is cut in half if the home is equipped with properly installed and working smoke alarms. The National Fire Protection Association recommends that smoke detectors be installed outside every bedroom or sleeping area and on each level of the home. Smoke detectors should be tested regularly—as often as once a week or at least once a month. Batteries should be replaced every year. The proper way to test a smoke detector is to expose it to smoke or steam or to use a commercial spray product that is specifically designed for testing smoke detectors.

Source: *National Fire Protection Association*

For more background, visit the **Webliography** in Teacher Resources at **www.harcourtschool.com/health** **Keyword** safety

Suppose you can't escape from your home during a fire. The exits are completely blocked by fire and smoke. These pictures show several steps you can take to protect yourself.

DRAW CONCLUSIONS Why should you close up cracks around a door and close vents?
to keep out the smoke

Step 1 Keep a closed door between you and the smoke. If the door is open, crawl quickly to it and close it to keep the smoke out. Breathe through your hand or a damp cloth.

Step 2 Stuff clothes or towels into the cracks under and around the door. Also close vents in the walls or floor.

Step 3 Open a window to let in fresh air. If smoke or flames come in, close the window.

Step 4 Stay by a window where you can be seen. Yell for help, and signal by waving your hand, a flashlight, or a sheet.

162

TEACH *continued*

Content-Area Reading Support

Using Text Format Direct attention to the boxes of text to the left of the illustration. Indicate to students that text set this way is known as *callout text*. Callout text often is used to describe the steps in a process or the parts of a diagram. Comment that students should study a picture and then look to the callouts for a detailed explanation of the parts or the process.

Interpret Visuals—Pictures

Ask students to study the numbered pictures and callouts. Ask them to describe what the boy in the pictures is doing to stay safe. Remind students that everyone in the house should be able to unlock and open all doors and windows easily and quickly. Families may want to practice this in the dark, because fires often occur at night. In addition, smoke can make it difficult or impossible for a person to see, even during the day.

Teacher Tip

Stop, Drop, and Roll Point out to students that if their clothes catch on fire, they should immediately stop where they are, drop to the floor or ground, cover their faces with their hands, and roll over and over slowly to put out the flames. You may wish to clear a space in the classroom and have students practice this technique.

Social Studies

Fire Prevention Week
Encourage students to use the Internet to find and print resources to research and report on the history of Fire Prevention Week in North America, first observed the week of October 4, 1925. As part of the research, ask students to discover how their own community, region, or state plans to participate in the next Fire Prevention Week.

What to Do After You Escape a Fire

Having a plan for what to do after escaping a fire is important. Once you're outside, go right away to your family meeting place. This may be under a certain tree, at a certain street lamp, or at the end of a driveway. Having a specific location is important so no one gets hurt looking for someone who has already safely escaped the fire. If you wander around, others may not know that you have gotten out of the burning building.

Once you are out of the building, don't go back inside for any reason. Use a neighbor's phone or a cellphone to call 911, your local emergency number, or your local fire department. The emergency operator will need answers to the following questions:

- What is the location of the fire? Give the street address and the nearest cross streets.
- What type of fire is it? For example, is the fire in a house, in an apartment, in some trash, or in a car?
- Is anyone in danger? Is anyone still inside a burning building? Are pets inside?
- How big is the fire? Can you see flames or just smell smoke? How much of the building is burning?

Remember: When you are reporting an emergency, do not hang up until the operator tells you to do so. He or she may need more information. Allow firefighters and rescue workers to do their jobs. They have the equipment and training to deal with emergency situations.

CAUSE AND EFFECT **What is the effect of going directly to your family's meeting place after escaping a fire?** Your family will know that you are safe, and no one will get hurt looking for you.

All family members should be able to quickly call for help, using a neighbor's home phone or a cellphone. ▼

163

Interpret Visuals—Pictures

Focus students' attention on the picture of the family practicing an escape plan. Ask students to describe what has probably happened before this point. Each member of the family has followed the escape plan; everyone has met outside at the agreed-upon meeting place.

Remind students that firefighters are trained to rescue people and pets. The protective clothing and gear that firefighters wear help them withstand the heat and smoke of a burning building.

Problem Solving **What should you do if you escape a fire in your home and then realize that your pet cat is still inside?** Do not go back into the house. Let firefighters rescue the cat. Either tell the 911 operator or dispatcher that your pet is trapped inside when you report the fire, or tell the firefighters when they arrive.

TEACH *continued*

Discuss

Ask students if they are familiar with the term *natural disaster*. Then discuss the kinds of natural disasters that have occurred or may occur in your region of the country. Ask students who have witnessed or lived through a natural disaster to describe what they observed.

Problem Solving **Why might the plans you make to be safe during a hurricane be different from the plans you would make to be safe during an earthquake?** Hurricanes involve fierce winds and relentless rain, while earthquakes result in broken buildings, gas mains, and water mains.

Content-Area Reading Support

Using Typographic Clues Draw attention to the information under the heading Plan for Other Emergencies. Discuss the functions of the boldface and lightface type. Tell students that the major parts of the plan are in boldface type. These statements form the outline of a universal emergency plan. The lightface type offers explanations and examples of how to execute the universal plan.

Point out that boldface type is used to draw attention to words and ideas. Recommend that students pay special attention to words, phrases, and sentences in boldface type.

Some natural disasters, such as hurricanes and winter storms, can be predicted. Other, such as tornadoes, earthquakes, and wildfires, can be very unexpected. See pages 402–403 for tips on safety during natural disasters.

Plan for Other Emergencies

By having a plan, your family can protect itself during other emergencies, such as natural disasters. **Natural disasters** are powerful events of nature that often result in the destruction of buildings and other structures. Earthquakes, tornadoes, hurricanes, floods, and volcanic eruptions are all examples of natural disasters.

To plan for these types of emergencies, your family must gather information and make some choices. All family members should understand and practice the parts of the plan.

Know What Could Happen

Learn about the kinds of natural disasters that can happen in your area. Emergency plans may differ, depending on the type of disaster. For example, the way you would protect yourself during an earthquake is different from what you would do during a tornado.

Have Two Meeting Places

Choose two places where you can meet in the event of an emergency. The first place should be where your family decided to meet in case of a house fire. The second location should be farther away.

Know Your Family Contact

Choose someone who lives far away to be a contact person. This person will help your family stay in touch. If a family member becomes lost during an emergency, he or she can call the contact person.

It's important that all family members are comfortable and familiar with the emergency plan. This helps reduce stress during an emergency situation.

164

Meeting Individual Needs
Leveled Activities

BELOW-LEVEL **Disaster Drills** Have a small group draw up a list of rules for leaving the classroom in the event of a fire or other disaster. Post the rules for all to see.

ON-LEVEL **FEMA** Make arrangements for a representative of the local office of the Federal Emergency Management Agency (FEMA) to visit the class. Have students prepare questions to ask about ways in which FEMA functions in an emergency. Have students role-play the interview.

CHALLENGE **Helping Disaster Victims** Have students brainstorm ways they can help schools in communities that have been damaged by natural disasters.

Practice Evacuating

During a fire, you need to evacuate, or get out of, your home right away. Think of the natural disasters you identified for your area. Do you know what to do in the event of a tornado? An earthquake? In some cases, your entire community may have to be evacuated. The threat of hurricanes, floods, and wildfires may make it unsafe to remain in the area. Listen to the radio or television during an emergency to find out if your community is being evacuated. Be familiar with your community's evacuation procedures.

▲ Part of your emergency plan should include evacuation.

Learn How to Turn Off Utilities

Services that provide water, electricity, and gas are utilities. An emergency may damage utility pipes or wires and make them dangerous. They can damage or even destroy a home. With an adult's help, learn when and how to turn off utilities. CAUTION: If you turn off the gas, a professional must turn it back on.

SUMMARIZE Name three things you can do to prepare for an emergency. Any three: Learn possible area emergencies; choose two meeting places; choose a family contact; practice evacuating; learn how to turn off utilities.

Myth and Fact

Myth: Natural gas smells like rotten eggs.

Fact: Natural gas is colorless, odorless, and tasteless. For safety reasons the scent of sulfur, which smells like rotten eggs, is added to natural gas. Natural gas is highly flammable, so it's important to know if there is a leak.

◄ Leaking gas and live electrical wires can lead to fires. If tools are needed to turn off a utility, they should be stored close by.

165

Math

Recent Floods Have students make double-bar graphs using the data below. Ask them to identify the cities in which peak stages were about twice normal flood stage.

Mississippi River Floods

City	Flood Stage (ft)	Peak Stage (ft)
St. Paul, MN	14	19.2
Estherville, IA	7	15.4
Des Moines, IA	12	26.7
St. Charles, MO	25	40.0
Grafton, IN	18	38.2
Quincy, IL	17	32.1
Jefferson City, MO	23	38.6

3. WRAP UP

Lesson 3 Summary and Review

1. natural disasters; utilities; evacuate; flammable; emergency supply

2. Accept all reasonable answers, including material covered in the illustration on pages 158–159.

3. If the candles are wax, tell your friend that candles are too dangerous to leave in windows. If the candles are electric with cords, tell your friend to make sure that the cords are not worn or frayed and not placed under rugs or where someone might trip over them.

4. Answers may include the following:

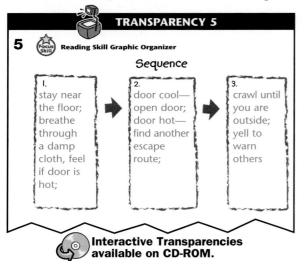

TRANSPARENCY 5

5 Reading Skill Graphic Organizer

Sequence

1. stay near the floor; breathe through a damp cloth, feel if door is hot;

2. door cool— open door; door hot— find another escape route;

3. crawl until you are outside; yell to warn others

Interactive Transparencies available on CD-ROM.

5. Have students draw the floor plans on grid paper. Suggest that they show the escape routes in red or another bright color.

 For **writing models** with examples, see *Teaching Resources* pp. 47–61. Rubrics are also provided.

 When Minutes Count ...

Quick Study Students can use *Activity Book* pp. 21–22 (shown on p. 139) as they complete each lesson in this chapter.

Make an Emergency Supply Kit

After an emergency or natural disaster, you may not have access to everyday services. You may not have water, electricity, or gas service for several days or longer. You may not be able to get to the store. It's important to have an emergency supply kit for your family. The American Red Cross recommends that the following items be included in an emergency supply kit:

▲ Other items for an emergency supply kit include a blanket, soap, and books and games for entertainment.

- a three-day supply of drinking water (6 quarts per person), stored in plastic containers
- a three-day supply of canned food and a manual can opener
- a first-aid kit and extra prescription medications
- a fire extinguisher, tools, a flashlight with extra batteries, candles, matches, and a battery-operated radio
- money and important family papers

MAIN IDEA AND DETAILS Why is having an emergency supply kit important?
Utilities may be off; you may not be able to get to a store.

Lesson 3 Summary and Review

① Summarize with Vocabulary

Use vocabulary and other terms from this lesson to complete the statements.

Earthquakes and tornadoes are examples of _____. In the event of an emergency, it may be necessary to turn off _____, such as water and gas. You also may have to quickly _____ your home. Paper is _____, which means it will burn. Blankets, food, and water belong in a(n) _____ kit.

② Name four ways to reduce fire hazards at home.

③ Critical Thinking A friend wants to keep a lighted candle in every window at holiday time. What should you tell her?

④ SEQUENCE Draw and complete the graphic organizer to show the steps involved in escaping from a fire.

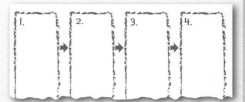

| 1. | 2. | 3. | 4. |

⑤ Write to Inform—Description

Describe where your family could meet after escaping a fire. Include the steps you should follow once you have escaped.

ACTIVITY BOOK P. 25

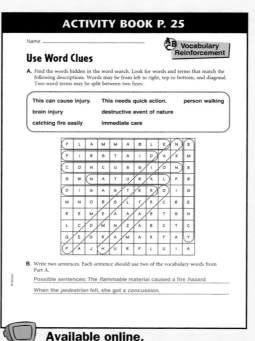

Name _____

Use Word Clues

Vocabulary Reinforcement

A. Find the words hidden in the word search. Look for words and terms that match the following descriptions. Words may be from left to right, top to bottom, and diagonal. Two-word terms may be split between two lines.

This can cause injury.	This needs quick action.	person walking
brain injury	destructive event of nature	
catching fire easily	immediate care	

B. Write two sentences. Each sentence should use two of the vocabulary words from Part A.

Possible sentences: The *flammable* material caused a fire *hazard*.

When the *pedestrian* fell, she got a *concussion*.

Available online. www.harcourtschool.com/health

ACTIVITIES

Physical Education

Walk for Safety Take a safety walk around your community. As you walk, make notes about hazards you find, such as holes in sidewalks and street signs hidden by trees. Then ask a parent to contact someone in authority about the unsafe conditions.

Science

Research Skin Why is the skin an important body organ? What are the functions of skin? How do burns affect skin? Find information about skin. Then make a poster that explains the functions of skin and how the three types of burns affect it. On your poster, include a labeled diagram of skin.

Technology Project

Make a Video Produce a video that shows how to make your home fire-safe. Include information about household fire hazards and how to prevent fires in the home. If a video camera is not available, use a software program to make a pamphlet with this information.

 For more activities, visit **The Learning Site.** www.harcourtschool.com/health

Home & Community

Communicating With a parent, look around your neighborhood for possible fire hazards. Then talk with your family about how to communicate with your neighbors about these hazards.

Career Link

Paramedic Paramedics provide first aid and medical treatment to injured people. They transport injured people to the hospital and work closely with fire and police departments. Suppose you are a paramedic. You arrive at the scene of a car accident. List the steps you would take to help the injured people.

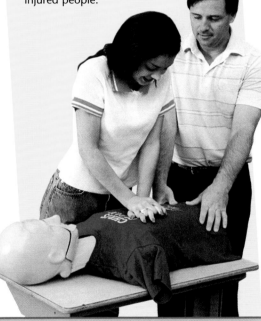

Career Link

Paramedic Students should recognize that many of the steps taken by paramedics are similar to the steps they themselves might take at an accident scene. First, paramedics survey the scene, determining what happened, how many people are injured, and which people need immediate assistance. Next, the paramedics give first aid for the most serious wounds. They keep injured persons from further injury by securing them to a stretcher and placing a safety collar around the neck of anyone who may have suffered a head, neck, or back injury. Of course, they also work to stop a victim's bleeding and administer medicines or apply techniques to keep a patient's vital signs (heartbeat and breathing rate) stable.

For more information on health careers, visit the **Webliography** in Teacher Resources at **www.harcourtschool.com/health** **Keyword** health careers

---

Activities

Physical Education
Direct students to walk in groups of three or four. Remind students to tell their parents or guardians where they are planning to walk and when they will return home. Urge students to avoid unsafe locations such as alleys and dead-end streets. Encourage students to call home once or twice during their walks.

Science
The skin protects the body in many ways. It's waterproof and keeps in body fluids. It protects against many bacteria and chemicals, and shields internal tissues from the sun's harmful UV rays. Skin also helps maintain normal body temperature. Finally, skin is sensitive to cold, heat, pain, pressure, and touch.

The skin has three layers: (1) epidermis, (2) dermis, and (3) subcutaneous tissue.

First-degree burns: skin turns red, only epidermis affected, no scars. Second-degree burns: skin blisters, epidermis and part of the dermis are affected, and may leave slight scars. Third-degree burns: skin turns black, all three layers of skin damaged, necessitate surgery.

Home & Community
Remind students to use a respectful approach when speaking to neighbors. Don't blame anyone for the hazards; rather, concentrate on correcting or eliminating them.

 Supports the Coordinated School Health Program

Technology Project
Students can use presentation software for this project. Students who do not have access to a computer can create "slides" by using construction paper.

Chapter Review and Test Preparation

Pages 168–169

Reading Skill 3 pts. each

TRANSPARENCY 5

5 Reading Skill Graphic Organizer

Sequence

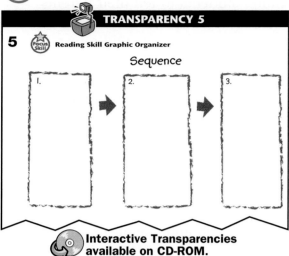

Interactive Transparencies available on CD-ROM.

1. Wash the cut.

2. Place a sterile bandage over the cut and apply pressure until bleeding stops.

3. Cover the cut with a sterile bandage.

Use Vocabulary 3 pts. each

4. B, hazard

5. A, flammable

6. D, emergency

7. C, concussion

8. E, pedestrian

Check Understanding 3 pts. each

9. C, emergencies

10. H, stop the bleeding

11. D, R.I.C.E.

12. H, sterile bandage

13. C

14. G, two

15. B, call 911

16. F, You may not ride your bike on this road.

17. D, a working smoke alarm

18. H, first aid

19. B, wait your turn

Think Critically 7 pts. each

20. Possible answers: If bones are broken or if there is a head or spinal injury, moving the injured person could cause additional damage or injury.

 Reading Skill

SEQUENCE

Draw and then use this graphic organizer to answer questions 1–3.

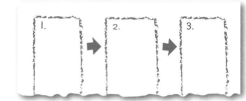

1. In the first box, write the first thing you would do to treat a cut.

2. In the second box, tell how to control the bleeding.

3. In the last box, tell what to do after the bleeding is stopped.

 Use Vocabulary

Match each term in Column B with its meaning in Column A.

Column A	Column B
4 Something in the environment or some person's action that can cause harm	A flammable
5 Easily catching fire	B hazard
6 Situation that calls for quick action	C concussion
7 Brain injury caused by a blow to the head	D emergency
8 Person who is walking	E pedestrian

Check Understanding

Choose the letter of the correct answer.

9 Drowning, poisoning, and choking are examples of _____. (p. 140)
  A spinal injuries
  B unconsciousness
  C emergencies
  D first aid

10 The first thing to do when someone is seriously injured is to _____. (p. 142)
  F call for help   H stop the bleeding
  G give oxygen   J wait your turn

11 Which of the following shows the correct order of steps for treating a bruise? (p. 145)
  A C.I.R.E.   C I.R.E.C.
  B E.R.I.C.   D R.I.C.E.

12 A bandage free of germs is a _____. (p. 142)
  F dirty bandage
  G wet cloth
  H sterile bandage
  J dry cloth

13 Which hand signal would you use if you wanted to make a right turn while riding your bike? (pp. 154–155)

168

Formal Assessment

ASSESSMENT GUIDE P. 31	ASSESSMENT GUIDE P. 32

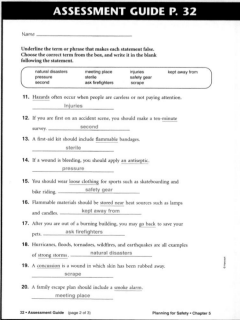

14 Each room in your home should have at least _____ escape route(s). (p. 160)
  F one   **H** three
  G two   **J** four

15 Which is the first step in the sequence of responding to an emergency? (p. 140)
  A Move the   **C** Give first aid.
  injured person.
  B Call 911.   **D** Call a friend.

16 What does this sign mean? (p. 156)

  F You may not ride your bike on this road.
  G Two-wheeled bikes are not allowed.
  H Only bikes can use the road.
  J No motorcycles.

17 All of the following are examples of fire hazards **EXCEPT** _____. (pp. 158–159)
  A an overloaded electrical outlet
  B a lighter left where a child can reach it
  C a newspaper left near a space heater
  D a working smoke alarm

18 The immediate care given to an injured person is _____. (p. 142)
  F a sterile bandage **H** first aid
  G an emergency   **J** stopping bleeding

19 Which is a playground safety rule? (pp. 148–149)
  A Run on wet surfaces.
  B Wait your turn.
  C Push and shove.
  D Go barefoot.

 Think Critically

20 Why should an injured person not be moved unless it's necessary for safety reasons?

21 How can human behavior lead to accidents? Give examples of accidents caused by human actions. Explain how these accidents can be prevented.

22 Why is it important to talk to your parents or other trusted adults about unsafe behaviors you have observed?

 Apply Skills

23 **BUILDING GOOD CHARACTER**
Caring Suppose you accidentally dropped a glass in your school cafeteria. The glass broke, and juice and pieces of glass are now on the floor. How can you show caring for your classmates by eliminating the hazards?

24 **LIFE SKILLS**
Make Responsible Decisions Your friends have found some firecrackers and want to play with them. You know that this is a hazard and that your parents do not allow you to play with firecrackers. Explain how you can make a responsible decision about playing with the firecrackers.

Write About Health

25 **Write to Inform—Explanation** Write a paragraph that compares the safety rules at your school with the safety rules you have at home. How are they similar? How are they different?

169

21. Possible answers: People who are showing off or playing dangerously can cause accidents. A fire can start if someone is careless with matches. A person running around a pool can slip and fall. People can prevent many accidents by following safety rules.

22. Possible answers: It's important to talk to parents or other adults about unsafe behaviors so that the behaviors can be stopped before there is serious injury.

 Apply Skills 7 pts. each

23. Possible answer: Place chairs or other barriers around the broken glass. Find the adult in charge of the cafeteria and ask for his or her help in cleaning up the juice and the broken glass.

24. Possible answers: "Sorry, I'm not allowed to play with firecrackers." "No, thank you. Those look dangerous. Besides, I'm fond of having fingers."

Write About Health 8 pts.

25. Accept all reasonable comparisons. Possible example: Do not run down stairs, do not run with a sharp object in hand, and do not play with matches are rules both at home and in school. Certain school rules, such as do not run in hallways and do not play rough in the cafeteria, apply only to school. In the same way, do not play with the oven and do not leave a candle burning in an empty room are home rules. Each place has rules to protect individuals in that place.

Performance Assessment

Use the Chapter Project and the rubric provided on the Project Evaluation Sheet. See *Assessment Guide* pp. 18, 58, 66.

Portfolio Assessment

Have students select their best work from the following suggestions:
• Leveled Activities, p. 144
• Quick Activity, p. 159
• Write to Inform, p. 156
• Activities, p. 167
See *Assessment Guide* pp. 12–16.

CHAPTER 6 Preventing Violence

Lesson	Pacing	Objectives	Reading Skills
Introduce the Chapter pp. 170–171		• Preview chapter concepts.	**Cause and Effect** p. 171; pp. 372–383
1 Violence in Your World pp. 172–174	1 class period	• Identify acts of violence. • Describe ways to avoid violence.	**Cause and Effect** pp. 173, 174 • Draw Conclusions, p. 174
★ **Building Good Character** p. 175		• Describe effective listening skills used in being fair.	
2 Avoiding Violence pp. 176–179	1 class period	• Explain strategies for avoiding violence, gangs, and weapons. • Identify alternatives to joining a gang.	**Cause and Effect** p. 179 • Sequence, p. 176 • Summarize, p. 177 • Compare and Contrast, p. 179
Life Skills pp. 180–181	1 class period	• Identify skills used to resolve conflicts. • Apply skills to resolve conflicts before conflicts become violent.	
3 Surviving Violence pp. 182–184	1 class period	• Demonstrate strategies for avoiding violence on the street and at school. • Describe safe ways to respond to a terrorist attack.	**Cause and Effect** p. 184 • Draw Conclusions, p. 182 • Main Idea and Details, p. 183 • Summarize, p. 184
Activities p. 185		• Extend chapter concepts.	
Chapter Review pp. 186–187	1 class period	• Assess chapter objectives.	

Vocabulary	Program Resources
	Music CD Teaching Resources, p. 33
violence terrorism	Transparency 3 Activity Book, pp. 26–28
	Poster 3
weapon bully gang	Transparency 3 Activity Book, pp. 26–27
	Activity Book, p. 29 Poster 11
zero-tolerance policy	Transparency 3 Activity Book, pp. 26–27, 30
	The Learning Site www. harcourtschool.com/health
	Assessment Guide, pp. 34–36

Interactive Transparencies available on CD-ROM.

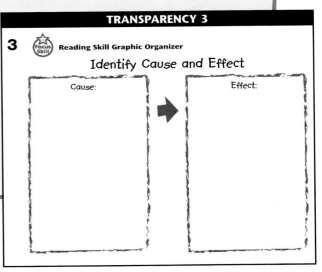

Reading Skill

These reading skills are reinforced throughout this chapter and one skill is emphasized as the Focus Skill.

Cause and Effect

- Draw Conclusions
- Compare and Contrast
- Identify Main Idea and Details
- Sequence
- Summarize

TRANSPARENCY 3

3 **Reading Skill Graphic Organizer**
Identify Cause and Effect

Cause: Effect:

Life Skills

Life Skills are health-enhancing behaviors that can help students reduce risks to their health and safety.

Six Life Skills are reinforced throughout *Harcourt Health and Fitness.* The skill emphasized in this chapter is Resolve Conflicts.

POSTER 11

Resolve Conflicts

The girls are resolving a conflict by negotiating politely.

Steps to Resolve Conflicts

1. Use I-messages to tell how you feel.
2. Listen to each other. Consider the other person's view.
3. Negotiate.
4. Find a way for both sides to win.

How do YOU RESOLVE CONFLICTS?
POSTER 11

Building Good Character

Character education is an important aspect of health education. When students behave in ways that show good character, they promote the health and safety of themselves and others.

Six character traits are reinforced throughout *Harcourt Health and Fitness.* The trait emphasized in this chapter is Fairness.

POSTER 3

Fairness

The children are showing fairness by being good sports.

DO	DON'T
▶ Play by the rules.	▶ Don't take more than your share.
▶ Be a good sport.	▶ Don't be a bad loser or a bad winner.
▶ Share.	▶ Don't take advantage of others.
▶ Take turns.	▶ Don't blame others without cause.
▶ Listen to the opinions of others.	▶ Don't cut in front of others in line.

How have YOU shown FAIRNESS today?
POSTER 3

Coordinated School Health Program

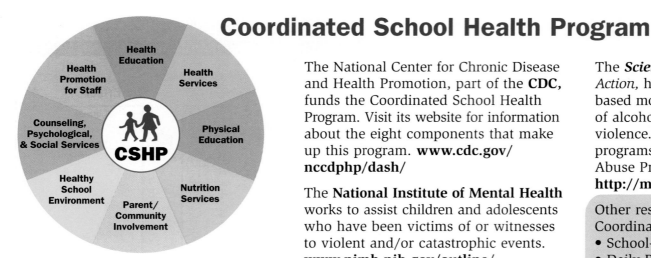

A Coordinated School Health Program endeavors to improve children's health and, therefore, their capacity to learn through the support of families, schools, and communities working together. The following information is provided to help classroom teachers be more aware of these resources.

The National Center for Chronic Disease and Health Promotion, part of the **CDC,** funds the Coordinated School Health Program. Visit its website for information about the eight components that make up this program. **www.cdc.gov/nccdphp/dash/**

The **National Institute of Mental Health** works to assist children and adolescents who have been victims of or witnesses to violent and/or catastrophic events. **www.nimh.nih.gov/outline/traumatic.cfm**

The **American Red Cross** offers opportunities for students to offer their services by participating in Youth Volunteer programs in the event of emergencies or other disasters. **www.redcross.org/services/youth/**

The **Science-Based Program,** *Positive Action,* has been identified as a research-based model program for the prevention of alcohol and tobacco use and violence. For this and other exemplary programs, visit the Center for Substance Abuse Prevention: Model Programs. **http://modelprograms.samhsa.gov/**

Other resources that support a Coordinated School Health Program:
• School-Home Connection
• Daily Physical Activity
• Daily Fitness Tips
• Activities: Home & Community
• Health Background: Webliography
• *Be Active! Resources for Physical Education*

Media Resources

100 lessons and activities to help students work out conflicts.

Books for Students

Schulson, Rachel Ellenberg. **Guns: What You Should Know.** Albert Whitman and Company, 1999. Warns of the danger of guns. **EASY**

Sanders, Pete, and Steve Myers. **Bullying (What Do You Know About).** Millbrook Press, 1996. Looks at why people bully others and offers solutions. **AVERAGE**

Goedecke, Christopher J., and Rosmarie Hausherr. **Smart Moves: A Kid's Guide to Self-Defense.** Simon & Schuster, 1995. Offers alternatives to violence. **ADVANCED**

Books for Teachers and Families

Giggans, Patricia Occhiuzzo, and Barrie Levy. **50 Ways to a Safer World.** Seal Press, 1997. A safety guide.

Teolis, Beth. **Ready-to-Use Conflict Resolution Activities for Elementary Students.** Center for Applied Research in Education, 1999. More than

Free and Inexpensive Materials

Elkind + Sweet/Live Wire Media
Request a free preview of their video titled *Prevent Violence with Groark.*

Bureau of Alcohol, Tobacco, and Firearms
The GREAT (Gang Resistance Education and Training) Program provides classroom instruction on preventing youth violence.

U.S. Department of Health & Human Services
Ask for "Safe Schools/Healthy Students" (#SVP-0005) posters on preventing school violence.

To access free and inexpensive resources on the Web, visit **www.harcourtschool.com/health/free**

Videos

The Truth About Violence. AIMS Multimedia, 2000.

Wasted! Guns & Dreams, Lives and Dreams. Educational Video Network, 1996.

Bully Dance. Bullfrog Films, 2000.

These resources have been selected to meet a variety of individual needs. Please review all materials and websites prior to sharing them with students to ensure the content is appropriate for your class. Note that information, while correct at time of publication, is subject to change.

Visit **The Learning Site** for related links, activities, resources, and the health **Webliography.**

www.harcourtschool.com/health

Meeting Individual Needs

Below-Level

Have students focus on text structure. Before they read a section, have them preview it by looking at the headings, the pictures, and the questions at the end. Have students predict what the section will be about and write one question they want to answer from the reading.

Activities
- Identify School Groups, p. 178

On-Level

Using prior knowledge can help students set a purpose for reading. Have them think about what they already know about the selection. Write their comments on a chart, and discuss areas where more information is needed. Ask students what they would like to learn more about.

Activities
- Volunteer, p. 178

Challenge

Write vocabulary words on cards and place them face down. Have students take turns choosing a card and pantomiming or illustrating the word without speaking or writing. The other students try to guess the word.

Activities
- Form a Club, p. 178

ESL/ELL

Learning Log

After reading a paragraph aloud, encourage students to develop language skills through paraphrasing. Select one student to retell ideas presented by the text. Have other students check the retelling for accuracy and add any other information that should be included.

Activities
- Comprehensible Input, p. 176
- Language and Vocabulary, p. 182

Curriculum Integration

Integrated Language Arts/Reading Skills
- Public Service Announcement, p. 183

Math
- Calculating Percentages, p. 183

Music
- Anti-Gang Rap, p. 179

Use these topics to integrate health into your daily planning.

Physical Education
- Daily Fitness Tip, pp. 172, 176, 182
- Daily Physical Activity, p. 171

Art
- Laugh Lines, p. 177

CHAPTER SUMMARY

In this chapter students
► recognize and describe how to respond to threatening situations.
► practice ways to avoid violence.

 Life Skills
Students *resolve conflicts* about the use of resources.

 Building Good Character
Students *demonstrate fairness* by practicing effective listening skills.

 Consumer Health
Students *access valid health information* about violence and *analyze media messages* about gangs.

 Literature Springboard

Use the article "Defusing Difficult Situations" to spark interest in the chapter topic. See the Read-Aloud Anthology on page RA-7 of this *Teacher Edition*.

Prereading Strategies

SCAN THE CHAPTER Have students preview the chapter content by scanning the titles, headings, pictures, graphs, and tables. Ask volunteers to predict what they will learn. Use their predictions to determine their prior knowledge.

PREVIEW VOCABULARY Arrange students in six groups, and assign each group one vocabulary term from this chapter. Give students three to five minutes to write what they know about the terms and what they would like to know.

What We Know	What We Want to Know	What We Learned

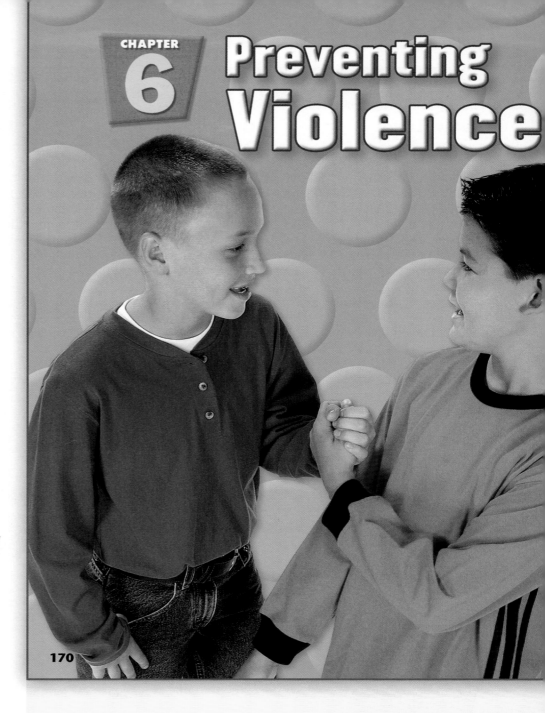

Preventing Violence

170

 Reading Skill

IDENTIFY CAUSE AND EFFECT To introduce or review this skill, have students use the Reading in Health Handbook, pp. 372–383. Teaching strategies and additional activities are also provided.

Students will have opportunities to practice this skill throughout this chapter.

• Focus Skill Reading Mini-Lesson, p. 172
• Reading comprehension questions identified with the
• *Activity Book* p. 28 (shown on p. 174)
• Lesson Summary and Review, pp. 174, 179, 184
• Chapter Review and Test Preparation, pp. 186–187

Reading Skill

IDENTIFY CAUSE AND EFFECT When you identify cause and effect, you tell what happens and why. An effect is what happens. A cause is the reason, or why, it happens. Use the Reading in Health Handbook on pages 372–383 and this graphic organizer to help you read the health facts in this chapter.

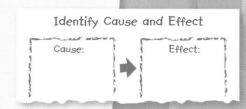

Identify Cause and Effect

Cause: → Effect:

Health Graph

INTERPRET DATA Young people commit more crimes and acts of violence on school days than on nonschool days. At what time during school days are young people most likely to commit crimes?

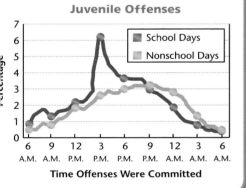

Juvenile Offenses

- School Days
- Nonschool Days

Time Offenses Were Committed

Daily Physical Activity

Staying away from potentially violent situations is one way to stay healthy. Being physically active every day is another way.

Be Active!
Use the selection, Track 6, **Muscle Mambo**, to move your heart and other muscles toward good health.

171

School-Home Connection

Distribute copies of the School-Home Connection (in English or Spanish). Have students take the page home to share with their families as you begin this chapter.

Follow Up Have volunteers share the results of their activities.

 Supports the Coordinated CSHP School Health Program

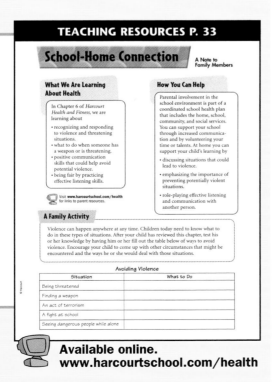

TEACHING RESOURCES P. 33

School-Home Connection A Note to Family Members

What We Are Learning About Health

In Chapter 6 of *Harcourt Health and Fitness*, we are learning about
- recognizing and responding to violence and threatening situations.
- what to do when someone has a weapon or is threatening.
- positive communication skills that could help avoid potential violence.
- being fair by practicing effective listening skills.

Visit www.harcourtschool.com/health for links to parent resources.

How You Can Help

Parental involvement in the school environment is part of a coordinated school health plan that includes the home, school, community, and social services. You can support your school through increased communication and by volunteering your time or talents. At home you can support your child's learning by
- discussing situations that could lead to violence.
- emphasizing the importance of preventing potentially violent situations.
- role-playing effective listening and communication with another person.

A Family Activity

Violence can happen anywhere at any time. Children today need to know what to do in these types of situations. After your child has reviewed this chapter, test his or her knowledge by having him or her fill out the table below of ways to avoid violence. Encourage your child to come up with other circumstances that might be encountered and the ways he or she would deal with those situations.

Avoiding Violence

Situation	What to Do
Being threatened	
Finding a weapon	
An act of terrorism	
A fight at school	
Seeing dangerous people while alone	

Available online.
www.harcourtschool.com/health

INTRODUCE THE CHAPTER

Health Graph

Interpret Data

Ask a volunteer to explain what the different-colored lines mean.

On school days, at what time of day are young people most likely to commit crimes? around 3 p.m.

What percent of all crimes by young people are committed around this time? about 6.5 percent

When are young people least likely to commit crimes? around 6 a.m. on school and nonschool days

Daily Physical Activity

Use *Be Active! Music for Daily Physical Activity* with the Instant Activity Cards to provide students with movement activities that can be done in limited space. Options for using these components are provided beginning on page TR2 in this *Teacher Edition*.

Chapter Project

Dealing with Violence (*Assessment Guide* p. 58)

ASSESS PRIOR KNOWLEDGE Use students' initial ideas for the project as a baseline assessment of their understanding of chapter concepts. Have students complete the project as they work through the chapter.

PERFORMANCE ASSESSMENT The project can be used for performance assessment. Use the Project Evaluation Sheet (rubric), *Assessment Guide* p. 67.

Objectives
► Identify acts of violence.
► Describe ways to avoid violence.

When Minutes Count . . .
Assign the Quick Study, Lesson 1, Activity Book pp. 26–27 (shown on p. 173).

Program Resources
► Activity Book pp. 26–28
► Transparency 3

Vocabulary
violence p. 172, **terrorism** p. 173

Daily Fitness Tip

Tell students that using alcohol not only has health and legal consequences but also plays a key role in violent acts. Roughly half the people who committed murders, assaults, and robberies had been drinking alcohol. Students can reduce their risk of violence by not using alcohol.

 For more guidelines on alcohol, drugs, and movement, see *Be Active! Resources for Physical Education,* p. 171.

1. MOTIVATE

Ask students to name violent behaviors, and list their responses on the board. Keep the items general, such as "slapping." Don't include details. Make sure students understand that violent acts include more than injuring a person physically; violence also is making threats, stealing, or damaging public or private property.

Students should also be aware that helping to rid their school of violence is the first step to making their community safe and a healthy place to live. Have students describe how a safe school environment relates to a healthy community.

Violence in Your World

Lesson Focus
Identifying violent acts can help you reduce the risk of harm to yourself and others.

Why Learn This?
What you learn can help you protect yourself from harm and lead to a secure school environment.

Vocabulary
violence
terrorism

Violence and Terrorism

If you watch television, you might get the idea that bad things happen most of the time. Some TV shows are based on the lives of crime-fighting police officers. Other shows highlight violence. **Violence** is any act that harms or injures people. Acts of violence include fights, certain crimes, and threats. A person who threatens violence is acting violently. Although the average person is unlikely to experience violence, it can happen anywhere and any time. That's why it's important to understand what violence is and how it can affect you. It's also important to know how to prevent and avoid violence.

Many acts of violence begin with violent thoughts, feelings, or words. Violence never solves problems. It's dangerous and harmful to everyone involved.

Consumer Activity

Accessing Valid Health Information Violence costs everyone money—even those not directly involved. Many schools and communities now spend money on new safety procedures. Do research to find the cost of keeping schools safe. Summarize your findings.

A school resource officer helps make a school environment safe. How might this lead to a safe, healthy community? ▼

172

Reading Skill

Mini-Lesson

CAUSE AND EFFECT Remind students that identifying cause and effect means that you tell what happens and why. Have students practice this skill by responding to the Focus Skill question on page 173. Have students draw and complete the graphic organizer as you model it on the transparency.

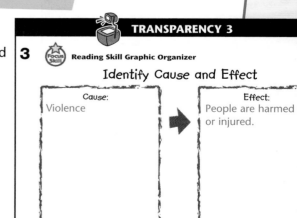

TRANSPARENCY 3

3 Reading Skill Graphic Organizer

Identify Cause and Effect

Cause:	Effect:
Violence	People are harmed or injured.

Interactive Transparencies available on CD-ROM.

Sometimes, violent acts happen between individuals or small groups of people who know each other, such as classmates getting into fights. At other times the people involved in violence may not know each other. For example, you may remember the acts of terrorism that occurred on September 11, 2001. **Terrorism** is the use of force and violence against people or property for a political or social goal. Terrorism can happen in any country in the world.

Sometimes you can't avoid violence, such as during a terrorist attack. But you can do many things to reduce your chance of being harmed by violence. Learning safe ways to communicate is an important tool for preventing violence. Learning nonviolent ways to resolve conflicts, or disagreements, is another important tool. You also can help any organizations in your school and community that work to make these places safe and nonviolent.

 CAUSE AND EFFECT **What is one effect of violence?**
Possible response: People are harmed or injured.

Health & Technology

Cargo Security Devices
Many types of security devices are used to help protect people from violence and terrorism. One type of security device uses X rays to check cargo entering the country. X rays are high-energy waves that can be used to "see" what's inside trucks and containers. X-ray devices enable security officers to find weapons, bombs, and other dangerous items hidden among legal cargo.

173

QUICK STUDY, ACTIVITY BOOK PP. 26–27

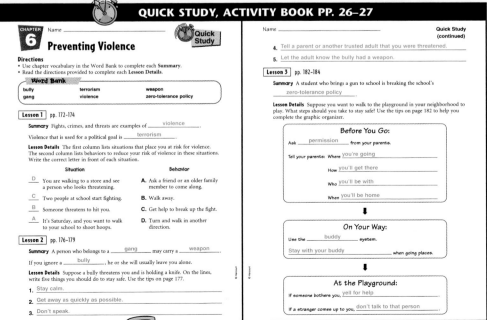

 Available online.
www.harcourtschool.com/health

---

2. TEACH

Interpret Visuals—Pictures

Direct students' attention to the picture of the security equipment. Ask students to describe what is happening.

Critical Thinking **How do X-ray devices and other security measures make us safer?** When the security devices find weapons or other dangerous items, security officers can seize them before they can be used to hurt or threaten people.

Assure students that these precautions make people safer than before the measures were in place and that the government takes many steps to prevent terrorist attacks.

Content-Area Reading Support

Using Sentence Structure Ask a volunteer to read the last paragraph on this page. Call attention to the next-to-last sentence. Point out that the sentence begins with *Learning*. Students may think that *Learning* is the verb in this sentence, but it is a gerund, a verb form used as a noun. Help students identify *Learning* as the subject of the sentence.

Health Background

TV Violence and Children By the end of elementary school, the average child has seen 100,000 acts of violence on TV, including 8,000 murders. Teens who watch more than three hours of TV daily are more likely to behave aggressively as adults.

Source: *Science*

For more background, visit the **Webliography** in Teacher Resources at **www.harcourtschool.com/health** **Keyword** violence prevention

Plans should include an explanation of strategies for avoiding violence, such as:

• Determine more than one route home.
• Know the location of the nearest trusted adult and the nearest phone.

3. WRAP UP

Lesson 1 Summary and Review

1. violence, threats, terrorism, alcohol
2. Possible answers: violent thoughts, feelings, or words
3. Possible answers: An adult helps keep the student safe, knows how to handle the problem better, and knows whether to call the police.
4. Answers may include the following:

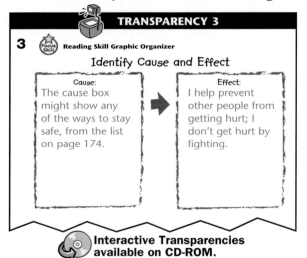

TRANSPARENCY 3

3 Reading Skill Graphic Organizer

Identify Cause and Effect

Cause:
The cause box might show any of the ways to stay safe, from the list on page 174.

Effect:
I help prevent other people from getting hurt; I don't get hurt by fighting.

 Interactive Transparencies available on CD-ROM.

5. Writing should describe the situation and should present supporting facts and details about resolving the problem.

 For **writing models** with examples, see *Teaching Resources* pp. 47–61. Rubrics are also provided.

When Minutes Count ...

Quick Study Students can use *Activity Book* pp. 26–27 (shown on p. 173) as they complete each lesson in this chapter.

Personal Health Plan ▶

Real-Life Situation
Violence can occur in any neighborhood. Suppose you walk home from school every day.

Real-Life Plan
Write three ways you could reduce the risk of violence as you walk home from school.

In the Know About Violence

The more you know about violence, the easier it is to avoid it. You can reduce your chance of being harmed by violence by avoiding gangs, staying away from weapons, and not using drugs or alcohol. Follow these tips to avoid violence:

• Be aware of what's going on around you.
• Avoid going places by yourself.
• Never try to break up a fight. If you see a violent act, tell a parent or another trusted adult.
• Walk away if someone threatens you.
• If you are walking and see people who look threatening, turn and walk in another direction.
• Tell your parents or another trusted adult if someone threatens you.

DRAW CONCLUSIONS How can paying attention to what is around you help you avoid violence?
Possible answer: Paying attention helps you identify dangerous situations so you can walk the other way.

Lesson 1 Summary and Review

❶ Summarize with Vocabulary

Use vocabulary and other terms from this lesson to complete the statements.

Any act that harms or injures someone is called _____. Acts of violence include fights, crimes, and _____. The use of violence for a political or social cause is _____. You can reduce your risk of harm from violence by not using drugs or _____.

❷ How do many acts of violence begin?

❸ Critical Thinking In a violent situation, why is it better to ask an adult for help instead of trying to solve the problem yourself?

❹ CAUSE AND EFFECT Draw and complete this graphic organizer to show how the tips for avoiding violence can help you stay safe.

Cause: → Effect:

❺ Write to Express— Solution to a Problem

Write about an argument you heard. How could the conflict have been avoided?

174

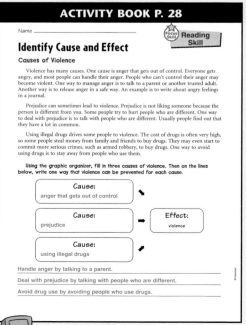

ACTIVITY BOOK P. 28

Name _____

Reading Skill

Identify Cause and Effect

Causes of Violence

Violence has many causes. One cause is anger that gets out of control. Everyone gets angry, and most people can handle their anger. People who can't control their anger may become violent. One way to manage anger is to talk to a parent or another trusted adult. Another way is to release anger in a safe way. An example is to write about angry feelings in a journal.

Prejudice can sometimes lead to violence. Prejudice is not liking someone because the person is different from you. Some people try to hurt people who are different. One way to deal with prejudice is to talk with people who are different. Usually people find out that they have a lot in common.

Using illegal drugs drives some people to violence. The cost of drugs is often very high, so some people steal money from family and friends to buy drugs. They may even start to commit more serious crimes, such as armed robbery, to buy drugs. One way to avoid using drugs is to stay away from people who use them.

Using the graphic organizer, fill in three causes of violence. Then on the lines below, write one way that violence can be prevented for each cause.

Cause: anger that gets out of control

Cause: prejudice → Effect: violence

Cause: using illegal drugs

Handle anger by talking to a parent.
Deal with prejudice by talking with people who are different.
Avoid drug use by avoiding people who use drugs.

 Available online. www.harcourtschool.com/health

Fairness

Listen to Others

Often, violence happens because people have conflicts, or disagreements. Good communication can help people work out a solution before a conflict turns violent. To be fair, each side must listen to the other. Fairness means giving both sides a chance to explain their points of view.

- **Give the other person time to share his or her feelings and thoughts.**
- **Don't interrupt. Wait until the person is finished before you speak.**
- **Use appropriate body language. Face the person, and make eye contact. Don't let your eyes wander. Keep your attention on the speaker.**
- **If you don't understand what the person is saying, ask questions or ask the person to say it again.**
- **Try to understand the other person's point of view. If you don't agree with it, don't say that the person is foolish or stupid. Respect the opinions of others, even if those opinions are different from yours.**

Activity

With a small group, think of a conflict that might occur between friends. Prepare and perform a skit in which the friends don't listen to each other. Then change the skit so that the friends do listen to each other.

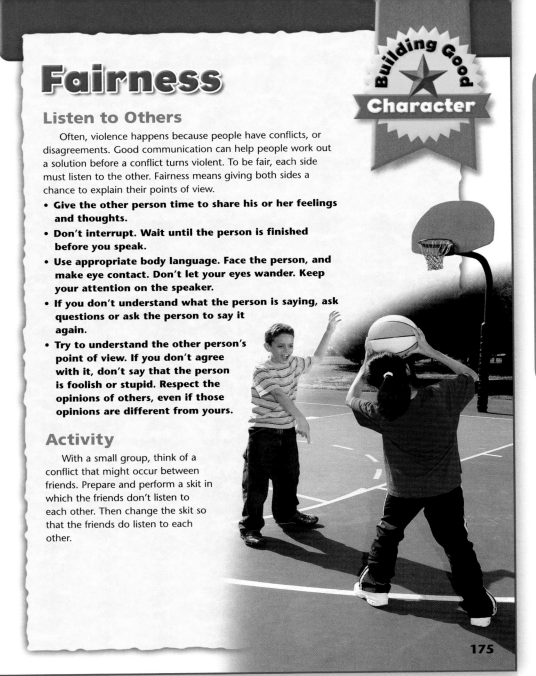

175

Building Good Character

Caring
Citizenship
Fairness
Respect
Responsibility
Trustworthiness

Objective

► Describe effective listening skills used in being fair.

Program Resources

► Poster 3

BEFORE READING

Present this scenario: **Suppose you borrow a video from a friend and accidentally misplace it. You try to explain to your friend that you will pay for the video, but your friend does not listen to you and says angry, mean things instead. Do you think your friend is treating you fairly?** Discuss students' responses with the class.

DISCUSS

After students have read the list, ask: **What can you do if you and the other person have very different points of view?** Lead students to recognize that a compromise that is acceptable to both parties is fair.

ACTIVITY

Advise students to write out scripts for both skits. After students perform their skits, ask each group to describe how the behavior in the second skit demonstrated fairness.

Using the Poster

Activity After students have reviewed the poster, ask them to write at least two more rules to follow when listening to another person's side of a story.

Display Poster 3 to remind students to be fair. The poster can be displayed in the classroom, the cafeteria, or another common area.

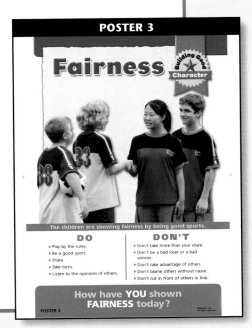

POSTER 3

Fairness

The children are showing fairness by being good sports.

DO
► Play by the rules.
► Be a good sport.
► Share.
► Take turns.
► Listen to the opinions of others.

DON'T
► Don't take more than your share.
► Don't be a bad loser or a bad winner.
► Don't take advantage of others.
► Don't blame others without cause.
► Don't cut in front of others in line.

How have **YOU** shown **FAIRNESS** today?

POSTER 3

Objectives

► Explain strategies for avoiding violence, gangs, and weapons.
► Identify alternatives to joining a gang.

When Minutes Count . . .

Assign the Quick Study, Lesson 2, Activity Book pp. 26–27 (shown on page 173).

Program Resources

► Activity Book pp. 26–27
► Transparency 3

Vocabulary

weapon p. 176, **bully** p. 177, **gang** p. 178

Daily Fitness Tip

Carrying a toy gun can be illegal. Emphasize that any kind of gun, including a toy gun or a BB gun, is not allowed in school.

 For more guidelines on safety rules, see *Be Active! Resources for Physical Education*, p. 177.

1. MOTIVATE

Share with the class two or three news stories about children who were killed or injured by guns that they had found and were playing with.

After reading each story, ask students to tell how the tragedy happened and how it could have been prevented. Survey students to find out how many safety rules they know concerning weapons. Then have them explain several strategies for avoiding weapons.

Help Prevent Violence

Lesson Focus

You can take steps to reduce violence in your community and avoid being harmed yourself.

Why Learn This?

What you learn can reduce your risk of getting hurt if you are in a violent situation.

Vocabulary

weapon
bully
gang

What to Do If Someone Has a Weapon

Even if you try to avoid violent situations, you still may find yourself faced with one. For example, a classmate may bring a weapon to school. A **weapon** is anything that can be used to harm someone. Guns and knives are weapons. Anytime a weapon is present, you are in danger.

Suppose that you find a gun while at a friend's home. To stay safe, follow these steps:

• Stop. Don't touch the gun. If your friend wants to pick it up, try to talk him or her out of it.
• Leave the room or the area right away. If your friend doesn't go with you, leave anyway. Don't wait to see what happens.
• Tell an adult. Make sure the adult knows where you found the gun.

In schools, guns and knives are not allowed. Students can be suspended or expelled for taking weapons to school.

SEQUENCE List in order the steps you should follow if you find a gun.
1. Stop; don't touch the gun. 2. Leave the area immediately. 3. Tell an adult.

◄ More than 20,000 people under the age of twenty are accidently killed or injured by gunshots each year in the United States. Guns should always be locked away, such as in a gun safe like the one shown here.

176

ESL/ELL Support

COMPREHENSIBLE INPUT Help students understand the rules for staying safe from guns.

Beginning Have students role play the steps they should take if they find a gun.

Intermediate Ask students to make a poster that lists *dos* and *don'ts* if a child finds a gun.

Advanced Help students write a dialogue between two students who find a gun. Allow volunteers to act out their dialogue for the class.

What to Do If Someone Threatens You

A **bully** is someone who hurts or frightens others. Bullies usually pick on people who are alone or who seem different in some way. Staying with a group can help you avoid bullies. However, if a bully threatens you, you may be in physical danger. Here are some tips that can help you reduce your risk of harm:

- Calmly and confidently ask the person to stop.
- Ignore the bully. A bully will usually leave you alone if you don't seem angry or frightened.
- If someone tries to get you to fight, leave the area. A person who walks away from a violent situation is stronger and smarter than a person who doesn't.
- If the bully has a weapon, stay calm and get away as quickly as possible. You don't have to speak. Don't try to be brave.
- Tell a parent or a trusted adult that you were threatened. If the bully had a weapon, let the adult know.

SUMMARIZE Tell three things you can do to reduce your risk of harm from a bully.
Students should summarize any three of the tips.

177

Personal Health Plan

Real-Life Situation
A bully at school begins calling you names and daring you to fight.
Real-Life Plan
In advance, list things you could do to avoid getting into a fight with a bully.

ACTIVITY

Life Skills

Make Responsible Decisions Tiago is at Spencer's house. Spencer wants to show his parents' gun to Tiago. What should Tiago do to stay safe?

Teacher Tip

Dispelling Blame Tell students that the victim of bullying is never to blame for the bully's behavior. Being treated with disrespect does not mean a person has done anything wrong. Some people are nasty or mean because they don't like themselves or they are jealous of others. Teach students phrases to use if someone is verbally abusive, such as "I will talk to you when you show me respect."

Art

Laugh Lines Explain that sometimes using humor may cause a bully to back off. (Be sure to discuss situations in which this is not appropriate—such as if the bully has a weapon or makes a threat.) Have students create cartoons showing humorous comebacks that a person could use if he or she is called a name or is made fun of. Display the cartoons in your classroom or elsewhere in the school to benefit all students.

---

2. TEACH

Interpret Visuals—Pictures

Have groups of students create a story about what is happening in the picture. Then have the groups think of ways to deal with the bullies. Allow groups to present their stories and solutions to the class.

Discuss

Critical Thinking What other forms can bullying take? Possible answers: spreading rumors; excluding others

 Activity

Make Decisions Students should respond that the best decision is to not go along with Spencer. Tiago could talk to Spencer first and tell him they shouldn't go near the gun. If Spencer persists, Tiago should leave quickly and tell an adult.

Personal Health Plan ▶

Students could do the following for their plans:

- List possible verbal responses.
- List possible actions or body language.
- Choose three options they would feel most comfortable with. They should think about the possibility that the bully has a weapon.

Health Background

Bullying in Schools About 16 percent of schoolchildren are victims of bullying. Children are more likely to be targets of bullying if they're socially isolated and have trouble making friends. Bullies are more likely to focus on a person's appearance or behavior than on race or religion. Boys are more likely to be hit, slapped, or pushed by bullies, and girls are often bullied through sexual comments and rumors.

Source: *Journal of the American Medical Association*

 For more background, visit the **Webliography** in Teacher Resources at **www.harcourtschool.com/health Keyword** violence prevention

TEACH *continued*

Content-Area Reading Support

Using Reference Words Direct students' attention to the second sentence in the second paragraph on this page: *Being in a gang can seem to fill these needs.* Explain that the phrase *these needs* refers to an idea stated earlier. Have a volunteer identify the idea. the needs for a sense of family and belonging

Point out to students that when they come across phrases using the word *these,* they should be certain they understand what the phrases refer to before they continue reading.

Discuss

Explain that another reason people join a gang is that they think it will protect them and they will be respected. Have students explain strategies for avoiding gangs.

Critical Thinking Does a person really get protection and respect from joining a gang? Explain your answer.
Possible answer: No. Gangs often fight rival gangs, and weapons and drugs are involved. A gang member might get respect from another gang member but not from people outside the gang.

Cause and Effect What are the possible effects of joining a gang?
fighting, being harmed, being exposed to drugs, being exptected to commit crimes, putting friends and family in danger

Consumer Activity

Analyze Media Messages Suggest that students compare the ways gangs are portrayed in different movies and TV programs. What are some common characteristics of the gangs? Ask students if they think those characteristics are true.

Quick Activity

Evaluate a Leader Have the whole group brainstorm a list of leaders. Pair students to build on each other's ideas. Suggest leadership characteristics such as "encourages people" and "treats people with respect."

Making Schools and Communities Less Violent

It is important for people to feel safe in their communities or their schools. Yet violence affects many places across the nation. Some communities have gangs that make neighborhoods or schools unsafe. A **gang** is a group of people who have a close social relationship. Recently, the word *gang* has come to refer to a group that uses violence. Gang members typically commit crimes, use drugs, and carry weapons.

Most people need a sense of family and belonging. Being in a gang can seem to fill these needs. Some people join gangs because older family members belong to one. Others join because they think membership will give them power. Some join because they are bullied or threatened if they don't become a gang member.

People who join gangs often don't understand all the consequences of being a gang member. Gangs are dangerous, and being in one usually involves fighting, drugs, weapons, crime, and going to jail. Fights between rival gangs put the members, their families, and their neighbors in danger of injury or death.

You don't have to join a gang to belong to a group. You can find positive ways to spend your time. A few ideas are listed on the next page.

Myth and Fact
Myth: Gang activity happens only in low-income neighborhoods.
Fact: Gangs can form in any community—and especially in schools. About one-fourth of the violence that occurs in schools is gang-related. Safe, gang-free schools lead to safe, healthy communities.

Being part of a group doesn't mean being part of a gang. ▶

178

Meeting Individual Needs
Leveled Activities

BELOW-LEVEL Identify School Groups Have students list clubs, sports, and other organized after-school activities at your school.

ON-LEVEL Volunteer Encourage students to brainstorm ideas for volunteer activities in your community. Provide telephone directories for locating organizations that might use volunteers. Ask students to get parental permission for contacting organizations in which they are interested and finding out if people their age can volunteer.

CHALLENGE Form a Club Have students create an after-school group based on their interests, such as exercise, games, or arts and crafts. Ask students to identify adults who might organize and lead the group.

◀ A parent, teacher, or other trusted adult can help you find ways to stay safe in your school and community.

- Get involved with a community group or start one of your own. Think about what you would like to change about your community to make it safer. Identify a person or a group that can help you.
- Join a school club or a sports team.
- Become a leader in your school's student government or become a member of your school's conflict resolution group.
- Volunteer for a good cause in your community. Encourage your classmates to join you.

COMPARE AND CONTRAST How are gangs and community groups alike? How are they different?

Alike—People in both have a sense of belonging. Different— Gangs involve violence; community groups do not.

Quick Activity

Evaluate a Leader Think about a leader in your community or school. What makes him or her a good leader? Write a paragraph telling how you could be a leader and help improve your community.

Lesson 2 Summary and Review

❶ Summarize with Vocabulary

Use vocabulary and other terms from this lesson to complete the statements.

A _____ is something that can be used to harm someone. Someone who hurts or frightens others is a _____. Fighting, drugs, crime, and going to jail often are part of being a member of a _____. You can join a positive group in your school or _____ to gain a sense of belonging.

❷ What happens to students who take weapons to school?

❸ Critical Thinking Why might a bully stop calling you names if you ask him or her to stop?

❹ **CAUSE AND EFFECT**

Draw and complete this graphic organizer to show some effects of being a gang member.

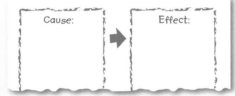

❺ Write to Entertain—Poem

Write a poem telling how to prevent violence.

179

---

3. WRAP UP

Lesson 2 Summary and Review

1. weapon, bully, gang, community

2. The students may be suspended or expelled.

3. Answers will vary. Possible answer: When you stand up to a bully, you show that you are not afraid. Bullies want to feel that they are frightening others.

4. Possible answers may include the following:

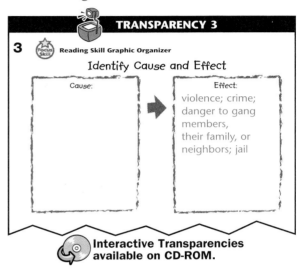

TRANSPARENCY 3

3 Reading Skill Graphic Organizer

Identify Cause and Effect

Cause:

Effect: violence; crime; danger to gang members, their family, or neighbors; jail

Interactive Transparencies available on CD-ROM.

5. Students' poems should focus on preventing violence and should include details about staying safe.

 For **writing models** with examples, see *Teaching Resources* pp. 47–61. Rubrics are also provided.

 When Minutes Count . . .

Quick Study Students can use *Activity Book* pp. 26–27 (shown on p. 173) as they complete each lesson in this chapter.

 Music

Anti-Gang Rap Have students create a rap song that promotes anti-gang activities. Arrange for students to perform the song for the school.

Teacher Tip

Identifying Gang Members

Tell students that gang members identify each other by wearing a particular color of clothing or a logo, by using certain hand signals, and by drawing gang symbols and using gang handwriting. Students should never try to copy or imitate any of these symbols or signals.

Life Skills

Communicate
Make Responsible Decisions
Manage Stress
Refuse
Resolve Conflicts
Set Goals

Objectives
► Identify skills used to resolve conflicts.
► Apply skills to resolve conflicts before conflicts become violent.

Program Resources
► Activity Book p. 29
► Poster 11

1. MOTIVATE

Write *win/win* and *negotiate* on the board, and ask if anyone knows what these terms mean. Lead students to understand that negotiation is a give-and-take process used when two sides have a disagreement. It allows each side to get something it wants or needs; both sides win.

2. TEACH

Direct students' attention to the photos of Shawn and Mark. Ask a student volunteer to read the first paragraph.

Step 1
What "I" message might Shawn use?
Possible answer: I need to finish my project on the computer. I'll be done in a little while.

Step 2
What do Shawn and Mark learn from listening to each other? They learn that both of them need to use the computer to finish a school project.

Resolve Conflicts
to Prevent Violence

It's normal for friends or classmates to disagree from time to time. However, if people don't resolve their disagreements, or conflicts, the result can be angry feelings and even fights. You can use the steps for **Resolving Conflicts** to prevent violence.

Sam is using a school computer to do research. Mark comes into the computer lab and wants to use the computer. When Sam doesn't leave the computer right away, Mark gets angry.

1 **Use "I" messages to tell how you feel.**

> I need to finish my work. I'm almost done.

When Sam turns around, Mark looks angry. Sam speaks calmly and tells Mark how he feels.

2 **Consider the other person's point of view.**

> I've missed a lot of school, and this is the best way for m to get caught up.

Sam and Mark talk about why they need to use the computer.

180

Teacher Tip

Communicating Wants and Needs Explain that it's important to express wants and needs clearly so that both people can start working on a solution. Saying "I'm angry because you're on the computer" isn't helpful because it doesn't let the other person know that you need the computer. Ask students how they would respond to such a statement. They will probably say they would feel defensive or confused. Have students practice making requests in a way that promotes good communication.

ACTIVITY BOOK P. 29

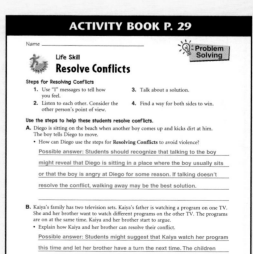

Name _____

Life Skill
Resolve Conflicts

Steps for Resolving Conflicts
1. Use "I" messages to tell how you feel.
2. Listen to each other. Consider the other person's point of view.
3. Talk about a solution.
4. Find a way for both sides to win.

Use the steps to help these students resolve conflicts.

A. Diego is sitting on the beach when another boy comes up and kicks dirt at him. The boy tells Diego to move.
• How can Diego use the steps for **Resolving Conflicts** to avoid violence?
  Possible answer: Students should recognize that talking to the boy might reveal that Diego is sitting in a place where the boy usually sits or that the boy is angry at Diego for some reason. If talking doesn't resolve the conflict, walking away may be the best solution.

B. Kaiya's family has two television sets. Kaiya's father is watching a program on one TV. She and her brother want to watch different programs on the other TV. The programs are on at the same time. Kaiya and her brother start to argue.
• Explain how Kaiya and her brother can resolve their conflict.
  Possible answer: Students might suggest that Kaiya watch her program this time and let her brother have a turn the next time. The children might flip a coin to see who goes first. They also might talk with their parents to try to find another solution.

Available online.
www.harcourtschool.com/health

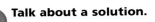

3 Talk about a solution.

If you can wait just a few minutes, I'll be finished with my assignments.

I need an hour to do my research.

Sam and Mark explain how much time they each need. The boys listen to one another without interrupting.

4 Find a way for both sides to win.

Thanks. I'm sorry I got angry.

Sam and Mark work out a plan that enables both of them to finish their assignments by sharing the computer.

Problem Solving

A. At school Matt bullies Jonah by calling him names. One day while Jonah is walking home from school, Matt walks up behind Jonah and shoves him.
- Use the steps for **Resolving Conflicts** to help Jonah prevent violence.

B. Laura and Anne used to be best friends. They got into an argument, and now they don't talk to each other. Last week Anne started to make angry phone calls to Laura at home. Laura knows she needs to do something about the problem before it gets worse.
- Explain a responsible decision that Laura could make to resolve the conflict with Anne.

181

Using the Poster

Activity Have students study the poster and review the steps shown here for resolving conflicts. Have students write a paragraph on how the steps not only prevent violence but also help promote healthy relationships with other people.

Display the poster to remind students of the steps for resolving conflicts.

POSTER 11

Resolve Conflicts

The girls are resolving a conflict by negotiating politely.

Steps to Resolve Conflicts

1 Use I-messages to tell how you feel.
2 Listen to each other. Consider the other person's view.
3 Negotiate.
4 Find a way for both sides to win.

How do YOU RESOLVE CONFLICTS?

POSTER 11

Step 3

How do Shawn and Mark show that they are listening to each other? They listen without interrupting.

Critical Thinking **How does talking about what they need help Shawn and Mark come up with a solution?** Each has to understand the needs of the other person before the two of them can come up with a solution that's helpful to both.

Step 4

How do Shawn and Mark both win? Both get the time they need to work on their projects, and they have prevented possible violence, either physical or verbal.

Building Good Character Remind students that fairness means you take turns and share. You treat others the way you want to be treated. Being fair helps prevent violence and keep friendships.

3. WRAP UP

Problem Solving

A Students should recognize that Jonah should not hit Matt or shove him back. The best solution for dealing with a bully who physically attacks someone would be to involve the parents.

B Laura should tell her parents that Anne is making threatening phone calls. Laura's parents can help the girls resolve the conflict by using the steps described on these pages. Students should show how the steps could help resolve the conflict.

Objectives

► Demonstrate strategies for avoiding violence on the street and at school.

► Describe safe ways to respond to a terrorist attack.

 When Minutes Count . . .

Assign the Quick Study, Lesson 3, Activity Book pp. 26–27 (shown on p. 173).

Program Resources

► Activity Book pp. 26–27, 30

► Transparency 3

Vocabulary

zero-tolerance policy p. 183

 **Daily Fitness Tip**

Anger plays a key role in violence. Remind students to express their anger in healthful ways, such as by talking honestly with the other person, trying to resolve disagreements peacefully, and talking to their parents and other trusted adults, such as the school counselor.

 For more guidelines about exercise for stress relief, see *Be Active! Resources for Physical Education,* p. 157.

1. MOTIVATE

Optional Activity Materials

transparency showing a newspaper headline about violence in schools

Be sure students have their books closed. Show them the headline, and ask them to estimate the percentage of violent deaths of children that occur on school grounds. Write their estimates on the board. Then have them open their books and read Did You Know? on page 183. Students may be surprised that the percentage is not higher. Point out that even with this low percentage and despite school policies, violence can still occur at school. This chapter will provide guidelines for staying safe at school.

 LESSON

3 Surviving Violence

Street Violence

Violence can sometimes take place in your own neighborhood. Street violence can involve gangs, drugs, theft, or *hate crimes*. Hate crimes are crimes based on race, religion, nationality, and other reasons.

The best way to protect yourself from street violence is to think ahead and follow these guidelines:

- Before you go out, ask permission. Tell a parent where you're going, how you'll get there, who you'll be with, and when you'll be home.
- Avoid places where violence occurs. Don't talk to strangers who come up to you. Yell for help if someone bothers you.
- Use the buddy system. Stay with other people when going places or just hanging out.

DRAW CONCLUSIONS How does each guideline for protecting yourself help you stay safe?

Lesson Focus
You can take steps to protect yourself from violence.

Why Learn This?
What you learn can reduce your risk of being harmed by violent acts, including terrorism.

Vocabulary
zero-tolerance policy

Possible answer: An adult knows where you are in case he or she needs to find you; you keep away from people who might harm you; if you are with someone else, he or she can help if you have a problem.

Quick Activity

Learn from Graphs Study this circle graph. What is the biggest reason for hate crimes? What percent of hate crimes are committed because of nationality? How many more crimes are committed because of race than nationality?

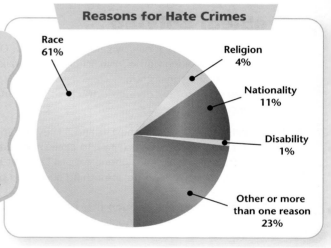

Reasons for Hate Crimes

Race 61%
Religion 4%
Nationality 11%
Disability 1%
Other or more than one reason 23%

182

 ESL/ELL Support

LANGUAGE AND VOCABULARY Help students understand compound nouns used as adjectives.

Beginning Help students figure out the meaning of *anger, management, zero,* and *tolerance.* Have each student work with an English-proficient partner to see how the words are put together and used as adjectives.

Intermediate Ask students to write two sentences using *anger-management* and *zero-tolerance* as adjectives.

Advanced Have students write a paragraph that describes the concept of anger-management skills or a zero-tolerance policy.

◀ Many schools expel students for having weapons, drugs, or alcohol; for fighting; or for making threats.

School Violence

Another place where you need to think about safety is at school. Almost half of all elementary schools report one or more violent situations each year. That's why many schools have zero-tolerance policies. A **zero-tolerance policy** means that no violence and no weapons of any kind are allowed in the school. It also promises punishments for students who don't follow the policy. These policies help keep students safe from weapons and threats. Students learn better when they aren't afraid.

Anger that gets out of control can lead to violence. Some schools have programs that help students learn how to manage anger and conflicts. You can learn more about dealing with anger and other emotions on pages 314–316.

Some schools take additional measures to reduce violence. Visitors must sign in before entering the school. School grounds and play areas may have fences around them. Some schools have security guards or resource officers.

MAIN IDEA AND DETAILS Give three details about how schools help keep students safe.
Any three of the following: zero-tolerance policies; anger-management programs; security guards, schoolyard fencing, signing in visitors

ACTIVITY

Building Good Character

Citizenship At school, José sees a knife sticking out of someone's coat. Explain how José can show good citizenship and help prevent school violence.

183

Integrated Language Arts/ Reading Skills

Public Service Announcement
Have students work together to prepare several messages about school rules that help keep students safe. The messages should include the school's policies on weapons and violence. Get permission from the principal to have several students present the messages over the school's public-address system. You might have students demonstrate other ways to communicate health information, such as posters, videos, and brochures.

Math

Calculating Percentages When reading the Did You Know? feature, students may wonder how many violent deaths the 1 percent figure represents. In 2000, according to CDC, 2,285 homicides occurred among children ages five to nineteen. Have students calculate 1 percent of this number (about 23). Of the total number of homicides, 1,736 were caused by firearms. What percentage of the homicides were caused by firearms? (76 percent)

2. TEACH

Discuss

Read to students your school's policy on reducing violence, and discuss its meaning. Point out the school standards for student behaviors. Explain that anger that gets out of control can lead to violence. As children get older, they are expected to have more self-control. They should also be able to demonstrate strategies for preventing deliberate injuries.

Critical Thinking What does it mean to have self-control? You control your actions and words so that you do not hurt anyone physically or verbally.

Problem Solving How can you get control over your anger? Possible answers: Talk to your parents; exercise; try to resolve your conflicts peacefully.

Content-Area Reading Support
Using Signal Words Direct students' attention to the first sentence on this page. Point out that the word *another* signals that there are at least two or more facts, ideas, or things. When students come across this word, they should pause briefly to recall the information that preceded it—in this case, information about the neighborhood.

Quick Activity
Learn from Graphs race; about 11 percent; about 5.5 times

Activity
Citizenship Students should recognize that being a good citizen means obeying rules and laws. Jose can be a good citizen by telling his teacher about the knife. Emphasize that students should always report a serious threat of violence. This is not tattling—students could be keeping someone from getting seriously hurt.

3. WRAP UP

Lesson 3 Summary and Review

1. hate crimes, zero-tolerance policy, buddy

2. Answers may include telling a parent where you are going before you leave home; not talking to strangers; and traveling with a friend.

3. Possible answers: Don't carry a weapon to school; follow school rules; don't get into fights or threaten others.

4. Possible answers are shown below:

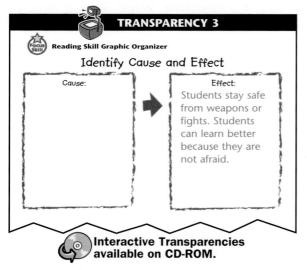

TRANSPARENCY 3

Reading Skill Graphic Organizer

Identify Cause and Effect

Cause:

Effect: Students stay safe from weapons or fights. Students can learn better because they are not afraid.

Interactive Transparencies available on CD-ROM.

5. Student writing should include details about where you will be going, how you will get there, who will be going with you, and when you will be back.

For **writing models** with examples, see *Teaching Resources* pp. 47–61. Rubrics are also provided.

When Minutes Count ...

Quick Study Students can use *Activity Book* pp. 26–27 (shown on p. 173) as they complete each lesson in this chapter.

Terrorism

Another kind of violence that can affect people's safety is terrorism. If a terrorist attack occurs, you can reduce your risk of injury by doing the following:

Information Alert!

Department of Homeland Security After September 11, 2001, the United States government formed the Department of Homeland Security to protect the nation from attacks.

GO ONLINE For the most up-to-date information, visit The Learning Site. www.harcourtschool.com/health

- Stay calm. Panic can cause people to get hurt.
- Listen to the directions from the person in charge. At school, teachers and the principal will give instructions to help students stay safe. Outside of school, community leaders, police, and other officials will try to keep everyone free from harm.
- Have an emergency plan. An emergency plan for terrorism might include going to a secure place inside and staying away from doors and windows.

SUMMARIZE Tell what you should do if a terrorist situation happens.
Stay calm, follow the directions of the person in charge, and carry out an emergency plan.

Lesson 3 Summary and Review

❶ **Summarize with Vocabulary**

Use vocabulary and other terms from this lesson to complete the statements.

Crimes based on race, religion, nationality, disability, and so on, are called _____. A school policy that does not allow any drugs or weapons is called a _____. Protecting yourself by hanging out with others is called the _____ system.

❷ What is one thing you can do to protect yourself from street violence?

❸ **Critical Thinking** What can individual students do to help reduce the risk of violence in their schools?

❹ **IDENTIFY CAUSE AND EFFECT**
Draw and complete this graphic organizer to show causes and effects of a school zero-tolerance policy.

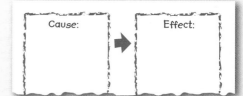

Cause:

Effect:

❺ **Write to Inform—Explanation**

Suppose a friend's family invites you to go to the mall. What should you tell your parents when you ask permission to go?

ACTIVITY BOOK P. 30

Name _____

AB Vocabulary Reinforcement

Find the Secret Words

A. Fill in the words or phrases that fit the definitions in the squares below. Then copy the letters from the numbered boxes into the matching numbered boxes at the bottom of the page.

1. anything that can be used to harm someone
2. a school policy that means no violence and no weapons of any kind are allowed in school
3. someone who hurts or frightens others
4. the use of force and violence against people or property for a political or social goal
5. a group of people who have a close social relationship
6. any act that harms or injures people

1. W E A P O N
2. Z E R O - T O L E R A N C E
3. B U L L Y
4. T E R R O R I S M
5. G A N G
6. V I O L E N C E

B. Use each secret word in a sentence that answers the question.

1. How can you avoid violence? A W A R E
   Possible answer: Be aware of what's going on around you.

2. How should you deal with a bully? I G N O R E
   Possible answer: Ignore the bully.

Available online. www.harcourtschool.com/health

Math

Keep a Record In a small notebook, make an entry each time you have a disagreement with someone. Then describe the problem or conflict. Think about whether you handled the situation well. If you didn't, write what you could have done differently. After one week, count the number of conflicts you have each day to see if they're increasing or decreasing. Share your notebook with a parent or other trusted adult.

Art

Organize a Community Mural Project Organize or help to organize a community art project. Talk with a community leader to find a place for a mural, or large painting, on a wall or building. Post fliers to encourage people from your community to get involved with painting the mural.

Technology Project

Research Community Youth Groups Identify local groups that are for kids your age. Use a computer to make a chart listing the groups and activities that young people can participate in. Which group would you like to join? Why? Explain how having young people active in local groups can help keep communities safe and healthy.

 For more activities, visit The Learning Site. www.harcourtschool.com/health

Home & Community

Discuss Conflicts on TV Keep a TV log with your family. As you watch each show, record any conflicts that you see. Later, discuss whether the conflicts could have been handled better. Record your observations in your log.

Career Link

Baggage Screener Baggage screeners check the bags that people carry onto airplanes. They also screen passengers' luggage that is carried onto the plane. Suppose that you're a baggage screener at an airport. Write a security report telling how you help keep people safe when they fly. Explain what you like about your job and why your job is important.

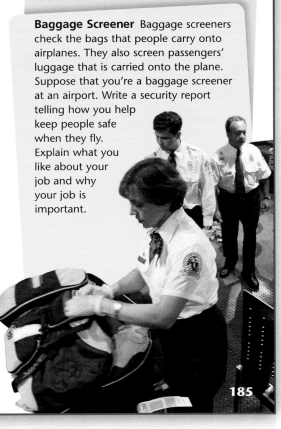

185

Activities

Math
Advise students to write the Steps to Resolve Conflicts in the front of their notebooks and refer to them as needed. Suggest that they ask their parents to help them if they experience a conflict they cannot resolve peacefully.

Art
Have students identify adults who can help with this project. One student's parent may be a member of the city council, for example. Tell students that they must have permission before painting community property.

Home & Community
Encourage students to also discuss conflicts that were handled well. Suggest that students analyze those conflicts for tone of voice, choice of words, body language, and listening skills. Ask students to write a brief paragraph describing what they learned.

 Supports the Coordinated School Health Program

Technology Project
Post the charts so that students can share information. Consider asking representatives of the groups to speak to your class. Encourage students to talk with their parents about joining a group.

Career Link

Baggage Screener Tell students that the qualifications for being a baggage screener were tightened after the terrorist attacks in September 2001. Some of the qualifications now include that the person must be a U.S. citizen, speak fluent English, and be able to deal well with the public.

Tell students to explain how baggage screeners help protect people's health. Students should also describe why it is important that baggage screeners know how to deal well with people.

 For more information on health careers, visit the **Webliography** in Teacher Resources at **www.harcourtschool.com/health** **Keyword** health careers

Chapter Review and Test Preparation

Pages 186–187

 Reading Skill 8 pts. each

1. Possible answers: Ask the bully to stop. Laugh it off.

2. Possible answer: The bully will leave you alone because he or she can see that you are not frightened or angry.

 Use Vocabulary 2 pts. each

3. C, weapon

4. E, gang

5. A, violence

6. F, hate crime

7. B, terrorism

8. D, bully

 Check Understanding 3 pts. each

9. B, zero-tolerance policy

10. G, Guns are not allowed in schools.

11. C, get away as quickly as possible

12. F, solving problems

13. D, Tell a teacher or principal.

14. H, protection from harm

15. B, a hairbrush

16. G, Terrorism can happen anywhere in the world.

17. A, Speak calmly to strangers.

18. J, all of the above

19. C, stay with a buddy when going places

 Think Critically 6 pts. each

20. Violence happens in communities around the world each day, so you need to know how to stay safe if a violent situation happens.

Chapter Review and Test Preparation

 Reading Skill

CAUSE AND EFFECT
Draw and then use this graphic organizer to answer questions 1 and 2.

1 Write about an action you can take if a bully calls you names.
2 Write about a possible effect of your action on the bully's behavior.

 Use Vocabulary

Match each term in Column A with its meaning in Column B.

Column A	Column B
3 Object used to harm someone is a _____.	**A** violence
4 Joining a _____ often leads to violence.	**B** terrorism
5 Any act that harms a person is _____.	**C** weapon
6 A crime based on race is a _____.	**D** bully
7 _____ is the use of violence for a political or social goal.	**E** gang
8 A _____ is someone who hurts or frightens others.	**F** hate crime

186

Check Understanding

Choose the letter of the correct answer.

9 A school's policy of not allowing any weapons is called a _____. (p. 183)
 A just-say-no policy
 B zero-tolerance policy
 C no-weapons policy
 D drug-free-zone policy

10 Which is **TRUE** about gun safety? (p. 176)
 F Toy guns are OK to bring to school.
 G Guns are not allowed in schools.
 H Guns should be stored loaded.
 J If a bully has a gun, take it away.

11 If a bully threatens you, _____. (p. 177)
 A kick the bully and get away
 B tell the bully he or she is stupid
 C get away as quickly as possible
 D laugh at the bully

12 Violence is **NOT** related to _____. (p. 172)
 F solving problems H stealing
 G hate crimes J fighting

13 Which of the following is the **BEST** way to prevent violence between the students in the picture? (p. 177)

 A Try to break up the argument.
 B Get them to talk about a solution.
 C Call the police.
 D Tell a teacher or principal.

14 Which of the following is **NOT** part of gang membership? (p. 178)
 F jail H protection
 G crime J sense of belonging

Formal Assessment

ASSESSMENT GUIDE P. 34

6 Name _____ Chapter Test

Preventing Violence

Match each phrase in Column A with the sentence part in Column B that makes a true statement.

		Column A		Column B
j	1.	A zero-tolerance policy means	a	is acting violently.
h	2.	Some teens join gangs	b	who are different in some way.
e	3.	Acts of violence include	c	by joining a school club or sports team.
g	4.	Never try to	d	leave the area right away.
b	5.	Bullies often target people	e	fights, crimes, and threats.
c	6.	Some students avoid gangs	f	walk away.
a	7.	A person who threatens you	g	break up a fight.
f	8.	If someone wants to fight you,	h	because they think it makes them strong.
d	9.	To be safe around a gun,	i	to stress a political point of view.
i	10.	Terrorists use violence	j	no weapons of any kind are allowed in school.

ASSESSMENT GUIDE P. 35

Name _____

Underline the term or phrase that makes each statement false. Choose the correct term from the box, and write it in the blank following the statement.

gang	expelled	communicate	terrorism	anger
weapon	bully	violence	hate crimes	

11. A concussion is anything that can be used to harm people. _____ weapon

12. A person who hurts or frightens others is a pedestrian. _____ bully

13. Students can be suspended or graduated for bringing weapons to school. _____ expelled

14. Any act that harms or injures people is antiseptic. _____ violence

15. Homeland crimes are based on race, religion, disability, and other reasons. _____ hate crimes

16. A community is a group of people who have a close social relationship and often commit crimes and carry weapons. _____ gang

17. A zero-tolerance policy means that no vehicles and no weapons of any kind are allowed. _____ violence

18. Learning ways to handle a gun is an important tool for preventing violence. _____ communicate

19. Tolerance is the use of violence for a political goal. _____ Terrorism

20. Children should learn how to settle disputes without laughing. _____ violence

15 Which of the following is **NOT** a cause for being suspended or expelled if it's carried to school? (p. 183)

A
B
C
D

16 Which is **TRUE** of terrorism? (p. 184)

F There is nothing you can do to stay safe during a terrorist attack.

G Terrorism can happen anywhere in the world.

H Terrorists use peaceful means to achieve social goals.

J Terrorists always know their victims.

17 Which of the following is **NOT** a detail about staying safe? (p. 182)

A Speak calmly to strangers.

B Don't play alone.

C Tell your parents where you will be.

D Avoid places where violence occurs.

18 At which of the following places would you need to watch out for violence? (pp. 172)

F school

G your community

H your neighborhood

J all of these places

19 In the buddy system, you _____. (p. 182)

A tell your parents where you're going

B make friends with strangers

C always stay with another person

D call your friends on the telephone

Think Critically

20 Why do you need to know about violence?

21 Suppose you're walking down the street and see a group of people who look threatening. What should you do to protect yourself from harm?

22 How could joining a community group help keep other kids in your neighborhood from joining a gang?

Apply Skills

23 **BUILDING GOOD CHARACTER**

Fairness A friend wants you to come home with her after school. When you tell her that you have other plans, and she gets angry. How can you handle the problem fairly?

24 **LIFE SKILLS**

Resolve Conflicts Your parents are away for the evening, and your older brother has been on the phone a long time. You're expecting a call from a friend. Your brother gives you an angry look when you signal that you need to use the phone. How could you resolve the conflict?

Write About Health

25 **Write to Inform—Explanation** Explain why preventing violence is an important part of staying healthy.

187

---

21. Possible answer: Turn and walk in the opposite direction.

22. Joining a community group could help others stay out of gangs by showing that community groups are fun, safe, and give people a sense of belonging.

Apply Skills 7 pts. each

23. Possible answer: Allow your friend to talk about her anger. Then make plans to do something else together.

24. Answers will vary. Students should demonstrate that they understand all four steps for resolving conflicts.

Write About Health 7 pts.

25. Students should recognize that preventing violence helps keep people from getting injured. Students also may recognize that preventing violence helps a person's mental and social health by helping maintain good relationships with family and friends.

Performance Assessment

Use the Chapter Project and the rubric provided on the Project Evaluation Sheet. See *Assessment Guide* pp. 18, 58, 65.

Portfolio Assessment

Have students select their best work from the following suggestions:

- Leveled Activities, p. 178
- Quick Activity, p. 178
- Write to Inform, p. 184
- Activities, p. 185

See *Assessment Guide* pp. 12–16.

ASSESSMENT GUIDE P. 36

Name _____

21. What three steps should you take if you find a weapon, such as a gun or knife?
(1) Stop what you are doing. Don't touch the weapon. (2) Get out of the area immediately. Don't wait to see what happens or try to talk a friend into leaving with you. (3) Tell an adult.

22. A neighborhood gang wants Daryl to join them. Daryl likes the idea of having a group of close friends that will support him, but he wants to avoid the gang. What might Daryl do instead of joining the gang?
Possible answer: Daryl could join a school club, sports team, or neighborhood organization. He could also volunteer in the community.

23. Nina thinks that fighting is the only way to win an argument. What suggestions could you make to help her settle disagreements without violence?
Possible answer: Nina could use the steps for Resolving Conflicts to avoid violence. First she could explain how she feels about a situation. Then Nina could talk with others, listening to their points of view. Nina could work with her friends to think of a solution that lets both sides win the argument

24. What kinds of things do you think are taught in an anger management class?
Possible answer: Anger management classes are likely to include exercises or role-playing that gives students practice communicating their points of view and discussing opposing points of view without yelling, name calling, or threatening. There might be class exercises in listening, as well as problem-solving exercises.

25. How has your school worked to prevent violence? What kinds of rules and safety measures are in place? Explain why you think your school took these actions. Write your answers on another sheet of paper.
Check students' answers.

Lesson	Pacing	Objectives	Reading Skills
Introduce the Chapter pp. 188–189		• Preview chapter concepts.	**Summarize** p. 189; pp. 372–383
1 Causes of Disease pp. 190–193	1 class period	• Identify the two types of disease. • Explain how lifestyle choices affect the risk of contracting some diseases. • Develop respect for people with disabilities.	**Summarize** pp. 190, 193 • Main Idea and Details, p. 191 • Cause and Effect, p. 192
2 Pathogens and Communicable Diseases pp. 194–199	1 class period	• Identify four kinds of pathogens that can cause communicable diseases. • Learn how to protect yourself from these pathogens.	**Summarize** p. 199 • Compare and Contrast, p. 194 • Draw Conclusions, p. 195 • Main Idea and Details, p. 196 • Cause and Effect, p. 197 • Sequence, p. 199
3 Disease and the Immune System pp. 200–205	1 class period	• Understand how the body defends itself from disease by blocking and destroying pathogens. • Understand how vaccines and antibiotics can fight disease.	**Summarize** p. 205 • Compare and Contrast, p. 201 • Draw Conclusions, p. 202 • Cause and Effect, p. 203
4 When Someone Gets Ill pp. 206–209	1 class period	• Understand the importance of seeking treatment from health-care professionals. • Learn the role and importance of immunizations.	**Summarize** pp. 207, 209 • Cause and Effect, p. 209
Life Skills pp. 210–211	1 class period	• Identify steps to manage stress. • Practice steps to manage stress to keep your body healthy.	
5 Noncommunicable Diseases pp. 212–218	2 class periods	• Identify the causes and symptoms of noncommunicable diseases. • Understand the difference between chronic and acute diseases.	**Summarize** pp. 216, 218 • Cause and Effect, pp. 213, 217 • Compare and Contrast, p. 214 • Draw Conclusions, pp. 215, 218
Building Good Character p. 219		• Learn how to take responsibility for your own health.	
6 Choosing a Healthful Lifestyle pp. 220–222	1 class period	• Learn how to make healthful choices to reduce your risk of disease. • Understand the importance of eating well, exercising, and avoiding tobacco.	**Summarize** p. 222 • Main Idea and Details, p. 221 • Cause and Effect, p. 222
Activities p. 223		• Extend chapter concepts.	
Chapter Review pp. 224–225	1 class period	• Assess chapter objectives.	

Vocabulary	Program Resources
	Music CD Teaching Resources, p. 35
communicable disease noncommunicable disease	Transparency 6 Activity Book, pp. 31–33
symptoms pathogens infection viruses bacteria fungi protozoa abstinence	Transparency 6 Activity Book, pp. 31–33
antibodies immunity vaccine antibiotic resistance	Transparency 6 Activity Book, pp. 31–32
immunization	Transparency 6 Activity Book, pp. 31–32
	Activity Book, p. 34 Poster 9
chronic acute insulin seizure	Transparency 6 Activity Book, pp. 31–32
	Poster 5
	Transparency 6 Activity Book, pp. 31–32, 35
	The Learning Site www. harcourtschool.com/health
	Assessment Guide, pp. 37–39

Interactive Transparencies available on CD-ROM.

Reading Skill

These reading skills are reinforced throughout this chapter and one skill is emphasized as the Focus Skill.

Summarize

- Draw Conclusions
- Identify Cause and Effect
- Identify Main Idea and Details
- Sequence
- Compare and Contrast

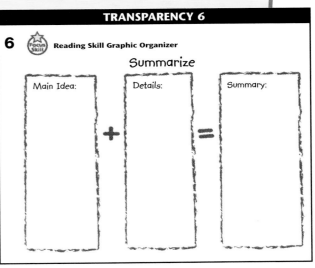

TRANSPARENCY 6

6 Reading Skill Graphic Organizer

Summarize

Main Idea: + Details: = Summary:

Life Skills

Life Skills are health-enhancing behaviors that can help students reduce risks to their health and safety.

Six Life Skills are reinforced throughout *Harcourt Health and Fitness.* The skill emphasized in this chapter is Manage Stress.

POSTER 9

Manage Stress

The girl is visualizing herself making new friends.

Ways to Manage Stress

1 Know what stress feels like and what causes it.
2 Do something active to make yourself feel better.
3 Talk with someone you trust about the way you are feeling.
4 Visualize yourself doing well in a stressful situation.

How have **YOU** MANAGED STRESS today?

POSTER 9

Building Good Character

Character education is an important aspect of health education. When students behave in ways that show good character, they promote the health and safety of themselves and others.

Six character traits are reinforced throughout *Harcourt Health and Fitness.* The trait emphasized in this chapter is Responsibility.

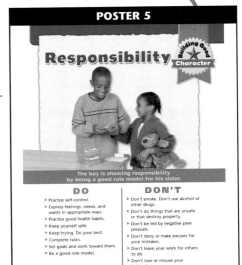

POSTER 5

Responsibility

The boy is showing responsibility by being a good role model for his sister.

DO
▸ Practice self-control.
▸ Express feelings, needs, and wants in appropriate ways.
▸ Practice good health habits.
▸ Keep yourself safe.
▸ Keep trying. Do your best.
▸ Complete tasks.
▸ Set goals and work toward them.
▸ Be a good role model.

DON'T
▸ Don't smoke. Don't use alcohol or other drugs.
▸ Don't do things that are unsafe or that destroy property.
▸ Don't be led by negative peer pressure.
▸ Don't deny or make excuses for your mistakes.
▸ Don't leave your work for others to do.
▸ Don't lose or misuse your belongings.

How have **YOU** shown RESPONSIBILITY today?

POSTER 5

Coordinated School Health Program

A Coordinated School Health Program endeavors to improve children's health and, therefore, their capacity to learn through the support of families, schools, and communities working together. The following information is provided to help classroom teachers be more aware of these resources.

The National Center for Chronic Disease and Health Promotion, part of the **CDC**, funds the Coordinated School Health Program. Visit its website for information about the eight components that make up this program. **www.cdc.gov/nccdphp/dash/**

Children, including babies, can have high blood pressure. The **American Heart Association** recommends that all children have yearly blood pressure checks. *The AHA Kids Cookbook* contains recipes for dishes that are low in fat and cholesterol. **www.americanheart.org/**

BAM! (Body and Mind) from the **CDC** contains various health topics for kids. *Disease Detectives* provides students with information about germs and preventing disease.

Myths and facts about influenza and the common cold are explained by the American Lung Association **(ALA)** along with guidelines for the prevention and treatment of these common illnesses. **www.lungusa.org/**

Other resources that support a Coordinated School Health Program:
- School-Home Connection
- Daily Physical Activity
- Daily Fitness Tips
- Activities: Home & Community
- Health Background: Webliography
- *Be Active! Resources for Physical Education*

Media Resources

Books for Students

Benziger, John. ***The Corpuscles Meet the Virus Invaders.*** Corpuscles Intergalactica, 1990. Fun facts about colds and the immune system. **EASY**

Yount, Lisa. ***Antoni van Leeuwenhoek: First to See Microscopic Life.*** Enslow Publishers, 2001. A biography of the scientist. **AVERAGE**

Parker, Steve. ***Medicine (Eyewitness).*** Dorling Kindersley Publishers, 2000. Looks at medicine around the world. **ADVANCED**

Books for Teachers and Families

American Lung Association Advisory Group and Norman Edelman. ***The American Lung Association Family Guide to Asthma and Allergies.*** Little, Brown and Company, 1997. A guide to symptoms and treatments.

Phibbs, Brendan, M.D. ***The Human Heart: A Basic Guide to Heart Disease.*** Lippincott Williams &

Wilkins, 1997. A text on types and prevention of heart disease.

Free and Inexpensive Materials

Federal Citizen Information Center
Ask for #507K, *Got a Sick Kid?*, which explains how to give the right medication in the right dosage.

The American Heart Association
Receive up to five free copies of *What Every Teacher Should Know*, #65-3535.

The American Lung Association
Subscribe to free e-mail newsletter on topics such as *Asthma Buster Alerts.*

Johnson & Johnson Companies
Receive e-mails with information on promotions and diabetes news.

American Institute for Cancer Research
Request brochures such as *Simple Steps to Prevent Cancer.*

To access free and inexpensive resources on the Web, visit **www.harcourtschool.com/health/free**

Videos

Immune System. Schlessinger Media, 2001.

Pumping Life: The Heart and Circulatory System. Rainbow Educational Media, 1989.

The Body's Defenses Against Disease. Rainbow Educational Media, 1996.

These resources have been selected to meet a variety of individual needs. Please review all materials and websites prior to sharing them with students to ensure the content is appropriate for your class. Note that information, while correct at time of publication, is subject to change.

Visit **The Learning Site** for related links, activities, resources, and the health **Webliography.**

www.harcourtschool.com/health

Meeting Individual Needs

ESL/ELL

Below-Level

Have students sort vocabulary words into categories. Categories might be based on similarities or differences in letter or syllable patterns, word meanings, parts of speech, or ways words are used. You may want to extend the activity by including other similar words.

Activities
- Lifestyle Choices, p. 192
- Flash Cards, p. 196
- Immunization Schedule, p. 202
- Medical Instruments, p. 208
- Healthful Lifestyle Songwriter, p. 214

On-Level

Using reference sources when reading can help students' understanding. Display resources, such as a dictionary or a computer. Have students identify a new word or idea in the chapter and write the meaning. Verify that meaning, using one of the resources.

Activities
- Design a Disease, p. 192
- Childhood Diseases, p. 196
- Travel Tips, p. 202
- Vaccine Research, p. 208
- Skin Cancer, p. 214

Challenge

Challenge students to locate information in the text quickly. Give students a list of vocabulary terms and provide self-stick notes. Have students race a partner to skim the selection for the terms, placing a note on each word after locating it.

Activities
- Noncommunicable Diseases, p. 192
- Food Poisoning, p. 196
- Epidemics, p. 202
- Diagnostic Tools, p. 208
- Cancer Research, p. 214

Learning Log

Provide students with graphic organizers to help them summarize ideas and concepts from the chapter. Model for students a possible main idea statement. Have students fill in the graphic organizer with three details to support that main idea.

Activities
- Comprehensible Input, pp. 198, 216
- Background and Experience, p. 204

Curriculum Integration

Integrated Language Arts/Reading Skills
- Character Study, p. 193
- Defenders Against Pathogens, p. 201
- Defining Instruments, p. 206
- Dramatic Choices, p. 220

Math
- Estimation and Calculation, p. 194
- Taking a Pulse, p. 206
- Allergy Surveys, p. 217

Physical Education
- Daily Fitness Tip, pp. 190, 194, 200, 206, 212, 220
- Daily Physical Activity, p. 189
- Staying Fit, p. 221

Use these topics to integrate health into your daily planning.

Science
- The Circulatory System, p. 203

Social Studies
- Worldwide Connections, p. 195
- Vaccine Development Time Line, p. 203
- Exploring the Globe, p. 212

Art
- Pathogens, p. 197
- Selling Immunizations, p. 207
- Television Commercials, p. 213

CHAPTER
7
Pages 188–225

CHAPTER SUMMARY

In this chapter students
► learn about communicable and noncommunicable diseases.
► find out that different kinds of pathogens can cause communicable diseases.
► discover how the body's immune system helps fight disease.
► learn to prevent and manage disease by making healthful lifestyle choices.

Life Skills

Students practice defending themselves against disease by learning to *manage stress*.

Building Good Character

Students show *responsibility* by practicing healthful behaviors to fight disease.

Consumer Health

Students *analyze* advertising and media messages.

Literature Springboard

Use the article "Vaccines—Then and Now" to spark interest in the chapter topic. See the Read-Aloud Anthology on page RA-8 of this *Teacher Edition*.

Prereading Strategies

SCAN THE CHAPTER Have students preview the chapter content by scanning the titles, headings, pictures, graphs, and tables. Ask volunteers to speculate on what they will learn. Use their predictions to determine their prior knowledge.

PREVIEW VOCABULARY As students scan the chapter, invite them to sort vocabulary into three groups: Words I Know; Words I've Seen or Heard; New Words.

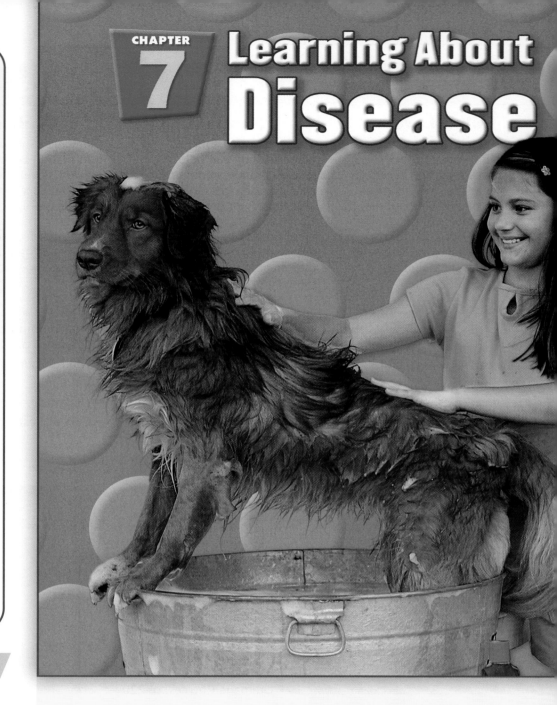

Reading Skill

SUMMARIZE To introduce or review this skill, have students use the Reading in Health Handbook, pp. 372–383. Teaching strategies and additional activities are also provided.

Students will have opportunities to practice and apply this skill throughout this chapter.

- Focus Skill Reading Mini-Lesson, p. 190
- Reading comprehension question identified with the
- *Activity Book* p. 33 (shown on p. 193)
- Lesson Summary and Review, pp. 193, 199, 205, 209, 218, 222
- Chapter Review and Test Preparation, pp. 224–225

Reading Skill

SUMMARIZE When you summarize, you state the main idea and the most important details. Use the Reading in Health Handbook on pages 372–383 and this graphic organizer to help you read the health facts in this chapter.

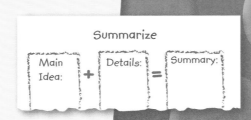

Summarize

Main Idea: + Details: = Summary:

Health Graph

INTERPRET DATA Humans can get Lyme disease from the bites of infected deer ticks. Describe how the number of cases of Lyme disease changed over the time period shown on the graph.

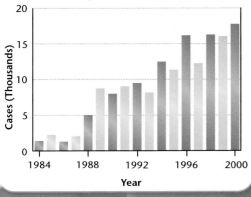

Cases of Lyme Disease in the U.S.

Cases (Thousands) — 20, 15, 10, 5, 0

Year — 1984, 1988, 1992, 1996, 2000

Daily Physical Activity

Eating healthful foods, getting plenty of sleep, and being physically active are lifestyle choices that can help fight disease.

 **Be Active!**
Use the selection, Track 7, **Moovin' and Groovin'**, to beef up your body's protection.

189

School-Home Connection

Distribute copies of the School-Home Connection (in English or Spanish). Have students take the page home to share with their families as you begin this chapter.

Follow Up Have volunteers share the results of their activities.

 Supports the Coordinated School Health Program

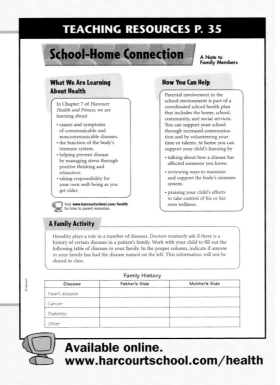

TEACHING RESOURCES P. 35

School-Home Connection A Note to Family Members

What We Are Learning About Health

In Chapter 7 of *Harcourt Health and Fitness*, we are learning about

- causes and symptoms of communicable and noncommunicable diseases.
- the function of the body's immune system.
- helping prevent disease by managing stress through positive thinking and relaxation.
- taking responsibility for your own well-being as you get older.

Visit www.harcourtschool.com/health for links to parent resources.

How You Can Help

Parental involvement in the school environment is part of a coordinated school health plan that includes the home, school, community, and social services. You can support your school through increased communication and by volunteering your time or talents. At home you can support your child's learning by

- talking about how a disease has affected someone you know.
- reviewing ways to maintain and support the body's immune system.
- praising your child's efforts to take control of his or her own wellness.

A Family Activity

Heredity plays a role in a number of diseases. Doctors routinely ask if there is a history of certain diseases in a patient's family. Work with your child to fill out the following table of diseases in your family. In the proper column, indicate if anyone in your family has had the disease named on the left. This information will not be shared in class.

Family History

Disease	Father's Side	Mother's Side
Heart disease		
Cancer		
Diabetes		
Other		

Available online.
www.harcourtschool.com/health

INTRODUCE THE CHAPTER

Health Graph

Interpret Data

Have students look at the graph on this page. Ask a volunteer to describe the data shown on the graph. The graph shows the numbers of cases of Lyme disease found in the United States from 1984 to 2000.

What does the number 10 represent on the graph? 10,000 cases of Lyme disease **Approximately how many cases of Lyme disease were discovered between 1992 and 1994?** about 4,000 Point out that Lyme disease is transmitted by ticks. Assure students that Lyme disease is rarely fatal, although it can be a very serious and unpleasant disease.

Daily Physical Activity

Use *Be Active! Music for Daily Physical Activity* with the Instant Activity Cards to provide students with movement activities that can be done in limited space. Options for using these components are provided beginning on page TR2 in this *Teacher Edition*.

Chapter Project

Have a Healthy Heart (*Assessment Guide* p. 59)

ASSESS PRIOR KNOWLEDGE Use students' initial ideas for the project as a baseline assessment of their understanding of chapter concepts. Have students complete the project as they work through the chapter.

PERFORMANCE ASSESSMENT The project can be used for performance assessment. Use the Project Evaluation Sheet (rubric), *Assessment Guide* p. 68.

Objectives

► Identify the two types of disease.
► Explain how lifestyle choices affect the risk of contracting some diseases.
► Develop respect for people with disabilities.

When Minutes Count . . .
Assign the Quick Study, Lesson 1, Activity Book pp. 31–32 (shown on p. 191).

Program Resources
► Activity Book pp. 31–33
► Transparency 6

Vocabulary
communicable disease p. 190,
noncommunicable disease p. 190

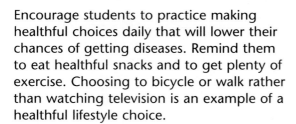

Daily Fitness Tip

Encourage students to practice making healthful choices daily that will lower their chances of getting diseases. Remind them to eat healthful snacks and to get plenty of exercise. Choosing to bicycle or walk rather than watching television is an example of a healthful lifestyle choice.

 For more guidelines on food, calories, and activity, see *Be Active! Resources for Physical Education,* p. 153.

1. MOTIVATE

Have students share what they already know about diseases—how they are spread and what causes them. (Be aware that some students might be unwilling to contribute to the discussion; these students should not be pushed to do so.)

Have you ever "caught" a disease such as a cold or a minor skin infection? How do you think you caught it? How did you manage it?

What are some diseases that cannot be spread? How or why would people get these diseases?

Causes of Disease

Types of Disease

Lesson Focus
There are two main types of disease and many causes of disease.

Why Learn This?
Learning about disease will help you know how to avoid it.

Vocabulary
communicable disease
noncommunicable disease

Terri's head aches, and her throat is sore. She feels weak. Although her illness isn't serious, there are things she should do to get better. She needs to rest, eat healthful foods, and drink lots of fluids. Terri is ill with influenza, or flu. Flu is a *disease*, a condition that damages or weakens part of the body.

There are two kinds of disease. One kind spreads from person to person. The other kind does not. A **communicable disease** (kuh•MYOO•nih•kuh•buhl dih•ZEEZ) is a disease that can be spread from person to person. Flu is a communicable disease because it spreads. Terri probably caught her flu from a classmate. Colds are also communicable diseases.

Other diseases do not spread from person to person. For example, Terri's best friend has diabetes. A disease that does not spread from one person to another is called a **noncommunicable disease**.

 SUMMARIZE How would you summarize the information you have just read about disease? There are two types of disease—communicable and noncommunicable.

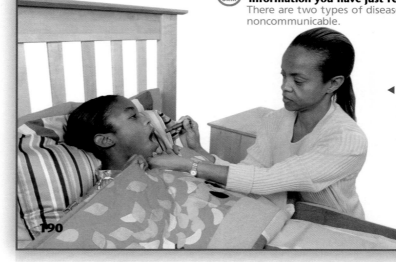

◄ Terri cooperates with her parents when she doesn't feel well. That makes it easier for them to help her get better.

190

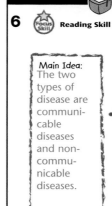 **Reading Skill**

Mini-Lesson

SUMMARIZE Remind students that when they summarize, they state the main idea and the most important details. Have them practice this skill by responding to the Focus Skill question on this page. Have students draw and complete the graphic organizer as you model it on the transparency.

 TRANSPARENCY 6

6 **Reading Skill Graphic Organizer** Types of Disease

Summarize

Main Idea:	Details:	Summary:
The two types of disease are communicable diseases and noncommunicable diseases.	Communicable diseases are spread from person to person. Noncommunicable diseases cannot be spread from person to person.	Communicable diseases, which can be spread from person to person, and noncommunicable diseases, which cannot be spread from person to person, are the two types of disease.

(with **+** and **=** symbols between boxes)

 Interactive Transparencies available on CD-ROM.

◀ Children can inherit many things from their parents—hair color, eye color, and even some diseases.

Some Diseases Can Be Inherited

Noncommunicable diseases can be caused partly by things like smoking tobacco, breathing polluted air, and eating an unhealthful diet. Some noncommunicable diseases can even be inherited. *Heredity* is the passing of characteristics from parents to their children. For example, your hair might be the same color as your dad's, or your eye color might be the same as your mom's.

Sickle cell anemia is an inherited blood disease. It causes attacks of pain, often in the chest, abdomen, and bones. Over time it can damage many parts of the body. Children can inherit sickle cell anemia from parents who don't show any signs of the disease.

Other diseases, including heart disease and some kinds of cancer, can be partly caused by heredity. People who have close relatives with one of these diseases are more likely to get the disease than people who have no relatives with it.

MAIN IDEA AND DETAILS What is an inherited disease? Give one example.
An inherited disease is a disease that is passed from parents to their children. Possible example: sickle cell anemia

▲ The smooth, doughnut-shaped red blood cells in the top picture are normal red blood cells. The odd-shaped red blood cells in the bottom picture are from a person who has sickle cell anemia.

191

2. TEACH

Interpret Visuals—Pictures

Direct students' attention to the images of red blood cells on this page. Explain that these images were made using an electron microscope. Electron microscopes enable us to see in great detail things that are extremely small. The red blood cells in the image are only about .007 millimeter across. Scientists use instruments such as microscopes to learn more about diseases. Doctors use them to diagnose diseases like sickle cell anemia. Sickle cell anemia gets its name from the shape of the cells—they look like sickles, the crescent-shaped tools used to cut tall grasses and weeds.

Discuss

Problem Solving Suppose you have a friend who is sick. You are not sure whether you should visit him. How can you make your decision? First, find out exactly what's wrong by asking your friend or his parents. Then find out whether the illness is communicable. If so, it is best not to visit until he is no longer contagious. If the disease is not communicable, you will not catch it if you visit. However, before going to visit, ask him and his parents if it is ok. Your friend might be feeling too sick to see anyone.

Health Background

ETS. Also called environmental tobacco smoke, ETS is the unfiltered smoke from a burning cigarette, pipe, or cigar or the exhaled smoke from a smoker's lungs. ETS, or passive smoking, is known to cause cancer in humans. Each year it causes approximately 3,000 lung cancer deaths in nonsmokers and 150,000 to 300,000 infections of the lower respiratory tract in children. Health risks associated with passive smoking can be reduced by ventilating the area in which smoking takes place.

Source: *Environmental Protection Agency*

For more background, visit the **Webliography** in Teacher Resources at **www.harcourtschool.com/health Keyword** diseases

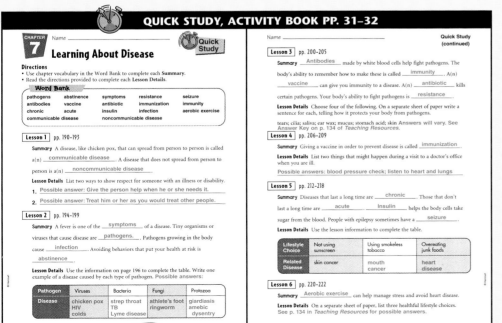

QUICK STUDY, ACTIVITY BOOK PP. 31–32

CHAPTER **7** Name _____ Quick Study
Learning About Disease

Directions
• Use chapter vocabulary in the Word Bank to complete each **Summary**.
• Read the directions provided to complete each **Lesson Details**.

Word Bank

pathogens	abstinence	symptoms	resistance	seizure
antibodies	vaccine	antibiotic	immunization	immunity
chronic	acute	insulin	infection	aerobic exercise
communicable disease		noncommunicable disease		

Lesson 1 pp. 190–193

Summary A disease, like chicken pox, that can spread from person to person is called a(n) communicable disease . A disease that does not spread from person to person is a(n) noncommunicable disease .

Lesson Details List two ways to show respect for someone with an illness or disability.
1. Possible answer: Give the person help when he or she needs it.
2. Possible answer: Treat him or her as you would treat other people.

Lesson 2 pp. 194–199

Summary A fever is one of the symptoms of a disease. Tiny organisms or viruses that cause disease are pathogens . Pathogens growing in the body cause infection . Avoiding behaviors that put your health at risk is abstinence .

Lesson Details Use the information on page 196 to complete the table. Write one example of a disease caused by each type of pathogen. Possible answers:

| Pathogen | Viruses | Bacteria | Fungi | Protozoa |
| Disease | chicken pox HIV colds | strep throat TB Lyme disease | athlete's foot ringworm | giardiasis amebic dysentry |

Name _____ Quick Study (continued)

Lesson 3 pp. 200–205

Summary Antibodies made by white blood cells help fight pathogens. The body's ability to remember how to make these is called immunity . A(n) vaccine can give you immunity to a disease. A(n) antibiotic kills certain pathogens. Your body's ability to fight pathogens is resistance .

Lesson Details Choose four of the following. On a separate sheet of paper write a sentence for each, telling how it protects your body from pathogens.
tears; cilia; saliva; ear wax; mucus; stomach acid; skin Answers will vary. See Answer Key on p. 134 of *Teaching Resources*.

Lesson 4 pp. 206–209

Summary Giving a vaccine in order to prevent disease is called immunization .

Lesson Details List two things that might happen during a visit to a doctor's office when you are ill.
Possible answers: blood pressure check; listen to heart and lungs

Lesson 5 pp. 212–218

Summary Diseases that last a long time are chronic . Those that don't last a long time are acute . Insulin helps the body cells take sugar from the blood. People with epilepsy sometimes have a seizure .

Lesson Details Use the lesson information to complete the table.

| Lifestyle Choice | Not using sunscreen | Using smokeless tobacco | Overeating junk foods |
| Related Disease | skin cancer | mouth cancer | heart disease |

Lesson 6 pp. 220–222

Summary Aerobic exercise can help manage stress and avoid heart disease.

Lesson Details On a separate sheet of paper, list three healthful lifestyle choices. See p. 134 in *Teaching Resources* for possible answers.

Available online. www.harcourtschool.com/health

TEACH *continued*

Personal Health Plan ▶

Plans should include:

- choosing meals and snacks that are more healthful
- getting more exercise or redesigning exercise routines
- keeping clean
- getting enough sleep
- staying away from people with communicable diseases

The Personal Health Plan should not be used to evaluate or assess students, nor should the results be shared among students.

Content-Area Reading Support

Using Paragraph Structure Direct students' attention to the following sentences in the first paragraph on this page: *That means Terri has a greater chance than the average person of developing this disease. However, Terri makes several healthful choices to lower her risk.* Point out that *however* is a signal word indicating a contrast. Have students identify what is being contrasted. Explain that when students see *however* at the beginning, middle, or end of a sentence, they should pay attention to the contrast being made.

Health Background

Diabetes is a disease in which the body does not produce or properly use the hormone insulin, needed to convert sugar, starches, and other food into energy. Diabetes can affect the heart, eyes, feet, and kidneys but can be controlled with lifestyle changes and medication. Approximately 17 million Americans have diabetes. Of these, about 90 to 95 percent have Type 2 diabetes, the result of the body's inability to properly use insulin.

Source: *American Diabetes Association*

 For more background, visit the **Webliography** in Teacher Resources at **www.harcourtschool.com/health** **Keyword** diseases

Personal Health Plan ▶

Real-Life Situation
You were ill five times during the past year, and you want to stay healthy this year.
Real-Life Plan
Plan things you might do this year to decrease your chances of becoming ill.

Healthful Choices Help Protect You from Disease

Terri's mother and grandmother both have heart disease. That means Terri has a greater chance than the average person of developing heart disease. However, Terri makes several healthful choices to lower her risk. She chooses foods that are low in fat, and she gets plenty of exercise. After school, instead of eating potato chips, Terri has an apple or some yogurt. Instead of getting a ride to school, she bicycles or walks.

Small daily choices such as these make up your *lifestyle*—the way you live your life. Your lifestyle and your health are closely related. People who make healthful lifestyle choices are less likely to become ill.

Choosing not to use tobacco is one of the most important lifestyle choices you can make. When you choose not to use tobacco, you lower your chances of getting lung cancer and heart disease.

CAUSE AND EFFECT **Name two things that affect your risk for heart disease.**
heredity and lifestyle

Members of the Rodriguez family are rarely ill. What lifestyle choices are they making to stay healthy?▼

192

Meeting Individual Needs
Leveled Activities

BELOW-LEVEL **Lifestyle Choices** Have pairs of students find examples of healthful and unhealthful lifestyle choices in magazines. Ask the students to position the pictures on a poster to compare and contrast these lifestyle choices.

ON-LEVEL **Design a Disease** Have students imagine they are scientists who have just discovered a disease. Have partners work together to write a report describing the disease. They should include information about how they discovered the disease, how it affects people, how people get it, whether it is communicable or not, and what causes it.

CHALLENGE **Noncommunicable Diseases** Have groups of students research the effects of lifestyle choices on one noncommunicable disease. Reports should include the causes of the disease, how it affects the body, and the positive effects of healthful lifestyle changes on the disease.

Respecting People with Illnesses and Disabilities

Thomas uses a wheelchair. Things that are simple for other people, such as riding a bus, taking a shower, and opening a door, are more complicated for Thomas to do. Thomas's disability also affects how others treat him and how he feels about himself.

You may feel awkward around people with disabilities or serious illnesses. However, a classmate who is ill with cancer or is disabled in some way may be just like you in every other way. You should always respect people who have serious illnesses or disabilities. Give them help when they need it, but otherwise treat them with respect, as you would anyone.

▲ People with disabilities can still be physically active.

Treat them with respect and help them when asked or needed; otherwise treat them as you might treat everyone else.

 SUMMARIZE How should you treat classmates who have disabilities or serious illnesses?

Lesson 1 Summary and Review

❶ **Summarize with Vocabulary**

Use vocabulary and other terms from this lesson to complete the statements.

There are two types of disease. A _____ disease can be passed from person to person. A _____ disease cannot. One factor that can increase your chances of getting a disease is _____, or the passing of characteristics from parents to their _____. Your _____ also affects your chances of getting certain diseases.

❷ What determines whether you develop sickle cell anemia or not?

❸ **Critical Thinking** Some people dislike sports. In what other ways can they be active to reduce their risks of becoming ill?

❹ **SUMMARIZE** Draw and complete this graphic organizer to show key information about the risks of disease.

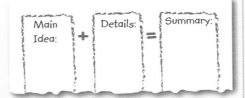

❺ **Write to Inform—Explanation**

Two of the children next door have diabetes. Explain to your little brother why he can't catch diabetes and how his behavior might affect the children.

193

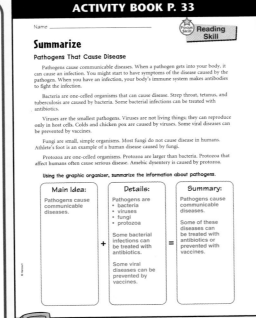

ACTIVITY BOOK P. 33

Name _____

Summarize

Pathogens That Cause Disease

Pathogens cause communicable diseases. When a pathogen gets into your body, it can cause an infection. You might start to have symptoms of the disease caused by the pathogen. When you have an infection, your body's immune system makes antibodies to fight the infection.

Bacteria are one-celled organisms that can cause disease. Strep throat, tetanus, and tuberculosis are caused by bacteria. Some bacterial infections can be treated with antibiotics.

Viruses are the smallest pathogens. Viruses are not living things; they can reproduce only in host cells. Colds and chicken pox are caused by viruses. Some viral diseases can be prevented with vaccines.

Fungi are small, simple organisms. Most fungi do not cause disease in humans. Athlete's foot is an example of a human disease caused by fungi.

Protozoa are one-celled organisms. Protozoa are larger than bacteria. Protozoa that affect humans often cause serious disease. Amebic dysentery is caused by protozoa.

Using the graphic organizer, summarize the information about pathogens.

Main Idea:	Details:	Summary:
Pathogens cause communicable diseases.	Pathogens are • bacteria • viruses • fungi • protozoa	Pathogens cause communicable diseases.
	Some bacterial infections can be treated with antibiotics.	Some of these diseases can be treated with antibiotics or prevented with vaccines.
	Some viral diseases can be prevented by vaccines.	

Available online. www.harcourtschool.com/health

3. WRAP UP

Lesson 1 Summary and Review

1. communicable; noncommunicable; heredity, children; lifestyle

2. Whether a person develops sickle cell anemia is determined by heredity.

3. Possible response: play active games; go bicycling, walking, or swimming; do chores like sweeping, mowing grass, and cleaning rooms

4. Possible answers are shown below:

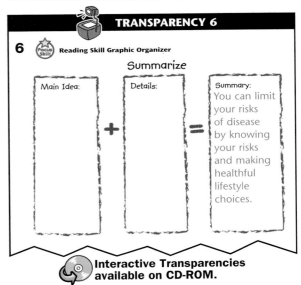

TRANSPARENCY 6

6 **Reading Skill Graphic Organizer**

Summarize

Main Idea:	Details:	Summary: You can limit your risks of disease by knowing your risks and making healthful lifestyle choices.

Interactive Transparencies available on CD-ROM.

5. Answers will vary but should include the fact that diabetes is a noncommunicable disease, so it cannot be passed from one person to another. Responses should also point out that you show respect when you treat someone with a serious illness as you would other people.

 For **writing models** with examples, see *Teaching Resources* pp. 47–61. Rubrics are also provided.

 When Minutes Count . . .

Quick Study Students can use *Activity Book* pp. 31–32 (shown on p. 191) as they complete each lesson in this chapter.

Objectives

► Identify four kinds of pathogens that can cause communicable diseases.

► Learn how to protect yourself from these pathogens.

 When Minutes Count . . .

Assign the Quick Study, Lesson 2, Activity Book pp. 31–32 (shown on p. 191).

Program Resources

► Activity Book pp. 31–32

► Transparency 6

Vocabulary

symptoms p. 194, **pathogens** p. 195,

infection p. 195, **viruses** p. 196,

bacteria p. 196, **fungi** p. 196,

protozoa p. 196, **abstinence** p. 197

Daily Fitness Tip

Encourage students to practice positive health behaviors to help prevent communicable disease. Remind students to cover their mouths while coughing and to wash their hands frequently.

 For more guidelines on fitness, see *Be Active! Resources for Physical Education*, p. 159.

1. MOTIVATE

Write the word *pathogen* on the board. Then write:

pathos—from Greek, meaning "suffering" or "disease"

genes—from Greek, meaning "born" or "producer"

Ask students to analyze the word *pathogen* and, based on its roots, explain what they think it means. Pathogen means "producer of disease" or "producer of suffering."

Pathogens and Communicable Diseases

Lesson Focus

Many different kinds of pathogens can cause communicable diseases.

Why Learn This?

You can practice positive health behaviors to prevent communicable diseases.

Vocabulary

symptoms
pathogens
infection
viruses
bacteria
fungi
protozoa
abstinence

Signs of Communicable Diseases

Julia had a cold but went to school anyway. In class she forgot to cover her mouth when she coughed. Rob sat at a desk near Julia and didn't notice her cough. Later that week Rob felt sick when he woke up. He had a cough and a sore throat, which are symptoms of a cold. **Symptoms** (SIMP•tuhmz) are the signs and feelings of an illness.

When you have a communicable disease, the symptoms of the disease usually identify it. One day you might wake up with a headache, a runny nose, and a cough. You might also be sneezing. These symptoms tell you that you probably have a cold. If you also have a fever and muscle aches, you probably have the flu.

A common symptom of many communicable diseases is fever. When you have a fever, your body temperature is a few degrees higher than normal.

COMPARE AND CONTRAST How are the symptoms of a cold and the flu alike and different? Fever, headache, runny nose, cough, sneezing, and muscle aches are symptoms of both. Flu symptoms are often worse than cold symptoms.

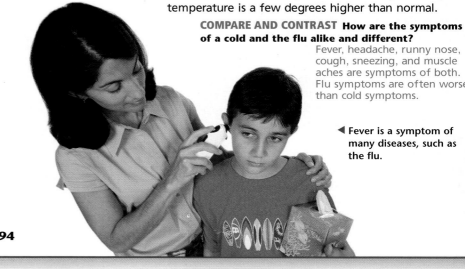

◄ Fever is a symptom of many diseases, such as the flu.

194

Math

Estimation and Calculation

Have students look at the illustrations of viruses on page 195. Explain that viruses are actually much smaller than they appear on the page. They are on the order of one hundred-thousandths (or 0.00001) of a centimeter across. Ask students first to estimate how much bigger the virus is in the illustration than it really is. They should then measure the illustration with a ruler and round the measurement to the nearest half-centimeter. Then they can calculate how many times it has been magnified.

Pathogens

Diseases that you can get from other people, such as colds and the flu, are spread by pathogens. **Pathogens** (PATH•uh•juhnz) are tiny organisms or viruses that cause diseases. Pathogens are all around you, but they are too small to see with your eyes. They can be seen only with a microscope. Their tiny size makes it difficult for people to tell when pathogens are being spread.

Pathogens can enter your body when you eat, drink, or just breathe. They can also enter your body through an open cut. Pathogens that get past your body's defenses and multiply can cause infection. **Infection** (in•FEK•shuhn) is the rapid growth of pathogens in the body.

Some pathogens kill body cells. Other pathogens produce substances that harm your body in other ways. Diseases caused by pathogens include athlete's foot, flu, food poisoning, chicken pox, and polio.

DRAW CONCLUSIONS Use what you read about pathogens to explain why Rob caught Julia's cold.
Rob breathed in pathogens that entered the air when Julia coughed without covering her mouth. The pathogens multiplied in his body and caused his cold.

Information Alert!

New Diseases Emerging infectious diseases (EIDs) are diseases that have recently become common or are expected to in the future. Discuss any EIDs that you have heard about in the news.

For the most up-to-date information, visit The Learning Site. www.harcourtschool.com/health

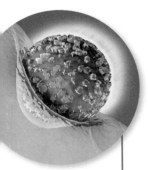

A virus is a pathogen that needs a host cell to reproduce. Here, a virus invades a host cell.

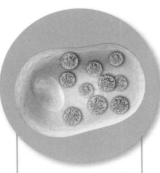

Once inside the cell, the virus takes over, forming new viruses.

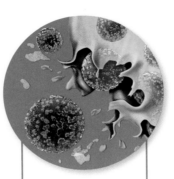

The new viruses burst out of the host cell, killing it. They move on to invade other cells.

195

Social Studies

Worldwide Connections
Provide students with a world map or globe, library resources, and a list of some diseases (such as amebic dysentery, malaria, and West Nile virus) that originated or occur more frequently in other countries. Have groups of students locate the countries where these diseases originated or occur most frequently. Ask students to find out about the conditions in these countries that contribute to the transmission and spread of the diseases.

2. TEACH

Interpret Visuals—Pictures

Call on volunteers to read aloud the captions on this page. Use the illustrations to discuss how viruses replicate to infect other cells in the body and cause disease. Explain that this illustration shows only one kind of virus. Different viruses have different shapes and sizes. All are very small—from 20–300 nanometers (billionths of a meter). Some are spherical, some look like sausages, some look like spiders, and some look like "alien" spacecraft.

Discuss

When a new disease is first noticed, scientists work very hard to figure out exactly what causes the disease and how the pathogen infects people.

Critical Thinking **Why is it important for scientists to figure out exactly how a virus or other pathogen infects a person?** It is much easier to find a cure or a vaccine for a disease if they know exactly what pathogen is causing it and how that pathogen is infecting people.

Health Background

Athlete's foot is a skin disease caused by a fungus that attacks the feet and usually occurs between the toes. Symptoms include drying skin, itching, scaling, inflammation, and blisters. Fungi thrive in a warm, dark, moist environment. To prevent infection, keep your feet clean and dry, change shoes and socks regularly, and avoid walking barefoot in places like public showers, where fungi may live.

Source: *American Podiatric Medical Association*

For more background, visit the **Webliography** in Teacher Resources at **www.harcourtschool.com/health Keyword** diseases

TEACH continued

Interpret Visuals—Tables

Have students use the table on this page to answer the following questions: **Which pathogen can reproduce only in host cells?** viruses **Which pathogen is the most common cause of food poisoning?** bacteria

Critical Thinking How could you add to this table to give readers more information? You could add more information, such as more diseases, to each column. You could also add more columns, such as a column for a photo or illustration, a column about how to fight these pathogens, and a column about how people discovered these pathogens.

Content-Area Reading Support

Using Respellings Direct students' attention to the phonetic respelling of *bacteria*: bak•TIR•ee•uh. Explain that respellings show how words are pronounced. Point out that the dots within the respelling divide the word into syllables and that small capital letters indicate the stressed, or accented, syllable. To emphasize this point, ask volunteers to pronounce the word *bacteria* with the emphasis on each of the other three syllables.

Discuss

Point out that the information in the table was learned through many years of hard work by scientists and doctors.

Problem Solving Suppose you are a medical scientist. A new disease has been noticed in your community. How can you figure out what is causing the disease? You could examine the people who have the disease, find out what their symptoms are, and figure out what all the people have in common. You could take blood or tissue samples to examine under a microscope to look for pathogens.

Kinds of Pathogens

Communicable diseases are caused by several kinds of pathogens. There are four main kinds of pathogens: *viruses* (VY•ruh•suhz), *bacteria* (bak•TIR•ee•uh), *fungi* (FUHN•jy), and *protozoa* (proh•tuh•ZOH•uh).

Diseases Caused by Pathogens

Pathogen	Characteristics	Diseases
Viruses	The smallest pathogens; the ones that cause most infectious diseases	Colds, chicken pox, AIDS, infectious hepatitis, influenza (flu), measles, mumps, polio, rabies, rubella (German measles)
Bacteria	One-celled living things that can—but do not always—cause disease; make people ill by producing harmful wastes	Strep throat, pertussis (whooping cough), some kinds of pneumonia, Salmonella food poisoning, tetanus, tuberculosis (TB), Lyme disease
Fungi	Small, simple living things like yeasts and molds; most often invade the skin or respiratory system	Ringworm, athlete's foot
Protozoa	One-celled organisms somewhat larger than bacteria; often cause serious diseases	Amebic dysentery, giardiasis

MAIN IDEA AND DETAILS Name four kinds of pathogens, and tell what they do.
Viruses, bacteria, fungi, and protozoa cause various communicable diseases.

196

Meeting Individual Needs
Leveled Activities

BELOW-LEVEL Flash Cards Have students make flash cards for each of the four kinds of pathogens. Ask them to write on the back of each card two or three diseases caused by the pathogen.

ON-LEVEL Childhood Diseases Have students research one of the childhood diseases listed in the table on this page and prepare oral or written reports. The reports might include causes and effects of the disease and how to treat someone with the disease.

CHALLENGE Food Poisoning Have groups of students do research to prepare oral or written reports about the causes of food poisoning. Students should identify examples of cases occurring in the United States during the last decade and tell about health laws concerning the handling of food by distributors and restaurant employees. Reports should also include information about the safe handling of food at home.

▲ Mosquitoes spread a number of pathogens, including West Nile virus, shown at the right.

How Pathogens Spread

Different pathogens spread in different ways. Some spread through the air when people sneeze or cough. Other pathogens spread when infected animals or insects bite people. For example, a bite from an infected raccoon or skunk can spread the virus that causes rabies. Tick bites can spread Lyme disease and Rocky Mountain spotted fever.

Pathogens can spread when you touch things such as doorknobs, pens, and telephones. They can also spread in food and water.

Other pathogens spread in other ways. HIV, the virus that causes AIDS, can be spread by intimate contact or by sharing needles. Some types of hepatitis pathogens can also be spread by sharing needles, including those used to draw tattoos. The best way to prevent the spread of HIV and hepatitis is abstinence. **Abstinence** (AB•stuh•nuhns) is the avoidance of behaviors that put your health at risk.

> **CAUSE AND EFFECT What could happen when a mosquito bites a bird infected with the West Nile virus?**
>
> Possible response: The mosquito can become infected and then transmit the virus to a human through its bite.

Myth and Fact

Myth: Only adults get HIV.

Fact: HIV can infect people of any age. Worldwide, there are more than 3 million people under the age of fifteen who have HIV. Children of mothers with HIV can even be born with the virus.

197

Discuss

Viruses cause many deadly diseases, including SARS and West Nile virus. Although these diseases are not common in the United States, they do occur here. Have students list the effects of other harmful viruses on the body, such as flu and cold viruses.

Critical Thinking How might you protect yourself from these diseases when traveling in other countries?

Possible answers: by taking preventive medicines before traveling; by using mosquito repellent and netting; by drinking only bottled or boiled water

Discuss

Direct students' attention to the Myth and Fact on this page. Have them distinguish between the myth that only adults get HIV and the fact that young people can also be infected.

Critical Thinking How can you and others help control the number of mosquitoes in your community?

Possible answers: Keep yards clean of debris and clutter; empty standing water in your yard; change water in birdbaths weekly; use sprays or insecticides

Growth, Development, and Reproduction Optional lessons about HIV/AIDS are provided in this supplement on pp. 63–72. Use this component in compliance with state and local guidelines.

Health Background

West Nile virus, discovered in Africa in 1937, is cycled between birds and mosquitoes and is transmitted to mammals by infected mosquitoes. It affects the central nervous system and is a form of encephalitis. It first appeared in North America in 1999 in New York. Dead birds are an indicator that the virus is in a particular area. The presence of dead birds should be reported to the local health department.

Source: *Centers for Disease Control and Prevention*

TEACH *continued*

 **Activity**

Refuse Lindsay should explain politely that sharing her drink is not a good idea because diseases can be spread through sharing food or drink. Lindsay might suggest that they go back to the store and ask for a cup for Beth or return home to get a cup so they can share without drinking from the same container. They could also pool their money to buy Beth a drink.

Discuss

One of the most important things you can do to keep from catching diseases is to wash your hands often.

Critical Thinking Why do you think washing your hands often is important? Possible responses: People touch things all day without thinking about it. Then they touch their mouths, noses, or eyes, causing the spread of pathogens.

Have students try to remember everything they have touched since entering the classroom. **How could pathogens have been spread when you touched these things?** Possible responses: After touching the doorknob, desk, papers, pencils, or water fountain (handled by many others), I touched my mouth, nose, or eyes and infected my body with the pathogens.

Quick Activity

Possible responses: Refuse to share food or drink with others. Use a tissue to cover your mouth when you cough or sneeze. Wash and cover cuts and scrapes. Avoid touching your eyes, mouth, or nose when you have a cut or scrape.

ACTIVITY

Life Skills

Refuse Beth buys veggie chips, and Lindsay buys fruit juice at a snack shop. Beth, who is sick with a cold, asks Lindsay for a sip of juice. Lindsay knows that this is not a good idea. Write a script to help her explain why she won't share her drink with Beth.

How Pathogens Enter the Body

Pathogens can enter your body in several ways. They can get in through your skin, your eyes, or the mucous membranes lining your nose and mouth. A cut or scrape on your skin can also let in pathogens.

Pathogens on your fingers or on a pen can enter your body if you put these things into your mouth. Pathogens can enter your eyes if you rub your eyes with your fingers.

The pathogens that cause food poisoning can enter your body through your digestive system when you eat spoiled or undercooked food. Pathogens can also enter if you drink water that has pathogens in it or you share a drink with someone who is sick. For example, protozoa called *Giardia* (jee•AR•dee•uh) can enter your digestive system if you drink untreated water from a

198

ESL/ELL Support

COMPREHENSIBLE INPUT Have students discover ways to protect themselves and others from getting a disease.

Beginning Write the words *colds* and *flu* on the board, and have students copy the words onto a large sheet of paper. Direct students to find magazine pictures or to draw pictures that illustrate things they could do to protect themselves from getting a disease. Pictures may include washing hands, covering the mouth with tissues, and refusing to share food and drinks.

Intermediate Have students draw pictures or find magazine pictures that show things they could do to protect themselves from getting a disease. Ask students to place the pictures on a poster and label them.

Advanced Have students draw or find pictures that show things they could do to protect themselves from getting a disease, place the pictures on a large sheet of paper, and write a paragraph about why these preventive measures are necessary.

stream. These protozoa cause a disease whose symptoms include diarrhea, stomach cramps, and fever.

SEQUENCE You come down with food poisoning after a picnic. What probably happened?

You drank some water with *Giardia* protozoa in it. The *Giardia* multiplied.

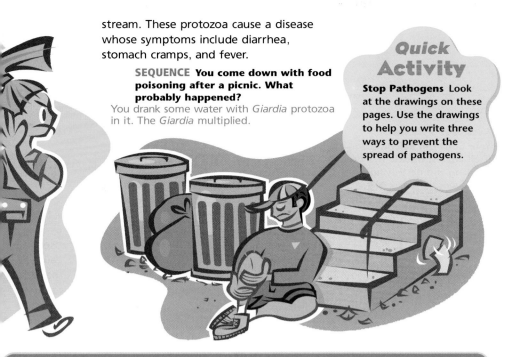

Lesson 2 Summary and Review

1 Summarize with Vocabulary

Use vocabulary from this lesson to complete the statements.

Diseases are caused by four main types of pathogens: _____, _____, _____, and _____. If one of these multiplies in your body, you may get a(n) _____. If you are ill, you may notice certain signs or feelings, which are known as _____.

2 Critical Thinking Why is washing your hands regularly with soap a good way to stop the spread of disease?

3 When do people get fevers?

4 SUMMARIZE Draw and complete this graphic organizer to show details about pathogens entering the body.

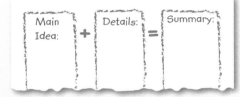

5 Write to Explain— Solution to a Problem

Your best friend asks you to play a game, but you have a cold. Write a story about the problem and what you decide to do.

199

Teacher Tip

Botulism Food-borne botulism is a type of food poisoning caused by rod-shaped bacteria known as *Clostridium*. Botulism can occur when a person ingests a canned food that was not properly sterilized. Botulism bacteria are able to grow in canned foods because the organisms are anaerobes—they don't need oxygen to survive. Food-borne botulism can be prevented if the food is prepared according to strict hygienic procedures and is properly stored and refrigerated.

3. WRAP UP

Lesson 2 Summary and Review

1. viruses, bacteria, fungi, protozoa; infection; symptoms

2. People touch many things every day that may have pathogens and then touch their noses, mouths, or eyes without thinking about it. Washing hands often can reduce the spread of diseases.

3. when they have a communicable disease, such as a cold or flu

4. Possible answers are shown below:

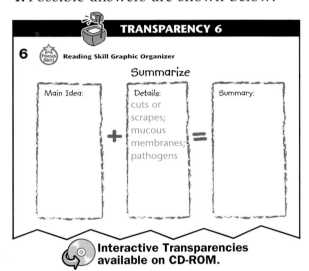

Interactive Transparencies available on CD-ROM.

5. Answers will vary but should include the fact that colds can be spread by touch, by sharing food or drinks, and by breathing in pathogens. Students may suggest that the game be rescheduled for another time when both friends are well.

For **writing models** with examples, see *Teaching Resources* pp. 47–61. Rubrics are also provided.

When Minutes Count . . .

Quick Study Students can use *Activity Book* pp. 31–32 (shown on p. 191) as they complete each lesson in this chapter.

LESSON 3

Pages 200–205

Objectives

► Understand how the body defends itself from diseases by blocking and destroying pathogens.

► Understand how vaccines and antibiotics can fight disease.

 When Minutes Count . . .

Assign the Quick Study, Lesson 3, Activity Book pp. 31–32 (shown on p. 191).

Program Resources

► Activity Book pp. 31–32
► Transparency 6

Vocabulary

antibodies p. 202, **immunity** p. 202, **vaccine** p. 203, **antibiotic** p. 203, **resistance** p. 204

Daily Fitness Tip

Remind students that any time they are prescribed oral antibiotics (those taken by mouth) for an infection, they must follow the instructions to finish all of the medicine. Many people think they can stop taking antibiotics once they start feeling better. As a result, they get sick again because the antibiotics have not had time to kill all the pathogens. The pathogens that have survived are generally more resistant to antibiotics than those that were killed first. Because many people use antibiotics improperly, some diseases are becoming harder and harder to treat.

 For more guidelines on activity, inactivity, and your health, see *Be Active! Resources for Physical Education*, p. 155.

1. MOTIVATE

As a class, brainstorm the different parts of the body that fight disease. Challenge students to name the largest and smallest parts of the body that fight disease. They might be surprised to learn that the largest part is the skin. On the average-size person, skin covers about 1.7 square meters. The smallest parts that fight infection are white blood cells. One cubic millimeter of blood contains 5,000 to 10,000 white blood cells.

200 Chapter 7 • Learning About Disease

LESSON 3

Disease and the Immune System

Lesson Focus

Your body can defend itself against disease by blocking and destroying pathogens.

Why Learn This?

Knowing how your immune system works can help you fight disease.

Vocabulary

antibodies
immunity
vaccine
antibiotic
resistance

First Line of Defense

There are millions of pathogens all around you. Fortunately, your body has ways to keep most pathogens out and to destroy most of the ones that do get in. Your body is a lot like a fort protected by many defenses. Even if pathogens get past one defense, they must overcome several others before they can cause an infection. Some defenses are physical barriers that block pathogens. Others are chemical defenses that kill or weaken pathogens.

Your skin is a thick barrier to pathogens. The outer layers are so tough that pathogens cannot pass through them unless the skin is broken in some way. Your skin also produces sweat, which contains chemicals that kill some pathogens.

Tiny hairs called *cilia* trap pathogens and keep them out of your lungs. ►

▲ Your eyes are protected from pathogens by tears. Tears wash pathogens out of your eyes. Tears also contain chemicals that kill some pathogens.

200

Teacher Tip

Immune Deficiencies Be aware that some students in the class might have medical conditions that suppress their immune systems. Some diseases, like AIDS, are acquired. Others, like Bruton's disease and Wiskott-Aldrich syndrome, are inherited. Many medications suppress the immune system (which is why they work — they suppress symptoms, i.e., the body's response to an infection). Students with these conditions may or may not be willing to discuss them with the class or participate in discussion.

Pathogens that enter through your nose must overcome mucus and cilia. *Mucus* (MYOO•kuhs) is a thick, sticky substance that traps pathogens. It covers the inside of your nose, throat, and trachea.

Tiny hairlike structures called *cilia* (SIL•ee•uh) line your breathing passages. Cilia move in waves. They push pathogens toward body openings, where your body gets rid of the pathogens. For example, the cilia in your throat push pathogens toward your mouth, where you get rid of them by coughing.

Saliva is a strong defense against pathogens that enter through your mouth. The chemicals in saliva kill many pathogens. If any survive, strong acid in the stomach usually kills them.

COMPARE AND CONTRAST **As defenses, how are skin and tears alike? How are they different?**
Alike: Both are defenses against pathogens; both keep pathogens from entering the body. Different: Skin is a physical barrier that keeps pathogens from entering the body. Tears wash away many pathogens and are a chemical barrier because they can kill some pathogens.

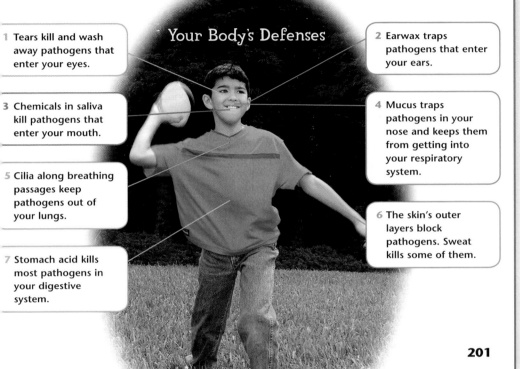

Your Body's Defenses

1 Tears kill and wash away pathogens that enter your eyes.

2 Earwax traps pathogens that enter your ears.

3 Chemicals in saliva kill pathogens that enter your mouth.

4 Mucus traps pathogens in your nose and keeps them from getting into your respiratory system.

5 Cilia along breathing passages keep pathogens out of your lungs.

6 The skin's outer layers block pathogens. Sweat kills some of them.

7 Stomach acid kills most pathogens in your digestive system.

201

Integrated Language Arts/ Reading Skills

Defenders Against Pathogens
Every living thing has natural defenses against pathogens. The defenses depend on the environment, the types of pathogens, and the lifestyle. Have students draw a creature of their own invention, labeling all its defenses. Students should also include a paragraph explaining why the creature needs these defenses.

2. TEACH

Interpret Visuals—Pictures
Direct students' attention to the diagram on this page. Ask volunteers to read the captions aloud.

Critical Thinking Why do you think we get runny or stuffed-up noses when we have colds? Mucus traps pathogens. When there are more pathogens than normal, our noses make more mucus to trap and wash away the pathogens. A runny nose is a sign that the immune system is working.

Discuss
Problem Solving Suppose you are a health-care professional working in a burn center in a hospital. The patients have all been severely burned. Why should you be particularly concerned about infection? You should be concerned because the patients have large patches of damaged skin (or no skin), and skin is the first line of defense the body has against pathogens.

Quick Activity
Possible responses: mucus, cilia, and saliva in the nose, throat, trachea, and mouth

Content-Area Reading Support
Using Signal Words Direct attention to the following sentence in the first paragraph: *If pathogens get past the first line of your body's defenses, they must face your blood.* Point out that *if* is a signal word indicating a requirement or condition. Getting past the first line of defense is the requirement that pathogens must fulfill before facing your blood. Ask students how they would logically end the sentence: *If pathogens don't get past the first line of your body's defenses . . . they won't face your blood.*

TEACH *continued*

Interpret Visuals—Pictures

Direct students' attention to the picture on this page. Ask a volunteer to read the caption. Explain that white blood cells represent only 1 percent of a person's blood but that they play a vital role in the body's defense system. Explain that *lymphocytes* are white blood cells that make antibodies. *Macrophages* are white blood cells that surround and destroy pathogens. **Which type of white blood cell is shown in the picture?**
macrophage

Health Background

The average adult has about 5 quarts of blood inside his or her body. Red blood cells contain hemoglobin, which enables the cells to pick up and deliver oxygen to all parts of the body. White cells provide a defense against infection. They can move out of the bloodstream to fight infection in the body.

White blood cells attack pathogens in a variety of ways. Some produce antibodies, and some surround and devour the bacteria. These cells live from a few days to a few weeks. A drop of blood can contain between 7,000 and 25,000 white cells at a time. When an infection is present, that number increases significantly to help you get well.

Source: *Puget Sound Blood Center*

For more background, visit the **Webliography** in Teacher Resources at **www.harcourtschool.com/health Keyword** diseases

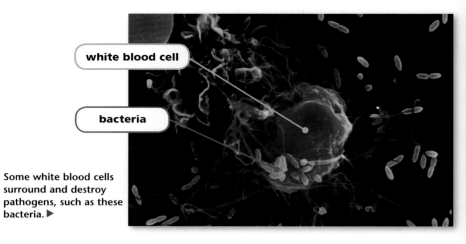

white blood cell

bacteria

Some white blood cells surround and destroy pathogens, such as these bacteria. ▶

How the Blood Fights Disease

If pathogens get past the first line of your body's defenses, they must face your blood. Blood contains white blood cells which circulate through your body and destroy pathogens. White blood cells are produced by the *immune system*, the body system that fights disease.

Antibodies (AN·tih·bahd·eez) are substances made by white blood cells to help fight pathogens. A different antibody is made for each kind of pathogen. When an antibody attaches itself to a pathogen, it can kill the pathogen, prevent it from entering body cells, or mark it to be killed by a white blood cell.

When a particular kind of pathogen enters your body for the first time, you show symptoms of disease while the pathogens multiply. After making antibodies, your body recovers and never "forgets" how to make them. The next time similar pathogens attack, antibodies can be made more quickly to keep the pathogens from multiplying. The body's ability to "remember" how to make antibodies quickly is called **immunity** (ih·MYOON·uh·tee).

DRAW CONCLUSIONS One winter you get the flu. A month later the same type of flu virus invades your body. Will you get sick again? Explain.
Probably not; your body will recognize the virus and make antibodies against it before it can cause the disease.

Did You Know?

A single drop of blood can contain 7,000 to 25,000 white blood cells. That number increases greatly when your body is fighting an infection. Lab workers count white blood cells in a small blood sample to determine whether a person has an infection.

202

Meeting Individual Needs
Leveled Activities

BELOW-LEVEL Immunization Schedule Have students find out which vaccines are required for students to attend public schools. Suggest that they talk with their parents or the school nurse. Have them report their findings to the class.

ON-LEVEL Travel Tips Have students choose a country and find out which vaccines are advised or required for Americans who plan to travel there. Then ask them to find out if the same vaccines or different ones are required for travel anywhere outside the United States. Have them report their findings to the class.

CHALLENGE Epidemics Have students research what factors need to be present for a disease to become an epidemic. Have them write a report about the plague, or Black Death, which killed millions of people in the 14th century, or the flu, which killed millions of people in the 20th century.

How Vaccines and Antibiotics Fight Disease

People can also become immune to diseases through the use of vaccines. A **vaccine** (vak•SEEN) is a medicine that can give you immunity to a disease. In most cases, a vaccine is a killed or weakened version of the pathogen that causes the disease.

Most vaccines protect people from certain diseases caused by viruses. If you get a flu shot, the vaccine will cause your body to make antibodies against certain flu viruses. The next time you are exposed to those viruses, your body will "remember" how to make the antibodies to fight the viruses and keep you healthy.

Antibiotics also help your body fight diseases. An **antibiotic** (an•ty•by•AHT•ik) is a medicine that kills certain organisms, especially bacteria. Antibiotics can't kill viruses, so they can't fight diseases like colds and flu. However, scientists have developed a few medicines that destroy certain viruses.

CAUSE AND EFFECT Nellie's sister has the flu. What do you need to know to decide whether Nellie is likely to catch the flu from her sister?
if Nellie has had the flu already or has been vaccinated against it

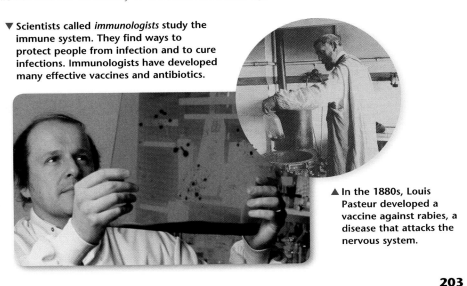

▼ Scientists called *immunologists* study the immune system. They find ways to protect people from infection and to cure infections. Immunologists have developed many effective vaccines and antibiotics.

▲ In the 1880s, Louis Pasteur developed a vaccine against rabies, a disease that attacks the nervous system.

203

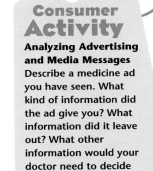

Consumer Activity

Analyzing Advertising and Media Messages Describe a medicine ad you have seen. What kind of information did the ad give you? What information did it leave out? What other information would your doctor need to decide whether this medicine is right for you?

Consumer Activity

Analyzing Advertising and Media Messages Medicine ad choices will vary, but the information needed by your doctor may include: If you had the disease, your doctor might need to know if you have had the disease before, if you have been with someone who had the disease, if you have been vaccinated against the disease, and if you are allergic to any medicines.

Discuss

After students read the text, refer them again to the table on page 196. Ask a volunteer to read aloud the characteristics of both fungi and viruses. Explain that penicillin is an antibiotic produced by a fungus. It keeps certain bacteria from multiplying by preventing these microbes from forming cell walls.

Critical Thinking Why do you think immunizations (vaccines) are important in disease prevention? They can make people immune to certain diseases.

Health Background

Louis Pasteur's most important discoveries were that most infectious diseases are caused by germs and that vaccines can be used to prevent diseases. His work led to improvements in hospital practices, such as sterilization of instruments and antiseptic medicine and surgery. Through his study of rabies, he discovered the rabies virus that causes it and developed the rabies vaccine. Pasteur also developed pasteurization, a process that uses heat to destroy microbes in perishable food products.

Source: *HyperLab*

For more background, visit the **Webliography** in Teacher Resources at **www.harcourtschool.com/health Keyword** diseases

---

Science

The Circulatory System Have students research the role of the circulatory system as part of the body's defenses against pathogens. Ask students to trace the path of white blood cells, using bones, other body tissues, and organs as reference points. Partners or small groups of students can make labeled drawings on posters to display in the classroom. Ask for volunteers to share their findings with the class.

Social Studies

Vaccine Development Time Line Divide the class into groups to research and develop a time line about vaccines. Ask students to begin with Pasteur's development of the first artificially produced vaccine for anthrax in 1881 and to end with the current year. Assign individuals or pairs in each group the tasks of doing the research, writing a brief report using the research, drawing the time line, and giving an oral report to the class.

Activity

Possible responses: Wash hands more frequently. Eat nutritious foods and drink lots of water. Exercise regularly and get plenty of sleep. See a doctor for regular checkups.

Discuss

Explain that AIDS stands for *A*cquired *I*mmune *D*eficiency *S*yndrome. When people who have AIDS die, they do not actually die of AIDS—they die of other diseases, such as cancer or pneumonia.

Critical Thinking **Why do you think people with AIDS are more susceptible to diseases than people who do not have AIDS?** Their immune systems do not function properly, so their bodies can't fight diseases as well as other people's bodies can.

AIDS is not the only immune deficiency disease. People with immune deficiencies must be particularly careful to protect themselves from other communicable diseases.

Problem Solving **Suppose you have a friend with an immune deficiency disease. How would you treat her differently from your other friends?** You would be particularly careful not to spread any of your own illnesses, such as colds, to your friend. You would look out for her and be aware that she can pick up infections more easily than you can. Other than that, you would treat her just like any other friend.

ACTIVITY

⭐ Building Good Character

Responsibility By practicing healthful behaviors, you can help your body fight disease and stay well. List two or three behaviors that you can change or improve to help your body fight disease.

Helping Your Body Fight Disease

Practicing good hygiene is one way to keep pathogens out of your body. Always wash your hands before you eat and after you use the bathroom or handle a pet. Be sure to use plenty of soap and warm water. This will help remove pathogens from your skin.

To fight disease, you need to keep your resistance high. **Resistance** (rih•ZIS•tuhns) is your body's ability to fight pathogens on its own. The higher your resistance, the less often you will become ill and the sooner you will recover from an illness. You can boost your resistance by eating a variety of nutritious foods. Also, drink lots of water.

Other ways to build resistance are through regular exercise and plenty of sleep. Most young people need at least eight hours of sleep each night.

Jane and her dad get regular exercise by playing softball. Exercise helps them deal with stress and keep up their resistance to disease. ▼

204

ESL/ELL Support

BACKGROUND AND EXPERIENCE Invite students to discuss healthful habits needed to fight disease.

Beginning Have students pantomime or draw pictures of themselves or others practicing healthful habits to fight disease.

Intermediate Have students draw and label pictures of someone practicing healthful habits. Ask volunteers to share their pictures with the class.

Advanced Have students present short oral reports about healthful habits that help them manage minor illnesses, such as colds or skin infections. Reports may include pictures or other visual aids.

Too much stress in your life can lower your resistance. Trying to do too many things or worrying about problems for too long can cause stress. You can manage stress by doing something relaxing. For example, you can talk with a parent or a friend, listen to music, play a game, read a book, or exercise.

Another way to manage stress is to get rid of things that cause stress. Instead of worrying about something, try to find a solution that will help you reduce your stress.

 SUMMARIZE How can you boost your resistance to disease?
Possible response: Keep clean, eat a healthful diet, get regular exercise, get plenty of sleep, and manage stress.

Keep clean to stay healthy. Use a fresh washcloth and warm—not hot—water. Using a towel to dry also gets rid of pathogens. ▶

Lesson 3 Summary and Review

1 Summarize with Vocabulary

Use vocabulary and other terms from this lesson to complete the statements.

You have many defenses against disease. For example, your breathing passages are lined with a thick, sticky substance called _____, which traps pathogens. An entire system in your body, the _____ system, fights disease. You can get _____ to some diseases either on your own or with the help of a _____. Medicines called _____ may help you recover from bacterial infections.

2 Where in the body are antibodies made?

3 Critical Thinking In what way is getting a vaccine like having a disease?

4 **SUMMARIZE** Draw and complete this graphic organizer to show how your body fights pathogens.

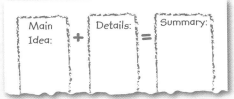

5 Write to Inform—Explanation
Sara seems to catch every cold that her classmates get. She has no idea how to avoid disease-causing pathogens. Write a paragraph explaining how Sara can avoid pathogens and stay well.

205

Lesson 3 Summary and Review

1. mucus; immune; immunity, vaccine; antibiotics

2. in white blood cells

3. Vaccines are killed or weakened forms of the pathogens that cause the disease.

4. Possible answers are shown below:

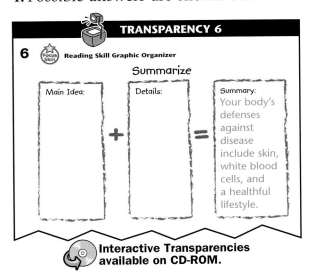

 Interactive Transparencies available on CD-ROM.

5. Possible response: Sara can practice good hygiene and wash her hands frequently with soap and water to remove pathogens from her skin. She can eat nutritious food, drink lots of water, and get plenty of sleep and regular exercise. She can reduce stress by doing something relaxing and finding solutions to things that worry her.

For **writing models** with examples, see *Teaching Resources* pp. 47–61. Rubrics are also provided.

 When Minutes Count . . .

Quick Study Students can use *Activity Book* pp. 31–32 (shown on p. 191) as they complete each lesson in this chapter.

Pages 206–209

Objectives
► Understand the importance of seeking treatment from health-care professionals.
► Learn the role and importance of immunizations.

When Minutes Count . . .
Assign the Quick Study, Lesson 4, Activity Book pp. 31–32 (shown on p. 191).

Program Resources
► Activity Book pp. 31–32
► Transparency 6

Vocabulary
immunization p. 208

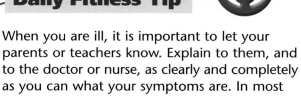

Daily Fitness Tip

When you are ill, it is important to let your parents or teachers know. Explain to them, and to the doctor or nurse, as clearly and completely as you can what your symptoms are. In most cases, the most important information doctors have is the information you give them. Without it, they may have a difficult time figuring out what is wrong and how to treat it.

 For more guidelines on fitness, see *Be Active! Resources for Physical Education.*

1. MOTIVATE

Have three volunteers role-play a sick patient, a parent, and a doctor to portray a child's illness from the time the parent realizes the child is sick through a visit to the doctor. Have the patient describe his or her symptoms to the parent and then to the doctor. The doctor should verify the symptoms and perform diagnostic "tests." The doctor should prescribe a medication if necessary, give instructions for home care, and make sure medical records are updated and filed. Allow students time to read the material on these pages, plan the role-playing activity, and make simple props.

When Someone Becomes Ill

Treating Disease

Jay had a bad headache, and his throat felt very scratchy. Jay's dad felt his head and said that it seemed hot. He took his temperature and found out that he had a fever. Jay's dad usually gives him medicine for minor illnesses, such as colds, but this time he thought Jay should see Dr. Phillips.

The doctor asked Jay to describe his symptoms. She then examined Jay, looking for signs of infection. She took his temperature and blood pressure. She listened to Jay's heart and lungs and examined his eyes, ears, and nose. She also looked at his throat and, using a swab, took a cell sample from it to test at the lab.

When Dr. Phillips finished her exam, she said Jay might have strep throat, a bacterial infection. She told Jay that he should drink plenty of fluids, like juice, and get extra rest. She asked Jay's dad to give him medicine

Lesson Focus
Many diseases can be prevented or treated, especially when detected early.

Why Learn This?
You can use what you learn to prevent illness and speed recovery from disease.

Vocabulary
immunization

◄ It's important to let a parent know when you feel ill.

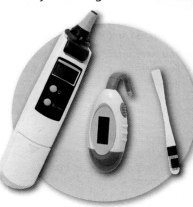

▲ All these thermometers measure body temperature. A fever may be a symptom of an infection.

206

Math

Taking Pulse Have students find their pulse by lightly placing the first two fingers of one hand over the inside of the wrist on the other arm. Have them count the pulse beats for exactly ten seconds while you keep track of the time. Then ask them to calculate how many times their hearts beat in one minute, one hour, one day, and one year. Ask volunteers what their pulse rates are per minute, and write those numbers on the board. Then, as a class, find the average pulse of those who volunteered their results.

Integrated Language Arts/ Reading Skills

Defining Instruments Students are probably familiar with some medical instruments (stethoscopes, thermometers, sphygmomanometers, and ophthalmoscopes). Have students examine the words closely and separate each one into its various components, such as *thermo* and *meter*. They can then use a dictionary to find the meaning of each word part. Have students write a definition for each word based on the meanings of the individual word parts.

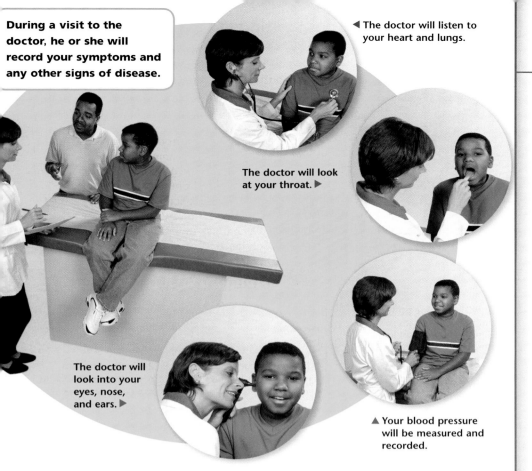

During a visit to the doctor, he or she will record your symptoms and any other signs of disease.

◀ The doctor will listen to your heart and lungs.

The doctor will look at your throat. ▶

The doctor will look into your eyes, nose, and ears. ▶

▲ Your blood pressure will be measured and recorded.

for his cough, fever, and headache. Dr. Phillips said she would prescribe an antibiotic if the lab results showed Jay had a bacterial infection.

As Dr. Phillips said goodbye to Jay and his dad, she gave Jay's medical record to Ms. Anders, a medical records technician. It is her job to keep patients' records. Jay's record contains information such as notes Dr. Phillips made during Jay's visits. The record also contains Jay's lab results and medical history.

 SUMMARIZE Why is it important to cooperate with a doctor both during an exam and after?

Describing your symptoms during an exam can help your doctor decide what's wrong. Following your doctors instructions after an exam can help you get well faster.

207

---

2. TEACH

Discuss

Have students describe health-related situations that require parent or adult assistance, such as going to a doctor. Although many minor illnesses, such as colds, flu, stomachaches, and skin infections, can be treated at home, doctors recommend that you have a checkup at least once a year. Many schools even require that you have a checkup before school starts.

Critical Thinking **Why is it important that you go to a doctor for routine examinations?** Doctors can get information about how your body works when it is healthy. This information can help them make an accurate diagnosis when you are feeling sick. The doctor may also find the symptoms of a disease in its early stages, which gives you a better chance of recovering from the disease.

Health Background

Normal blood pressure in healthy adults is below 120/80. The first number, called the systolic blood pressure, is the pressure (in millimeters of mercury) exerted on the walls of the blood vessels when the heart beats. The second number, called the diastolic pressure, is the pressure exerted between beats, when the heart rests. It is important that blood pressure be checked regularly because there are no direct symptoms of high blood pressure, also called hypertension. Low blood pressure, on the other hand, causes lightheadedness and dizziness. Blood pressure in children tends to be lower than in adults. The exact value depends on age, size, and gender. The systolic pressure of babies, for example, is around 90. Contrary to popular belief, hypertension does occur in children and can be a sign of serious illness such as kidney disease. One common form of high blood pressure among all groups is "white coat syndrome." This is simply an elevation of blood pressure due to the stress of having the blood pressure checked.

Source: *American Heart Association*

Teacher Tip

X-Ray Safety X rays are needed to diagnose and treat certain diseases, but they can damage healthy cells, tissues, and organs. Explain to students the importance of wearing the lead shield provided by the doctor or health professional to protect parts of the body that are not being examined with X rays.

Art

Selling Immunizations Have pairs or groups of students choose one disease from the table on page 208. Ask them to design a newspaper or magazine advertisement that stresses the importance of being immunized against that disease. Students may also choose to produce a television commercial, using their artwork and original scripts. Ask each pair or group of students to share its work with the class.

Interpret Visuals—Tables

Direct students' attention to the table on this page. **Which vaccine needs to be given every 10 years?** tetanus **Which vaccines are given just before a child enters preschool or kindergarten?** DTP, MMR, and IPV

The number of cases of measles and mumps among children and young adults increased in the 1980s and early 1990s.

Critical Thinking **What are some possible reasons for this increase in the number of cases of measles and mumps?** Possible responses: Some parents thought the diseases had been eradicated and did not have their children immunized against them; some people think that all immunizations provide them with lifetime immunity and do not get boosters or have boosters given to their children.

Discuss

Explain that when you visit a doctor's office for the first time, you are given a medical history form to fill out. The form asks what illnesses you've had in the past, what vaccinations you've had, what medications you are taking, whether you are allergic to anything, and what illnesses other people in your family have had.

Critical Thinking **Why do you think this form is important? Why is it important to fill it out as completely and honestly as you can?** Knowing your medical history will help the doctor diagnose your problem. (For example, if you have already had chicken pox and you've had the measles vaccine, the doctor will know it is unlikely you will get those diseases again.) Knowing what illnesses your family has had will help the doctor determine whether you might have an inherited disease. The doctor needs to know what medicines you are taking and which ones you are allergic to so he or she can prescribe the right ones for you. (Some medicines can interact with each other and make people very sick.)

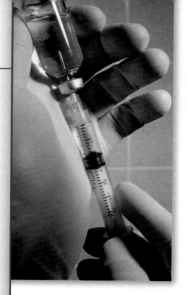

▲ The DTP vaccine protects against three diseases: diphtheria, tetanus, and pertussis (whooping cough). Before this vaccine was developed, many people died from diphtheria.

Preventing Disease

When the results from Jay's lab test came in, they showed no signs of a bacterial infection. Dr. Phillips concluded that a virus must be causing Jay's symptoms. Jay didn't need an antibiotic. He just needed to help his body fight the virus. After more rest and plenty of fluids, Jay felt much better.

To prevent some viruses from causing diseases, doctors use immunization. **Immunization** (im•yoo•nuh•ZAY•shuhn) is the giving of vaccines to people to prevent them from getting diseases. Immunization can prevent some diseases that spread easily. Before immunization was possible, most children got measles. When Jay's mom was young, measles spread through her class. However, no one in Jay's class

Immunization Schedule

Vaccine	When Needed
Hepatitis B Protects against hepatitis B virus	birth–2 months, 4 months, 6–18 months
DTP Protects against diphtheria, tetanus, and pertussis bacteria	2 months, 4 months, 6 months, 15–18 months, 4–6 years, 11–16 years (tetanus and diphtheria only); tetanus booster every 10 years
MMR Protects against measles, mumps, and rubella viruses	12–15 months, 4–6 years
HIB Protects against *Haemophilus influenza* bacteria	2 months, 4 months, (6 months), 12–15 months
IPV Protects against polio virus	2 months, 4 months, 6–18 months, 4–6 years
Pneumococcal conjugate Protects against pneumococcal bacteria	2 months, 4 months, 6 months, 12–15 months
Varicella Protects against chicken pox	12–18 months

208

Meeting Individual Needs
Leveled Activities

BELOW-LEVEL **Medical Instruments** Have students research instruments, such as a stethoscope, sphygmomanometer, or ophthalmoscope, used by doctors during regular examinations. Have each student choose one of these instruments and draw a diagram with labels explaining how the instrument works.

ON-LEVEL **Vaccine Research** Have students write a report about one of the vaccines from the table on this page. Reports should include information about how the vaccine was discovered and developed, when it was first used, and some details about the diseases it prevents.

CHALLENGE **Diagnostic Tools** Have students research diagnostic tools, such as an EKG, an ultrasound, or a CT scan. Reports may include what the tool looks like, how it works, the illnesses or diseases it helps diagnose, how it is used to diagnose diseases, and how it has changed the procedure for diagnosing diseases.

has had measles. All the students were immunized against it. The vaccine they received is called MMR. It protects against measles, mumps, and rubella.

Jay will need a booster soon for diphtheria and tetanus. A *booster* is an extra dose of vaccine given to maintain immunity.

CAUSE AND EFFECT Throughout life, Jay will need tetanus boosters. How will they affect his immunity?
The boosters will maintain Jay's immunity to tetanus.

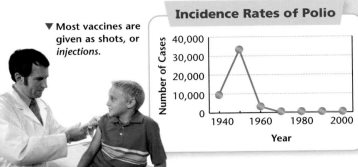
▼ Most vaccines are given as shots, or *injections*.

Incidence Rates of Polio

Number of Cases / Year

Quick Activity

Beating Polio Polio is caused by a virus that disabled and killed many children until a vaccine was developed in the 1950s. Find out how the number of people with polio has changed since the use of polio vaccines.

Lesson 4 Summary and Review

❶ **Summarize with Vocabulary**

Use vocabulary and other terms from this lesson to complete the statements.

Just after she was born, Serena's baby sister got a hepatitis B _____, which gave her immunity to that disease. In another few months, she will need a _____ to keep her immunity up. _____, which is the giving of vaccines, is an important part of disease prevention. Bacterial diseases can be treated with _____, but diseases caused by _____ cannot.

❷ Why does a doctor examine you even if you tell him or her your symptoms?

❸ **Critical Thinking** Why is it especially important to develop vaccines for diseases caused by viruses?

❹ **SUMMARIZE** Draw and complete this graphic organizer to show how communicable diseases can be treated or prevented.

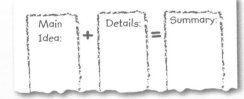

Main Idea: + Details: = Summary:

❺ **Write to Inform—Description**

Think about the last time you were ill. How could describing your symptoms help your doctor determine what is wrong?

209

Teacher Tip

Take Care with Medicines
Discuss the role of over-the-counter medicines—medicines that adults can buy without a prescription. Many of these medicines are used to treat symptoms of diseases, not the diseases themselves. Discuss the positive and negative effects of using medicines like these. For example, medicines such as aspirin reduce fevers, which can help you feel better. However, there is evidence that moderate fevers (under 102°F) actually fight infection and stimulate other parts of the immune system to go into action.

Content-Area Reading Support
Using Typographic Clues Direct students' attention to the word *booster* on this page. Explain that the typeface used is called *italics*. The writer has used italics to draw attention to the word. In this case the word is emphasized because it is being defined.

3. WRAP UP

Lesson 4 Summary and Review

1. vaccine; booster; immunization; antibiotics, viruses

2. to decide whether you have the disease or not and to prescribe the proper treatment by checking your temperature, listening to your heart and lungs, and examining your eyes, nose, and throat

3. Most communicable diseases are caused by viruses. Viruses can't be cured with antibiotics, so it is important to develop vaccines to prevent them.

4. Possible answers are shown below:

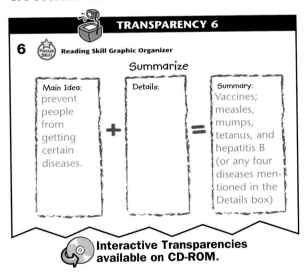

TRANSPARENCY 6

6 Reading Skill Graphic Organizer

Summarize

Main Idea: prevent people from getting certain diseases. + Details: = Summary: Vaccines; measles, mumps, tetanus, and hepatitis B (or any four diseases mentioned in the Details box)

Interactive Transparencies available on CD-ROM.

5. Students' lists of symptoms will vary. The doctor is familiar with the symptoms of most diseases. Some of your symptoms could cause the doctor to order special tests or prescribe particular treatments for a certain disease.

For **writing models** with examples, see *Teaching Resources* pp. 47–61. Rubrics are also provided.

Life Skills

Communicate
Make Responsible Decisions
Manage Stress
Refuse
Resolve Conflicts
Set Goals

Objectives
► Identify steps to manage stress.
► Practice steps to manage stress to keep your body healthy.

Program Resources
► Activity Book p. 34
► Poster 9

1. MOTIVATE

Have students describe strategies for stress management. Ask volunteers to share their experiences with stress. What caused their stress? How did it affect them emotionally? How did it affect them physically? Did they do anything about it? Explain that the physical effects of stress are real, not just "in your mind," and that it is important to deal with them.

2. TEACH

Step 1
Critical Thinking Why is it important to know what stress feels like? People need to recognize the feelings of stress so that they can identify the causes and find a solution before becoming ill.

Step 2
Critical Thinking Why do you think Michael is afraid he will do badly on the test? Responses will vary but will probably include some personal anecdotes about testing fears. **Do you think he's the only one in the class who is nervous?** No; probably most of the students feel stressed.

Manage Stress
to Prevent Disease

Each of us feels stress in certain situations. Some stress can help us perform better. However, all stress feels uncomfortable, and people who feel stress over a long time are more likely to become ill. Using the steps for **Managing Stress** can help you get through a stressful situation.

On Monday, everyone in fifth grade will take a standardized reading test. On the Friday before the test, Michael starts to worry. He is nervous and upset, and he has a hard time sleeping. What should Michael do?

1 **Know what stress feels like.**

Michael's stomach hurts, and he feels jittery. He figures out that the feelings he has are due to stress.

2 **Try to determine the cause of the stress.**

Michael recognizes that he is feeling stress because he's afraid of doing badly on the test.

210

Teacher Tip

Watching for Stress There are times of year when most of the students will be under stress: during standardized testing, near the holidays, and when distressing events have occurred locally, nationally, or internationally. Young people show their stress in different ways. Some will become ill. Some will become very quiet. Others will become boisterous or violent. When this happens, take time out from class to allow them to relieve some of their stress. Go outside for a game or a walk, or practice stress-relief exercises.

ACTIVITY BOOK P. 34

Name _____

Problem Solving

Life Skill
Manage Stress

Steps for Managing Stress

1. Know what stress feels like.
2. Try to determine the cause of the stress.
3. Do something that will help you relieve the feeling of stress. Talk to someone you trust about how you feel.
4. Think positively rather than negatively.

Use the steps to help these students manage stress.

A. Keisha is feeling stressed because she has a violin recital, a track meet, and a gymnastics meet—all next week. She knows she also has to study for several tests that are coming up. Keisha has a headache from the stress she is feeling.
• How can Keisha manage her stress to protect her health?
   Possible answer: Keisha's stress is caused by doing too much. She
   should talk to a parent or another trusted adult about reducing her
   activities or rearranging her schedule. She should think positively
   about doing well at the activities she chooses to continue.
   _____

B. Nate is a talented artist. He has entered drawings in a citywide competition. After he enters his drawings, he feels sick to his stomach. He is sure his drawings won't be as good as others entered in the competition.
• How can Nate stop feeling sick?
   Possible answer: Nate's stress is making him feel sick to his stomach.
   He should talk to his parents or his art teacher and share his worries
   about his drawings. He should think about the benefits of competing.
   _____
   _____

 Available online.
www.harcourtschool.com/health

3 Do something that will help you relieve the feeling of stress. Talk to someone you trust about how you feel.

I'm really worried about that test on Monday.

You're a good reader. You'll do fine on the test.

Michael tells his mom that he's nervous about the test.

4 Think positively rather than negatively.

Michael knows that he reads well. There's no reason to think that the test won't show that. "I can do it!" he thinks to himself. Now he can relax and sleep.

Problem Solving

A. Jocelyn has just learned that her grandfather is very ill. She is upset and worried about her grandfather.
- Use the steps for **Managing Stress** to help Jocelyn manage her stress and deal with her grandfather's illness.

B. Rick is becoming friends with a popular group at school. He has noticed that many of those in the group smoke. He is feeling stress because he thinks they won't like him unless he smokes, too.
- How can Rick manage his stress and show responsibility by not smoking?

211

Using the Poster

Activity Have students use the Poster 9 as a guide to make illustrations of things they do to manage stress.

Display the poster to remind students of the steps for managing stress.

Step 3
Critical Thinking **What else can Michael do to relieve his stress?** He can ride his bike or play soccer. He can do something to relax, such as read a good book or go to a friend's house.

Step 4
Critical Thinking **How can thinking positively help to relieve stress?**
Thinking positively makes you feel better. It's better to think about the things you *can* do rather than the things you *can't* do.

Critical Thinking **How does realizing that he reads well help Michael relax?**
Michael knows that the test will show that he reads well, so he does not need to worry. He is prepared for the test.

3. WRAP UP

Problem Solving

A Jocelyn can recognize the feelings of stress and determine the cause of those feelings. She can talk with her parents about her feelings and can find ways to express her feelings for her grandfather through cards, letters, or visits.

B Rick can manage his stress by talking with a parent about his feelings. He may think about what he has learned about the dangers of smoking and about making good decisions. He can remind himself that true friends would respect his decision not to smoke.

Objectives

▶ Identify the causes and symptoms of noncommunicable diseases.

▶ Understand the difference between chronic and acute diseases.

When Minutes Count . . .

Assign the Quick Study, Lesson 5, Activity Book pp. 31–32 (shown on p. 191).

Program Resources

▶ Activity Book pp. 31–32

▶ Transparency 6

Vocabulary

chronic p. 212, **acute** p. 212, **insulin** p. 215, **seizure** p. 218

Daily Fitness Tip

Playing sports and engaging in other physical activities is not only fun but also decreases your chances of developing chronic diseases. Exercise can also help people manage chronic diseases.

(CSHP) For more guidelines on choosing activities for fitness, see *Be Active! Resources for Physical Education,* p. 137.

1. MOTIVATE

Ask for volunteers to tell about a time they had a cold or flu. Ask them to talk about the length of time it took them to get well. Explain that colds are considered acute diseases because they do not last very long. Discuss the difference between acute and chronic diseases. Ask students to name some chronic diseases.

What do you think is the most common fatal disease in the United States? Students might be surprised that heart disease is the number one cause of death in this country.

Discuss

Have students distinguish between the myth that suntans look healthy, and the fact that a suntan means damaged skin and the possibility of getting skin cancer.

LESSON 5 — Noncommunicable Diseases

Lesson Focus

Noncommunicable diseases have many causes.

Why Learn This?

Knowing the causes and symptoms of noncommunicable diseases can help you prevent these diseases, treat them, and show concern for people who have them.

Vocabulary

chronic
acute
insulin
seizure

Myth and Fact

Myth: **A suntan shows that you are healthy.**
Fact: **A suntan shows that your skin has been damaged. And sunburns can lead to skin cancer.**

Chronic and Acute Diseases

Darla has asthma. Her piano teacher has arthritis. These are two examples of noncommunicable diseases. Others include cancer, diabetes, heart disease, and epilepsy.

Many noncommunicable diseases are chronic. Chronic (KRAHN•ik) diseases are diseases that affect a person for a long time. But some noncommunicable and most communicable diseases are acute. Acute diseases don't last very long. For example, most colds are acute diseases. They usually affect a person for less than a week or two.

Doctors have discovered the causes of many noncommunicable diseases. They have learned that sometimes the causes are found in the environment. For example, too much exposure to sunlight can lead to skin cancer.

Darla's piano teacher has arthritis, which causes pain and stiffness in her joints. However, this doesn't stop her from teaching piano. ▶

212

Social Studies

Exploring the Globe Have groups of students choose a country other than the United States and research the diseases commonly found there. Students should identify the disease that causes the most deaths in that country; the causes and effects of that disease; and any bacterial, environmental, and hereditary factors contributing to the spread of the disease. They may also refer to efforts to eradicate or control the disease. Have students report their findings to the class.

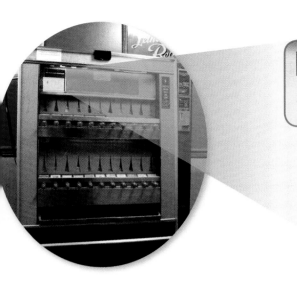

WARNING: THE U. S. SURGEON GENERAL
FINDS THAT SMOKING CAUSES LUNG CANCER

WARNING: The U.S. Surgeon General finds that
smoking causes lung cancer

The sale of tobacco
products to persons
under age 18 is
strictly prohibited
by state law. If you are under
18, you could be penalized for
purchasing a tobacco product;
photo ID required.

▲ **Why are there warning
labels on tobacco
vending machines?**

Tobacco smoke can bring about lung cancer. Air pollution might have caused Darius's asthma.

Lifestyle choices can affect your chances of getting some noncommunicable diseases. Unhealthful habits such as using tobacco, drinking alcohol, and eating fatty foods increase your risk. So does having too much stress and getting too little exercise.

Using any form of tobacco puts you at greater risk for cancer and heart disease. Smokeless tobacco, for example, can give you cancer of the mouth. Drinking too much alcohol makes liver disease more likely.

People who overeat or eat a lot of junk food place themselves at risk for heart disease. People who get very little exercise also increase this risk.

Other factors, such as heredity, can affect your chances of getting a noncommunicable disease. Unlike lifestyle choices, you have little or no control over hereditary factors.

CAUSE AND EFFECT List three noncommunicable diseases and their possible causes.

Possible answer: asthma—substances in the environment; heart disease—unhealthful lifestyle choices; diabetes—heredity

213

ACTIVITY

Life Skills

Make Responsible Decisions One day a teenager offers Christa a cigarette. Use what you know about tobacco and noncommunicable diseases to help Christa decide what to say. Write a script for her to follow.

2. TEACH

Interpret Pictures—Visuals

Direct students' attention to the picture on this page. Explain that the United States government requires that warning labels be placed on all cigarette packages, advertisements, and in places that sell cigarettes.

Discuss

Have students research the effect of media on health-promoting behaviors.

Critical Thinking **Why do you think the government requires warning labels on cigarettes?** Without them, many people wouldn't know how dangerous cigarettes can be or exactly what the dangers are. The government is concerned about the health effects of smoking.

Ask students if they have ever seen a television ad for cigarettes. Unless they have been to another country, they likely have not seen any, because TV and radio ads for cigarettes have been banned in the United States since 1971. Point out that print ads never actually show people with cigarettes in their mouths. This is against the law as well.

Activity

Students' responses may include that using any form of tobacco can cause cancer and heart disease. Students might also mention the adverse effects of secondhand smoke and suggest that Christa ask the person not to smoke around her. Point out that all Christa has to say is "No, thanks." She does not need to justify her decision. Explain that it can be very difficult to "just say *no*," even for adults, but that being able to do so can be very powerful. If the teenager is mature, he or she will respect Christa's decision and not bother her about it.

Content-Area Reading Support

Using Tables and Graphs Direct attention to the clipboard graphic on this page. Explain that the graphic provides additional detailed information on the symptoms of cancer in children. Notice that the beginning letters of the symptoms combine to spell the word *children*. Recommend that students pause to study tables, diagrams, and graphic aids such as this, since the information they provide is often as important as the information in the paragraphs of text.

Discuss

Explain to students that there are two types of tumors. Malignant tumors are cancerous and can be fatal if left untreated. Benign tumors are noncancerous and are usually not fatal.

Critical Thinking Why do some benign tumors cause health problems?
Possible response: Because of their size or location, benign tumors may cause discomfort or interfere with normal body functions.

Health Background

Leukemia, a cancer of the white blood cells, starts in the bone marrow–the soft, inner part of bones. It can then spread to the blood, lymph nodes, spleen, liver, central nervous system, and other organs. Cancer is more common in adults, but it is the second-leading cause of death in children under the age of fourteen. Children's cancer centers have been established to meet the special needs of children who have cancer and their families. These centers have health professionals who support and educate the whole family. These usually include doctors, nurses, psychologists, social workers, and dietitians.

Source: *American Cancer Society*

 For more background, visit the **Webliography** in Teacher Resources at **www.harcourtschool.com/health Keyword** diseases

---

Eight Warning Signs of Possible Childhood Cancer

1. **Continued, unexpected weight loss**
2. **Headaches with vomiting in the morning**
3. **Increased swelling or persistent pain in bones or joints, sometimes accompanied by limping**
4. **Lump or mass in abdomen, neck, or elsewhere**
5. **Development of a whitish appearance in the pupil of the eye or a sudden change in vision**
6. **Recurrent fevers not due to infections**
7. **Excessive bruising or bleeding (often sudden)**
8. **Noticeable paleness or prolonged tiredness**

From the Physician Oncology Education Program, Texas Medical Association

Many people with cancer lead active lives. Bill has leukemia (loo•KEE•mee•uh), a cancer of the white blood cells. ▶

214

Cancer

Cancer is a noncommunicable disease that can take many forms. All forms of cancer occur when body cells that are not normal start to multiply in an uncontrolled way. In most cancers, cells clump together and form abnormal masses called tumors. However, not all cancers form tumors, and not all tumors are cancerous.

A cancerous tumor can kill normal cells around it and can damage healthy body tissues. Cancer can spread from one part of the body to another. The symptoms of cancer vary. Skin cancer can cause sores that don't heal. Lung cancer can cause a cough that doesn't go away.

The sooner a cancer is found, the greater the chances that it can be removed or treated. By learning the warning signs of cancer, you might be able to detect cancer in yourself or in someone else. (The disease occurs much more often in adults than in children.) Cancer can be detected earlier and treated more quickly through regular checkups by a doctor.

COMPARE AND CONTRAST
How are different forms of cancer alike and different?

Alike—All forms of cancer are caused by abnormal multiplying of cells. Different— Symptoms of different types of cancer vary.

 Meeting Individual Needs
Leveled Activities

BELOW-LEVEL Healthful Lifestyle Songwriters Have students research the dangers of smoking and write songs about those dangers.

ON-LEVEL Skin Cancer Have students find out about the risks of too much sun exposure and the dangers of using tanning beds or salons. Ask students to write short reports that include information about the types of skin cancers and precautions people should take to limit their risks.

CHALLENGE Cancer Research Have students contact the American Cancer Society for current research and information about cancer. Have students write reports that discuss the differences between normal and cancerous cells, some diagnostic tests used to detect cancer, the work that cancer labs are doing, and the services provided by the American Cancer Society.

Diabetes

Diabetes is a disease in which body cells don't get the sugar they need for energy. There are two types of diabetes. In people with Type 1 diabetes, the body doesn't make enough **insulin** (IN·suh·lin), a hormone that helps body cells take sugar from the blood. In people with Type 2 diabetes, insulin does not work as it should. Over time, the body gradually loses the ability to use insulin.

When people have diabetes, their body cells get too little sugar. Body cells "starve." This causes the people to feel weak and tired. Because sugar cannot enter body cells, it stays in the blood. The high level of blood sugar can cause a number of health problems, such as blindness, poor blood circulation, and frequent infections.

With proper treatment, people can manage diabetes. They must follow a balanced diet, control their blood sugar levels, and get regular exercise. People with Type 1 diabetes must give themselves daily shots of insulin. Type 2 diabetes can often be controlled with diet, exercise, and medicines.

DRAW CONCLUSIONS
Why must some people with diabetes take insulin?

Their bodies do not make enough insulin or cannot use the insulin that they do make.

Marcus, who has diabetes, is checking his blood sugar level. ▶

Health & Technology

Sugar Watches Today some people with diabetes can test their blood sugar levels without drawing blood. The monitor shown below, which looks like a wristwatch, painlessly collects fluid from under the skin. Sensor pads measure sugar levels in the fluid and show them on the dial.

215

TEACH *continued*

Discuss

Problem Solving If you were a doctor, how could you determine whether someone had a tumor and whether it was cancerous or benign? I could take an X ray or use some other kind of imaging technique (such as an MRI) to find out if there is a tumor. Then I would take a sample of the tumor and look at the cells under the microscope to find out whether the tumor is cancerous or benign.

Personal Health Plan ▶

Plans may include initiating a family discussion about developing more healthful eating habits. Students may suggest some healthful alternatives for after-school treats or offer to go grocery shopping with their parents to help make those choices.

Discuss

Explain that many noncommunicable diseases are hereditary. Some people are born with them, and some develop them later in life. In many cases there is nothing a person could have done to avoid getting the disease. Point out that it can take many years of research to determine the cause of a disease and that many diseases have a number of causes.

Discuss

Critical Thinking Why do you think a low-fat diet and regular exercise are essential to maintaining a healthy heart? Possible responses: Fat can build up in the linings of the arteries and block the flow of blood to the heart, causing a heart attack. Exercise helps you maintain a healthful weight and lessen the stress and strain on your heart muscle.

Personal Health Plan ▶

Real-Life Situation
Your family has some cookies, ice cream, and chips in the kitchen for special treats. These are always tempting when you come home from school. But you want to develop healthful eating habits that will help prevent heart disease when you get older.
Real-Life Plan
Write a plan for dealing with this temptation.

Blocked arteries have fatty substances that limit the flow of blood. With high blood pressure (hypertension), the heart must work harder to pump the needed blood to the body's tissues.

Doctors recommend regular exercise as a way to prevent heart disease. ▶

216

Heart Disease

Heart disease is a leading cause of death in the United States. One of the most common forms of heart disease is blocked arteries. People with this condition have fatty substances lining their arteries and blocking the flow of blood. If the flow to part of the heart muscle is completely cut off, a heart attack occurs.

Blocked arteries usually get worse over time. However, the advance of the condition can be slowed with medicine. Lifestyle choices, such as eating a low-fat diet and getting exercise, also help control the condition.

High blood pressure is another common disease of the circulatory system. If your blood pressure is too high, your heart must work harder to get blood to all your body tissues. Over time, this strains your heart and damages blood vessels. High blood pressure can usually be managed by weight control, medicine, a low-salt diet, and exercise.

SUMMARIZE Identify and describe two forms of heart disease.

ESL/ELL Support

COMPREHENSIBLE INPUT Have students use graphic organizers to show how to help prevent or manage some noncommunicable diseases.

Beginning Have students copy a word web from the board. The summary circle should read "How to prevent or manage noncommunicable diseases." Students should draw pictures in the surrounding circles to illustrate prevention techniques.

Intermediate Have students copy the web from the board. Students should draw and label pictures in the surrounding circles to illustrate ways to prevent or manage noncommunicable diseases.

Advanced Have students copy the web from the board or design a graphic organizer of their own choosing and complete it, using information from the text.

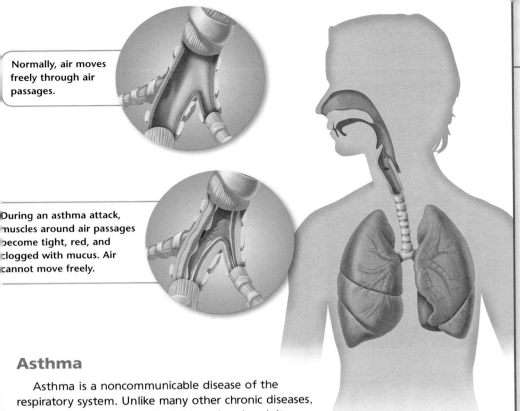

Normally, air moves freely through air passages.

During an asthma attack, muscles around air passages become tight, red, and clogged with mucus. Air cannot move freely.

Asthma

Asthma is a noncommunicable disease of the respiratory system. Unlike many other chronic diseases, asthma is more common in children than in adults. Many children who have asthma outgrow it.

When a person has an asthma attack, he or she coughs a lot and has trouble breathing. Some attacks are triggered by infections such as colds and bronchitis. Allergies, cold air, smoke, and air pollution can also cause asthma attacks.

The first step in treating asthma is to find out what things trigger the attacks. Those things might then be avoided. Medicines can also help. Some asthma medicines are swallowed, and some are given in shots. However, most asthma medicines are breathed in through devices called inhalers.

CAUSE AND EFFECT A girl in your class has an asthma attack. What could have caused it?
Possible responses: smoke; allergies; cold air; pollution; bronchitis; a cold

Students with asthma should cooperate with health-care professionals, such as the school nurse, to help manage their asthma.

217

 Math

Allergy Surveys Have students use library resources or interview an allergy specialist to find out about common allergies and how they affect the body. Have pairs or groups of students interview five people who have allergies. Have the class graph the data to determine which allergens are most common among the people surveyed.

Discuss

After students read the text, direct their attention to the diagrams on this page. Ask a volunteer to read the captions. Use the diagram of the respiratory system to explain what asthma is and how it affects the person. Asthma occurs when the airways carrying air to the lungs become inflamed. During an asthma attack, muscles tighten around the airways, causing the tubes to constrict. Excess mucus is produced when membranes inside the air tubes swell. The airways become clogged, and the person has difficulty breathing and coughs a lot.

Problem Solving Why is it important to identify the cause of an asthma attack? Possible response: so the person can avoid the things that cause it

Problem Solving What are some treatments for asthma? Possible responses: medicines, such as inhalers; avoiding things that trigger attacks

Direct students' attention to the pictures on page 218, and have volunteers read the captions aloud. Ask volunteers to talk about their knowledge of such medical devices. Have volunteers read aloud the text on page 218.

Discuss

Problem Solving When someone seems to be having a seizure, how might you find out how to help that person? Possible response: Look for a medical ID bracelet or tag to understand what is happening to the person; look for devices containing medicines to treat allergic reactions. Explain that it is particularly important for people with epilepsy or diabetes to wear medical bracelets because their conditions can cause them to lose consciousness.

3. WRAP UP

Lesson 5 Summary and Review

1. chronic; acute; responses may include asthma, arthritis, cancer, diabetes, epilepsy; insulin, medical IDs

2. If found early, cancer may be removed or treated quickly through regular checkups by a doctor.

3. to control the blood sugar levels in their bodies

4. Possible answers are shown below:

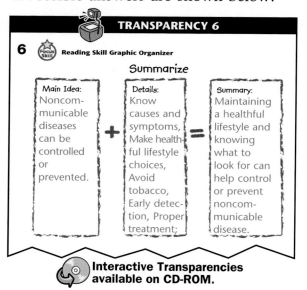

TRANSPARENCY 6

6 Reading Skill Graphic Organizer

Summarize

Main Idea:	Details:	Summary:
Noncommunicable diseases can be controlled or prevented.	Know causes and symptoms, Make healthful lifestyle choices, Avoid tobacco, Early detection, Proper treatment;	Maintaining a healthful lifestyle and knowing what to look for can help control or prevent noncommunicable disease.

Interactive Transparencies available on CD-ROM.

5. Letters to the real or imaginary friend may include an understanding of how the disease affects the friend's body and lifestyle and some knowledge about the precautions or medicines the friend must take to control the disease.

For **writing models** with examples, see *Teaching Resources* pp. 47–61. Rubrics are also provided.

When Minutes Count . . .

Quick Study Students can use *Activity Book* pp. 31–32 (shown on p. 191) as they complete each lesson in this chapter.

Some people with chronic diseases wear medical ID bracelets or necklaces. These make it easier to get the right medical help if it is needed. ▼

Medical IDs

Epilepsy is a chronic disease of the brain. In people with epilepsy, signals between brain cells are sometimes out of control. The result is a **seizure** (SEE•zher), or sudden attack of unconsciousness or uncontrolled body movement.

People who have epilepsy can wear identification bracelets so that others can understand what is wrong during a seizure. People with certain other chronic diseases, such as asthma, diabetes, or serious allergies, may also wear medical IDs. If the people are unable to explain what might be wrong, the IDs can help explain their conditions.

DRAW CONCLUSIONS What might happen if someone with epilepsy had a seizure but was not wearing a medical ID?
The person might not get proper medical treatment.

This pen-shaped device contains medicine to treat severe allergic reactions. Many people with life-threatening allergies carry such devices. ▶

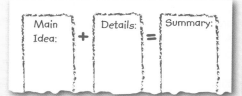

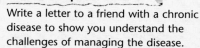

Lesson 5 Summary and Review

❶ **Summarize with Vocabulary**

Use vocabulary and other terms from this lesson to complete the statements.

Many noncommunicable diseases are _____, which means that they cause health problems over a long time. In contrast, most communicable diseases are _____. Noncommunicable diseases include heart disease and _____. People with Type 1 diabetes inject _____ so that body cells can get sugar for energy. People with serious allergies sometimes wear _____.

❷ Why is it important to find cancer early?

❸ **Critical Thinking** Why do people with diabetes have to control what they eat?

❹ **SUMMARIZE** Draw and complete this graphic organizer to show how noncommunicable diseases can be controlled or prevented.

Main Idea:	Details:	Summary:

❺ **Write to Express—Letter**

Write a letter to a friend with a chronic disease to show you understand the challenges of managing the disease.

218

Teacher Tip

Epilepsy is the tendency of the brain to produce sudden bursts of electrical energy that disrupt other normal brain functions. Having seizures can be one symptom of epilepsy, but seizures can also be caused by other factors, such as fever, head injury, or lack of oxygen. Epilepsy is never contagious and can develop at any time of life. Of the 125,000 new cases diagnosed each year, 30 percent begin in childhood or early adolescence.

Responsibility

Take Responsibility for Your Own Health

There are many ways to lower your chances of getting a disease. As you get older, it becomes more important for you to take responsibility for your wellness. Here are some tips to help you get started.

At play:

- Warm up your muscles by stretching before you exercise. This helps get you ready for activity.
- Wear safety gear to keep you from getting hurt when you play sports.
- Make sure that the safety gear fits you properly and that you use it correctly.

At home and at school:

- Drink lots of water. Water is better for you than drinks containing caffeine or sugar. Most people drink too little plain water.
- Go to bed on time. Getting enough sleep is especially important while you're still growing. People your age need at least eight hours of sleep each night.
- Don't let others talk you into doing things that you believe are wrong or that can harm your health.

Activity

Keep track of how much sleep you get each night and how many glasses of water or juice you drink during the day. Make a table that you can mark each day. At the end of the week, evaluate this table to see if you can improve your health by changing your habits.

219

Using the Poster

Activity Have students make posters illustrating activities that are part of healthful lifestyles. Encourage students to be creative but realistic.

Display Poster 5 to remind students of ways to show responsibility. The poster can be displayed in the classroom or in the hallway.

POSTER 5

Responsibility

The boy is showing responsibility by being a good role model for his sister.

DO
- Practice self-control.
- Express feelings, needs, and wants in appropriate ways.
- Practice good health habits.
- Keep yourself safe.
- Keep trying. Do your best.
- Complete tasks.
- Set goals and work toward them.
- Be a good role model.

DON'T
- Don't smoke. Don't use alcohol or other drugs.
- Don't do things that are unsafe or that destroy property.
- Don't be led by negative peer pressure.
- Don't deny or make excuses for your mistakes.
- Don't leave your work for others to do.
- Don't lose or misuse your belongings.

How have **YOU** shown **RESPONSIBILITY** today?

POSTER 5

Caring
Citizenship
Fairness
Respect
Responsibility
Trustworthiness

Objective

► Learn how to take responsibility for your own health.

Program Resources

► Poster 5

BEFORE READING

Provide pictures of people doing healthful activities, such as eating well-balanced meals and exercising. Ask students to describe what is happening in the pictures and to name the wellness activities that should occur before and after the event. For example, students would need to warm up before exercising and wash their hands before preparing food. Lead students to the conclusion that they must take responsibility for their own health and wellness.

DISCUSS

Discuss the fact that it can be very difficult to have a healthful lifestyle if the people around you don't. For example, if all your friends watch TV and eat fast food every day after school, it can be hard to maintain a healthful lifestyle. Discuss ways that students can overcome this sort of obstacle.

ACTIVITY

Remind students that taking responsibility for their own healthful habits is essential for maintaining wellness. Assign the Activity. At the end of the week, ask volunteers to share what they discovered about their own wellness habits and the changes they can make to improve those habits.

LESSON 6
Pages 220–222

Objectives
▶ Learn how to make healthful choices to reduce your risk of disease.
▶ Understand the importance of eating well, exercising, and avoiding tobacco.

When Minutes Count . . .
Assign the Quick Study, Lesson 6, Activity Book pp. 31–32 (shown on p. 191).

Program Resources
▶ Activity Book pp. 31–32, 35
▶ Transparency 6

Daily Fitness Tip

Encourage students to avoid secondhand smoke. Explain that, according to the American Cancer Society, children of smokers are hospitalized during the first year of life for pneumonia and bronchitis more often than are children of nonsmokers. Tell children that leaving the room when smokers light up will reduce their risks of developing diseases associated with secondhand smoke.

 For more guidelines on smoking and exercise, see *Be Active! Resources for Physical Education,* p. 169.

1. MOTIVATE

Have a class discussion about sports and other physical activities. Ask students what their favorite sports are, and list them on the board. Ask students why they like the particular sport, how they feel when they are playing it, and how they feel afterward. Make a bar graph of the activities and the number of students who enjoy them. Note that some students might not be enthusiastic about physical activities. Explain that you don't have to be good at an activity to enjoy it and get something out of it. It can take a lot of practice to become skilled at an activity. When you first start out, it might not be much fun because you'll get tired very quickly.

LESSON 6
Choosing a Healthful Lifestyle

Lesson Focus
The choices you make about food, activity, and tobacco have a major impact on your health.

Why Learn This?
By making healthful choices, you can reduce your risk of disease.

Healthful Eating and Exercise

You don't have any control over your heredity. You have only some control over your environment. But you can definitely control your lifestyle through smart and healthful choices. You can decide to eat right, exercise regularly, and not use tobacco. These choices will reduce your risk of getting many diseases.

Heart disease is more likely to affect people who eat a lot of foods that are high in fat. High-fat foods include ice cream, doughnuts, potato chips, French fries, and other foods at the top of the Food Guide Pyramid on pages 78–79. Which foods on the Food Guide Pyramid are low in fat?

Fats should be eaten only in small amounts. You don't have to completely cut them out of your diet in order to stay healthy. However, if you eat more foods from the Fats, Oils, and Sweets Group than from the Vegetable and Fruit Groups, you

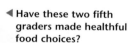 Have these two fifth graders made healthful food choices?

220

 **Integrated Language Arts/ Reading Skills**

Dramatic Choices Have groups of students write scripts and perform plays about healthful lifestyle choices. Students may choose to focus on one choice or several lifestyle choices. Scripts should include information from the text and from other approved sources. Students may choose to make simple sets or props. Allow time for students to prepare and practice before presenting their plays to the class.

◄ Regular aerobic exercise can lower your chances of getting some diseases.

may be more likely to develop heart disease. It is important to eat the right amounts of bread, cereal, rice, and pasta, too. These foods should make up the largest part of your diet.

Regular aerobic exercise can reduce your risk of heart disease and also help you manage stress. Aerobic exercise is any activity that makes your heart pump faster, causing you to breathe deeply. Aerobic activities include swimming, cycling, jogging, and active team sports such as soccer. Aerobic exercise gives your heart muscle a workout, which makes it stronger. It also improves the flow of blood. People with high blood pressure can often lower their blood pressure through exercise and diet.

MAIN IDEA AND DETAILS Give three reasons why you should eat a healthful diet and get regular aerobic exercise.

Possible answer: to avoid chronic disease, to strengthen your heart muscle, to manage stress

Quick Activity

Analyze Foods Make a list of possible lunch foods. Then compare your list with the Food Guide Pyramid on pages 78–79. On your list, mark the foods that are lowest in fat. Draw a star next to foods that would be healthful choices.

221

2. TEACH

Interpret Visuals—Pictures

Direct students' attention to the picture on this page. Ask a volunteer to read the caption aloud. Ask students if they know what the word *aerobic* means. Point out the word part *aer,* and make sure students understand that *aerobic* means "using oxygen" or "living in the presence of oxygen." Aerobic activities involve temporarily increasing the heart and respiration rates. Aerobic exercise strengthens the heart and lungs.

Critical Thinking How can you tell if an activity is aerobic? If it makes you breathe harder and makes your heart beat faster, it is aerobic.

Discuss

There are two kinds of fats—unsaturated and saturated. Unsaturated fats usually come from plants and are less harmful than saturated fats, which usually come from animals.

Critical Thinking What are some sources of unsaturated fats? Examples: corn oil, canola oil, low-fat milk, vegetables, fruits, fish What are some sources of saturated fats? Examples: meats, butter, cheese

Physical Education

Staying Fit Have students survey at least five adults to find out about their exercise habits, including how often they exercise. Have students record their findings on a chart and classify each exercise as aerobic or anaerobic. Students should also determine the body systems that benefit from each type of exercise. Students should report their findings to the class and draw conclusions about what is meant by "regular" exercise.

Teacher Tip

Exercise Aerobic exercise, which involves increasing the breathing and heart rates over an extended period of time, is efficient at burning fat. The name *aerobic* comes from the fact that your body requires extra oxygen to perform these activities. Anaerobic exercise, on the other hand, is efficient at building muscle. It involves short bursts of exertion followed by periods of rest. Weight lifting and swinging a baseball bat are examples of anaerobic exercise.

Health Background

Anorexia nervosa and bulimia are examples of eating disorders and are common among adolescent girls. Anorexia nervosa is characterized by deliberate self-starvation, and bulimia is characterized by binge eating followed by purging. Without intervention, these conditions can be fatal. Research indicates that about 1 percent of young women between the ages of ten and twenty are anorexic. Although anorexia and bulimia primarily affect people in their teens and twenties, these disorders have been reported in children as young as six.

Source: *National Eating Disorders Association*

For more background, visit the **Webliography** in Teacher Resources at **www.harcourtschool.com/health Keyword** eating disorders

Lesson 6 • Choosing a Healthful Lifestyle **221**

Consumer Activity

Students could point out that the ad isn't telling them everything about the dangers of smoking. Students could also explain that the ad was designed to take advantage of young people. The person who thinks smoking is cool from looking at this ad has fallen for it.

3. WRAP UP

Lesson 6 Summary and Review

1. heredity; lifestyle; fat, aerobic, tobacco
2. Aerobic exercise is any activity that causes you to breathe deeply and your heart to pump faster. Activities may include swimming, cycling, jogging, and participating in active team sports.
3. Possible responses: People who smoke are more likely to get lung, throat, and mouth cancer and heart disease than people who do not smoke. Nonsmokers will live healthier lives and are less likely to get these diseases.
4. Possible answers are shown below:

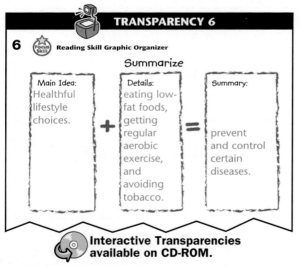

TRANSPARENCY 6

6 Reading Skill Graphic Organizer

Summarize

| Main Idea: Healthful lifestyle choices. | + | Details: eating low-fat foods, getting regular aerobic exercise, and avoiding tobacco. | = | Summary: prevent and control certain diseases. |

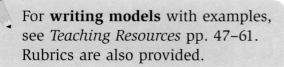
Interactive Transparencies available on CD-ROM.

5. Possible responses: The e-mail should include facts about the diseases that can be caused by smoking and that are the leading causes of death in the United States.

> For **writing models** with examples, see *Teaching Resources* pp. 47–61. Rubrics are also provided.

Consumer Activity

Analyze Advertisements and Media Messages List several arguments against smoking that you could use for someone who thinks smoking is cool because of advertisements like the one below.

Tobacco Use Harms Your Health

Using tobacco can cause a number of chronic diseases. It can cause lung, throat, and mouth cancer and heart disease. These diseases are the leading causes of death in the United States today. In spite of this, people still use tobacco. Why? Some use tobacco because they think it makes them look grown-up. Others want to fit in. Many people cannot stop—they have become addicted to tobacco.

It's easy to prevent tobacco from harming you. All you have to do is avoid tobacco and tobacco smoke. Refuse to use tobacco if it is offered to you. Using tobacco is a bad health habit and should be avoided.

CAUSE AND EFFECT **What effects can smoking tobacco have on someone later in life?**
A person can develop serious health problems such as cancer and heart disease.

Lesson 6 Summary and Review

1 **Summarize with Vocabulary**

Use terms from this lesson to complete the statements.

One factor that affects chances of getting a noncommunicable disease is _____, the passing of characteristics from parents to children. Your _____ plays a major role in whether you develop diseases. Eating low-_____ foods, getting regular _____ exercise, and not using _____ can decrease your risk of getting many chronic diseases.

2 What is aerobic exercise? Give examples.

3 **Critical Thinking** Explain why people who use tobacco are more likely to die at a younger age than people who don't.

4 **SUMMARIZE** Draw and complete this graphic organizer to show important parts of a healthful lifestyle.

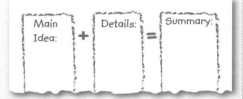

| Main Idea: | + | Details: | = | Summary: |

5 **Write to Express—Idea**

Suppose you have a friend who smokes cigarettes. Write an e-mail to your friend, warning about the dangers of using tobacco. Try to convince him or her that smoking is not cool. Use facts.

222

ACTIVITY BOOK P. 35

Name _____

Vocabulary Reinforcement

Use Word Meanings

In each of the following sentences, the italicized term makes the sentence incorrect. Find the term in the box that makes the sentence correct. Write the correct term on the line. Use each term only once.

| immunity | resistance | acute | bacteria | fungi |
| antibodies | seizures | insulin | noncommunicable disease | symptoms |

1. Most colds are *chronic* diseases, lasting about a week or less.
   acute
2. Diabetes can't be spread from person to person; it is a *communicable disease*.
   noncommunicable disease
3. Strep throat is a disease caused by *viruses*.
   bacteria
4. Your body has a natural *abstinence* to disease.
   resistance
5. Fever and sore throat can be *pathogens* of disease.
   symptoms
6. Your white blood cells make *antibiotics* to fight disease.
   antibodies
7. You body's ability to remember how to make antibodies is called *immunization*.
   immunity
8. *Infections* can be caused by the disease epilepsy.
   Seizures
9. People with diabetes can't make or use *vaccines* properly.
   insulin
10. Athlete's foot is caused by *protozoa*.
    fungi

Available online.
www.harcourtschool.com/health

ACTIVITIES

Social Studies

Research Sanitation and Health
Florence Nightingale was a British nurse who lived in the nineteenth century. She is best known for her role in slowing the spread of communicable diseases by making hospitals more sanitary. Research Florence Nightingale's work during the Crimean War, which began in 1854. How did her work affect wounded soldiers?

Science

List Touched Objects You know that communicable diseases spread from person to person. This can happen by touching objects that were touched by a person with a communicable disease. Make a list of classroom objects you touched today that may have been touched by a classmate. What does this information tell you about how quickly diseases can be spread?

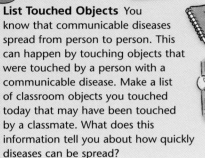

Technology Project

Use a computer to make a brochure that tells people how to keep their hearts healthy. Share your brochure with your family, and offer a copy to your school library. If a computer is not available, use construction paper and colored pencils or markers.

For more activities, visit The Learning Site.
www.harcourtschool.com/health

Home & Community

Show Food Preparation Rules With a partner, make a poster about preparing food in a school cafeteria or at home. Show rules for preventing the spread of disease during food preparation. Decide where to display the poster in your home or community.

Career Link

Physician Assistant Physician assistants work closely with doctors. They help relieve the work of busy doctors by treating patients who have minor or chronic health problems. Suppose you are a physician assistant. One of your patients is a young boy with Type 1 diabetes. What should you ask his parents about his diet?

223

Career Link

Physician Assistant Explain that physician assistants (or PAs for short) work under the supervision of a physician. They take medical histories, examine and treat patients, order and interpret laboratory tests and X rays, make diagnoses, and prescribe medication. To become a PA, you need at least two years of college plus a degree from a PA program, which usually lasts about two years.

If you were a physician assistant aiding a twelve-year-old boy with Type 2 diabetes, you should ask him about his diet and exercise. What foods does he typically eat? How much sugar is he eating? Is he getting enough exercise? You would stress that these things are very important.

For more information on health careers, visit the **Webliography** in Teacher Resources at **www.harcourtschool.com/health**
Keyword health careers

Activities

Science
Provide time for students to share their lists. Write the names of these objects on the board, and make a tally of the number of students in the class who touched each object. Talk about how easily and quickly pathogens can spread. Encourage students to wash their hands frequently with soap and warm water before touching their eyes, nose, or mouth.

Social Studies
Students might be encouraged to research the contributions of Florence Nightingale and Louis Pasteur to antiseptic and sanitary conditions in hospitals and operating rooms. Have students share their reports with the class.

Home & Community
Students should get permission to display their posters with others outside the classroom. Have students share their posters with the class.

Supports the Coordinated School Health Program

Technology Project
To complete this project, students should be encouraged to use what they learned from reading Chapter 7 and to look for information in approved library sources. Research topics might include the effects on the heart of hypertension, atherosclerosis, diet, exercise, smoking, alcohol abuse, and stress. Have students share their brochures with the class.

Reading Skill 3 pts. each

1. pathogens
2. heredity
3. lifestyle

 Use Vocabulary 3 pts. each

4. immune system
5. viruses
6. Insulin
7. Antibiotics
8. infection
9. immunity
10. acute
11. protozoa

 Check Understanding 3 pts. each

12. C, heredity
13. J, cancer
14. B, resistance
15. F, bacteria
16. C, cilia
17. H, booster
18. A, mucus
19. J, fried chicken
20. C, treatment

 Think Critically 8 pts. each

21. Ana can tell her brothers that diseases are spread by pathogens. Pathogens cause disease and can enter the body through the skin, eyes, nose, or mouth and can be spread through sharing food or drinks.

22. He could find out if there is a history of diabetes in his family and ask a doctor to check his blood sugar level.

 Reading Skill

SUMMARIZE

Draw and then use this graphic organizer to answer questions 1–3.

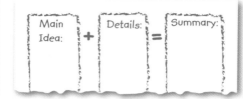

1. What causes communicable diseases?
2. What can cause a child to get a noncommunicable disease such as sickle cell anemia?
3. What kinds of choices help determine your risk for chronic diseases?

 Use Vocabulary

Use a term from this chapter to complete each sentence.

4. The _____ is the body system that fights disease.
5. _____ are the pathogens that cause colds.
6. _____ is a hormone that helps body cells get sugar from the blood.
7. _____ are medicines that kill bacteria.
8. If pathogens have multiplied quickly in the body, _____ has occurred.
9. The condition in which antibodies protect a person from a disease is called _____.
10. Diseases that don't last long are _____.
11. The organisms that cause diseases such as amebic dysentery are _____.

224

 **Check Understanding**

Choose the letter of the correct answer.

12. This boy and his mom look very much alike because of _____. (p. 191)
    A resemblance   C heredity
    B lifestyle   D transmission

13. Which disease occurs when body cells multiply out of control? (p. 214)
    F asthma   H heart disease
    G diabetes   J cancer

14. Your body's natural ability to fight off disease on its own is called _____. (p. 204)
    A antibiotic   C defense
    B resistance   D immunity

[Graphic organizer: Pathogens — Fungi, Protozoa, Viruses]

15. Which kind of pathogen is missing from the graphic organizer? (p. 196)
    F bacteria
    G vaccines
    H *Giardia*
    J antibodies

Formal Assessment

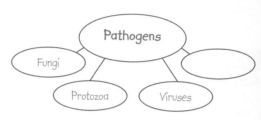

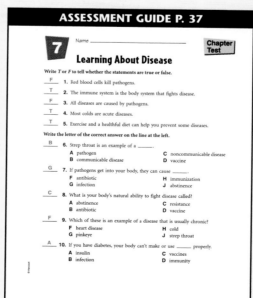

ASSESSMENT GUIDE P. 37

7 Learning About Disease

Name _____

Chapter Test

Write T or F to tell whether the statements are true or false.

__F__ 1. Red blood cells kill pathogens.
__T__ 2. The immune system is the body system that fights disease.
__F__ 3. All diseases are caused by pathogens.
__T__ 4. Most colds are acute diseases.
__T__ 5. Exercise and a healthful diet can help you prevent some diseases.

Write the letter of the correct answer on the line at the left.

__B__ 6. Strep throat is an example of a _____.
    A pathogen   C noncommunicable disease
    B communicable disease   D vaccine

__G__ 7. If pathogens get into your body, they can cause _____.
    F antibiotic   H immunization
    G infection   J abstinence

__C__ 8. What is your body's natural ability to fight disease called?
    A abstinence   C resistance
    B antibiotic   D vaccine

__F__ 9. Which of these is an example of a disease that is usually chronic?
    F heart disease   H cold
    G pinkeye   J strep throat

__A__ 10. If you have diabetes, your body can't make or use _____ properly.
    A insulin   C vaccines
    B infection   D immunity

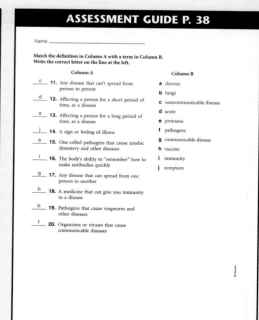

ASSESSMENT GUIDE P. 38

Name _____

Match the definition in Column A with a term in Column B. Write the correct letter on the line at the left.

Column A

__c__ 11. Any disease that can't spread from person to person
__d__ 12. Affecting a person for a short period of time, as a disease
__a__ 13. Affecting a person for a long period of time, as a disease
__j__ 14. A sign or feeling of illness
__e__ 15. One-celled pathogens that cause amebic dysentery and other diseases
__i__ 16. The body's ability to "remember" how to make antibodies quickly
__g__ 17. Any disease that can spread from one person to another
__h__ 18. A medicine that can give you immunity to a disease
__b__ 19. Pathogens that cause ringworm and other diseases
__f__ 20. Organisms or viruses that cause communicable diseases

Column B

a chronic
b fungi
c noncommunicable disease
d acute
e protozoa
f pathogens
g communicable disease
h vaccine
i immunity
j symptom

16 Which are the tiny hairlike structures that push trapped pathogens toward a body opening? (p. 201)

  A antibodies   **C** cilia
  B white blood   **D** saliva
     cells

17 An extra dose, or a _____ , of a vaccine is given to maintain immunity. (p. 209)

  F shot
  G injection
  H booster
  J antibiotic

18 Which of these body defenses is a thick, sticky substance that traps pathogens? (pp. 200–201)

  A mucus
  B sweat
  C tears
  D urine

19 If you are trying to eat a healthful diet, which of these foods will you eat **LEAST** often? (pp. 220–221)

F

H

G

J

20 The special care you get when you are ill is called medical _____. (pp. 206–207)

  A vaccination
  B stress
  C treatment
  D heredity

21 Ana's younger brothers often share licks from their ice-cream cones. What can Ana tell her brothers to make them understand that each boy should eat his own ice cream?

22 Juan wonders if he is more likely than the average person to get diabetes. What is one thing he could find out to help him answer his question?

Apply Skills

23 **LIFE SKILLS**
  Manage Stress Tests make Dante feel jittery, so he puts off studying until the last minute. What would be a better way for Dante to manage the stress of tests?

24 **BUILDING GOOD CHARACTER**
  Responsibility You have just switched doctors, and your new doctor doesn't have your medical records. You think you might be due for a tetanus booster shot, but your new doctor hasn't mentioned it. What should you do?

Write About Health

25 Write to Entertain—Poem Write a funny and informative poem to explain to a younger student how the body fights pathogens.

225

Apply Skills 8 pts. each

23. Dante could develop a habit of studying every day at the same time. Then he will not be stressed, because he will feel prepared to take the test.

24. You should talk with your parents about the need for a booster shot and ask them to call or make an appointment with your doctor to discuss your booster shot schedule.

Write About Health 8 pts.

25. Songs may include information about the skin as the first layer of defense; the protective roles of sweat, mucus, cilia, and saliva; the production of antibodies by white blood cells; and the development of immunity.

Performance Assessment

Use the Chapter Project and the rubric provided on the Project Evaluation Sheet. See *Assessment Guide*, pp. 18, 59, 68.

Portfolio Assessment

Have students select their best work from the following suggestions:

- Leveled Activities, p. 214
- Quick Activity, p. 201
- Write to Inform, p. 218
- Activities, p. 223

See *Assessment Guide* pp. 12–16.

ASSESSMENT GUIDE P. 39

Name _____

Complete the diagram below by naming the parts of the body indicated by the arrows. Then tell how each helps to keep pathogens from entering the body.

21. Possible answer: Earwax traps pathogens that try to enter your body through the ears.

22. Possible answer: Tears wash away and kill pathogens that enter the eyes.

23. Possible answer: Chemicals in saliva kill pathogens that enter your mouth.

Lifestyle choices can have a big impact on your health. For each lifestyle choice below, tell whether it is a healthful choice or an unhealthful choice. Then explain how the lifestyle choice could impact your health.

24. Getting regular exercise
Healthful choice. Possible answer: Getting regular exercise can help reduce the risk of heart disease. It also helps you manage stress, which reduces the risk of getting many diseases.

25. Using tobacco
Unhealthful choice. Possible answer: Using tobacco products is harmful to your health. It can cause lung, throat, and mouth cancer, as well as heart disease.

CHAPTER 8 Legal and Illegal Drugs

Lesson	Pacing	Objectives	Reading Skills
Introduce the Chapter pp. 226–227		• Preview chapter concepts.	🔵 **Cause and Effect** pp. 227; 372–383
1 How Medicines Help the Body pp. 228–233	1 class period	• Explain that medicines are drugs that cause helpful changes in the body when used correctly. • Differentiate between OTC and prescription medicines. • Interpret information on how to use a medicine.	🔵 **Cause and Effect** pp. 229, 233 • Summarize, p. 230 • Compare and Contrast, p. 231 • Sequence, p. 232
2 Medicine Use, Misuse, and Abuse pp. 234–237	1 class period	• Discuss how to use medicines safely. • Interpret a medicine label. • Distinguish between medicine misuse and medicine abuse.	🔵 **Cause and Effect** p. 237 • Main Idea and Details, p. 235 • Draw Conclusions, p. 237
3 Illegal Drugs pp. 238–244	2 class periods	• Explain how the use of illegal drugs can harm the body. • Describe crack and cocaine and analyze their short-term and long-term effects on the body. • Describe marijuana and inhalants and analyze their short-term and long-term effects on the body.	🔵 **Cause and Effect** pp. 239, 244 • Summarize, p. 241 • Draw Conclusions, p. 243 • Main Idea and Details, p. 244
★ **Building Good Character** p. 245		• Identify ways to be trustworthy about not using drugs.	
4 Staying Away from Drugs pp. 246–249	1 class period	• Describe the negative consequences of illegal drug use. • Analyze how illegal drug use can interfere with activities and goals. • Explain strategies for saying *no* to illegal drug use.	🔵 **Cause and Effect** p. 249 • Draw Conclusions, p. 247 • Main Idea and Details, p. 248
Life Skills pp. 250–251	1 class period	• Identify refusal skills. • Use refusal skills to stay drug-free.	
5 How Drug Users Can Get Help pp. 252–254	1 class period	• Recognize when someone needs help refusing or getting off drugs. • Describe methods for getting help about illegal drug use.	🔵 **Cause and Effect** p. 254 • Compare and Contrast, p. 252 • Draw Conclusions, p. 254
Activities p. 255		• Extend chapter concepts.	
Chapter Review pp. 256–257	1 class period	• Assess chapter objectives.	

Vocabulary	Program Resources
	Music CD Teaching Resources, p. 37
drug medicine prescription medicines over-the-counter medicines side effects	Transparency 3 Activity Book, pp. 36–39
dosage expiration date self-medication medicine misuse medicine abuse addiction anabolic steroids	Transparency 3 Activity Book, pp. 36–37
illegal drugs overdose withdrawal inhalants	Transparency 3 Activity Book, pp. 36–37
	Poster 6
refuse	Transparency 3 Activity Book, pp. 36–37
	Activity Book, p. 43 Poster 10
	Transparency 3 Activity Book, pp. 36–37, 40
	The Learning Site www. harcourtschool.com/health
	Assessment Guide, pp. 40–42

 Reading Skill

These reading skills are reinforced throughout this chapter and one skill is emphasized as the Focus Skill.

Cause and Effect

- Draw Conclusions
- Compare and Contrast
- Identify Main Idea and Details
- Sequence
- Summarize

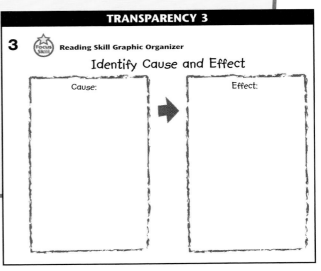

TRANSPARENCY 3

3 Reading Skill Graphic Organizer
Identify Cause and Effect

Cause: → Effect:

 Life Skills

Life Skills are health-enhancing behaviors that can help students reduce risks to their health and safety.

Six Life Skills are reinforced throughout *Harcourt Health and Fitness*. The skill emphasized in this chapter is Refuse.

POSTER 10

Refuse

The girl is refusing to use drugs.

Ways to Refuse

1. Say *no*, and state your reasons for saying no.
2. Say *no*, and suggest something else to do.
3. Say *no*, and change the subject.
4. Say *no*, and walk away.
5. Say *no*, and make a joke or use any other nonviolent way.

How do YOU REFUSE?

POSTER 10

 Building Good Character

Character education is an important aspect of health education. When students behave in ways that show good character, they promote the health and safety of themselves and others.

Six character traits are reinforced throughout *Harcourt Health and Fitness*. The trait emphasized in this chapter is Trustworthiness.

POSTER 6

Trustworthiness

The older girl is showing trustworthiness by taking good care of the children.

DO	DON'T
► Be honest. Tell the truth.	► Don't tell lies.
► Do the right thing.	► Don't cheat.
► Report dangerous situations.	► Don't steal.
► Be dependable.	► Don't break promises.
► Be loyal to your family, friends, and country.	► Don't borrow without asking first.
► Take care of things you borrow, and return them promptly.	

How have YOU shown TRUSTWORTHINESS today?

POSTER 6

Interactive Transparencies available on CD-ROM.

Coordinated School Health Program

A Coordinated School Health Program endeavors to improve children's health and, therefore, their capacity to learn through the support of families, schools, and communities working together. The following information is provided to help classroom teachers be more aware of these resources.

The National Center for Chronic Disease and Health Promotion, part of the **CDC,** funds the Coordinated School Health Program. Visit its website for information about the eight components that make up this program. **www.cdc.gov/ nccdphp/dash/**

The School Health Policies and Programs Study of the **CDC** is a national survey periodically conducted to assess all eight Coordinated School Health Programs at the state, district, school, and classroom levels. **www.cdc.gov/nccdphp/dash/ shpps/**

The National Institute of Drug Abuse, an arm of the National Institutes of Health **(NIH)**, offers a guide on *Preventing Drug Use Among Children and Adolescents.*

The **American Junior Red Cross** invites students to participate in Youth Volunteer programs, including Community Services, where they can serve as mentors to peers or younger children on substance abuse prevention and other major youth issues. **www.redcross.org/services/youth/**

Other resources that support a Coordinated School Health Program:
- School-Home Connection
- Daily Physical Activity
- Daily Fitness Tips
- Activities: Home & Community
- Health Background: Webliography
- *Be Active! Resources for Physical Education*

Books for Students

Berry, Joy. ***Substance Abuse (Good Answers to Tough Questions).*** Gold Star Publishing, 2000. An in-depth look at drug abuse. **EASY**

Gutman, Bill. ***Harmful to Your Health.*** Twenty-First Century Books, 1996. Straightforward presentation on the dangers of drug abuse. **AVERAGE**

Gates, Phil. ***The History News: Medicine.*** Gareth Stevens, 2001. History of medicine presented in a newspaper-like style. **ADVANCED**

Books for Teachers and Families

Donjon, Richard P. ***Medicine Cabinet Medicines: Over-the-Counter Drugs.*** Mosby Year Book, 1996. A guide to commonly asked questions.

Kuhn, Cynthia; Scott Swartzwelder, Ph.D.; Wilkie Wilson, Ph.D. ***Just Say Know: Talking with Kids About Drugs and Alcohol.*** W. W. Norton

Media Resources

& Company, 2002. What kids should know to make informed decisions.

Free and Inexpensive Materials

National Clearinghouse for Alcohol and Drug Information
Ask for copies of *Preventing Drug Use Among Children and Adolescents.*

Social Studies School Service
Request its Health Education catalog containing health topics.

Central Intelligence Agency
Has a Homepage for Kids on topics such as heroin and CIA drug-related publications, such as *From Flowers to Heroin.*

To access free and inexpensive resources on the Web, visit **www.harcourtschool.com/health/free**

Videos

Getting High on Life: Alternatives to Drugs. Rainbow Educational Media, 1993.

The Truth About Inhalants. Sunburst Communications, 1998.

Drugs: Tough Questions, Straight Answers. Rainbow Educational Media, 1997

These resources have been selected to meet a variety of individual needs. Please review all materials and websites prior to sharing them with students to ensure the content is appropriate for your class. Note that information, while correct at time of publication, is subject to change.

Visit **The Learning Site** for related links, activities, resources, and the health **Webliography.**

www.harcourtschool.com/health

Meeting Individual Needs

Below-Level

Tell students that SQ3R is a study strategy in which you survey the material, form questions, read, recite what was learned, and review information. As you name each step, have volunteers tell when it should be completed: before, during, or after reading.

Activities
- Staying Healthy, p. 230
- Medicine Disposal, p. 234
- In the News, p. 238
- Just Say *No*, p. 246
- Radio Announcements, p. 252

On-Level

Understanding new words is easier when students use context to confirm the word's meaning. Have partners determine a new word's meaning from context clues. Then have them substitute a word for the new word and read the sentence to see if it still makes sense.

Activities
- Medicinal Plants, p. 230
- Children's Diseases, p. 234
- Drug Laws, p. 238
- Refusal Poetry, p. 246
- Drugs, p. 252

Challenge

To help students acquire problem-solving skills, have them identify a problem relating to the topic of this chapter. Have students use construction paper, craft sticks, glue, and scissors to make puppets. Then have them act out the problem and possible solutions.

Activities
- Alternative Medicine, p. 230
- Overdose, p. 234
- Crack vs. Cocaine, p. 238
- Drug Pain, p. 246
- Drug Treatment, p. 252

Learning Log

Students can use a Learning Log to help them summarize a section using five key points. After reading a section aloud, ask students to tell five things they learned. On the board, write the five most important facts in clear, simple language. Have students copy them into their Learning Logs.

Activities
- Comprehensible Input, p. 232
- Background and Experience, p. 236, 240, 248

Curriculum Integration

Integrated Language Arts/Reading Skills
- Write an Essay, p. 235
- Compare Medicines and Street Drugs, p. 239
- Amotivational Syndrome, p. 242
- Role Models, p. 247

Science
- Commonly Abused Medicines, p. 237
- Drug Use Statistics, p. 253

Use these topics to integrate health into your daily planning.

Physical Education
- Daily Fitness Tip, pp. 228, 234, 238, 246, 252
- Daily Physical Activity, p. 227

Art
- Medicine Collage, p. 231
- Marijuana *No!* Poster, p. 243
- Self-Esteem Collages, p. 249

CHAPTER SUMMARY

In this chapter students

► compare and contrast the effects medicines and drugs have on the body.

► describe the safe use of over-the-counter and prescription medicines.

► learn that illegal drugs, such as marijuana and cocaine, are harmful and should be avoided.

 Life Skills
Students practice *refusing* to use illegal drugs.

 Building Good Character
Students practice *trustworthiness* about not using drugs.

 Consumer Health
Students *make buying decisions*.

 ### Literature Springboard

Use the article "Learn How to Refuse" to spark interest in the chapter topic. See the Read-Aloud Anthology on page RA-9 of this *Teacher Edition*.

Prereading Strategies

SCAN THE CHAPTER Have students preview the chapter content by scanning the titles, headings, pictures, graphs, and tables. Ask volunteers to predict what they will learn. Use their predictions to determine prior knowledge.

PREVIEW VOCABULARY As students scan the chapter, point out the vocabulary terms listed at the beginning of each lesson. Invite students to sort the terms into two groups—familiar and unfamiliar terms.

Familiar Terms	Unfamiliar Terms

 ### Reading Skill
Focus Skill

IDENTIFY CAUSE AND EFFECT To introduce or review this skill, have students use the Reading in Health Handbook, pp. 372–383. Teaching strategies and additional activities are also provided.

Students will have opportunities to practice and apply this skill throughout this chapter.

• Focus Skill Reading Mini-Lesson, p. 228

• Reading comprehension questions identified with the

• *Activity Book* p. 39 (shown on p. 233)

• Lesson Summary and Review, pp. 233, 237, 244, 249, 254

• Chapter Review and Test Preparation, pp. 256–257

Focus Skill — Reading Skill

IDENTIFY CAUSE AND EFFECT An effect is what happens. A cause is the reason, or why, it happens. Use the Reading in Health Handbook on pages 372–383 and this graphic organizer to help you read the health facts in this chapter.

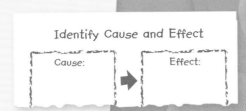

Identify Cause and Effect

Cause: → Effect:

Health Graph

INTERPRET DATA Anabolic steroids are prescription medicines, but some people abuse them—that is, they use them for a purpose other than what was intended. About what percentage of high school students have used anabolic steroids?

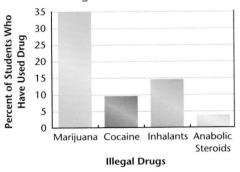

Illegal Drug Use by High School Students

Percent of Students Who Have Used Drug — Marijuana, Cocaine, Inhalants, Anabolic Steroids

Illegal Drugs

Daily Physical Activity

Staying away from illegal drugs is a good way to stay healthy. So is getting some physical activity every day.

 Be Active!
Use the selection, Track 8, **Jumping and Pumping**, to make your body feel better.

227

School-Home Connection

Distribute copies of the School-Home Connection (in English or Spanish). Have students take the page home to share with their families as you begin this chapter.

Follow Up Have volunteers share the results of their activities.

 Supports the Coordinated School Health Program

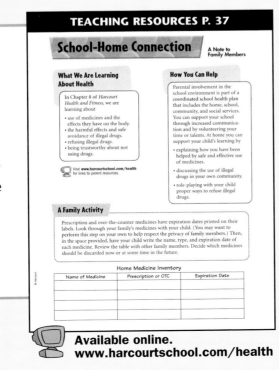

TEACHING RESOURCES P. 37

School-Home Connection — A Note to Family Members

What We Are Learning About Health

In Chapter 8 of *Harcourt Health and Fitness*, we are learning about
- use of medicines and the effects they have on the body.
- the harmful effects and safe avoidance of illegal drugs.
- refusing illegal drugs.
- being trustworthy about not using drugs.

Visit **www.harcourtschool.com/health** for links to parent resources.

How You Can Help

Parental involvement in the school environment is part of a coordinated school health plan that includes the home, school, community, and social services. You can support your school through increased communication and by volunteering your time or talents. At home you can support your child's learning by
- explaining how you have been helped by safe and effective use of medicines.
- discussing the use of illegal drugs in your own community.
- role-playing with your child proper ways to refuse illegal drugs.

A Family Activity

Prescription and over-the-counter medicines have expiration dates printed on their labels. Look through your family's medicines with your child. (You may want to perform this step on your own to help respect the privacy of family members.) Then, in the space provided, have your child write the name, type, and expiration date of each medicine. Review the table with other family members. Decide which medicines should be discarded now or at some time in the future.

Home Medicine Inventory

Name of Medicine	Prescription or OTC	Expiration Date

Available online.
www.harcourtschool.com/health

INTRODUCE THE CHAPTER

Health Graph

Interpret Data

Have students describe the abuse of prescription medications. Ask volunteers to explain what information the graph is presenting.

What percent of high school students have used illegal anabolic steroids? 3.7 percent

What percent of high school students have never used cocaine? 90.5 percent

From looking at this graph, would you say that most high school students have or have not used illegal drugs? Most high school students have not used illegal drugs.

Daily Physical Activity

Use *Be Active! Music for Daily Physical Activity* with the Instant Activity Cards to provide students with movement activities that can be done in limited space. Options for using these components are provided beginning on page TR2 in this *Teacher Edition*.

Chapter Project

Illegal Drugs Affect Body Organs (*Assessment Guide* p. 59)

ASSESS PRIOR KNOWLEDGE Use students' initial ideas for the project as a baseline assessment of their understanding of chapter concepts. Have students complete the project as they work through the chapter.

PERFORMANCE ASSESSMENT The project can be used for performance assessment. Use the Project Evaluation Sheet (rubric), *Assessment Guide* p. 69.

LESSON 1

Pages 228–233

Objectives
► Explain that medicines are drugs that cause helpful changes in the body when used correctly.
► Differentiate between OTC and prescription medicines.
► Interpret information on how to use a medicine.

 When Minutes Count . . .
Assign the Quick Study, Lesson 1, Activity Book pp. 36–37 (shown on p. 229).

Program Resources
► Activity Book pp. 36–37, 39
► Transparency 3

Vocabulary
drug p. 228, **medicine** p. 228, **prescription medicines** p. 230, **over-the-counter (OTC) medicines** p. 231, **side effects** p. 232

Daily Fitness Tip

Being physically fit involves more than exercising and eating healthful foods. It also means using medicines only as directed by a parent or doctor.

 For more guidelines about alcohol, drugs, and movement, see *Be Active! Resources for Physical Education,* p. 171.

1. MOTIVATE

Write the word *medicine* on the board.

Name three medicines. Answers will vary. Record all the correct responses on the board under the word *medicine*.

Have students examine the finished list of medicines. Ask students if they know what any of the listed medicines are used for. Students may recognize medicines that are used to relieve pain, calm upset stomachs, soothe itching skin, and so on.

 LESSON 1

How Medicines Help the Body

Drugs and Medicines

Lesson Focus
Medicines can help you stay healthy if they are used correctly. They can be harmful if they are used incorrectly.

Why Learn This?
Learning how to use medicines safely will help you stay healthy.

Vocabulary
drug
medicine
prescription medicines
over-the-counter
 medicines
side effects

Everyone becomes ill or gets hurt. Harmful bacteria in food can give you an upset stomach. An allergy can make you sneeze, and a scraped knee can be painful. Sometimes a medicine, which is a kind of drug, can help you feel better or heal you more quickly, but only if it is used the right way.

A **drug** is a substance, other than food, that affects the way your body or mind works. A **medicine** is a drug used to prevent, treat, or cure an illness. Illegal drugs, such as cocaine and marijuana, also cause changes in the body. But unlike medicines, illegal drugs cause changes that do not improve your health. Illegal drugs are harmful to use and can even be deadly.

Many medicines come from plants like these that live in rain forests. ▶

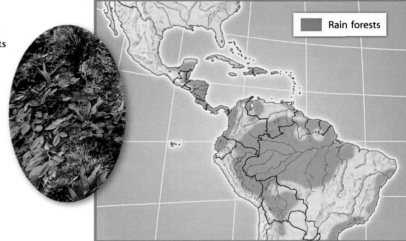

Rain forests

228

 **Reading Skill**

Mini-Lesson

CAUSE AND EFFECT Remind students that an effect is what happens. A cause is the reason, or why, it happens. Have students practice this skill by responding to the Focus Skill question on page 229. Have students draw and complete the graphic organizer as you model it on the transparency.

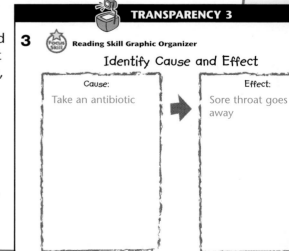

TRANSPARENCY 3

3 Reading Skill Graphic Organizer

Identify Cause and Effect

Cause:	Effect:
Take an antibiotic	Sore throat goes away

 Interactive Transparencies available on CD-ROM.

▼ Today, many medicines are made in laboratories.

▲ Some rainforest plants have been used to treat illnesses for many years.

Different medicines improve health in different ways. Vaccines help prevent diseases such as polio, measles, and chicken pox. Antibiotics kill organisms that cause infections, such as strep throat. Pain relievers help reduce aches and pains. Some people take medicines to control health problems such as allergies, asthma, diabetes, and high blood pressure.

Scientists working for drug companies are always developing new, more effective medicines. They make many new medicines in laboratories by using chemicals. They also find new medicines in plants, animals, and minerals. Before a new medicine can be sold, however, the government must approve it. Scientists who work for the government test every new medicine to make sure it is safe and effective. It often takes years of testing before a new medicine can be sold.

 CAUSE AND EFFECT **What effect does an antibiotic have on an infection, like strep throat?**
An antibiotic kills the organisms causing the infection. That helps the person get well.

Health & Technology

Laboratory Drugs
When scientists find useful new drugs in plants, they then usually try to make the drugs in a lab. It's often easier to do that than to grow large numbers of the plants that the drugs came from. Laboratory-made drugs are also safer than natural drugs. For example, different soils and weather conditions can change the chemicals in plants. Drugs made in labs are always the same.

229

2. TEACH

Content-Area Reading Support
Using Word Parts Have students scan this page for words they may not be familiar with. Tell them to figure out the meanings of the words by analyzing word parts. For example, *anti-* means "against" and *bio* means "life." Students could use these two word parts to guess the meaning of *antibiotic*. After students use word parts to understand unfamiliar terms, have them look up the words in a dictionary to see how close their guesses are to the actual definitions.

Health Background

Drug Research Drug research is a multibillion-dollar business. Of perhaps 100,000 synthesized chemicals tested, only one or two may get through to trials on patients. During initial trials on human volunteers, all effects of a drug are carefully monitored. If the tests go well, the drug is then further tested to determine the safest and most effective dosages.

Source: *U.S. Food and Drug Administration; U.S. Department of Labor*

 For more background, visit the **Webliography** in Teacher Resources at **www.harcourtschool.com/health** **Keyword** medicines

---

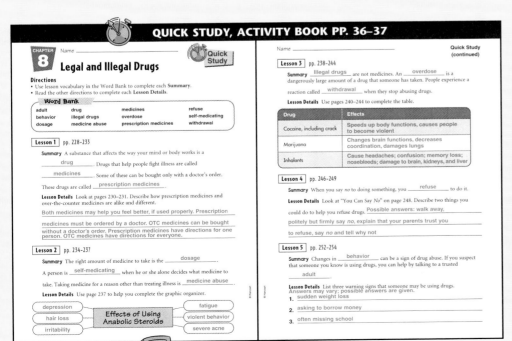

QUICK STUDY, ACTIVITY BOOK PP. 36–37

Available online.
www.harcourtschool.com/health

Discuss

After students have read about prescription medicines, discuss why they should never use other people's prescriptions.

Critical Thinking **What factors might affect how an individual responds to a medicine?** age, gender, weight, severity of the illness, health status (especially nutritional status), and even mood

Why shouldn't you use someone else's prescription medicine? You may not share all of the factors listed above with the other person.

Why might a person react differently to the same medicine at different times? He or she might have changed in age or weight, may not have the same severity of the illness, might have a different health status, or might be in a different mood.

Why should you throw away leftover prescription medicines and not use them again? Each medicine was prescribed for a particular situation, and only a doctor can tell if it is suitable in another situation.

Consumer Activity

Making Buying Decisions Generic medicines (medicines without brand names) are less costly than brand-name medicines, and are usually just as effective. Select several brand-name medicines that are also available as generics. Make a chart to compare active ingredients and prices.

A prescription medicine has a label that may also have special directions, such as "Take with food" or "Do not take with other medicines." ▼

Prescription Medicines

Suppose you go to the doctor about a sore throat. The doctor examines you, decides what's wrong, and prescribes a medicine. Following the doctor's orders, a pharmacy prepares a prescription medicine for you.

Prescription medicines are medicines that can be bought only with a doctor's order. They are strong and can be harmful if not used correctly. That's why you should always have a parent or other trusted adult give you any prescription medicine.

A doctor considers many things before writing a prescription. These include the patient's symptoms, age, weight, other medicines being taken, and any allergies.

Your doctor writes your prescription for you only. It's dangerous to take a medicine prescribed for someone else, even if both of you have the same health problem.

SUMMARIZE **Why is it important to take medicines prescribed for you only?**

230 A doctor considers a person's age, weight, other medicine's being used, and so on, before prescribing a certain medicine. The medicine may not be appropriate or safe for another pers

---

Meeting Individual Needs
Leveled Activities

BELOW-LEVEL **Staying Healthy** Ask students to write on one side of a folded sheet of paper four things they do to keep themselves healthy. On the other side they should list four things they should avoid doing, such as using medicine improperly.

ON-LEVEL **Medicinal Plants** Have students research plants used for treating diseases and draw pictures of the plants on poster board. Ask them to label the different parts of each plant as well as the disease for which each plant is indicated. Encourage students to include a map showing places each plant is found.

CHALLENGE **Alternative Medicine** Have students interview an alternative medicine specialist. Suggest that they learn the history and development of the particular branch of alternative medicine, and the forms of treatment used. Students should report their findings to the class.

◄ Pharmacies and supermarkets sell many OTC medicines, such as pain relievers, nasal sprays, eye drops, cough syrups, and acne creams.

Over-the-Counter Medicines

If you have a slight headache, you probably don't need to see a doctor. Instead, your parent can give you an over-the-counter pain reliever. **Over-the-counter (OTC) medicines** are medicines that can be bought without prescriptions. OTC medicines usually treat minor health problems. They are for short-term use. Some cough medicines, nasal sprays, and pain relievers are OTC medicines.

Like prescription medicines, OTC medicines can be harmful if not used correctly. That's why it's important to always have a parent or other trusted adult help you with an OTC medicine.

The label on an OTC medicine tells what the medicine treats and how it should be taken. The label also tells the length of time to take the medicine. In addition, it lists warnings for people who should not take the medicine. For example, an aspirin label might say, "Children and teens should not use this medicine for flu symptoms."

ALLERGY SINUS
1 PILL EVERY 4 to 6 HOURS
20 Coated Tablets
Reliever Runny Nose, Nasal Congestion, Sneezing, Itchy, Watery Eyes, Headache and Sinus Pressure

Did You Know?

Hundreds of OTC medicines were once prescription medicines. After a prescription medicine has been used safely for many years, the government may reclassify it as an OTC medicine.

COMPARE AND CONTRAST What are the similarities and differences between prescription medicines and OTC medicines?
Both OTC and prescription medicines help to prevent or cure illnesses. However, prescription medicines are usually more powerful and can be bought only with a doctor's order.

231

Discuss
Tell students that doctors in the United States write about 3 billion prescriptions each year. This is the equivalent of 10 medicines for every American. In addition, people in the United States consume countless doses of over-the-counter (OTC) medicines, which can be purchased without a doctor's prescription.

Critical Thinking What do these figures tell you? Possible answer: Many people in the United States depend on medicines to help keep them healthy. People may also be using medicines instead of adopting healthful lifestyles.

Discuss
Have students describe the use of prescription and non-prescription medications.

Interpret Visuals—Pictures
Ask students to compare the prescription medicine on page 230 to the OTC medicines on this page.

Critical Thinking How are these medicines the same? Both are for specific illnesses.

How are they different? Prescription medicines can only be purchased with a doctor's order, while OTC medicines can be purchased by anyone.

TEACH *continued*

Discuss

After students have read this page, discuss different ways in which drugs can be administered.

Critical Thinking **What would probably be the fastest way of getting a drug for asthma to where it is needed—swallowing it, injecting it, or inhaling it?** Inhaling would be fastest, because it delivers the drug directly to the area where it is needed—tiny airways in the lungs.

How would breathing the drug in help minimize side effects? Less of the drug would go to other parts of the body, where it might cause unwanted reactions.

What would be the most effective way to administer a drug that is needed quickly throughout the body? by injection **A drug that is needed gradually throughout the body?** by swallowing

Quick Activity

Have students work in pairs to write their dialogues. They can focus on one kind of information on the medicine's label, such as questions about precautions to take when using the drug, or they can address the fact sheet in a more general way by asking a question about each of the areas. After they have finished writing their dialogues, ask volunteers to use their scripts to perform skits for the rest of the class.

Myth and Fact

Myth: All medicines made with "natural" ingredients are safe.

Fact: "Natural" does not always mean "safe." Always consult a doctor before using natural medicines. For example, ephedra, or ma huang, is a dangerous herbal drug that can cause heart attacks and strokes.

How Medicines Affect the Body

Medicines come in many forms. Some are creams rubbed on the skin. Others are drops placed in the eyes, ears, or nose. Most medicines are pills or liquids that are swallowed. From the small intestine, a medicine enters the bloodstream and is carried to all parts of the body.

Different medicines have different side effects. **Side effects** are unwanted effects of a medicine. For example, an allergy medicine might make you sleepy. Most side effects are not serious. But if you ever feel strange after taking a medicine, tell a parent or other trusted adult right away.

You should also avoid taking two or more different medicines at the same time without your doctor's directions. This can cause side effects that are different from those listed on either medicine's label. These effects can be very dangerous. That's why it's important for your parent to ask your doctor or pharmacist before giving you more than one medicine at a time.

SEQUENCE **After you swallow a pill, how does the medicine reach different parts of your body?**
The medicine goes to your stomach and intestines, where it is absorbed into your bloodstream. The bloodstream carries the medicine to every part of the body.

232

ESL/ELL Support

COMPREHENSIBLE INPUT Familiarize students with different types of medicines.

Beginning Help students brainstorm a list of prescription and OTC medicines. Have them tell or role-play what each medicine is used for.

Intermediate Have students do the Beginning activity. Then help them make a two-column table of the medicines and their uses.

Advanced Have students collect news articles that describe advances in medical science made possible by the use of medicines. Post the articles on the bulletin board, and lead a group discussion on articles of interest.

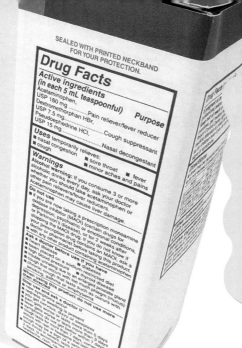

SEALED WITH PRINTED NECKBAND FOR YOUR PROTECTION.

Drug Facts

Active ingredients
(in each 5 mL teaspoonful) | **Purpose**
Acetaminophen,
USP 160 mg .... Pain reliever/fever reducer
Dextromethorphan HBr,
USP 7.5 mg .... Cough suppressant
Pseudoephedrine HCl,
USP 15 mg .... Nasal decongestant

Uses temporarily relieves:
■ nasal congestion ■ sore throat ■ fever
■ cough ■ minor aches and pains

Warnings

Quick Activity

Read Labels The OTC medicine shown here has important information printed on the side of its box. It's important to read this information before taking the medicine. Use the information on this box to write a dialogue between a pharmacist and a patient who has questions about this medicine.

Lesson 1 Summary and Review

❶ **Summarize with Vocabulary**

Use vocabulary from this lesson to complete these statements.

A _____ is a _____ that is used to treat an illness. Some medicines are _____ medicines, and others are _____, both of which can cause _____, such as sleepiness.

❷ What is the difference between over-the-counter medicines and prescription medicines?

❸ **Critical Thinking** How do medicines benefit people, and how can they harm people?

❹ 🌟 **CAUSE AND EFFECT** Draw and complete this graphic organizer to show the effects of antibiotics on the body.

Cause:	Effect:

❺ **Write to Inform—Description**

Write a paragraph describing some effects of helpful drugs and harmful drugs.

233

---

3. WRAP UP

Lesson 1 Summary and Review

1. medicine, drug; OTC, prescription, side effects

2. Prescription medicines are more powerful than OTC medicines and should be used only under a doctor's supervision.

3. Medicines help people recover from illnesses, but they can hurt people if they are used incorrectly.

4. Possible answers are shown.

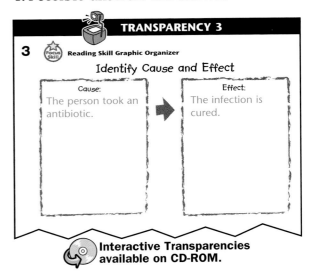

TRANSPARENCY 3

3 🌟 **Reading Skill Graphic Organizer**

Identify Cause and Effect

| Cause:
The person took an antibiotic. | ➡ | Effect:
The infection is cured. |

 Interactive Transparencies available on CD-ROM.

5. Students' paragraphs should note that both helpful and harmful drugs affect the body in some way but that harmful drugs hurt a person's health.

For **writing models** with examples, see *Teaching Resources* pp. 47–61. Rubrics are also provided.

 **When Minutes Count . . .**

Quick Study Students can use *Activity Book* pp. 36–37 (shown on p. 229) as they complete each lesson in this chapter.

Objectives
► Discuss how to use medicines safely.
► Interpret a medicine label.
► Distinguish between medicine misuse and medicine abuse.

When Minutes Count . . .
Assign the Quick Study, Lesson 2, Activity Book pp. 36–37 (shown on p. 229).

Program Resources
► Activity Book pp. 36–37
► Transparency 3

Vocabulary
dosage p. 235,

expiration date p. 235,

self-medication p. 236,

medicine misuse p. 236,

medicine abuse p. 236,

addiction p. 236,

anabolic steroids p. 237

Daily Fitness Tip

Knowing how to read medicine labels and use medicines correctly is an important part of being physically fit.

 For more guidelines about drugs, alcohol and movement, see *Be Active! Resources for Physical Education,* p. 171.

1. MOTIVATE

Write the number 300,000 on the board or on a large sheet of paper. Tell students that this is the number of people in the United States who are hospitalized each year because they experience severe reactions to medicines.

What does this statistic tell you? People should know the hazards as well as the benefits of taking medicines.

Medicine Use, Misuse, and Abuse

Lesson Focus
Medicines can be abused if they are not taken correctly.

Why Learn This?
Learning the dangers of medicine abuse will help you use medicines safely.

Vocabulary
dosage
expiration date
self-medication
medicine abuse
addiction
anabolic steroids

Use Medicines Safely

It's important to remember that medicines can have strong effects on your body. Always make sure you talk with a parent or other trusted adult before taking any medicine. Medicines will help you only if you use them correctly. If you take medicines incorrectly, they can harm you. To use a medicine safely, always read the directions on the label. It tells you when and how to take the medicine and when not to take it. Never use a medicine that is not labeled. You might take the wrong medicine or take it incorrectly.

It is also important to store medicines as directed. If you store them incorrectly, they might not work the way they should or they could make you ill.

Most medicines should be kept in a cool, dark place, away from moisture. Some medicines must be kept in the refrigerator. Check medicine labels for storage directions.

Never take any medicine without the direction of a parent or other trusted adult. ▶

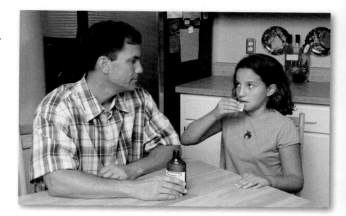

234

Meeting Individual Needs
Leveled Activities

BELOW-LEVEL Medicine Disposal Have students talk to a pharmacist to learn the proper ways to dispose of leftover prescription medicines or expired medicines. Have them make a poster explaining what they learned.

ON-LEVEL Children's Diseases Have students read articles and interview pediatricians about childhood diseases. Ask them to write letters addressed to the parents of young children telling about the history, immunization, symptoms, and treatment of one disease. Letters should also tell how a person gets the disease and how long it lasts.

CHALLENGE Overdose Have students choose three different kinds of OTC medicines. Then have them make graphs comparing the number of milligrams of medicine contained in a regular adult dose. Direct students to the "Do Not Exceed Recommended Dosage" warning on each label. Have students calculate what this would mean for each medicine. Ask them to consider why the recommended dosages for OTC medicines vary.

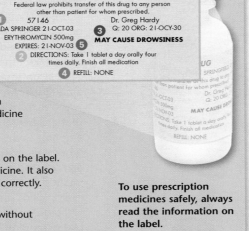

1 Patient's name
A doctor writes a prescription for one patient. The doctor considers the symptoms, age, weight, and allergies of the patient. Never take someone else's medicine or give your medicine to someone else.

2 Directions
Follow the directions that come with your medicine. Be sure to take it at the right time and in the right dosage. The **dosage** is the amount of medicine to take.

3 Warnings
Pay attention to the warnings and cautions printed on the label. This can help you avoid some side effects of a medicine. It also helps ensure that the medicine is stored and given correctly.

4 Refills
This tells you if you can get more of the medicine without getting a new prescription.

5 Date
This is the date the prescription was filled. The label might include an **expiration date**, the last date the medicine should be used.

TOWN DRUG
49 HARDING RD. PHONE 555-8531 SPRINGFIELD, OH 46203
Federal law prohibits transfer of this drug to any person other than patient for whom prescribed.
1   57146   Dr. Greg Hardy
ADA SPRINGER 21-OCT-03   Q: 20 ORG: 21-OCY-30
ERYTHROMYCIN 500mg
EXPIRES: 21-NOV-03   **MAY CAUSE DROWSINESS**
2 DIRECTIONS: Take 1 tablet a day orally four times daily. Finish all medication
4 REFILL: NONE

To use prescription medicines safely, always read the information on the label.

You must also be careful about the foods you eat when taking some medicines. Some foods stop medicines from working. For example, some antibiotics shouldn't be taken with fruit juice. The acid in the juice reduces the ability of the antibiotics to kill bacteria.

Using medicines safely requires a great deal of care and caution. That's why it's important never to make decisions on your own about medicines. A parent or other trusted adult should always help you use medicines.

MAIN IDEA AND DETAILS Make a list of rules you can follow to always use medicines safely.

Possible answer: I always have a parent or other trusted adult help me take medicine; I always follow the label directions; I never take medicine if I don't really

ACTIVITY

Life Skills

Communicate
Christina has a prescription for a new medicine. Her mother isn't sure how often Christina should take it or what side effects to expect. What could Christina's mother do to learn more about the medicine?

235

---

2. TEACH

Interpret Visuals—Pictures
Direct students' attention to the prescription medicine label on this page, and ask students to describe the use of prescription medication.

Problem Solving **What information is given on a prescription label?** warnings and cautions, patient's name, directions for taking, whether the prescription is or is not refillable, and date

Are there any special warnings or directions on this label?

For whom is this medicine prescribed?

Activity

Communicate Have students write their answers to the question, and then discuss their answers as a class. Christina's mother could find and read the directions on the label, on the insert, or on the printout, if it has been provided. She could also question the doctor or pharmacist about the medicine. Encourage students to brainstorm a list of questions Christina's mother should ask. Questions might include: What is the purpose of the medicine? What side effects might it have? Which side effects should be reported to a doctor if they occur? How should the medicine be taken, and what, if any, precautions should be followed when taking it? When should results be expected, and how soon should the doctor be called if no improvement occurs?

TEACH *continued*

Content-Area Reading Support

Using Context Clues Remind students that by reading the sentences that precede, include, and follow highlighted vocabulary, they can get important clues to a term's meaning. Draw a three-column table on the board, labeling the first column *Highlighted Term*, the second column *What I Think It Means*, and the third column *What It Really Means*. Ask volunteers to locate each highlighted vocabulary term and enter it in the first column. Have them read each term in context and fill in the second column. Students can complete the third column by listing each word's meaning as it appears in the Glossary.

Discuss

Most people have medicine cabinets in the bathroom, and take non-prescription medications as they need them.

Critical Thinking Describe the possible abuse of non-prescription medications from this practice. People may take too much medication, or take it when it is not necessary.

Where would be the best place to store medicines in your home? in a cool, dry place away from direct sunlight, children, and pets

Health Background

Aspirin Aspirin is the nation's most useful and most often used OTC, but it can also have unwanted interactions with other medicines. People should not use aspirin if they are allergic to it, have ulcers, are pregnant, have been drinking alcohol (alcohol irritates the stomach lining and increases the amount of internal bleeding that aspirin can cause), or are taking other medicines such as anticoagulants, oral diabetes medicines, or anti-arthritis medicines. Children and teenagers should not take aspirin for chicken pox or flu symptoms.

Source: *Bayer Consumer Care*

 GO **ONLINE** For more background, visit the **Webliography** in Teacher Resources at **www.harcourtschool.com/health** **Keyword** medicines

Medicine Misuse and Abuse

Jason's head hurts and he feels warm. He finds some aspirin in the medicine cabinet. The label says, "Relieves pain and fever." What should he do?

Jason should NOT take the aspirin. Doing so would be self-medication. **Self-medication** is deciding on your own what medicine to take. Children and teens should never take asprin unless a doctor orders it.

If Jason took the aspirin, he would also be misusing a medicine. *Medicine misuse* is taking a medicine without following the directions. The directions warn that children and teens should never take aspirin unless a doctor says it's all right. Aspirin can cause Reye's syndrome, a serious condition that can lead to brain damage and even death. Using leftover prescription medicines or taking too much of a medicine are also examples of medicine misuse.

Some people abuse medicines. **Medicine abuse** is taking medicine for some reason other than treating an illness. The medicines people abuse most are those that cause changes in the brain and nervous system. People who abuse medicines can even develop an addiction. An **addiction** is the constant need for and use of a drug, even though it is not medically necessary. People addicted to drugs sometimes feel they need the drugs, much as other people need food and sleep. Addiction is dangerous. It can lead to serious illness or death.

◄ Sometimes you don't really need medicine. Sarah has a stomachache from eating too many snacks. She thinks she needs some medicine to feel better. However, her mother has her lie down with a warm water bottle, and soon she is feeling well again. ►

236

ESL/ELL Support

BACKGROUND AND EXPERIENCE Invite students to discuss times they have followed safety rules when using medicines. Remind students that the first rule for using medicine safely is *never* to take medicine without adult supervision.

Beginning Help students make a list of medicine-use rules they have read in this lesson and rules they have learned at home.

Intermediate Have students write a pamphlet that could be kept in a pediatrician's office to teach children about medicine safety.

Advanced Have students write short skits that describe ways non-prescription medications can be abused or misused. Students can perform the skits in front of the class, and their classmates can guess which term (*abuse* or *misuse*) they think each skit represented.

Some OTC medicines can be abused. Prescription medicines, especially those for pain, can also be abused. **Anabolic steroids** are prescription medicines that are used to treat certain health problems. But they are also abused by some people. Anabolic steroids have unpleasant and dangerous side effects. These include hair loss, irritability, depression, fatigue, severe acne, and violent behavior. Longtime use of anabolic steroids can cause liver and heart disease and kidney failure.

DRAW CONCLUSIONS Why are anabolic steroids dangerous?

Anabolic steroids cause side effects such as hair loss, irritability, depression, fatigue, severe acne, and violent behavior.

This man is gaining muscle strength the proper way—by exercising, not by taking drugs. ▶

Personal Health Plan ▶

Real-Life Situation
Exercise can help you in several ways. Suppose you want to be stronger.
Real-Life Plan
Make a list of exercises you enjoy that can increase your strength.

Lesson 2 Summary and Review

1 Summarize with Vocabulary

Use vocabulary and other terms from this lesson to complete the statements.

Children and teenagers should never _____ because they can easily _____ medicine by taking the wrong _____. When a person starts using medicines for a reason other than treating an illness, he or she is _____ medicine. This can lead to _____. One commonly abused medicine is _____.

2 What are three things you can do to make sure you use medicine safely?

3 Critical Thinking What is the difference between medicine misuse and medicine abuse?

4 IDENTIFY CAUSE AND EFFECT
Draw and complete this graphic organizer to show the effects of medicine abuse and addiction.

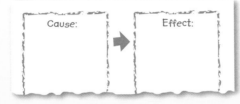

5 Write to Entertain—Short Story

Write a story describing a person who has started abusing medicines. Include in your description the consequences of the abuse.

237

Science

Commonly Abused Medicines
Have students do research to find out what prescription and non-prescription medicines are commonly abused, which types of medicines they are, and what harm they do to the body when abused. Have students describe the abuse of prescription and non-prescription medications in written reports.

Personal Health Plan ▶

Plans should include the following:
- lifting weights
- running
- doing curl-ups
- doing push-ups

This feature is designed to provide students with an opportunity to reflect on health decisions they are making in their personal lives. The Personal Health Plan should not be used to evaluate or assess students, nor should the results be shared among students.

3. WRAP UP

Lesson 2 Summary and Review

1. self-medicate, misuse, dosage; abusing; addiction; anabolic steroids

2. Sample answer: Store it properly, always read the instructions and warnings, and never take medicine without the supervision of a parent.

3. Medicine misuse occurs when people do not follow directions. Medicine abuse is taking medicine for something other than treating an illness.

4. Possible answers are shown.

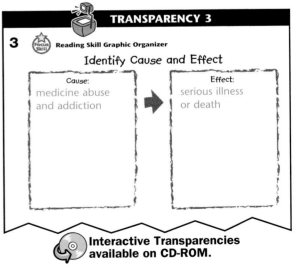

5. Students' stories should discuss the consequences of the abuse, including addiction and serious illness.

Objectives

► Explain how the use of illegal drugs can harm the body.

► Describe crack and cocaine and analyze their short-term and long-term effects on the body.

► Describe marijuana and inhalants and analyze their short-term and long-term effects on the body.

 When Minutes Count . . .

Assign the Quick Study, Lesson 3, Activity Book pp. 36–37 (shown on p. 229).

Program Resources

► Activity Book pp. 36–37
► Transparency 3

Vocabulary

illegal drugs p. 238,

overdose p. 239, **withdrawal** p. 239,

inhalants p. 244

 **Daily Fitness Tip**

Part of being physically fit is not doing things that harm your body, such as using illegal drugs.

 For more guidelines about alcohol, drugs, and movement, see *Be Active! Resources for Physical Education,* p. 171.

1. MOTIVATE

Optional Activity Materials small cardboard box

Hand out small slips of paper, and ask students to write any questions they have about illegal drugs. Collect the questions in the box. Tell students the questions can be anonymous and that they can add questions to the box at any time. If questions are not too personal, you could answer them in class or assign students to research the answers.

 LESSON 3

Illegal Drugs

Illegal Drugs Harm the Body

Lesson Focus

Illegal drugs used in any amount can harm the body.

Why Learn This?

Learning about illegal drugs and their harmful effects can help you avoid them.

Vocabulary

illegal drugs
overdose
withdrawal
inhalants

Medicines are legal drugs if they are used correctly. But some drugs should never be used. They are **illegal drugs**—drugs that are not medicines and that are against the law to sell, buy, have, or use.

People who break the law by using or selling illegal drugs may be sent to prison. But even more serious than going to prison are the harmful effects that illegal drugs have on the body. Some illegal drugs can damage the body or even kill a person. Some illegal drugs can make the heart beat so fast that the user can have a heart attack and die. They can also make blood vessels burst in the brain and cause a stroke.

Illegal drugs also have long-term effects. For example, smoking one illegal drug can lead to memory loss, asthma, and lung cancer. Sniffing another illegal drug can damage the nose, causing sores to form

One of the jobs of the United States Coast Guard is to stop illegal drugs from coming into the country. Each year, the coast guard seizes billions of dollars' worth of illegal drugs. ▼

238

 Meeting Individual Needs
Leveled Activities

BELOW-LEVEL **In the News** Have students clip articles from newspapers and magazines that mention illegal drug use. Post the articles on the bulletin board. After a number of articles have been posted, review their contents with the class. Ask students what the display should be titled—for example, "The High Cost of Illegal Drug Use."

ON-LEVEL **Drug Laws** Have students learn about and list local laws against the possession, use, and sale of marijuana.

CHALLENGE **Crack and Cocaine** Have students write articles about the crack and cocaine laws in their area. Include the minimum and maximum penalties for first-time and repeat possessors, users, and sellers. Direct students to make a graph comparing the minimum and maximum sentencing for drug abuse for first-time and repeat offenders.

inside. It can even break down the septum, the wall that separates the nostrils.

Long-term illegal drug users often do not eat as they should. They may become thin and weak. They are also ill more often than people who don't use drugs. Using an illegal drug during pregnancy can cause birth defects or cause the baby to be born addicted to drugs.

Using some illegal drugs can lead to *tolerance*—the need to use more and more of a drug. A user's body gets used to a drug, and the user needs more of the drug to feel the same effect as before. As tolerance increases, so does the risk of an overdose. An **overdose** is a dangerously large dose of a drug. It can cause severe illness or even death.

The use of illegal drugs has serious effects on a person's life. Users of illegal drugs often become drug addicts. Drug addicts' lives are ruled by drugs. Addicts may no longer care about school or work, family, or friends. They care only about getting more drugs. They can't stop taking drugs because their bodies need the drugs. If the drugs are taken away, the users experience withdrawal. **Withdrawal** is the painful reaction that occurs when someone suddenly stops using a drug. Symptoms can include vomiting, shaking, seeing and hearing things that aren't there, seizures, and even death. Drug addicts usually need medical help to get through withdrawal.

 CAUSE AND EFFECT **What are the causes and effects of withdrawal?**

When a young person uses illegal drugs, his or her grades usually fall. He or she also may start to lose friends. ▶

Drug use and the Effect on Grades

■ = Grades   ■ = Drug use

Withdrawal is caused by a drug addict's discontinuance of drug use. It has various effects, including shaking, seeing and hearing things that aren't there, seizures, and even death. **239**

2. TEACH

Content-Area Reading Support
Using Tables and Graphs Have students examine the graph on this page. Ask for volunteers to describe what the graph's message is. Then have a volunteer read the page aloud. As the volunteer reads, ask other students to identify and write the sequence of events that may lead to addiction and overdose.

Discuss
Critical Thinking **Why do tolerance and dependence keep increasing with long-term drug use?** Tolerance grows because the body gets used to a drug, so the user needs more and more of the drug to produce the same effect. The body begins to need the drug to feel normal, so dependence grows.

Why do the risk of addiction and the risk of an overdose also increase? Eventually drug abusers can become so dependent on drugs that they are addicted. As tolerance and dependence grow, more and more of the drug must be taken to feel the drug's effect or to feel normal. When this happens, the risk of taking too much, or overdosing, also increases.

Health Background

Drugs and Crime Police statistics show that drugs are implicated in about one in four robberies. Drug-related robberies are committed by addicts seeking money to support their drug habit. The illegal drug trade has produced an underworld of drug traffickers and dealers for whom crime is a daily way of life. Additionally, many people are killed or hurt each year in car crashes due to people driving after taking drugs.

Source: *U.S. Department of Justice; Office of National Drug Control Policy*

 For more background, visit the **Webliography** in Teacher Resources at **www.harcourtschool.com/health** **Keyword** drug abuse

Teacher Tip

Tolerance and Addiction
Explain to students that regular drug use leads to increased tolerance. As tolerance builds, the user needs more and more of the drug, and the risk of overdose increases. Drug dependence leads to addiction and to withdrawal symptoms if the addict tries to stop using drugs without help. Have students illustrate this concept as a cycle. Post a few of the illustrations on a bulletin board.

 Integrated Language Arts/ Reading Skills

Compare Medicines and Street Drugs After students finish reading this lesson, have them compare and contrast the effects of medicines and street drugs (illegal drugs).

Quick Activity

There were 62,700 more visits caused by using cocaine.

Discuss

Have students analyze the short-term and the long-term harmful effects of substances, such as cocaine, on the function of the body systems. Students may think that cocaine causes no major health problems. In reality, several health problems are associated with cocaine. Some people who are hypersensitive to cocaine die when exposed to a small amount. Also, cocaine causes a sudden rise in blood pressure, which can cause seizures or heart attacks in some people.

Problem Solving What do you think might be the best way to stop the illegal use of cocaine in the United States?
Sample answers: Drug enforcement agents should address the problem on many fronts, including arresting users and dealers in the United States, catching drug runners, and extraditing drug criminals to the United States. Many educators believe that drug education is the most effective way to stop illegal drug use.

What can you do to stop the illegal use of cocaine? Possible answers: Learn about the harmful effects of cocaine; follow a healthful, drug-free lifestyle; try to help others avoid or stop use of drugs.

Cocaine and Crack

Cocaine is an illegal drug made from the leaves of the coca plant. It's usually sold as a white powder and sniffed through the nose. Sometimes it's injected into a vein. *Crack* is a rocklike form of cocaine that users smoke. The term *crack* refers to the crackling sound the drug makes when someone smokes it. All forms of cocaine are extremely harmful to the body.

Cocaine affects the user just minutes after it is sniffed. It increases blood pressure and speeds up breathing and heartbeat rates, making the user think he or she is more alert or has more energy. Cocaine is so addictive that it can make the user violent. Cocaine addicts have become violent enough to hurt or even kill people to get money to buy more cocaine.

▲ Coca plants, which grow in South America, are used to make cocaine and crack.

Did You Know?
In the late 1800s, many soft drinks were marketed as being medicinal, or good for the health. The so-called medicinal effects of one soft drink came from trace amounts of cocaine. When people started to realize how dangerous cocaine is, its use in the drink was stopped.

Quick Activity

Analyze Graphs Study the graph showing the number of emergency room visits related to illegal drug use. How many more emergency room visits were caused by using cocaine than by using the other three drugs combined?

Number of Emergency Room Visits Related to Cocaine and Other Drugs

Number of Visits: 0, 50,000, 100,000, 150,000, 200,000

Illegal Drugs: Cocaine, Marijuana, Heroin, Amphetamines

ESL/ELL Support

BACKGROUND AND EXPERIENCE Ask students to remember times when they have tried to find a solution to a problem or tried to help somebody.

Beginning Have students draw posters showing the dangers of using cocaine and crack. Encourage students to include an antidrug slogan on their posters in English and in their first language.

Intermediate Have students participate in a brainstorming session to list actions that can stop the use of illegal drugs such as cocaine. Write down all the ideas on the board.

Advanced Have students write a short script about an adult who wants to help a friend or family member stop using illegal drugs. Encourage students to perform the completed scene for the rest of the class.

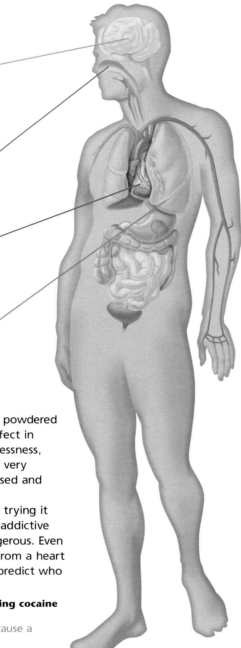

1 People who use cocaine sometimes hear and see things that are not there. Long-term cocaine use can lead to brain damage.

2 Sniffing cocaine over a long period can destroy the inside of the nose.

3 Cocaine and crack raise blood pressure, increase heartbeat rate, and can cause a heart attack.

4 When a person takes in cocaine or crack, he or she starts to breathe more rapidly.

The body absorbs crack even faster than powdered cocaine. The user gets a sudden, intense effect in seconds. Some users report feelings of restlessness, anger, and fear. The drug's effects wear off very quickly. The user then becomes very depressed and wants more crack.

Some crack users become addicted after trying it only once. It is considered one of the most addictive illegal drugs. It is also one of the most dangerous. Even a first-time user of crack can die suddenly from a heart attack or a seizure. And it is impossible to predict who might die from a first-time use of crack.

SUMMARIZE List three reasons why using cocaine is dangerous.
Possible answer: Using cocaine can harm the body, cause a person to become violent, and cause death.

241

Interpret Visuals—Illustrations

Draw students' attention to the illustration of the human body on this page. Have students trace the path cocaine takes when it is sniffed or injected. When cocaine is sniffed, it goes through blood vessels in the nose into the circulatory system, which carries it to all other parts of the body. Cocaine can also be injected directly into the circulatory system. It is a stimulant, so once it reaches the central nervous system, it speeds up all body processes. It can cause rapid heartbeat, convulsions, serious mental disorders, heart attacks, and death. Have students compare and contrast the effects of medications, such as asthma medicine, and street drugs, such as cocaine and crack, on body systems.

Health Background

From Coca to Cocaine Most coca is grown by farmers in South America. Coca is the only source of income for many of the farmers. After coca leaves are picked, they are dried in the sun. Sulfuric acid and kerosene are added, and the leaves are pressed into a coca paste. The coca paste is shipped to people who operate cocaine labs. Ether, alcohol, and hydrochloric acid are added to the paste to dissolve and remove any impurities. The result is crystals of cocaine hydrochloride, which are ground into white powder. Drug runners who work for the processors smuggle the cocaine into the United States. Then it is delivered to distributors, who get the cocaine to dealers.

Source: *U.S. Drug Enforcement Administration, U.S. Department of Justice*

For more background, visit the **Webliography** in Teacher Resources at **www.harcourtschool.com/health Keyword** drug abuse

Teacher Tip

Medical Use of Marijuana
In some states and in Canada, using marijuana for some medical reasons is legal. For example, marijuana is sometimes prescribed for people with cancer to ease the nausea caused by chemotherapy and for people with AIDS to increase their appetite.

Discuss

Have students analyze the short-term and long-term effects of substances, such as marijuana, on the function of the body systems. The health effects of marijuana remain controversial because it is difficult to do controlled studies. The immediate effects on the brain are the least controversial and best defined of marijuana's hazards. What is also known is that marijuana smoke contains 150 chemicals in addition to the active ingredient tetrahydrocannabinol (THC). The effects of most of these are not known. One ingredient is benzopyrene, a known cancer-causing agent that is 70 percent more abundant in marijuana smoke than in the smoke of high-tar cigarettes.

Critical Thinking **What are marijuana's effects on the brain?** Marijuana interferes with memory, coordination, speech, reading comprehension, and problem solving.

How would smoking marijuana affect performance in school? School performance would suffer because students would be unable to comprehend or remember what they have read or heard. They would be unable to solve problems or speak normally.

How would smoking marijuana affect performance in sports or driving? Driving a car would be dangerous because the drug would interfere with reaction time, coordination, and visual perception. A user would probably not perform well in sports because of those same effects.

Marijuana

Marijuana (mair•uh•WAH•nuh) is an illegal drug that comes from a tall, leafy plant with small white and yellow flowers. Marijuana is made from the crushed, dried leaves and flowering tops of the plant. Marijuana is usually smoked. Some users put it into foods and eat it. Marijuana is sometimes called grass, pot, or weed. The plant's thick, sticky resin, called *hashish* (HASH•eesh), is a powerful drug that is smoked or eaten.

Marijuana contains more than 400 substances that affect the body. Some of the chemicals affects the brain, changing the way a user sees, hears, and feels things.

Marijuana affects different people in different ways. It can even affect one person differently at different times. In general, people who smoke marijuana feel relaxed at first. They may also have a fast heartbeat and a dry mouth and feel hungry. Marijuana affects the mind in strange ways. Time may seem to move more slowly than usual or everything may seem funny for no reason. Marijuana users often do things that embarrass themselves. Sometimes marijuana causes sudden feelings of panic.

Marijuana users often find it hard to concentrate and to remember things. Marijuana disrupts nerve cells in the part of the brain that forms memories. This makes it difficult to learn and do schoolwork. Young people who smoke marijuana tend to lose interest in school and get poor grades.

Heavy marijuana use affects coordination. This makes it hard to do physical things, like playing sports and exercising.

Information Alert!
Marijuana Research
As scientists learn more about marijuana, other dangerous effects of this drug on the human body may become known.

GO ONLINE For the most up-to-date information, visit The Learning Site. www.harcourtschool.com/health

Myth and Fact
Myth: Marijuana is a safe drug.
Fact: Marijuana is addictive and is more harmful to the lungs than tobacco. One marijuana cigarette has more tar than one pack of regular cigarettes.

242

Integrated Language Arts/ Reading Skills

Amotivational Syndrome Some researchers have described what they call amotivational syndrome in young marijuana smokers who use the drug frequently. They tend to lose interest in school, friends, and family. Have students write stories about a fictional character who hurts himself or herself by experimenting with marijuana and eventually develops amotivational syndrome.

Teacher Tip

Sensitivity Issues The discussion of drugs and drug use may make some students uncomfortable, especially those who may have drug use problems or have family members or friends who do. Other students may be experiencing peer pressure to try drugs. Respect students' privacy and present the information in a factual, nonjudgmental way.

◀ Growing marijuana is illegal in the United States. Each year, law enforcement officers find and destroy tons of marijuana plants. People who grow the plants can be fined or jailed.

A person who has smoked marijuana has slower reflexes, making it dangerous for him or her to drive a car or even ride a bike.

Marijuana use can also damage the lungs. Marijuana smoke contains many of the same harmful chemicals found in tobacco smoke, but in larger amounts. People who use a lot of marijuana face many of the same health problems as people who smoke cigarettes. These problems include asthma, heart disease, and lung cancer. Marijuana use may also lower the body's defenses against other diseases. So, marijuana smokers tend to be ill more often than nonsmokers.

DRAW CONCLUSIONS How can smoking marijuana lead to getting hurt in an accident?

Smoking marijuana affects the mind, reduces coordination, and slows the reflexes, which can cause you to have an accident.

Quick Activity

Research Use the Internet to research the effects of marijuana smoke on the body. Then make a diagram of the body to show all of the effects you learned about.

243

Quick Activity

You may wish to have students refer to the diagram of the respiratory system on page 7. Have them trace the path of THC from the mouth, through the trachea and bronchi to the lungs, and into the capillaries surrounding the air sacs of the lungs. Then have them refer to the diagram of the circulatory system on page 5 and trace the path of THC from the lungs to the heart, and from the heart out to the rest of the body, including the brain.

Once students have done this, encourage them to complete their diagrams. Students' diagrams can show such effects as damaged lungs, short-term memory loss, slowed reflexes, and dilated pupils.

Health Background

THC in the Body After marijuana smoke is inhaled, it takes only six or seven seconds for the heart to pump the THC to every part of the body. In about ten minutes the THC is changing the way the brain works. Reflexes slow down, time seems to slow down, short-term memory is impaired, and moods change. These effects may last between five minutes and three hours, depending on how strong the marijuana is and how much is smoked. A user may have a feeling of depression for a few hours after this. The THC stays in the body's fatty tissues, especially in the kidneys, lungs, and reproductive organs, for up to a month.

Source: *Office of the U.S. Attorney General; Florida Alcohol and Drug Abuse Association*

For more background, visit the **Webliography** in Teacher Resources at **www.harcourtschool.com/health Keyword** drug abuse

---

Art

Marijuana *No!* Poster Have students use the material in this lesson and any other information they find to design and make posters giving young people reasons *not* to use marijuana. Each poster should include a catchy slogan to help communicate its message.

Teacher Tip

Illegal Drugs Speaker Invite a health expert to be a guest speaker in your class. He or she can talk about the effects of illegal drugs, especially on children's growth and development. Before the guest arrives, have your students list questions that they want answered. (You might want to give this list to the health expert before he or she arrives.)

3. WRAP UP

Lesson 3 Summary and Review

1. inhalants, addicted; tolerance; overdose; withdrawal

2. Sample answer: Cocaine in the short term speeds up the heart rate and breathing rate. In the long term, cocaine damages the inside of the nose and causes brain damage. Inhalants in the short term cause nosebleeds and headaches. In the long term, inhalants damage the brain, liver, and kidneys.

3. Legal drugs are medicines that can be used to help treat or cure illnesses. Illegal drugs are drugs that can severely harm the body and are against the law to use.

4. Possible answers are shown.

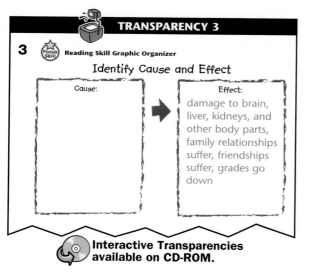

TRANSPARENCY 3

3 Reading Skill Graphic Organizer

Identify Cause and Effect

Cause:

Effect: damage to brain, liver, kidneys, and other body parts, family relationships suffer, friendships suffer, grades go down

Interactive Transparencies available on CD-ROM.

5. Opinion articles should discuss possible reasons for drug use, how drugs affect a person's behavior, and consequences of drug use.

For **writing models** with examples, see *Teaching Resources* pp. 47–61. Rubrics are also provided.

When Minutes Count ...

Quick Study Students can use *Activity Book* pp. 36–37 (shown on p. 229) as they complete each lesson in this chapter.

Inhalants

If you look around most homes, you will find chemicals that give off fumes. In many cases, the fumes are poisonous. In fact, some chemical products have warnings that say breathing the fumes can be very harmful. Those products should be used only in places with a lot of fresh air.

As dangerous as these chemical products are, some people breathe the fumes on purpose. Chemicals that people breathe on purpose are called inhalants. **Inhalants** are common products that some people abuse by breathing their fumes. Inhalants are very addictive. Effects of breathing inhalants include nosebleeds, headaches, confusion, memory loss, nausea, and changes in heartbeat and breathing rates. Long-term use of inhalants can damage the brain, kidneys, liver, and lungs and can even cause death.

▲ Many chemicals give off fumes that are dangerous to breathe.

MAIN IDEA AND DETAILS **What are some ways to avoid breathing dangerous fumes?**
If you use products that give off fumes, use the products only in places where there is fresh air.

Lesson 3 Summary and Review

❶ Summarize with Vocabulary

Use vocabulary and other terms from this lesson to complete the statements.

_____ are chemicals whose fumes are breathed. They are particularly dangerous when used for a period of time, because people become _____ to them. When someone has a _____ for drugs, it is easier to _____ on the drugs. If drug users suddenly stop taking the drugs they are addicted to, they go through _____.

❷ Critical Thinking Analyze the short-term and long-term effects of two different illegal drugs.

❸ What are the differences between legal and illegal drugs?

❹ IDENTIFY CAUSE AND EFFECT Draw and complete this graphic organizer to show the physical and social effects of taking illegal drugs.

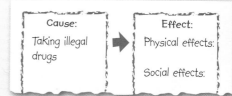

Cause: Taking illegal drugs

Effect: Physical effects:

Social effects:

❺ Write to Inform—Explanation
Write an article explaining why people might try illegal drugs, and the consequences of illegal drug use.

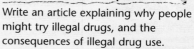

244

Teacher Tip

Inhalants Ask students why they think the possession of solvents and aerosols is not prohibited by law. Guide them to understand that these products have many legitimate household and industrial uses. Then have students discuss different ways to prevent the abuse of inhalants by young people.

Trustworthiness

Be Trustworthy About Not Using Drugs

People who are trustworthy are honest, tell the truth, and keep promises—and other people can trust them. Not using drugs shows your parents that you are trustworthy. Here are some tips on how to be trustworthy about not using drugs:

- **Talk with your parents about illegal drugs.**
- **Don't become friends with people who abuse medicines or who use illegal drugs.**
- **Make friends with people who respect your decision not to use illegal drugs.**
- **Play sports or develop other healthful hobbies.**
- **Avoid events that might involve using illegal drugs.**
- **Practice different ways of refusing to abuse medicines and choosing not to use illegal drugs.**
- **Tell your parents, a teacher, or other trusted adult if someone ever offers you illegal drugs.**

Activity

With a friend, role-play a conversation between a parent and a child about using illegal drugs. Plan a conversation opener. For example, as the "child," you could start by asking your friend—the "parent"—if he or she has ever known somebody who used illegal drugs. After role-playing, try a similar conversation with your mom, dad, or other trusted adult.

245

Using the Poster

Activity Have students make lists of five things they can do to be trustworthy today.

Display Poster 6 to remind students of ways to be trustworthy. The poster can be displayed in the classroom, cafeteria, or another common area.

Building Good Character

Caring
Citizenship
Fairness
Respect
Responsibility
Trustworthiness

Objective
▶ Identify ways to be trustworthy about not using drugs.

Program Resource
▶ Poster 6

BEFORE READING
Brainstorm with students some ways to show trustworthiness. After a discussion of showing trustworthiness in various situations, guide students to discuss ways to be trustworthy about not using illegal drugs. List some ideas on the board.

DISCUSS
After students have read the page, ask them to identify and describe alternatives to drug use. For example, students may realize that if they are friends with people who do not use illegal drugs, these friends will encourage them to avoid illegal drugs.

ACTIVITY
Before students role-play a conversation between a child and a parent about illegal drugs, have them write down anything they would want to include in the conversation. Also have students write down three different ways they can start the conversation. For example, students could mention that they are learning about illegal drugs in school right now and want to talk about the family's rules on illegal drugs.

Objectives

► Describe the negative consequences of illegal drug use.

► Analyze how illegal drug use can interfere with activities and goals.

► Explain strategies for saying *no* to illegal drug use.

 When Minutes Count . . .

Assign the Quick Study, Lesson 4, Activity Book pp. 36–37 (shown on p. 229).

Program Resources

► Activity Book pp. 36–37
► Transparency 3

Vocabulary

refuse p. 246

 **Daily Fitness Tip**

Part of being physically fit is learning to avoid things that harm your body, such as illegal drugs.

 For more guidelines about alcohol, drugs, and movement, see *Be Active! Resources for Physical Education,* p. 171.

1. MOTIVATE

Optional Activity Materials large sheet of mural paper, poster paints, brushes

Hang the mural paper in the classroom, and have each student draw activities he or she likes to do. (As an alternative, students can draw their pictures on individual sheets of paper.)

How would illegal drug use interfere with your favorite activities? Answers will vary. For example, drugs slow reaction time, disrupt coordination, and distort the senses, making it difficult to play sports, play a musical instrument, or paint.

 LESSON 4

Staying Away from Drugs

Lesson Focus

You can avoid drugs by knowing about them and by having a plan for how to refuse them.

Why Learn This?

Knowing how to refuse drugs is an important part of staying healthy and drug-free.

Vocabulary

refuse

You Should Refuse Illegal Drugs

To **refuse** something is to say *no* to it. There are many reasons you should refuse to use illegal drugs. If you buy, sell, or use drugs or you simply have an illegal drug in your possession, you are breaking the law.

Using drugs can prevent you from doing well in school and sports. They can stop you from caring about anything except getting more drugs. Drugs can ruin your health, too. They can lead to addiction and overdose. Drugs can even kill you.

Drugs hurt not only the users but also everybody around them. Drug users often stop making positive contributions to their families, friendships, and communities. The use of illegal drugs often leads to

Some kids use drugs to "fit in." What they don't realize is that most kids never use illegal drugs. To really fit in, say *no* to drugs.

246

 Meeting Individual Needs
Leveled Activities

BELOW-LEVEL Just Say No Have students make brochures about saying *no* to illegal drugs. Suggest they include information on the dangers of drug use (including statistics), ways to say *no,* and healthful alternatives to drug use.

ON-LEVEL Refusal Poetry Have students write poems about drugs, peer pressure, how to say *no,* and why saying *no* is the wise thing to do. Encourage them to read their poems aloud to the class. Then display the poems around the room.

CHALLENGE Drug Pain Have students read stories about former drug users who describe the pain of addiction and the process of going through treatment. Then have them draw pictures depicting the difficulties of addiction and have them write slogans encouraging people to say *no* to drugs. Post the pictures around the school.

Having fun doesn't need to include using drugs.

violence and crimes. Many innocent people become victims of crimes committed by drug users.

People have many good reasons for refusing drugs. They want to stay out of jail. They want to stay in control and healthy. They want to do well in school or in sports. They don't want to disappoint or embarrass their parents or teachers. They have plans for the future, such as sports or college, and they know that drug use can ruin those plans.

Drugs can interfere with your ability to enjoy most activities. How well can you play basketball, ride a bike, read a book, enjoy an amusement park, or take photographs when your mind and body are out of control?

DRAW CONCLUSIONS Describe how family, friends, and school influence a person's choice to refuse illegal drugs.
Possible answer: A person who wants to avoid disappointing his or her family, who wants to keep strong friendships, and who wants to do well in school will refuse illegal drugs

Consumer Activity

Analyze Media Messages Many TV ads encourage young people to decide what is more important to them than taking drugs. Research current anti-drug campaigns on TV and other places. How effective do you think the campaigns are in helping people refuse drugs?

247

Interpret Visuals—Pictures

Have students read the list of reasons not to use illegal drugs that the student is writing on the flip-board. Ask students which of the responses they would use if someone asked them to use drugs. Then direct them to write other possible responses they could use. Write "Ways to Say *No*" on a large sheet of paper, and hang it in the classroom as a reminder for students.

Discuss

Have students describe health-related situations that require parent or adult assistance, such as a discussion of health-related consequences of high-risk health behaviors. Many young people do not say *no* when someone offers them illegal drugs because they do not know how to or because they are afraid of being teased or excluded by other people.

Problem Solving How can you refuse illegal drugs without offending someone? Answers will vary but could include telling the person that your parents would disapprove, telling him or her you need to do or be somewhere else, or making a joke.

Content-Area Reading Support

Using Paragraph Structure Direct attention to the first sentence of the first paragraph. Point out that the sentence states the topic of the paragraph—in this case, that students have the right and responsibility to refuse illegal drugs. Explain that paragraphs in textbooks often begin with topic sentences that tell what the other sentences are about.

 Personal Health Plan ▶

Plans might include the following:
- I want to do well in school.
- I plan to excel in sports.
- I want to learn a new hobby.
- I want to make my family happy.

You Can Say *No*

You have the right and a responsibility to refuse drugs. Remember that drug users are the ones who are not cool. Get advice from a parent about how to avoid drugs. Make friends with other drug-free students. Plan ahead for how you will respond if someone asks you to take a drug. You don't have to give excuses, and you don't have to argue with people who want you to use illegal drugs.

Learn from a parent about the harmful effects of drugs. Remember that using drugs is illegal. Think about how drugs can ruin your relationships with your family and friends. Drugs can take over your whole life. They can make you ill and can kill you.

MAIN IDEA AND DETAILS Where can you get good information about the harmful effects of illegal drugs?
Possible answer: I can get information in this book and from my parents.

Personal Health Plan ▶

Real-Life Situation
There are a lot of different reasons to refuse to use illegal drugs.
Real-Life Plan
Make a list of reasons you would use to refuse illegal drugs.

248

ESL/ELL Support

BACKGROUND AND EXPERIENCE Have students remember times when they have refused to do something that their friends were encouraging them to do.

Beginning Have students pantomime scenes in which one person is offering another person something illegal or dangerous, and the other person is refusing.

Intermediate Have students write down simple sentences that they could use to refuse drugs if somebody offered drugs to them.

Advanced Have students write a short story about a student who has just been offered illegal drugs. The story should describe why the student refused the drugs, how he or she refused the drugs, and how the student felt afterward.

WHY SAY NO
1.

What reason do you have for not using drugs?

Quick Activity

Reasons for Saying *No*
Make a poster that shows at least one reason to avoid illegal drugs. Include an alternative to drug use, such as learning to play a musical instrument. After you make your poster, make of list of other ways you can communicate information about drugs.

Lesson 4 Summary and Review

❶ **Summarize with Vocabulary**
Use vocabulary and other terms from this lesson to complete the statements.

"I'm going to _____ drugs because I want to stay _____ and live a long life. If I take _____, I might go to prison. I have too many plans for that. I want to go to college."

❷ **Critical Thinking** List two social effects and one legal effect that might result from using drugs.

❸ What are three things you can do to avoid using drugs?

❹ **CAUSE AND EFFECT**
Draw and complete this graphic organizer to show some effects on Josh's decision about illegal drugs.

Cause:
Josh has decided not to use illegal drugs.

Effect:

❺ **Write to Inform—Explanation**
Suppose you are a parent. Write a letter to your children, explaining how peer pressure can influence their views about illegal drugs.

249

Quick Activity

Students' posters will vary. You may want to hang the posters in your classroom or school hallways. Students' lists may include songs, T-shirts, and commercials.

3. WRAP UP

Lesson 4 Summary and Review

1. refuse, healthy, illegal

2. Possible answer: Social consequences— lose friends and disappoint family; Legal consequence—go to prison

3. Possible answer: Take advice from my parents, avoid negative peer pressure, and plan what to say if somebody offers me drugs.

4. Possible answers are shown.

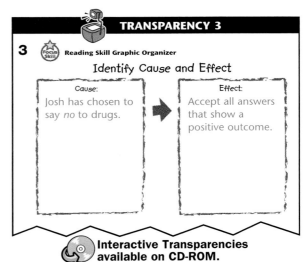

TRANSPARENCY 3

3 **Reading Skill Graphic Organizer**
Identify Cause and Effect

Cause:
Josh has chosen to say *no* to drugs.

Effect:
Accept all answers that show a positive outcome.

Interactive Transparencies available on CD-ROM.

5. Students' letters will vary. Some students may note that positive peer pressure can help the child avoid drugs, while negative peer pressure can make him or her curious about drugs.

For **writing models** with examples, see *Teaching Resources* pp. 47–61. Rubrics are also provided.

 When Minutes Count . . .

Quick Study Students can use *Activity Book* pp. 36–37 (shown on p. 229) as they complete each lesson in this chapter.

Teacher Tip

Peer Pressure Write these categories on the board: *Brand of Jeans, Type of Shoes, Kind of Music,* and *Movies.* Ask students to copy the headings onto their own paper and to write the names of their favorite items in categories. Then have them review their lists and circle the answers they gave because they knew most of their friends felt the same way. Explain that peer pressure is the pressure felt among friends to do the same thing or think the same way in order to be accepted.

Art

Self-Esteem Collages Have students make self-esteem collages. Each student should paste a photo or draw a picture of himself or herself in the middle of the collage. Students can look through magazines to find pictures that represent their favorite things to add to the collages. They can also draw or paste photos of other important things in their lives. Display the collages around the room to demonstrate that each student is special and doesn't have to be like everyone else.

Life Skills

Communicate
Make Responsible Decisions
Manage Stress
Refuse
Resolve Conflicts
Set Goals

Objectives
► Identify refusal skills.
► Use refusal skills to stay drug-free.

Program Resources
► Activity Book p. 39
► Poster 10

1. MOTIVATE

There's a good chance you'll be asked to use or buy illegal drugs in the future. Perhaps some of you have already been approached. It's important to learn refusal skills so you won't be pressured into doing something you don't want to do.

2. TEACH

Direct students' attention to the photos of George and Ned. Have them assess the role of refusal skills on decision making.

Step 1
What is George's first option for refusing the marijuana Ned offers him? George could say *no* and explain why he isn't interested ("My mom trusts me not to take drugs.").

Critical Thinking What are other reasons George could have given for refusing the marijuana? Possible answer: Using marijuana is illegal and dangerous.

Step 2
What is George's second option for refusing the marijuana? George can suggest doing something else instead (playing basketball).

Refuse
Illegal Drugs

At some time you may be asked if you want to use illegal drugs. You need to have your decision made and your answers ready ahead of that time. Learning several different ways to **Refuse**, such as the ones shown here, will help you stay drug-free.

George is walking home from school when he sees Ned, another student in his class. Ned waves George over and asks if he wants to smoke some marijuana. George has many different options for how to refuse Ned. Which one of the following four options would you choose?

1 **Say *no* and tell why not.**

When Ned offers George the marijuana, George says, "No way! My mom trusts me not to use drugs."

2 **Suggest something else to do.**

George says, "No thanks. Why don't we go play basketball instead?"

250

Teacher Tip

Singing *No* Have students make up songs, poems, or posters that express why a person will feel good about himself or herself when he or she says *no* to drugs.

ACTIVITY BOOK P. 39

Name _____

Problem Solving

Life Skill
Refuse

Steps for Refusing to Use Drugs
1. Say *no* and tell why not.
2. Suggest something else to do.
3. Reverse the peer pressure.
4. Just turn and walk away. You can create an opportunity for the other person to join you.

Use the steps to tell how these students could refuse to use drugs.

A. Jerry and Mike were walking home from the park. On their way, they ran into some boys from school who were smoking marijuana. The boys offered marijuana to Jerry and Mike. How could the boys say *no* to smoking marijuana?
• Describe how Jerry and Mike could use refusal skills to tell the boys *no*.
Possible answer: Jerry and Mike could say *no* to the boys and tell them that the reason they refuse to smoke marijuana is that it can cause short-term memory loss, slow reaction time, and harm the immune system. It can also cause unpleasant side effects, is illegal, and is against their families' rules.

B. Lakisha went over to Kendra's house to study for a test. While she was there, Kendra opened a can of something and inhaled the fumes. She then handed the can to Lakisha and told her that it would help her concentrate as they studied. How could Lakisha say *no* to using inhalants?
• Describe how Lakisha could use refusal skills to say *no* to Kendra.
Possible answer: Lakisha could say *no* to Kendra's idea and suggest that they get started studying. In the future, Lakisha could choose to spend her time with people who don't make harmful decisions.

Available online.
www.harcourtschool.com/health

③ Reverse the peer pressure.

After Ned suggests they smoke marijuana, George shakes his head and says, "Not on your life! Only losers use drugs."

④ Just turn and walk away. You can create an opportunity for the other person to join you.

Hey! Wait up!

George rolls his eyes and starts to walk away. He says over his shoulder as he is leaving, "Ned, I'm going home to shoot some hoops. You can come if you want to, but you've got to get rid of those drugs first."

Problem Solving

A. Sophia's older brother uses marijuana. One day Sophia walks into the backyard and finds her brother smoking some marijuana. He offers to share it with her. Sophia does not want to use drugs.
   • Tell how Sophia can use ways to **Refuse** in this situation.

B. Craig and Bob are cleaning up Craig's father's workshop. Craig tells Bob that he often sniffs fumes from some of the chemicals in the workshop. He offers to show Bob how to do it. Bob knows that his parents trust him not to sniff chemicals.
   • Explain the most trustworthy decision for Bob to make to show that he won't disappoint his parents.

251

Using the Poster

Activity Suggest that students look at the poster to come up with other ways George could refuse the marijuana.

Display Poster 10 to remind students of ways to refuse. The poster can be displayed in the classroom, cafeteria, or another common area.

POSTER 10

Refuse

The girl is refusing to use drugs.

Ways to Refuse

❶ Say *no*, and state your reasons for saying no.
❷ Say *no*, and suggest something else to do.
❸ Say *no*, and change the subject.
❹ Say *no*, and walk away.
❺ Say *no*, and make a joke or use any other nonviolent way.

How do YOU REFUSE?

POSTER 10

What is George's third option? George could reverse the pressure by telling Ned that only losers use marijuana.

🎖 Building Good Character

Remind students that when making any decision, they should consider whether a decision shows their trustworthiness. Ask students to discuss how George is showing his trustworthiness by refusing to use marijuana.

Step 4

What is the fourth way George could refuse marijuana? George could simply leave and offer to let Ned join him if Ned gets rid of the drugs.

Which of the four options would you choose? Why? Answers will vary, based on students' personal preferences.

3. WRAP UP

Problem Solving

A Students' suggestions for how Sophia can handle this situation may include saying and repeating the word *no*, using humor, and walking away to do something more healthful or more productive (such as taking a walk or doing her homework).

B Have students assess the role of refusal skills on problem solving. Students should mention that Bob can handle this situation by saying *no* to Craig, repeating the word *no*, using humor, or suggesting they do something else. He can also leave the situation.

Objectives
► Recognize when someone needs help refusing or getting off drugs.
► Describe methods of getting help for using illegal drug use.

When Minutes Count . . .
Assign the Quick Study, Lesson 5, Activity Book pp. 36–37 (shown on p. 229).

Program Resources
► Activity Book pp. 36–37, 40
► Transparency 3

Daily Fitness Tip

Part of family fitness is learning to help others avoid things that can harm them, such as using illegal drugs.

 For more guidelines about alcohol, drugs, and movement, see *Be Active! Resources for Physical Education,* p. 171.

1. MOTIVATE

Ask students to draw pictures of illegal drug users. Call on volunteers to show and explain their pictures to the rest of the class. Introduce the idea that people often have stereotypes, or images of a type of person that may or may not be true. There are stereotypes about what men are like and what women are like, for example. There are also stereotypes about what illegal drug users are like. Some people believe that all drug users dress in dirty, ragged clothes and spend their days hanging out on the streets. In fact, many drug abusers look quite normal.

Critical Thinking How do you know if someone needs help with a drug problem? Changes in behavior are often warning signs that signal a drug problem.

LESSON 5 How Drug Users Can Get Help

Lesson Focus
Drug users and their families can get help from sources at home, at school, and in the community.

Why Learn This?
If you or someone you know needs help to refuse drugs or to stop using drugs, it is important to know where to get help.

When Someone Needs Help

You might know someone who needs help in refusing drugs. Or you might know someone who actually may be abusing medicines or using illegal drugs. How can you help the person? To help someone who is abusing drugs, you must first know what the signs of drug abuse are. One of the signs is changes in behavior. If you know anyone who shows some of the signs listed below, he or she might have a drug problem.

COMPARE AND CONTRAST Compare and contrast normal behaviors with the signs that a person might be using drugs.
Possible answer: People normally take care of their health, go to school or work, and get along with others. Drug users may not care about their health, may miss school or work often, and may withdraw from or become angry at others.

Some of the warning signs of medicine abuse or illegal drug use are listed on the notepad. If you know someone who shows some of these warning signs, you can help by telling a parent or other trusted adult. ▶

Drug Abuse Warnings

A person who displays some of the following signs may be abusing drugs.

❶ Neglects personal health.

❷ Becomes secretive.

❸ Suddenly loses weight without trying.

❹ Frequently misses school or work.

❺ Is anxious and nervous.

❻ Has trouble being responsible.

❼ Explodes in anger without reason.

❽ Often asks to borrow money.

252

Meeting Individual Needs
Leveled Activities

BELOW-LEVEL Radio Announcements Have students write radio announcements about how to recognize whether someone has a problem with drugs and where to go for help. Allow students to perform their announcements for the class.

ON-LEVEL Drugs Have students choose three illegal drugs. For each drug, students should find out the effects, specific warning signs of use, and where users can get help. Direct them to make the information available in an easy-to-read manner on sheets of poster board. Then have them present their findings to the class and display their posters.

CHALLENGE Drug Treatment Have students contact a drug treatment counselor to learn about the recovery process for someone addicted to an illegal drug. Suggest they ask what the treatment process involves, how long it lasts, and what the success rate is. Encourage students to write newspaper articles based on what they learn.

Getting Help

There are many people who can help someone who has a problem with drugs. The drug user can talk to a parent, teacher, school nurse, or school counselor. If you are worried about a family member who may have a drug problem, talk to another adult in your family. Don't worry about getting someone in trouble. You could actually be helping a person with a drug problem.

Many communities have programs to help people who are abusing medicines or using illegal drugs. Drug users can call local drug prevention and treatment centers or community drug hotlines. The people who work there can provide information or counseling to help drug users stop abusing drugs.

Many county and state governments also have drug treatment programs. You could check with the media specialist at your school or the librarian at your local library for the names, phone numbers, and addresses of these programs.

Talk to a parent, grandparent, older brother or sister, teacher, counselor, or other trusted adult if you or someone you know has a drug problem. ▼

ACTIVITY

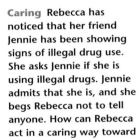

Building Good Character

Caring Rebecca has noticed that her friend Jennie has been showing signs of illegal drug use. She asks Jennie if she is using illegal drugs. Jennie admits that she is, and she begs Rebecca not to tell anyone. How can Rebecca act in a caring way toward Jennie?

253

Science

Drug-Use Statistics Have students look in an almanac or other reference source to find statistics on young people's use of marijuana, cocaine, and other drugs. Work with students to organize the information into a bar graph. Be sure to include a bar to represent the young people who don't use drugs at all.

Teacher Tip

Help Lines Many help lines and national organizations are available for people who want to get help with quitting drugs. For help with cocaine addiction, people can call 1-800-COCAINE. For narcotics addiction, people can call Narcotics Anonymous. For information on other drug and alcohol addictions, people can call the National Clearinghouse for Alcohol and Drug Information.

Content-Area Reading Support

Using Tables and Graphs Direct students' attention to the table on page 252 showing warning signs of illegal drug use. Explain that text set off in a table often contains important information. Have a volunteer read aloud the contents of the table.

Discuss

After students have read this page, lead a discussion on how they would feel about trying to get help for a friend who is in trouble with drugs. **How do you think you would feel if you told a trusted adult that you thought a friend had a drug problem?** Answers will vary, but many may feel that they would be "snitching." They might also be afraid that they would get the friend into trouble with the law.

How would you feel if your friend got angry at you for telling a trusted adult about his or her drug problem? Answers will vary, but many students may feel that they have somehow betrayed the friend.

What could you tell yourself if you were worried about how your friend felt about you? You could remind yourself that you are not harming or betraying him or her, but helping. By intervening, you are keeping your friend from harming himself or herself further and getting into deeper trouble.

Activity

Caring Possible answer: Rebecca should first talk to her own parents about the situation to get their advice. Then she can talk to Jennie to let her know about the different resources that are available for help.

3. WRAP UP

Lesson 5 Summary and Review

1. warning signs, money; counselor, nurse

2. Students' answers should include three of the following: A person neglects his or her health; behaves secretively; loses weight; misses school; has mood swings; is always nervous; has trouble with friends and family; is not responsible; is angry for no reason; borrows money; has red eyes and runny nose; repeatedly denies having a drug problem.

3. Possible answers: You are helping to prevent the family member from hurting himself or herself further; you are preventing the family member from possibly ending up in prison.

4. Possible answers may include:

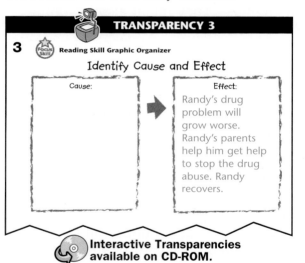

TRANSPARENCY 3

3 Reading Skill Graphic Organizer

Identify Cause and Effect

Cause:

Effect: Randy's drug problem will grow worse. Randy's parents help him get help to stop the drug abuse. Randy recovers.

Interactive Transparencies available on CD-ROM.

5. Students' letters should state the nature of the problem and the type of information and/or help the writer is requesting.

For **writing models** with examples, see *Teaching Resources* pp. 47–61. Rubrics are also provided.

When Minutes Count . . .

Quick Study Students can use *Activity Book* pp. 36–37 (shown on p. 229) as they complete each lesson in this chapter.

There are several national groups that can provide information to help drug users stop abusing drugs. They include the National Clearinghouse for Alcohol and Drug Information, the National Council on Alcoholism and Drug Dependence, and Narcotics Anonymous. Your parents or another trusted adult can help you contact one of these groups for information.

DRAW CONCLUSIONS How can you help a friend or family member who is using illegal drugs to take responsibility for his or her health?

Help Line

If you or someone you know has a problem with drugs, help can be just a phone call away.

Lesson 5 Summary and Review

❶ **Summarize with Vocabulary**

Use terms from this lesson to complete the statements.

If you are worried that a friend is using drugs, watch for _____, such as weight loss and often asking to borrow _____. You can help your friend handle the problem if you talk to a _____.

❷ List three warning signs of drug use.

❸ **Critical Thinking** Suppose you tell a parent about a family member who shows some signs of drug use. Explain how you are really helping the family member.

❹ **CAUSE AND EFFECT** Draw and complete this graphic organizer to show the effects of choosing to get help for a drug problem or choosing not to get help.

Cause:

Effect:

❺ **Write to Express—Business Letter**

Write a letter to an organization that deals with drug problems. Request information for a friend who might be abusing drugs.

Possible answer: You can help the person by talking to a parent or other trusted adult.

254

ACTIVITY BOOK P. 40

Name _____

Vocabulary Reinforcement

Match the Meanings

A. Find the term in Column B that matches the definition in Column A. Write the letter of the correct term on the line. Use each term only once.

Column A		Column B
d	**1.** drugs that are against the law to have or use	a. dosage
e	**2.** a painful reaction when a person stops taking drugs	b. medicine
b	**3.** a drug used to prevent an illness	c. self-medicating
h	**4.** a constant need for and use of a harmful drug	d. illegal drugs
c	**5.** deciding on one's own how much medicine to take	e. withdrawal
g	**6.** taking a medicine for a reason other than treating an illness	f. overdose
a	**7.** the correct amount of a medicine to take	g. medicine abuse
f	**8.** a dangerously large amount of a drug taken by someone	h. addiction

B. Choose two of the vocabulary terms from Part A. Use each term correctly in a sentence. Check students' sentences.

_____
_____
_____
_____
_____
_____
_____

Available online.
www.harcourtschool.com/health

Language Arts

To Tell or Not to Tell Work in a team of five to eight students. Write a skit about a situation in which someone you know has a drug problem. Perform the skit for your classmates.

Home & Community

Promote Health Ask a parent for permission to survey your family's medicine cabinet. List the names of the medicines, their uses, whether they are prescription or OTC medicines, and their side effects.

Science

Reaction Time With a partner, explore how reaction time might be affected by drug use. Have your partner hold the top of a yardstick so that the zero mark is hanging between your open thumb and forefinger. Your partner should drop the yardstick without warning. You should try to catch it. Record the number of inches that dropped before you caught the stick. Repeat this exercise several times. What do you think might happen to a person's reactions if he or she were using drugs?

Technology Project

Use a computer to make a database containing drug information, such as the effects of drugs on the body. Present your information to your family or classmates.

 For more activities, visit The Learning Site. www.harcourtschool.com/health

Career Link

School Resource Officer Imagine you are a school resource officer. A school resource officer is a police officer who provides information to people at schools. Make a pamphlet that can teach the students at your school about illegal drug use. Include information about how and where people can get help if they have drug problems or if they know others who do.

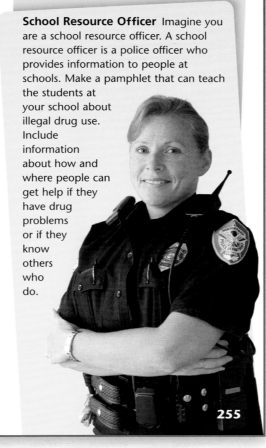

255

Career Link

School Resource Officer Remind students that the pamphlets they are making are for students their age. Explain that they should always consider who their audience is before writing or designing something. For example, they would write in very different ways if they were writing letters to their grandmothers than if they were writing to businesses or government representatives.

Encourage students to emphasize the positive effects of not using illegal drugs rather than the negative effects of using them. Help them understand that people tend to react better to encouragement than to warnings.

For more information on health careers, visit the **Webliography** in Teacher Resources at **www.harcourtschool.com/health** **Keyword** health careers

---

Activities

Science

After students conduct their experiments, hold a discussion about situations in which it is important to have quick reactions, such as when driving a car and riding a bicycle.

Language Arts

If students have difficulty coming up with situations, you might suggest one such as the following. A friend begins to use illegal drugs, loses interest in school and friends, and becomes more and more dependent on drugs. You must decide whether to tell someone about the friend's drug problem. You finally decide to tell a responsible adult, but the friend—instead of being grateful—is resentful. However, after the friend is on the road to recovery, he or she thanks you.

Home & Community

After students examine and list the contents of their home medicine cabinets, you might want to encourage them to compare their lists with the American Red Cross's list of suggested first-aid supplies.

 Supports the Coordinated School Health Program

Technology Project

Explain to students that a database is a collection of information that is arranged for ease and speed of retrieval. There are many types of databases. When students search for a book through a library's computer, they are using a database. When they look up an unfamiliar term in a dictionary, they are also using a database.

Chapter Review and Test Preparation

Pages 256–257

 Reading Skill 8 pts. each

1. Answers may include such effects as damaged nose and brain, increased breathing and heartbeat rates, memory loss, and even death.

2. Addiction can be caused by things such as abusing medicines, using cocaine or marijuana, or trying crack cocaine.

 Use Vocabulary 2 pts. each

3. A, drug

4. C, medicine misuse

5. E, side effect

6. B, medicine abuse

7. D, overdose

8. F, withdrawal

 Check Understanding 3 pts. each

9. D, OTC medicines

10. J, all of these

11. B, gasoline

12. J, all of these

13. A, self-medication

14. J, doing well in school

15. D, both A and B

16. F, marijuana

17. B, may cause drowsiness

18. G, when they stop using drugs they are addicted to

19. C, cool, dark place

 Think Critically 6 pts. each

20. If you know the warning signs of drug use, you have a better chance of knowing if the people around you are using drugs. Then you can better understand their behavior, take appropriate action, and be able to help them get help.

21. Drug users often enjoy the feelings they have when they use drugs, and their bodies and minds react negatively when they stop using them. Some drugs make users feel confident, and it's hard for them to realize they can be just as confident without drugs.

 Reading Skill

IDENTIFY CAUSE AND EFFECT
Draw and then use this graphic organizer to answer questions 1 and 2.

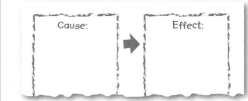

1 Write three effects of drug use.
2 Write three causes of addiction.

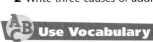 **Use Vocabulary**

Match each term in Column B with its meaning in Column A.

Column A	Column B
3 Chemical that changes the way the body or mind works	**A** drug
	B medicine abuse
	C medicine misuse
4 Taking a medicine without following the directions	**D** overdose
	E side effect
	F withdrawal
5 Unwanted reaction to a medicine	
6 Taking a medicine for a reason other than an illness	
7 Dangerously large dose of a drug	
8 Reaction that occurs when someone suddenly stops using a drug	

256

Check Understanding

Choose the letter of the correct answer.

9 Medicines you can buy without a doctor's prescription are called _____. (p. 231)
A illegal drugs   C anabolic steroids
B drugs   D OTC medicines

10 Illegal drugs include _____. (pp. 240–243)
F crack
G marijuana
H cocaine
J all of these

11 Which of the following gives off dangerous fumes? (p. 244)
A paper paste   C soda
B gasoline   D watercolor paints

12 Which information should be on a prescription medicine label? (pp. 235–235)
F how much of the medicine to take
G the name of the patient
H the number of refills left
J all of these

13 Deciding what medicine to take without asking a doctor is _____. (p. 236)
A self-medication
B medicine misuse
C medicine abuse
D overdosing

14 Which of the following is **NOT** a warning sign of drug abuse? (p. 252)
F missing a lot of school
G borrowing money often
H getting angry for no reason
J doing well in school

Formal Assessment

ASSESSMENT GUIDE P. 40	ASSESSMENT GUIDE P. 41

ASSESSMENT GUIDE P. 40

8 Name _____   Chapter Test

Legal and Illegal Drugs

Write the letter of the best answer on the line at the left.

_C_ 1. If you want to know how much medicine to take, what must you know?
A an overdose   C the dosage
B the medicine name   D a refill

_F_ 2. Which describes self-medication?
F taking aspirin for a headache
G taking medicine for "fun"
H taking a vaccine
J taking medicine from a doctor

_D_ 3. Which is an effect of using marijuana?
A changes in your hearing   C feelings of panic
B trouble playing sports   D all of the above

_F_ 4. Which is NOT a good reason to refuse drugs?
F You want everyone to like you.
G You want to stay healthy.
H You want to do well in school.
J You want to show trustworthiness to your parents.

_C_ 5. Why is crack cocaine especially dangerous?
A It can cause hair loss.   C It is highly addictive.
B It causes memory problems.   D It can harm your liver.

Write T or F to show if the statements are true or false.

_T_ 6. A drug is a substance that affects how the body or mind works.
_F_ 7. A medicine is a drug that is used to make the user feel good.
_T_ 8. An over-the-counter medicine can be bought without a doctor's order.
_T_ 9. A prescription medicine can be bought only with a doctor's order.
_T_ 10. Side effects are unwanted effects of a medicine.

ASSESSMENT GUIDE P. 41

Name _____

_T_ 11. It may not be safe to take a medicine after its expiration date.
_F_ 12. Taking medicine that a parent gives you is medicine abuse.

Match each term in Column B with its meaning or example in Column A.

Column A	Column B
_b_ 13. Painful reaction that happens when someone stops using a drug	a illegal drugs
	b withdrawal
_c_ 14. Substances that some people abuse by breathing in fumes	c inhalants
	d addiction
_h_ 15. An illegal drug made from a leafy plant and usually smoked	e overdose
	f anabolic steroids
_f_ 16. Prescription medicines that are sometimes abused	g cocaine
	h marijuana
_e_ 17. A dangerously large dose of a drug	
_g_ 18. An illegal drug that is sniffed or injected, and is made from the coca plant	
_a_ 19. Drugs that are not medicines and are against the law to sell, buy, have, or use	
_b_ 20. The constant need for and use of a drug, even though it is not medically necessary	

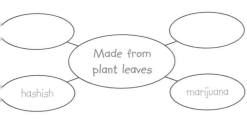

hashish — Made from plant leaves — marijuana

15 Which illegal drugs are missing in the graphic organizer? (p. 240)

A cocaine
C neither A nor B
B crack
D both A and B

16 Which drug is related to hashish? (p. 242)

F marijuana
G crack
H anabolic steroids
J cocaine

17 Which warning on a label relates to a side effect of a medicine? (p. 235)

A Take with food.
B May cause drowsiness.
C Shake well.
D No refills.

18 When do drug users begin suffering from withdrawal? (p. 239)

F when they take too much of a drug
G when they stop using drugs they are addicted to
H when they have a high tolerance to a drug
J when they start using drugs

19 Most medicines should be stored in a _____. (p. 234)

A warm, bright place
B place that children can get to easily
C cool, dark place
D bottle without a label

Think Critically

20 Why is it important to know the warning signs of drug use?

21 Why is it difficult for drug users to quit using drugs?

22 Look at this prescription label. Tell what each piece of information means and why it is on the label.

TOWN DRUG
49 HARDING RD. PHONE 555-8531 SPRINGFIELD, OH 46203
Federal law prohibits transfer of this drug to any person other than patient for whom prescribed.
57146   Dr. Greg Hardy
ADA SPRINGER 21-OCT-03   Q: 20 ORG: 21-OCY-30
ERYTHROMYCIN 500mg
EXPIRES: 21-NOV-03   **MAY CAUSE DROWSINESS**
DIRECTIONS: Take 1 tablet a day orally four times daily. Finish all medication
REFILL: NONE

Apply Skills

23 **BUILDING GOOD CHARACTER**
Trustworthiness Suppose you have a stomachache. Your parents are not at home, but you know where they keep the medicine that they take for stomach problems. Should you take the medicine? Explain what you should do to show that you are trustworthy.

24 **LIFE SKILLS**
Refuse A friend has started to use drugs. She wants you to try them, too. She says that if you're a good friend, you'll join her. Describe two ways you could say *no* to her.

Write About Health

25 **Write to Inform—Explanation** Why do people use drugs, and what are some reasons not to do so?

257

---

22. Name of person for whom the prescription was written—this is the only person who should take the drug; name of doctor who prescribed the drug—for any questions or problems; prescription number—for pharmacy records; date of prescription—so you can tell how old the medicine is; refill information—tells if you can refill or if you have to go back to the doctor before you can get more of this medicine; directions and dose—tells you how to take the medicine; name of drug—so you know what it is; name and address of pharmacy—for questions or problems.

Apply Skills 7 pts. each

23. You should not take the medicine without talking to a parent or another trusted adult first. Only if your parents give you permission should you ever take any medicine.

24. You could say that you want to remain a good friend and do things with her but that you won't do drugs. You could try humor and make the situation less serious. If that doesn't work, walk away.

Write About Health 7 pts.

25. Some people use illegal drugs because the drugs make them feel confident, cool, and mature. Others use them because of peer pressure. Drug users are harming their bodies and their minds. Drug users are also breaking the law.

Performance Assessment

Use the Chapter Project and the rubric provided on the Project Evaluation Sheet. See *Assessment Guide* pp. 18, 59, 68.

Portfolio Assessment

Have students select their best work from the following suggestions:

- Leveled Activities, p. 246
- Quick Activity, p. 249
- Write to Inform, p. 237
- Activities, p. 255

See *Assessment Guide* pp. 12–16.

About Tobacco and Alcohol

Lesson	Pacing	Objectives	Reading Skills
Introduce the Chapter pp. 258–259		• Preview chapter concepts.	**Draw Conclusions** p. 259; pp. 372–383
1 Tobacco Affects Body Systems pp. 260–265	1 class period	• Name three harmful substances in tobacco smoke. • Describe the harmful effects of tobacco use on parts of the body. • Identify reasons people use tobacco.	**Draw Conclusions** pp. 260, 265 • Summarize, p. 261 • Cause and Effect, p. 263
2 Alcohol Affects Body Systems pp. 266–272	2 class periods	• Explain what blood alcohol level is and what it measures. • Describe how alcohol affects health, abilities, and body functions. • Explain what alcoholism is and who might suffer from it.	**Draw Conclusions** p. 272 • Sequence, p. 267 • Main Idea and Details, p. 269 • Compare and Contrast, p. 271 • Summarize, p. 272
Building Good Character p. 273		• Identify ways to be a good citizen by showing respect for authority.	
3 Refusing Alcohol and Tobacco pp. 274–279	1 class period	• List reasons for choosing not to use alcohol or tobacco. • Develop strategies for dealing with peer pressure. • Analyze advertisements for alcohol and tobacco products.	**Draw Conclusions** pp. 275, 279 • Main Idea and Details, p. 277 • Summarize, p. 279
Life Skills pp. 280–281	1 class period	• Identify ways to say *no*. • Use refusal skills to say *no* to alcohol and tobacco.	
4 Where Users Can Find Help pp. 282–284	1 class period	• Identify the warning signs of a problem with alcohol. • Explain why people who are addicted to alcohol or tobacco need help to stop using these drugs. • Identify sources of support available to people who want to stop using alcohol or tobacco.	**Draw Conclusions** p. 284 • Cause and Effect, p. 283 • Summarize, p. 284
Activities p. 285		• Extend chapter concepts.	
Chapter Review pp. 286–287	1 class period	• Assess chapter objectives.	

Vocabulary

carcinogens
nicotine
carbon monoxide
tar
environmental
    tobacco smoke
    (ETS)

blood alcohol level
    (BAL)
intoxicated
alcoholism

Program Resources

🎵 Music CD
Teaching Resources, p. 39

📀 Transparency 2
Activity Book, pp. 41–43

📀 Transparency 2
Activity Book, pp. 41–42

Poster 2

📀 Transparency 2
Activity Book, pp. 41–42

Activity Book, p. 44
Poster 10

📀 Transparency 2
Activity Book, pp. 41–42, 45

🖥 The Learning Site
**www.
harcourtschool.com/health**

Assessment Guide,
pp. 43–45

💿 **Interactive Transparencies**
available on CD-ROM.

 Reading Skill

These reading skills are reinforced throughout this chapter and one skill is emphasized as the Focus Skill.

Draw Conclusions

- Compare and Contrast
- Identify Cause and Effect
- Identify Main Idea and Details
- Sequence
- Summarize

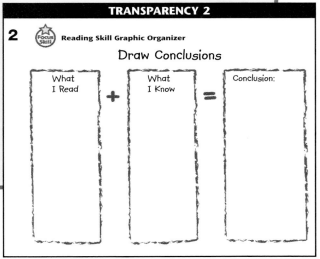

TRANSPARENCY 2

2 **Reading Skill Graphic Organizer**

Draw Conclusions

| What I Read | + | What I Know | = | Conclusion: |

 Life Skills

Life Skills are health-enhancing behaviors that can help students reduce risks to their health and safety.

Six Life Skills are reinforced throughout *Harcourt Health and Fitness.* The skill emphasized in this chapter is Refuse.

POSTER 10

Refuse

The girl is refusing to use drugs.

Ways to Refuse

1. Say *no*, and state your reasons for saying *no*.
2. Say *no*, and suggest something else to do.
3. Say *no*, and change the subject.
4. Say *no*, and walk away.
5. Say *no*, and make a joke or use any other nonviolent way.

How do YOU REFUSE?

Building Good Character

Character education is an important aspect of health education. When students behave in ways that show good character, they promote the health and safety of themselves and others.

Six character traits are reinforced throughout *Harcourt Health and Fitness.* The trait emphasized in this chapter is Citizenship.

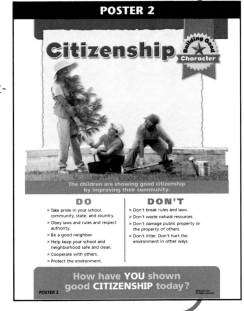

POSTER 2

Citizenship

The children are showing good citizenship by improving their community.

DO
- Take pride in your school, community, state, and country.
- Obey laws and rules and respect authority.
- Be a good neighbor.
- Help keep your school and neighborhood safe and clean.
- Cooperate with others.
- Protect the environment.

DON'T
- Don't break rules and laws.
- Don't waste natural resources.
- Don't damage public property or the property of others.
- Don't litter. Don't hurt the environment in other ways.

How have YOU shown good CITIZENSHIP today?

Coordinated School Health Program

A Coordinated School Health Program endeavors to improve children's health and, therefore, their capacity to learn through the support of families, schools, and communities working together. The following information is provided to help classroom teachers be more aware of these resources.

The National Center for Chronic Disease and Health Promotion, part of the **CDC**, funds the Coordinated School Health Program. Visit its website for information about the eight components that make up this program. **www.cdc.gov/nccdphp/dash/**

State governors have renewed their commitment to reducing disease and death from tobacco use. The National Governor's Association **(NGA)**, Center for Best Practices, affiliated with the Coordinated School Health Program, identifies smoking issues. **www.nga.org/center/divisions/**

The *Science-Based Program, Keep a Clear Mind,* has been identified as a research-based model program for the prevention of alcohol and tobacco use. For this and other exemplary programs, visit the California Healthy Kids Resource Center: Research-Validated Programs. **www.california healthykids.org**

Other resources that support a Coordinated School Health Program:
- School-Home Connection
- Daily Physical Activity
- Daily Fitness Tips
- Activities: Home & Community
- Health Background: Webliography
- *Be Active! Resources for Physical Education*

Media Resources

Books for Students

Sanders, Pete, and Steve Myers. **Smoking (What Do You Know About).** Copper Beech Books, 1996. Features children dealing with situations related to the topic. **EASY**

Aronson, Virginia. **How to Say No.** Chelsea House, 2000. Graphs and text describe drug abuse. **AVERAGE**

Clayton, Lawrence. **Alcohol Drug Dangers.** Enslow Publishers, 1999. Discusses the popularity and the social impact of alcohol. **ADVANCED**

Books for Teachers and Families

Schwebel, Robert. **Keep Your Kids Tobacco-Free: Smart Strategies for Parents of Children Ages 3 Through 19.** Newmarket Press, 2001. Advises parents on how to deal with the influence of the tobacco industry.

Claypool, Jane. **Alcohol and You.** Franklin Watts, Inc. 1997. Examines the causes of underage alcohol use.

Free and Inexpensive Materials

National Clearinghouse for Alcohol and Drug Information
Ask for *Preventing Drug Use Among Children and Adolescents.*

Social Studies School Service
Request its activity books and a poster on the dangers of smoking.

Texas Commission on Alcohol and Drug Abuse
Provides activities and a "Red Ribbon Pledge" sheet that encourages children to take a stand against alcohol and drug abuse.

To access free and inexpensive resources on the Web, visit **www.harcourtschool.com/health/free**

Videos

The Trouble with Tobacco. Rainbow Educational Media, 1996.

Ad-Libbing It. Comprehensive Health Education Foundation, 1993.

Don't Even Try It. United Learning, 1997.

These resources have been selected to meet a variety of individual needs. Please review all materials and websites prior to sharing them with students to ensure the content is appropriate for your class. Note that information, while correct at time of publication, is subject to change.

Visit **The Learning Site** for related links, activities, resources, and the health **Webliography.**

www.harcourtschool.com/health

Meeting Individual Needs

ESL/ELL

Below-Level

Study strategies help students retain what they've read. Make cards showing the letters **K, W,** and **L** to stand for *What I Know, What I Want to Know,* and *What I Learned.* Hold up a card at the proper time during a lesson as students write their responses.

Activities

- Effects of ETS on Pets, p. 262
- Decision Maze, p. 268
- Rap, p. 276
- Write an Editor, p. 283

On-Level

If students are having a difficult time reading a selection, encourage them to continue reading until they get to the end. The meaning may become clearer when more information is available. Have them skim the selection before reading and reread as needed.

Activities

- News Bulletin, p. 262
- Write Stories, p. 268
- Write Fables, p. 276
- Make Art, p. 283

Challenge

Have students write idiomatic expressions related to health topics. Idioms might include *being green with envy, feeling blue, having a bone to pick,* or *being chilled to the bone.* Have students illustrate both the figurative and literal meanings.

Activities

- Addicted Brains, p. 262
- Give Your Input, p. 268
- Make Web Pages, p. 276
- Write Articles, p. 283

Learning Log

Have students use context to determine word meanings. Draw two columns on the board, one with vocabulary words and one with their definitions. Read a paragraph, pausing after each vocabulary word. Ask volunteers to draw a line connecting the word with its definition.

Activities

- Language and Vocabulary, pp. 264, 267
- Comprehensible Input, p. 270
- Background and Experience, p. 278

Curriculum Integration

Integrated Language Arts/Reading Skills

- Positive Peer Pressure Role-Play, p. 275
- Write a Dialogue, p. 280

Math

- How Many Servings, p. 266
- Comparing Pulse Rates, p. 269

Physical Education

- Daily Fitness Tip, pp. 260, 266, 274, 282
- Daily Physical Activity, p. 259
- Breathing and Exercise, p. 263

Use these topics to integrate health into your daily planning.

Science

- Fetal Alcohol Syndrome, p. 282

Social Studies

- Prohibition, p. 274

Art

- Write a Skit, p. 277

CHAPTER SUMMARY

In this chapter students
► examine the risks of using tobacco and alcohol.
► analyze conditions and situations that lead people to use these drugs.
► learn about resources available to people who want to quit using these drugs.

Life Skills
Students practice ways to *refuse* tobacco and alcohol.

Building Good Character
Students practice good *citizenship* by showing respect for authority.

Consumer Health
Students *analyze* the costs and consequences of using tobacco and alcohol products.

 Literature Springboard

Use the excerpt "Tobacco" from *Turtle Island Alphabet* to spark interest in the chapter topic. See the Read-Aloud Anthology on page RA-10 of this *Teacher Edition*.

Prereading Strategies

SCAN THE CHAPTER Have students preview the chapter content by scanning the titles, headings, pictures, graphs, and tables. Ask volunteers to predict what they will learn. Use their predictions to determine their prior knowledge.

PREVIEW VOCABULARY As students scan the chapter, have them sort the vocabulary into categories. Students should look up unfamiliar terms in the Glossary.

Disease	Drug	Ingredient	Behavior	Person	Measurement

258

 Reading Skill

DRAW CONCLUSIONS To introduce or review this skill, have students use the Reading in Health Handbook pp. 372–383. Teaching strategies and additional activities are also provided.

Students will have opportunities to practice and apply this skill throughout this chapter.

• Focus Skill Reading Mini-Lesson, p. 260
• Reading comprehension questions identified with the
• *Activity Book* p. 43 (shown on p. 265)
• Lesson Summary and Review, pp. 265, 272, 279, 284
• Chapter Review and Test Preparation, pp. 286–287

DRAW CONCLUSIONS Sometimes authors don't directly tell you all the information in what you read. You have to use information from a passage plus what you already know to draw a conclusion. Use the Reading in Health Handbook on pages 372–383 and this graphic organizer to help you read the health facts in this chapter.

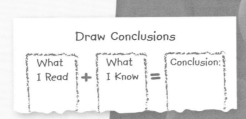

Draw Conclusions

What I Read + What I Know = Conclusion:

Health Graph

INTERPRET DATA The costs of smoking go far beyond the price of cigarettes. Look at the graph below. How much per year are the combined medical and social costs of smoking?

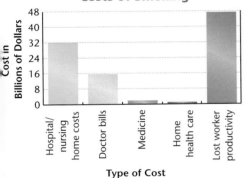

Costs of Smoking

Cost in Billions of Dollars

Type of Cost

Hospital/ nursing home costs • Doctor bills • Medicine • Home health care • Lost worker productivity

Daily Physical Activity

You should keep alcohol and tobacco out of your life. They can harm your growing body. However, physical activity should be part of your life every day.

Be Active!
Use the selection, Track 9, **Hop To It**, to practice some healthful activity choices.

259

School-Home Connection

Distribute copies of the School-Home Connection (in English or Spanish). Have students take the page home to share with their families as you begin this chapter.

Follow Up Have volunteers share the results of their activities.

Supports the Coordinated School Health Program

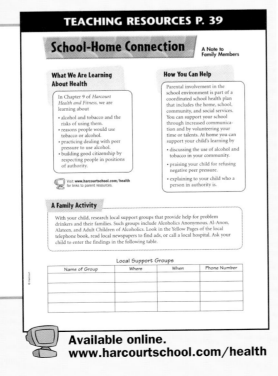
INTRODUCE THE CHAPTER

Health Graph

Interpret Data

Ask for volunteers to explain what information the graph is presenting.

How much are the yearly combined medical and social costs of smoking? $97.2 billion **What is the greatest cost of smoking as represented by the data in the graph?** $47.2 billion lost in worker productivity

Do you think this graph represents all the costs of smoking? No; many of the costs of smoking would be difficult, if not impossible, to calculate. For example, nobody can put a price on a person's life after that person dies from a tobacco-related illness.

Daily Physical Activity

Use *Be Active! Music for Daily Physical Activity* with the Instant Activity Cards to provide students with movement activities that can be done in limited space. Options for using these components are provided beginning on page TR2 in this *Teacher Edition*.

Chapter Project

It's Nothing to Laugh About (*Assessment Guide* p. 60)

ASSESS PRIOR KNOWLEDGE Use students' initial ideas for the project as a baseline assessment of their understanding of chapter concepts. Have students complete the project as they work through the chapter.

PERFORMANCE ASSESSMENT The project can be used for performance assessment. Use the Project Evaluation Sheet (rubric), *Assessment Guide* p. 70.

Objectives

► Name three harmful substances in tobacco smoke.
► Describe the harmful effects of tobacco use on parts of the body.
► Identify reasons people use tobacco.

When Minutes Count . . .

Assign the Quick Study, Lesson 1, Activity Book pp. 41–42 (shown on p. 261).

Program Resources

► Activity Book pp. 41–43
► Transparencies 2, 8

Vocabulary

carcinogens p. 261, **nicotine** p. 261, **carbon monoxide** p. 261, **tar** p. 261, **environmental tobacco smoke (ETS)** p. 263

Daily Fitness Tip

Burning cigarettes are a leading cause of fire in homes and other buildings. Review fire safety, including tips on what to do during a fire. For example, remind students to avoid elevators and to feel a door for heat before opening it.

 For more guidelines on fitness, see *Be Active! Resources for Physical Education.*

1. MOTIVATE

Ask students to imagine they are taking a walk with a friend. Suddenly the friend stops, bends down, picks up what looks like a handful of dried leaves and grass, and suggests smoking or chewing this material. **What would you say?** Many students will respond that they would be disgusted by the idea. Some might worry that the leaves and grass would make them sick. Others might want to know exactly what kinds of leaves and grass were being offered.

Have students analyze the short-term harmful effects of tobacco on the function of the body systems.

Tobacco Affects Body Systems

Lesson Focus

Using tobacco, even for a short period of time, can have harmful effects on the body.

Why Learn This?

Understanding the harmful effects will help you avoid using tobacco.

Vocabulary

carcinogens
nicotine
carbon monoxide
tar
environmental tobacco smoke (ETS)

Many people will not want to be around a person who smells bad. A smoker's difficulty in breathing makes it hard to play sports with friends.

Quick Activity

Examine Effects of Tobacco Use Look at the picture. Write down other ways in which smoking is ugly.

Short-Term Effects of Using Tobacco

In the last fifty years, people have learned more and more about the harm tobacco does to the human body. Many people believe that tobacco will harm them only if they use it for a long time. This just isn't true. There are also many short-term effects of tobacco use.

One of the first effects of smoking tobacco is a bad smell. A smoker's hair and clothes often smell of stale cigarette smoke. A smoker's breath usually smells bad, too. Tobacco smoke makes the eyes and nose burn. People who chew tobacco have bad breath, also, and chewing tobacco turns teeth yellow or brown.

Smoking makes it hard to breathe. People who have trouble breathing have a hard time playing sports and doing other activities. There is another danger that can result from smoking. Ashes from a smoker's cigarette can fall on clothing, carpets, and furniture. Sometimes these ashes burn little holes or even start fires.

DRAW CONCLUSIONS How can using tobacco affect a person's relationships with others?

Smoking makes people smell bad—and look bad, too. ►

260

Mini-Lesson

DRAW CONCLUSIONS

Remind students that drawing conclusions is a skill to use when authors don't supply all the information. Have them practice this skill by responding to the Focus Skill question on this page. Have students draw and complete the graphic organizer as you model it on the transparency.

TRANSPARENCY 2

2 Reading Skill Graphic Organizer

Draw Conclusions

What I Read		What I Know		Conclusion:
Smoking makes it hard to breathe.	+	My best friend has asthma.	=	If I smoke, my best friend won't be able to b near me.

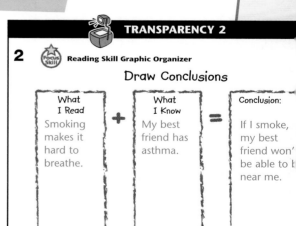 Interactive Transparencies available on CD-ROM.

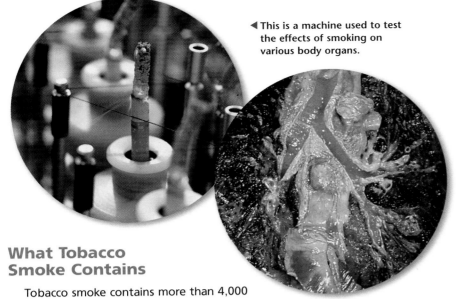

◀ This is a machine used to test the effects of smoking on various body organs.

What Tobacco Smoke Contains

Tobacco smoke contains more than 4,000 substances. More than 50 of these are linked to cancer. Substances that cause cancer are called **carcinogens** (kar·SIN·uh·juhnz).

One substance tobacco contains is nicotine. **Nicotine** (NIK·uh·teen) is a poison. In fact, in the past it was used to kill insects. Nicotine speeds up the nervous system. It also makes the blood vessels smaller. As a result, the heart must work harder to move blood through the body.

Tobacco smoke contains a poisonous gas called **carbon monoxide** (KAR·buhn muh·NAHK·syd). This gas takes the place of oxygen in the blood. A little carbon monoxide makes you tired. Too much can kill you.

Tobacco smoke also contains **tar**, a dark, sticky paste. When people smoke, tar coats the air passages in their lungs. The tar builds up and makes breathing difficult. In time, some smokers are not able to get enough oxygen to keep their bodies working. They may even get lung cancer, because tar is a carcinogen.

▲ These lungs are black because of the tar in cigarettes. Tar causes cancer.

Information Alert!

Chemicals in Tobacco Researchers keep finding new chemicals in tobacco smoke that harm the body.

GO ONLINE For the most up-to-date information, visit The Learning Site. www.harcourtschool.com/health

SUMMARIZE Identify three harmful substances in tobacco smoke, and describe their effects on the body.

Tobacco smoke contains nicotine, which speeds up the nervous system; carbon monoxide, which takes the place of oxygen in the blood; and tar, which coats the air passages and makes

261

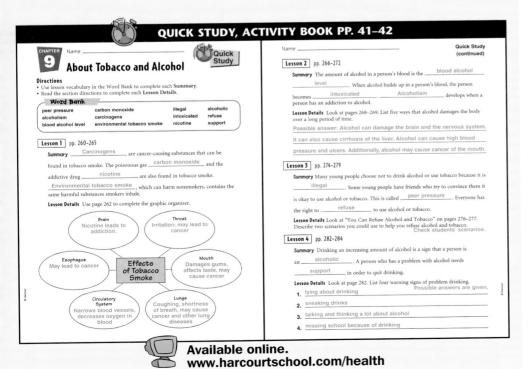

QUICK STUDY, ACTIVITY BOOK PP. 41–42

Available online.
www.harcourtschool.com/health

Quick Activity

Students might suggest the following: bad teeth, ruined clothes, shreds of tobacco in pockets, and poor posture. Accept any answers that show logical conclusions.

Interpret Visuals—Pictures

Have students closely examine the two lungs in the pictures. Invite a volunteer to read the caption. Remind students why the lungs are so important to the body: they take in air, which contains oxygen essential to body cells. The lungs also act as an air filter, removing impurities before the oxygen enters the bloodstream.

Critical Thinking Which of these lungs would do a better job of taking in oxygen and cleaning impurities from the air? The normal lung would do a better job because the air passages are unclogged.

Content-Area Reading Support

Using Text Format Tell students that all vocabulary terms in this textbook are highlighted in yellow at the point where the term is defined. Remind students that by reading the sentences that precede, include, and follow highlighted vocabulary, they can get important clues to the terms' meanings.

Invite volunteers to locate the vocabulary terms on this page (*carcinogens, nicotine, carbon monoxide, tar*). Have them read each term in context and then guess the term's meaning from the clues provided by the context. Have other volunteers look up the terms in the Glossary and read the definitions aloud.

TEACH *continued*

Discuss

The tobacco used in the manufacture of some cigarettes has a high sugar content.

Critical Thinking What is a possible harmful effect of the sugar in tobacco? The sugar can cause tooth decay.

Interpret Visuals—Illustrations

Have students analyze the long-term harmful effects of tobacco on the function of the body systems. Explain that the respiratory system takes oxygen into the body and rids the body of carbon dioxide. Have students look at the illustration and examine all the parts of the respiratory system affected by smoking tobacco.

Extend this activity by pointing out the close relationship between the circulatory system and the respiratory system. Be sure students understand that poisons taken into the respiratory system will be carried to every part of the body. Have students draw flowcharts that show the path oxygen follows from the time it enters the nose or mouth. The flowchart should show oxygen entering through the nose or mouth, traveling down the trachea, entering the lungs, passing into the air sacs, and moving from those into the blood vessels. The blood then travels to the heart and is pumped through the entire body.

When Minutes Count . . .

Transparency 8: The Respiratory System can be used to present material in this lesson. *Interactive Transparencies available on CD-ROM.*

Did You Know?

Bidis are cigarettes that come in flavors such as wild berry and chocolate. Bidis are sweet smelling, but they are also deadly! They contain low-quality tobacco that harms body functions and leads to many different types of cancer.

Long-Term Effects of Using Tobacco

The respiratory system is the body system that is harmed the most by smoking tobacco. Breathing in tobacco smoke over and over again irritates the nose, throat, trachea, and lungs. Eventually, these irritations cause smokers to cough a lot.

Smokers are much more likely to die of *chronic bronchitis* and *emphysema* than nonsmokers. Chronic bronchitis starts with a buildup of tar in the respiratory system. The buildup causes the breathing tubes leading to the lungs to produce excess mucus and to swell. This makes it hard for the person to breathe.

Emphysema destroys the tiny air sacs in the lungs. When these air sacs are destroyed, it takes longer for the lungs to do their job. People with emphysema have a hard time breathing. Often they can't

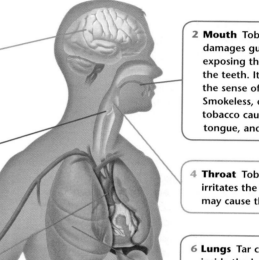

1 Brain Nicotine reaches the brain 10 seconds after being inhaled. Taking in nicotine leads to addiction.

2 Mouth Tobacco juice damages gums, exposing the roots of the teeth. It also affects the sense of taste. Smokeless, or "spit," tobacco causes mouth, tongue, and lip cancer.

3 Esophagus Smokers get about 80 percent of all cases of cancer of the esophagus.

4 Throat Tobacco smoke irritates the throat and may cause throat cancer.

5 Circulatory System Chemicals in tobacco smoke decrease the amount of oxygen in the blood and narrow the blood vessels. This makes the heart work harder, leading to heart diseases.

6 Lungs Tar collects inside the lungs, causing coughing and shortness of breath. Long-term smoking is the leading cause of cancer and other lung diseases.

262

Meeting Individual Needs
Leveled Activities

BELOW-LEVEL Effects of ETS on Pets Ask students to choose a type of pet and interview a veterinarian about how ETS affects this animal. Students should make diagrams of the animal's internal organs, with labels describing how the organs and systems are affected.

ON-LEVEL News Bulletin Divide the class into groups. Have each group research a different disease caused by smoking and develop a news bulletin about it. Encourage the students to use as many facts as possible, as well as interview quotes and drawings of healthy and diseased tissues.

CHALLENGE Addicted Brains Suggest that students contact three sources to learn how nicotine affects the brain, what it means to have an addiction, and how addiction affects a person's social relations. Encourage students to creatively display what they learn.

◀ This woman has to breathe through a hole in her neck because smoking caused a cancer in her throat.

▲ Using smokeless tobacco causes sores to form in the mouth. These sores often turn into cancer.

get enough oxygen to exercise or even walk short distances.

Lung cancer is the disease most people relate to smoking. Cancer destroys healthy tissues and organs. The longer a person smokes cigarettes, the more likely he or she is to get lung cancer. Smokers are also at risk of getting cancer of the mouth, esophagus, larynx, throat, and digestive system.

Heart diseases caused by smoking kill people every year. Chemicals in cigarette smoke make the heart work faster and harder. Smokers are four times more likely to die of heart disease than are nonsmokers.

Tobacco smoke also harms nonsmokers. People who are around smokers breathe **environmental tobacco smoke (ETS)**—tobacco smoke in the air. ETS has the same harmful poisons that smokers inhale. People who breathe ETS all the time can end up with lung diseases, cancer, and heart disease. They also have more allergies, asthma, and respiratory infections than people who stay in smoke-free places.

CAUSE AND EFFECT List four possible long-term effects of using tobacco.

Possible answer: developing heart disease, emphysema, chronic bronchitis, and cancer

Myth and Fact

Myth: Smokeless tobacco is harmless.
Fact: People who use smokeless tobacco are fifty times more likely to get oral cancer than people who don't. Oral cancer is cancer of the mouth, lips, gums, tongue, or inside of the cheeks.

263

Discuss

Have students explain how to maintain the healthy status of body systems, such as avoiding smoking to protect the lungs. Tell students that environmental tobacco smoke is also known as secondhand smoke or sidestream smoke. Explain that the act of breathing ETS is also known as passive smoking or involuntary smoking. Emphasize the words *secondhand*, *passive*, and *involuntary* in these terms.

Critical Thinking Does calling ETS *secondhand smoke* change the way you think about it? Why or why not? Students might answer that the term *secondhand smoke* makes breathing ETS sound more unappealing because they are breathing in something that is "used."

Critical Thinking Why might someone who wanted stronger laws against smoking in public places use terms like *passive smoking* or *involuntary smoking*? Using those terms emphasizes the idea that the people who breathe this type of smoke are not doing it intentionally.

Health Background

Lung Cancer In the 1920s, when cigarette smoking was not as widespread as it would later become, lung cancer was such a rare disease that a doctor might see it only once in a lifetime. Within a few decades, however, when the use of cigarettes had spread among the United States population, a typical thoracic surgeon, or specialist in chest surgery, had begun to see hundreds of cases of lung cancer each year.

Source: *Journal of Cancer Detection and Prevention; University of California, San Francisco, News Service*

 For more background, visit the **Webliography** in Teacher Resources at **www.harcourtschool.com/health** **Keyword** tobacco

 **Physical Education**

Breathing and Exercise
Invite students to research three types of exercises. Have them choose individual exercises from at least two of these categories: aerobic, strength training, stretching, and relaxation. Have them consult teachers or books about these exercises to find out what breathing patterns are recommended or how oxygen affects the ability to perform the activity. Have students present their findings to classmates.

Teacher Tip

Sources for Information
- National Center for Tobacco-Free Kids (202) 296-5469
- American Cancer Society (800) 227-2345
- American Heart Association (800) 242-8721
- American Lung Association (212) 315-8700
- National Cancer Institute Publications (800) 4-CANCER
- Action on Smoking and Health (202) 659-4310

TEACH *continued*

Personal Health Plan ▶

Reasons to try tobacco might include
- curiosity
- peer pressure
- influence of the media
- wish to appear grown up

Reasons to avoid tobacco might include
- yellowing of teeth
- bad-smelling breath
- breathing problems
- diseases, including cancer

Discuss

Tell students that being addicted to nicotine is like being addicted to any other drug. Review with students what they learned about addiction in Chapter 8. Point out that, like other drug users, most people who quit smoking feel miserable at first.

Critical Thinking **Should people who are trying to quit smoking interpret feeling miserable as a sign that they should continue smoking? Explain.** No, smoking is an addiction. People experience unpleasant symptoms whenever they try to stop using anything to which they are addicted.

Problem Solving **If you knew someone who was experiencing the discomforts of quitting smoking, what could you say to help the person keep trying to quit?** Answers will vary, but students might mention that those discomforts are temporary, whereas the discomforts of smoking get worse with time and could result in death.

Consumer Activity

Make Buying Decisions Suggest that students also figure out the costs for someone who smokes two packs a day. Extend this activity by having students think of other ways they could spend the money saved by not buying cigarettes.

Consumer Activity

Make Buying Decisions How expensive is it to smoke? Find out how much a pack of cigarettes costs. Then figure out how much a person who smokes one pack a day spends in a week, a month, and a year. If a one-pack-a-day smoker decided to quit, how many CDs (at $15 each) could he or she buy in a year?

Personal Health Plan ▶

Real-Life Situation You are curious about tobacco. Your mom smokes, and you want to try it, too.
Real-Life Plan Write down a list of five reasons why you might want to try tobacco. Next to each of your reasons, write two reasons why you should avoid tobacco.

264

Stop—Or Don't Start

Most people who use tobacco continue to do so because they can't stop. So why do people start? Some young people start using tobacco because they wonder what it's like. Others start because their friends urge them to start.

Many young people think using tobacco makes them look grown-up and cool. But the facts are that most grown-ups don't use tobacco and that cigarettes make people sick! Also, in most states a person under the age of eighteen who is caught buying tobacco can be arrested or fined.

Don't think you can smoke a cigarette once in a while or quit whenever you want. Nicotine is an addictive drug. When you smoke a cigarette, you will soon want another. People who are addicted to nicotine become nervous, depressed, and irritable if they don't use tobacco often. The best way to avoid this is to never use tobacco in the first place!

Most adults who smoke want to quit. As soon as a smoker quits, his or her body begins to heal. The chances of developing cancer, lung diseases, and heart diseases go down.

Nicotine Withdrawal and Recovery

After 12 Hours	After a Few Days	After a Few Weeks
Carbon monoxide and nicotine levels decline	Senses of smell and taste return	Heart and lungs begin to repair themselves
Person feels hungry, tired, edgy, short-tempered	Person often eats more and experiences temporary weight gain	Risk of death from disease, stroke, cancer, emphysema is reduced
Coughing increases	Mouth and tongue are dry	More healthy, productive days
	Most nicotine is gone from the body	Chances for a longer life improve

---

ESL/ELL Support

LANGUAGE AND VOCABULARY Some students may find the terms *bronchitis* and *emphysema* difficult to pronounce and use.

Beginning Assist students by breaking these words into their Greek roots and discussing their meanings. *Bronchitis* comes from the Greek word *bronkhos*, meaning "windpipe," and the suffix *-itis*, meaning "inflammation or disease." *Emphysema* comes from *emphsēma*, meaning "inflation." Have students organize this information in a table that shows each word, its roots, the meaning of the roots, and the definition of the word.

Intermediate Have students research bronchitis and emphysema and then make a list of words that describe each disease.

Advanced Give students the information in the Beginning section. Tell students that *inflated* means "filled with air," like a balloon. Have students write a sentence explaining why *inflation* is a good word to describe emphysema.

Many people need help to quit smoking. Hospitals, support groups, and health organizations are sources that offer help. Also, doctors can suggest special medicines to help smokers get over their addiction.

 DRAW CONCLUSIONS Why does taking responsibility for your own health mean not smoking?

Possible answer: Taking responsibility for my health means taking care of my body. Tobacco use harms a person's body, so not using tobacco is acting responsibly.

◀ You can be cool and have fun with friends without smoking!

Lesson 1 Summary and Review

❶ Summarize with Vocabulary

Use vocabulary from this lesson to complete the statements.

Tobacco smoke contains cancer-causing substances, or _____, such as the sticky substance known as _____. Tobacco smoke also contains the addictive drug _____ and the poisonous gas _____. Even nonsmokers can be hurt by tobacco by way of _____.

❷ Describe two ways in which nicotine affects the body.

❸ Critical Thinking Once a person has started using tobacco, why should he or she stop?

❹ **DRAW CONCLUSIONS** Draw and complete this graphic organizer to show how you might arrive at the following conclusion.

| What I Read | + | What I Know | = | Conclusion: No tobacco helps body systems stay healthy. |

❺ Write to Inform—Description

Write a paragraph describing how to avoid tobacco products and ETS. Also describe how avoiding tobacco helps reduce health problems.

265

3. WRAP UP

Lesson 1 Summary and Review

1. carcinogens, tar, nicotine, carbon monoxide, environmental tobacco smoke

2. Possible answers: makes the nervous system work faster, makes blood vessels smaller, forces the heart to work harder

3. Possible answer: Once a person stops, the body begins to heal and has less chance of developing lung disease, heart disease, and cancer. Also, stopping will save money.

4. Possible answers include:

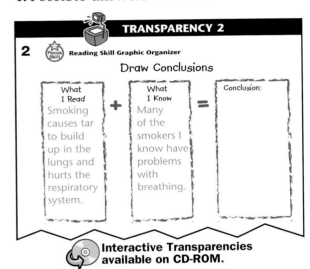

TRANSPARENCY 2

2 Reading Skill Graphic Organizer
Draw Conclusions

| What I Read Smoking causes tar to build up in the lungs and hurts the respiratory system. | + | What I Know Many of the smokers I know have problems with breathing. | = | Conclusion: |

Interactive Transparencies available on CD-ROM.

5. Students' paragraphs should list ways to avoid tobacco, such as refusing to try tobacco products or leaving a place where other people are smoking. Students should also explain that avoiding tobacco would help them breathe better, play sports better, and avoid many deadly diseases.

 For **writing models** with examples, see *Teaching Resources* pp. 47–61. Rubrics are also provided.

 When Minutes Count ...

Quick Study Students can use *Activity Book* pp. 41–42 (shown on p. 261) as they complete each lesson in this chapter.

Objectives

► Explain what blood alcohol level is and what it measures.

► Describe how alcohol affects health, abilities, and body functions.

► Explain what alcoholism is and who might suffer from it.

 ### When Minutes Count . . .

Assign the Quick Study, Lesson 2, Activity Book pp. 41–42 (shown on p. 261).

Program Resources

► Activity Book pp. 41–42
► Transparency 2

Vocabulary

blood alcohol level (BAL) p. 266,

intoxicated p. 267,

alcoholism p. 270

Daily Fitness Tip

Drinking and driving is dangerous, but so is drinking and walking. About half the adult pedestrians killed in traffic accidents had some alcohol in their bodies; more than a third had blood alcohol levels above the legal limit for driving. Remind students that someone who has been drinking should not walk outside alone.

 For more guidelines about alcohol, drugs, and movement, see *Be Active! Resources for Physical Education*, p. 171.

1. MOTIVATE

Give an index card to each student. Ask students to write *What I Know About Alcohol* at the top of one side. Then ask them to list the things they know about alcohol. Tell them to put the cards in a safe place. At the end of the lesson, ask students to review what they wrote on their cards. Then have them turn the cards over and write the heading *What I Learned About Alcohol*. Have them list the things they have learned.

 # Alcohol Affects Body Systems

LESSON 2

Lesson Focus

Alcohol is a drug that can cause immediate and long-term effects.

Why Learn This?

Knowing the effects of alcohol will help you make good decisions about its use.

Vocabulary

blood alcohol level (BAL)
intoxicated
alcoholism

Short-Term Effects of Using Alcohol

You may see alcohol being served at family gatherings, in restaurants, or even in church. When used by adults in small amounts, alcohol can even have positive effects on the circulatory system. However, drinking too much alcohol can be dangerous or even deadly. Even small amounts of alcohol can harm a young person.

Alcohol is a drug. It is found in beer, wine, and liquor. Alcohol changes the way a person feels, acts, and thinks. It also changes the way the body works. How much a person is affected by alcohol depends on the person's blood alcohol level. **Blood alcohol level (BAL)** is a measure of the amount of alcohol in a person's blood. The more alcohol a person drinks, the higher the person's BAL. The higher the BAL, the more the person is affected by alcohol.

Each of these drinks contains about $\frac{1}{2}$ ounce of alcohol.

266

 ### Math

How Many Servings? Have students use the illustration on this page to figure out how many servings of alcohol are in a 12-oz. can of ale ($1\frac{1}{2}$); in a mixed drink, such as a strawberry daiquiri, that has 10 oz. of juice and sugar water and $1\frac{1}{2}$ oz. of rum (1); in a wine cooler that has 7 oz. of juice and sugar water and 5 oz. of wine (1).

Teacher Tip

SADD Invite a representative from Students Against Destructive Decisions to talk to your class about how the organization educates young people and adults about the dangers of drinking and driving.

◀ It is dangerous for someone who has been drinking a lot to drive a car! It is also illegal. An intoxicated person who drives could have his or her license taken away or even be put in jail.

Alcohol affects the parts of the brain that control speech, balance, and coordination. People who drink a lot of alcohol sometimes have trouble speaking and even standing.

Alcohol also affects the parts of the brain that control judgment, attention, and memory. Drinking a lot of alcohol causes people to make bad decisions. They may do things they would otherwise never do. They may also forget what they have done.

As alcohol builds up in a person's body, the person becomes drunk, or intoxicated. Being **intoxicated** (in•TAHK•sih•kay•tuhd) means being strongly affected by a drug. This happens to different people at different rates. A small or young person will become intoxicated faster than a large adult. Some people become loud, angry, or violent when intoxicated. Some become sleepy, sad, or silly. Others may vomit.

Alcohol slows down a person's breathing. If a person's BAL is high enough, he or she may fall asleep or become unconscious. Alcohol is a poison. Too much alcohol can kill a person.

Did You Know?

Every year in the United States, more than 17,000 people die in car crashes linked to drinking alcohol. That's about two people killed every hour.

SEQUENCE What are some of the short-term effects a person experiences as his or her BAL increases?
Possible answer: The person may lose the ability to speak clearly, walk easily, make good judgments, and remember things. If the person continues to drink, he or she may become ill, fall unconscious, or die.

267

ESL/ELL Support

LANGUAGE AND VOCABULARY The term *intoxicated* may be unfamiliar to many students. Help students understand its meaning by examining the structure of the word and its origin. The root of the word—*toxic*—comes from the Latin word *toxicum*, which means "poison."

Beginning Help students divide the word *intoxicated* into its individual syllables: *in-tox-i-cat-ed*. Ask students to repeat the words *intoxicate, intoxicated*, and *intoxication* to practice hearing different forms of the word.

Intermediate Ask students to write two or three simple sentences using the word *intoxicated*. Have students explain how the meaning of the word is shown in the sentence.

Advanced Prepare two or three sentences that use forms of the word *intoxicate*. Read each sentence to the students, omitting that word. Ask students to write the form of the word that is missing from the sentence.

2. TEACH

Content-Area Reading Support

Using Related Words As students read this lesson, have them identify terms that describe a connection between people and alcoholic beverages. Vocabulary words include *intoxicated* and *alcoholism*. Students may also find or think of other terms, such as *drunk, problem drinker, social drinking, alcohol abuse,* and *heavy drinker.*

Have students make a two-column table that lists each term in the first column and its meaning in the second column. After students have completed their tables, have them identify relationships between the terms. For example, *problem drinkers* probably suffer from *alcoholism*.

Discuss

Tell students that some states have laws about the sale of beer and wine that are different from those regarding liquor. For example, in some states, beer and wine can be sold in a grocery store, but liquor must be sold in specially licensed stores.

Critical Thinking Does it make sense to have different laws for when and where beer and wine and when and where liquor can be sold or used? Why or why not? Some students may say that it does because liquor is stronger; others may say it does not because alcohol is still being purchased.

Discuss

As students read this section, have them analyze the short-term harmful effects of alcohol on the function of the body systems.

Lesson 2 • Alcohol Affects Body Systems **267**

The liver cleans the blood. A healthy liver (left) is a network of smooth tissue. Over time, abusing alcohol can cause scar tissue to form in the liver (right).

TEACH continued

Interpret Visuals—Pictures

Have students examine the picture of the healthy liver and the diseased liver. Ask students to analyze the long-term harmful effects of alcohol on the function of the body systems.

Discuss

Are you surprised at the difference in appearance between a diseased liver and a normal liver? Why or why not? Accept all reasonable answers. Encourage students to think about the damage that alcohol does to the liver.

Why do you think alcohol can cause so much damage to the liver? The liver is the body's primary organ for processing alcohol, so it's affected directly by the alcohol circulating in the bloodstream.

Health Background

Alcohol and Nutrition Heavy drinking affects the body's ability to absorb important vitamins and minerals. Physicians often find nutritional deficiencies in alcohol abusers. Deficiencies of vitamins A and C, potassium, magnesium, calcium, folic acid, and thiamine cause weakness in muscles and bones, reduced resistance to disease, reduced ability to heal, and anemia.

Source: *National Institute of Alcohol Abuse and Alcoholism; Alpha Nutrition Health Education Series*

For more background, visit the **Webliography** in Teacher Resources at **www.harcourtschool.com/health** **Keyword** alcohol

Long-Term Effects of Using Alcohol

Drinking alcohol causes changes in a person's brain and body. These changes can cause the person to become addicted to alcohol.

People who start drinking alcohol at a young age become addicted more quickly than people who begin as adults. In fact, a young person can become addicted after drinking alcohol for only a few months. That's one reason why it's against the law for people under the age of twenty-one to buy alcohol.

Drinking a lot of alcohol over a long time can cause many health problems. Alcohol can damage nerve cells in the brain and other parts of the nervous system. This can make it hard for people to remember things or to think clearly.

Drinking alcohol for a long time can also cause damage to the liver, an important organ that cleans the blood of certain wastes. Liver damage due to alcohol or other drugs is called *cirrhosis*.

Myth and Fact

Myth: Alcohol hurts only the people who drink it.
Fact: Each year thousands of nondrinkers are killed in alcohol-related violence or car crashes.

268

Meeting Individual Needs
Leveled Activities

BELOW-LEVEL **Decision Mazes** Have each student make a simple maze about decisions that may lead to drinking and alcoholism. Instruct students to place a question at each junction of the maze, with arrows pointing in different directions for different answers. Suggest making exits for answers such as *Never Starting, Quitting,* and *Going Through Treatment.*

ON-LEVEL **Write Stories** Ask each student to write a short story about someone who is addicted to alcohol. Have students include the pain the alcoholic feels, the pain the alcoholic's family feels, and the process of getting help.

CHALLENGE **Give Your Input** Ask students to brainstorm tactics used to discourage underage drinking. How effective are they? What others could be used? What is the best way to discourage underage drinking? How do students feel about media representations of alcohol use? How do those representations affect them and those around them?

Alcohol keeps some people from feeling hungry. So a person who drinks a lot of alcohol may not eat enough. As a result, the body may not get the nutrients it needs. This makes the body less fit and less able to protect itself from disease.

MAIN IDEA AND DETAILS Describe how alcohol affects the body.

Possible answer: Alcohol damages parts of the brain and is an addictive drug. It damages the liver, makes the heart beat faster, and can cause stomach ulcers.

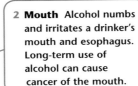

1 Brain Alcohol slows nerve activity that controls speech, motor skills, judgment, thinking, and memory. Alcohol makes the blood vessels in the brain expand, causing headaches. Long-term alcohol use can cause permanent brain damage.

3 Heart Alcohol makes the heart beat faster. It also causes blood pressure to rise. Heavy drinking can cause lasting high blood pressure.

2 Mouth Alcohol numbs and irritates a drinker's mouth and esophagus. Long-term use of alcohol can cause cancer of the mouth.

4 Stomach Alcohol causes the stomach to secrete juices for digestion. If there is no food in the stomach, these juices irritate the stomach, causing small sores, called *ulcers*, to form.

5 Liver The poisons in alcohol collect in the liver and form blisters. Over time these blisters form scar tissue that keeps the liver from cleaning the blood. Eventually the liver stops working.

269

Math

Comparing Pulse Rates Explain to students that pulse rate tells how fast the heart is beating. Every time the heart beats, it forces blood through the arteries. This force is felt as a pulse. Have students work in pairs to take each other's pulses at the wrist. First, have students count the beats for fifteen seconds. Then, have them multiply the number by four to get the number of beats per minute. Students can compare the pulse rates of all students by constructing a bar graph.

Teacher Tip

Alcohol's Effect on Body Organs Ask students to find "before" and "after" photos that show normal organs and organs that have been affected by alcohol. These might include photos of livers, hearts, brains, and stomachs. Students might find these photos in books on the effects of alcohol, in reference materials, and in pamphlets and other literature offered by many organizations.

Interpret Visuals—Illustrations

Have students look at the illustration of the body organs affected by alcohol. Then have them list the body systems affected and summarize how alcohol affects each system.

Remind students that a body system consists of organs that work together to perform a process. Point out that when one organ is affected, other organs and systems might be affected as well. For example, a problem with the stomach could affect the entire digestive system, the muscular system, and the skeletal system by making it difficult for the body to get proper nutrients to maintain these systems.

Discuss

Explain that blood pressure is a measure of the amount of pressure blood puts on the walls of arteries. Blood pressure is measured with two numbers. Blood pressure below 120/80 is considered normal for adults. High blood pressure increases the risk of stroke, heart attack, and kidney disease.

Critical Thinking How can alcohol-related damage to the heart affect the blood vessels? Help students understand that alcohol causes the heart to beat faster, increasing blood pressure. The increased pressure weakens the walls of blood vessels over time.

Quick Activity

The graph indicates that 41 percent of car-crash deaths are related to alcohol use.

Discuss

The National Highway Traffic Safety Administration estimates that raising the drinking age to 21 in 1975 saved more than 12,000 lives and reduced teen traffic deaths by 13 percent within twenty years. Still, in 2001 more than 14,000 teens were killed in alcohol-related traffic crashes. Traffic crashes involving drunk drivers are the number-one killer of people between the ages of 5 and 22.

The National Transportation Safety Board advises states to take away the license of any teen with any measurable alcohol in his or her blood. It also recommends that teenagers 17 and under be prohibited from driving between midnight and 5:00 A.M.

Critical Thinking **Is it fair to have stricter laws governing alcohol and driving for teens than for adults? Why or why not?** Some students might agree that it is fair, arguing that teens are less experienced and less mature than adults and so are more likely to drink and drive. Others might argue that it is unfair to have different laws because alcohol impairs the ability of anyone to drive, or that laws prohibiting teens from driving at certain hours assume that teens will be drinking.

Many students may think that alcoholics are people that are homeless or look a certain way. Emphasize that many alcoholics look like average people.

▲ Alcohol use causes more car-crash deaths than any other factor.

Other Problems Caused by Alcohol

Health effects are not the only risks connected to alcohol use. Remember that alcohol affects the brain in many ways. Intoxicated people may say hurtful things, take foolish risks, and damage property. They may also injure or kill themselves and others. Thousands are killed in car crashes each year because of people who think they can drive safely after drinking.

People who can't stop drinking have a disease called alcoholism. **Alcoholism** (AL·kuh·hawl·iz·uhm) is an addiction to alcohol. People who suffer from alcoholism are *alcoholics*

Quick **Activity**

Analyze Data Look at the bar graph at the right. What percent of car-crash deaths are related to alcohol use?

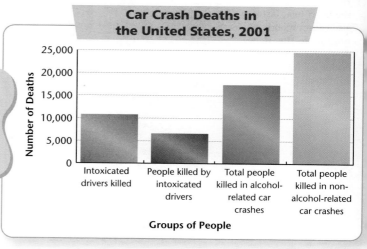

Car Crash Deaths in the United States, 2001

270

COMPREHENSIBLE INPUT The term *alcoholism* is a noun, but it does not represent a concrete object. Clarify with students the concept of alcoholism.

Beginning Show pictures of sick people. Explain that alcoholism is a type of illness that people can get when they drink too much alcohol. Have students list other illnesses they know about.

Intermediate Have students describe how the symptoms of an illness feel. For example, nausea makes your stomach feel funny, fever makes you feel hot, and fatigue makes you feel tired.

Advanced Suggest that students write a story about an alcoholic, showing how the alcoholic's family members are affected by their loved one's disease.

(al·kuh·ʜᴀᴡʟ·iks). Alcoholism can affect people of any age, any race, and either gender.

Many alcoholics want to stop drinking. When they try to stop, though, they go through withdrawal. Recall from Chapter 8 that withdrawal is the physical and emotional changes addicts go through when they stop using an addictive drug.

Withdrawal is different for different people. Some sweat a lot or become very confused. Some see or hear things that aren't there. Some get severe headaches or feel sick to the stomach. Others get nervous and are unable to sleep. Nearly all alcoholics in withdrawal want to drink to feel better.

Trained health-care workers at hospitals and treatment centers can help alcoholics going through withdrawal. The workers can offer counseling and medicine to lessen the effects of withdrawal.

Going through withdrawal is not the end for an alcoholic. He or she may still need help for months or years to keep away from alcohol. Most alcoholics can't stop drinking by themselves. They need help from doctors or from organizations that understand alcoholism and know how to treat it.

COMPARE AND CONTRAST Compare and contrast the health risks of an alcohol user with the health risks of a non-user.

ACTIVITY

Building Good Character

Trustworthiness You trust people not to use alcohol or other drugs while they are working. For example, a school-bus driver should never drink alcohol before going to work. Name other jobs that require workers to be trustworthy about not using alcohol while they are working.

Possible answer: An alcohol user faces heart disease, liver disease, alcoholism, car accidents, and legal problems. A non-user doesn't face the alcohol-related diseases but could be in an accident caused by an intoxicated driver.

You may think that all alcoholics look dirty and wear ragged clothes. The truth is that most alcoholics are ordinary people with a problem.

271

Building Good Character

Trustworthiness Sample answers include dentists, teachers, taxi drivers, police, doctors, airplane pilots, mechanics, firefighters, and construction workers.

Discuss

It's important for alcoholics and their families to get help. According to the National Council on Alcoholism and Drug Dependence, the family is key. If a family enters treatment, there is about a 90 percent chance that the alcoholic will also enter treatment.

Some people who have drinking problems think they can quit drinking through their own efforts. Most alcoholics and problem drinkers need support from other people to quit drinking. Support can come from trained health-care workers, counselors, or other recovering alcoholics.

Critical Thinking Why do some people think it is more admirable to do something alone than with help from others? Some students might respond that doing something alone shows strength, courage, or discipline.

Do you agree with this attitude? Some students might respond that although they know people need help and support from others, they can't help admiring those who "go it alone." Others might indicate that it takes a strong person to admit that he or she needs help.

Why do most people who want to stop drinking need support from others? People need the reinforcement of new behaviors others can provide. Also, feeling lonely, isolated, and afraid to acknowledge difficult feelings is what drives many people to drink. Knowing that others have similar problems or that they accept the person, even if they can't accept the drinking problem.

3. WRAP UP

Lesson 2 Summary and Review

1. alcohol, intoxicated, blood alcohol level, alcoholic

2. The more alcohol a person drinks, the higher the person's BAL.

3. Students' charts will vary. You might want to refer them to the Life Skills feature on pp. 280–281 for ideas.

4. Possible answers include:

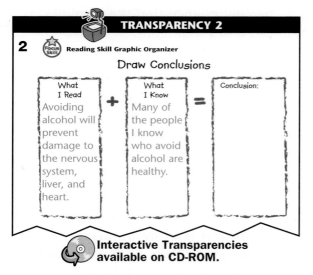

Interactive Transparencies available on CD-ROM.

5. Students' how-to guides should include reasons for a young person to avoid alcohol.

 For **writing models** with examples, see *Teaching Resources* pp. 47–61. Rubrics are also provided.

 When Minutes Count . . .

Quick Study Students can use *Activity Book* pp. 41–42 (shown on p. 261) as they complete each lesson in this chapter.

Alcohol Affects Others, Too

Alcoholism doesn't affect just the alcoholic. It causes problems for the alcoholic's family and friends, too. Alcoholics may not always notice others. Their moods may go up and down a great deal, depending on how much they have been drinking. They buy alcohol with money that should be used for family needs. Family members get used to being treated badly. They adjust their lives around the alcoholic's behavior. They lose their sense of worth. Al-Anon is an organization that sponsors support groups for people close to an alcoholic. Alateen support groups are for teens and younger children who have an alcoholic friend or relative.

SUMMARIZE List two programs of support groups for family members of alcoholics.
Al-Anon and Alateen

◄ Alateen offers support groups in most communities. Find out where Alateen groups meet in your community.

Lesson 2 Summary and Review

❶ Summarize with Vocabulary

Use vocabulary and other terms from this lesson to complete the statements.

When a person drinks a lot of _____, he or she can become _____ and have a high _____. A person who continues to drink too much alcohol can become a(n) _____.

❷ Critical Thinking How is a person's blood alcohol level (BAL) affected by the number of drinks he or she has had?

❸ Make a table showing times or places in which you might be offered alcohol. For each situation, list a reason not to drink.

❹ DRAW CONCLUSIONS Draw and complete this graphic organizer to show how you might arrive at the following conclusion.

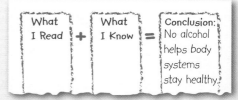

❺ Write to Inform—How-To

Write a short how-to guide that teaches young people how to reduce health risks related to alcohol use.

272

Cultural Connection

Write a Public Service Announcement Invite students to make up tunes and write lyrics to remind people not to drink alcohol and drive. Encourage them to choose a tempo and a melody that express their message. Some students may choose a slow tempo and a scary-sounding melody to emphasize the danger of this behavior; others might choose a bouncy, upbeat tempo and melody to suggest that choosing safe behavior can bring happiness.

Teacher Tip

Alcohol in Religious Rituals Some religions use small amounts of alcohol in rituals. For example, some Christians use wine in the Communion service; some Jews use wine in the seder celebration and on the Sabbath and holy days. Explain that although alcohol has many negative effects if it is abused, when used properly it can add to the solemnity of a religious event. Ask students to describe any ceremonial uses of alcohol with which they are familiar.

Citizenship

Showing Respect for Authority

Being a good citizen means helping to keep your community safe, clean, and a good place to live. There are many ways that you can be a good citizen. One way is to show respect for people who have authority, including parents, teachers, police officers, firefighters, bus drivers, store security guards, and crossing guards. Here are some ways to show respect:

- **Always follow instructions given to you by people in authority.**
- **If you see others not following instructions given by a person in authority, tell the person about it.**
- **When you're outside and you see a person in authority, pay attention in case he or she needs to signal you to stop or come over.**
- **If you see people breaking the law, such as a young person using alcohol or tobacco, tell a parent or report it to someone in authority.**

Activity

Working with a partner, make a list of people in authority, who need respect in order to do their jobs. Then role-play some of these people as they try to enforce rules. Decide how both the authorities and the people they direct should act. Make sure everyone involved shows respect.

273

Using the Poster

Activity Suggest that students design and display their own posters about citizenship and showing respect for authority.

Display Poster 2 to remind students of ways to show citizenship. The poster can be displayed in the classroom, the school cafeteria, or other common areas.

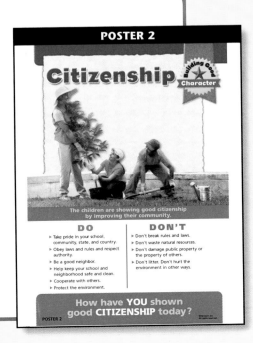

Building Good Character

Caring
Citizenship
Fairness
Respect
Responsibility
Trustworthiness

Objective
▶ Identify ways to be a good citizen by showing respect for authority.

Program Resources
▶ Poster 2

BEFORE READING

Have students brainstorm a list of people in positions of authority. Point out that many of these people (such as police officers, firefighters, crossing guards, and bus drivers) wear uniforms and badges that identify them.

DISCUSS

After students have read the passage, have them discuss reasons for respecting and obeying the instructions of people in authority. Help students understand that one job of people in authority is to keep others safe from danger. You may want to have a police officer, a firefighter, or another authority figure visit the class to talk about his or her work.

ACTIVITY

To help students complete the practice activity, bring in pictures of people in different positions of authority so that students can see how their uniforms and badges vary.

Objectives
► List reasons for choosing not to use alcohol or tobacco.
► Develop strategies for dealing with peer pressure.
► Analyze advertisements for alcohol and tobacco products.

When Minutes Count . . .
Assign the Quick Study, Lesson 3, Activity Book pp. 41–42 (shown on p. 261).

Program Resources
► Activity Book pp. 41–42
► Transparency 2

Daily Fitness Tip

Drinking alcohol interferes with a person's ability to operate any vehicle, regardless of where it travels. Most students know that they should not get into a car with a driver who has been drinking. Remind them that the same is true for boats, snowmobiles, and other forms of transportation.

 For more guidelines about alcohol, drugs, and movement, see *Be Active! Resources for Physical Education,* p. 165.

1. MOTIVATE

Ask students the following questions:
• What are some foods you don't like?
• What are some foods you would never eat?
• What are some activities you don't like and would never do?

Explain that just as students have the right to refuse foods they don't like, they also have the right to refuse alcohol, tobacco, and other drugs.

Ask the following questions:
• Why are there school rules about the use of tobacco and alcohol?
• What are those rules?

Lesson Focus
Refusing alcohol and tobacco is easier if you know the facts and plan ahead.

Why Learn This?
Many young people face peer pressure to use alcohol and tobacco. But it is illegal, dangerous, and unhealthful for young people to use these drugs.

Some People Choose Not to Use Alcohol and Tobacco

Sometimes it might seem as if you have to use alcohol and tobacco to have fun. You see adults smoking and drinking in movies, videos, magazines, and TV shows. The media make the people using these drugs look glamorous, healthy, and full of energy. However, this image is *not true*. Adults who use tobacco and too much alcohol are harming their bodies. That is why most adults have chosen to avoid tobacco and large amounts of alcohol.

There are many reasons not to use alcohol. Some people find that alcohol makes them feel tense, sad, or worried. Other people are allergic to chemicals in some alcoholic drinks. People may also avoid alcohol because they regret how they act when they drink.

Young people may choose not to use alcohol because it's illegal or because of family rules. They may

Follow your family rules! This will keep you healthy and show your parents that you are trustworthy. ►

274

 ### Social Studies

Prohibition In 1920 so many Americans were concerned about the harmful effects of alcohol that a law was passed making it illegal to make, sell, or ship alcohol anywhere in the United States. The time when that law was in effect is called Prohibition. Alcohol was everywhere, but gangsters and criminals controlled it. In 1933 Prohibition was repealed. Have students further research Prohibition and write short papers telling how they think such a law would work today.

also want to do well in school. They know that alcohol affects their ability to think and remember. They know about the health risks linked to alcohol use, too.

Most people also choose not to use tobacco. For them it's more important to avoid the health risks, like cancer, heart disease, and respiratory diseases. They also know that using tobacco would make it harder for them to enjoy sports and other activities.

The cost of tobacco is also a concern to many people. Smokers may buy a pack or two of cigarettes a day. Users of smokeless tobacco may buy a pouch or tin every day or two. That's a lot of money to spend on things that makes people ill!

Many young people don't want to get hooked on a behavior that not only costs a lot of money but also is dangerous. Young people may decide not to use tobacco because it's against the law for them. Bad breath, smelly clothes, and stained teeth may also keep them from smoking or chewing tobacco. Even friends don't want to be around people who smoke or chew.

 DRAW CONCLUSIONS How do family, school, and peers influence your choice not to use alcohol and tobacco?

Possible answer: Family and school rules do not allow use of alcohol or tobacco. It would be hard to participate in sports with my peers if I used alcohol or tobacco.

These students are proud of their good grades. How might using alcohol and tobacco keep them from doing well in school? ▶

275

Personal Health Plan ▶

Real-Life Situation
You're hanging out with your best friends, and all of you are bored. One of your friends suggests you go to her house to drink a few beers.
Real-Life Plan
Make a list of fun activities you and your friend could do that don't involve alcohol.

2. TEACH

Interpret Visuals—Pictures
Point out the photos of the students at the bottom of the page. After a class discussion of possible goals of each of those students, ask the caption question. Then have students identify and describe alternatives to substance (alcohol and tobacco) use.

Personal Health Plan ▶

Personal plans may include:
- inline skating
- listening to music
- going to movies
- dancing
- drawing

Discuss
Point out that people who want to achieve their goals know that making a good impression is important. People who make decisions about scholarships, internships, jobs, admissions to schools, and so forth look for students who seem to be serious about their futures.

Critical Thinking How might knowing that a young person uses or gives others alcohol or tobacco products affect someone's opinion of that person?
Accept all reasonable answers. Some students may say that the person's willingness to break the law shows that the person is untrustworthy.

 Integrated Language Arts/ Reading Skills

Positive Peer Pressure Tell students that peer pressure can be negative, encouraging behaviors that are harmful, dangerous, or illegal. It can also be positive. For example, one student might encourage friends to form a study group, learn the rules of a game, or refuse harmful substances. Have students brainstorm ways they could influence their peers.

Ways to Say *No*

1. Politely say *no*, and walk away.

2. Explain that you would rather do something else.

3. Explain that you choose not to use alcohol or tobacco because of the risks.

4. Change the subject.

5. Make a joke.

6. Express surprise that your friend would be so foolish.

7. Express disappointment that your friend would want to do something so unpleasant.

You Can Refuse Alcohol and Tobacco

At some time most young people must decide whether to use or refuse alcohol and tobacco. People your age might try to pressure you to use these products. This is called *peer pressure*. Choosing to say *no* to alcohol and tobacco is one of the most important decisions you can make. Preparing for peer pressure can help you stick to your decision to refuse.

It's important to practice ways of saying *no*. There are many ways to do it. You can simply say "No thanks" and walk away. You can explain that you would rather do something else. You can explain that you don't want to use these drugs because of their health and safety risks. You can also simply change the subject. Any way you can think of to say *no* will be better than using tobacco and alcohol!

Knowing the serious health risks of tobacco and alcohol can help you refuse them. But there are serious safety risks, too. Cigarettes are the main cause of fires

276

TEACH *continued*

Content-Area Reading Support

Using Tables And Graphics Direct students' attention to the table on this page, which lists ways of saying *no*. Invite students to give specific examples of what someone might say for each strategy.

Problem Solving **What would you say if you used one of these refusal strategies and the person who had offered you alcohol or tobacco called you a name like "chicken" or "baby"?** Possible answers: "Doing what's best for my health isn't babyish"; "I'm too smart to do something risky like trying alcohol or tobacco"; "Yes, I'm too young to use something that's illegal for people under 21 to buy or use."

Discuss

Describe the following situation to students: Tina goes to a swimming party with some of her friends. An hour into the party, Tina realizes that some people there have been drinking alcohol. One group that has been drinking wants to have a diving contest. **What advice would you give Tina?** Possible answer: Call the police or a responsible adult to come take control of the situation.

Meeting Individual Needs
Leveled Activities

BELOW-LEVEL **Rap** Groups of students can compose rap songs advising people how to deal with peer pressure and how to refuse alcohol and tobacco. Have students perform their songs for the class. Encourage them to tape the songs and submit them to a local radio station for broadcast.

ON-LEVEL **Write Fables** Ask students to write fables about refusing alcohol and tobacco. Suggest they look at Aesop's fables for guidelines. They can read their fables to the class and can submit them to a newspaper or magazine for publication.

CHALLENGE **Make Web Pages** Divide the class into groups to develop web pages with tips to help young people refuse alcohol and tobacco and deal with peer pressure. Have groups include hyperlinks to websites with further information—for example, the sites of MADD and the American Cancer Society.

◄ Young people who want to stay healthy say *no* to cigarettes. How can friends help each other say *no*?

in homes, hospitals, and hotels. Alcohol is a leading cause of car crashes.

One of the most important reasons to refuse alcohol and tobacco is to feel good about yourself. When you feel good about yourself, you won't want to follow the bad habits of others. You won't need alcohol or tobacco to feel grown-up.

You can also avoid places where you know there will be drinking or smoking. Parties where there are no responsible adults are often places where young people feel they can get away with drinking or smoking. You can also protect yourself by making friends with young people who don't drink or smoke.

MAIN IDEA AND DETAILS Identify ways to resist peer pressure to use alcohol and tobacco.

Possible answer: Stay around friends and other people who don't use alcohol or tobacco; tell a trusted adult if somebody is pressuring you to use alcohol or tobacco; avoid places where tobacco and alcohol are used.

277

ACTIVITY

Life Skills

LIFE SKILLS **Communicate**

Colette is watching television with her older brother Jim when a beer commercial comes on. Jim says, "Hey, we have some of that in the refrigerator! Want one?" What are some ways Colette can say *no*?

Activity

Communicate Suggest that students write scripts or scenarios for different refusal strategies. The list below gives some suggestions.

- Colette could refuse by simply saying *no* and leaving the room.
- Colette could say that she needs to get homework done or that she is supposed to get dinner started.
- Colette could say that she's read that the younger people are when they start using alcohol, the more likely they are to have problems with it later.

Discuss

Surveys show that if most of a teen's friends drink alcohol, that teen has a much greater chance of being a moderate or heavy drinker. Studies also show that teenagers are much more likely to drink with other teenagers than with their parents, with other relatives, or by themselves. These studies demonstrate that most drinking takes place outside the home, in such settings as cars and outdoor areas. Have students assess the role of peer pressure on decision making.

Critical Thinking **How can this information help you avoid using alcohol?** Students might respond that it reminds them to choose friends who do not drink.

Problem Solving **What might you do if a good friend starts using alcohol?** Possible answers: tell the friend the dangers of using alcohol and try to persuade him or her to get help; decide not to be friends with that person

Consumer Activity

Analyze Advertisements and Media Messages Commercials should present some of the ways that alcohol can harm either the individual who is drinking or innocent bystanders.

Discuss

The alcohol and tobacco industries contribute billions of dollars to the American economy. This money goes to people who grow tobacco; to people who make alcohol and tobacco products; to people who sell the products in stores; to restaurants and bars; to people who drive or own trucks that deliver the products; to people who make advertising, packages, and products with company logos; and to many others. When people buy alcohol and tobacco, they also pay taxes to the government of the United States and to the state where they bought the product. These taxes help keep governments running and fund services.

Critical Thinking **Why might it be hard to pass or enforce laws that make it more difficult for young people to buy alcohol or tobacco products?** Since so many people earn all or some of their income from these products, they may oppose cutting back on the sale of the products.

Discuss

Many insurance companies charge smokers more than nonsmokers. They say that smokers need more medical services, have shorter life spans, and have more unintended injuries and fires than nonsmokers.

Critical Thinking **Do you think this is a fair policy? Why or why not?** Accept all reasonable answers. Many students will think it is fair for smokers to pay more to cover the additional costs their smoking causes.

Consumer Activity

Analyze Advertisements and Media Messages Watch a TV commercial for an alcoholic beverage. Write down the ways the commercial tries to make drinking alcohol seem fun or cool. Then work with a partner to make a commercial that tells the truth about alcohol.

Analyze Advertising Messages

Companies that make and sell tobacco and alcohol products spend a lot of money on advertising. Their ads suggest that people who use their products are rich, cool, and always have fun. They want you to think that using alcohol or tobacco products will make you popular and fun to be with.

People who see these ads should remember the harmful effects of alcohol and tobacco. These ads never show how hard it is to quit using the products. They never tell how much money the products cost. You would never know by looking at the ads that people become ill and die from using alcohol and tobacco.

The style may have changed over the years, but the messages in cigarette ads are still the same—even now that we know how dangerous smoking is. ▶

278

ESL/ELL Support

BACKGROUND AND EXPERIENCE Familiarize students with the word *advertisement*.

Beginning Show students advertisements for and against the use of alcohol and tobacco. Have students draw their own advertisements for refusing tobacco or alcohol. Emphasize that words are not necessary as long as the picture gets the meaning across.

Intermediate Have students find an alcohol or tobacco advertisement and write two or three sentences describing how the ad is misleading.

Advanced Have students write a 30-second radio commercial explaining why a young person should avoid tobacco or alcohol.

Ads for alcohol and tobacco often show young adults using these products. Alcohol and tobacco companies know that young people want to be like adults. These companies also know that people who start drinking and smoking have a hard time stopping.

Beer companies often show their commercials during sporting events. The commercials are designed to make people think that drinking beer is as exciting as playing sports. Cigarette companies are no longer allowed to advertise on TV. But they still get the names of their products on TV by sponsoring sporting and cultural events. When you see the names of alcohol and tobacco products or ads for them, be sure to think about what's not being shown.

SUMMARIZE List ways the media influence a person's view of alcohol and tobacco.

Possible answer: The media make using alcohol and tobacco seem cool, fun, and glamorous. They don't show the health risks of using these drugs.

Lesson 3 Summary and Review

❶ Summarize with Vocabulary

Use terms from this lesson to complete the statements.

TV, magazines, and other _____ often encourage young people to use alcohol and _____. They don't show how _____ these products are. An honest media message would encourage people to _____ rather than use alcohol and tobacco.

❷ Why do you think it's illegal for young people to buy or use tobacco and alcohol?

❸ Critical Thinking Why is it a good idea to think of reasons for refusing alcohol and tobacco before you are offered these drugs?

❹ (Focus Skill) **DRAW CONCLUSIONS** Draw and complete this graphic organizer to show a conclusion you might make about using alcohol and tobacco.

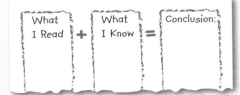

❺ Write to Inform—How-To

Write a how-to manual that teaches young people the attitudes and skills for making responsible decisions about tobacco and alcohol.

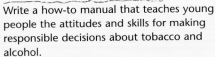

279

3. WRAP UP

Lesson 3 Summary and Review

1. media, tobacco, dangerous (or harmful), refuse

2. Possible answer: Tobacco and alcohol are powerful drugs that have an even stronger effect on the minds and bodies of young people; young people may also be less capable of making good decisions about whether to use tobacco or alcohol and how much.

3. You will be prepared and know what you want to say before you are actually offered the drugs.

4. Possible answers include:

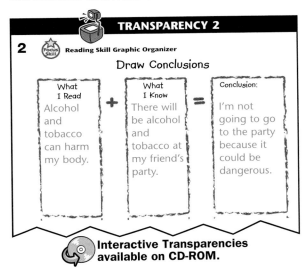

TRANSPARENCY 2

2 (Focus Skill) **Reading Skill Graphic Organizer**

Draw Conclusions

What I Read		What I Know		Conclusion:
Alcohol and tobacco can harm my body.	+	There will be alcohol and tobacco at my friend's party.	=	I'm not going to go to the party because it could be dangerous.

Interactive Transparencies available on CD-ROM.

5. Students' how-to guides should include a discussion of self-esteem and confidence.

 For **writing models** with examples, see *Teaching Resources* pp. 47–61. Rubrics are also provided.

 When Minutes Count . . .

Quick Study Students can use *Activity Book* pp. 41–42 (shown on p. 261) as they complete each lesson in this chapter.

Life Skills

Communicate
Make Responsible Decisions
Manage Stress
Refuse
Resolve Conflicts
Set Goals

Objectives
► Identify ways to say *no*.
► Use refusal skills to say *no* to alcohol and tobacco.

Program Resources
► Activity Book p. 44
► Poster 10

1. MOTIVATE

Discuss the following scenario with students: Your soccer team has a game early tomorrow morning. Your older sister has rented a scary video and doesn't want to watch it alone. She asks you to watch it with her. It's already well past your bedtime. You want to feel fresh and alert for the soccer game tomorrow. **How can you refuse your sister's offer but let her know you're pleased that she wanted to include you?**

2. TEACH

Direct students' attention to the photos of Cory and Nicki walking home.

Step 1
What is the first way Cory can refuse Nicki's offer? She can say *no* and give a reason.

Critical Thinking What are some other reasons not to drink? It's against family rules to drink. It can harm the user physically.

Step 2
How does Cory use humor to make her point? Cory laughs about getting a beer belly.

Refuse
Alcohol

There will be times when you need to make decisions for yourself about alcohol and tobacco use. Learning ways to **Refuse** will help you stay healthy.

Cory and Nicki had been playing tennis together. When the game was over, they headed to Nicki's house. Nicki's parents weren't home at the time. Nicki said, "Hey, my dad bought a six-pack of beer last night. Do you want to try one?" Cory may want to drink alcohol but knows she shouldn't. Here are some ways she can say *no*.

1 **Say *no*, and tell why not.**

2 **Use humor to make your point.**

> No way! It's illegal for us to drink!

> Girl, I don't want to get a beer belly!

Cory can say *no* and explain why they shouldn't be drinking alcohol.

Cory can make a joke, hoping Nicki will forget about drinking.

Integrated Language Arts/ Reading Skills

Write a Dialogue Students can practice refusing tobacco and alcohol by writing a dialogue that includes ways to refuse. For example: Suggestion—"C'mon. Just take one puff." Response—"Nah, I know I can't take just one!" Let students continue the dialogue by showing how they would cope with peer pressure.

ACTIVITY BOOK P. 44

Name _____

Life Skill
Refuse

Steps for Refusing Alcohol and Tobacco
1. Say *no* and say why not.
2. Use humor to make your point.
3. Suggest something else to do.
4. Just ignore what the person has said.

Use the steps to help these students refuse alcohol and tobacco.

A. Before the school dance, Ryan goes to his friend Aaron's house with several other friends. Aaron takes a bottle of alcohol from his parents' cupboard and offers it to everyone.
• Describe how Ryan can refuse the alcohol that Aaron has offered him.
Possible answers: Before the bottle of alcohol reaches Ryan, he can suggest that everyone get ready to leave for the dance so they are not too late. He could also say *no* when the bottle reaches him and tell his friends that he has chosen not to drink and that it is against his family's rules.

B. Julie and Jorge are studying for a math test when Jorge gets up and takes a pack of cigarettes out of his backpack. He tells Julie that cigarettes help him relax when he feels tense and asks her to come outside to have one with him.
• Describe how Julie can refuse the tobacco that Jorge has offered her.
Possible answers: Julie can tell Jorge *no* and explain that she does not smoke cigarettes because they can cause serious damage to her body. She might also tell him that cigarette smoke gives her a headache, which makes it hard for her to study. She could also tell him that smoking is against her family's rules.

Available online.
www.harcourtschool.com/health

3 Suggest something else to do.

> Nah, let's go see that new spy movie.

Cory can suggest something else for them to do instead of drinking alcohol.

4 Just ignore what the person has said.

> Did you see that TV show last night?

Cory can just not respond to Nicki's suggestion and can change the subject.

 ## Problem Solving

A. Anna and Kay are looking at a magazine. They see a picture of a beautiful woman advertising cigarettes. Kay suggests that they smoke some cigarettes so they can look like the model. Anna does not want to smoke.
- Choose and explain one way to **Refuse** in Anna's situation.

B. Dave and his older friend Chuck are camping out. As Chuck is unpacking the food, Dave notices a six-pack of beer. Dave doesn't want to drink alcohol, and he doesn't want to be around if Chuck is going to drink.
- What are some ways Dave can get out of this situation? How can Dave show respect for his family's rules about not using alcohol?

281

Life Skills

Activity Help students think of slogans that could accompany the poster. The slogans could be written on strips of poster board and displayed around the poster.

Display the poster to remind students of the different ways of refusing alcohol or tobacco.

Critical Thinking What other ways can humor be used to refuse beer? Possible answer: Make a funny face or a funny noise as if to say, "That's not for me!"

Step 3

What does Cory suggest that she and Nicki do? go to a movie

Critical Thinking **What other suggestions might work?** visiting friends or playing a game

Building Good Character
Remind students that when making any decision, they should consider how the decision shows citizenship. Have them discuss how refusing beer shows that Cory is a good citizen.

Step 4

How do we know that Cory is refusing Nicki's offer? Cory doesn't respond to the offer.

Do you think that was a smart move on Cory's part? Yes. It shows Nicki that she isn't interested in drinking alcohol.

3. WRAP UP

Problem Solving

A Students might suggest that Anna say *no* and explain why she isn't interested in smoking cigarettes. It's not healthy for the body, and smoking won't make anyone look like a model.

B Have students assess the role of peer pressure on problem solving. Students might suggest that Dave express his concerns to Chuck. If Chuck won't listen, Dave might walk away from the situation and possibly get back home on his own. He might also call an older sibling or an adult and ask for a ride home.

Objectives

► Identify the warning signs of a problem with alcohol.

► Explain why people who are addicted to alcohol or tobacco need help to stop using these drugs.

► Identify sources of support available to people who want to stop using alcohol or tobacco.

 When Minutes Count . . .

Assign the Quick Study, Lesson 4, Activity Book pp. 41–42 (shown on p. 261).

Program Resources

► Activity Book pp. 41–42, 45
► Transparency 2

 **Daily Fitness Tip**

Students already know not to ride in any kind of vehicle when the driver has been drinking. Remind them that they should never ride in a car without using a safety belt. Tell them that for anyone under the age of 12, the safest position in a car is in the back seat.

 For more guidelines on fitness, see *Be Active! Resources for Physical Education.*

1. MOTIVATE

Using a pencil or some other object, tap out the Morse code for SOS (three short/three long/three short). Ask students if they recognize the signal. Explain that SOS is an international code requesting urgent help. Ask students to suggest other signals used to ask for help. They may know about signal flags used on sailboats, high-intensity flares that hikers and explorers use in remote regions, signs that people put in the back windows of stalled cars, and burglar or smoke alarms. Ask students what kinds of situations might require these signals. Explain that signals for help can be just as important from someone who is in trouble with alcohol or tobacco.

 LESSON **4**

Where Users Can Find Help

When Someone Needs Help

"I want to do it myself!" You've probably heard small children say this. Maybe you've said it, too. It expresses a natural feeling. You feel proud when you do something without any help. But everyone needs help sometimes. Asking for help when it's needed is a sign of being responsible.

Overcoming a problem with alcohol or tobacco is difficult. Most people need help with it. Fortunately, there are many kinds of help for overcoming alcohol or tobacco addiction.

How much alcohol use is too much? You may be worried about the drinking habits of someone you know. Maybe you've noticed someone drinking more alcohol now than he or she used to. Maybe you've seen someone drinking alone. In both cases, the person might need help.

Lesson Focus

Smokers, alcohol users, and their families can get help at home and in the community.

Why Learn This?

Finding sources of help for users of alcohol and tobacco may help you, your family, or your friends.

Did You Know?

Most people who decide to quit using alcohol or tobacco have to try several times before they succeed. Just because a person tries and fails doesn't mean he or she will never be able to quit.

Warning Signs of Problem Drinking

1. Drinking more now than in the past
2. Hiding alcohol or sneaking drinks
3. Forgetting things as a result of drinking
4. Missing school or work as a result of drinking
5. Lying about drinking
6. Needing a drink to have fun or to relax
7. Drinking alone
8. Thinking and talking about alcohol a lot

282

 Science

Fetal Alcohol Syndrome Mothers who drink alcohol when they are pregnant may give birth to babies with fetal alcohol syndrome (FAS). Ask students to find out what FAS is and how it affects the baby. Have them use this information to prepare a short video presentation for the rest of the class.

Teacher Tip

Support Sourcebook Students might be interested in compiling a book that lists sources of support in the community for people who want to quit using alcohol or tobacco. Encourage students to locate sources and find out what services they offer. Students should include in their sourcebook the information about services, along with the name, address, and telephone number of each source.

Drinking more and more alcohol can mean that the person has become an alcoholic. A person who drinks alone may be using alcohol to deal with feelings such as anger, sadness, or grief. To the person who is drinking, alcohol seems to make these feelings go away. In fact, however, alcohol will only make the feelings worse. With the right help, a person can learn to deal with his or her feelings in healthful ways.

If someone's drinking worries you, chances are that the person needs help. To know for sure, check the warning signs listed on page 282. These signs can help you know whether someone needs help.

Anyone who uses tobacco should also get help. Most people who use tobacco want to quit. They know how dangerous and expensive the habit is. But quitting is hard, especially for someone who tries to do it alone. Medicine is available now to help people quit smoking. Encouragement from family and friends helps, too.

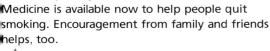
Quick Activity

Be a Friend The attitudes of friends can make a big difference to people who are trying to quit using tobacco. Make a list of ways you could help a person close to you who wants to stop smoking.

 CAUSE AND EFFECT **Describe a situation that might lead a person to drink too much alcohol.**

If somebody is trying to quit using tobacco or alcohol, you should support that person by encouraging his or her efforts. ▶

Possible answer: A person might be feeling sad or angry about something and think that drinking will help those feelings go away.

283

Meeting Individual Needs
Leveled Activities

BELOW-LEVEL **Write the Editor** Have students read a magazine article about alcohol or tobacco. Then ask them to write letters to the editor with their thoughts about the article. How accurately do they feel it addressed the problem of addiction to these substances? Is there anything they would add? Did it address the concerns of young people?

ON-LEVEL **Make Art** Have students use a variety of media (charcoal, pencil, pastels, oil paints, mosaic) to make works of art. The art pieces should suggest why people who are addicted to alcohol or tobacco need help to stop using these drugs.

CHALLENGE **Write Articles** Suggest that students write articles about problem drinking, its warning signs, and actions to take if you suspect someone has a problem. Have them send the articles to a local newspaper or a magazine and ask that the articles be published.

2. TEACH
Quick Activity
Be a Friend Students' lists might include the following: encouraging the person to explain his or her reasons for quitting and helping that person find sources of help or information about quitting; suggesting activities in places where smoking is not allowed or where there are few smokers.

Content-Area Reading Support
Using Tables and Graphs Have students examine the table Warning Signs of Problem Drinking on page 282. Point out that both the text and the table contain important information. Help students understand that the text gives general information about problem drinkers. The table gives specific information on recognizing a problem drinker.

Discuss
Explain that many drinkers believe they are successfully hiding their behavior when, in fact, they are not.

Which of the warning signs might be easy to spot in another person? It might be easy to spot drinking more than in the past, needing a drink to have fun or to relax, thinking and talking about alcohol a lot, forgetting things, or missing school or work.

Which signs would be more difficult? Signs that might be harder to spot are hiding alcohol or sneaking drinks, making excuses or breaking promises, forgetting small things, lying about drinking, and drinking alone.

Critical Thinking Do you think it's possible for someone to show only a few of these warning signs? Why or why not? Possible answer: yes, because alcoholism takes different forms in different drinkers

3. WRAP UP

Lesson 4 Summary and Review

1. problem drinkers, addicted, feelings (or problems), help, trusted adult

2. Sample answer: a hospital, a religious institution, the school counselor

3. People who feel stress may drink because the alcohol helps them forget their problems. But forgetting will not help for long. They are only increasing their problems by becoming addicted to alcohol.

4. Possible answers include:

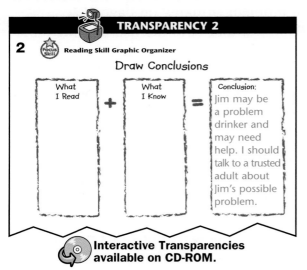

TRANSPARENCY 2

2 Reading Skill Graphic Organizer

Draw Conclusions

What I Read + What I Know = Conclusion: Jim may be a problem drinker and may need help. I should talk to a trusted adult about Jim's possible problem.

 Interactive Transparencies available on CD-ROM.

5. Students' answers should note that these people would give a young person good, trustworthy advice and they would try to help the young person with his or her problems.

 For **writing models** with examples, see *Teaching Resources* pp. 47–61. Rubrics are also provided.

When Minutes Count . . .

Quick Study Students can use *Activity Book* pp. 41–42 (shown on p. 261) as they complete each lesson in this chapter.

If you know somebody who has a problem with alcohol or tobacco, one of the best people to go to is a parent. ▼

Getting Help

If someone close to you has a problem with alcohol or tobacco, talk about the problem with a parent or another adult you trust. You might worry that telling someone will get the person who needs help in trouble. The truth is that people who have an alcohol or tobacco problem need help before they do more harm to themselves. Telling someone about a person's problem will let the person know that you care about him or her. It will also give you the chance to share your concerns with someone else.

Talking with someone can also help the person with the problem find other kinds of support. For example, your community may have clinics, hospitals, or community organizations that help people deal with alcohol and tobacco problems.

SUMMARIZE Describe a plan for getting help for a person who has an alcohol or tobacco problem.
Talk with a trusted adult, such as a parent, teacher, or doctor, who can find sources of help.

Lesson 4 Summary and Review

1 **Summarize with Vocabulary**
Use terms from this lesson to complete the statements.

To recognize when a person has a problem with drinking, know the _____. Some people drink because they think it will get rid of unwanted _____. They need _____ to stop drinking. If you know a problem drinker, you should talk with a (an) _____.

2 Suppose you are looking for help for a person with an alcohol or tobacco problem. Name some people and groups in your community that you might call.

3 **Critical Thinking** Why do you think some people drink when they are feeling stress?

4 **DRAW CONCLUSIONS** Draw and complete this graphic organizer to show what you can conclude from the following facts.

What I Read Warning signs of problem drinking + What I Know Jim misses school. He talks about drinking. = Conclusion:

5 **Write to Inform—Description**
Describe the importance of seeking advice from parents, teachers, or school counselors about unsafe behaviors such as using alcohol and tobacco.

ACTIVITY BOOK P. 45

Name _____

Vocabulary Reinforcement

Word Puzzle

A. Use each clue to complete the word puzzle.

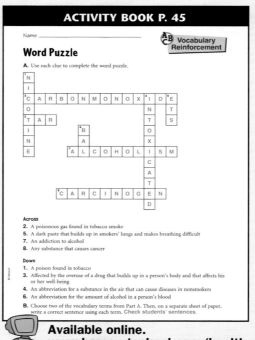

Across
2. A poisonous gas found in tobacco smoke
5. A dark paste that builds up in smokers' lungs and makes breathing difficult
7. An addiction to alcohol
8. Any substance that causes cancer

Down
1. A poison found in tobacco
3. Affected by the overuse of a drug that builds up in a person's body and that affects his or her well-being
4. An abbreviation for a substance in the air that can cause diseases in nonsmokers
6. An abbreviation for the amount of alcohol in a person's blood

B. Choose two of the vocabulary terms from Part A. Then, on a separate sheet of paper, write a correct sentence using each term. Check students' sentences.

Available online.
www.harcourtschool.com/health

ACTIVITIES

Language Arts

Smoking Skit Write a humorous skit about why some people don't smoke cigarettes. Include several scenes so you can show the many different reasons people have for not smoking. Perform the skit for your class.

Science

Effects of Alcohol Take two leaves from a living plant. Cover one leaf with water. Have your teacher or a parent cover the other leaf with clear alcohol. Keep a log of your observations of what happens to the two leaves over the next three days. At the end of the three days, try to explain some of the changes you observed.

Technology Project

Identify at least ten local athletes who do not use tobacco. Ask them to give their top two reasons for not using tobacco. Use a spreadsheet on a computer to record your results. If you don't have a computer, use a paper spreadsheet.

For more activities, visit The Learning Site.
www.harcourtschool.com/health

Home & Community

Analyze Ads Find three or more magazine ads that feature alcohol or tobacco products. Analyze them by listing the negative results of smoking or drinking that the ads don't show and by describing why the ads are misleading. Then discuss your findings with a parent.

Career Link

Magazine Editor Imagine you are the chief editor for a top-rated teen magazine. You'd like your next issue to include a two-page feature article that gives readers positive and effective tools for refusing tobacco and alcohol. The article should offer readers things they can do and things they can say. As the editor of the magazine, what other guidelines will you give the writer of this article?

285

Activities

Language Arts
If you have several teams of students working on this, suggest that each team choose a different reason for not smoking and then develop one scene that focuses on that reason. Allow time for teams to present their skits in class.

Science
Tell students that they should observe the leaves at regular intervals at least once a day over the three-day period. Each time they make observations, they should describe them in a notebook. If students have a camera available, suggest they take a photo of the leaves every time they make an observation. They can paste the photos into their observation notebooks.

Home & Community
Have each student write a summary of the discussion he or she had with a parent. You may want to have the parents sign the summaries.

Supports the Coordinated School Health Program

Technology Project
Have students identify top local athletes in sports such as swimming, track, football, basketball, or tennis. These could be college-level or serious amateur athletes. Have students present their findings to the class in the form of a poster.

Career Link

Magazine Editor Remind students that the article will be for teenagers. Because of this, the guidelines about the article should focus on that age group.

Encourage students to include in their guidelines some of the benefits of staying tobacco- and alcohol-free. Also, the guidelines could tell the writer to describe refusing alcohol and tobacco as the cool thing to do.

For more information on health careers, visit the **Webliography** in Teacher Resources at **www.harcourtschool.com/health**
Keyword health careers

Chapter Review and Test Preparation

Pages 286–287

 Reading Skill 8 pts. each

1. Sample answer: Tobacco is illegal for young people to use. Tobacco harms every major organ in the body. Tobacco makes it hard to breathe and participate in sports.

2. Sample answer: Alcohol is illegal for young people to use. Alcohol makes it hard to remember things, and thus hard to learn new things in school. Alcohol leads to deadly car crashes.

 Use Vocabulary 3 pts. each

3. G, nicotine
4. A, tar
5. E, carbon monoxide
6. C, intoxicated
7. D, carcinogens
8. H, alcoholic
9. F, blood alcohol level
10. B, environmental tobacco smoke (ETS)

 Check Understanding 3 pts. each

11. D, nicotine
12. F, cirrhosis
13. D, juice
14. G, a person who drinks only at religious celebrations
15. B, environmental tobacco smoke (ETS)
16. H, Most adults do not smoke cigarettes.
17. B, carcinogens
18. J, oxygen
19. C, respiratory
20. J, all of the above

 Think Critically 6 pts. each

21. Possible answer: The adult probably has a problem with drinking because he is thinking and talking about alcohol and probably drinks more than he did in the past.

 Reading Skill

DRAW CONCLUSIONS
Draw and then use this graphic organizer to answer questions 1 and 2.

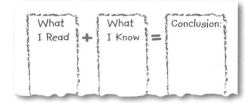

1 Write three facts that lead the conclusion that tobacco can be dangerous.
2 Write three facts that lead to the conclusion that alcohol can be dangerous.

 Use Vocabulary

Match each term in Column B with its meaning Column A.

Column A	Column B
3 Poison that speeds up the nervous system	**A** tar
4 Sticky, dark paste in tobacco smoke	**B** environmental tobacco smoke (ETS)
5 Poisonous gas from burning tobacco	**C** intoxicated
6 Affected by alcohol	**D** carcinogens
7 Causes of cancer	**E** carbon monoxide
8 A person who is addicted to alcohol	**F** blood alcohol level (BAL)
9 Amount of alcohol in the bloodstream	**G** nicotine
10 Tobacco smoke in air	**H** alcoholic

286

 Check Understanding

Choose the letter of the correct answer.

11 All forms of tobacco contain a poison called _____. (p. 261)
A tar
B a tumor
C carbon dioxide
D nicotine

12 The only disease below that is **NOT** a serious risk for smokers is _____. (pp. 262–263)
F cirrhosis   **H** emphysema
G cancer   **J** heart disease

13 Alcohol is found in all of the following products **EXCEPT** _____. (p. 266)

 A   C

 B   D

14 Who probably does **NOT** have a problem with alcohol? (p. 282)
F a person who hides his or her drinking
G a person who drinks only at religious celebrations
H a person who thinks about alcohol often
J a person who drinks alone

15 People who don't smoke can suffer from respiratory problems and other diseases if they breathe a lot of _____. (p. 263)
A smokeless tobacco
B environmental tobacco smoke (ETS)
C carbon dioxide
D unfiltered air

Formal Assessment

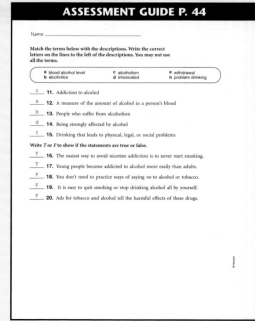

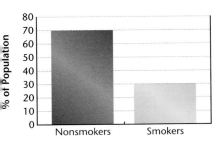

16 Look at the graph above. Which of the following statements is **TRUE** according to the data in the graph? (p. 274)
  F Most adults smoke.
  G Almost half of all adults are smokers.
  H Most adults do not smoke.
  J Most adults who smoke are able to quit.

17 Cigarette smoke contains many _____, or substances that cause cancer. (p. 261)
  A poisons
  B carcinogens
  C depressants
  D fibers

18 Carbon monoxide makes the heart work harder because it takes the place of _____ in the blood. (p. 261)
  F tars   **H** nicotine
  G air sacs   **J** oxygen

19 The _____ system is the body system **MOST** damaged by smoking tobacco. (p. 262)
  A digestive   **C** respiratory
  B circulatory **D** nervous

20 Alcohol affects a person's _____. (pp. 267–269)
  F judgment
  G personality
  H memory
  J all of these

Think Critically

21 You overhear two adults talking. One of them says, "Alcohol is not a problem for me. I drink only a few beers each night." Review the warning signs of problem drinking. Then tell whether you agree with this person or not. Explain your answer.

22 Someone you know quit smoking two days ago. "Wow," he says, "I thought my cough was caused by smoking. But I'm coughing worse than ever now that I've quit." What would you tell him?

Apply Skills

23 **BUILDING GOOD CHARACTER**
  Citizenship You arrive at a party where an adult was supposed to be in charge. However, only young people are there, and many of them have been drinking. Some of them are intoxicated and talking about going swimming. What should you do to be a good citizen?

24 **LIFE SKILLS**
  Refuse You've been working hard all season because you want your team to make it to the state finals. One day a teammate takes out a pouch of chewing tobacco and offers you some. What would you do or say?

Write About Health

25 Write to Explain—How-To Explain what you should do if you know someone who has a problem with drinking.

287

22. The coughing will get better within a few weeks. The coughing is caused by his having smoked and is a sign that his lungs are cleaning themselves out.

 Apply Skills 8 pts. each

23. Sample answer: Leave the party immediately. Tell my parents what is happening at the party and suggest they call to report the problem to the police.

24. Possible answers: politely say *no* and walk away, explain that I have something else to do (such as practice), explain that I prefer not to use tobacco because of the health risks, change the subject, make a joke, express surprise that my teammate would be so foolish, and express disappointment that he or she would do something so unpleasant. I could also remind my teammate of how hard the team has worked to get to the state finals and the disappointment everyone will feel if the team doesn't make it because of the side effects of some team members' use of tobacco.

Write About Health 8 pts.

25. Answers should include first telling a trusted adult.

Performance Assessment

Use the Chapter Project and the rubric provided on the Project Evaluation Sheet. See *Assessment Guide*, pp. 18, 60, 70.

Portfolio Assessment

Have students select their best work from the following suggestions:
- Leveled Activities, p. 276
- Quick Activity, p. 283
- Write to Inform, p. 284
- Activities, p. 285

See *Assessment Guide* pp. 12–16.

CHAPTER
10 Dealing with Feelings

Lesson	Pacing	Objectives	Reading Skills
Introduce the Chapter pp. 288–289		• Preview chapter concepts.	**Compare and Contrast** p. 289; pp. 372–383
1 Your Self-Concept pp. 290–293	1 class period	• Recognize that each person shapes his or her own self-concept. • Realize that a positive self-concept helps a person make healthful decisions.	**Compare and Contrast** pp. 291, 293 • Cause and Effect, p. 293
2 Setting Goals pp. 294–297	1 class period	• Distinguish between needs and wants. • Identify practical strategies for setting and achieving short-term and long-term goals. • Identify sources of help in setting and working toward goals.	**Compare and Contrast** p. 297 • Summarize, p. 294 • Draw Conclusions, p. 295 • Sequence, p. 297
3 Friends and Feelings pp. 298–302	1 class period	• Identify strategies for making and keeping friends. • Explain how to deal with peer pressure. • Practice communication skills. • Distinguish between healthful and unhealthful relationships.	**Compare and Contrast** p. 302 • Main Idea and Details, p. 299 • Compare and Contrast, p. 301 • Cause and Effect, p. 302
Building Good Character p. 303		• Recognize the importance of respecting individual differences, including speech problems.	
4 Actions, Reactions, and Stress pp. 304–307	1 class period	• Identify three ways in which people communicate their feelings. • Explain and practice effective strategies for stress management.	**Compare and Contrast** p. 307 • Draw Conclusions, p. 305 • Cause and Effect, p. 307
Life Skills pp. 308–309	1 class period	• Identify steps to cope with and manage stress. • Use the stress management skills to deal with stress.	
5 Resolving Conflicts pp. 310–313	1 class period	• Learn effective strategies for resolving conflicts. • Explain the importance of respecting differences. • Analyze respectful ways of communicating with others.	**Compare and Contrast** p. 313 • Sequence, p. 311 • Cause and Effect, p. 313
6 Uncomfortable Feelings pp. 314–316	1 class period	• Define boredom, anger, loneliness, grief, and shyness, and identify possible sources of these feelings. • Learn effective strategies for coping with uncomfortable feelings.	**Compare and Contrast** p. 316 • Main Idea and Details, p. 314 • Summarize, p. 316
Activities p. 317		• Extend chapter concepts.	
Chapter Review pp. 318–319	1 class period	• Assess chapter objectives.	

Vocabulary	Program Resources
	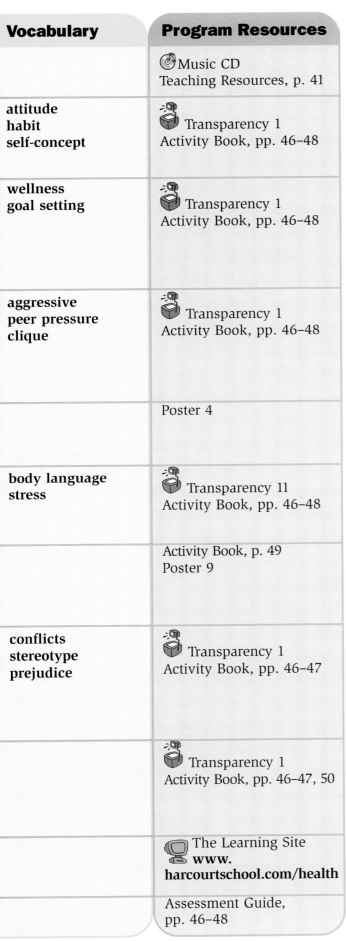 Music CD Teaching Resources, p. 41
attitude habit self-concept	Transparency 1 Activity Book, pp. 46–48
wellness goal setting	Transparency 1 Activity Book, pp. 46–48
aggressive peer pressure clique	Transparency 1 Activity Book, pp. 46–48
	Poster 4
body language stress	Transparency 11 Activity Book, pp. 46–48
	Activity Book, p. 49 Poster 9
conflicts stereotype prejudice	Transparency 1 Activity Book, pp. 46–47
	Transparency 1 Activity Book, pp. 46–47, 50
	The Learning Site **www.** **harcourtschool.com/health**
	Assessment Guide, pp. 46–48

Interactive Transparencies available on CD-ROM.

Focus Skill — Reading Skill

These reading skills are reinforced throughout this chapter and one skill is emphasized as the Focus Skill.

Compare and Contrast

- Draw Conclusions
- Identify Cause and Effect
- Identify Main Idea and Details
- Sequence
- Summarize

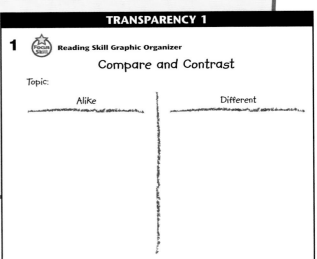

TRANSPARENCY 1

1 **Focus Skill** Reading Skill Graphic Organizer
Compare and Contrast

Topic:

Alike	Different

Life Skills

Life Skills are health-enhancing behaviors that can help students reduce risks to their health and safety.

Six Life Skills are reinforced throughout *Harcourt Health and Fitness.* The skill emphasized in this chapter is Manage Stress.

POSTER 9

Manage Stress

The girl is visualizing herself making new friends.

Ways to Manage Stress

1 Know what stress feels like and what causes it.
2 Do something active to make yourself feel better.
3 Talk with someone you trust about the way you are feeling.
4 Visualize yourself doing well in a stressful situation.

How have **YOU** **MANAGED STRESS** today?

Building Good Character

Character education is an important aspect of health education. When students behave in ways that show good character, they promote the health and safety of themselves and others.

Six character traits are reinforced throughout *Harcourt Health and Fitness.* The trait emphasized in this chapter is Respect.

POSTER 4

Respect

The children are showing respect by sharing their different interests.

DO
- Treat others the way you want to be treated.
- Accept people who are different from you.
- Be polite and use good manners.
- Be considerate of the feelings of others.
- Stay calm when you are angry.
- Develop self-respect and self-confidence.

DON'T
- Don't use bad language.
- Don't insult or embarrass anyone.
- Don't threaten or bully anyone.
- Don't hit or hurt anyone.

How have **YOU** shown **RESPECT** today?

Coordinated School Health Program

A Coordinated School Health Program endeavors to improve children's health and, therefore, their capacity to learn through the support of families, schools, and communities working together. The following information is provided to help classroom teachers be more aware of these resources.

Books for Students

Moser, Adolph. ***Don't Feed the Monster on Tuesdays! The Children's Self-Esteem Book.*** Landmark Editions, 1991. Looks at self-esteem and positive attitudes. **EASY**

Romain, Trevor, and Elizabeth Verdick. ***Stress Can Really Get on Your Nerves!*** Free Spirit Publishing, 2000. Explains stress and solutions to it. **AVERAGE**

Sneddon, Pamela Shires. ***Body Image: A Reality Check.*** Enslow Publishers, 1999. Discusses society's influence on self-perception and self-acceptance. **ADVANCED**

Books for Teachers and Families

Schrumpf, Fred, Donna K. Crawford, and Richard J. Bodine. ***Peer Mediation: Conflict Resolution in Schools.*** Research Press, 1997. The six steps of mediation are clearly spelled out.

Schmitt, Barton D. ***Your Child's Health:***

The National Center for Chronic Disease and Health Promotion, part of the **CDC,** funds the Coordinated School Health Program. Visit its website for information about the eight components that make up this program. **www.cdc.gov/nccdphp/dash/**

The **American Red Cross** provides information to help families prepare for any type of disaster. *How Do I Deal With My Feelings?* (available in sixteen languages) explains how to deal with feelings of loss and anger, and gives tips on how to recover from traumas or disasters such as terrorism. **www.redcross.org/**

The **CDC** monitors statistics on a state-by-state basis on topics such as the Youth Risk Behavior Surveillance

Media Resources

The Parent's Guide to Symptoms, Emergencies, Common Illnesses, Behavior and School Problems. Bantam, 1999. An excellent guide on topics from birth through adolescence.

Free and Inexpensive Materials

Federal Citizen Information Center Receive free express e-mail on the FirstGov for Kids site. This informative government site has a wide range of topics on its KidsHealth page that deals with topics such as feelings and related emotional and social issues. Also has information about social groups such as the National 4-H web page.

LifeSkills4kids Has free health lesson plans and a free *Life Skills* newsletter for teachers and parents—topics are on life skills and character education.

To access free and inexpensive resources on the Web, visit **www.harcourtschool.com/health/free**

System (YRBSS). **www.cdc.gov/nccdphp/dash/state_info/**

The National Association of State Boards of Education **(NASBE),** the founder of *Character Counts!,* reviews the history of character education and its place in public schools and is featured in the publication, *Fit, Healthy, and Ready to Learn! A School Health Policy Guide.* **www.nasbe.org/**

Other resources that support a Coordinated School Health Program:
- School-Home Connection
- Daily Physical Activity
- Daily Fitness Tips
- Activities: Home & Community
- Health Background: Webliography
- *Be Active! Resources for Physical Education*

Videos

Understanding, Controlling and Preventing Anger, Parts 1 and 2. Rainbow Educational Media, 1997.

Too Much to Handle: Living with Stress. Rainbow Educational Video, 1993.

Everybody Wants to Be Popular. Rainbow Educational Media, 1993.

These resources have been selected to meet a variety of individual needs. Please review all materials and websites prior to sharing them with students to ensure the content is appropriate for your class. Note that information, while correct at time of publication, is subject to change.

Visit **The Learning Site** for related links, activities, resources, and the health **Webliography.**

www.harcourtschool.com/health

Meeting Individual Needs

ESL/ELL

Below-Level

Before reading a section of the text, ask students to think about how the topic relates to them personally. Have students write their responses in their health journals and include what they hope to learn about the topic. Remind students that their journals are private.

Activities
- Accept Compliments, p. 292
- Identifying Actions, p. 300
- Exercise Stress Away, p. 306
- Make Posters, p. 311

On-Level

Students can increase their understanding by asking questions during reading. Point out the questions at the end of each section. Explain that good readers ask themselves *who*, *what*, *when*, *where*, or *why* questions as they read. Have students pause during reading to ask questions.

Activities
- Gather Quotes, p. 292
- Use Positive Peer Pressures, p. 300
- Control Stress, p. 306
- Act Out a Conflict, p. 311

Challenge

Have students explore their perspectives on a health-related topic, such as the importance of exercise. Have them write seven descriptive words, each on a puzzle piece, about the topic. They can then exchange puzzles with a partner, solve them, and compare ideas.

Activities
- Share Heroes, p. 292
- Model Listening, p. 300
- Chart Stress, p. 306
- Research Conflicts, p. 311

Learning Log

After reading a section of the text, have students think of two questions to ask a volunteer seated in the "answer chair." Students take turns asking the questions. When the student in the "answer chair" has answered two questions correctly, another student can take a turn.

Activities
- Background and Experience, pp. 296, 303
- Language and Vocabulary, p. 302
- Comprehensible Input, p. 314

Curriculum Integration

 Integrated Language Arts/Reading Skills
- Building Castles, p. 295
- Friendship Cinquain, p. 299
- Acrostics and Concrete Poetry, p. 315

 Math
- Make a Laugh Graph, p. 293
- Using Different Graphs, p. 313

 Physical Education
- Daily Fitness Tip, pp. 290, 294, 298, 304, 310, 314
- Daily Physical Activity, p. 289
- Stress, Injuries, and Disease, p. 308

Use these topics to integrate health into your daily planning.

 Science
- Writing a Hypothesis, p. 297
- Newton Was Right!, p. 304

 Social Studies
- Needs Around the World, p. 294
- Saying *No*, p. 301
- Common Ground, p. 310

 Art
- Image of Friendship, p. 298

CHAPTER SUMMARY

In this chapter students
► analyze how positive thinking and goal setting help establish a healthy and realistic self-concept.
► discuss effective ways to express feelings and to form and maintain positive friendships.
► learn and practice effective strategies for managing stress, dealing with feelings, and resolving conflicts.

Life Skills
Students practice *managing stress at school*.

Building Good Character
Students learn that accepting individual differences is a way to show *respect*.

Consumer Health
Students *analyze* advertisements.

Literature Springboard

Use the article "Dealing with Diversity" to spark interest in the chapter topic. See the Read-Aloud Anthology on page RA-11 of this *Teacher Edition*.

Prereading Strategies

SCAN THE CHAPTER Have students preview the chapter content by scanning the titles, headings, pictures, graphs, and tables. Ask volunteers to predict what they will learn.

PREVIEW VOCABULARY As students scan the chapter, invite them to sort the vocabulary into three groups.

Words I Know	Words I've Seen or Heard	New Words

Reading Skill
Focus Skill

COMPARE AND CONTRAST To introduce or review this skill, have students use the Reading in Health Handbook, pp. 372–383. Teaching strategies and additional activities are also provided.

Students will have opportunities to practice and apply this skill throughout this chapter.

• Focus Skill Reading Mini-Lesson, p. 290
• Reading comprehension questions identified with the
• *Activity Book* p. 48 (shown on p. 293)
• Lesson Summary and Review, pp. 293, 297, 302, 307, 313, 316
• Chapter Review and Test Preparation, pp. 318–319

Reading Skill

COMPARE AND CONTRAST When you compare things, you tell how they are alike. When you contrast things, you tell how they are different. Use the Reading in Health Handbook on pages 372–383 and this graphic organizer to help you read the health facts in this chapter.

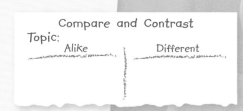

Compare and Contrast
Topic:
Alike   Different

Health Graph

INTERPRET DATA Not everyone has the same feelings in the same situation. Students in one class wrote on slips of paper how they feel about going to school. Then the students made a graph of their feelings. How many of the students have positive feelings about going to school?

Feelings About Going to School

Number of Students / Feeling

Excited Happy Unsure Nervous

Daily Physical Activity

Knowing when and how to relieve stress can help keep you healthy. Getting some physical activity every day can help with stress, too.

 Be Active!
Use the selection, **Super Stess Buster**, to relax you and give your mood a boost.

289

School-Home Connection

Distribute copies of the School-Home Connection (in English or Spanish). Have students take the page home to share with their families as you begin this chapter.

Follow Up Have volunteers share the results of their activities.

 Supports the Coordinated School Health Program

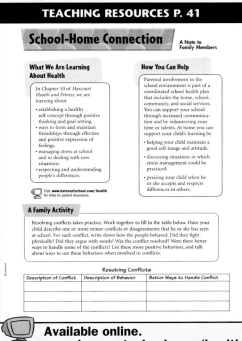

TEACHING RESOURCES P. 41

School-Home Connection — A Note to Family Members

What We Are Learning About Health

In Chapter 10 of *Harcourt Health and Fitness,* we are learning about
• establishing a healthy self-concept through positive thinking and goal setting.
• ways to form and maintain friendships through effective and positive expression of feelings.
• managing stress at school and in dealing with new situations.
• respecting and understanding people's differences.

How You Can Help

Parental involvement in the school environment is part of a coordinated school health plan that includes the home, school, community, and social services. You can support your school through increased communication and by volunteering your time or talents. At home you can support your child's learning by
• helping your child maintain a good self-image and attitude.
• discussing situations in which stress management could be practiced.
• praising your child when he or she accepts and respects differences in others.

Visit www.harcourtschool.com/health for links to parent resources.

A Family Activity

Resolving conflicts takes practice. Work together to fill in the table below. Have your child describe one or more minor conflicts or disagreements that he or she has seen at school. For each conflict, write down how the people behaved. Did they fight physically? Did they argue with words? Was the conflict resolved? Were there better ways to handle some of the conflicts? List these more positive behaviors, and talk about ways to use these behaviors when involved in conflicts.

Resolving Conflicts

Description of Conflict	Description of Behavior	Better Ways to Handle Conflict

**Available online.
www.harcourtschool.com/health**

Health Graph

Interpret Data

Invite volunteers to explain what the graph shows.

How many of these students have positive feelings about coming to school? 20

How do you think this group compares with our class? Students may think the students represented on this graph feel more enthusiastic or less enthusiastic about school than their own classmates.

What are some other feelings that students might have about coming to school? Possible answers: contentment, determination, anger, embarrassment, fright

Daily Physical Activity

Use *Be Active! Music for Daily Physical Activity* with the Instant Activity Cards to provide students with movement activities that can be done in limited space. Options for using these components are provided beginning on page TR2 in this *Teacher Edition.*

Chapter Project

Something to Laugh About (*Assessment Guide* p. 60)

ASSESS PRIOR KNOWLEDGE Use students' initial ideas for the project as a baseline assessment of their understanding of chapter concepts. Have students complete the project as they work through the chapter.

PERFORMANCE ASSESSMENT The project can be used for performance assessment. Use the Project Evaluation Sheet (rubric), *Assessment Guide* p. 71.

Objectives

► Recognize that each person shapes his or her own self-concept.

► Realize that a positive self-concept helps a person make healthful decisions.

When Minutes Count . . .

Assign the Quick Study, Lesson 1, Activity Book pp. 46–47 (shown on p. 291).

Program Resources

► Activity Book pp. 46–48

► Transparency 1

Vocabulary

attitude p. 290, **habit** p. 290, **self-concept** p. 290

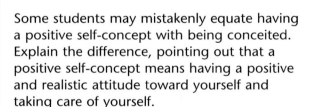

Daily Fitness Tip

Some students may mistakenly equate having a positive self-concept with being conceited. Explain the difference, pointing out that a positive self-concept means having a positive and realistic attitude toward yourself and taking care of yourself.

 For more guidelines on principles of good posture, see *Be Active! Resources for Physical Education*, p. 145.

1. MOTIVATE

Remind students that in science, things are always described objectively, without making judgments. Ask students to use twenty words to write objective descriptions of themselves—physical, emotional, social, and mental. For example, they might describe themselves as having brown hair, being thoughtful, and being good at math.

Would someone else use different adjectives to describe you? Why or why not? Possible answers: Someone else might notice different things or be more positive.

Was it difficult to be objective about yourself? Why or why not? Possible answer: Yes, because I tend to be critical of myself and focus on my faults.

Your Self-Concept

Lesson Focus

Your attitude toward yourself plays a big part in how you act every day.

Why Learn This?

A healthy self-concept—a positive attitude toward yourself—helps you enjoy life and do your best.

Vocabulary

attitude
habit
self-concept

Think Positively

You probably know people who always seem to be in a good mood. These people enjoy life. They have a good **attitude**, or feeling, toward themselves and toward life in general. In this lesson you will learn ways to strengthen or develop a good attitude.

First, remember that you are in charge of your thoughts. You are a powerful person. You can use this power to make healthful choices about how you think.

Each person tends to develop a habit of thinking positively or negatively about things. A **habit** is something you do again and again without thinking about it. If you have a habit of thinking positively about yourself, you will probably have a good self-concept. If you think negatively about yourself, you may have a poor self-concept. Your **self-concept** is how you see yourself *most* of the time.

I've become a good bike rider!

290

Reading Skill

Mini-Lesson

COMPARE AND CONTRAST
When you compare, you tell how things are alike. When you contrast, you tell how they are different. Have students practice this skill by responding to the Focus Skill question on page 291. Have students draw and complete the graphic organizer as you model it on the transparency.

TRANSPARENCY 1

1 Reading Skill Graphic Organizer

Compare and Contrast

Topic: Positive and negative self-concept

Alike	Different
They are both ways to think about yourself.	A positive self-concept means you think well of yourself.
	A negative self-concept means you think poorly of yourself.

Interactive Transparencies available on CD-ROM.

I know how to play the saxophone.

Quick Activity

Make a List Draw yourself doing something you are good at and like to do. Then make a list that includes six positive qualities of yourself. Relate these qualities to things you do a lot.

I have a good sense of humor.

As you begin to think about yourself positively, you might find ways to help your family and friends. You might want to do your best on your homework and to get higher grades on tests!

As your self-concept becomes more positive, you might decide to try something new. Maybe you will try out for a team, for the school band, or for a school play. Maybe you will learn a new skill or take up a new hobby. You might develop the courage to make some important changes in your life. Maybe you will get more exercise or eat more healthful meals.

As you make such changes, your self-concept gets even better. You become proud of yourself. You also enjoy life and the people around you. And they, in turn, enjoy being around you.

 COMPARE AND CONTRAST How are a positive self-concept and a negative self-concept alike? How are they different?

Alike: Both are our pictures of ourselves, or what we think of ourselves most of the time. Different: A positive self-concept can help us do our best, but a negative one can keep us from doing things we might be able to do.

291

2. TEACH

Interpret Visuals—Pictures

Have students study the pictures on these pages. Ask why they think these images were chosen to begin a lesson on self-concept. The pictures show young people doing things that can help build their self-concept.

Describe some other images that could have been used on these pages. any pictures of young people showing skills that help strengthen their concept of themselves as valuable, competent people

Content-Area Reading Support

Using Typographic Clues Have students locate the words on page 290 that are highlighted in yellow. Point out that each highlighted word is a vocabulary term and is followed by its definition. Advise students to pay special attention to highlighted terms and their definitions since they will need to know and understand them.

Discuss

Problem Solving How could you help someone else build a positive self-concept? Possible answers: help the person recognize things he or she does well; do not be critical; encourage him or her to learn new skills

Problem Solving How could you turn negative thoughts about yourself into positive ones? Possible answers: I can focus on what I can do, not on my weaknesses; I can strengthen a weak area by practicing or learning a new skill.

Quick Activity

Students might incorporate some of the twenty adjectives they used to describe themselves at the beginning of this lesson. Monitor students as they complete this activity, and discreetly help any who have trouble thinking of six positive qualities.

QUICK STUDY, ACTIVITY BOOK PP. 46–47

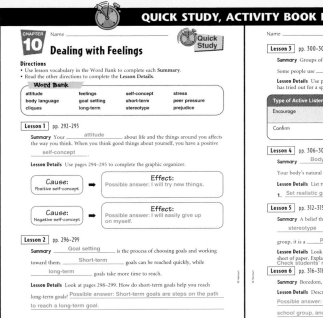

Available online.
www.harcourtschool.com/health

Discuss

Critical Thinking Why do people sometimes treat others better than they treat themselves? They feel that they do not deserve to be treated well.

Problem Solving What can you do if you realize you are treating yourself badly? Possible answers: Focus on my strengths; remember that I am a unique person who has many skills and positive qualities.

Problem Solving What are some things young people can do if their positive attitude is slipping? Possible answers: tell someone, especially a parent or another trusted adult, how they feel; do something nice for others, which will help young people feel appreciated, needed, and competent

Consumer Activity

Discuss students' analyses. Help them recognize the ways the media influence how young people—and adults—see themselves. Explore ways consumers might affect advertising, such as by writing to sponsors and by boycotting unhealthful products.

Health Background

Thinning Trend Since WWII, women in the media have been getting thinner. This trend has greatly affected American children, who watch 20,000 to 40,000 TV commercials a year. Many commercials focus on beauty and appearance, leading even children to become dissatisfied with their bodies. In a study of 9- and 10-year-old girls, 40 percent have tried to lose weight. The more young girls are exposed to media, including movies and music videos, the more unhappy they tend to be with their bodies.

Sources: *National Institute on Media and the Family, Children Now, Teen Health and the Media*

 For more background, visit the **Webliography** in Teacher Resources at **www.harcourtschool.com/health Keyword** eating disorders

---

Maintain a Positive Attitude

Cars need tuneups to keep them running smoothly. A regular "tuneup" can also help you keep a positive attitude toward yourself. As part of your tuneup, ask yourself these questions:

- Am I treating my friends better than I treat myself? Do I forgive them more easily than I forgive myself? Do I stand by them but give up on myself?

Don't be your own enemy! Forgive yourself for mistakes and stand by yourself, no matter what.

- Do I remember that no one is perfect? Making mistakes does not make me a failure. If I am trying new things and learning new skills, I will make mistakes.

Don't worry about your mistakes. Mistakes are part of living. Laugh at them!

- Am I sharing my thoughts and feelings with people who care about me? These people could include my parents, other relatives, a teacher, or close friends.

Treat yourself as well as you treat your friends. ▼

292

Meeting Individual Needs
Leveled Activities

BELOW-LEVEL **Accept Compliments** Help students learn ways to accept compliments graciously. Have them write scripts that show different ways to be courteous when someone says nice things about them.

ON-LEVEL **Gather Quotes** Ask students to find quotations about being positive, taking care of oneself, or having a strong self-concept. For example, Will Rogers said, "Don't let yesterday use up too much of today." Have students share their favorite quotations.

CHALLENGE **Share Heroes** Have students write one-page reports about a person they think is an excellent role model. This person might be living or deceased and may be someone they know or have only read about. Have them post their reports for others to read.

You can also share your thoughts by talking to yourself. When you say out loud what is bothering you, it might be easier to identify the real problem.

- Do I remember that each person is unique, or different from others? If I am quieter or more outgoing than my friends, do I think, "This is me! I am the way I am."

When you have a positive self-concept and treat yourself well, it's easy to be unique.

CAUSE AND EFFECT What might be one effect of giving your self-concept a tuneup?

Possibel answer: You might treat yourself better.

Being willing to try new things is one of the outcomes of a positive self-concept. ▶

Lesson 1 Summary and Review

❶ Summarize with Vocabulary

Use vocabulary from this lesson to complete the statements.

Your _____ toward life influences how you think about yourself. A person's way of looking at life is an example of a _____. If you look at yourself in a positive way, you will develop a positive _____.

❷ What shapes your self-concept?

❸ Critical Thinking How can laughing at yourself help you maintain a positive self-concept?

❹ (Focus Skill) **COMPARE AND CONTRAST** Draw and complete this graphic organizer to show how a student with a positive attitude and a student with a negative attitude prepare for a test.

Topic:
| Alike | Different |

❺ Write to Express—Business Letter

Write a business letter to the owners of a company, asking them to use "real" people instead of "perfect" people in ads.

293

Math

Make a Laugh Graph Have students construct a bar graph to keep track of how often they laugh at their own mistakes. Instruct them to make a column on the graph for each day of the week. Encourage them to keep their graphs in their notebooks so they can quickly mark each time they laugh at themselves. At the end of the week, ask students to review their graphs and write a paragraph about what they have learned about themselves.

ACTIVITY BOOK P. 48

Name _____

(Focus Skill) **Reading Skill**

Compare and Contrast

Self-Concept

Mrs. Stokes assigns each of her students the name of a former President and gives students two weeks to prepare an oral report to present to the class. During the school day, she allows students to work on their reports in their free time. She has also blocked out time to meet with students who would like to practice their oral reports one-on-one before presenting them to the class.

José is assigned President Grover Cleveland. José has not studied anything about President Cleveland before, but he thinks that it will be fun to learn about someone new. He takes some of his free time each day to work on his project and has a rough draft completed by the end of the first week. He then practices his oral report with Mrs. Stokes. She thinks he has a good start, but she suggests some changes. José then spends more free time during the second week revising his presentation. When it is José's turn to present his report, he feels confident and ready to go.

Maggie is assigned President Woodrow Wilson. When she learns that, she thinks the project will be impossible because she has not even heard of him. During her free time, she doodles on her notebook and complains to her friends that the project is too hard. Finally, at the end of the week, she looks up some information about President Wilson and writes it down. When Mrs. Stokes looks at her notes, she offers Maggie some ideas of where to look for more information. Maggie thinks Mrs. Stokes is unhappy with her efforts and gives up. When it is Maggie's turn to give her report, she feels extremely nervous walking up to the front of the room.

Using the graphic organizer, fill in the things that are alike and different about these two students—one with a positive self-concept and one with a negative self-concept.

Alike	Different
• Both have to give an oral report.	• José thinks it will be fun, while Maggie thinks it will be too difficult.
• Both students have topics that are new to them.	• José takes feedback in a positive way, while Maggie takes it as criticism.
• Both students talk to the teacher about their report.	• José is ready to give his report, while Maggie is unprepared.

Available online.
www.harcourtschool.com/health

3. WRAP UP

Lesson 1 Summary and Review

1. attitude; habit; self-concept
2. Your attitude toward life and your thoughts and feelings about yourself shape your self-concept.
3. Laughing at your mistakes can help you not be upset about them. It may also release your tension and help you find ways to correct the mistakes.
4. Examples may include:

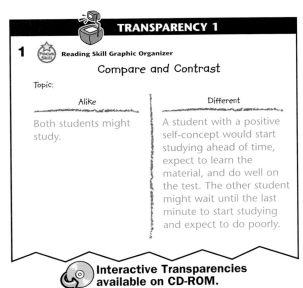

TRANSPARENCY 1

1 (Focus Skill) **Reading Skill Graphic Organizer**

Compare and Contrast

Topic:

Alike	Different
Both students might study.	A student with a positive self-concept would start studying ahead of time, expect to learn the material, and do well on the test. The other student might wait until the last minute to start studying and expect to do poorly.

Interactive Transparencies available on CD-ROM.

5. Students' letters should clearly express their opinions. They might explain that using very attractive and thin people in ads provides unrealistic role models for young people. Their letters should also include a heading, inside address, salutation, body, closing, and signature.

For **writing models** with examples, see *Teaching Resources* pp. 47–61. Rubrics are also provided.

When Minutes Count . . .

Quick Study Students can use *Activity Book* pp. 46–47 (shown on p. 291) as they complete each lesson in this chapter.

Objectives

► Distinguish between needs and wants.

► Identify practical strategies for setting and achieving short-term and long-term goals.

► Identify sources of help in setting and working toward goals.

When Minutes Count . . .

Assign the Quick Study, Lesson 2, Activity Book pp. 46–47 (shown on p. 291).

Program Resources

► Activity Book pp. 46–47

► Transparency 1

Vocabulary

wellness p. 294, **goal setting** p. 295

Daily Fitness Tip

Basic human needs are shelter, food, water, love, security, and acceptance. If one of these things is missing, a person may become physically, emotionally, or mentally ill. Reinforce the idea that love, security, and acceptance are as important to wellness as shelter, food, and water are.

 For more guidelines on continuing to try, see *Be Active! Resources for Physical Education*, p. 179.

1. MOTIVATE

Ask students if they remember saying this rhyme when they were younger:

Star light, star bright,
First star I see tonight,
I wish I may, I wish I might
Have the wish I wish tonight.

Invite students to offer examples of wishes that young children sometimes make. Possible examples: to have a pony, a million dollars, a brother/sister; to be a star athlete Point out that as people grow older, they stop making wishes. Instead, they set goals and work toward achieving those goals. Emphasize that this lesson will help students learn to set and work toward their own goals.

Setting Goals

Needs and Wants

Lesson Focus

To get things you want, take responsibility for yourself by setting and working toward goals.

Why Learn This?

When you know how to set goals, you can make good things happen in your life.

Vocabulary

wellness
goal setting

We all have the same physical *needs*: shelter, food, water, air. To stay alive, we must meet these needs. We also have emotional needs, including love, security, and a place to belong and to be accepted.

For most people, physical and emotional needs are met within the family. When our physical and emotional needs are met, we feel good. We have **wellness**, a state of good health.

In addition to needs, we have *wants*. These are the things we would like to have but do not need to stay alive. For example, we *need* food, but we might *want* pizza with all the toppings.

We sometimes confuse wants with needs. We think we need something, but we really only want it. It's not wrong to want things. If our wants are important to us, we can set goals and work toward reaching them.

SUMMARIZE How can you tell the difference between a need and a want?

Something you must have to stay alive is a need. Something you would like to have but can live without is a want.

Needs and Wants

Needs	Wants

Quick Activity

Needs and Wants As the table shows, people's needs include food and clothing. Make lists of the foods you like and want to eat and the clothing you want to wear. List any other wants for the needs you have.

294

Teacher Tip

Unmet Needs As you discuss physical and emotional needs that are usually met by families, remember that this is not true for all children. Even children from well-to-do families may have unmet needs.

Be sensitive to the individual situation of each student by not requiring everyone to participate in discussions and not implying that all families meet all their children's needs.

 Social Studies

Needs Around the World Encourage small groups of students to choose different countries in developing regions of the world and find out whether people's basic needs are being met there. For example, is there enough food and clean water for everyone? Can families stay together, or must some people travel or live far away to find work to support their families? Students should also find out about any organizations that are trying to help these people meet their basic needs.

Set Goals

When you were younger, you probably wished for the things you wanted, such as a special present for your birthday. Now that you are older, you are more responsible for what happens in your life. You can still wish for things, but now you can set goals and try to make those wishes come true. **Goal setting** is the process of choosing goals and working toward them.

You can set goals to make many kinds of positive changes in your life, but you should choose your goals carefully. If you set a goal that is unrealistic, you may not be able to reach it. Then you might decide that setting goals is a waste of time. Your goals should be

- realistic and within your abilities.
- important to you—things you really want to do.
- things you can do yourself, not things that depend on someone else's actions. You can ask for help, but you should be the one working toward your goals.

DRAW CONCLUSIONS **What is likely to happen if you choose a goal that's not very important to you?**

ACTIVITY

Life Skills

Set Goals Set a goal you would like to reach within one week. Make sure it's realistic, important to you, and something you can achieve by yourself. After one week, decide whether you have reached your goal.

You are likely to lose interest in reaching this goal and may quit working toward it.

◀ Kaley has a goal of being a member of her school's jazz group.

295

Integrated Language Arts/ Reading Skills

Building Castles Tell students that author Henry David Thoreau once wrote, "If you have built castles in the air, your work need not be lost; that is where they should be. Now put the foundations under them." Ask what students think Thoreau meant by building castles in the air. dreaming, wishing

---

Teacher Tip

Have students explain the importance of having a parent or trusted adult help them set some long-range goals. Be sure they understand that it is hard to set goals for the future with the limited experiences they have. This is where the guidance of a parent or another trusted adult becomes important.

---

2. TEACH

Interpret Visuals—Table
Have students suggest ways to complete the table on page 294.

Content-Area Reading Support
Using Text Format Draw students' attention to the bulleted list at the bottom of this page. Explain that these ideas could have been included in a paragraph but that they were presented in a bulleted list to bring more attention to them. Remind students to read bulleted lists carefully because they often contain important information.

Discuss
Critical Thinking **What are some things about people that cannot be changed?** Possible examples: height, eye color, certain other aspects of appearance

What are some things about people that can be changed? Possible examples: how they relate to friends and family members; interests; skills; attitudes

Problem Solving **What might happen if you set a long-range goal without the guidance of a parent or other trusted adult?** Possible answers: You might become discouraged and unhappy; you might set unrealistic goals.

Activity
Set Goals Have students describe the benefits of setting short-term goals. Students might begin by brainstorming possible goals that can be met within one week. Examples might include finishing all math homework assignments, practicing a musical instrument for 20 minutes each day, reading a certain book, and learning a certain athletic skill. Then have students describe the benefits of implementing short-term goals.

Interpret Visuals—Pictures

Point out the picture and caption about Kaley's goal of being in her school's jazz band. Discuss which steps toward her goal are listed on this page. practicing; taking lessons **What other steps might she take to reach her goal?** Possible answers: learning to play songs that the jazz band plays; talking to the band's director to find out more about the requirements to join the band

Discuss

Have students explain the importance of perseverence to achieve goals. Point out that the goal of finishing a book report by Friday can be broken down into even shorter goals, such as reading the book by Tuesday and writing a first draft of the report by Wednesday.

What are some examples of unrealistic goals? Possible answers: trying to change something that cannot be changed, such as height; trying to do something that takes extraordinary skills, such as becoming an NBA star; trying to do something too quickly, such as learning how to play the piano in one week; trying to learn something you are not old enough to learn

Why might someone set an unrealistic goal? Possible answers: the person has not received any guidance from a parent or other trusted adult; the person doesn't really want to reach the goal and wants an excuse; the person is feeling pressure from peers or from himself or herself to be outstanding

If you do not reach your goal, what should you do? Possible answers: determine whether it was a realistic goal for you; think about other ways you might reach it; ask for help from a trusted adult

Discuss

Have students describe the benefits in setting and implementing short-term goals.

Reaching a Goal

When you say, "I'm going to finish my book report by Friday," you are setting a *short-term* goal. When you say, "I plan to be a teacher," you are setting a *long-term goal*. You don't have to set goals by yourself. You can ask parents, other family members, teachers, religious leaders, and counselors to help you.

After setting a goal, think about what you need to do to reach it. You might break down a long-term goal into several short-term goals. Write down the short-term goals you decide on, and list them in the order you will tackle them. Then set a deadline for each one. This will serve as a guide to help you reach your final goal. As you work toward your goal, check your progress. Do you need to change a short-term goal or even your final goal?

▲ One step toward Kaley's goal is practicing every day.

Did You Know?

Animal horns and conch shells were the world's first trumpets. The ancient Egyptians made silver and bronze trumpets with long, straight tubes. In today's American elementary and middle schools, more students are involved in music than any other activity except sports.

Another step toward Kaley's goal is taking trumpet lessons.

296

 ESL/ELL Support

BACKGROUND AND EXPERIENCE Invite students to discuss goals they or someone they know has set and worked toward. However, caution students not to share information that might embarrass themselves or someone else.

Beginning Pantomime scoring points in soccer, football, or another sport to help students understand that a goal is something you want to reach.

Intermediate Help students choose a realistic goal for themselves, and then ask them to explain or act out how they would work toward reaching it. Write the steps they suggest on the board.

Advanced Ask students to compare two goals—one realistic and one unrealistic. Encourage partners to create skits that illustrate the difference between the goals.

After you reach your goal, feel proud of yourself! Then review your experience. Did this goal turn out to be a good one for you? Will you do anything differently next time? Use what you have learned when you set your next goal.

SEQUENCE What are the steps in goal setting?
Possible steps: Choose a goal carefully; break it down into short-term goals and set a deadline for each one; check your progress; evaluate the experience.

◀ Kaley has reached her goal! For her it was worth all the hard work.

Lesson 2 Summary and Review

❶ **Summarize with Vocabulary**

Use vocabulary and other terms from this lesson to complete the statements.

You must meet your basic _____ in order to have good health, or _____. Your _____ are things you would like to have. _____ is a way to get the things you would like to have. Learning how to shoot baskets is a _____ goal. Becoming a professional athlete is a _____ goal.

❷ How can reaching short-term goals help you reach a long-term goal?

❸ **Critical Thinking** Why should you choose a goal that depends on your own actions and not on the actions of others?

❹ (Focus Skill) **COMPARE AND CONTRAST** Draw and complete this graphic organizer to show how these two goals are alike and different.

Goal 1: Win a gold medal in swimming.

Goal 2: Take 5 seconds off my best time.

Topic:
Alike   Different

❺ **Writing to Entertain—Short Story**
Write a short story about someone who set a goal and how he or she reached it.

297

Personal Health Plan ▶

Real-Life Situation
Getting in physical shape is a good goal to set. Suppose you want to play soccer this year.
Real-Life Plan
Choose a physical fitness goal that you think you can reach within one month. Then plan steps for meeting that goal.

Personal Health Plan ▶

Each student's plan should include:
- a clear and realistic fitness goal.
- realistic steps that should allow him or her to reach the goal.

This feature is designed to provide students with an opportunity to reflect on health decisions they are making in their personal lives. The Personal Health Plan should not be used to evaluate or assess students, nor should the results be shared among students.

3. WRAP UP

Lesson 2 Summary and Review

1. needs, wellness; wants, Goal setting; short-term; long-term
2. Short-term goals can help you break a long-term goal into steps.
3. If your goal depends on someone else, you cannot control whether you reach it.
4. Examples may include:

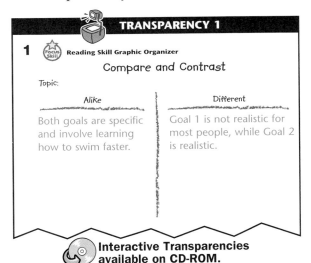

TRANSPARENCY 1

1 (Focus Skill) **Reading Skill Graphic Organizer**
Compare and Contrast

Topic:

Alike   Different

Both goals are specific and involve learning how to swim faster.

Goal 1 is not realistic for most people, while Goal 2 is realistic.

Interactive Transparencies available on CD-ROM.

5. The main character in students' stories should set a goal that is realistic, important to him or her, and dependent on the character's actions. The character should then make a plan for reaching the goal and carry it out.

For **writing models** with examples, see *Teaching Resources* pp. 47–61. Rubrics are also provided.

Science

Writing a Hypothesis Tell or remind students how scientists solve problems. First, they state the problems and gather information. Next, they write hypotheses—predictions that can be tested. Then they set up experiments that test the hypotheses. They analyze the results to see if they support the hypotheses. If not, they revise the hypotheses and test them again. Scientists' goals are to prove or disprove hypotheses. Scientists' plans are experiments that test hypotheses.

Teacher Tip

Sharing Learning Goals Research has shown that students absorb more and perform better when teachers share the learning objectives with them. When students understand what is expected of them, they are better able to focus their attention, stay on task, and understand and remember new concepts. Sharing a limited number (not a long list) of specific objectives at the beginning of a lesson, chapter, or unit helps students set learning goals.

Pages 298–302

► Identify strategies for making and keeping friends.
► Explain how to deal with peer pressure.
► Practice communication skills.
► Distinguish between healthy and unhealthy relationships.

 When Minutes Count . . .

Assign the Quick Study, Lesson 3, Activity Book pp. 46–47 (shown on p. 291).

Program Resources

► Activity Book pp. 46–47
► Transparency 1

Vocabulary

aggressive p. 299,

peer pressure p. 300, **clique** p. 302

Daily Fitness Tip

It is often difficult to stand up to what is right when faced with peer pressure. Remind students that true friends will not pressure them to do things that are unsafe or against the rules.

 For more guidelines on playing by the rules, see *Be Active! Resources for Physical Education.*

1. MOTIVATE

Ask students to look through the textbook to identify a picture of someone they would like to have as a friend. Invite volunteers to share their choices and explain why they chose that picture. Then ask students how they would go about becoming friends with this person.

Quick Activity

Ask students to review what they have written. Have students discuss whether acceptable methods for gaining attention from a friend are the same as acceptable methods for a friend gaining attention from them.

Your Actions Affect Others

When you were very young, you may have learned that to have a friend, you need to be a friend. No matter how old we are, this advice still works.

We all try to treat our friends well, but sometimes we hurt their feelings. Suppose you want to walk home with a new student in class instead of your old friends. How can you avoid hurting your friends' feelings? Think about how you would feel if your friends did something without you. You might feel hurt and left out, the same way your friends might feel. By thinking ahead, you can make sure your actions and words strengthen your friendships.

Lesson Focus

To be a good friend, you must pay attention to how you affect your friends and how they affect you.

Why Learn This?

As you learn more about yourself, you will be better able to make and keep friends.

Vocabulary

aggressive
peer pressure
clique

Being a friend means being aware of others' feelings. ▼

Quick Activity

Write a Letter During class one of your friends talks out loud—trying to be the center of attention. Write a note to this friend, explaining why his or her method for getting attention is not acceptable.

298

Teacher Tip

New Students Students who are new to the school or who have difficulty making friends might hesitate to share their feelings about friendship. Protect their privacy and self-respect during these discussions by calling on volunteers only. At the same time, encourage the class to help everyone feel like part of the group.

 ### Art

Image of Friendship Challenge students to use any available art media to create an image of friendship. This image, however, should not include written words or pictures of people. Students may use chalk, charcoal, watercolors, pieces of torn paper, clay, found objects, or any other medium.

Friends' actions affect us in many ways. Friends make us laugh, listen to our thoughts and feelings, and help us feel accepted. Sometimes our friends tease us or do things that make us feel angry or hurt.

When you're angry, you might feel like saying mean things or even hitting another person. Feeling this way is normal. Acting on these feelings is not. Acting in ways that can hurt other people on purpose is being **aggressive**. Aggressive words and actions can end friendships. Later in this chapter you will learn to deal with anger and other uncomfortable feelings.

Think about what you want in a friend. Do you want someone who talks a lot or someone who is a good listener? Maybe you'd like to have both kinds of friends. You certainly want friends who care about you. Knowing what makes a good friend can help you be a good friend to others.

ACTIVITY

Life Skills

Responsibility
David has lost a CD he borrowed from his friend Chandra. Role-play how he can be responsible and save this friendship.

MAIN IDEA AND DETAILS Explain the most important thing about making and keeping friends. Then describe two ways to keep friendships strong.

The most important way to make and keep friends is to be a friend. Possible ways to keep friendships strong: Show respect, be a good listener, do not be aggressive, keep angry feelings under control.

◀ Friends can help each other learn new skills.

299

 Integrated Language Arts/ Reading Skills

Friendship Cinquain Have partners work together to write a poem called a cinquain. Here is the format:

Line 1—One word naming the topic (some aspect of friendship). Line 2—Two words describing the topic. Line 3—Three action words about the topic. Line 4—A four- or five-word phrase describing the topic. Line 5—One word that is a synonym for the topic or that restates it in some way.

Teacher Tip

Coping with Crises Disasters and crises, whether natural or caused by people, can disrupt students' lives and cause much worry. One way to reassure students after a disaster or crisis is to provide structure and routine so that part of their lives seems predictable and familiar. Discourage students from telling classmates about frightening incidents that happened during the disaster. Instead, help them focus on sources of help and support.

---

2. TEACH

Interpret Visuals—Pictures

Draw students' attention to the picture and caption on page 298. Ask students how they think these young people are feeling. **How are the two students in front affecting the feelings of the students behind them?** They are helping the students feel accepted and respected.

Then have students study the picture on this page. **How do you think these three people feel? How might they affect each other's feelings?** Possible answer: They can help each other feel skillful by offering praise instead of making fun of mistakes. They can help each other feel comfortable by being patient.

Discuss

Have students describe the characteristics of healthy and unhealthy friendships.

Critical Thinking The subheading on page 298 is *Your Actions Affect Others*. **What are some actions that can affect others, positively and negatively?** Possible examples: including others in a group or ignoring them; showing respect by asking for someone's opinion; helping someone deal with uncomfortable feelings by being a good listener; making someone feel bad by forgetting to call or meet him or her when you said you would; losing someone's trust by sharing private information

Problem Solving **What can you do when someone's actions have hurt your feelings?** Possible answers: Tell the person how you feel; find another friend if this happens too many times; talk over the situation with a trusted adult.

Activity

Responsibility Accept any reasonable responses. David should apologize. He might also buy Chandra a new CD.

Interpret Visuals—Pictures

What other examples of positive peer pressure could be shown on these pages? Possible examples: studying together; working on a project; playing on a sports team or in the school band; helping with a community project

Discuss

Have students distinguish between healthy and harmful influences of friends and others. **Why do peers become more important as you enter your teen years?** Possible answers: You want to feel independent and grown up; you become more separate from your family, but you still want to be part of a group who like and appreciate you.

Critical Thinking Do you think the influence of peer pressure becomes stronger or weaker as young people grow older? Guide the class to recognize that young teens who are unsure of themselves are very susceptible to peer pressure. As they grow older and gain confidence, most teenagers learn to make their own decisions and not just follow the crowd. That's why nearly all people who smoke cigarettes begin before age 21. By the time they reach adulthood, they are better able to resist peer pressure to smoke because they don't need to prove that they are "cool."

Critical Thinking Why is it important to think for yourself, even if you are part of a group? If you don't follow your own values and family rules, you will lose self-respect and confidence in your ability to make wise decisions. You may end up in situations that are embarrassing, harmful, or illegal. When you think for yourself, you can make decisions based on your own values and family rules.

Discuss

Have students explain the importance of communication skills as a major influence on the social health of the individual.

▲ Peer pressure is good when friends encourage each other to do helpful things, such as washing cars.

Friends Help You

Friends are always important, but friends will become especially important as you enter your teen years. Teenagers want to be accepted by their friends and want to be part of a group. To belong to a group, teenagers may feel they must dress, act, and think like others in the group. However, if you have a strong, positive self-concept, you will make different choices when you don't agree with the rest of the group.

Teenagers who do not have a strong self-concept let friends make decisions for them. They go along with the group even when they know certain actions are wrong or harmful. They're afraid they'll be left out if they make their own decisions. These teenagers are giving in to peer pressure. **Peer pressure** is the influence a group has over the actions or decisions of group members.

300

Meeting Individual Needs
Leveled Activities

BELOW-LEVEL Identify Actions Have students work with a partner to make two lists: actions that help others feel good and actions that hurt others' feelings. Have pairs share and compare their lists.

ON-LEVEL Use Positive Peer Pressure Invite small groups to act out situations in which they demonstrate positive peer pressure—that is, situations in which they encourage others to do helpful, healthful things.

CHALLENGE Model Listening Ask pairs of students to demonstrate active listening. The class should watch and listen to the conversation and then point out the actions and words that show respectful listening.

Active Listening Techniques

Technique	Example
Encourage	"Good for you! What did you do next?"
Clarify	"Was your brother there, too?"
Restate	"So Jeff said he would meet you, but he didn't show up?"
Reflect	"That must have been scary."

Often, teenagers who are not sure of themselves do something because "everyone is doing it." They are afraid to disagree. They are afraid to say *no*.

On the other hand, good friends respect one another's right to have different opinions. They talk things over and listen carefully to each other.

Practice using active listening techniques to show your friends and family members that you are listening. Soon, good listening will be a habit for you. If you learn to listen respectfully, your friends and family members will be ready to listen to you!

 COMPARE AND CONTRAST How are expressing a different opinion and arguing alike? How are they different?

Work is fun when you do it with a friend. ▶

Did You Know?

Friends never give up on each other—even animal friends. A family from Ohio lost its dog while vacationing in Oregon. Months later the dog arrived back in Ohio. It had traveled hundreds of miles to find its home.

Alike: Both are ways to tell others how you think and feel. Different: People who express opinions that differ respect each other's right to have different ideas. People who argue try to change each other's ideas.

301

What are some examples of negative peer pressure? pressure to do anything that will lead to trouble and is against school rules, family rules, laws, or your own values

Critical Thinking How can giving in to negative peer pressure make you feel worse instead of better? Possible answers: You can lose confidence in yourself; you can be embarrassed if someone finds out what you did; your friends may lose respect for you; your family may no longer trust you.

Good friends listen to each other. Should a friend just sit quietly and listen? Why or why not? Guide students to recognize that a good listener is an active listener. He or she should ask questions and make comments such as the ones in the box on this page to show that he or she is interested and wants to hear more.

How do you feel when you know that someone is really listening to you? Possible answers: appreciated, liked, respected, accepted

Problem Solving Suppose someone suggests an activity that will hurt a friend's feelings or is against your school's or family's rules. Should you be an active listener then too? Assure students that they have the right to say *no* as soon as they realize that the suggested activity is wrong and will lead to trouble. This is not a time for a long discussion—or for a compromise. If the other person continues to apply negative peer pressure, the student should consider changing friends.

Social Studies

Saying No To help students learn how to resist peer pressure, have small groups each choose a different language and learn ways of refusing or saying *no* in that language. Some students might be fluent in another language or have friends or family members who are. Have each group teach the class what it has learned. Also have the group describe the country where the language is spoken and point out on a map where the country is located.

Teacher Tip

Nonverbal Listening Help students realize that their body language can also show whether they are listening. If they are looking around the room, leafing through a book, or watching television, the speaker will know that their attention is elsewhere. Demonstrate how to maintain a comfortable level of eye contact and lean toward the speaker to show interest in what the speaker is saying.

Discuss

Have students describe the characteristics of unhealthy friendships.

Critical Thinking The textbook points out that if you are in a clique, you might be pressured to tease a new student. What are some other reasons being in a clique can be unhealthy?

Possible answers: You may not get to know many people outside the clique; others may think you are unfriendly and snobbish.

3. WRAP UP

Lesson 3 Summary and Review

1. healthy; clique, unhealthy; peer pressure; aggressive

2. Possible answers: Calmly explain your feelings; find friends who are kind and respectful.

3. A strong self-concept helps you respect your own ability to make decisions, even when they are different from

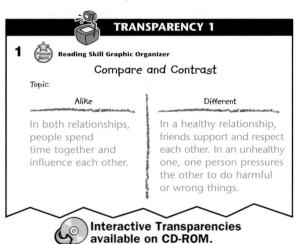

TRANSPARENCY 1

1 Reading Skill Graphic Organizer

Compare and Contrast

Topic:

Alike	Different
In both relationships, people spend time together and influence each other.	In a healthy relationship, friends support and respect each other. In an unhealthy one, one person pressures the other to do harmful or wrong things.

Interactive Transparencies available on CD-ROM.

those of your friends.

4. Examples may include:

5. Students' poems should relate to

When Minutes Count ...

Quick Study Students can use *Activity Book* pp. 46–47 (shown on p. 291) as they complete each lesson in this chapter.

Healthy and Unhealthy Relationships

In a *healthy* relationship, friends have fun together, respect each other, help each other solve problems, and learn new things. Some relationships, like those in cliques, are *unhealthy*. A **clique** is a group that leaves other people out. People in cliques rarely make new friends.

Being *in* a clique can be just as harmful as being *left out* of a clique. For example, one clique member might pressure another member to tease a new student. If you find yourself in an unhealthy relationship, remember your positive self-concept. Say *no!*

▲ Being in a clique is unhealthy, because someone is always left out.

CAUSE AND EFFECT What might cause someone to join a clique?

A person's poor self-concept and lack of confidence about making friends on his or her own might lead to the person's joining a clique to try to become popular.

Lesson 3 Summary and Review

❶ Summarize with Vocabulary

Use vocabulary and other terms from this lesson to complete the statements.

A friendship in which two people help each other is _____. However, a _____, which leaves others out, is _____. Some young people use _____ to get others to dress and act in certain ways. A(an) _____ person might threaten to hurt anyone who disagrees.

❷ What can you say or do if you or your friends are teased by members of a clique?

❸ Critical Thinking How can having a strong self-concept help you make choices that are different from those of your friends?

❹ COMPARE AND CONTRAST Draw and complete this graphic organizer to show how a healthy relationship and an unhealthy relationship are alike and how they are different.

Topic:

Alike	Different

❺ Writing to Entertain—Poem

Write a poem about friendship. You might write about an ideal friend, about someone who wants a new friend, or about someone who has had the same good friend for a long time.

ESL/ELL Support

LANGUAGE AND VOCABULARY The word *peer* has two main meanings, and the words *clique* and *click* can be confused.

Beginning Pantomime the two main meanings of *peer*—"someone your own age" and "to look." Write *clique* and *click* on the board, and pantomime their meanings.

Intermediate Have students find a partner. Assign each pair the word *click*, *clique*, or one meaning of *peer*. Have the pair make up a sentence that uses the word. Invite each pair to say its sentence for the class.

Advanced Ask pairs of students to write four sentences, one for each key word—*peer* ("to look"), *peer* ("someone your own age"), *click*, and *clique*. As the pairs take turns reading one of their sentences aloud, have the class determine whether the key word is used correctly.

Respect

Accept Individual Differences

Friends recognize and respect ways that they are different from each other. No two people on Earth are exactly the same. People are tall or short, pale or dark. They wear different kinds of clothes, and they eat different foods.

Different people also speak different languages, and some speak English with an accent. Some people have difficulty speaking because of a hearing loss or other reasons.

If you have difficulty understanding someone, you might repeat what you think you heard. For example, you might ask, "Did you say you forgot your homework?" If you can't understand a certain word, think of other words, related to the topic you are discussing. Then you might use those words to make sure you understand what your friend is saying.

Don't miss out on having good friends just because other people are different from you. Remember: You are also different from them! You wouldn't want them to pass you by because you are different, would you?

Activity

Some people who have a hearing loss communicate with sign language instead of spoken words. They use their hands to express their ideas. Work with a small group to learn some words and phrases in American Sign Language. Practice your signs until you can use them to communicate with other group members. Then describe some other ways to adapt class activities people with hearing losses.

303

Using the Poster

Activity Have students make up slogans that could go along with the poster. The slogans can be printed neatly on strips of paper and attached to the poster, or they could stand alone in a separate display.

Display Poster 4 to remind students that people are more alike than they are different. The poster can be displayed in the classroom, school cafeteria, or another common area.

Building Good Character

Caring
Citizenship
Fairness
Respect
Responsibility
Trustworthiness

Objective

▶ Recognize the importance of respecting individual differences, including speech problems.

Program Resource

▶ Poster 4

BEFORE READING

Have two self-confident friends sit in front of the room. Ask the class how these two students are the same. Then ask how they are different. For example: One is a girl, one is taller, one has curly hair, one has freckles. Ask: **These two people are different in many ways. Can they still be friends?** Yes, of course they can.

DISCUSS

Have students analyze respectful ways to communicate with adults. After students read the page, ask why people sometimes let differences keep them from getting to know each other. Possible answer: They are a little uncomfortable around someone who is not quite like them in some way.

Discuss ways to overcome the urge to avoid being around someone who is slightly different. For example, doing a fun activity together helps people find out what they have in common.

ACTIVITY

Have students demonstrate ways of communicating with individuals who communicate in unique ways. Provide time for groups to practice their signs and teach them to the class. Have groups describe to you ahead of time the activity they would like to show the class.

Objectives

► Identify three ways in which people communicate their feelings.

► Explain and practice effective strategies for stress management.

When Minutes Count . . .

Assign the Quick Study, Lesson 4, Activity Book pp. 46–47 (shown on p. 291).

Program Resources

► Activity Book pp. 46–47
► Transparency 1

Vocabulary

body language p. 304, **stress** p. 306

Daily Fitness Tip

When students are under a lot of stress, they are much more likely to act out their anger and frustration. Encourage students to begin each school morning with a few deep breathing exercises to clear their minds and reduce stress.

 For more guidelines on exercises to reduce stress, see *Be Active! Resources for Physical Education,* p. 157.

1. MOTIVATE

Ask students if they have ever heard people say that they are "blue." What does this mean? They feel sad or depressed.

What colors could we connect with other feelings? What color might happy be? Scared? Angry? Worried? Stressed? Accept reasonable responses.

Would you like it if people turned colors to show how they feel? Why or why not?

Point out that we do not always want others to know how we are feeling. Sometimes we have unpleasant feelings that we prefer to keep to ourselves. Still, we do show those feelings, even if we say nothing about them.

Tell students that this lesson will help them understand the different ways we express our feelings. They will also learn how to manage the uncomfortable feeling called stress.

LESSON 4
Actions, Reactions, and Stress

Lesson Focus

You express your feelings in actions, words, and body language. You can control how you express those feelings.

Why Learn This?

When you express your feelings clearly and respectfully, you have a better chance of meeting your needs and wants.

Vocabulary

body language
stress

Your Feelings Show

Did you ever believe that if you didn't cry, no one would know you were sad? Have you ever thought that if you didn't say anything, no one would know you were scared—or angry? The truth is, your feelings show, no matter how quiet you are.

Your feelings show in your actions, which can range from smiling to shaking your head to stomping out of a room. Your feelings show in your words, too. They show in both what you say and how you say it. You might explain what is bothering you, or you might try to hide your feelings. You might speak by whispering or by shouting.

You might not realize that your feelings also show in your body language. **Body language** is the way your body expresses your feelings. Body language includes your posture and facial expressions, the clothes you choose to wear, the way you take care of yourself, and much more. Are you surprised that your body gives away your feelings?

◄ What does the body language of these three people tell you? Which person is angry, and which person is excited? Which one is not even listening?

Science

Newton Was Right! Explain that one of Sir Isaac Newton's laws of motion states that for every action there is an equal and opposite reaction. Ask students how this law seems to apply to people. If you act in a forceful way, what do others do? (They might push back at you or move away, but they do react.) How can you get people to react to you in a positive way?

Teacher Tip

Body Language and Learning You might remind students that our use of gestures is learned partly from our parents and partly from our backgrounds. People of some cultural backgrounds are naturally more expressive, using their hands and bodies to communicate their feelings. People of other cultures are more reserved. Caution students not to make assumptions about someone based on his or her gestures. Instead, they should first get to know the individual.

When you fold your arms across your chest, your body language may be saying, "I won't do it, and you can't make me do it." When the teacher asks for volunteers and you stare at the floor, your body language says, "Please don't call on me!"

Sometimes our words say one thing but our body language says another. For example, did you ever tell a friend you were not angry anymore, but you stared at the wall instead of looking at him or her? Your body language was showing that you *were* still angry. You were sending your friend a "mixed message."

We communicate clearly when our words, actions, and body language all express the same thing. When we show our feelings clearly, others understand them. And people are more likely to respond in the way we want them to.

We must also express our feelings calmly and remember that others have feelings, too. If we shout in anger, people will move away from us. If we calmly explain what is wrong, without blaming or insulting anyone, others will be more willing to listen and understand.

DRAW CONCLUSIONS Why are "mixed messages" confusing and unfair?
Possible answer: Mixed messages are confusing because if your words and your actions say two different things, the other person

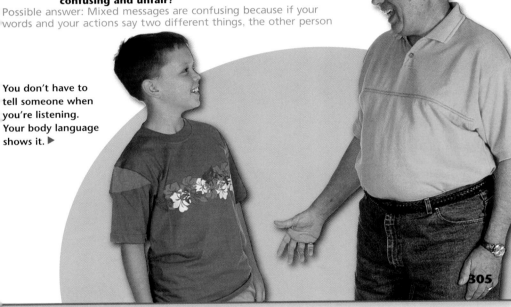

You don't have to tell someone when you're listening. Your body language shows it. ▶

Quick Activity

Show Your Feelings
Work with a partner to act out feelings. Take turns using body language to show a positive or negative feeling. See if your partner can guess which feeling you are showing.

Teacher Tip

Modeling Body Language
Remember that students use your body language to determine your feelings and reactions. Make sure the messages in your body language match the messages in your words. It's better to admit to being annoyed or frustrated than to try to hide it behind a smile. Your body language will give you away!

Cultural Connection

A Simple Handshake The act of shaking hands can convey anything from a simple greeting to an international treaty agreement. The origin of the handshake dates back to ancient Greece, when it was used as a sign of hospitality. In medieval times, the handshake is thought to have been a sign of trust—that no weapons were being held in the hands. Have students research customary greetings used in other countries. Then have students practice greeting each other by using them.

2. TEACH

Interpret Visuals—Pictures
Have students study the young people on these pages. **What message does each person's body language send?** Then focus on the two listeners on page 304. Imagine that one of them is sending a mixed message. **What might that person be saying?** something that contradicts his or her body language

Content-Area Reading Support
Using Signal Words Have students find this sentence on page 304:

You might not realize that your feelings also show in your body language.

Point out that the word *also* suggests that the text has already explained at least one way in which your feelings show. Have students identify the other way or ways. two ways: actions and words Explain that when students see the word *also*, they should make sure they understand what was explained earlier.

Quick Activity
Have each pair demonstrate an example of body language, and discuss whether everyone interprets it the same way. For example, point out that one person may think a shrug of the shoulders means "I don't know," while someone else might think it means "I don't care."

Discuss
Critical Thinking Why might a person's body language not match his or her words? The person may be trying to hide something or deny having unpleasant feelings.

Problem Solving What can you do if someone sends you a mixed message?
Possible answers: You might ask if the person is angry or worried. You could let the person know that you are confused.

Discuss

Have students describe strategies for stress management.

How are the symptoms of stress, such as a faster heartbeat, a form of body language? Symptoms of stress are your body's way of telling you that you are trying to do too much or that you are very worried about something.

How can you tell that someone else is feeling stress? Possible answers: The person might be jumpy, nervous, in a hurry, unable to concentrate, or have a stomachache or a headache.

Consumer Activity

Help students recognize that a long bath, for example, can be relaxing, even without adding expensive preparations to the water. Alcohol and cigarette ads seem to imply that using the products will help people relax. However, alcohol and cigarettes definitely do not reduce feelings of stress.

Health Background

Fight-or-Flight Response The symptoms of stress prepare the body to protect itself and are sometimes called the fight-or-flight response. When we experience stress, our bodies release adrenaline and other chemicals into our bloodstream. Our hearts beat faster to increase the blood flow to our muscles. The increase in blood flow raises our body temperature, causing sweaty palms. We breathe faster so that our blood can get extra oxygen to our cells. Our muscles receive extra energy—fuel for running or fighting. Digestion shuts down so that energy can be used by our muscles, leaving us with a queasy feeling. If stress continues, our bodies stay in this defensive mode, which wears down our body systems.

Sources: *MSN Health, Anxiety and Panic Disorder Center of Los Angeles, Mind/Body Education Center*

Health & Technology

Biofeedback Biofeedback uses machines to help people "listen" to their bodies. One kind of machine picks up electrical signals from muscles and changes the signals into beeps. When the muscles relax, the beeps slow down. When the muscles get tense, the beeps speed up. In this way, people learn to recognize what is going on within their bodies. Some therapists use biofeedback machines to help people learn to relax.

Manage Stress

You probably know what stress feels like. **Stress** is a feeling of tension in your body, your mind, or both. Your heart might beat faster, or your palms might get sweaty. "Butterflies" might flutter around in your stomach. Stress is your body's natural reaction to challenges.

A little stress can be helpful. Good stress can give you extra energy to play well in a game or do well on a test. However, when stress is too great or lasts too long, it can be harmful. Bad stress can harm your health and interfere with your life. Bad stress can be caused by

- trying to do too much and leaving no time to relax.
- putting too much pressure on yourself.
- worrying about problems at home or at school.
- coping with the changes of puberty.
- keeping a problem inside instead of talking to someone.

music lessons

meet with friends

soccer practice

science project

306

Meeting Individual Needs
Leveled Activities

BELOW-LEVEL **Exercise Stress Away** Ask students to choose and demonstrate exercises or other vigorous activities that might help reduce stress.

ON-LEVEL **Control Stress** Have students make posters that offer tips for controlling stress, such as time management and exercise. Display the posters in the common areas of the school to help other students learn to deal with stress.

CHALLENGE **Chart Stress** Encourage students to record their stress levels for a week. They might divide each day into one-hour periods and mark each period 1 (low stress) to 10 (high stress). Have them note their activities during that hour so they can determine what seems to cause the most and least stress.

To reduce the stress in your life, set realistic goals. Don't try to do too many things in a short time. Eating healthful foods, getting enough sleep, and getting enough exercise all help reduce stress. Be sure to allow time for fun, too.

Talk with a parent or other trusted adult about anything that's bothering you. He or she may be able to help you understand things in a way you had not thought of before.

CAUSE AND EFFECT How can talking to a parent or another adult about a problem help you reduce stress?

Myth and Fact

Myth: Trying to eat well only adds stress to your life.

Fact: The quality and amount of food you eat influence how your body handles stress. When you eat well, your body gets the nutrients it needs to help you bounce back from stressful events.

Possible answers: When you talk about problems, you often see them more clearly; an adult might suggest good ways to deal with a

When to Get Help for Stress

If you feel any of the symptoms below, ask a parent for help.		
frequent tiredness	trouble sleeping	frequent headaches
eating problems	trouble concentrating	

Lesson 4 Summary and Review

1 Summarize with Vocabulary

Use vocabulary and other terms from this lesson to complete the statements.

Our actions, words, and _____ show our feelings. When we have too much to do, we feel _____. Stress that helps you do well on a test is called _____. Stress that makes you feel sick is called _____.

2 Critical Thinking How can body language get in the way of communication?

3 What are two ways to manage stress?

4 COMPARE AND CONTRAST Draw and complete this graphic organizer to compare and contrast good stress and bad stress.

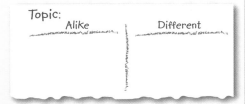

Topic:
Alike   Different

5 Writing to Inform—Narration

Write a story that tells how a fifth grader becomes stressed about something and then learns how to handle the stress.

307

ESL/ELL Support

BACKGROUND AND EXPERIENCE Invite students to name some causes of stress for fifth graders.

Beginning Have students pantomime how they feel when they are stressed and when they are not stressed.

Intermediate Ask students to draw pictures of a young person in a situation that causes stress. Have them share and explain their pictures.

Advanced Have students write four or five tips for avoiding or dealing with stress.

Interpret Visuals—Table

Have students add examples to the list titled *When To Get Help.* Discuss the different adults whom they might ask for help, either by category or by name.

Discuss

What is your favorite way of reducing stress? Possible answers: playing a sport, talking with a friend, petting my dog, reading, listening to music

3. WRAP UP

Lesson 4 Summary and Review

1. body language; good stress; bad stress
2. If your body language does not match your words and actions, you send a confusing message to listeners.
3. Possible answers: Try not to do too much, take time to relax, set realistic goals, allow time for fun, exercise, talk with a trusted adult.
4. Examples may include:

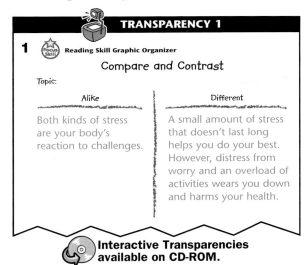

TRANSPARENCY 1

1 Reading Skill Graphic Organizer

Compare and Contrast

Topic:

Alike	Different
Both kinds of stress are your body's reaction to challenges.	A small amount of stress that doesn't last long helps you do your best. However, distress from worry and an overload of activities wears you down and harms your health.

Interactive Transparencies available on CD-ROM.

5. Students' stories should incorporate what they have learned about the causes and symptoms of stress and should tell ways to reduce it.

For **writing models** with examples, see *Teaching Resources* pp. 47–61. Rubrics are also provided.

Life Skills

Communicate
Make Responsible Decisions
Manage Stress
Refuse
Resolve Conflicts
Set Goals

Objectives
▶ Identify steps to cope with and manage stress.
▶ Use the stress management skills to deal with stress.

Program Resources
▶ Activity Book p. 49
▶ Poster 9

1. MOTIVATE

Without any warning, ask students to move to a new seating arrangement. Urge them to hurry, giving them little time to gather their things. When students are in their new seats, ask them how it felt to move. Have they ever moved with their families? How did that feel? Point out that these feelings are caused by stress.

2. TEACH

Step 1
How does stress feel for Erin? Her heart beats faster and she feels shaky.

Critical Thinking Does everyone feel the same symptoms of stress? Guide students to realize that different people can have different symptoms and that the same person might have different symptoms at different times.

Step 2
Would most students feel stress if they were Erin? Why or why not? Most students probably would be stressed because of the uncertainty of the situation.

Manage Stress
At School

Stress is part of everyday life. A little stress is OK, but too much can make you sick and unhappy. Fortunately, you can learn how to handle stress so it does not become a problem. Using the steps for **Managing Stress** can help you keep the stress in your life at a reasonable level.

Erin is starting her first day at a new school. She doesn't know anyone at the school, and she's worried about making new friends there. How can she manage the stress she's feeling?

1 **Know what stress feels like.**

As Erin waves goodbye to her father, her heart starts beating faster and she feels a little shaky. She knows these are symptoms of stress.

2 **Try to determine the cause of the stress.**

It's lunchtime, and Erin knows the cause of her stress—she's worried about fitting in. Should she sit by herself? Will others ask her to sit with them?

308

Physical Education

Stress, Injuries, and Disease

When people are under stress, they may not pay full attention to their environment and are more likely to become injured. A study of farmers, for example, found that those who were under economic stress were two to three times more likely to become injured than farmers who were not under stress. The stressed farmers were thinking about paying their bills and were not focusing on their work.

ACTIVITY BOOK P. 49

Name _____

 Life Skill
Manage Stress

🔆 Problem Solving

Steps for Managing Stress at School

1. Know what stress feels like.
2. Try to determine the cause of the stress.
3. Do something that will help relieve you of stress.
4. Visualize yourself doing well in the stressful situation.

Use the steps to help these students manage stress at school.

A. Tomorrow Tyron has a unit test in science class. Tyron enjoys science class and has done well on his chapter tests. However, every time he thinks about the unit test, he becomes shaky and his palms get sweaty.

• Describe how Tyron can manage the stress he feels before taking the unit test.

   Possible answer: Tyron can reduce his stress by going for a long run
   after school. He can then imagine himself getting his test back with a
   very good grade on it.

B. Cora tried out for the softball team and made it. Practices have been going well, and her teammates think she is a great addition to the team. However, this afternoon is Cora's first game, and every time she thinks about it she has a sick feeling in her stomach.

• Describe how Cora can manage the stress she feels before her first game.

   Possible answer: Cora can reduce her stress by finding a quiet area to
   relax and taking deep breaths before the game. She can visualize
   herself catching the ball for the other team's third out.

 Available online.
www.harcourtschool.com/health

3 Do something that will help relieve you of stress.

Erin reduces her stress by taking a deep breath and relaxing her shoulders and other muscles.

4 Visualize yourself doing well in the stressful situation.

Erin pictures herself sitting with others from her class, talking with her new friends. After picturing that, she joins a group of students at a table.

Problem Solving

A. This morning it's Jacob's turn to present his oral book report. He enjoyed reading the book and has prepared a good report, but he feels a little sick in his stomach.
- Use the steps for **Managing Stress** to tell how Jacob can handle the stress he feels.

B. Mackenzie wants to be in the school play, but the thought of trying out for a part gives her a headache. Maybe she should forget trying to be in the play and just go see it when it's presented. No one would even know that she ever thought about trying out.
- Using what you know about stress and responsibility, explain what Mackenzie could do to handle her stress.

309

Using the Poster

Activity Have students make mini-posters to accompany the big poster. The mini-posters can represent some sources of stress that fifth graders commonly encounter.

Display the poster to remind students of ways they can deal with stress.

POSTER 9

Manage Stress

The girl is visualizing herself making new friends.

Ways to Manage Stress

1 Know what stress feels like and what causes it.
2 Do something active to make yourself feel better.
3 Talk with someone you trust about the way you are feeling.
4 Visualize yourself doing well in a stressful situation.

How have YOU MANAGED STRESS today?

POSTER 9

What else could Erin do to relieve her stress? Possible answers: help another person, think positively, tell someone how she feels

 Building Good Character
Remind students that they need to be responsible as they manage their stress. They should not simply avoid situations or tasks as a way of reducing stress.

Step 4
How well do you think Erin handled this situation? Would you have done something differently? If so, what?

Critical Thinking Did you ever worry about something and later discover that you had little to worry about? Volunteers may describe times when they worried more than necessary. **How do we sometimes cause stress for ourselves?** Possible answer: We imagine the worst and assume that something bad will happen.

3. WRAP UP

Problem Solving

A Possible answer: Jacob needs to recognize that his upset stomach is caused by stress over presenting his report. Then he should do something to relieve the stress, such as deep breathing and visualizing himself doing well as he presents the report.

B Possible answer: Mackenzie should manage her stress and not let it keep her from trying out. She has a responsibility to herself to do her best and try new experiences. She should identify what part of trying out is bothering her and do something to reduce this stress, such as telling someone about it, exercising before trying out, or taking a friend with her.

LESSON 5

Pages 310–313

Objectives

► Learn effective strategies for resolving conflicts.

► Explain the importance of respecting differences.

► Analyze respectful ways of communicating with others.

 When Minutes Count . . .

Assign the Quick Study, Lesson 5, Activity Book pp. 46–47 (shown on p. 291).

Program Resources

► Activity Book pp. 46–47

► Transparency 1

Vocabulary

conflicts p. 310, **stereotype** p. 312, **prejudice** p. 313

 **Daily Fitness Tip**

When forming opinions, young people are naturally influenced by the opinions of their parents or guardians whether those opinions are fair or not. Stress the importance of treating each person as an individual, of keeping an open mind, and of avoiding generalizations about entire groups of people.

 For more guidelines about learning to relate well to others, see *Be Active! Resources for Physical Education*, p. 181.

1. MOTIVATE

Ask students to imagine a school in which there are no arguments, no disagreements, no differences of opinion, and no conflicts.

What would it be like to go to school there? Possible answers: It would be boring, especially with no differences of opinion.

Next, ask students to list some things students typically disagree about during the school day. Point out that conflicts are normal but students can learn how to resolve them in ways that everyone involved can accept. Have students analyze respectful ways to communicate with adults and peers.

 LESSON 5

Resolving Conflicts

Dealing with Conflicts at School

Conflicts are struggles that result from people's differing needs and wants. It takes practice to resolve conflicts. Handling conflicts at school can be very hard. When groups of friends take sides, a conflict can quickly involve a large number of students. A problem that starts at school can become a conflict outside of school as well.

How should you deal with conflicts at school? If you find yourself too angry to talk about a problem, just walk away. Give yourself time to cool off. When you are calmer, you will be more in control. Then it will be easier to work toward a peaceful solution.

Lesson Focus

Our lives are full of conflicts. Some of them result from cultural differences. We need to respect our differences and find peaceful ways to resolve conflicts.

Why Learn This?

Resolving conflicts peacefully takes practice and requires respect for people's differences.

Vocabulary

conflicts
stereotype
prejudice

Did the soccer ball go out of bounds? These players learn how to resolve this conflict peacefully. ▶

310

Teacher Tip

Win/Win The steps for resolving a conflict are designed so that both parties win. However, some people, regardless of age, have only one goal in a conflict—to win and to make sure the other person loses. Stress that resolving a conflict fairly means that both people cooperate and compromise, rather than compete. That way, all parties win!

 Social Studies

Common Ground Explain that when we work to resolve conflicts, we look for "common ground." This term dates back to colonial America, in which most towns set aside space—a common—in the center of town for livestock to graze. Everyone shared the common. Ask students to identify common areas in their school, such as the hallways, cafeteria, and media center. Discuss the need to find common ground in conflicts.

Conflict resolution is a respectful way to solve problems. It helps people find solutions that everyone involved can accept. Using the five steps in conflict resolution can help you resolve disagreements in ways that respect each person's needs.

Conflict Resolution

❶ As calmly as possible, tell what happened and how you feel about it.

❷ Share your feelings without blaming or criticizing the other person.

❸ Listen to the other person with an open mind. Respect his or her feelings.

❹ Take responsibility for your actions. Ask what you can do to help solve the problem.

❺ Find a solution that you and the other person can both accept.

The first thing to do in conflict resolution is to stop arguing. Try to talk calmly about the problem. Allow each person to tell his or her side of the conflict without interruption. Use "I" messages, such as this one: "I feel angry because I did most of the work on our project. I had to write the whole report."

Listen respectfully to the other person's "I" message. He or she might say, "I feel angry, too, because I think I did my share. I worked hard on the map for the project, but it took a lot longer than I expected. I just didn't have enough time to finish it."

After everyone involved understands what the problem is, you can work together to find a solution. Perhaps you can help finish the map to meet the deadline for the project.

SEQUENCE When you want to resolve a conflict, what should you do before you discuss the problem?
Stop arguing and calm down.

ACTIVITY

Life Skills

Resolve Conflicts

You and Corey find a baseball lying on the ground. He thinks it's his ball, and you think it's yours. You both begin arguing and trying to grab the ball. Use the conflict resolution steps on this page to find a solution to this problem.

311

311

Meeting Individual Needs
Leveled Activities

BELOW-LEVEL Make Posters Have students make posters showing the steps in resolving conflicts. Display the posters in the school's common areas.

ON-LEVEL Act Out a Conflict Have small groups each choose a typical conflict at school and act it out using the steps of conflict resolution to find a solution.

CHALLENGE Research Conflicts Assign each small group a well-known war or conflict, or have each group choose one. Ask students to research reasons the war started. After students complete their research, provide time for them to share what they have learned, and discuss ways that the war or conflict might have been resolved peacefully.

---

2. TEACH

Interpret Visuals—Table
Have students identify ways to enhance personal communication skills. Discuss the table on this page.

In which steps could you use "I" messages? Steps 1 and 2 **How would doing so help?** "I" messages would help by explaining your feelings without blaming the other person and making him or her angry.

How could you use active listening in Step 3? Possible answer: You could ask questions, maintain eye contact, and nod to show that you are listening.

What would probably happen during Step 4 if you made excuses for your actions? Possible answer: The other person might become angry or angrier.

What does the word *compromise* mean? How could a compromise help in Step 5? A compromise is an agreement in which both people give up something they want in order to reach a solution.

Discuss
Have students analyze respectful ways to communicate with peers. Explain that some schools have a peer mediation process. (If your school has one, describe it.) A peer mediator asks each person involved in a conflict what happened and how he or she feels about it. Then the mediator restates what he or she heard. Next, each person explains what he or she wants. The mediator again restates each position. Then the mediator asks what each person can do to solve the problem. After the students agree on a solution, the mediator writes an agreement, and each person signs it.

Activity
Resolve Conflicts Admitting that you may be mistaken would be a good start in resolving this conflict.

Discuss

Ask students to imagine that they have never seen red apples—only yellow ones. One day someone offers them a red apple. It looks strange to them, so they throw it away the first chance they get.

Critical Thinking **How is this story similar to the way people make judgments about other people?** We sometimes make judgments based on appearances, without getting to know the real person.

Can you think of a group of people in which every member is the same? If students suggest that they do, help them recognize important differences among the members.

Critical Thinking **Why might people with a positive attitude and a strong self-concept have an easier time making friends with someone from a different culture?** People who respect themselves and have a positive attitude are far more able to accept and respect people of different cultures than people who are unsure of themselves and who are worried about what others think about them.

Respect Cultural Differences

People from other cultures often speak different languages, celebrate different holidays, and wear various kinds of clothes. They may even look different. We should respect these differences, but sometimes they lead to conflicts.

For example, Joy wants to be friendly toward a new boy in class, so she asks him about his family. In his culture, questions about one's family are considered impolite, so he doesn't answer. Now Joy thinks the new student is unfriendly. She might even decide that all the people in his culture are unfriendly. A belief based on thinking that everyone in a certain group is the same is a **stereotype**.

Can you think of any group in which every member is exactly the same? All groups are made up of people with differences. This is why stereotypes are often incorrect and usually unfair.

One result of being a nation of many cultures is the variety of delicious foods we have. ▶

312

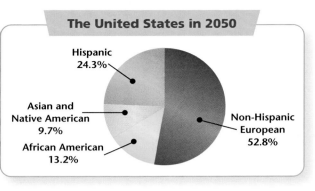

The United States in 2050

- Hispanic 24.3%
- Asian and Native American 9.7%
- African American 13.2%
- Non-Hispanic European 52.8%

Because of Joy's misunderstanding, she may now have a prejudice against the boy's culture. A **prejudice** is an unfair negative attitude toward a whole group.

How can we avoid stereotypes and prejudice? We should look at people as individuals, too, not just as members of a group.

CAUSE AND EFFECT How can believing a stereotype lead to conflict? If you believe a stereotype, you might act badly because of it. For ~~[ex]~~mple, you might think everyone from a certain group is rude and then treat someone from that ~~[grou]~~p in a rude way

Myth and Fact

Myth: The ancestors of most people in the United States came here from Europe.

Fact: By 2050 nearly half of the people will have ancestors who were not from Europe. They will have ancestors from South and Central America, Asia, Africa, India, and Pacific and Caribbean islands.

Lesson 5 Summary and Review

1 Summarize with Vocabulary

Use vocabulary and other terms from this lesson to complete the sentences.

When people have different needs, they might have a _____. The steps of _____ can help them solve the problem peacefully. Expecting bad behavior from someone who belongs to a certain group is a _____. This can lead to _____ toward the entire group.

2 Critical Thinking What is a stereotype that some people have about teenagers? Why do you think this belief may be incorrect?

3 Why is it important to find a peaceful resolution to a conflict?

4 COMPARE AND CONTRAST Draw and complete this graphic organizer to show how a prejudice and a stereotype are alike and different.

Topic:
Alike	Different

5 Write to Express— Solution to a Problem

Think of a stereotype that may cause conflicts in school. Describe this problem and suggest ways to avoid conflicts.

313

Math

Using Different Graphs Challenge students to use the figures in the circle graph to make a bar graph. Have them label the populations along the bottom of the graph and show percentages along the left side of the graph. Ask students if these figures could also be used to make a line graph. (No, because they do not show changes over time; each population is separate. A line connecting them would be meaningless.)

Teacher Tip

Clarifying Meanings Help students differentiate between the meanings of *resolution*. This word can refer to a promise made to oneself to improve in some way. It can also refer to an acceptable solution to a conflict. Some students may also know that *resolution* can refer to a formal expression of an opinion, such as a council's resolution, and to the point in a story at which the problem is solved.

Interpret Visuals—Graph

Have students study the graph and list the population predictions for 2050 in order from greatest to least size. Non-Hispanic white, Hispanic, black, Asian, and Native American

Critical Thinking Why is a circle graph a good way to compare these populations? The circle graph shows what part of the entire population each group represents.

3. WRAP UP

Lesson 5 Summary and Review

1. conflict; conflict resolution; stereotype; prejudice

2. Possible answer: Some people think that all teenagers like loud, harsh music, but many teenagers do not.

3. If one person wins and one loses, the loser will not be happy and the conflict might continue.

4. Examples might include:

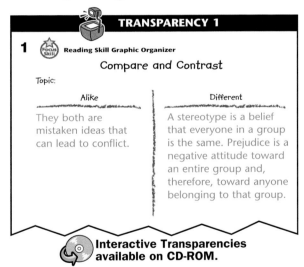

TRANSPARENCY 1

1 Reading Skill Graphic Organizer

Compare and Contrast

Topic:

Alike	Different
They both are mistaken ideas that can lead to conflict.	A stereotype is a belief that everyone in a group is the same. Prejudice is a negative attitude toward an entire group and, therefore, toward anyone belonging to that group.

Interactive Transparencies available on CD-ROM.

5. Students' solutions should include opportunities for everyone involved in the conflict to get to know and understand each other better.

For **writing models** with examples, see *Teaching Resources* pp. 47–61. Rubrics are also provided.

LESSON 6

Pages 314–316

▶ Define *boredom, anger, loneliness, grief,* and *shyness,* and identify possible sources of these feelings.

▶ Learn effective strategies for coping with uncomfortable feelings.

 When Minutes Count . . .

Assign the Quick Study, Lesson 6, Activity Book pp. 46–47 (shown on p. 291).

Program Resources

▶ Activity Book pp. 46–47, 50
▶ Transparency 1

 **Daily Fitness Tip**

Some students may feel that it is wrong or a sign of weakness to experience uncomfortable feelings, such as anger and shyness. Emphasize that everyone experiences uncomfortable feelings from time to time and that people can take effective steps to deal with such feelings.

 For more guidelines on choosing physical activities, see *Be Active! Resources for Physical Education,* p. 135.

1. MOTIVATE

Optional Activity Materials: slips of paper

Give everyone a slip of paper, and ask students to write down the feeling that makes them most uncomfortable—the one that they least like to feel. They may write one feeling or two. (Tell students not to put their names on the papers so the activity is anonymous.)

Collect the slips of paper, and then read the names of the feelings and list each different feeling on the board. You might keep track of how many times each feeling was mentioned to emphasize that many students experience—and dislike— the same uncomfortable feelings.

Point out that all people have unpleasant feelings as well as pleasant ones.

Uncomfortable Feelings

Lesson Focus
Knowing how to recognize and deal with uncomfortable feelings is part of taking good care of yourself.

Why Learn This?
When you know how to deal with your uncomfortable feelings, you feel more in control of yourself.

Dealing with Feelings

In this lesson, you will learn ways to deal with five uncomfortable feelings: boredom, anger, loneliness, shyness, and grief. These feelings are not good or bad, right or wrong. They are simply feelings. You decide how to express them and how to deal with them.

Being in control of your feelings makes you strong and confident. Learning how to deal with your feelings is an important part of growing up.

MAIN IDEA AND DETAILS What are some uncomfortable feelings?
Uncomfortable feelings include boredom, anger, loneliness, shyness, and grief.

Boredom

When you are bored, you feel tired and restless. You might sit and stare into space. You might feel most bored when you are sick or when all your friends are busy.

Strategies: Exercise can help. So can finding something unusual to do by yourself or thinking of a way to help someone in your family or community. Doing something for someone else is an excellent way to fight boredom.

Anger

Anger can rage out of control, or it can stay bottled up inside you. You can be angry with other people or with yourself.

Strategies: Admit you are angry, and then calm down. Leave the situation, or count to ten. Take several deep breaths. Then express your feelings in an "I" message without blaming others or being critical. Just telling someone what is bothering you can help you feel better. If you're angry with someone, ask how he or she feels. Then listen carefully to the answer. Be ready to forgive someone who has hurt your feelings—and be ready to forgive yourself, too. If you are angry for a long time, talk to a parent.

314

 ESL/ELL Support

COMPREHENSIBLE INPUT The names of the five feelings in this lesson are nouns, but they are not concrete objects. Help clarify the meanings with students.

Beginning Help students pantomime boredom, anger, loneliness, grief, and shyness. Have students draw pictures of someone their age having each feeling.

Intermediate Have students explain situations that might lead to each of the five feelings named on this page.

Advanced Organize five groups of students, and assign each group a feeling word. Ask each group to write a paragraph describing someone who is experiencing the assigned feeling. Provide time for each group to read its paragraph aloud.

Loneliness

Loneliness is a painful, empty feeling of isolation. It could be the result of an argument with a friend or a move to a new neighborhood. Having a negative self-concept can make loneliness seem worse. You may think that no one wants to be your friend, so there is no point in trying to find one.

Strategies: First, name your feeling. If you have argued with a friend, use the steps of conflict resolution to make peace. If you have just moved, remember that making new friends takes time. Joining an after-school activity might help you meet a new friend who shares one of your hobbies or interests. If your loneliness continues, talk to a parent or other trusted adult.

Shyness

If you are shy, you avoid talking to other people, especially in groups or in unfamiliar situations. At these times, your shyness may make you blush, give you sweaty hands, or make your heart beat faster. When you have to talk to someone new, you may end up with "butterflies" in your stomach.

Strategies: Remember that there is nothing wrong with you. Some people are naturally shy. To help overcome your shyness, ask another student how he or she feels about a situation that bothers you, such as giving an oral report. You may be surprised to learn that the same situations that bother you also bother other people!

Grief

Grief is a sad feeling that lasts for a long time. It may come after the death of a pet, a friend, or a family member or after a change in the family. You may cry often and find it hard to concentrate. Some people have trouble sleeping. You might not enjoy the things you used to.

Strategies: Grief can go on for a while, so be patient with yourself. Talking about your loss with a parent or other adult you trust can help you start to feel better. Writing about it can also help. The pain will lessen over time.

Personal Health Plan ▶

Real-Life Situation
All people have feelings from time to time that make them uncomfortable. Suppose you have just moved to a new neighborhood.
Real-Life Plan
Write about how you feel. Make a list of ways you can deal with your feelings.

315

Teacher Tip

Battling Boredom Many of today's young people are susceptible to boredom because they are accustomed to television and electronic games, and are not used to entertaining themselves. Challenge your students to spend some time each day away from electronic sources of amusement. Encourage them to try activities like reading, writing, drawing, and playing board games as ways to express and share their ideas and to develop positive relationships with others.

Integrated Language Arts/ Reading Skills

Acrostics and Concrete Poetry
Have students use one or all of the names of feelings in this lesson to create acrostics. They should use the letters in the name to begin words, phrases, or sentences that help explain the feeling.

Students might also try creating concrete poetry. They can arrange words and phrases on the page to help express a feeling.

---

2. TEACH

Content-Area Reading Support
Using Text Format Draw students' attention to the word *Strategies* in each box. Ask what kind of information they expect to read after that word. ways to deal with that feeling Explain that subheadings like this show how information is organized and can help students locate specific points quickly.

Discuss
Have students explain the importance of communication skills as a major influence on the emotional health of the individual.

Critical Thinking Do you think boredom was more of a problem long ago, before many homes had a television and video games? Why or why not? Guide students to realize that many children in the past were used to finding their own fun activities and probably were not bored.

Why is calming down important when you are angry? It allows you to cool off so you won't be tempted to lash out at someone verbally or physically.

Do people always cry when they are grieving? Why or why not? Guide students to recognize that people grieve in different ways. Some cry, and some don't. There are no rules for grieving.

Does everyone feel shy at times? Students may be surprised to learn that very friendly people are sometimes trying to cover up feelings of shyness.

Personal Health Plan ▶

Students' plans could name loneliness, anger, sadness, shyness, frustration, or other unpleasant feelings. New ways of dealing with the feeling might include talking to a parent, a counselor, or another trusted adult; writing about the feeling; or exercising.

3. WRAP UP

Lesson 6 Summary and Review

1. anger; boredom; grief; shyness; loneliness

2. Possible answers: Cool off before reacting; explain your feelings calmly; listen to the other person's point of view; seek help from a trusted adult.

3. Possible answers: Be a good listener; include the person in fun activities; be patient and kind; encourage the person to seek help from a trusted adult.

4. Examples might include:

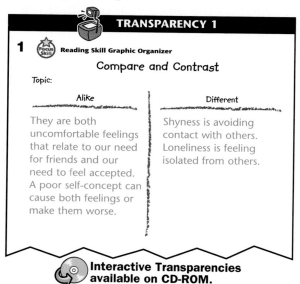

TRANSPARENCY 1

1 Reading Skill Graphic Organizer

Compare and Contrast

Topic: _____

Alike	Different
They are both uncomfortable feelings that relate to our need for friends and our need to feel accepted. A poor self-concept can cause both feelings or make them worse.	Shyness is avoiding contact with others. Loneliness is feeling isolated from others.

Interactive Transparencies available on CD-ROM.

5. Students should name an uncomfortable feeling, suggest some causes, and explain how strategies they have learned in this lesson can help someone deal with it. Their work should show that they understand the strategies and know how to apply them.

For **writing models** with examples, see *Teaching Resources* pp. 47–61. Rubrics are also provided.

When Minutes Count ...

Quick Study Students can use *Activity Book* pp. 46–47 (shown on p. 291) as they complete each lesson in this chapter.

Dealing with Uncomfortable Feelings

Students might mention strategies from pages 314–315 or the tips on page 316.

Pretending that uncomfortable feelings do not exist will not make them go away. Instead, face those feelings and deal with them in positive ways. Change the situation if you can, or change the way you think about it. Try the tips listed below. You are in control!

SUMMARIZE Explain two or three of the most important tips in this list.

❶ Be aware of your feelings.

❷ Speak up. Ask a parent for help if the feeling lasts a long time or hurts too much.

❸ Tell a friend.

❹ Make a plan of action for changing the situation.

❺ Get some vigorous exercise.

❻ Get involved in a fun activity or group.

Lesson 6 Summary and Review

❶ **Summarize with Vocabulary**

Use the terms discussed in this lesson to complete the statements.

When you rage out of control, you are feeling _____. When you can't think of anything to do, you are feeling _____. When you feel sad about the death of a pet, you are feeling _____. When you can't bring yourself to speak to a new student, you are feeling _____. When you are sick in bed and wish someone would visit you, you are feeling _____.

❷ Name at least four ways to cope with anger. Explain which one works best for you.

❸ **Critical Thinking** How could you help someone who is feeling grief?

❹ **COMPARE AND CONTRAST** Draw and complete this graphic organizer to compare and contrast the feelings of shyness and loneliness.

Topic: _____

Alike	Different

❺ **Write to Inform—Explanation**

Think of an uncomfortable feeling not discussed in this lesson, such as fear, or guilt. Explain what the feeling is like and some things that might cause it.

316

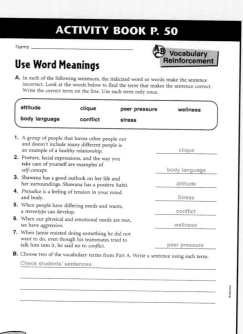

ACTIVITY BOOK P. 50

Name _____

AB Vocabulary Reinforcement

Use Word Meanings

A. In each of the following sentences, the italicized word or words make the sentence incorrect. Look at the words below to find the term that makes the sentence correct. Write the correct term on the line. Use each term only once.

attitude	clique	peer pressure	wellness
body language	conflict	stress	

1. A group of people that leaves other people out and doesn't include many different people is an example of a *healthy relationship*. — clique

2. Posture, facial expressions, and the way you take care of yourself are examples of *self-concept*. — body language

3. Shawana has a good outlook on her life and her surroundings. Shawana has a positive *habit*. — attitude

4. *Prejudice* is a feeling of tension in your mind and body. — Stress

5. When people have differing needs and wants, a *stereotype* can develop. — conflict

6. When our physical and emotional needs are met, we have *aggression*. — wellness

7. When Jamie resisted doing something he did not want to do, even though his teammates tried to talk him into it, he said no to *conflict*. — peer pressure

B. Choose two of the vocabulary terms from Part A. Write a sentence using each term.

Check students' sentences. _____

Available online.
www.harcourtschool.com/health

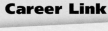

ACTIVITIES

Math

Spreading Smiles Let's say you smile at two people, and those two people each spread your smile to two more people. If those four each spread the smile to two more people, how many people are smiling?

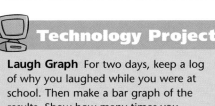
Art

What Does a Friend Look Like? Draw a symbolic picture of an ideal friend. For example, an ideal friend might have large ears so he or she can be an excellent listener. An ideal friend might have super-strong muscles for playing basketball with you or have extra-long arms to give you big hugs when you need them. An ideal friend might have a large heart, also, to be able to forgive you if you hurt his or her feelings.

Technology Project

Laugh Graph For two days, keep a log of why you laughed while you were at school. Then make a bar graph of the results. Show how many times you laughed because you were happy and how many times you laughed because you were nervous. If you laughed for other reasons, show them, too.

 For more activities, visit The Learning Site. www.harcourtschool.com/health

Home & Community

Posters for Peace Make a series of posters that will help other students at your school learn ways to resolve their conflicts peacefully. Display your posters in a hallway or the cafeteria.

Career Link

Martial Arts Instructor Imagine that you teach one of the martial arts, such as karate, kung fu, or tae kwon do. What would you teach your students about resolving conflicts? What would you tell them to do and not to do? What is the most important piece of advice you would give your students?

317

Career Link

Martial Arts Instructor *Karate*, which means "empty hand," originated in China as a method of self-defense for unarmed people. *Kung fu*, also a Chinese martial art, means "disciplined person." It involves not only self-defense but also meditation, breathing, and concentration. *Tae kwon do* is a modern Korean martial art. The name means "to strike or block with the foot and hand."

Students might suggest that an instructor tell students to make every effort to resolve conflicts by talking about them before resorting to any kind of violence. The instructor's most important advice may vary, but it might be to listen with an open mind or to be ready to compromise.

For more information on health careers, visit the Webliography in Teacher Resources at **www.harcourtschool.com/health** **Keyword** health careers

Activities

Math
The answer is 15. If students have trouble figuring this out, draw a diagram on the board. Place one person at the top, linked to two at the second level. Each of those two will be linked to two more at the third level, and so on. Students might also act out this math problem for fun.

Arts
If possible, provide large sheets of poster board for students' drawings. Students might work in groups of two or three. Display the completed drawings around the classroom to remind students of the qualities of a good friend.

Home & Community
Be sure to obtain necessary permission to display posters in locations outside of your classroom. When the study of this topic is complete, have students take their posters home to serve as a reminder of ways to resolve conflicts peacefully.

CSHP **Supports the Coordinated School Health Program**

Technology Project
If computers are available, students might use them to create their bar graphs. They might use multiple-bar graphs, with two side-by-side bars of different colors for each day. One bar can show how many times they laughed out of happiness, while the other bar for the same day can show how many times they laughed out of nervousness.

Chapter Review and Test Preparation

Pages 318–319

 Reading Skill 5 pts. each

1. Possible answer: In both relationships, people provide companionship and influence each other.

2. Possible answer: In a healthy relationship, friends respect each other; in an unhealthy one, one person does not respect the other. Healthy relationships involve positive activities. Unhealthy ones tend to involve harmful activities.

 Use Vocabulary 3 pts. each

3. A, goal setting

4. E, self-concept

5. D, body language

6. B, clique

7. C, attitude

8. F, stereotype

9. G, prejudice

Check Understanding 3 pts. each

10. C, wellness

11. G, anger

12. B, a conflict

13. F, stress

14. C, listening

15. G, a habit

16. C, need

17. F, push someone to get his or her own way

18. B, do not expect to meet their goals

19. G, peer pressure

 Think Critically 6 pts. each

20. Audrey's goal is so general that she will not be able to tell when she reaches it. She needs to set a more specific goal, such as raising her science grade from a C to a B.

 Chapter Review and Test Preparation

Reading Skill

COMPARE AND CONTRAST
Draw and then use this graphic organizer to answer questions 1 and 2.

Topic:
Alike   Different

1 Write at least two ways that healthy and unhealthy relationships are alike.

2 Write at least two ways that healthy and unhealthy relationships are different.

 Use Vocabulary

Match each term in Column B with its meaning in Column A.

Column A	Column B
3 A way to get what you want	**A** goal setting
4 How you see yourself	**B** clique
5 A way you show your feelings	**C** attitude
	D body language
6 A group that leaves others out	**E** self-concept
7 How you feel about life	**F** stereotype
8 A belief based on thinking that everyone in a group is the same	**G** prejudice
9 Bad feelings about people because they belong to a certain group	

318

Check Understanding

Choose the letter of the correct answer.

10 A state of good health is _____. (p. 294)
   A self-concept   C wellness
   B habit   D attitude

11 This boy is demonstrating one way to deal with _____. (p. 314)

   F loneliness   H shyness
   G anger   J grief

12 Wanting to do a different project than the rest of the group is _____. (pp. 310–311)
   A prejudice   C a stereotype
   B a conflict   D body language

13 If your heart is pounding and your hands feel sweaty, you are probably experiencing _____. (pp. 308–309)
   F stress   H boredom
   G a habit   J loneliness

14 This girl's body language shows that she is _____. (pp. 304–305)

   A bored   C listening
   B angry   D prejudiced

Formal Assessment

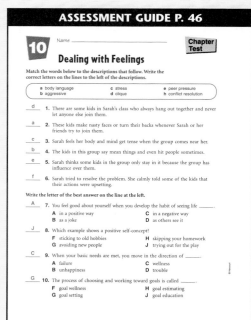

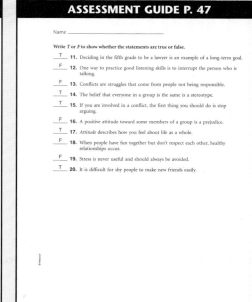

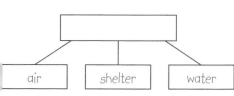

| air | shelter | water |

15 Which word belongs in the top box? (p. 294)
F wants **H** needs
G habits **J** goals

16 When you do something over and over, it becomes _____. (p. 292)
A an attitude **C** a goal
B a habit **D** a clique

17 An aggressive person is likely to _____. (p. 299)
F push someone to get his or her own way
G listen carefully to others
H set goals that are difficult to reach
J resolve conflicts peacefully

18 People who have a negative self-concept _____. (pp. 292–293)
A can easily make changes in their lives
B do not expect to meet their goals
C can usually resist peer pressure
D can't help how they feel

19 A so-called friend is trying to get you to steal a lunch from someone's backpack. This is an example of _____. (p. 300)
F prejudice
G peer pressure
H a stereotype
J managing stress

Think Critically

20 Audrey has set a goal of improving her grades. Explain why she should adjust her goal, and suggest one for her.

21 At lunchtime, a friend sighs and says, "I'm really having a bad day." Describe at least two ways you could use active listening to help this friend.

22 A neighbor your age wants you to take some of your uncle's cigarettes so you both can find out what smoking is like. The neighbor says, "If you're really my friend, you'll do this with me." How would you describe this relationship? What can you say to this person?

Apply Skills

23 **BUILDING GOOD CHARACTER**
Accept Individual Differences A new girl at school has trouble saying certain words. You hear a student making fun of her. What can you do?

24 **LIFE SKILLS**
Manage Stress Your science report is due tomorrow, so you go to the library to use a computer. When you get there, all five computers are being used. The library will close in an hour. You might not have time to finish your report—or even start it! Your stomach feels upset, and your hands are sweaty. How can you deal with this situation?

Write About Health

25 **Write to Inform** Explain why dealing with feelings is an important part of maintaining good health.

319

Performance Assessment

Use the Chapter Project and the rubric provided on the Project Evaluation Sheet. See *Assessment Guide* pp. 18, 60, 71.

Portfolio Assessment

Have students select their best work from the following suggestions:
- Leveled Activities, p. 311
- Quick Activity, p. 298
- Write to Inform, p. 316
- Activities, p. 317

See *Assessment Guide* pp. 12–16.

---

21. Possible answers: You could encourage the friend to share more about the problem by saying, "Why do you say that?" You could reflect the friend's feelings by saying, "You surely seem sad."

22. This is an unhealthy relationship that includes negative peer pressure. You could say, "No. I'm not going to steal from my uncle because it's wrong, and he wouldn't trust me if he found out. I am definitely not going to smoke. If you were really my friend, you wouldn't ask me to do this."

Apply Skills 7 pts. each

23. You could quietly tell the teaser that you overheard him or her and that the new girl might overhear too and feel hurt and embarrassed. You could show respect for the new girl by listening to her and ignoring her speech problem.

24. First, you can realize that stress is causing your upset stomach and sweaty hands. Then you can identify the cause: You are afraid that you will not get your report done in time. Next, you can think of ways to handle your stress, such as taking deep breaths and planning alternative ways to type your report. Then you can visualize handing in your completed report the next day.

Write About Health 7 pts.

25. Possible answer: Our feelings directly affect the health of our bodies, including the digestive system, nervous system, respiratory system, and cardiovascular system. If we are upset and unhappy, we will not feel well or do our best. When we know how to identify, control, and deal with our feelings, we are happier and healthier.

11 Supporting Your Family

Lesson	Pacing	Objectives	Reading Skills
Introduce the Chapter pp. 320–321		• Preview chapter concepts.	**Main Idea and Details** p. 321; pp. 372–383
1 Changing Families, Changing Roles pp. 322–326	1 class period	• Identify some kinds of changes that families experience. • Describe how children's responsibilities change as they mature.	**Main Idea and Details** pp. 323, 326 • Draw Conclusions, p. 325 • Summarize, p. 326
Building Good Character p. 327		• Recognize the importance of caring by supporting and forgiving family members.	
2 Communication in Families pp. 328–333	2 class periods	• Describe ways to communicate effectively with family members. • Identify causes of conflicts in the family and ways to resolve them. • Explain what to do if something bad happens in the family.	**Main Idea and Details** p. 333 • Cause and Effect, p. 329 • Summarize, p. 331 • Compare and Contrast, p. 333
Life Skills pp. 334–335	1 class period	• Identify the steps used to communicate effectively. • Use communication to solve problems.	
3 Families Working Together pp. 336–340	1 class period	• Explain why the family should be the focal point for seeking health advice and promoting good health. • Recognize the importance of developing a family health plan.	**Main Idea and Details** pp. 337, 340 • Sequence, p. 339 • Draw Conclusions, p. 340
Activities p. 341		• Extend chapter concepts.	
Chapter Review pp. 342–343	1 class period	• Assess chapter objectives.	

Vocabulary	Program Resources
	Music CD Teaching Resources, p. 43
empathy negotiate	Transparency 4 Activity Book, pp. 51–55
	Poster 1
communicate exploitation neglect	Transparency 4 Activity Book, pp. 51–52
	Activity Book, p. 54 Poster 7
health maintenance	Transparency 4 Activity Book, pp. 51–52
	The Learning Site www. harcourtschool.com/health
	Assessment Guide, pp. 31–33

Reading Skill

These reading skills are reinforced throughout this chapter and one skill is emphasized as the Focus Skill.

Main Idea and Details

- Draw Conclusions
- Identify Cause and Effect
- Compare and Contrast
- Sequence
- Summarize

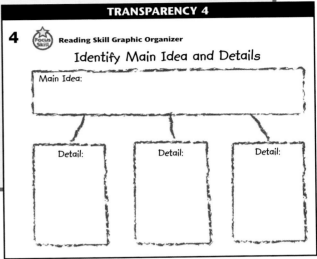

TRANSPARENCY 4

4 Reading Skill Graphic Organizer
Identify Main Idea and Details

Main Idea:

Detail: Detail: Detail:

Life Skills

Life Skills are health-enhancing behaviors that can help students reduce risks to their health and safety.

Six Life Skills are reinforced throughout *Harcourt Health and Fitness.* The skill emphasized in this chapter is Communicate.

POSTER 7

Communicate

The boy is communicating with his parents.

Steps for Communicating

1 Understand your audience.
2 Express your message in a clear, organized way.
3 Listen carefully, and answer any questions.
4 Gather feedback.

How well have **YOU** COMMUNICATED today?

Building Good Character

Character education is an important aspect of health education. When students behave in ways that show good character, they promote the health and safety of themselves and others.

Six character traits are reinforced throughout *Harcourt Health and Fitness.* The trait emphasized in this chapter is Caring.

POSTER 1

Caring

The girls are showing caring by helping each other.

DO
- Support and value family members.
- Be a good friend and share your feelings in appropriate ways.
- Show concern for others.
- Thank people who help you.
- Help people in need.

DON'T
- Don't be selfish.
- Don't expect rewards for being caring.
- Don't gossip about people.
- Don't hurt anyone's feelings.

How have **YOU** shown CARING today?

Coordinated School Health Program

A Coordinated School Health Program endeavors to improve children's health and, therefore, their capacity to learn through the support of families, schools, and communities working together. The following information is provided to help classroom teachers be more aware of these resources.

The National Center for Chronic Disease and Health Promotion, part of the **CDC,** funds the Coordinated School Health Program. Visit its website for information about the eight components that make up this program. **www.cdc.gov/ nccdphp/dash/**

Parent/Community Involvement is one of the eight components of the Coordinated School Health Program. The **YMCA of the USA** offers support to parents with *Building Strong Families* summary, fact sheet, and parenting quiz. **www.ymca.net/**

The goal of the **California Department of Education,** School Health Connections and Child Development Division, is to link schools with parents and community members to use the Coordinated School Health Program to promote a positive lifestyle for children. **www.cde.ca.gov/ cyfsbranch/lsp/**

Health Is Academic: A Guide to Coordinated School Health Programs, developed in collaboration with more than seventy national organizations and funded by the **CDC,** summarizes the concepts and the eight components of a Coordinated School Health Program. **www2.edc.org/MakingHealthAcademic/**

Other resources that support a Coordinated School Health Program:
- School-Home Connection
- Daily Physical Activity
- Daily Fitness Tips
- Activities: Home & Community
- Health Background: Webliography
- *Be Active! Resources for Physical Education*

Media Resources

Books for Students

Ransom, Candice F. *Fire in the Sky.* Carolrhoda Books, 1997. A child deals with relationships. **EASY**

Rosenberg, Liz, Ed. *Roots and Flowers: Poets and Poems on Family.* Henry Holt, 2001. Forty poets make statements about families. **AVERAGE**

Schwartz, Linda. *What Do You Think? A Kid's Guide to Dealing with Daily Dilemmas.* Learning Works, 1993. Presents situations requiring decision-making skills. **ADVANCED**

Books for Teachers and Families

Canfield, Jack. *Chicken Soup for the Kid's Soul.* Health Communications, 1998. Short stories foster discussions on issues that children face.

McLanahan, Sara, and Gary D. Sandefur. *Growing Up with a Single Parent— What Hurts, What Helps.* Harvard University Press, 2001. Describes the impact of divorce on children.

Free and Inexpensive Materials

Sylvan Learning Center
Request their brochure, *Seven Days of Activities for Family Learning Fun.*

U.S. Food and Drug Administration
Has articles on topics of interest such as "The Fright of the Iguana," which deals with the risk of infection from pets.

Federal Citizen Information Center
Request their poster "My History Is America's History" (#360K) on how to discover family history.

Mead Five-Star
Ask for *How to Have a Productive Teacher-Parent Conference* booklet.

To access free and inexpensive resources on the Web, visit **www.harcourtschool.com/health/free**

Videos

What's Right for Me: Making Good Decisions. Rainbow Educational Video, 1993.

Manners for Young Moderns. Educational Video Network, 1996.

Positive Critical Thinking. Educational Video Network, 1996

These resources have been selected to meet a variety of individual needs. Please review all materials and websites prior to sharing them with students to ensure the content is appropriate for your class. Note that information, while correct at time of publication, is subject to change.

Visit **The Learning Site** for related links, activities, resources, and the health **Webliography.**

www.harcourtschool.com/health

Meeting Individual Needs

ESL/ELL

Below-Level

Read a vocabulary word or chapter concept aloud. Have one student give the meaning of the word or concept. If the meaning is correct, the player draws one part of a Word Bug's body on the board. Continue play until the Word Bug has six legs, a body, a head, and two antennas.

Activities

- Acting Out, p. 324
- Acting Out, p. 330
- Family Health Poster, p. 338

On-Level

If students are having difficulty explaining what a paragraph is about, work with a small group to discuss how summarizing helps with comprehension. Have them tell or list the main points of the section. This will help them understand and remember what they read.

Activities

- Brainstorm, p. 324
- Conflict Solutions, p. 330
- Fun Things for the Family, p. 338

Challenge

Have students write a cinquain poem from the text. Have students follow this pattern in their poems: Line 1: a one-word title; Line 2: two adjectives describing the title; Line 3: three action verbs; Line 4: four words expressing feelings; Line 5: a one-word synonym for the title.

Activities

- Discuss Responsibility, p. 324
- Writing a Short Story, p. 330
- A Short Play, p. 338

Learning Log

Before reading, write each new vocabulary term on the board, pronounce it, and have students repeat it. Give the meanings and cite examples. Then whisper each term to a different volunteer. The volunteers act out their terms or draw pictures about them for others to guess.

Activities

- Comprehensible Input, p. 329
- Background and Experience, pp. 331, 337
- Language and Vocabulary, p. 332

Curriculum Integration

Integrated Language Arts/Reading Skills

- Books About Growth, p. 325
- Role-Play Feelings, p. 326
- Poem, p. 328
- Be a Mime, p. 334

Math

- Data on Injuries, p. 336
- Using Calories, p. 339

Use these topics to integrate health into your daily planning.

Physical Education

- Daily Fitness Tip, pp. 322, 328, 336
- Daily Physical Activity, p. 321

Art

- Family Fun, p. 340

CHAPTER SUMMARY

In this chapter students

► learn that family members help support each other in times of change.

► learn that families that communicate regularly stay close in good times and bad.

► learn that a family is a good source of health information and advice.

Life Skills

Students *communicate* with their family members.

Building Good Character

Students support family members by *caring*.

Consumer Health

Students *access valid information* on the nutritional values of foods.

 Literature Springboard

Use the article "Family Ties to Your Health" to spark interest in the chapter topic. See the Read-Aloud Anthology on page RA-12 of this *Teacher Edition*.

Prereading Strategies

SCAN THE CHAPTER Have students preview the chapter content by scanning the titles, headings, pictures, graphs, and tables. Ask volunteers to predict what they will learn. Use their predictions to determine their prior knowledge.

PREVIEW VOCABULARY Have students fold a sheet of paper in half lengthwise. In the left column, have them write definitions of the terms that they know.

Terms I Know	Terms I Don't Know

 Reading Skill

MAIN IDEA AND DETAILS To introduce or review this skill, have students use the Reading in Health Handbook, pp. 372–383. Teaching strategies and additional activities are also provided.

Students will have opportunities to practice and apply this skill throughout this chapter.

• Focus Skill Reading Mini-Lesson, p. 322

• Reading comprehension questions identified with the

• *Activity Book* p. 53 (shown on p. 326)

• Lesson Summary and Review, pp. 326, 333, 340

• Chapter Review and Test Preparation, pp. 342–343

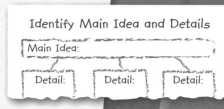

Focus Skill: Reading Skill

IDENTIFY MAIN IDEA AND DETAILS

The main idea is the most important thought in a reading passage. Details help you understand the main idea. They usually tell about *who*, *what*, *when*, *where*, *why*, and *how*. Use the Reading in Health Handbook on pages 372–383 and this graphic organizer to help you read the health facts in this chapter.

Identify Main Idea and Details

Main Idea:

Detail: Detail: Detail:

Health Graph

INTERPRET DATA In the past most American families with children had a father who worked and a mother who stayed home. Study the graph below to find out how things have changed. What trend is shown in the graph?

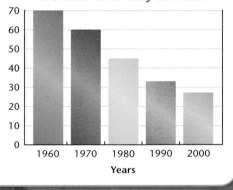

Mothers Who Stay at Home

(bar graph with values approximately)
- 1960: 70
- 1970: 60
- 1980: 45
- 1990: 33
- 2000: 27

Years

Daily Physical Activity

Supporting your family includes helping with chores. Some chores, like washing windows and raking leaves, provide physical activity.

Be Active!
Use the selection, Track 11, **Funky Flex**, to practice exercises you can share with your family.

321

School-Home Connection

Distribute copies of the School-Home Connection (in English or Spanish). Have students take the page home to share with their families as you begin this chapter.

Follow Up Have volunteers share the results of their activities.

Supports the Coordinated School Health Program (CSHP)

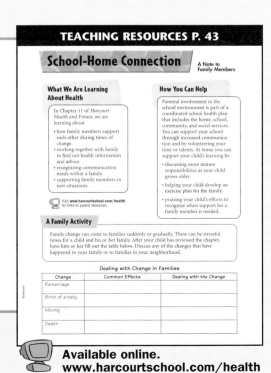

TEACHING RESOURCES P. 43

School-Home Connection — A Note to Family Members

What We Are Learning About Health

In Chapter 11 of *Harcourt Health and Fitness*, we are learning about

- how family members support each other during times of change.
- working together with family to find out health information and advice.
- recognizing communication needs within a family.
- supporting family members in new situations.

Visit www.harcourtschool.com/health for links to parent resources.

How You Can Help

Parental involvement in the school environment is part of a coordinated school health plan that includes the home, school, community, and social services. You can support your school through increased communication and by volunteering your time or talents. At home you can support your child's learning by

- discussing more mature responsibilities as your child grows older.
- helping your child develop an exercise plan for the family.
- praising your child's efforts to recognize when support for a family member is needed.

A Family Activity

Family change can come to families suddenly or gradually. These can be stressful times for a child and his or her family. After your child has reviewed the chapter, have him or her fill out the table below. Discuss any of the changes that have happened to your family or to families in your neighborhood.

Dealing with Change in Families

Change	Common Effects	Dealing with the Change
Remarriage		
Birth of a baby		
Moving		
Death		

Available online.
www.harcourtschool.com/health

INTRODUCE THE CHAPTER

Health Graph

Interpret Data

Have students answer the question in the graph. There are fewer families in which the father works and the mother stays home. **If the trend continues, what prediction could you make about American families in the future?** Possible response: The percent of families in which the father works and the mother stays home will be less than 27 percent.

Daily Physical Activity

Use *Be Active! Music for Daily Physical Activity* with the Instant Activity Cards to provide students with movement activities that can be done in limited space. Options for using these components are provided beginning on page TR2 in this *Teacher Edition*.

Chapter Project

Getting Personal
(*Assessment Guide* p. 61)

ASSESS PRIOR KNOWLEDGE Use students' initial ideas for the project as a baseline assessment of their understanding of chapter concepts. Have students complete the project as they work through the chapter.

PERFORMANCE ASSESSMENT The project can be used for performance assessment. Use the Project Evaluation Sheet (rubric), *Assessment Guide* p. 72.

Objectives
► Identify some kinds of changes that families experience.
► Describe how children's responsibilities change as they mature.

 When Minutes Count . . .
Assign the Quick Study, Lesson 1, Activity Book pp. 51–52 (shown on p. 323).

Program Resources
► Activity Book pp. 51–53
► Transparency 4

Vocabulary
empathy p. 324, **negotiate** p. 324

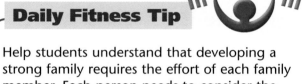

Daily Fitness Tip

Help students understand that developing a strong family requires the effort of each family member. Each person needs to consider the health and happiness of the other members. This may mean placing family first from time to time. Making sacrifices, sharing goals, and creating traditions help families stay strong.

 For more guidelines about fitness, see *Be Active! Resources for Physical Education.*

1. MOTIVATE

Ask students to imagine how they might feel if they had to move.

Did you want to move? Why? Did the whole family feel the same way?

Moving can be stressful for everyone in a family. Have students imagine that their families are moving.

What could you do to help make the move easier? Possible answer: Help pack and unpack; accept the change; look at the positive aspects of the move; help other children cope with the change.

 LESSON

1 Changing Families, Changing Roles

Lesson Focus
Family members can help and support each other during times of change.

Why Learn This?
Being a responsible member of your family will help you feel good about yourself.

Vocabulary
empathy
negotiate

Family Changes

Change is something that you can depend on happening regularly. Some changes happen with little or no effort on your part. You grow taller. A new student joins your class. You get a new soccer coach.

Other changes require your effort. If a new person joins your family, for example, you will need to do things in new ways. Some of the new ways will be challenging. You might have to share your room. Or you might have to do more chores. A new family member is a big change for the whole family.

Family members need to help each other when important changes happen. As you *mature*, or grow older, you become more responsible. You can be more helpful to your family. You can especially help younger brothers and sisters deal with big changes.

◄ Losing a pet can be a painful experience. A parent or other family member can help you deal with the loss.

322

 Focus Skill **Reading Skill**

Mini-Lesson

MAIN IDEA AND DETAILS
Remind students that the main idea is the paragraph's most important idea and that details tell about the main idea. Have them practice this skill by responding to the Focus Skill question on page 323. Have students draw and complete the graphic organizer as you model it on the transparency.

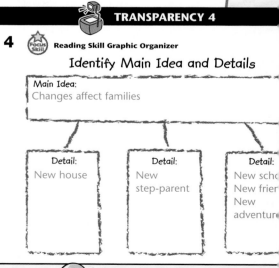

TRANSPARENCY 4

4 **Reading Skill Graphic Organizer**
Identify Main Idea and Details

Main Idea:
Changes affect families

Detail:	Detail:	Detail:
New house	New step-parent	New scho New frier New adventure

Interactive Transparencies available on CD-ROM.

Dealing with Change in Families

Change	Common Effects	Dealing with Change
Remarriage	Confusion about how to fit into a new family	Take time to adjust, and be patient with each other.
Birth of a baby	More responsibilities for parents; older children may feel jealous and left out	Find ways to help out so parents will have more time to spend with you.
Moving	Happiness about your new home but sadness about leaving old friends and old school	Make friends in your new neighborhood and school.
Death	Sadness, loneliness, and anger	Talk about your feelings; write about your feelings.

Sharing things with new family members helps them feel welcome. ▼

Pleasant Changes Many of the changes you experience through the years are pleasant. For example, you might discover that you enjoy singing, so you might become part of a choir. Your whole family may experience pleasant changes together. Your family may decide to take a special vacation, try new foods, or start a new activity that is fun for everyone. These changes can help your family grow closer.

Difficult Changes Families sometimes experience big changes that are hard to deal with. A new baby, divorce, remarriage, and death are all difficult changes. Such changes put stress on families. During these times, family members need to support each other.

 MAIN IDEA AND DETAILS **Write about ways that changes affect families. Describe pleasant and difficult changes, and include details.**

Possible answer: Changes can result in more responsibilities. They can help family members grow closer together. When difficult changes occur, family members need to help and support each other. Pleasant changes may include vacations and new family activities; difficult changes may include divorce, death, birth of a new baby, remarriage, and moving.

323

QUICK STUDY, ACTIVITY BOOK PP. 51–52

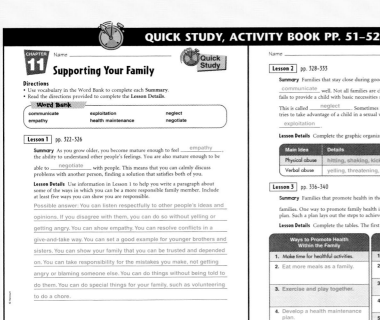

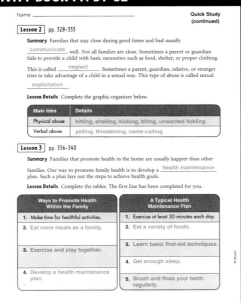

Available online.
www.harcourtschool.com/health

2. TEACH

Interpret Visuals—Pictures

Direct attention to the photograph on this page. Tell students that the picture shows a man and child welcoming the man's new wife and her child to their home. Such families are called blended families.

Critical Thinking **What evidence suggests that the woman and her child feel welcome?** They are both smiling. The girl has a pet hamster, which indicates that her new stepfather has agreed to allow her to have a pet. Allowing her to keep her pet probably makes her feel welcome.

Interpret Visuals—Table

Tell students to read the table on this page. **What are some other common effects of a move?** having to get used to new stores, new school, different living arrangements

Discuss

Problem Solving Have students imagine that their best friend is having difficulty dealing with his or her parents' recent divorce.

What can you do to help your friend cope with this difficult change? Possible answer: Be patient and understanding; be a good listener.

Health Background

A child who lives in a family with only one parent generally has fewer economic resources available than does a child with two parents. One-parent households are substantially more likely to have family incomes below the poverty line than are two-parent households.

Source: *ChildStats*

GO ONLINE For more background, visit the **Webliography** in Teacher Resources at **www.harcourtschool.com/health** **Keyword** family life

TEACH *continued*

Content-Area Reading Support

Using Typographic Clues Direct students' attention to the phonetic respellings that follow the highlighted words on this page. Tell students that new words often are followed by respellings. The syllables in small capital letters indicate where the main emphasis should be placed when the word is spoken. Have students identify additional respelled terms in this chapter. Help students who are having difficulty pronouncing the words.

Discuss

Talk about some of the ways people accept greater responsibility as they mature.

Do all people mature at the same rate? Everyone matures at a different rate.

What factors might cause one person to mature earlier than others? Possible answer: A child with only one parent could mature earlier than other children if he or she is expected to accept additional family responsibilities.

What factors might cause a person to mature later than most others? Possible answer: A child who has been given few responsibilities might mature later than other children.

Discuss

Critical Thinking Sean, a friend of yours, shows empathy for you after your pet dies. **How will you likely treat Sean when something bad happens to him?** Possible answer: I will likely show empathy and will treat him the same way that he treated me.

Consumer Activity

Analyze Media Messages

TV families often argue. Watch one of your favorite shows. When family members argue, write down the cause. Then write how they settled the argument. Did they negotiate a solution that made both sides happy?

Family Responsibilities

When you were a baby, your parents took care of all your needs. They fed you, dressed you, and kept you safe. Now you are older. You are mature enough to be responsible for yourself and others in many ways.

You can help and support your family by being respectful. Listen respectfully to other people's ideas and opinions. If you disagree, do so without yelling or getting angry. You are also mature enough to feel **empathy** (EM·puh·thee), which means you can understand other people's feelings. When you have empathy, you are able to imagine that you are in someone else's place. You can relate to how the person feels. When you know how a person feels, you can treat him or her the way that you would like to be treated in the same situation.

You are also old enough to be able to negotiate (nih·GOH·shee·ayt). When you **negotiate**, you discuss and resolve a conflict with another person.

You'll never forget to do a chore if you make a list of what to do. Check off your chores as you do them. ▼

MY CHORES
Feed the cat.
Clean the litter box.
Take out the trash.
Set the table.

324

Meeting Individual Needs
Leveled Activities

BELOW-LEVEL Resolve Conflict Have groups of students act out situations in which they resolve a conflict or show responsibility at home or at school. Have other students identify the specific strategies used in each presentation.

ON-LEVEL Brainstorm Have students work in pairs to brainstorm ways to ease the trauma of moving to a new home and school. Have them illustrate their suggestions and share the results with the class.

CHALLENGE Discuss Responsibility Have pairs of students discuss how the level of responsibility grows as a person's skills and abilities increase.

For example, if you and your sister both want to use the computer at the same time, you can negotiate a solution that both of you can accept.

As you become more responsible, your family begins to trust and depend on you. You do your regular chores without being reminded. You try to do your chores better, and you accept suggestions for improvement. Doing your chores well helps the whole family.

You even do things without being asked. For example, if you see a bike left in the driveway, you move it to a safe place. When someone is behind on chores, you offer to help. Sometimes you help the family by doing a special job, like cleaning up the kitchen after a party.

As a responsible family member, you are a good model for younger brothers and sisters. For example, when you make a mistake, you are mature enough to take responsibility for it. You also learn from your mistakes.

▲ Caring about his older sister is one way this boy shows he is a responsible family member.

DRAW CONCLUSIONS Why is it important to feel empathy?
Possible answer: If you understand a person's feelings and needs, you will be able to get along with him or her better.

Quick Activity

List Responsibilities Think about the types of jobs you do for your family now. Could you have done these jobs five years ago? What types of jobs will you be able to do in a few years? Write your answers in a chart.

◄ This furry family member depends on other family members to feed him.

325

Teacher Tip

Job Loss Loss of a job by one family member can be stressful for all other members. Make sure students understand that a person who loses a job may sometimes blame himself or herself even though he or she did nothing wrong. As a result, the person may become depressed or feel inadequate. Students should understand that families need to be very supportive of a family member who loses a job.

Quick Activity
Possible answer: I can do many jobs that I wasn't able to do five years ago. A few years from now, I may cook meals for the family. When I am a teenager, I may run errands with the family car.

Discuss
What are some ways people your age can set a good example for brothers and sisters? Possible answer: using good table manners; listening to and obeying parents; doing jobs without being reminded; showing respect to family members

Discuss
Critical Thinking Why is it important to make an effort to learn from your mistakes? Possible answer: so that you don't repeat the same mistakes

Discuss
Have students discuss the importance of communication skills as a major influence in the social health of the family. Talk about the importance of being trusted by your family.

Problem Solving How does a person gain another person's trust? Possible answers: by doing jobs well and on time; by doing what the person promises to do **How can you lose someone's trust?** Possible answers: by lying; by failing to do what you promise to do

Consumer Activity
Students should report on family arguments dramatized in one or two television programs they have watched. They should indicate the cause of each argument, how the characters resolved it, and whether the resolution made both sides or only one side happy.

3. WRAP UP

Lesson 1 Summary and Review

1. mature, responsible; empathy; negotiate; volunteer

2. Possible answer: *p*leasant: new friends, new traditions; *un*pleasant: divorce, death

3. Set a good example for younger brothers and sisters; do jobs without being reminded; take responsibility for mistakes.

4. Possible answers are shown below.

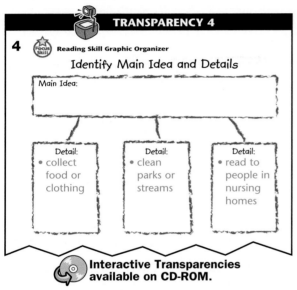

TRANSPARENCY 4

4 Reading Skill Graphic Organizer

Identify Main Idea and Details

Main Idea:

| Detail: • collect food or clothing | Detail: • clean parks or streams | Detail: • read to people in nursing homes |

Interactive Transparencies available on CD-ROM.

5. Poems will vary but should demonstrate the process or experiences of growth.

For **writing models** with examples, see *Teaching Resources* pp. 47–61. Rubrics are also provided.

When Minutes Count ...

Quick Study Students can use *Activity Book* pp. 51–52 (shown on p. 323) as they complete each lesson in this chapter.

Volunteering in the Community

Some families do *volunteer* work. Volunteers give their time to good causes without being paid. Many families collect food for people who don't have enough. Some families help clean up parks or lakes. Still others read to people in nursing homes.

Volunteering has many benefits. It meets needs in your community. It is also a way to spend time with your family. Working together toward a common goal can be very satisfying for all of you. Volunteer work also helps you as you mature by showing you how to care for others. As a volunteer, you become a more responsible person.

SUMMARIZE List several types of volunteer work that families can do.

Answers will vary but may include collecting food for those who don't have enough, cleaning up parks, and reading to people in nursing homes.

◀ **Families often help community or religious organizations collect food.**

Lesson 1 Summary and Review

❶ **Summarize with Vocabulary**

Use vocabulary and other terms from this lesson to complete the statements.

As you _____, or grow older, you can become more _____ and helpful in your family. As you continue to grow, you can feel _____, which is an understanding of other people's feelings. You are also able to _____. This means that you can help resolve conflicts through discussion. Some families _____, or help out in their neighborhoods.

❷ What are two pleasant and two difficult changes that a family can experience?

❸ **Critical Thinking** How can you become a more responsible member of your family?

❹ **MAIN IDEA AND DETAILS** Draw and complete this graphic organizer to show three details related to the main idea described in the box.

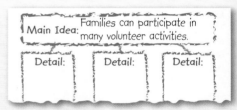

Main Idea: Families can participate in many volunteer activities.

| Detail: | Detail: | Detail: |

❺ **Write to Entertain—Poem**

Write an eight-line poem that is titled "I'm Nearly Grown Up Now."

326

ACTIVITY BOOK P. 53

Name _____

Reading Skill

Identify Main Idea and Details

Family Time

Families may have very busy schedules. How do they find time to communicate? Some families have discovered that mealtime is a good time to talk about family news. Some even make it a point to cook dinner together. Sometimes schedules do not permit sharing regular family meals. In this case, work with your family to find a time when everyone can be together. Perhaps you can plan a fun activity such as playing a game together or going to a park or beach.

Writing letters and notes is another way for family members to stay in touch. You can write a note to say you are sorry for something you said or did. Your parents may have given you permission to go next door after school. You can write a note to tell your parents where you are and that you will set the table when you get home. Such notes show you care about your family. You don't want them to worry.

You don't always need words to communicate. Doing something special for a family member shows you care, too. A hug, a smile, a wink, or a pat on the back can also communicate feelings.

1. What is the main idea in paragraph 1?
   Even busy families can find time to be together and communicate.

2. What details support the main idea in paragraph 1?
   Some families talk about family news at mealtimes. Some families cook together. Some families plan a fun activity to do together.

3. What details in paragraph 2 answer this question: Why might you want to write a note to your parents or another family member?
   You might want to say you are sorry for something you said or did. You might want to make sure your parents know where you are and when you will be home so they won't worry.

4. How can you communicate that you care about your family without using words?
   You can do something special for a family member. You can also communicate feelings with a hug, a smile, a wink, or a pat on the back.

Available online. www.harcourtschool.com/health

Integrated Language Arts/ Reading Skills

Role-Play Feelings Have students work in groups of three to role-play the feelings and actions surrounding the birth of a sibling. Students can choose to play the roles of parents or children. Have them express themselves verbally and with body language.

Caring

Support Family Members

Changes in the makeup of your family can be stressful. This is especially true for a new family member or a family member who moves away. A new family member may not feel welcome or accepted. A family member who moves away, such as a grandparent who moves to a nursing home, needs your support more than ever. Here are a few simple ways to show these family members that you really care about them:

- **Include all family members in family traditions.**
- **Do something special for a family member.**
- **Show family members things you think might interest them. For example, you can show a grandparent photos or movies on a computer.**
- **Be a good listener.**
- **Respect the opinions of all family members, even though you might disagree with them.**
- **Be responsible by doing your chores and helping out, even when you're not asked to.**
- **Be understanding.**

Activity

With a classmate, write a short skit for the class. You can play the role of a boy or girl whose family has just adopted a twelve-year-old. Your classmate can play the role of the adopted child. Write a dialogue for the two children. The adopted child should express his or her fears about joining the new family. You should show how to welcome him or her through words and actions.

327

Using the Poster

Activity Suggest that students design and display their own posters about supporting and caring for family members.

Display Poster 1 to remind students of ways to show they care. The poster can be displayed in the classroom, school cafeteria, or another common area.

POSTER 1

Caring

The girls are showing caring by helping each other.

DO	DON'T
► Support and value family members.	► Don't be selfish.
► Be a good friend and share your feelings in appropriate ways.	► Don't expect rewards for being caring.
► Show concern for others.	► Don't gossip about people.
► Thank people who help you.	► Don't hurt anyone's feelings.
► Help people in need.	

How have **YOU** shown **CARING** today?

POSTER 1

Caring
Citizenship
Fairness
Respect
Responsibility
Trustworthiness

Objective
► Recognize the importance of caring by supporting and forgiving family members.

Program Resource
► Poster 1

BEFORE READING
Write this phrase on the board: "Caring means . . ." Have students complete the sentence on a small piece of paper, fold it, and hand it in unsigned. Read and discuss the definitions.

DISCUSS
Talk about the ways to show caring toward a family member who has been affected by change.

What are some special things that you can do for a family member? Possible answer: help with chores, take him or her to a movie, hug him or her.

ACTIVITY
Make sure students understand what the skits should show. You may want to model some dialogue so that students are aware of an appropriate type of writing. Tell students to refer to the list on this page to get ideas for ways to show that they care.

Objectives

► Describe ways to communicate effectively with family members.

► Identify causes of conflicts in the family and ways to resolve them.

► Explain what to do if something bad happens in the family.

 When Minutes Count . . .

Assign the Quick Study, Lesson 2, Activity Book pp. 51–52 (shown on p. 323).

Program Resources

► Activity Book pp. 51–52

► Transparency 4

► Growth, Development, and Reproduction pp. 32–33

Vocabulary

communicate p. 328,

exploitation p. 332, **neglect** p. 332

 Daily Fitness Tip

Emphasize to students that communication and family health go hand in hand. Family members who do not share feelings, good or bad, run the risk of creating health problems for themselves. Physical, emotional, or mental problems can result when a person keeps things inside. In addition, the rest of the family suffers when one member does not communicate effectively.

CSHP For more guidelines about fitness, see *Be Active! Resources for Physical Education.*

1. MOTIVATE

Have students identify ways to enhance personal communication skills. Tell students that effective communication does not necessarily involve words. Encourage students to brainstorm different ways to nonverbally communicate *yes* and *no.* yes: nodding head up and down, giving the OK signal, thumbs up; no: shaking head sideways, thumbs down

 LESSON 2

Communication in Families

Lesson Focus

Families that communicate well stay close during good times and bad.

Why Learn This?

Good communication skills will help you resolve many conflicts.

Vocabulary

communicate
exploitation
neglect

How Families Communicate

Why are some families close? They're close because they communicate (kuh•MYOO•nih•kayt) well. Family members **communicate** by sharing views, thoughts, and feelings with each other. They also listen carefully. As a result, the family stays close during bad times as well as good.

A family's well-being depends on good communication. When you are happy, tell your family why. If you hit a home run or get a good grade in school, let everybody know about it. You should also let family members know when you are sad. Tell them what is troubling you. They will listen to you and let you know they care. They may even have a solution to your problem. If not, they can help you work on one. Just talking about a problem with a parent or another family member is helpful.

Good communication isn't only about you. It includes showing you care about others. Find ways to

Busy families can communicate while they prepare meals together. ▶

 *Quick* **Activity**

Communicate Good Things Write three good things that have happened to you in the last week. Share your list with your family.

328

 Integrated Language Arts/ Reading Skills

Poem Have pairs of students write a poem that explores the importance of communication in families. Before students begin writing, you might want to have them read the first section in the lesson. Encourage students to illustrate their poems. Post the poems on the bulletin board.

Teacher Tip

Dealing with Change Make sure students understand that they should ask their parents or other family members for help when they are trying to deal with a difficult change. Remind them that a large part of being responsible is knowing how and when to ask for help and advice. Talking to parents is particularly important in times of change.

tell family members how much you love them. Saying something nice helps spread good feelings through the whole family. Also, listen respectfully when other family members talk to you. Listening carefully is another way to show you care.

Many families have busy schedules. How do they find time to communicate? Many families talk things over at mealtimes. Some families even make it a point to cook dinner together.

Sometimes, schedules do not allow regular family meals. In this case, work with your family to find a time when all of you can be together. Maybe you can plan an activity you'll all enjoy, such as playing a game together or going to a park or beach.

You can even communicate with family members in writing. Writing letters is a way for family members to stay in touch when they might be apart. Try writing a note to say you are sorry for something you said or did. You can also use a note to tell a parent where you are and when you will be home. Such notes show that you care about and respect your family.

You don't always need words to communicate. Doing something special for a family member also shows you care.

CAUSE AND EFFECT **What is the effect of telling people you are proud of them?**
Positive comments help spread good feelings through the whole family.

Personal Health Plan ▶
Real Life Situation
You realize that you should communicate better with your family members. You want to take action immediately.
Real-Life Plan
Make a list of some of the good things you like about each family member. Share your list with your family.

One way families communicate is by planning a vacation together, even if everyone isn't happy with the plan. ▼

329

ESL/ELL Support

COMPREHENSIBLE INPUT The term *communication* is a noun, but it does not represent a concrete object. Clarify with students the concept of communication.

Beginning Collect pictures in which people are communicating verbally or nonverbally and others in which no communication seems to be taking place. Have students put the pictures that show communication in one pile and the ones that do not show communication in a separate pile.

Intermediate Have students describe situations that involve verbal and nonverbal communication and other situations that do not.

Advanced Have students write a story in which characters communicate verbally and nonverbally.

2. TEACH

Quick Activity
Tell students that the good things in their lists do not have to be major events.

Interpret Visuals—Pictures
What does this photograph tell you about effective communication? Possible answer: Sometimes people communicate effectively through actions rather than words. Helping a family member with a chore shows him or her that you care.

Content-Area Reading Support
Using Paragraph Structure Direct attention to the third paragraph, which begins on page 328 and ends on page 329. Tell students that the main idea is stated in the first two sentences. The details—ways to show you care—follow the main idea.

What are the details in this paragraph? saying something nice, listening carefully and respectfully Tell students that reading the first sentence or two of each paragraph is a good way to find out what a lesson is about. Encourage them to use this pre-reading strategy before reading each lesson.

Discuss
Have students explain the importance of communication skills as a major influence on the emotional health of the family.

Problem Solving In what types of situations would it be helpful to talk to a parent or guardian about a problem? if you are experiencing anger, sadness, stress, or grief

Why is it helpful to talk with a trusted adult when you have a problem? Adults have experienced many of the problems that you are likely to experience. Thus, they may be able to offer good suggestions on how to deal with the problems. In addition, they can listen to you without judging you.

Plans should include lists of
- each family member
- some good things about each family member

 Activity

Possible answer: She could go home and leave a note on the refrigerator or family bulletin board; she could call again; she could decide to have dinner with her friend another day; she could go home and start preparing dinner.

Discuss

What is the difference between a disagreement and an argument? Possible answer: When people disagree, they express differing opinions or viewpoints on a topic. They may or may not accept the other person's viewpoint. When people argue, they disagree about something but express their disagreement with anger or are unwilling to consider that the other person might have some valid points.

Content-Area Reading Support
Using Signal Words Direct attention to the last sentence in the first paragraph on this page: *But they should be resolved before they grow.* Tell students that *but* is a signal word. It qualifies the preceding sentence: *Such conflicts are normal.* Other words such as *although*, *yet*, *however*, and *nevertheless* also qualify phrases or sentences. Students should be aware of these qualifying words as they read.

Resolving Family Conflicts

Conflicts happen in every family. They often result from misunderstandings. Failure to communicate also causes conflicts. You might argue with a brother about the use of a game or toy. You might disagree with a parent about how late you can stay outdoors after dinner. Such conflicts are normal, but they should be resolved before they grow.

Family members need to work together to resolve conflicts. Understanding the other person's point of view is important. If you have a conflict with someone, listen carefully and quietly to what that person is saying. To be sure you understand the person's thinking, ask questions. Then calmly give your point of view. Clearly tell your wants, needs, and feelings with "I" messages, such as "I feel badly when I can't watch my favorite TV show about animals. Someday I want to be a vet."

ACTIVITY

 Building Good Character

Responsibility Tina usually comes home right after band practice. Her dad has dinner ready around 5:00 P.M. Today, however, she wants to have dinner with a friend. She calls home at 4:30 to ask permission, but no one answers. Describe at least two ways Tina can show responsible behavior.

Being a responsible family member means thinking how your actions will affect others. ▶

330

Meeting Individual Needs
Leveled Activities

BELOW-LEVEL Have students work in groups to act out a situation in which they resolve a conflict or show responsibility at home or in school. Have other students identify the specific strategies used in each presentation.

ON-LEVEL Have pairs make up a conflict that could occur at school. Students should brainstorm as many solutions to the conflict as possible. After the list is complete, have them record whether each solution might work for all parties involved and *why* it would or would not.

CHALLENGE Students could write short stories that feature a conflict that is peacefully resolved.

After you and the other person give your points of view, work toward a solution. It should be one that makes both of you happy. Giving in on some points, or *compromising*, is part of becoming a mature person. But sometimes a compromise is not possible. The differences between the people are too great. In those cases, a parent or another family member may suggest a fair solution.

At times, your parents may tell you that you can't do something you'd like to do because it isn't safe. You should accept their decision. They probably have good reasons for making it. Accepting a decision you can't change shows that you are mature.

Some families resolve conflicts by holding family meetings. These meetings give all family members the chance to tell their points of view. This may help avoid more serious conflicts by settling disagreements before they go too far. Good communication helps keep families happy and strong.

> **SUMMARIZE** What are three things you can do to resolve small disagreements before they grow into larger ones?

ry to understand the other person's point of view; calmly give your point of view; work toward a compromise.

331

▲ Many families like to keep a note board in the kitchen. They write schedules and dates on the board. They may also leave important messages there.

ACTIVITY
Life Skills
Resolve Conflicts
Bill says it's his sister Jo's turn to walk the dog, but she tells him she wants to play a computer game first. Write down two ways to help them resolve this conflict. How can writing possible solutions help you resolve your own conflicts?

Activity

Sample answer: Jo's parents might want her to walk the dog before it gets dark or because the dog is used to being walked right after dinner. Jo might reason that it doesn't make any difference when the dog is walked just as long as it happens. A possible solution would be to walk the dog right after dinner. Jo's parents presented her with good reasons. Besides, she doesn't want to argue with her parents over such a trivial matter.

Interpret Visuals—Pictures
Have students look at the illustration on page 330.

How is the student's behavior affecting her younger siblings? They are disturbed because the music is too loud. **Why is this behavior irresponsible?** A responsible person cares how his or her actions affect others.

Discuss
Problem Solving Have students imagine that an older sister is using the basketball court in the driveway. Although you have asked nicely, your sister refuses to let you use the court for a half hour. You are on your school's basketball team, and you would like to practice for a big game.

What "I" messages could you use to clearly state your wants, needs, and feelings to your sister? Possible answer: "I really need to practice. I don't want to let my teammates down. You're so good at basketball; would you please help me practice for the game?"

TEACH *continued*

Discuss

Tell students that some children do not report incidents of abuse because they are afraid or feel that they are partly to blame for the abuse. Emphasize that an abused person is *never* at fault. Sometimes abused children are afraid to report abuse because the abuser threatens them. For example, the abuser might say he or she will harm a family member if the abused person tells. Students should understand that an abused person should never believe such threats. An abused child should tell a trusted adult about the incident immediately. Have students explain the impact of neglect and abuse.

Discuss

Problem Solving Make sure that students understand the difference between a proper touch and an improper touch.

Would any of the following be considered abuse—a family doctor examining a child; a mother giving a young child a bath; an uncle who kisses a child on the cheek as a greeting? None are abuse. None would make the child feel uncomfortable or confused.

Health Background

Children who are the victims of extended sexual abuse usually develop low self-esteem, feelings of worthlessness, and abnormal views of sex. They often become withdrawn, do not trust adults, and may exhibit suicidal behavior. Sexually abused children and their families should seek immediate help from a qualified psychiatrist who specializes in children and adolescents.

Source: *American Academy of Child and Adolescent Psychiatry*

For more background, visit the **Webliography** in Teacher Resources at **www.harcourtschool.com/health Keyword** family life

---

Abuse and Neglect

Bad things can happen in all types of families. These bad things may include abuse. *Abuse* is the harmful treatment of another person.

Abuse can be physical or verbal. Physical abuse may include hitting, shaking, kicking, and biting. Even tickling can be physical abuse. It's abuse when the person who is doing the tickling does not stop when asked.

Sexual abuse is another form of physical abuse. It's an act of touching a person in a way that makes the person feel uncomfortable or confused. Sexual exploitation (ex•ploy•TAY•shuhn) is a form of sexual abuse. **Exploitation** means "taking advantage of someone." Sexual exploitation is taking advantage of someone in a sexual way.

Verbal abuse may include yelling, threatening, and name-calling. This type of abuse can hurt a person just as much as physical abuse. People who are verbally abused often lose self-esteem.

Neglect is another form of abuse. **Neglect** is failure to take care of a person's basic needs, such as food and clothing. Sometimes family members are guilty of neglect of another family member.

Myth and Fact

Myth: You should never talk to a stranger.
Fact: You may need to ask a stranger for help in an emergency. Always remember to use common sense. If you feel uncomfortable with a stranger, leave immediately and ask someone else for help.

◄ Your school counselor can help you learn about forms of abuse.

332

ESL/ELL Support

LANGUAGE AND VOCABULARY Help students understand that *abuse* can be used as a noun and as a verb.

Beginning Have students pronounce the noun form and verb form of the word *abuse* several times.

Intermediate Tell students to write simple sentences using *abuse* as a noun and as a verb. Provide models if necessary.

Advanced Have students create a simple table that shows some of the forms of abuse.

Abuse, exploitation, and neglect are against the law. If someone is doing something to you against your will or is doing something to you that you don't like, tell the person "No!" in a firm voice. Then get away from the person as quickly as you can. As soon as possible, tell a parent or another trusted adult about the abuse.

COMPARE AND CONTRAST What is the difference between good tickling and bad tickling?

Good tickling is wanted and fun. Bad tickling is tickling that continues after you ask the person to stop.

Having your fingerprints on file can help police if you become lost or are kidnapped. ▶

Health & Technology

Safe-Kids Kit The National Crime Prevention Council says that safe-kids identification kits can help prevent many crimes against kids. The kits feature instructions and ink for making fingerprints. They also have booklets with tips for handling emergencies.

Lesson 2 Summary and Review

1 Summarize with Vocabulary

Use vocabulary and other terms from this lesson to complete the statements. Families stay close when they _____. When conflicts arise, it is important to be able to _____, or give in on some points. Bad things sometimes happen in families. One of these is _____, which is a failure to take care of a person's basic needs. Another bad thing is sexual _____.

2 Critical Thinking What are some ways family members can communicate good feelings without using words?

3 How can families resolve small conflicts before they get worse?

4 MAIN IDEA AND DETAILS Draw and complete this graphic organizer to show details related to the main idea described in the box.

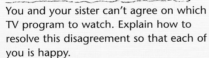

Main Idea:	Abuse sometimes happens in families.

Detail:	Detail:	Detail:

5 Write to Inform—Explanation

You and your sister can't agree on which TV program to watch. Explain how to resolve this disagreement so that each of you is happy.

333

Teacher Tip

Lessons that provide strategies for teaching about child abuse, including sexual exploitation, are provided on pages TR30–TR33. Lessons are also provided in the optional component *Growth, Development, and Reproduction*, pp. 26–33. Use these lessons and components in compliance with state and local guidelines.

3. WRAP UP

Lesson 2 Summary and Review

1. communicate; compromise; neglect; exploitation
2. They can do special things for family members. Hugs and smiles can also be used to communicate feelings without using words.
3. They can regularly set aside time to talk together.
4. Possible answers are shown below.

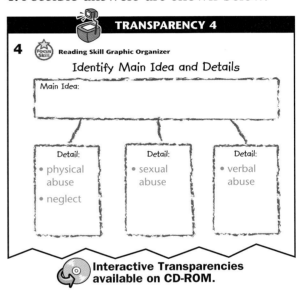

TRANSPARENCY 4

4 Reading Skill Graphic Organizer

Identify Main Idea and Details

Main Idea:

Detail:	Detail:	Detail:
• physical abuse • neglect	• sexual abuse	• verbal abuse

Interactive Transparencies available on CD-ROM.

5. Possible answer: My sister can pick the first program, and I'll pick the second one.

For **writing models** with examples, see *Teaching Resources* pp. 47–61. Rubrics are also provided.

When Minutes Count . . .

Quick Study Students can use *Activity Book* pp. 51–52 (shown on p. 323) as they complete each lesson in this chapter.

Life Skills

Communicate
Make Responsible Decisions
Manage Stress
Refuse
Resolve Conflicts
Set Goals

Objectives
► Identify the steps used to communicate effectively.
► Use communication to solve problems.

Program Resources
► Activity Book p. 54
► Poster 7

1. MOTIVATE

Talk with students about a story that is in the news. The story should be familiar to students and should feature a problem faced by two people, two groups, or two countries. Ask students to offer solutions to the problem. Then talk about the fact that all solutions require the two sides to communicate effectively.

2. TEACH

Step 1

How could Kendra communicate with her mother that she knows she will need to help more? She could offer to help her mother with more family chores.

Building Good Character

Remind students that when communicating with family members, they should consider ways to show that they care. **What evidence suggests that Kendra is a caring person?** She acknowledges that her mom is busy and needs more help from the family. This shows that Kendra cares about her mother.

Communicate
with Your Family

Communicating with other people is not always easy, but it is important. Communication skills help you express your feelings in healthful ways. Using the steps for **Communicating** can help you build better relationships with the people in your family.

Kendra's mom has just taken a job. Kendra wonders about coming home to an empty house after school. Her older brother gets home an hour after Kendra arrives. She worries about who will drive her to dance lessons and help her with her homework. How can Kendra use communication skills to help her talk to her parents?

1 **Understand your audience.**

Kendra knows that her mom will be away from home more often, so her mom will need help from the whole family.

2 **Give a clear message.**

After dinner Kendra talks to her parents. "I'm worried about being home alone after school. Who will help me with my homework?"

334

Integrated Language Arts/ Reading Skills

Be a Mime Have teams of students take turns using pantomime, body language, hand signals, and other nonverbal clues to communicate short health messages to the class. If you wish, you could prepare the messages in advance and let the teams draw the messages out of a bag. The class should try to guess the message that is being communicated.

ACTIVITY BOOK P. 54

Name _____

 Life Skill
Communicate

Steps for Communicating with Your Family
1. Understand your audience.
2. Give a clear message.
3. Listen actively.
4. Gather feedback.

Use these steps to help these students communicate with their families.

A. Mahesh's mother has remarried. Mahesh is upset because his new stepfather takes a long shower each morning. He takes the shower at the time Mahesh used to take his shower. As a result, Mahesh doesn't have enough time to get ready for school. He has been late several times.
• How can Mahesh use communication skills to solve his problem?
Possible answer: Mahesh likes his stepfather, but he doesn't feel he is ready to talk with him one-on-one. At dinner, he decides to talk with his mother and stepfather. He states his problem clearly, telling them about being late for school. Mahesh then listens carefully as his mother and stepfather offer suggestions. Finally, they agree that his stepfather will shower in the evening.

B. Cheryl recently injured her ankle while she was playing softball after school. She wants to tell her parents about the injury, but she is afraid to do so because she was supposed to be home at the time, doing her homework.
• How can Cheryl use communication skills to solve her problem?
Possible answer: Cheryl realizes that her parents are concerned about her health. She decides to tell them about her injury at breakfast. She also apologizes for disobeying them. She listens carefully as her parents tell her that she did the right thing by telling them. The family doctor treats her ankle.

Available online.
www.harcourtschool.com/health

③ Listen actively.

"Rusty can keep me company."

"You could do homework after supper."

"I think those are good ideas."

The family listens, and everyone makes suggestions. They agree that Kendra can let the dog in to keep her company and do her homework after supper.

④ Gather feedback.

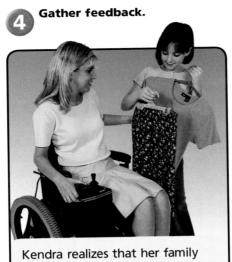

Kendra realizes that her family cares about her and will help her adjust to the changes.

💡 Problem Solving

A. Mandy shares a computer with her older brother. She is upset because he seems to want to use the computer whenever she wants to. She must finish a research paper in two days, and she needs to use the computer for at least three or four hours.
  - Use the steps for **Communicating** to help resolve Mandy's problem. Be sure the resolution is fair.

B. Julio often forgets to do things he promises. As a result, his older sister usually has to do more chores around the house.
  - How can Julio's older sister be fair while helping her brother learn not to be forgetful?

335

Using the Poster

Activity Suggest that students design and display their own posters about communicating.

Display Poster 7 to remind students of the steps used to communicate effectively.

Display the poster in the classroom, school cafeteria, or another common area.

POSTER 7

Communicate

The boy is communicating with his parents.

Steps for Communicating

❶ Understand your audience.   ❸ Listen carefully, and answer any questions.

❷ Express your message in a clear, organized way.   ❹ Gather feedback.

How well have YOU COMMUNICATED today?

POSTER 7

Step 2
Utilize critical thinking in problem solving.

Critical Thinking **Why is it important for Kendra to clearly communicate her concerns to her family?** Kendra's family won't be able to help if they can't fully comprehend her concerns.

Step 3
What suggestions and offers does Kendra hear and make when she actively listens to her family? help with homework, time to spend together, a ride to dance class, the dog for company

Problem Solving **What could Kendra do if she didn't like any of her family's suggestions?** She could develop other ideas and see if her family agrees with them.

Step 4
What does Kendra learn by gathering feedback? She learns that her family cares about her concerns and will help her adjust to the changes.

3. WRAP UP

Problem Solving

A Possible answer: Mandy knows that her brother's friend rarely uses his computer. She suggests that her brother ask to use this computer for the next two nights. In return, she offers to stay off their computer when he has a paper due. Mandy listens to her brother without interrupting. Her brother finally agrees. Mandy realizes that her brother cares about her.

B Possible answer: She understands that Julio is a good brother except for his forgetfulness. She tells him how his forgetfulness affects her. She listens to his apologies. Then she suggests that he keep a small notebook in his back pocket so he can write down things he needs to do. He agrees. Julio rarely forgets anymore.

Objectives

► Explain why the family should be the focal point for seeking health advice and promoting good health.

► Recognize the importance of developing a family health plan.

 When Minutes Count . . .

Assign the Quick Study, Lesson 3, Activity Book pp. 51–52 (shown on p. 323).

Program Resources

► Activity Book pp. 51–52, 55
► Transparency 4

Vocabulary

health maintenance p. 340

 **Daily Fitness Tip**

Many young people are anxious or self-conscious about asking their family doctors or even their parents or guardians about health concerns. Remind students that health-care professionals and their parents or guardians are there to help them.

 For more guidelines about fitness, see *Be Active! Resources for Physical Education.*

1. MOTIVATE

Have students describe daily and weekly activities that promote the health of the family. Possible answer: by exercising, eating good foods, learning first-aid and safety techniques, avoiding dangerous situations, getting enough sleep, regularly brushing and flossing teeth

What are some of the benefits of promoting health in the family? Possible answers: living longer; living a fuller life—being able to do the things you want to do because you are physically able to do so

---

3 Families Working Together

Lesson Focus

Your family can give you information and advice about health and can promote good health within the family.

Why Learn This?

You can live a happier, healthier, longer life if you work with your family toward achieving health goals.

Vocabulary

health maintenance

Seeking Health Advice from Family Members

We all have questions about our health from time to time. For example, have you ever wondered if a new snack food is bad for you? Or have you ever wanted to learn more about exercising to keep a healthful weight? Information about these and many other health topics can often be found at home.

Your parents may not be doctors or nurses, but they can probably answer many of your health questions. When they decided to raise a family, your parents may have read books about family health. They probably have also asked your family doctor many questions.

Parents should be the first people you talk to about health matters. They can help you decide what exercises to do. They can also help you choose the right foods to eat. They can even give you medicines for a cold or a fever.

 **Myth and Fact**

Myth: You should play through pain.

Fact: If you feel pain while you are exercising or playing, you should stop immediately. Pain tells you that the activity is hurting you. If you ignore the pain, you may seriously injure yourself.

▲ If you injure yourself, tell a parent or another trusted adult right away.

336

Teacher Tip

Medicine Safety Make sure students understand that they should never take any medicine without the permission of a parent or trusted adult. This applies even to vitamins and ordinary pain relievers such as acetaminophen. Vitamins and pain relievers can be toxic if too many are taken or if they interact with other medicines.

 ## Math

Data on Injuries Have students use the graph on page 337 as a guide to survey friends, classmates, and family members under the age of fourteen to find out which injuries they have suffered in the last year. Students should record their findings in a circle graph. Assist any students who have difficulties calculating percents.

Your parents may not have all the answers. But they can help you look for them, and they know when to ask a doctor. Together with your parents you might find health information by searching the Internet. Your local library also has books, magazines, and other health-related resources you can use together.

Some health questions that you have might be personal. You should never be embarrassed to ask your parents these types of questions. They care for you and understand your feelings because they were once your age, too. Not asking these types of questions may be putting your health at risk.

 MAIN IDEA AND DETAILS
Your parents can help you find health information. Name two places where you might find this type of information.
the Internet and the library

Leading Causes of Injuries

Fire/burns 2%
Dog bite 2%
Poison 2%
Bicycle 4%
Motor vehicle 4%
Cut/pierce 6%
Struck by object 22%
Other 22%
Falls 36%

Quick **Activity**

According to the graph, what is the leading cause of injuries? List the causes in order, from most common to least common.

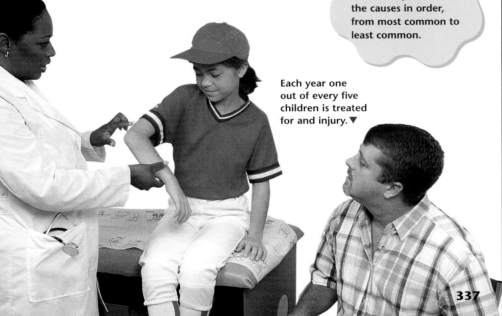

Each year one out of every five children is treated for and injury. ▼

337

2. TEACH

Quick Activity
Falls are the leading cause of injuries. List: falls, being struck by object, other, cut/pierce, motor vehicle occupant, bicycle, fire/burns, dog bite, poison

Interpret Visuals—Graph
What percent of children fourteen and under are treated for an injury shown in the graph? 20 percent

Interpret Visuals—Pictures
Have students look at the pictures on these pages.

What do these pictures tell you about the role parents play in keeping their children healthy? Possible answer: When children are injured, parents can often tell what treatment is needed or if a visit to a doctor is necessary.

Discuss
Have students analyze the components of a personal health maintenance plan for families.
Problem Solving Have students look at the graph. Talk about things that can be done to prevent some of the injuries.

What steps could you take to reduce your chances of being injured while riding a bicycle? wear a helmet; use a light at night; wear knee pads; use proper directional signals

Health Background

People should never continue to exercise if they are injured. They should follow the advice given in the acronym R.I.C.E.: Rest (stop playing and rest), Ice (apply ice to the injured area), Compression (wrap injured area with a supportive bandage), and Elevate (raise the injured part to reduce swelling).

Source: *KidsHealth*

 For more background, visit the **Webliography** in Teacher Resources at **www.harcourtschool.com/health** **Keyword** injury prevention

TEACH *continued*

Content-Area Reading Support

Using Titles and Headings Direct attention to the headings on these pages. Point out that the first heading, Promoting Health Within the Family, identifies the overall topic. It is in larger type than the other headings. The other headings are subheadings. They provide information about ways to promote health within the family.

What are some of these ways? holding family meetings, eating more family meals, exercising and playing together Encourage students to use headings and subheadings when they are creating an outline of a reading passage or a lesson.

Discuss

Talk with students about the concept of time management. Emphasize that people who are busy need to manage their time so that they are able to do everything that they want and need to do.

What are some ways you manage your time? Possible answer: write important dates or things to do on a calendar or in a notebook.

Interpret Graphics—Pictures

Have students look at the picture on this page.

What types of things do you think the younger children learn by taking walks with their family? Possible answer: They learn that participating in activities with the family can be fun; they learn that you feel good after you exercise; they can learn about a wide variety of topics by listening to parents and siblings.

Promoting Health Within the Family

You and your family can meet many challenges if you work together. Staying healthy is a big challenge. However, it is a challenge that is worth the effort to meet. Families that promote health are usually happier and more likely to live long, active lives.

Families can do many things to promote health in the home. The problem, however, is finding time. Families today are very busy. Often, both moms and dads have jobs. Older brothers and sisters may have jobs or activities after school. You probably have many activities, too. On the next page are ways a family can promote health.

Did You Know?

Only one out of three children participates in daily physical activity. About one out of four adults gets no vigorous exercise at all. Encourage your family to exercise together. Studies show that people should get at least 30 minutes of moderate activity each day.

Families who take walks together get good exercise. Walks also provide a time for families to communicate. ▶

338

Meeting Individual Needs
Leveled Activities

BELOW-LEVEL Family Health Poster Have students create a poster that shows one or two ways to promote health in the family.

ON-LEVEL Fun Things for the Family Students could create a list of fun, healthful activities that they would like to do with their families. Encourage students to share their lists with their families at dinner or during a family walk or meeting.

CHALLENGE A Short Play Small groups of students could create a short play about a family that holds a family meeting and plans several healthful activities.

◀ Picking fresh vegetables or fruit with your family is good exercise and fun. Fresh foods also taste great and add variety to your diet.

Make time for healthful activities

Talk about healthful activities that family members can enjoy together. Making time for family activities may be hard. If one person is always busy, offer to do one or more of his or her chores. If the jobs are divided evenly, your family will have a better chance to find time for things that are healthful and fun.

Eat more meals as a family

Eating meals with your family helps you develop good eating habits. Children who have regular family meals usually eat foods that are more healthful than do children who eat alone. They usually eat fewer snacks, too. Eating together also gives everyone a chance to suggest family activities.

Exercise and play together

Regular exercise helps keep you healthy. Your family can enjoy exercising and playing together. Walking, biking, hiking, swimming, and just playing ball in the park are activities that can be enjoyed by the whole family.

SEQUENCE Make a list of three things that your family can do to promote health within the family. List your ideas in order of importance to you.

Possible answers: exercising and playing together; holding family meetings; eating more meals together

Consumer Activity

Access Valid Health Information Eating healthful, balanced meals is important. With a parent, use the Internet or the library to research the nutritional value of different foods. Then use your research to plan and write out a healthful menu for your family for a week.

339

3. WRAP UP

Lesson 3 Summary and Review

1. communicate; health maintenance
2. family members
3. Possible answer: They have busy schedules.
4. Possible answers are shown below.

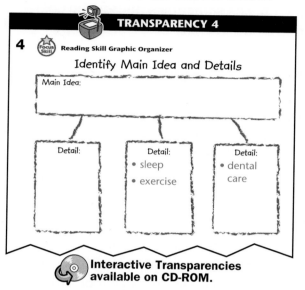

TRANSPARENCY 4

4 Reading Skill Graphic Organizer

Identify Main Idea and Details

Main Idea:

Detail:

Detail:
• sleep
• exercise

Detail:
• dental care

 Interactive Transparencies available on CD-ROM.

5. Paragraphs might include changing the times of various activities and developing new activities.

 For **writing models** with examples, see *Teaching Resources* pp. 47–61. Rubrics are also provided.

When Minutes Count ...

Quick Study Students can use *Activity Book* pp. 51–52 (shown on p. 323) as they complete each lesson in this chapter.

Personal Health Plan

Real-Life Situation
You realize you may not be doing everything you can for your health.

Real-Life Plan
Make a weekly chart with a personal health maintenance program. Provide spaces where you can check off each completed item.

Developing a Family Health Plan

When you set goals, you make a plan containing the steps that will lead you to the goals. That is why families that want to maintain, or keep, their health need a plan. A **health maintenance** (MAYNT•uhn•uhns) plan includes the steps to take to achieve goals for good health. A typical family health maintenance plan might include the following:

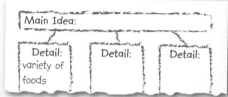

❶ Exercise at least 30 minutes each day.

❷ Eat a variety of foods.

❸ Learn basic first-aid techniques.

❹ Get enough sleep.

❺ Brush and floss your teeth regularly.

DRAW CONCLUSIONS **Can a family be healthy without developing a health maintenance plan?**
Possible answer: Probably, but it's easier to achieve a goal when you have a clear plan.

Lesson 3 Summary and Review

❶ **Summarize with Vocabulary**

Use vocabulary and other terms from this lesson to complete the statements.

Family meetings provide an opportunity for a family to _____, or share feelings and opinions about family health. Every family should develop a _____ plan. Such a plan lays out the steps the family should take to achieve its health goals.

❷ Who are the first people you should talk with when you have questions about health matters?

❸ **Critical Thinking** Why is it often difficult for families to promote health in the home?

❹ **MAIN IDEA AND DETAILS** Draw and complete this graphic organizer to show the missing details of a health maintenance plan.

Main Idea:

Detail: variety of foods

Detail:

Detail:

❺ **Write to Inform—Explanation**

Explain how to change a health maintenance plan as a family changes.

340

Art

Family Fun Have students create a collage showing families engaged in a variety of activities. Pictures can come from magazines and the Internet. The collage should show families doing things like talking, visiting parks and the zoo, cleaning house, and engaging in leisure activities and sports.

ACTIVITY BOOK P. 55

Name _____

Vocabulary Reinforcement

Word Meanings

Complete the sentences in the following paragraphs by using terms from the Word Bank. Use context to help you choose the correct term.

| neglect | negotiate | communicate |
| health maintenance | empathy | exploitation |

1. Sarah used to be very self-centered. She never thought about the feelings of her parents, brothers, sisters, and friends. She is more mature now. She is able to feel _____empathy_____ and can imagine herself in someone else's situation and understand that person's feelings.

2. Juan used to keep all of his problems to himself. As he grew older, he discovered how to _____communicate_____ with his family. He is glad that he has learned to share his viewpoints, thoughts, and feelings with his family during good times as well as bad.

3. There are many types of _____exploitation_____, the unfair use of someone. A person who takes advantage of someone in a sexual way is guilty of this type of behavior.

4. Sheena and her family discovered that they were neglecting their health. At a family meeting, they discussed steps they could take to improve and maintain their health. Sheena wrote down these steps and posted them on the family bulletin board. This _____health maintenance_____ plan has helped improve the health of everyone in the family.

5. Many children in this country are victims of _____neglect_____, a form of abuse. People guilty of this type of abuse fail to provide their children with proper clothing or enough food.

6. Darnell used to get into a lot of arguments with his brothers and sisters. Then, as he became more mature, he learned how to _____negotiate_____. Now he is able to resolve conflicts with his brothers and sisters in a give-and-take way.

 Available online.
www.harcourtschool.com/health

ACTIVITIES

Math

Survey Friends and Classmates Survey your friends and classmates to find out how many times their families have moved in the last ten years. Show your results in a bar graph. Then find the average number of times your classmates and friends have moved in the last five years.

Science

Observe Animal Communication Observe pets, such as dogs and cats, or wild animals, such as birds and squirrels. Notice how they communicate with other animals of their kind and with animals of different kinds. What parts of their bodies do they use? What do you think they are trying to communicate? Write a short report describing your observations.

Technology Project

Make a Leaflet Families can grow stronger when they volunteer to help people in the community. Find three or four activities in your community that a family could volunteer to do. Using a computer, make a leaflet that lists and briefly describes these activities. If a computer is not available, use construction paper and markers to make your leaflet.

 For more activities, visit The Learning Site. www.harcourtschool.com/health

Home & Community

Order Activities Ask your classmates what activities their families do together. Summarize the answers in a list showing the activities in order from the most common to the least common. Share your list with your classmates and teacher.

Career Link

Social Worker Social workers help families deal with difficult changes. Suppose you are a social worker. You have an appointment with a family of people who are stressed because of a new baby. Prepare a list of five suggestions that you think will help them deal with this change in their family.

Career Link

Social Worker Before students begin the activity, briefly discuss their conceptions of what social workers do. Students' suggestions could include scheduling times for people to help care for the baby; getting people to help shop for groceries and run errands; getting people to help with laundry and other household chores; getting people to baby-sit so that the parents can have some time to themselves; and getting the parents to schedule time to spend with their other child or children.

For more information on health careers, visit the **Webliography** in Teacher Resources at **www.harcourtschool.com/health** **Keyword** health careers

Activities

Math
If necessary, review with students the procedures for determining an average. Encourage students to illustrate their graphs.

Science
Tell students that they should not get too close to the animals. If binoculars are available, students should use them to view the animals. Students who have cameras might take pictures of some of the animals as they communicate. The photographs could be used to illustrate their reports.

Home & Community
Some students might like to show the results of their surveys in an illustrated graph.

 Supports the Coordinated School Health Program

Technology Project
Prior to the activity, discuss search words or search engines that students could use to find information on the Internet. Suggest that students create their leaflets from standard-size letter paper folded in half or in thirds. Encourage students to illustrate their leaflets with photographs or drawings.

Chapter Review and Test Preparation

Pages 342–343

 Reading Skill 8 pts. each

1. abuse
2. sexual abuse

 Use Vocabulary 2 pts. each

3. F, empathy
4. B, negotiate
5. D, volunteer
6. A, mature
7. C, communicate
8. E, neglect

 Check Understanding 3 pts. each

9. D, a new teacher
10. H, regularly
11. B, disagreeing
12. F, mature
13. C, getting good grades
14. J, bike
15. B, communication
16. F, conflict
17. C, telling no one about the abuse
18. F, self-esteem
19. B, rudeness

 Think Critically 6 pts. each

20. Answers will vary. Possible answers: You can listen respectfully to other people's ideas and opinions. You can feel empathy. You are able to negotiate conflicts through discussion. You do a job as well as possible. You don't make excuses, get angry over little things, or blame someone else for things you have done.

Chapter Review and Test Preparation

 Reading Skill

IDENTIFY MAIN IDEA AND DETAILS
Draw and then use this graphic organizer to answer questions 1 and 2.

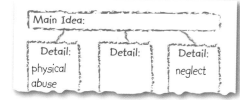

1 What main idea belongs in the graphic organizer above?
2 What detail is missing?

Use Vocabulary

Match each term in Column B with its meaning in Column A.

Column A	Column B
3 Understanding of others' feelings	A mature
4 To resolve conflicts through discussion	B negotiate
5 To work for a cause without being paid	C communicate
6 To become more responsible and helpful	D volunteer
7 To share thoughts, opinions, and feelings	E neglect
8 To fail to provide someone with basic needs, such as food or clothing	F empathy

Check Understanding

Choose the letter of the correct answer.

9 Which of these changes is **NOT** a difficult change that families sometimes face? (pp. 322–333)
   A a death   C a new baby
   B a move   D a new teacher

10 Change is something that happens _____. (p. 322)
   F once in a while   H regularly
   G hardly ever   J never

11 Which of these actions is **NOT** a form of abuse?
   A hitting   C name-calling
   B disagreeing   D neglect

12 Being able to compromise is part of being a(n) _____ person. (p. 331)
   F mature   H old
   G young   J unreasonable

13 Which of these changes requires some effort on your part? (p. 322)
   A getting older
   B getting taller
   C getting good grades
   D getting a new teacher

14 Which of the following items is **NOT** a basic need? (p. 332)

342

Formal Assessment

ASSESSMENT GUIDE P. 49

ASSESSMENT GUIDE P. 50

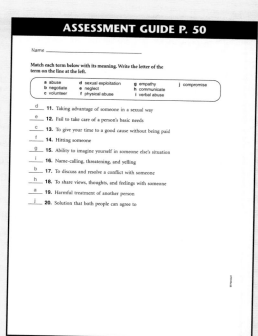

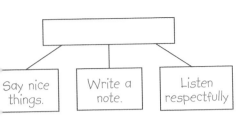

Say nice things. Write a note. Listen respectfully.

15 Which is the main idea of the graphic organizer above? (p. 328–329)
 A compromise **C** negotiation
 B communication **D** disagreement

16 Misunderstandings and poor communication can lead to ____. (p. 330)
 F conflicts **H** exploitation
 G solutions **J** compromises

17 Which of these actions would probably **NOT** be a good idea if you are abused? (pp. 332–333)
 A saying "No!" in a firm voice
 B quickly getting away from the abuser
 C telling no one about the abuse
 D calling an abuse hotline

18 People who are verbally abused often lose ____. (p. 332)
 F self-esteem **H** weight
 G their patience **J** their temper

19 The picture on page 330 is an example of ____. (p. 330)
 A politeness **C** caring
 B rudeness **D** sharing

 Think Critically

20 What are some signs that you are becoming more mature?

21 Why is it important for family members to communicate with each other on a regular basis?

22 What role does listening play when you are trying to resolve a conflict with someone?

Apply Skills

23 **BUILDING GOOD CHARACTER**
 Caring Your grandmother has just told you that she will be moving to a nursing home on the other side of town. She is very sad and confused. What can you do or say to show her that you care about her?

24 **LIFE SKILLS**
 Communicate Your parents are very special to you. Despite some disagreements, you respect them and the judgments they have made. What are some of the ways you can show your parents how much you appreciate them?

Write About Health

25 **Write to Inform—Explanation** Explain why it is important to support your family during good times as well as bad times.

343

---

21. Possible answers: Communication shows that you care. Communication helps families stay close during good times and bad.

22. Possible answers: You need to listen carefully in order to understand the other person's ideas and point of view. Once you understand the other person's viewpoint, you can work toward a resolution.

Apply Skills 7 pts. each

23. Possible answer: You could hug her and tell her that you love her. You could visit her often.

24. Possible answer: You could do extra chores. You could cook dinner one night. You could hug them both and tell them that you love them.

Write About Health 7 pts.

25. Possible answer: It is important to the health of your family members to support them during good times and bad. Family members need to know that you appreciate and care for them. They also need your support anytime they have problems.

Performance Assessment

Use the Chapter Project and the rubric provided on the Project Evaluation Sheet. See *Assessment Guide*, pp. 18, 61, 72.

Portfolio Assessment

Have students select their best work from the following suggestions:
- Leveled Activities, p. 338
- Quick Activity, p. 337
- Write to Inform, p. 340
- Activities, p. 341

See *Assessment Guide* pp. 12–16.

ASSESSMENT GUIDE P. 51

Name _____

21. A new baby can bring difficult changes to a family. A new baby can also present pleasant changes. Describe some of the pleasant changes.
 Possible answer: opportunities to watch a new member of the family grow; to teach things to the baby; to accept new responsibilities

22. Your grandfather is getting too old to take care of himself. He is moving into your family's home. Describe how you can make him feel welcome.
 Possible answers: Be understanding; be a good listener; do something special for him; play a board game with him; show him something I've made.

23. Write a paragraph about why communication is important in every family.
 Possible answer: Good communication shows that family members care about one another. Family members can help one another solve a variety of problems. Your family will be happy if you tell them about the good things that happen to you.

24. Complete the list below by adding two steps in a typical family health maintenance plan. Answers may vary slightly.

1. Exercise at least 30 minutes each day.	4. Get enough sleep.
2. Eat a variety of foods.	5. Brush and floss your teeth regularly.
3. Learn basic first-aid techniques.	

25. Tom's cousin touched him in a way that made him feel uncomfortable. Describe the steps that Tom should take.
 Possible answer: He should tell his cousin "No!" in a firm voice and get away as quickly as possible. He should then immediately tell a parent, guardian, or other trusted adult what happened.

12 Working Toward a Healthful Community

Lesson	Pacing	Objectives	Reading Skills
Introduce the Chapter pp. 344–345		• Preview chapter concepts.	🔵 **Summarize** p. 345; pp. 372–383
1 Groups That Protect Public Health pp. 346–349	1 class period	• Identify programs that promote community health. • Identify private groups as sources of health information. • Find out about roles of the World Health Organization and local health agencies in disease prevention.	🔵 **Summarize** pp. 346, 349 • Compare and Contrast, p. 347
2 Community Health Needs pp. 350–353	1 class period	• Explain the role of health agencies involved in community health. • Learn some ways to access health information. • Identify community sources of health services.	🔵 **Summarize** pp. 350, 353 • Sequence, p. 351 • Main Idea and Details, p. 353
3 Handling Community Emergencies pp. 354–358	2 class periods	• Identify sources of assistance in the event of an emergency. • List some causes of forest fires and explosions. • Demonstrate ways to help support positive family interactions.	🔵 **Summarize** pp. 355, 358 • Sequence, p. 357 • Compare and Contrast, p. 358
⭐ **Building Good Character** p. 359		• Participate in community efforts to address local issues.	
4 Protecting Land, Water, and Air pp. 360–363	1 class period	• Identify environmental factors that affect community health. • Analyze how environmental and personal health are related. • Identify environmental protection programs that promote community health.	🔵 **Summarize** pp. 360, 363 • Draw Conclusions, p. 361 • Cause and Effect, p. 363
🏃 **Life Skills** pp. 364–365	1 class period	• Describe how a safe school environment leads to a healthful community. • Identify when help is needed in making decisions and setting goals. • Identify ways in which communication skills enhance goal achievement.	
5 Protecting Consumers pp. 366–368	1 class period	• Identify methods of accessing valid health information. • Utilize critical thinking in decision-making and problem solving. • Cite ways of knowing if health information, products, and services are reliable.	🔵 **Summarize** pp. 367, 368 • Draw Conclusions, p. 368
Activities p. 369		• Extend chapter concepts.	
Chapter Review pp. 370–371	1 class period	• Assess chapter objectives.	

Vocabulary	Program Resources
	Music CD Teaching Resources, p. 45
public health **sanitation**	Transparency 6 Activity Book, pp. 56–57, 58
sewage **septic tank** **sanitary landfills**	Transparency 6 Activity Book, pp. 56–57
evacuation	Transparency 6 Activity Book, pp. 56–57
	Poster 2
natural resources **conserve**	Transparency 6 Activity Book, pp. 56–57
	Activity Book, p. 59 Poster 12
	Transparency 6 Activity Book, pp. 56–57, 60
	The Learning Site **www. harcourtschool.com/health**
	Assessment Guide, pp. 52–54

Interactive Transparencies
available on CD-ROM.

Reading Skill

These reading skills are reinforced throughout this chapter and one skill is emphasized as the Focus Skill.

Summarize

- Draw Conclusions
- Identify Cause and Effect
- Identify Main Idea and Details
- Sequence
- Compare and Contrast

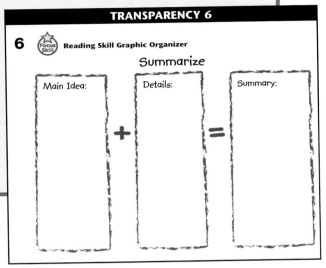

TRANSPARENCY 6

6 Reading Skill Graphic Organizer

Summarize

Main Idea: + Details: = Summary:

Life Skills

Life Skills are health-enhancing behaviors that can help students reduce risks to their health and safety.

Six Life Skills are reinforced throughout *Harcourt Health and Fitness*. The skill emphasized in this chapter is Set Goals.

POSTER 12

Set Goals

The girl is setting a goal to get more exercise.

Steps for Setting Goals

1 Choose a goal.
2 Plan steps to reach that goal. Determine whether you will need help.
3 Check your progress as you work toward the goal.
4 Evaluate the results of your work.

What **GOALS** have **YOU** SET?

POSTER 12

Building Good Character

Character education is an important aspect of health education. When students behave in ways that show good character, they promote the health and safety of themselves and others.

Six character traits are reinforced throughout *Harcourt Health and Fitness*. The trait emphasized in this chapter is Citizenship.

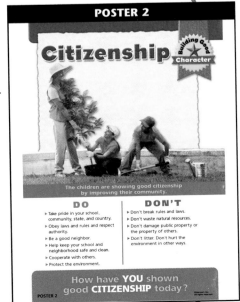

POSTER 2

Citizenship

The children are showing good citizenship by improving their community.

DO
► Take pride in your school, community, state, and country.
► Obey laws and rules and respect authority.
► Be a good neighbor.
► Help keep your school and neighborhood safe and clean.
► Cooperate with others.
► Protect the environment.

DON'T
► Don't break rules and laws.
► Don't waste natural resources.
► Don't damage public property or the property of others.
► Don't litter. Don't hurt the environment in other ways.

How have **YOU** shown good **CITIZENSHIP** today?

POSTER 2

Resources

Coordinated School Health Program

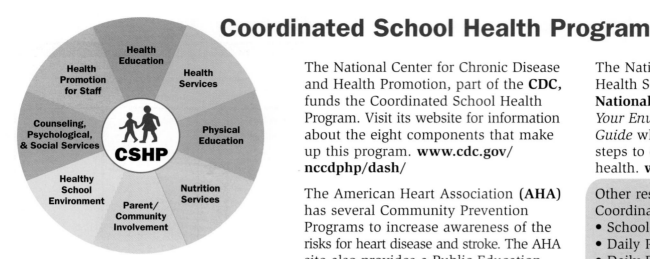

A Coordinated School Health Program endeavors to improve children's health and, therefore, their capacity to learn through the support of families, schools, and communities working together. The following information is provided to help classroom teachers be more aware of these resources.

The National Center for Chronic Disease and Health Promotion, part of the **CDC,** funds the Coordinated School Health Program. Visit its website for information about the eight components that make up this program. **www.cdc.gov/ nccdphp/dash/**

The American Heart Association **(AHA)** has several Community Prevention Programs to increase awareness of the risks for heart disease and stroke. The AHA site also provides a Public Education Material List of all their printed products. **www.americanheart.org/**

The **Baylor College of Medicine** and the National Institute of Environmental Health Services **(NIEHS)** offers activities for children and tips for parents on environmental health on their Kids' Pages.

The National Institute of Environmental Health Services, a branch of the **National Institutes of Health,** offers *Your Environment Is Your Health Family Guide* which identifies twenty easy steps to ensure personal environmental health. **www.health.nih.gov**

Other resources that support a Coordinated School Health Program:
- School-Home Connection
- Daily Physical Activity
- Daily Fitness Tips
- Activities: Home & Community
- Health Background: Webliography
- *Be Active! Resources for Physical Education*

Books for Students

Hooper, Meredith. *The Drop in My Drink: The Story of Water on Our Planet.* Viking Children's Books, 1998. Explains the importance of water conservation. **EASY**

Maze, Stephanie, and Catherine O. Grace. *I Want to Be an Environmentalist.* Harcourt, 2000. Describes ways to pursue a career in that field. **AVERAGE**

Beil, Karen Magnuson. *Fire in Their Eyes: Wildfires and the People Who Fight Them.* Harcourt, 1999. Depicts the real-life experiences of firefighters. **ADVANCED**

Books for Teachers and Families

Liverman, Catharyn T., Carrie E. Ingalls, and Carolyn E. Fulco. *Toxicology and Environmental Health Resources: The Role of the National Library of Medicine.* National Academy Press, 1997. Looks at hazardous waste and the changing trends in health practice.

Media Resources

Bartone, John C. *Human Body Encyclopedia of Exposures to Environmental Conditions for Ill Health, Sickness, & Disease Including Various Cancers.* 5 Vols. ABBE Publishers Association, 1997. Offers valuable health information.

Free and Inexpensive Materials

World Wildlife Fund
Ask for the Action Kit, which has free bookmarks and other items.

A&E Classroom
Will send *The Idea Book for Educators* containing the A&E Classroom Calendar and Teacher's Guides.

Health Information Network
Will provide free kits, brochures, and fact sheets such as "How Asthma-Friendly Is Your School?"

Federal Citizen Information Center
Request the pamphlet *Catch the Spirit: A Student's Guide to Community Service* (#501K).

To access free and inexpensive resources on the Web, visit **www.harcourtschool.com/health/free**

Videos

The Rotten Truth. Children's Television Workshop, 1990.

Power Up: Energy in Our Environment. Rainbow Educational Media, 1992.

Clean Water—The Earth at Risk. Schlessinger Video Productions, 1993.

These resources have been selected to meet a variety of individual needs. Please review all materials and websites prior to sharing them with students to ensure the content is appropriate for your class. Note that information, while correct at time of publication, is subject to change.

Visit **The Learning Site** for related links, activities, resources, and the health **Webliography.**

Meeting Individual Needs

ESL/ELL

Below-Level

To practice study strategies, students can fold a paper to form two columns. In the left column, they write questions they may have before or while they read. In the right column, they write the page number where they found the answer.

Activities

- Public Health Hotlines, p. 348
- Water Use, p. 350
- Be Prepared, p. 354
- The Three R's and You, p. 360

On-Level

Encourage students to jot down key words or concepts that are unclear. If something does not make sense, remind students that they may have missed an important point. Tell them to reread the passage, focusing on the context of the key words.

Activities

- Tobacco Road, p. 348
- Cycling Water, p. 350
- Consult the Pros, p. 354
- Recycling and You, p. 360

Challenge

To help students analyze content, have them make judgments on a health-related topic. Write scenarios on cards that could be considered right or wrong. Have students take turns pulling out a card, reading it aloud, and deciding if the action taken was, in their opinion, right or wrong.

Activities

- Disease Statistics, p. 348
- Sewage Treatment, p. 350
- Building Citizenship, p. 354
- Step Up Conservation Effort, p. 360

Learning Log

Read aloud a portion of the text as students echo what you read. You may wish to give students an opportunity to read aloud the quantity of text he or she is comfortable with. The student can give a signal word such as *popcorn* to indicate when he or she is ready for someone else to read.

Activities

- Background and Experience, pp. 352, 362
- Comprehensible Input, pp. 356, 366

Curriculum Integration

Math

- Rising Water, p. 355

 **Physical Education**

- Daily Fitness Tip, pp. 346, 350, 354, 360, 366
- Daily Physical Activity, p. 345

 **Use these topics to integrate health into your daily planning.**

 Science

- Tricky Treats, p. 351
- Plants That Need Fires, p. 357
- Xeriscaping, p. 361
- Recycling Flow Chart, p. 364

 Social Studies

- Research Disease, p. 349
- A Virtual Tour, p. 358

 Art

- Depicting Natural Disasters, p. 355
- Playing Safe, p. 367

CHAPTER SUMMARY

In this chapter students
► find out about groups that promote personal and environmental health.
► explain the role of health agencies involved in community health.
► identify sources of assistance in the event of an emergency.

Life Skills

Students practice *setting goals* to promote community health and to protect the environment.

Building Good Character

Students develop *citizenship* by showing pride in their community.

Consumer Health

Students access valid health information.

Literature Springboard

Use the poem "Litterology" to spark interest in the chapter topic. See the Read-Aloud Anthology on page RA-13 of this *Teacher Edition*.

Prereading Strategies

SCAN THE CHAPTER Have students preview the chapter content by scanning the titles, headings, pictures, graphs, and tables. Ask volunteers to speculate as to what they will learn. Use their predictions to determine their prior knowledge.

PREVIEW VOCABULARY Have students make a table with the headings shown below. Have students complete the first two columns before reading the chapter.

Vocabulary Word	What I Think It Means	What It Means

344

 Focus Skill Reading Skill

SUMMARIZE To introduce or review this skill, have students use the Reading in Health Handbook, pp. 372–383. Teaching strategies and additional activities are also provided.

Students will have opportunities to practice and apply the skill throughout this chapter.

- Focus Skill Reading Mini-Lesson, p. 346
- Reading comprehension questions identified with the
- *Activity Book* p. 58 (shown on p. 349)
- Lesson Summary and Review, pp. 349, 353, 358, 363, 368
- Chapter Review and Test Preparation, pp. 370–371

Reading Skill

SUMMARIZE A summary is a short statement that includes the main idea and the most important details in a passage. Use the Reading in Health Handbook on pages 372–383 and this graphic organizer to help you summarize the health facts in this chapter.

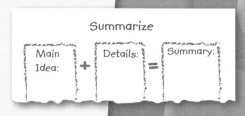

Summarize

Main Idea: + Details: = Summary:

Health Graph

INTERPRET DATA Bike helmets protect bike riders against head injuries. Many states have passed laws that require bike riders to wear helmets. What is the total percentage of bike riders that use helmets more than half of the time?

Survey of Helmet Use by Cyclists Age 16 and Under

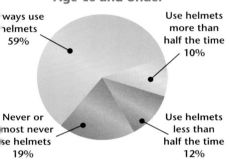

Always use helmets 59%

Use helmets more than half the time 10%

Never or almost never use helmets 19%

Use helmets less than half the time 12%

Daily Physical Activity

Picking up trash in your neighborhood or at school is a great way to get some exercise and improve your community.

 Be Active!
Use the selection, Track 12, **Broadway Bound**, to share some exercise time with your classroom community.

345

School-Home Connection

Distribute copies of the School-Home Connection (in English or Spanish). Have students take the page home to share with their families as you begin this chapter.

Follow Up Have volunteers share the results of their activities.

 Supports the Coordinated School Health Program

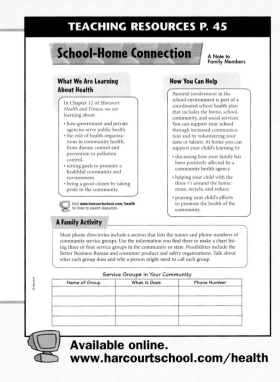

TEACHING RESOURCES P. 45

School-Home Connection   A Note to Family Members

What We Are Learning About Health

In Chapter 12 of *Harcourt Health and Fitness*, we are learning about

- how government and private agencies serve public health.
- the role of health organizations in community health, from disease control and prevention to pollution control.
- setting goals to promote a healthful community and environment.
- being a good citizen by taking pride in the community.

Visit www.harcourtschool.com/health for links to parent resources.

How You Can Help

Parental involvement in the school environment is part of a coordinated school health plan that includes the home, school, community, and social services. You can support your school through increased communication and by volunteering your time or talents. At home you can support your child's learning by

- discussing how your family has been positively affected by a community health agency.
- helping your child with the three r's around the home: reuse, recycle, and reduce.
- praising your child's efforts to promote the health of the community.

A Family Activity

Most phone directories include a section that lists the names and phone numbers of community service groups. Use the information you find there to make a chart listing three or four service groups in the community or state. Possibilities include the Better Business Bureau and consumer product and safety organizations. Talk about what each group does and why a person might need to call each group.

Service Groups in Your Community

Name of Group	What It Does	Phone Number

Available online.
www.harcourtschool.com/health

INTRODUCE THE CHAPTER

Health Graph

Interpret Data

Call on a volunteer to interpret the graph by telling what information it presents. The graph gives the results of a survey of bike riders 16 years old and under. It shows how often the bike riders surveyed use helmets. 69% of bike riders use helmets more than half the time.

How could you have conducted a better survey—that is, a survey that gives information that would be more useful? Possibilities include narrowing the age range, specifying the gender, or surveying cyclists in a single community (for example, all fifth-grade cyclists in your school).

Daily Physical Activity

Use *Be Active! Music for Daily Physical Activity* with the Instant Activity Cards to provide students with movement activities that can be done in limited space. Options for using these components are provided beginning on page TR2 in this *Teacher Edition*.

Chapter Project

Health Resources in My Community (*Assessment Guide* p. 61)

ASSESS PRIOR KNOWLEDGE Use students' initial ideas for the project as a baseline assessment of their understanding of chapter concepts. Have students complete the project as they work through the chapter.

PERFORMANCE ASSESSMENT The project can be used for performance assessment. Use the Project Evaluation Sheet (rubric), *Assessment Guide* p. 73.

Objectives
► Identify programs that promote community health.
► Identify private groups as sources of health information.
► Find out about the roles of the World Health Organization and local health agencies in disease prevention.

When Minutes Count . . .
Assign the Quick Study, Lesson 1, Activity Book pp. 56–57 (shown on p. 347).

Program Resources
► Activity Book pp. 56–57, 58
► Transparency 6

Vocabulary
public health p. 346,
sanitation p. 348

Daily Fitness Tip

Urge students to practice good personal hygiene to avoid spreading disease. Because most colds are spread by indirect contact, remind students to wash their hands with soap and warm water after blowing their noses and after covering their mouths with their hands to stifle a cough or sneeze.

 For more guidelines on fitness, see *Be Active! Resources for Physical Education.*

1. MOTIVATE

Point out that people living in communities often catch one another's colds.

Catching someone's cold may not be serious. Why? Most people tend to recover from colds fairly quickly. **When might catching a disease become everyone's problem?** when the disease is a serious one that can harm the health of a whole community

Use students' responses to introduce the concept of public health and to explain the roles of groups that work to promote it.

Chapter 12
346 • Working Toward a Healthful Community

Groups That Protect Public Health

LESSON 1

Lesson Focus
Both government and private groups work to protect public health.

Why Learn This?
You will know what information and services these groups can give you.

Vocabulary
public health
sanitation

Government Protects Public Health

People living in a community often catch each other's colds. Catching a cold from someone usually isn't serious. However, the spread of a serious disease, such as West Nile virus, is a public health problem. **Public health** is the health of all the people in a community. Government agencies and private groups work to keep communities healthy.

In the federal government three agencies of the Department of Health and Human Services (DHHS) protect public health.

- The National Institutes of Health (NIH) carries out and supports medical research.
- The Food and Drug Administration (FDA) makes sure that medicines work and are safe. The FDA also makes sure that foods are safe and that packaged foods are labeled with nutritional values.
- The Centers for Disease Control and Prevention (CDC) gathers information about communicable diseases. It tells doctors and other health-care workers what diseases to look for in communities where people are ill.

SUMMARIZE How does the federal government protect public health?
Agencies of the DHHS support and conduct medical research, make sure that medicines are safe and effective and that food is safe, and inform health-care workers about communicable diseases.

◄ Researchers at the CDC study communicable diseases. They share their findings with hospitals, doctors, and other health-care workers.

346

 Reading Skill

Mini-Lesson

SUMMARIZE Remind students that when they summarize a passage, they restate—in their own words—the most important information. Have students practice this skill by responding to the Focus Skill question on this page. Have students draw and complete the graphic organizer as you model it on the transparency.

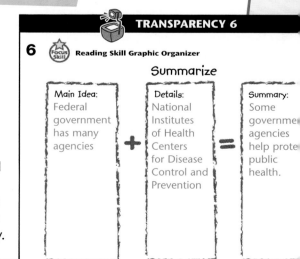

TRANSPARENCY 6

6 Reading Skill Graphic Organizer

Summarize

Main Idea:	Details:	Summary:
Federal government has many agencies	National Institutes of Health Centers for Disease Control and Prevention	Some governmen agencies help prote public health.

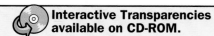 **Interactive Transparencies available on CD-ROM.**

Private Groups Protect Public Health

There are several large private groups in this country that help promote public health. They do this by educating the public and raising money for research. Many of these groups depend on unpaid workers, or *volunteers*, to do much of their work.

- The American Cancer Society (ACS) researches the causes and effects of all types of cancer. It also helps cancer patients get the information and treatment they need.
- The aim of the American Heart Association (AHA) is to reduce illness and death from heart disease and stroke by educating people about these problems.
- The American Diabetes Association (ADA) helps people with diabetes manage their disease.
- The purpose of the American Lung Association (ALA) is to help people with chronic lung diseases, such as asthma.

COMPARE AND CONTRAST **How are the ACS and the AHA alike and different?**
Possible answer: Alike: Both are large private groups that focus on particular diseases. Different: The ACS focuses on curing cancer; the AHA works to reduce heart disease and stroke.

▲ A private group sponsored this race as a fundraising event. The money raised will be used for research to find a cure for cancer.

Consumer Activity

Access Information About Health You have read about a few large private groups that focus on particular diseases. Find out more about similar but smaller groups. Make a chart showing the names of the groups and the diseases they focus on.

347

---

2. TEACH

Content-Area Reading Support

Using Text Format Direct students' attention to the list of private groups that serve public health. Point out that bullets draw attention to the individual groups. Explain that the groups could have been described one after the other in succeeding paragraphs but that this format helps readers quickly identify important individual points.

Consumer Activity

Access Valid Health Information Students may work in groups to do this activity. A school nurse, librarian, or some parents may be able to help students identify private groups that serve public health in your community.

Interpret Visuals—Pictures

Ask students why the tag icon is used for Consumer Activity features. If necessary, point out that it represents tags on products that consumers might buy. In this case, the "product" that one might buy is information.

Health Background

Prevent Heart Disease The American Heart Association (AHA) originated in 1915 as the Association for the Prevention and Relief of Heart Disease through the efforts of visionary New York City physicians and social workers. At that time, complete bed rest was the only treatment for heart disease. These health-care workers conducted studies that determined that heart patients could safely resume normal lives. The AHA, founded in 1924, aims to improve public and medical awareness of the disease.

Source: *American Heart Association*

For more background, visit the **Webliography** in Teacher Resources at **www.harcourtschool.com/health** **Keyword** community/environmental health

---

QUICK STUDY, ACTIVITY BOOK PP. 56–57

CHAPTER 12 Name _____ Quick Study

Working Toward a Healthful Community

Directions
- Use lesson vocabulary and other terms in the Word Bank to complete each **Summary**.
- Read the other directions to complete each **Lesson Details**.

Word Bank

conserve	evacuation	public health	septic tank
consumer	natural resources	sanitary landfills	sewage
emergency	protect	sanitation	water

Lesson 1 pp. 346–349

Summary The health of all the people in a community is known as __public health__. Both government and private groups work to study diseases, educate the public, and improve __water__ supplies and __sanitation__.

Lesson Details Use pages 346–348 to complete the graphic organizer.

| Detail: Government Groups: NIH, FDA, CDC | → | Main Idea: Many groups work to keep the people of a community healthy. | → | Detail: Private Groups: AHA, ACS, ADA, ALA, WHO |

Lesson 2 pp. 350–353

Summary Garbage and __sewage__ are waste materials. Sewage can be cleaned at a treatment plant or in a __septic tank__. Garbage can be burned or buried in __sanitary landfills__.

Lesson Details Use pages 352–353 to help you number the steps in order.

__3__ Water is piped to homes and businesses.

__1__ A community's water comes from wells, lakes, rivers, or reservoirs.

__2__ Water is cleaned, treated, and tested for bacteria at a treatment plant.

Name _____ Quick Study (continued)

Lesson 3 pp. 354–358

Summary Floods, fires, and explosions can affect a community. Sometimes the __emergency__ is so serious that people have to be sent from their homes to a safer place. This removal of people from their homes is called __evacuation__.

Lesson Details Use page 355 to fill in the blanks.

FEMA helps organize __federal__, __state__, and __local__ agencies to restore __services__ and __power__. It provides __transportation__ and __communication__ and assists with __medical__ care. FEMA also ensures a supply of __food__ and helps people apply for __funds__ to rebuild.

Lesson 4 pp. 360–363

Summary People use materials found in the environment, such as soil, water, and trees, in order to live. These materials are __natural resources__. It is important to __conserve__ natural resources by using them carefully.

Lesson Details Choose an item that you use regularly. It can be made of paper, aluminum, plastic, or glass. Tell how you can *reduce* your use of the item, how you can *reuse* it, and how you can *recycle* it. Explain how these actions would conserve natural resources.

Examples will vary but must include a way to reduce the usage, a way to reuse the item, and a way to recycle the item.

Lesson 5 pp. 366–368

Summary A __consumer__ is a person who buys a product or pays for a service. Government and private groups work to __protect__ consumers.

Lesson Details Reread pages 366–368. On a separate sheet of paper, write what the FDA and CPSC do. See p. 139 in *Teaching Resources* for answers.

Available online.
www.harcourtschool.com/health

Discuss

Inform students that the World Health Organization was established in 1948 to help people all over the world attain "a state of complete physical, mental, and social well-being."

Critical Thinking **Do you think this is a worthwhile goal? Why or why not?** Accept all reasonable responses. Many students will probably affirm the goal, which reflects an understanding of "health" as more than freedom from disease.

Draw students' attention to the information on this page, about how WHO has worked to improve sanitation.

Critical Thinking **What do you think happens if wastes are dumped directly into rivers or streams?** Pathogens enter the water and multiply, causing people who use the water to become ill.

Problem Solving Have students use information given in the text to calculate the percentage of people who have no sanitation facilities, assuming that the world population is 6.5 billion. 38 percent

Myth & Fact

Myth: Everybody in the world gets fresh water from a tap in his or her home.

Fact: In some places in the world, people walk for hours every day just to get water to drink.

WHO works with governments and private groups throughout the world to make clean water and good sanitation available to more people. ▼

The World Health Organization

The World Health Organization (WHO) provides public health services worldwide. One important goal of WHO is to make sure all children in the world are immunized against deadly diseases such as diphtheria, measles, polio, tetanus, typhoid, and whooping cough.

WHO also performs other important services around the world. It trains health-care workers and educates people about diseases. WHO also helps mothers and children get healthful food and good medical care. In addition, it makes sure that medicines sent between countries are pure. As the CDC does in the United States, WHO tracks the spread of communicable diseases worldwide.

Another aim of WHO is to improve water supplies and sanitation in parts of the world that do not have clean running water. **Sanitation** (sa•nuh•TAY•shuhn) is the safe disposal of human wastes. Diseases can spread quickly in places where water isn't clean and where human wastes aren't disposed of properly. Today almost two and a half billion people in the world have no sanitation facilities. Many of these people also lack clean water for drinking and cooking. WHO is working to change this.

348

Meeting Individual Needs
Leveled Activities

BELOW-LEVEL **Public Health Hotlines** Have students find and make a display of the toll-free numbers for the American Cancer Society (1-800-ACS-2345), American Heart Association (1-800-242-8721), and American Diabetes Association (1-800-342-2383).

ON-LEVEL **Tobacco Road** WHO is concerned about the health of people who use tobacco. Reinforce the disadvantages of using tobacco by listing them on the board after students state them. (Allow students to refer to Chapter 9.) Lists could include increased risk for cancer and heart disease, smelling like smoke, and discolored fingers and teeth.

ADVANCED **Disease Statistics** Have students research a disease of their choice to find out how many Americans have it. Ask them to find out what the current population of the United States is and to calculate what percent of the population has the disease. Students may also want to compare statistics for the United States with those for other countries.

WHO is also concerned about the rapid rise in tobacco use in many countries. In 2003 WHO sponsored the Framework Convention on Tobacco Control. This is a public health treaty that encourages countries around the world to work toward stopping the spread of tobacco use.

 SUMMARIZE What jobs does the World Health Organization do?

It tries to ensure the health of the world's children, trains health workers, educates the public about health, checks the safety of medicines, tracks diseases, works to provide clean water and sanitation facilities, and aims to reduce smoking.

WHO has held international conferences on smoking and health to discuss problems and look for solutions. ▼

Lesson 1 Summary and Review

1 Summarize with Vocabulary

Use vocabulary and other terms from this lesson to complete the statements.

Both government and private groups work to protect _____ health. Some workers are paid, and others are _____. Some groups work to prevent the spread of dangerous _____ diseases, such as typhoid. Many people in the world do not have clean water or _____ facilities.

2 Which public agencies track the spread of diseases?

3 Critical Thinking Why do you think educating people about diseases is a main goal of many public health groups?

4 **SUMMARIZE** Draw and complete this graphic organizer to summarize how government agencies and private groups protect public health.

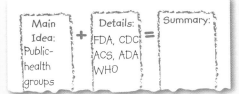

5 Write to Inform — Description

Write a news story about one of the public-health groups in this lesson.

349

Social Studies

Research Disease Smallpox is thought to have originated in India or Egypt more than 3,000 years ago. Epidemics of this acute communicable disease devastated human populations for centuries. One of the greatest achievements of the World Health Organization (WHO) was wiping out the "ancient scourge." Have students find out how smallpox affected people and how WHO abolished it.

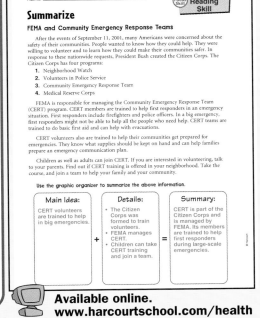

ACTIVITY BOOK P. 58

Name _____

Reading Skill

Summarize

FEMA and Community Emergency Response Teams

After the events of September 11, 2001, many Americans were concerned about the safety of their communities. People wanted to know how they could help. They were willing to volunteer and to learn how they could make their communities safer. In response to these nationwide requests, President Bush created the Citizen Corps. The Citizen Corps has four programs:

1. Neighborhood Watch
2. Volunteers in Police Service
3. Community Emergency Response Team
4. Medical Reserve Corps

FEMA is responsible for managing the Community Emergency Response Team (CERT) program. CERT members are trained to help first responders in an emergency situation. First responders include firefighters and police officers. In a big emergency, first responders might not be able to help all the people who need help. CERT teams are trained to do basic first aid and can help with evacuations.

CERT volunteers also are trained to help their communities get prepared for emergencies. They know what supplies should be kept on hand and can help families prepare an emergency communication plan.

Children as well as adults can join CERT. If you are interested in volunteering, talk to your parents. Find out if CERT training is offered in your neighborhood. Take the course, and join a team to help your family and your community.

Use the graphic organizer to summarize the above information.

Main Idea:	Details:	Summary:
CERT volunteers are trained to help in big emergencies.	• The Citizen Corps was formed to train volunteers. • FEMA manages CERT. • Children can take CERT training and join a team.	CERT is part of the Citizen Corps and is managed by FEMA. Its members are trained to help first responders during large-scale emergencies.

Available online.
www.harcourtschool.com/health

---

3. WRAP UP

Lesson 1 Summary and Review

1. public, volunteers, diseases, sanitation

2. the Centers for Disease Control and Prevention (CDC) and the World Health Organization (WHO)

3. Possible answer: If people understand the causes, spread, and effects of diseases, they will be better able to avoid getting ill.

4. Possible answers are shown.

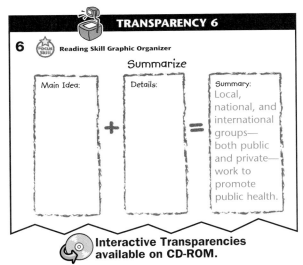

TRANSPARENCY 6

6 Reading Skill Graphic Organizer

Summarize

Main Idea:	Details:	Summary: Local, national, and international groups—both public and private—work to promote public health.

Interactive Transparencies available on CD-ROM.

5. Students should do independent research to learn about the groups and their choices. Stories will vary but should demonstrate understanding of each organization's mission and services.

 For **writing models** with examples, see *Teaching Resources* pp. 47–61. Rubrics are also provided.

 When Minutes Count ...

Quick Study Students can use *Activity Book* pp. 56–57 (shown on p. 347) as they complete each lesson in this chapter.

Objectives
▶ Explain the role of health agencies involved in community health.
▶ Learn some ways to access health information.
▶ Identify community sources of health services.

 When Minutes Count . . .

Assign the Quick Study, Lesson 2, Activity Book pp. 56–57 (shown on p. 347).

Program Resources
▶ Activity Book pp. 56–57
▶ Transparency 6

Vocabulary
sewage p. 352, **septic tank** p. 352, **sanitary landfills** p. 352

Daily Fitness Tip

Urge students to wear shoes when they go outdoors to protect themselves against pathogens that live in soil. After working in a yard or playing in soil, students should wash their hands thoroughly, using soap and warm water.

 For more guidelines on choosing proper clothing and shoes, see *Be Active! Resources for Physical Education,* p. 185.

1. MOTIVATE

Have students look at the photo on this page and read aloud the caption accompanying it.

Why is it important for communities to track Lyme disease and other communicable diseases? to understand how the diseases spread and learn to control the spread **How do we learn about the dangers of Lyme disease, how to prevent it, and the likelihood of its presence in our community?**

Use students' responses to introduce the concepts of health records and communication between local health departments and the CDC.

Community Health Needs

Lesson Focus
Each community has a system for taking care of its public health needs.

Why Learn This?
Health issues in your community can affect your life and the lives of your family members.

Vocabulary
sewage
septic tank
sanitary landfills

Medical Care and Health Records

Suppose you go for a hike in a nearby park. When you finish the hike, you find a deer tick on your leg. Deer ticks can carry Lyme disease, which makes people feel weak. What would you do?

Lyme disease is curable, but you would need prompt medical treatment. You might go to your doctor or see a doctor at a local health department clinic. The doctor would review records of all the tests, treatments, and illnesses you have had and any allergies you have. This information would help the doctor decide how best to treat you.

Doctors inform the local health department about illnesses that might affect the community. The health department keeps records of these illnesses. It uses the records to decide if an illness is spreading and threatening the public health. The records can also help other agencies study certain diseases.

SUMMARIZE Summarize how private doctors and public clinics meet community health needs.

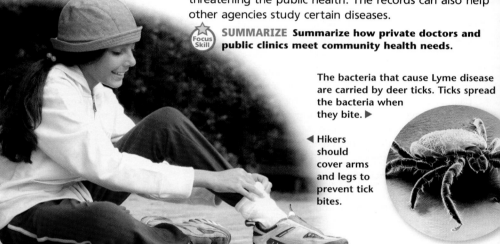

The bacteria that cause Lyme disease are carried by deer ticks. Ticks spread the bacteria when they bite. ▶

◀ Hikers should cover arms and legs to prevent tick bites.

Possible answer: The doctor passes the information along to the local health department. This department sends the information to the state health department and the CDC.

350

 Meeting Individual Needs
Leveled Activities

BELOW-LEVEL Water Use Have students brainstorm to identify ways people use water in a typical day. Ask small groups to make collages with pictures and drawings of water usage. Tell students to use red arrows to indicate uses for which it is especially important that water be clean (drinking, for example, as contrasted with washing cars).

ON-LEVEL Cycling Water Have students use the information on page 352 to diagram the path of water from clouds to reservoir to a treatment plant, to homes and businesses, back to a treatment plant, out to a body of water, and back into clouds. Ask students to find out where their community's water comes from and where it is treated.

CHALLENGE Sewage Treatment Have students research the main steps in sewage treatment. Tell students to present their findings by making a bulletin board that shows and describes each step. Students could use construction paper or butcher paper and paints, chalk, or markers.

◄ Often, raccoons and other wild mammals carry diseases. One of the most dangerous is *rabies*. Rabies is spread when an infected mammal bites another mammal.

Disease Control and Prevention

Health information that doctors send to local health departments is sometimes shared with state health departments and the CDC. The CDC tells health-care workers about where certain disease outbreaks are occurring. The CDC also tells health-care workers how to recognize certain diseases in their patients. With this information, workers can stop some communicable diseases before they spread very far.

The best way to control disease is to prevent it. Doctors and local health departments work to prevent the spread of disease by

- vaccinating children against serious diseases.
- vaccinating older people and others against the flu.
- inspecting restaurants and food stores to ensure they are clean and that food is handled properly.

SEQUENCE What happens after a doctor gathers medical records about a patient who has a communicable disease?
Doctors and clinics protect public health. They treat people with illnesses and diseases, keep health records, and tell the health department about illnesses that might affect the community.

Information Alert!

Smallpox Smallpox is a communicable disease that was eliminated in 1977. Recently, people began to fear that smallpox might be spread by terrorists. Now the United States has enough vaccine for everyone in the country.

 For the most up-to-date information, visit The Learning Site. www.harcourtschool.com/ health

351

2. TEACH

Discuss

Inform students that doctors don't routinely pass their patients' health information on to the health department. They do it only when the disease is, or could become, a threat not just to the patient they are seeing but to public health in general.

Critical Thinking **What are some diseases that could prompt doctors to report information to the public health department?** Possible responses: flu, West Nile virus, food poisoning, rabies

Interpret Visuals—Pictures

Have students identify the mammal in the photograph. Inform them that any mammal—skunk, raccoon, cat, dog, human, and so on—can get rabies. Knowing which animals in a given location are most likely to have rabies is essential to prevent exposure. That is why reporting occurrences of the disease to local health authorities is so important.

Critical Thinking **In what jobs are people most likely to be helped by a rabies vaccine?** Responses might include zookeeper, animal shelter worker, dogcatcher, veterinarian, park ranger.

Discuss

Explain that septic tank systems discharge sewage over large drainage fields. Soil filters out some pollutants as wastes percolate downward. Soil bacteria slowly decompose biodegradable wastes.

Critical Thinking **Septic tanks are common in rural and suburban areas, while sewer systems are used in urban areas. Why?** Septic tanks are impractical in urban areas, where much sewage is produced in a concentrated space and there is not room to bury large septic tanks or to lay large drainage fields. Sewer systems, which carry wastes through long pipes, are impractical in rural areas, where houses are far apart.

Critical Thinking **Why is it important to install septic tank systems away from freshwater wells and to clean tanks out every few years?** to avoid polluting drinking water and groundwater

Health Background

Dysentery Dysentery is a common illness in many parts of the world. Symptoms include stomach cramps, fever, and diarrhea that often contains blood. People contract dysentery by drinking water or eating food that has been contaminated by the feces of a human carrier of the disease. The disease is most often caused by *Shigella* bacteria. About 18,000 cases are reported in the United States annually.

Source: *Centers for Disease Control and Prevention*

 For more background, visit the **Webliography** in Teacher Resources at **www.harcourtschool.com/health** **Keyword** diseases

Machine Testing Machines can test water samples at regular time intervals, such as every hour. Then the data is transmitted to a central location. This costs less than having the water tested by people. It also enables more samples to be tested.

Protecting the Environment

The water you drink starts out in wells, lakes, rivers, or reservoirs. It is cleaned, treated, and tested for bacteria at a water treatment plant. Finally, it is piped to homes and businesses.

Much of the water we use simply goes down the drain. Some of it is flushed down the toilet. The mixture of wastewater and human wastes that leaves homes and businesses is called **sewage**. Sewage flows through pipes to a treatment plant. There it is cleaned and treated before being released into rivers, lakes, or oceans.

The sewage from some homes is sent into septic tanks. A **septic tank** is a concrete or steel tank buried in the ground. Bacteria in the tank change most of the human wastes into harmless substances that flow slowly out of the tank and into the soil.

Your local sanitation department collects garbage, or *solid waste*, and hauls it away to be burned or to be buried in sanitary landfills. **Sanitary landfills** (SAN•uh•tair•ee LAND•filz) are large holes dug in the

Workers record information gathered by water-sampling machines. They make sure wastewater is safe to release into the environment. ▼

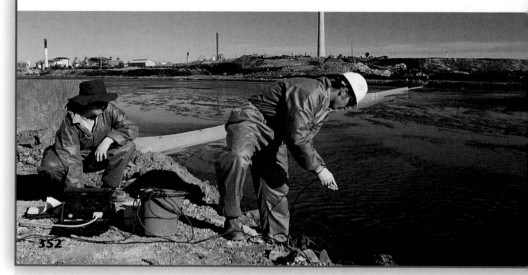

352

ESL/ELL Support

BACKGROUND AND EXPERIENCE Invite students to discuss methods of solid-waste disposal with which they are familiar.

Beginning Have students pantomime ways to dispose of trash. (Students might pantomime burning or burying trash in landfills, for example.)

Intermediate Ask students to draw and label pictures of sanitary landfills. Provide illustrated reference materials for them to use in addition to the information on these pages.

Advanced Have students present a short oral report about ways they already knew of to dispose of trash and ways they have learned of in this lesson. Challenge them to assess which ways are best for the environment.

▲ When a sanitary landfill is full, it can be covered and used for new purposes.

ground to hold trash. The holes are usually lined with plastic or clay. This keeps harmful materials in solid waste from polluting the land or the water that flows underground. Each day, the collected waste is covered with dirt to keep birds and other animals from spreading diseases to nearby communities.

MAIN IDEA AND DETAILS What are two types of community wastes? How do communities get rid of each type?

Did You Know?

When organic waste breaks down, it gives off a gas called methane. Some power plants use that methane. They burn it instead of coal or oil for running generators to make electricity. Unlike coal and oil, methane doesn't pollute the air. Since there's plenty of garbage, these power plants never run out of methane.

Lesson 2 Summary and Review

❶ Summarize with Vocabulary

Use vocabulary and other terms from this lesson to complete the statements.

Before we drink water from the tap, it is cleaned at a _____. The mixture of wastewater and human wastes that leaves our homes is called _____. Some homes collect this matter in a _____, where _____ change most of the human wastes into harmless substances. Sanitation departments often bury trash in _____.

❷ How does the CDC work to control disease?

❸ Critical Thinking If a landfill does not have a protective lining of clay or plastic, what effect might it have on public health?

❹ (Focus Skill) **SUMMARIZE** Draw and complete this graphic organizer to summarize how communities control and prevent disease.

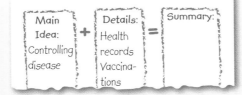

❺ Write to Inform—How-To

Write a short pamphlet about what people should do to avoid getting Lyme disease. Research the subject. Include what people should do in areas that have deer ticks.

Wastewater and solid waste; wastewater is cleaned, treated, and tested in treatment plants or purified in septic tanks; solid waste is incinerated, or it is buried in sanitary landfills. **353**

3. WRAP UP

Lesson 2 Summary and Review

1. water treatment plant, sewage, septic tank, bacteria, sanitary landfills

2. The CDC keeps health-care workers across the country informed about the spread and symptoms of diseases.

3. Pollutants could seep into groundwater and contaminate it.

4. Possible answers are shown.

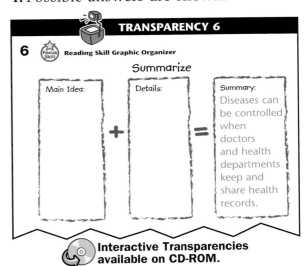

TRANSPARENCY 6

6 (Focus Skill) **Reading Skill Graphic Organizer**

Summarize

Main Idea: + Details: = Summary: Diseases can be controlled when doctors and health departments keep and share health records.

 Interactive Transparencies available on CD-ROM.

5. Pamphlets should include a description of the characteristic rash. They should advise people to wear clothing that covers their arms and legs, to use insect repellent, and to seek medical assistance if they suspect that an infected deer tick has bitten them.

For **writing models** with examples, see *Teaching Resources* pp. 47–61. Rubrics are also provided.

 When Minutes Count ...

Quick Study Students can use *Activity Book* pp. 56–57 (shown on p. 347) as they complete each lesson in this chapter.

Objectives

► Identify sources of assistance in the event of an emergency.

► List some causes of forest fires and explosions.

► Demonstrate ways to help support positive family interactions.

When Minutes Count . . .

Assign the Quick Study, Lesson 3, Activity Book pp. 56–57 (shown on p. 347).

Program Resources

► Activity Book pp. 56–57
► Transparency 6

Vocabulary

evacuation p. 352

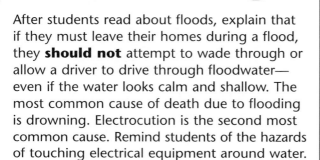

Daily Fitness Tip

After students read about floods, explain that if they must leave their homes during a flood, they **should not** attempt to wade through or allow a driver to drive through floodwater—even if the water looks calm and shallow. The most common cause of death due to flooding is drowning. Electrocution is the second most common cause. Remind students of the hazards of touching electrical equipment around water.

 For more guidelines on choosing proper clothing and shoes, see *Be Active! Resources for Physical Education,* p. 185.

1. MOTIVATE

Have students generate a list of emergencies that could require them to leave their homes. Write the list on the board.

If you had to evacuate, what five items would you want to take with you? Some students will want to take items of sentiment, such as journals or toys, while others will want to take practical items, such as food, flashlights, blankets, and clothing.

Use responses to tell students that this lesson will give them information about emergencies.

Handling Community Emergencies

Lesson Focus

A number of kinds of emergencies may affect your community, and many agencies can help your community handle them.

Why Learn This?

Knowing about possible emergencies can help you be prepared for an emergency in your community.

Vocabulary

evacuation

Disasters like floods can strike without warning. Often, however, people and communities have time to prepare for them. ▼

Floods

When streams, lakes, or rivers overflow with water, there is a flood. Floods usually occur when rain falls or snow melts faster than it can be soaked up by the soil or carried away by rivers. Floods can cause great damage. In farming areas, for example, a flood can destroy crops. In towns, floods can fill houses and businesses with water and mud, damaging furniture and machinery. In all areas, floodwater can pollute drinking water.

Sometimes, floods can be predicted. This gives communities time to get ready. The picture on the next page shows young people helping prepare for a flood by filling bags with sand. The sandbags will be stacked high along a river to keep the rising water from flooding the surrounding land.

354

Meeting Individual Needs
Leveled Activities

BELOW-LEVEL Be Prepared Guide students to formulate rules for readying the classroom for an evacuation such as a fire drill. Rules could include, for example, *Keep floor free of books so everyone can get out quickly.* Discuss and assess students' ideas. Help students choose the best rules to post in the classroom.

ON-LEVEL Consult the Pros Arrange for students to visit the local office of the American Red Cross, or have a Red Cross volunteer visit the class. Have students prepare questions to ask about ways the Red Cross serves the community in an emergency.

CHALLENGE Building Citizenship Have students brainstorm ways they could help schools in communities that have suffered a flood or other disaster. If feasible, have a small group plan and hold a fundraiser, clothing drive, or other kind of disaster relief activity.

◄ For a disaster such as a flood, local government agencies and private groups like the Red Cross organize volunteers who want to help.

What if the sandbags do not protect the community from the flood? It may be necessary for the local emergency manager to organize an evacuation. An **evacuation** (ee·vak·yoo·AY·shuhn) is the removal of people from their homes to safer places.

If the flood causes a great amount of damage, the state's governor and local officials may ask the President to declare the region a disaster area. The Federal Emergency Management Agency (FEMA) will then help the community. FEMA helps organize federal, state, and local agencies to

- restore public services and power.
- provide transportation and communication.
- assist with medical care.
- ensure a supply of food in the disaster area.
- help people apply for money to rebuild.

Personal Health Plan ▶

Real-Life Situation
Your family has decided to prepare a family emergency plan.

Real-Life Plan
Ask your parents to go to the FEMA website or the Department of Homeland Security website. Using the information there, help organize and write your family's emergency plan.

(Focus Skill) **SUMMARIZE How can a community prepare for and respond to a flood?**

...le can prepare by putting sandbags along a riverbank or moving belongings to higher
...nd. They can also evacuate. After a flood they can ask the government for help and get
...tance from FEMA.

355

Math

Rising Water "Flood stage" is the water height at which a river begins to cause damage. "Peak stage" is the highest that the water gets during one particular flood. The peak stages in the table at the right are from a major flooding of the Mississippi that occurred in 1993. Ask students to make a poster with a double-bar graph using the data in the table.

City	Flood Stage	Peak Stage
Des Moines, IA	12 ft	26.7 ft
Estherville, IA	7 ft	15.4 ft
Grafton, IN	18 ft	38.2 ft
Jeff. City, MO	23 ft	38.6 ft
Quincy, IL	17 ft	32.1 ft
St. Charles, MO	25 ft	40.0 ft

2. TEACH

Discuss

Explain that although floods can do tremendous damage to property, they are natural and are essential to some aspects of the environment. Floods add sediments (like mud) and fresh nutrients to the soil. In fact, without floods the fertile farmland along rivers like the Mississippi would not exist at all.

In addition to human-made flood barriers like levees, there are many natural ones.

Critical Thinking **What types of landforms give natural protection from floods?** Wetlands, parks, and open space, which allow floods to spread over large areas, offer flood protection. There are natural levees (high banks) along some rivers. Barrier islands protect coastlines from flooding during hurricanes.

Personal Health Plan ▶

Plans should include:
- identifying types of disasters that might happen
- creating a family disaster kit
- memorizing procedures to follow in an evacuation
- deciding where to meet family members in case of a fire in the home
- deciding whom family members should telephone to restore contact if they become separated during a disaster

TEACH *continued*

Interpret Visuals—Pictures

Direct students' attention to the photo of the fire-fighting robot. Inform students that robotic firefighters can remove flammable or dangerous chemicals from the heart of a fire. They can withstand temperatures of up to 1,475°F.

Critical Thinking **Why might human firefighters welcome the use of robots on the job?** Possible answers: Robots could save human firefighters' lives and prevent chemicals from spreading or exploding. Remind students that, in addition to responding to emergencies, firefighters work to prevent fires through education programs that promote community and environmental health. For example, they teach fire safety in schools and educate the public about the dangers of fires during dry weather conditions.

Content-Area Reading Support

Using Text Format Direct attention to the first paragraph on this page. Point out that the last sentence, *What happened next?*, introduces the main idea of the passage. The main idea is developed (that is, the question is answered) in the list that follows.

Students may be accustomed to looking for the most important idea in the first sentence of a paragraph. Explain that in some types of writing, the most important idea is presented after a "hook" that engages the reader's attention. The textbook writer is using a similar strategy.

Activity

Communicate Encourage students to make a list of emergency numbers and post a copy near each phone in their homes.

ACTIVITY

Life Skills
Communicate

Communicating clearly and quickly with emergency workers can save lives. You can prepare for this kind of communication. Make sure you know your community's emergency phone number. Keep important information, such as your address and nearby cross streets, near the phone.

Robots can be used in fires that are too dangerous for humans, such as fires in warehouses filled with chemicals. ▼

Fires

The fire shown in the picture on this page broke out in an empty warehouse. People in the area smelled smoke and called the fire department. What happened next?

1. Firefighters rushed to the scene. They sprayed the warehouse with water. They also sprayed the buildings next to the warehouse to keep them from catching fire. Firefighters evacuated nearby apartment buildings.

2. Red Cross volunteers set up an emergency shelter and mobile feeding units for firefighters and for people whose homes were damaged by the fire.

3. After the fire was out, officials from the fire department and police department dug through the rubble. They looked for evidence of the cause of the fire. Local businesses, churches, and schools raised money to help people affected by the fire.

This device helps firefighters see through dense smoke, enabling them to find trapped people. ▼

356

ESL/ELL Support

COMPREHENSIBLE INPUT Familiarize students with the personnel, businesses, and institutions referred to in the discussion of fires.

Beginning Write on the board *firefighters, Red Cross volunteers, police, restaurants,* and *churches.* Have students draw a picture to represent each one. For example, they might draw a helmet for a firefighter, a heart shape for Red Cross volunteers, a badge for police, a knife and fork for restaurants, and a steeple for churches.

Intermediate Write on the board as above. For each noun, have students list an adjective to describe it. For example, they might list *brave* for firefighter, *caring* for Red Cross volunteers, *helpful* for police, and *large* for government.

Advanced Write on the board as above. Have students write a sentence for each noun, explaining who or what it names.

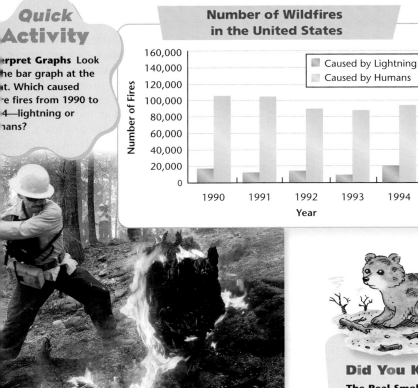

Number of Wildfires in the United States

Interpret Graphs Look the bar graph at the [ri]t. Which caused [mo]re fires from 1990 to [199]4—lightning or [hum]ans?

Legend:
- Caused by Lightning
- Caused by Humans

Y-axis: Number of Fires (0 to 160,000)
X-axis: Year (1990, 1991, 1992, 1993, 1994)

▲ To put out a forest fire, firefighters may set backfires, which burn up fuel needed for a fire to spread.

Forest fires are handled differently from fires in towns and cities. If local firefighters need help with a forest fire, specially trained firefighters from the United States Forest Service respond.

SEQUENCE In order, list steps that people threatened by fire can take to respond to the threat.
Possible answer: Contact emergency workers by using an emergency phone number; then evacuate the home.

Did You Know?

The Real Smokey Bear In 1950 a careless person started a forest fire in New Mexico. This fire injured a black-bear cub. The cub was rescued by firefighters and later given to the chief of the U.S. Forest Service to use in its forest fire prevention program. The bear was named Smokey Bear. When he "retired" from the Forest Service, Smokey Bear moved to the National Zoo, where he lived until 1975.

357

Science

Plants That Need Fire Have students research to identify trees and other plants that depend on fire. Examples include lodgepole pines, whose seed-containing cones often remain closed until opened by the heat of forest fires, and ponderosa pines, which flourish in areas that burn from time to time. Prairie grasses also benefit from fire, which keeps them from being crowded out by shrubs and trees.

Discuss

Explain that not all forest fires are bad. Wildfires are part of the natural cycle. Many forest ecosystems depend on fires to maintain a diversity of plant life; many plants depend on fires for reproduction. The U.S. Forest Service recognizes the benefits of setting controlled low-intensity forest fires, which burn out underbrush (fuel for large, destructive fires), leave most trees standing, and increase animal habitats. This is another example of a community program that protects the environment.

Critical Thinking In what situations might the needs of humans and the benefits of fire to a forest conflict?
Possible answer: A low-intensity fire could be good for a forest but disturbing to humans who live nearby.

Problem Solving Terri and her family are camping in a hot, dry forest. What can they do to make sure they do not start a forest fire? Possible answers: Avoid smoking; use a camp stove on bare ground, instead of an open fire, for cooking; make sure the camp stove flame is put out immediately after food is prepared.

Quick Activity

Humans cause more forest fires than lightning. Explain that forest fire investigators try to determine the causes of forest fires. They use techniques similar to those of crime scene investigators. They analyze burn patterns, interview people, and look for other evidence such as tire tracks and footprints to figure out where and how the fires started.

Discuss

Inform students that many bomb squads use specially trained dogs.

Critical Thinking Why might dogs be particularly useful to bomb squads?

A dog's sense of smell is much keener than that of other mammals, including humans. Dogs can be trained to recognize and respond to certain scents.

3. WRAP UP

Lesson 3 Summary and Review

1. flood, evacuation, forest fires, fire lanes, explosion

2. Federal, state, and local governments work with local emergency personnel and volunteers.

3. FEMA can organize and coordinate efforts across state or regional lines.

4. Possible answers are shown.

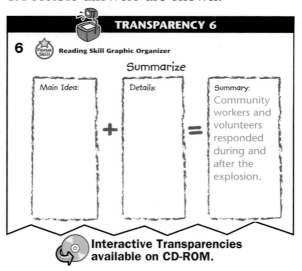

TRANSPARENCY 6

6 **Reading Skill Graphic Organizer**

Summarize

Main Idea: + Details: = Summary: Community workers and volunteers responded during and after the explosion.

 Interactive Transparencies available on CD-ROM.

5. Answers will vary. Students should give at least one example of a specific disaster or emergency and demonstrate an understanding of how people can respond to it in a caring way.

For **writing models** with examples, see *Teaching Resources* pp. 47–61. Rubrics are also provided.

Explosions

Explosions usually occur quickly and without much warning. They can destroy buildings, knock out power, and injure and kill people. Many explosions happen by accident. Natural gas explosions, for example, can happen when leaking gas comes in contact with a flame or spark. Gas companies add an unpleasant odor to natural gas so that people will notice any leaks.

Some explosions, however, are set off on purpose to hurt people or destroy property. Federal, state, and local governments all work hard to prevent disasters like these. Many police departments have bomb squads trained to stop explosives from going off.

 **COMPARE AND CONTRAST How are accidental disasters and deliberate disasters alike? How are they different?**

◀ In 1995 an explosion destroyed part of a government building in Oklahoma City, Oklahoma. The Oklahoma City National Memorial honors the 168 people who died.

Lesson 3 Summary and Review

❶ Summarize with Vocabulary

Use vocabulary and other terms from this lesson to complete the statements.

There are several kinds of emergencies. Too much rain can cause a _____. If this threatens homes, the local emergency manager will organize an _____. Specially trained teams from the U.S. Forest Service deal with _____ by setting _____. A bomb or a gas leak can cause an _____.

❷ What types of groups work together to help communities handle emergencies?

❸ Critical Thinking Why is FEMA helpful when a disaster affects a large area or several states?

❹ SUMMARIZE Draw and complete this graphic organizer to show a community's reaction to a gas explosion.

Main Idea: Community reaction + Details: 1. Fire. 2. Victims 3. Cleanup = Summary:

❺ Write to Inform—Narration

Write about how you and your family might help during a local emergency.

Possible response: Alike: Both cause destruction and create emergency situations; firefight rescue workers respond. Different: Accidental disasters can be caused by human error; deli **358** disasters are caused by the actions of criminals.

Social Studies

A Virtual Tour Encourage interested students to learn more about the Oklahoma City National Memorial Center by visiting its website. Students can take an online tour, which begins with images from the moments immediately following the bomb explosion and ends with images of rebuilding and community unity.

Teacher Tip

Talking About Terrorism When addressing students' questions about terrorism, refrain from lecturing or expressing your opinion about related issues (for example, about how the federal government should respond). Allow students who wish to do so to express their feelings while respecting the wishes of other students not to talk. Inform parents if a child seems especially anxious.

Citizenship

Taking Pride in Your Community

Your community is your neighborhood. You see it every day. You can probably think of some great ideas for how to make it a better place. One example might be helping out with a community garden. Here are some steps to get you started in improving your community. You can make a difference!

- **Look around. Ask yourself, "What would make my community a better place?"**
- **Write down your ideas. Include the locations of the improvements and what you think needs to be done.**
- **Show your list to a parent or another adult, such as a teacher. Work with that person to choose your best idea.**
- **Write up a plan. Say what you want to do and how you think it can happen. List any special equipment that will be needed. In your plan, show that you know all the safety rules for working with the equipment.**
- **If your plan involves fixing something, find out who owns it. You will need the owner's permission to carry out your plan.**

Activity

With your family or class, discuss your plan and others' plans for improving your community. As people share ideas, write each one down. At the end of the discussion, decide on something you can all do together as a family or class to show pride in your community.

Developing a garden is one way to take pride in your community. ▶

359

Building Good Character

Caring
Citizenship
Fairness
Respect
Responsibility
Trustworthiness

Objective

► Participate in community efforts to address local issues.

Program Resource

► Poster 2

BEFORE READING

Brainstorm with students to identify people or groups whose good citizenship is shown by the pride they take in their school or local community. Offer an example, such as a class or a scout troop that picks up litter on a stretch of highway. List students' examples on the board.

DISCUSS

Have students complete the first two bulleted steps in class. Call on volunteers to read their suggestions aloud. Guide students to make constructive suggestions for refining and implementing the ideas shared. Stress that as students carry out the activity, they should involve their parents and proceed only with parental permission. Also point out that projects don't need to be long or difficult. Small steps (for example, just picking a piece of trash off the sidewalk on the way to school) can make a difference.

ACTIVITY

Students will probably generate several good ideas. You might consider implementing one idea now, as a class, and encouraging students to implement another at a later time (perhaps in the summer with their families).

Using the Poster

Activity Have students design and display their own posters that show ways they could improve their school or home environment.

Display Poster 2 to remind students to show good citizenship. The poster can be displayed in the classroom, school cafeteria, or another common area.

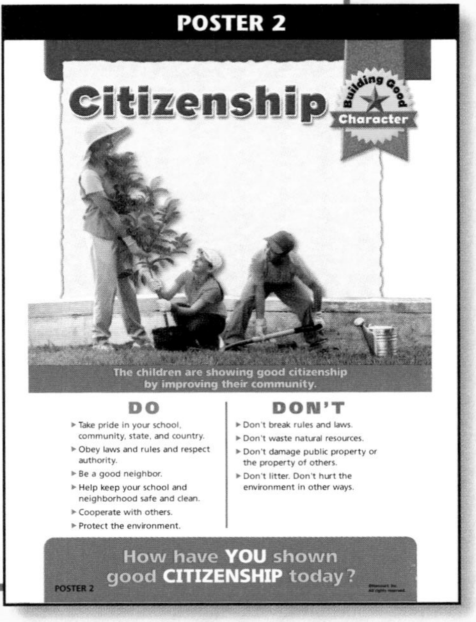

Objectives

► Identify environmental factors that affect community health.

► Analyze how environmental and personal health are related.

► Identify environmental protection programs that promote community health, such as recycling and waste disposal.

 When Minutes Count . . .

Assign the Quick Study, Lesson 4, Activity Book pp. 56–57 (shown on p. 347).

Program Resources

► Activity Book pp. 56–57
► Transparency 6

Vocabulary

natural resources p. 360,
conserve p. 361

Daily Fitness Tip

Suggest that students seek their parents' permission to open a window or two for a few minutes each day to let some fresh air into the home. Indoor air pollutants, such as fumes from household cleaning products, can be dangerous to human health.

 For more guidelines on fitness, see *Be Active! Resources for Physical Education.*

1. MOTIVATE

Copy on the board the table below, reordering the items under **Reuse**. Challenge students to match each material with a product that can be made after the material is recycled.

Material → Recycle →	Reuse
old clothes	dusting rags
old tires	car bumpers
plastics	cassette casings
aluminum foil	license plates
paper	egg cartons

Protecting Land Water, and Air

Lesson Focus

People can do many things to protect natural resources.

Why Learn This?

You and your family can help protect land, water, and air for future generations.

Vocabulary

natural resources
conserve

People can limit the need for landfills by reducing waste, by reusing some items they normally throw away after one use, and by recycling aluminum, paper, plastic, and glass.

 Personal Health Plan ▶

Real-Life Situation
You notice that a fast-food restaurant doesn't have a recycling bin for glass and plastic.
Real-Life Plan
Have a parent help you write a letter to the restaurant. Ask the manager to start a recycling program. Offer to tell everyone you know about the restaurant's new program.

360

Protecting Land

Land, water, and air are important natural resources and need to be protected. Natural resources are materials that people use from the environment. How can we protect these resources?

We need land to grow the crops and feed animals. We also need land for our homes, schools, factories, and businesses. We use landfills for disposing of our trash. However, land is limited. One way we can protect the land is by producing less trash. To do this, follow the three R's—reduce, reuse, and recycle. Here are some things to do at home and at school:

- Reduce the amount of paper you use.
- Reuse paper or plastic bags the next time you shop.
- Recycle aluminum cans, paper, plastic, and glass.

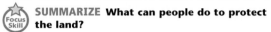 **SUMMARIZE** What can people do to protect the land?

One way to protect the land is by recycling. ▼

Meeting Individual Needs
Leveled Activities

BELOW-LEVEL **The Three R's and You** Have students fold sheets of paper into thirds. Tell them to write *Reduce, Reuse,* and *Recycle* as headings for the sections. Ask students to list or draw pictures of ways they apply the three R's in their daily lives.

ON-LEVEL **Recycling and You** Have students identify environmental protection programs that promote community health, such as recycling.

CHALLENGE **Step Up Conservation Efforts** Have students propose a plan for reducing, reusing, or recycling materials used in the classroom. Such materials could include pens, paper, folders, paper clips, and textbooks. Use students' plans to formulate class goals for reducing, reusing, and recycling. Appoint willing students to track the class's progress in achieving its goals.

There are may ways to conserve water. You can take showers instead of baths. You can also use a water-saving attachment on a garden hose.

Protecting Water

You can protect your community water supply by conserving water. You **conserve** (kuhn•SERV) when you save something or use it carefully. There are many ways you can conserve water at home and school:

- Don't let the water run when it's not in use. For example, turn off the faucet while you brush your teeth.
- Use low-flow shower heads to conserve water. These cut in half the amount of water you would use with other shower heads.
- Fix leaky pipes and faucets. A leak big enough to fill a cup in 10 minutes wastes more than 3,000 gallons a year.
- Cut back on activities that use water. For example, use a broom instead of a hose to clean the sidewalk. Water the lawn only when it looks dry.

DRAW CONCLUSIONS Why might people in dry areas want to grow plants that grow well in dry soil?

The people could conserve water by growing these plants.

ACTIVITY

Building Good Character

Respect Moira's research on saving water has shown her that small actions add up. She wants to tell her parents about ways to save water. However, she doesn't want to act as if she's telling them what to do. Write two ways that Moira can try to get her message across with respect.

361

Personal Health Plan ▶

Plans should include:
- upbeat, respectful approach
- reasons for recycling
- suggestions on how to start a recycling program
- business letter format

★ Activity

Respect Moira could introduce the topic by asking to share something she learned in school; Moira could ask her parents to help her apply what she has learned. She could be honest about her concern for the water supply and for her family's water bill.

Content-Area Reading Support

Using Respellings Direct students' attention to the phonetic respelling of conserve (kuhn•SERV). Remind or inform students that respellings show how words are pronounced. Point out that the dots in the middle of the respellings divide the words into syllables and that capital letters indicate the stressed, or accented, syllable.

Science

Xeriscaping Xeriscaping is a method of landscaping using plants that require very little water. Have students research Xeriscaping and write short reports about it. Ask them to include:

- what Xeriscaping is.
- plants that are ideal for Xeriscaping.
- reasons for Xeriscaping.
- places or environments where Xeriscaping is most useful.

Challenge students to find out why this approach is called "Xeriscaping."

Teacher Tip

Pronunciations When you discuss phonetic respellings, point out that word pronunciations vary within the United States and among English-speaking countries. As a result, many words have more than one correct pronunciation. For example, the word *resources* may be correctly pronounced as REE•sohr•suhz, as rih•SOHR•suhz, and as ruh•SOHR•suhz. Discourage students from making any judgments about the intelligence or education of people whose speech is different from their own.

TEACH *continued*

Discuss

After students have read the Did You Know? feature, pose the following question.

Critical Thinking Why could exercising outdoors on an Ozone Alert Day be harmful to your health? Exercise makes your respiratory rate increase, so pollutants are breathed in faster than when you are at rest.

Problem Solving What can people who exercise outdoors do to avoid the harmful effects of air pollution? Possible answer: Exercise when ozone levels are relatively low. Avoid areas of heavy vehicular traffic when exercising. Wear masks that filter at least some pollutants from the air.

Suggest that students watch for Ozone Alerts on radio and television broadcasts and in newspapers. Note that most such alerts occur during warmer months of the year, with ozone levels peaking in the warmest hours of the day.

Interpret Visuals—Pictures

Direct students' attention to the photo of a hybrid car.

Critical Thinking Do you think it is important for the automobile industry to produce more hybrid cars and for consumers to buy them? Why or why not? Possible answer: Yes, because hybrid cars can reduce dependence on fossil fuels and reduce the pollutants that cars release into air.

Health Background

Ozone Ozone (a molecule composed of three oxygen atoms) occurs naturally in the upper atmosphere, blocking out harmful ultraviolet light. Ozone builds up at ground level as a result of human activity—usually from burning fossil fuels. Accumulated ozone can harm human health, reducing lung capacity in everyone and making it hard for people with respiratory illness to breathe.

Source: *National Institute of Environmental Health Sciences (NIEHS)*

Protecting Air

Factories make most of the products we use every day. Unfortunately, some factories release pollution into the air. Motor vehicles and other gasoline-powered equipment also pollute the air.

People who breathe polluted air are more likely to have colds, flu, asthma, eye irritation, some kinds of cancer, and even heart attacks. Polluted air also damages grass, trees, flowers, and crops.

People have developed ways to cut down on air pollution. Many factory smokestacks now have devices that "scrub" the smoke by removing solids and harmful gases. The federal government has passed laws controlling the gases allowed in car exhaust. Cars built today produce far less pollution than cars built twenty years ago.

Did You Know?

Ozone is a poisonous gas that can cause severe respiratory problems. When there is too much ozone in the air (usually on hot, humid, hazy days), local governments can declare Ozone Action Days or Ozone Alert Days. People are advised to stay indoors and to cut back on activities that cause pollution, such as driving.

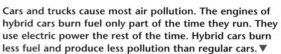

Cars and trucks cause most air pollution. The engines of hybrid cars burn fuel only part of the time they run. They use electric power the rest of the time. Hybrid cars burn less fuel and produce less pollution than regular cars. ▼

362

ESL/ELL Support

BACKGROUND AND EXPERIENCE Ask students to discuss air pollution that they have observed and (where relevant) ways they have tried to reduce or avoid air pollution.

Beginning Have students draw a picture of something they have seen that pollutes air. Challenge them to think about and pantomime a way they can reduce or avoid that source of pollution (for example, by riding a bicycle to reduce auto emissions).

Intermediate Ask students to draw pictures of three things that pollute air. Have them write short captions for their drawings.

Advanced Help students draw a comic strip to show sources of air pollution they have observed. Before they begin, display a comic strip—an educational one, if possible—to elucidate the task.

What can you and your classmates do to reduce air pollution? One way is to bike, walk, or use public transportation when you need to get around. Another is to follow the three R's. Less use of new products means less air pollution from factories.

CAUSE AND EFFECT For the desired effect of having clean air, what are some possible causes?

Possible answer: more people using public transportation; more factories using scrubbers; having greater controls on vehicle exhaust

Clean air helps us enjoy outdoor activities.

Quick Activity

Identify Resources for Recreation Make a list of outdoor activities that require clean land, clean water, or clean air. Describe the resources needed for each activity. Then explain why clean resources are important for good health.

Lesson 4 Summary and Review

1 **Summarize with Vocabulary**

Use vocabulary and other terms from this lesson to complete the statements.

Land, water, and air are _____. We must _____, or save them, by using them carefully. If we practice the three R's, _____, _____, and _____, we will help protect the environment.

2 Give an example of each of the three R's.

3 **Critical Thinking** Who do you think has the main responsibility for protecting land, water, and air—individual citizens or government agencies? Give reasons to support your answer.

4 **SUMMARIZE** Draw and complete this graphic organizer to show how to protect our water resources.

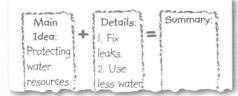

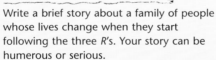

5 **Write to Inform—Narration**

Write a brief story about a family of people whose lives change when they start following the three R's. Your story can be humerous or serious.

363

Quick Activity

Possible answers: soccer, basketball, camping, hiking, swimming, jogging. All such activities require clean air to breathe and clean water to replenish the water lost while doing them; clean land is needed for all outdoor activities.

3. WRAP UP

Lesson 4 Summary and Review

1. natural resources, conserve, reduce, reuse, recycle

2. Possible answers: Reduce: use less paper and water; Reuse: use both sides of writing paper; Recycle: keep aluminum, glass, and plastic out of landfills by separating them for recycling.

3. Possible answer: Citizens are responsible for controlling the amount and type of resources they use. Government agencies are responsible for making and enforcing laws to protect natural resources.

4. Possible answers are shown.

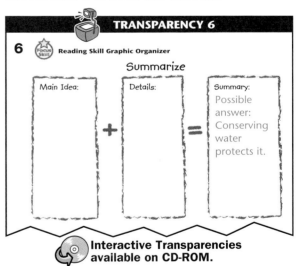

TRANSPARENCY 6

6 Reading Skill Graphic Organizer

Summarize

Main Idea:

Details:

Summary: Possible answer: Conserving water protects it.

Interactive Transparencies available on CD-ROM.

5. Stories should reflect understanding that natural resources are valuable and, in some cases, limited. They should include examples of the three R's.

For **writing models** with examples, see *Teaching Resources* pp. 47–61. Rubrics are also provided.

Life Skills

Communicate
Make Responsible Decisions
Manage Stress
Refuse
Resolve Conflicts
Set Goals

Objectives

► Describe how a safe school environment leads to a healthful community.
► Identify when help is needed in making decisions and setting goals.
► Identify ways in which communication skills enhance goal achievement.
► Explain the necessity of perseverance to achieve goals.

Program Resources

► Activity Book p. 59
► Poster 12

1. MOTIVATE

Write the three R's (reduce, reuse, recycle) on the board. Circle *recycle*.

What kinds of things do you see in trash cans and dumpsters? aluminum cans, glass bottles, newspapers, food wastes List on the board the things that students name. Challenge students to identify which things can be recycled and how. (Food wastes can be composted, for example.)

2. TEACH

Have students examine the photos of Carla using the Steps for Setting Goals to increase recycling. Then have them describe the benefits of setting short-term goals.

Step 1

Carla sets the goal of raising her schoolmates' interest in recycling. Which natural resource is Carla concerned about protecting? land, water, air

Chapter 12
364 • Working Toward a Healthful Community

Set Goals
to Protect Resources

All of us can help protect important resources. Using the steps for **Setting Goals** can make the job easier. You can use these steps to help protect resources such as land, water, and air.

Carla and her family recycle many things at home. However, people at her school seem to be less careful. She wonders if there is anything she can do about it.

1 **Set a goal. In this case, it is to get more people to recycle.**

Carla sets a goal. She wants her schoolmates to do more recycling.

2 **List and plan steps to meet the goal. Determine whether you will need help.**

Carla decides to make posters about recycling. She asks the principal for permission to hang the posters in the cafeteria.

364

Science

Recycling Flowchart Have students choose a recyclable material and find out how it is recycled. Ask them to make a flowchart that shows where the material goes, from being picked up by the recycling truck to reemerging as another product.

ACTIVITY BOOK P. 59

Name _____

Life Skill
Set Goals

Steps for Setting Goals

1. Set a goal.
2. List and plan steps to meet the goal. Determine whether you will need help.
3. Check your progress as you work toward the goal.
4. Reflect on and evaluate your progress toward the goal.

Tell how these students could use the steps to set goals.

A. Ned's class has been reading about the importance of protecting our natural resources. Ned's not sure how he can do his part. Then he remembers his mother's garden. Ned's mother uses chemicals to fertilize the soil and chemical sprays to get rid of insects that might damage her plants. Ned decides to try to persuade his mother to use fertilizers and insect repellents that will not pollute the environment.

• How could Ned persuade his mother to care for her garden without using chemicals?

Possible answer: Ned could explain to his mother that the chemicals she uses pollute natural resources. Together they could set a goal to find environmentally safe garden products. They could plan to do research and then buy nonpolluting materials to use in the garden.

B. Lea wants to know exactly how much trash her class makes in a single day. She needs the information to prove how important it is for people to reduce, reuse, and recycle every day in order to conserve natural resources.

• How could Lea plan to gather and share information about the three R's?

Possible answer: Lea could begin by explaining the plan to her teacher and asking for permission to talk to the class about helping with her project. Next, she could set up an area with containers in which the trash could be collected and sorted. Finally, Lea could prepare a report on her findings and share it with the class.

Available online.
www.harcourtschool.com/health

3 Check your progress as you work toward the goal.

4 Reflect on and evaluate the results of your work.

Carla makes one poster and then asks some friends to help her make and hang the other posters.

After a few days, Carla notices that the recycling bins are being used more often. She feels good about her success.

Problem Solving

A. José's father complains about the size of the water bill. José says that in school he has learned some simple ways to conserve water. His father asks for José's suggestions.
  • Use the steps for **Setting Goals** to help José and his father make a plan for conserving water.

B. Fatima packs her own lunch for school. She realizes that she throws away a lot of the packing materials. She wants to use the three *R*'s to be more responsible about the environment.
  • Suggest some steps Fatima can take to achieve her goal of making less trash.

365

What were the steps Carla planned to take to reach her goal? Carla decided to make posters explaining how and why to recycle; she asked the principal's permission to display the posters.

 Building Good Character
Point out that in setting the goal of increasing recycling, Carla exhibits the character trait of good *citizenship* by promoting school health.

Step 3
Critical Thinking **How did Carla make sure that she would progress toward her goal?** Carla involved her friends in the project. This saved her time and gave her friends a personal investment in recycling.

Step 4
Describe the benefits of implementing Carla's short-term goals. She and her friends felt good about their efforts because more students (and perhaps teachers) were recycling.

3. WRAP UP

Problem Solving

A Plans should reflect the Steps for Setting Goals. They could include setting the goal of reducing the water bill, listing steps to meet that goal (for example, taking shorter showers), checking on progress toward the goal (such as checking the next water bill), and evaluating their progress toward meeting the goal.

B Steps could include setting the goal (recycling packing materials), listing steps to meet the goal (e.g., reusing lunch bags), checking on progress (e.g., fewer trips to the trash can at lunch), and evaluating her progress (e.g., checking her perseverance from week to week).

 ## Using the Poster

Activity Have students use the poster to write stories or essays about a time that they or someone else set, worked toward, and reached a goal. Allow time for volunteers to read their stories to the class.

Display the poster to remind students of the steps for setting goals.

POSTER 12

Set Goals

The girl is setting a goal to get more exercise.

Steps for Setting Goals

1 Choose a goal.
2 Plan steps to reach that goal. Determine whether you will need help.
3 Check your progress as you work toward the goal.
4 Evaluate the results of your work.

What GOALS have YOU SET?

POSTER 12

Objectives

► Identify methods of accessing valid health information.

► Utilize critical thinking in decision making and problem solving.

► Cite ways of knowing if health information, products, and services are valid and reliable.

► Identify programs that promote community health through consumer protection.

 When Minutes Count . . .

Assign the Quick Study, Lesson 5, Activity Book pp. 56–57 (shown on p. 347).

Program Resources

► Activity Book pp. 56–57, 60
► Transparency 6

Daily Fitness Tip

Cyclists, in-line skaters, and skateboarders can avoid serious or even fatal injuries by wearing helmets. Remind students **always** to wear helmets when riding or skating, even if they are just going down the street. This lesson provides an opportunity to review bicycle safety rules.

 For more guidelines on safe cycling and skating, see *Be Active! Resources for Physical Education,* p. 187.

1. MOTIVATE

Optional Activity Materials several over-the-counter medicines with child safety closures or tamper-evident packaging

Show students OTC medicines with the safety features specified above (or have students describe medicine lids and packaging that they have seen).

Why do you think packaging like this was developed? to keep children from direct access to medicines; to prevent criminals from harming medicines

Help students identify environmental protection programs that promote community health, such as safe food packaging.

Protecting Consumers

Lesson Focus

Government agencies and private groups help protect consumers from unsafe products.

Why Learn This?

Information from this lesson can help you become a better health consumer.

Seals like the one on this bottle help protect food from tampering. ▶

The FDA makes and enforces rules to ensure that meat is safe to eat. ▶

Government Works to Protect Consumers

Whenever you pay for a product or service, you're a consumer. For example, you're a consumer when you buy a bike helmet at a store or get a checkup at the doctor's office. Some states have laws that help protect consumers. State licensing boards also help by making sure that health-care workers, such as doctors and nurses, are properly trained.

The federal government also protects consumers, through a number of agencies that make sure products and services are safe and effective. One such agency, the Food and Drug Administration (FDA), makes sure that foods, medicines, and cosmetics sold in the United

366

ESL/ELL Support

COMPREHENSIBLE INPUT Familiarize students with public and private groups that work to protect consumers.

Beginning Write on the board the abbreviations FDA, CPSC, and BBB. Have students draw a picture to show the work of each group. For example, they might show a fast-food milkshake for the FDA, a stuffed animal for the CPSC, and an auto-body shop for the BBB.

Intermediate Draw a three-column chart with FDA, CPSC, and BBB as column heads. For each agency, have students supply phrases explaining what it does. Write these in the appropriate column.

Advanced Have students list several public and private groups that work to protect consumers. Students should and tell in a few words what each group does.

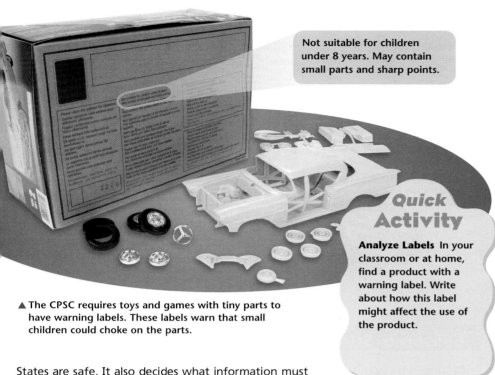

Not suitable for children under 8 years. May contain small parts and sharp points.

▲ The CPSC requires toys and games with tiny parts to have warning labels. These labels warn that small children could choke on the parts.

States are safe. It also decides what information must be on the labels of these products.

Another government agency that protects consumers is the Consumer Product Safety Commission (CPSC). It works to reduce the risk of injury by doing things such as

- setting safety standards for products.
- informing the public about unsafe products.
- working with manufacturers to fix unsafe products.

 SUMMARIZE Summarize the things that government agencies do to protect consumers.

Government agencies work to protect consumers from unsafe products. The FDA makes sure that foods, medicines, and cosmetics are safe and properly labeled. The CPSC sets safety standards, informs the public about unsafe products, and works with manufacturers to make unsafe products safe.

Quick Activity

Analyze Labels In your classroom or at home, find a product with a warning label. Write about how this label might affect the use of the product.

Myth and Fact

Myth: All products for sale at a store are safe to use.

Fact: During an average year, the CPSC finds hundreds of unsafe products. These products have to be recalled, or returned to the manufacturers.

367

 Art

Playing Safe Give students a catalog that includes toys. Have them make two different collages: (1) showing toys that children under three years old would like and that would not be hazardous to them, and (2) showing toys that would be dangerous to children under three. Remind students to be especially aware of toys with small parts. Suggest that students who have very young siblings share their collages with their families and display them in their homes.

---

2. TEACH

Content-Area Reading Support

Using Signal Words Direct attention to the first paragraph in the lesson. Point out that the first sentence states the main idea: *Whenever you pay for a product or service, you're a consumer.* Call on a volunteer to read aloud the second sentence: *For example, you're a consumer when you buy a bike helmet at a store or get a checkup at the doctor's office.*

Explain that *for example* signals that examples of the main idea will be provided. Point out that signal words such as *for example* give readers clues about how the information in a paragraph is organized.

Discuss

Students can read about the latest activities of the CPSC by checking *New This Week* on the agency's website.

Explain that if someone thinks that a product is unsafe, he or she needs to report it to the appropriate authority.

Critical Thinking If you had a complaint about the following items, who would you contact? hand cream (FDA), light bulbs (CPSC), over-the-counter medications (FDA), children's car seats (CPSC), fast-food hamburgers (FDA), portable heaters (CPSC), cough syrup (FDA), bicycles (CPSC), drain cleaner (CPSC), vitamins (FDA), the design of vitamin containers (CPSC)

Quick Activity

Analyze Labels Products with warning labels that students could examine include electrical appliances and devices such as clothes dryers, hair dryers, and blenders. Responses should focus on the effect of the warning label on the product's use.

Consumer Activity

Point out that there are many factors that you need to consider when calculating cost. For example, what is the real cost of *not* buying a helmet? You might save $30 at first, but a trip to the emergency room can cost several hundred dollars. You must also take into account things that are difficult to put a price on.

3. WRAP UP

Lesson 5 Summary and Review

1. consumer, licensing, Food and Drug Administration (FDA), Consumer Products Safety Commission (CPSC), consumer

2. The FDA makes sure that foods, drugs, and cosmetics are safe to use. It sets label requirements for these products.

3. They test products and publish their findings, check that businesses provide services they promise, and accept and file consumer complaints about businesses.

4. Possible answers are shown.

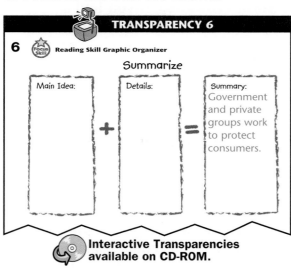

TRANSPARENCY 6

6 Reading Skill Graphic Organizer

Summarize

Main Idea: + Details: = Summary: Government and private groups work to protect consumers.

Interactive Transparencies available on CD-ROM.

5. Letters should state the problem clearly and respectfully and should be formatted correctly.

For **writing models** with examples, see *Teaching Resources* pp. 47–61. Rubrics are also provided.

Consumer Activity

Research What You Buy Suppose you want to buy a piece of safety equipment, such as a bike helmet. Look for an article about it in a consumer magazine or on a website. Then use this information to help decide which helmet to buy.

Private Groups Protect Consumers

Many private groups, also, work to protect consumers. Several of these groups test products and publish their findings in consumer magazines or on consumer websites. They also check to make sure that businesses provide the services they promise to consumers.

Another kind of consumer group is the Better Business Bureau (BBB) in your community. If you want to know whether to trust a local business, you can ask the BBB whether there are any complaints against the business. If you have your own complaint about a business, you can send it to the BBB. The complaint will be kept on file to help other consumers.

DRAW CONCLUSIONS What kinds of things might happen if consumer groups did not exist?

Products available to consumers might not be as safe, and the level of service from businesses might drop.

Lesson 5 Summary and Review

1 Summarize with Vocabulary

Use terms from this lesson to complete the statements.

Whenever you buy goods or services, you are a _____. Governments protect health consumers through state _____ boards. A government agency that makes sure foods and medicines are safe is the _____. A government agency that monitors product safety is the _____. You can find information about the safety and quality of products in _____ magazines.

2 Name two ways the Food and Drug Administration protects consumers.

3 Critical Thinking How do consumer groups, like the CPSC, help consumers?

4 SUMMARIZE Draw and complete this graphic organizer.

Main Idea: Government and private groups + Details: Set safety standards and test products = Summary:

5 Write to Express—Business Letter

Imagine that you have a complaint against a local business. Write a letter that might be sent to the Better Business Bureau to explain the problem and to ask for an investigation.

368

Teacher Tip

Cycle Safely According to the Centers for Disease Control and Prevention, if all cyclists between the ages of 4 and 15 were to wear safety helmets, more than 100 deaths and thousands of head injuries would be prevented each year. Many nonfatal head injuries produce lifelong disability from irreversible brain damage. Annual costs to society associated with bicycle-related head injury or death resulting from head injury have been estimated at more than $3 billion.

ACTIVITY BOOK P. 60

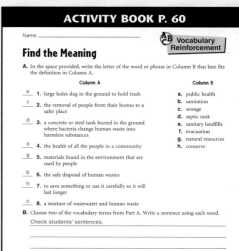

Name _____

Vocabulary Reinforcement

Find the Meaning

A. In the space provided, write the letter of the word or phrase in Column B that best fits the definition in Column A.

Column A	Column B
e 1. large holes dug in the ground to hold trash	a. public health
f 2. the removal of people from their homes to a safer place	b. sanitation
d 3. a concrete or steel tank buried in the ground where bacteria change human waste into harmless substances	c. sewage
d. septic tank
a 4. the health of all the people in a community	e. sanitary landfills
g 5. materials found in the environment that are used by people	f. evacuation
g. natural resources
b 6. the safe disposal of human wastes	h. conserve
h 7. to save something or use it carefully so it will last longer
c 8. a mixture of wastewater and human waste

B. Choose two of the vocabulary terms from Part A. Write a sentence using each word.

Check students' sentences.

Available online. www.harcourtschool.com/health

ACTIVITIES

Activities

 ## Math

Calculate Water Savings A person taking a shower uses about 5 gallons of water per minute. If a person shortens his or her daily shower by one minute, how much water could be saved in one week? In one month?

 ## Science

Wasted Water Fill a gallon jug with water, and put it in the refrigerator for an hour. Measure the water's temperature with a thermometer. Then gather a few more gallon jugs. Turn on the cold-water tap. Let the water run into the jugs until it is cold enough to enjoy as a drink. Measure the temperature. Is it warmer or colder than the refrigerated water? How much water was wasted before the tap water got cold enough to drink?

Technology Project

Make a Video With a partner, write a skit about steps to take during a community emergency, such as a severe storm. Act out the skit with your partner or classmates, and videotape the performance.

 For more activities, visit The Learning Site. www.harcourtschool.com/health

 ## Home & Community

Be Aware Design and prepare a reference card that people can keep near the phone. List the names and numbers of emergency agencies. Include a sentence about what each agency does. If possible, distribute copies of the card to other students so they can take them home.

Career Link

Industrial Hygienist Suppose you are an industrial hygienist. You look for health hazards that might affect workers in their jobs. Make a checklist that an industrial hygienist could use while inspecting your school. List any places, things, and activities that could be health hazards. You might ask a teacher for ideas.

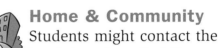

369

Career Link

Industrial Hygienist Explain that industrial hygienists are specialists in occupational safety and health, which means that they make sure people are working under safe conditions. They might inspect from a safety standpoint the air or noise conditions in a building, the structure of a building, or even the way a person is physically performing his or her job. Schools may employ industrial hygienists when an environmental problem, such as mold, causes illness. (Mold can infest carpeting and grow in concrete block walls if ventilation systems are not properly maintained.) Many industrial hygienists work in federal, state, and local government agencies, helping enforce rules governing worker health and safety.

 For more information on health careers, visit the **Webliography** in Teacher Resources at **www.harcourtschool.com/health** **Keyword** health careers

---

Activities

 ### Math
About 35 gallons of water could be saved each week; about 140 gallons could be saved in one month. Calculations:

5 gallons/day × 7 days/week = 35 gallons/week

35 gallons/week × 4 weeks/month = 140 gallons/month (or 5 gallons/day × 30 days/month = 150 gallons/month)

 ### Science
Some water may come from the tap at an enjoyable drinking temperature right away or shortly after running, so answers may vary greatly from no water wasted to gallons wasted. "Cold enough to enjoy as a drink" may vary from person to person. Was the gallon of water in the refrigerator cold enough after one hour? Reinforce the message that there are ways to reduce water waste, and that, perhaps, keeping drinking water in the refrigerator wastes less water than running it from the tap until it gets cold enough.

Home & Community
Students might contact the local American Red Cross or the Federal Emergency Management Agency (FEMA) to find out what help is available in their area. The FEMA website has a section for young people.

Supports the Coordinated School Health Program

Technology Project
If pressed for time, lead students in creating a single class skit. Call on volunteers to act in the skit. A parent volunteer might videotape it for you.

Chapter Review and Test Preparation

 Reading Skill 3 pts. each

1. Answers will vary. Example: Having a healthful community means protecting the community in different ways.

2. protect natural resources

 Use Vocabulary 3 pts. each

3. false, volunteers

4. true

5. false, evacuation

6. true

7. true

8. false, sanitation

9. false, Public health

10. true

 Check Understanding 3 pts. each

11. B, National Institutes of Health

12. J, BBB

13. D, sanitary landfill

14. F, reduce

15. A, food leftovers

16. F, preventing disease

17. C, water use

18. G, sanitation

19. A, checks cosmetics for safety

20. J, Consumer Product Safety Commission

 Think Critically 8 pts. each

21. Answers will vary but should reflect accurate analyses of the choices. Students should consider the cost of gas and the health threat of pollution as well as the relative costs of the cars.

22. A flood can damage physical facilities such as buildings, equipment, and vehicles, as well as water supplies and sanitation facilities.

 Reading Skill

SUMMARIZE
Draw and then use this graphic organizer to answer questions 1 and 2.

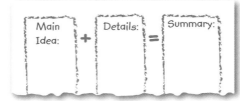

1 Write a summary sentence about groups that protect commumnity heralth.
2 Write details about ways to conserve natural resources.

 Use Vocabulary

Decide whether each statement is true or false. If it is false, replace the underlined part with a term that makes the statement true.

3 People who work without pay are called consumers.
4 Sewage contains water and human wastes.
5 An emergency is the removal of people from their homes to safe places.
6 To conserve something is to save it.
7 Materials that people use from the environment are called natural resources.
8 The safe disposal of human wastes is called recycling.
9 The environment is the health of all the people in the community.
10 Bacteria in septic tanks change wastes into harmless substances.

370

 Check Understanding

Choose the letter of the correct answer.

11 The _____ is a United States government group that carries out and supports health research. (p. 346)
A American Diabetes Association
B National Institutes of Health
C American Heart Association
D World Health Organization

12 Which group does **NOT** work to prevent and control disease? (p. 368)
F WHO   H ACS
G CDC   J BBB

13 Which of the following is the correct place to dispose of solid trash? (pp. 352–353)
A septic tank
B reservoir
C treatment plant
D sanitary landfill

14 Which of these terms refers to using fewer things so that you don't have as much to throw out? (p. 360)
F reduce   H recycle
G reuse   J receive

15 Which of these is **NOT** usually sent to community recycling centers? (p. 360)

A   B

C   D

Formal Assessment

Name _____

12 Chapter Test

Working Toward a Healthful Community

Match the words below to the sentences. Write the correct letters on the lines to the left of the sentences.

a sewage	d conserve	g septic tank	j sanitary landfill
b volunteers	e evacuation	h natural resources	
c sanitation	f public health	i health department	

d 1. You do this when you save something or use it more carefully.
i 2. People here keep records of illnesses.
f 3. This describes the health of all the people in a community.
b 4. These people work for no pay.
c 5. This is the safe disposal of human wastes.
h 6. We use these materials that are in the environment.
g 7. Bacteria in this place change most of the human wastes into harmless substances.
e 8. An emergency manager may organize this removal of people from their homes to safer places.
a 9. This mixture of wastewater and human waste flows through pipes to a treatment plant.
j 10. This large, clay-lined hole keeps harmful materials from polluting the land or the water that flows underground.

Name _____

Write T or F to show whether the sentence is true or false.

F 11. The World Health Organization has agencies that work to protect public health in the United States.
T 12. Diseases spread quickly where there is no sanitation.
T 13. Communicable diseases can spread from one person to another.
F 14. One way to save resources is to expand our landfills.
F 15. The Food and Drug Administration tests sanitation facilities.

Write the letter of the best answer on the line at the left.

C 16. Private groups such as the American Cancer Society _____
A test medicines for safety   C help promote public health
B teach people about heart disease   D study diseases that spread

J 17. The World Health Organization _____
F develops new medicines   H measures water pollution
G measures air pollution   J studies diseases that spread

A 18. A job of the Consumer Product Safety Commission is to _____
A tell people about unsafe products
B make sure food and drugs are safe
C help health-care workers recognize disease outbreaks
D support medical research

G 19. When you buy a product or a service, you are a(n) _____
F advertiser   H worker
G consumer   J patient

C 20. The Federal Emergency Management Agency _____
A tests drinking water   C aids people after disasters
B reports disease outbreaks   D distributes ozone to people

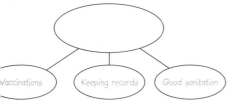

Which best states the main idea of this web? (pp. 350–353)
F preventing disease
G Lyme disease
H state licensing board
J consumer magazine

Low-flow shower heads limit _____. (p. 361)
A ozone   C water use
B land use   D water pollution

Of the four listed, which is the most important method of disease prevention? (pp. 348–349)
F vaccinations   H disease tracking
G sanitation   J smoking prevention

Which of the following does the World Health Organization **NOT** do? (p. 348)
A checks food for safety
B trains health-care workers
C vaccinates children
D improves water supplies

Which agency requires labels like these? (p. 367)

> Not suitable for children under 8 years. May contain small parts and sharp points.

F Better Business Bureau
G Department of Homeland Security
H Centers for Disease Control
J Consumer Product Safety Commission

Think Critically

21 If you had to choose between a car that uses very little gas but costs a lot and a car that uses a lot of gas but costs less, which would you choose? Explain your choice.

22 In what ways can a flood affect a community's public health facilities?

Apply Skills

23 **BUILDING GOOD CHARACTER**
Citizenship Suppose community officials predict that a flood will strike your community within a day or two. Describe what you could do to help prepare for the flood.

24 **LIFE SKILLS**
Set Goals All of your family members use a lot of paper for schoolwork and other work. The paper is made mostly from trees and often ends up in a landfill. State some steps for setting and reaching the goal of reducing your use of paper.

Write About Health

25 Write to Express—Solution to a Problem Suppose air pollution is a problem in your city. Write a short speech in which you try to persuade people to take steps to reduce air pollution.

371

Apply Skills 8 pts. each

23. Answers may include filling sand bags, working with emergency workers to set up shelters on high ground, and preparing for possible evacuation.

24. Possible answer: First, choose a goal for your family to reduce paper use by agreeing on how much to cut down; second, plan steps to meet the goal, for example, by ending some magazine subscriptions and reusing or recycling paper; third, check your progress toward the goal, perhaps by keeping track of paper disposal; finally, reflect on and evaluate your progress toward the goal by determining whether your family is moving toward the target goal.

Write About Health 8 pts.

25. Responses will vary. Speeches should be persuasive, accurately explain how air pollution harms the community, and offer practical strategies for reducing it.

Performance Assessment

Use the Chapter Project and the rubric provided on the Project Evaluation Sheet. See *Assessment Guide,* pp. 18, 61, 73.

Portfolio Assessment

Have students select their best work from the following suggestions:
- Leveled Activities, p. 350
- Quick Activity, p. 357
- Write to Inform, p. 363
- Activities, p. 369

See *Assessment Guide* pp. 12–16.

Objective

► Compare and contrast information given in expository text

1. TEACH/MODEL

Have students explain why it is helpful to compare and contrast text. (to understand how things are alike and how they are different) Point out the graphic organizer and discuss the Tips for Comparing and Contrasting. Have students read the paragraph in the example.

Read aloud the following model to help students see how to record in the graphic organizer information from the paragraph.

I know that my topic is Sheila and Maria. The girls are alike because they both are honest and have a good sense of humor. I will write that in the Alike column. I see the signal word *however* that is used to show what is different. Maria has a positive self-concept. Sheila has a negative self-concept. I will write that information in the Different column.

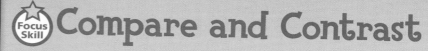

Compare and Contrast

Learning how to compare and contrast information can help you understand what you read. You can use a graphic organizer like this one to show information that you want to compare and contrast.

Topic: Name the topic—the two things you are comparing and contrasting.

Alike	Different
List ways the things are alike.	List ways the things are different.

Tips for Comparing and Contrasting

- To compare, ask: *How are people, places, objects, ideas, or events alike?*
- To contrast, ask: *How are people, places, objects, ideas, or events different?*
- When you compare, look for signal words and phrases such as *similar, both, too,* and *also.*
- When you contrast, look for signal words and phrases such as *unlike, however, yet,* and *but.*

Here's an example.

Compare → Contrast →

Maria sees herself as being honest, good at sports, and friendly. Sheila also thinks of herself as honest. However, her negative self-concept leads her to believe that she is clumsy and that Maria is her only friend. Both girls have a great sense of humor, which helps them stick together.

Here's what you could record in the graphic organizer.

Topic: Sheila and Maria

Alike	Different
Both—honest	Maria—positive self-concept
Both—good sense of humor	Sheila—negative self-concept

372

Skills in Context

COMPARE AND CONTRAST: ILLUSTRATE A DAYDREAM To compare and contrast is to notice how things are alike and how they are different. For this activity, review with students the differences between a positive and a negative self-concept.

What To Do

1. Draw a scene illustrating a person who has a positive self-concept facing a challenging situation. Include a speech balloon over the person's head. Write what you think that person might say to show how he or she might cope with the situation.
2. Then draw a person with a negative self-concept faced with the same challenging situation. Write in the speech baloon what that person might say.
3. Compare and contrast the pictures. How are the scenes alike? How are they different?

What You Need

- Paper
- Drawing tools

More About Comparing and Contrasting

Identifying how things are alike and how they're different can help you understand new information. Use the graphic organizer on page 372 to sort the following new information about Maria and Sheila.

| Maria | Enjoys going to movies | Fastest runner in her class | Enjoys playing baseball | Makes friends easily |
| Sheila | Doesn't enjoy baseball | Enjoys going to movies | Slowest runner in her class | Doesn't make friends easily |

Sometimes a paragraph compares and contrasts more than one topic. In the following paragraph, one topic of comparison is underlined. Find a second topic for comparison or contrast.

Justin and Zach are great friends. Zach loves basketball and Justin loves football. They take turns choosing which sport to play. Steven and Ben live next door to each other. Ben loves hockey and Steven loves kickball. They argue about which sport to play. The two don't get along well.

Skill Practice

Read the following paragraph. Use the Tips for Comparing and Contrasting to answer the questions.

Vitamins and minerals are nutrients. They help keep parts of your body strong and healthy. For example, vitamin A helps keep your skin and eyes healthy. Calcium is a mineral that helps build strong bones and teeth.

1. What are two ways vitamins and minerals are alike?
2. Explain a difference between vitamins and minerals.
3. Name two signal words that helped you identify likenesses or differences in this paragraph.

373

2. PRACTICE

More About Comparing and Contrasting

Have students work in small groups to sort the information given in the table.

Remind students that some paragraphs tell about ways a number of topics are alike and different. Read aloud the paragraph. Help students place the underlined information from the paragraph in a graphic organizer like the one used in the model. Have students identify the second topic being compared. Organize that information in a second graphic organizer.

3. APPLY

Skill Practice

Have students use the Tips for Comparing and Contrasting to answer the questions.

1. They are both nutrients. They help keep parts of your body strong and healthy.
2. Minerals help keep cells functioning normally and help keep bones strong. Vitamins help keep skin, eyes, blood, gums, and teeth healthy.
3. *Both* and *another* are signal words in this paragraph.

Meeting Individual Needs
Leveled Activities

BELOW-LEVEL Have students make lists of common breakfast foods and common lunch foods. Have them tell which foods promote good nutrition and which do not. Then tell students to compare and contrast their food lists with a partner's list. Discuss how the lists are alike and how they are different.

ON-LEVEL Give pairs of students a blank graphic organizer. Each partner has 30 seconds to list his or her favorite healthful foods. Ask partners to compare and contrast the foods found on both graphic organizers. Partners can share with the class the information from their completed graphic organizers.

CHALLENGE Have students fold sheets of construction paper into brochures. Have them write brief descriptions in their brochures to compare and contrast the different types of food service that are available in each of three restaurants in your area.

READING IN HEALTH HANDBOOK

Pages 374–375

Objective

► Use information from expository text and your own experience to draw conclusions

1. TEACH/MODEL

Have students explain why it is helpful to draw conclusions about text. (When not all of the information is given, readers must use text information and their own knowledge to understand what is written.) Point out the graphic organizer and discuss the Tips for Drawing Conclusions. Have students read the paragraph in the example.

Read aloud the following model to help students see how to record in the graphic organizer information from the paragraph.

I read that Matt chose not to brush his hair. I wrote this on the What I Read box. What I Know is that when you don't brush your hair, it can look messy. Even though it was not said, my Conclusion is that Matt's sister laughed at his hair, so he decided to go back upstairs to brush it.

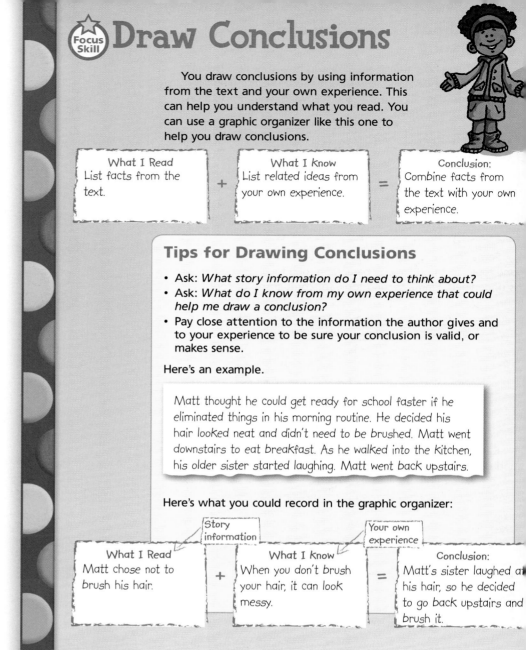

Focus Skill Draw Conclusions

You draw conclusions by using information from the text and your own experience. This can help you understand what you read. You can use a graphic organizer like this one to help you draw conclusions.

| What I Read List facts from the text. | + | What I Know List related ideas from your own experience. | = | Conclusion: Combine facts from the text with your own experience. |

Tips for Drawing Conclusions

• Ask: *What story information do I need to think about?*
• Ask: *What do I know from my own experience that could help me draw a conclusion?*
• Pay close attention to the information the author gives and to your experience to be sure your conclusion is valid, or makes sense.

Here's an example.

Matt thought he could get ready for school faster if he eliminated things in his morning routine. He decided his hair looked neat and didn't need to be brushed. Matt went downstairs to eat breakfast. As he walked into the kitchen, his older sister started laughing. Matt went back upstairs.

Here's what you could record in the graphic organizer:

| What I Read Matt chose not to brush his hair. | + | What I Know When you don't brush your hair, it can look messy. | = | Conclusion: Matt's sister laughed at his hair, so he decided to go back upstairs and brush it. |

374

Skills in Context

DRAW CONCLUSIONS: Design a Bumper Sticker As you read Chapter 9, think about some conclusions you can draw. Think of a catchy slogan based on one of your conclusions to use on a bumper sticker.

What To Do

1. Make a generalization based on a conclusion you drew about a topic found in Chapter 9.
2. Turn this generalization into a catchy slogan, and design a bumper sticker that features your slogan.
3. Make the bumper sticker from construction paper and colored markers, stick-on letters, and so forth. If you have access to a computer, you may want to use a word processing or drawing program.
4. Post your bumper sticker in the classroom.

What You Need

• Construction paper
• Writing and drawing tools

Say NO to Tobacco

More About Drawing Conclusions

Sensible conclusions based on the facts you read and on your experience are valid. For example, suppose the paragraph on page 374 had ended with the sentence *Matt glared at his sister and stormed out the door.* You might have come to a different conclusion about Matt's decision to brush his hair.

What I Read		What I Know		Conclusion:
Matt glared at his sister.	**+**	A glaring person is usually unhappy with another person.	**=**	Matt decided he didn't care what his sister thought about his hair.

Sometimes a paragraph might not contain enough information for drawing a valid conclusion. Read the paragraph below. Think of one valid conclusion you could draw. Then think of one invalid conclusion someone might draw from the given information.

> David was about to go swimming with his friends. His mom asked him to be sure to reapply sunscreen throughout the day. David rolled his eyes as the door slammed behind him. That evening a sunburned David couldn't go to the movies with his friends. His mom was unhappy with his behavior.

Skill Practice

Read the following paragraph. Use the Tips for Drawing Conclusions to answer the questions.

> Stephanie was afraid that her older sister, Alexa, had picked up a harmful habit. She noticed that her sister's hair and clothes smelled like smoke. She also smelled smoke on Alexa's breath. Stephanie wondered if she should tell her parents about the smell.

1. What conclusion did you draw about Alexa?
2. What information from your personal experience did you use to draw the conclusion?
3. What story information did you use?

375

2. PRACTICE

More About Drawing Conclusions

Have students compare the graphic organizer on page 374 with the one on this page. Lead students to see that a different conclusion has been drawn because of the additional information given.

Remind students that some paragraphs might not contain enough information to draw a valid conclusion. Read aloud the paragraph. Help students arrive at one valid conclusion. (David did not apply enough sunscreen.) Discuss with students other possible conclusions and why some may or may not be valid ones.

3. APPLY

Skill Practice

Have students use the Tips for Drawing Conclusions to answer the questions.

1. Alexa had been smoking.
2. I know that when someone smells of smoke, he or she usually has smoked cigarettes.
3. Alexa's habit was called "harmful"; her hair, clothes, and breath smelled of smoke.

Meeting Individual Needs
Leveled Activities

BELOW-LEVEL Write a conclusion on the board based on information found in Chapter 2. Have students identify the facts and details from the text that lead to that conclusion.

ON-LEVEL Have students design an advertisement about a health product that includes statements about the product. Have classmates draw conclusions about the product based on information given in the advertisement, and on their own experiences.

CHALLENGE Have students write skits about using a health-related product. The skits might reflect positive or negative responses to the product. Have them perform the skits for classmates. Have classmates draw conclusions about the product based on their interpretation of information given in the skits.

Objective

▶ Identify cause-and-effect relationships

1. TEACH/MODEL

Have students explain why it is helpful to understand cause-and-effect relationships. (to understand how and why things happen) Point out the graphic organizer and discuss the Tips for Identifying Cause and Effect. Have students read the paragraph in the example.

Read aloud the following model to help students see how to record in the graphic organizer information from the paragraph.

I know that Randy tripped over Albert's jacket. I think that is the cause. I will write that in the Cause box of the graphic organizer. The signal word *because* is given. I see that the effect is Albert's jacket got dirty. I will write that in the Effect box.

Identify Cause and Effect

Learning how to identify cause and effect can help you understand what you read. You can use a graphic organizer like this one to show cause and effect.

> **Cause:**
> A cause is an action or event that makes something happen.

➡️

> **Effect:**
> An effect is what happens as a result of an action or event.

Tips for Identifying Cause and Effect

- To find an effect, ask: *What happened?*
- To find a cause, ask: *Why did this happen?*
- Remember that events can have more than one cause or effect.
- Look for signal words and phrases, such as *because* and *as a result*, to help you identify causes and effects.

Here's an example.

> Randy and Albert were in a conflict because Randy tripped over Albert's jacket and it got dirty. The boys listened to each other. Randy said he didn't see the jacket because it was on the floor. Albert said he understood that it was an accident. Albert agreed to be more careful about hanging up his jacket. He said he was glad Randy hadn't been hurt.

Here's what you could record in the graphic organizer.

> **Cause:**
> Randy tripped over Albert's jacket.

> **Effect:**
> Albert's jacket got dirty.

376

Skills in Context

CAUSE AND EFFECT: A Stack of Causes Think about what causes and what effects violence has. Revisit Chapter 6 to make up a cause-and-effect game.

What To Do

1. Find six examples of cause-and-effect relationships in Chapter 6. Write each of the six causes on a separate Cause card. Write the six effects on separate Effect cards.
2. Play the game with three classmates. Shuffle the Cause cards, and place them facedown in a stack in the center of the table. Shuffle the Effect cards, and deal them to the players.
3. Each player in turn draws a Cause card. If a player is holding a matching Effect card, the two cards are placed face up on the table. If not, the Cause card is placed face down beside the stack on the table.
4. Continue playing until all of the Cause cards have been correctly matched.

What You Need

- Index cards
- Writing tools

More About Cause and Effect

Events can have more than one cause or effect. For example, suppose the paragraph on page 376 included the sentence *Randy sprained his ankle.* You could then identify two effects of Randy's tripping.

> Cause: Randy tripped over Albert's jacket.
>
> → Effect: Albert's jacket got dirty.
>
> → Effect: Randy sprained his ankle.

Some paragraphs contain more than one cause and effect. In the paragraph, one cause and its effect are underlined. Find a second cause and its effect.

> Nick and Emma were playing soccer at lunchtime. As Nick turned to look for the ball, <u>it hit him in the head and he fell.</u> Nick looked angrily at Emma. He got up to hurl the ball at her. She pleaded that hitting him was an accident. Nick wanted Emma to promise to be more careful. Emma said she would practice kicking straighter. Emma and Nick agreed on a solution that worked for both of them.

Skill Practice

Read this paragraph. Use the Tips for Identifying Cause and Effect to help you answer the questions.

> Illegal drugs have many harmful effects. As a result of using illegal drugs, a person can be harmed or even die. Marijuana can cause memory loss and lung problems. Cocaine or crack can make the heart beat so fast that the user may have a heart attack and die.

1. What can cause a person to have memory loss?
2. What are three other effects of illegal drugs?
3. What two signal words or phrases helped you identify the causes and effects in this paragraph?

377

2. PRACTICE

More About Cause and Effect

Have students compare the graphic organizer on page 376 with the one on this page. Lead students to see that the Effect box now has two things listed instead of one.

Remind students that some paragraphs might have more than one cause and effect. Read aloud the paragraph. Have students identify the given cause and effect. (Cause: The ball hit Nick; effect: He fell to the ground.) Have students find the second cause and effect in the paragraph. (Cause: Nick got up to hurl the ball; effect: Emma pleaded that it was an accident.)

3. APPLY

Skill Practice

Have students use the Tips for Identifying Cause and Effect to answer the questions.

1. Using marijuana can cause memory loss.
2. Three other effects of illegal drugs are lung problems, heart attacks, and death.
3. As a *result* and *cause* are signal words in this paragraph.

Meeting Individual Needs
Leveled Activities

BELOW-LEVEL Have students scan newspapers and magazines for a picture or headline about an event that shows a clear cause-and-effect relationship related to drugs or violence. Have students study the picture or headline and speculate about what happened, what caused it to happen, and what the effects of the event were.

ON-LEVEL Have students write about a real or imaginary disagreement that happened on the playground. Have them tell the cause and effect of that disagreement.

CHALLENGE Have students read an article related to drug abuse or violence. Ask them to identify the cause-and-effect relationships in the article.

READING IN HEALTH HANDBOOK

Pages 378–379

Objective

▶ Recognize the main idea of a selection and identify the details that support it

1. TEACH/MODEL

Have students explain why it is helpful to identify the main idea and details of a selection. (to know what a passage is mostly about) Point out the graphic organizer and discuss the Tips for Identifying Main Idea and Details. Have students read the paragraph in the example.

Read aloud the following model to help students see how to record in the graphic organizer information from the paragraph.

I read the entire paragraph and decided that it is mostly about exercise being important to good health. I put this in the Main Idea box. The details include that exercise helps you manage stress and maintain a healthful weight; exercise helps you keep your body systems strong; and doing a variety of activities in the right amount is important. I put these in the boxes marked Details.

Identify Main Idea and Details

Being able to identify the main idea and details can help you understand what you read. You can use a graphic organizer like this one to show the main idea and details.

Main Idea: The most important idea of a paragraph, several paragraphs, or a selection

Detail: Information that tells more about the main idea

Detail: Information that tells more about the main idea

Detail: Information that tells more about the main idea

Tips for Identifying Main Idea and Details

• To identify the main idea, ask: *What is this mostly about?*
• Remember that the main idea is not always stated in the first sentence.
• Be sure to look for details that help you answer questions such as *Who?, What?, Where?, When?, Why?,* and *How?*
• Use pictures as clues to help you figure out the main idea.

Here's an example.

Main Idea

Getting enough exercise is a key to good health. Daily physical activity helps you manage stress and maintain a healthful weight. It strengthens your body systems and boosts overall fitness. Doing a variety of activities helps, too.

Detail

You could record this in the graphic organizer.

Main Idea: Exercise is important to good health.

Detail: Exercise helps you manage stress and maintain a healthful weight.

Detail: Exercise helps you keep your body systems strong.

Detail: Doing a variety of activities is important.

378

Skills in Context

MAIN IDEA AND DETAILS: Main Idea Mobile A paragraph or a group of paragraphs usually has one main idea. Any paragraphs that follow usually include details that support the main idea. Make a mobile that illustrates the main idea and details of a section from Chapter 4 or 11.

What You Need

• 12" x 3" strip of poster board
• Index cards
• Pencil
• Hole punch
• String
• Drawing tools

What To Do

1. Choose a text section that interests you. Identify the main idea and several supporting details.

2. Write the main idea sentence on one side of the strip of poster board. On the other side, draw a picture to accompany your sentence.

3. Write each supporting detail on a separate index card. Draw a picture or symbol on the opposite side.

4. Punch a hole at the center top of the main idea poster board, and attach a loop of string as a hanger. Punch holes along the bottom, and attach each detail card. Then hang up your mobile.

More About Main Idea and Details

Sometimes the main idea of a passage is at the end instead of the beginning. The main idea may not even be stated. However, it can be understood from the details. Look at the following graphic organizer. What do you think the main idea is?

Main Idea: ?

Detail: Warm up your body before exercise.

Detail: Do aerobic exercise that lasts at least twenty to thirty minutes.

Detail: After exercise, give your body time to return to normal by doing low-level activity.

A passage can contain details of different types. In the following paragraph, identify each detail as a reason, an example, a fact, a step, or a description.

Some kinds of exercise do not build cardiovascular fitness. Activities that use oxygen faster than it can be replaced are anaerobic. For example, sprinting as fast as you can is anaerobic. So is carrying a heavy load. Anaerobic activities build strength, but they don't help your heart.

Skill Practice

Read this paragraph. Use the Tips for Identifying Main Idea and Details to answer the questions.

Being a responsible family member means people depend on you. You may have jobs to do, such as walking the dog. Doing your jobs sets a good example for younger brothers or sisters. As you mature, your responsibilities grow.

1. What is the main idea of the paragraph?
2. What supporting details give more information?
3. What details answer any of the questions *Who?, What?, Where?, When?, Why?,* and *How?*

379

2. PRACTICE

More About Main Idea

Have students work in small groups to look at the information given on the graphic organizer. Discuss with students what is most likely the main idea given the set of details provided. (There are three important steps to exercise.)

Read aloud the paragraph. Help students identify and analyze the details to determine in what category each detail would fall. (Reasons, facts, examples, and descriptions are given.)

3. APPLY

Skill Practice

Have students use the Tips for Identifying the Main Idea and Details to answer the questions.

1. Being a responsible member of a family means that people can depend on you.
2. Doing your jobs sets a good example for younger siblings.
3. *Possible answer:* When you mature, your responsibility grows.

Meeting Individual Needs
Leveled Activities

BELOW-LEVEL Have students listen to a passage from the text and tell their partners what they think it is mostly about. Have students reread the passage and write the main idea and the supporting details of the passage.

ON-LEVEL Give pairs of students a blank graphic organizer. Each partner should tell a short story about a supportive family. Partners should use the graphic organizer to fill in the main idea of each story and identify the important details. Partners can share with the class the information from their completed graphic organizers.

CHALLENGE Have students identify the main idea and four supporting details from a passage in Chapter 11. Have them draw four equal sections on each of two paper plates. They should cut away and discard one wedge on one plate. Have them write the main idea on this plate and then write and illustrate one supporting detail on each wedge of the other plate. With the main idea on top, attach the plates with a fastener.

READING IN HEALTH HANDBOOK

Pages 380–381

Objective

► Understand that time-order words signal the sequence of events in text

1. TEACH/MODEL

Have students explain why it is helpful to pay attention to the sequence of events. (Knowing the order in which things happen can help you understand what you read.) Point out the graphic organizer and discuss the Tips for Understanding Sequence. Have students read the paragraph in the example.

Read aloud the following model to help students see how to record in the graphic organizer information from the paragraph.

I know that my topic is how blood moves in the heart. I read that blood from the body and lungs enters *first* into the atria of the heart. The atria squeeze, and the blood *next* passes through two valves and enters the ventricles. The valves close and the ventricles squeeze. The signal word, *finally*, tells me the third thing that happens is that blood moves through two other valves to the lungs and the body. I write that in my graphic organizer.

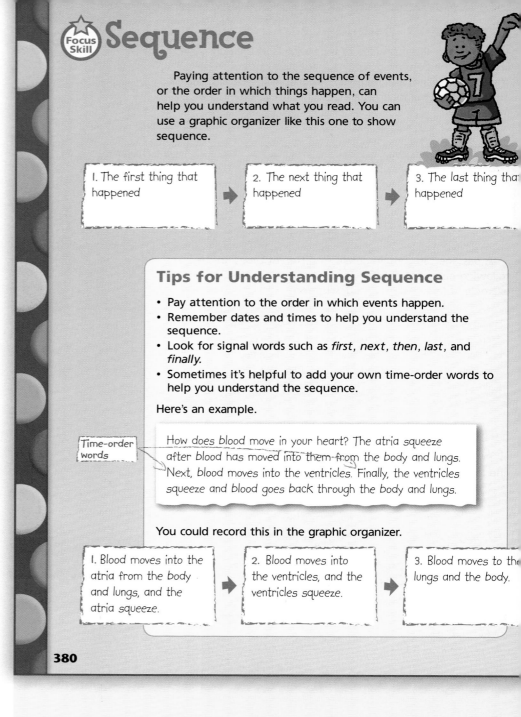

Sequence

Paying attention to the sequence of events, or the order in which things happen, can help you understand what you read. You can use a graphic organizer like this one to show sequence.

1. The first thing that happened → 2. The next thing that happened → 3. The last thing that happened

Tips for Understanding Sequence

- Pay attention to the order in which events happen.
- Remember dates and times to help you understand the sequence.
- Look for signal words such as *first, next, then, last,* and *finally.*
- Sometimes it's helpful to add your own time-order words to help you understand the sequence.

Here's an example.

Time-order words

How does blood move in your heart? The atria squeeze after blood has moved into them from the body and lungs. Next, blood moves into the ventricles. Finally, the ventricles squeeze and blood goes back through the body and lungs.

You could record this in the graphic organizer.

1. Blood moves into the atria from the body and lungs, and the atria squeeze. → 2. Blood moves into the ventricles, and the ventricles squeeze. → 3. Blood moves to the lungs and the body.

380

Skills in Context

SEQUENCE: Emergency Line Sequence is the order in which events take place. Revisit Chapter 5 to recall the steps to take in the event of an emergency.

What To Do

1. Use a separate index card to write a sentence about each step to follow in an emergency.
2. Add an illustration to each card.
3. Punch a hole at the top and bottom of each card.
4. Connect the cards in order by tying them together through the holes.
5. Hang up your emergency line.

What You Need

- Index cards
- Pencil or pen
- Crayons or markers
- String, cut into 6" lengths
- Scissors
- Hole punch

More About Sequence

Sometimes information is sequenced by dates or times. For example, in an emergency, authorities often need to know the exact times at which events occurred. Use the graphic organizer to sequence events that occurred during an emergency you experienced or read about.

> 1. My grandfather started getting chest pains at about 7:15 P.M.

> 2. My mom called 911 at about 7:17 P.M.

> 3. The ambulance arrived at 7:23 P.M, and my grandfather received CPR.

When time-order words are not given, add your own words to help you understand the sequence. In the paragraph below, one time-order word has been included and underlined. What other time-order words can you add to help understand the paragraph's sequence?

> Last week I saw my cousin Diane crash her bike into a tree. <u>First</u>, I performed a ten-second survey. I realized that Diane needed immediate help, so I quickly called 911. I made sure that Diane didn't move until the ambulance arrived. I tried to stay calm and confident so that I could help Diane.

Skill Practice

Read the following paragraph. Use the Tips for Understanding Sequence to answer the questions.

> One day at camp, Amy fell off her horse. First, I surveyed the situation. Next, I saw that she might have broken a bone, so I quickly dialed 911. Then, because of the possible broken bone, I told Amy to lie still. Finally, I calmly talked to Amy until the ambulance arrived.

1. What was the first thing Amy's friend did after Amy fell off the horse?
2. What might have happened if Amy's friend had left out the second step in the sequence of these events?
3. What four signal words helped you identify the sequence of events in this paragraph?

381

2. PRACTICE

More About Sequence

Have students look at the events written in sequence on the graphic organizer. Give students a blank graphic organizer. Have them use the graphic organizer to write, in order, the events that occurred during an emergency they have experienced or read about.

Remind students that some paragraphs don't include time-order words. This can make it harder to understand an event's sequence. Read the paragraph aloud. The time-order word *first* is given. Students should find places to add the other time-order words *next, then,* and *finally*.

3. APPLY

Skill Practice

Have students use the Tips for Understanding Sequence to answer the questions.

1. She surveyed the situation.
2. If she did not contact 911, she would risk not having emergency help when it was needed.
3. *First, then, next,* and *finally* are signal words in this paragraph.

Meeting Individual Needs
Leveled Activities

BELOW-LEVEL Have each student divide a sheet of paper into four sections. Ask students to draw a sequence of events and tell what happened *first, then, next,* and *last*.

ON-LEVEL Write on the board a series of steps that tells the sequence of events that occur as a body grows and changes. Write the steps out of order. Have students identify signal words and organize the sentences in sequence. Then have them write the sentences as a paragraph.

CHALLENGE Have students choose a subject from Chapter 1 or 5 that can be put into sequence. Have them write each step except for one on a separate sentence strip. Have a partner locate the information in the text and identify the missing step.

READING IN HEALTH HANDBOOK

Pages 382–383

Objective

▶ Identify the elements that make up a good summary.

1. TEACH/MODEL

Have students explain why it is important to summarize a passage. (to understand how to tell about the most important parts) Point out the graphic organizer and discuss the Tips for Summarizing. Have students read the paragraph in the example.

Read aloud the following model to help students see how to record in the graphic organizer information from the paragraph.

I know that the main idea of the paragraph is that healthful choices reduce your risk of disease. I write that in the Main Idea box. The paragraph includes details about exercising regularly, eating low-fat foods, and not smoking. I write those in the boxes marked Details. In my own words, I write in the box marked Summary that we should make healthful choices to live a longer life.

Summarize

Learning how to summarize helps you identify the most important parts in a passage. This can help you understand what you read. You can use a graphic organizer like this one to help you summarize.

| Main Idea: Tell about the most important information you have read. | + | Details: Add details that answer the questions Who?, What?, Where?, When?, Why?, and How? | = | Summary: Retell what you have just read, including only the most important details. |

Tips for Summarizing

- To write a summary, ask: *What is the most important information in the paragraph?*
- To include details with your summary, ask: *Who, what, when, where, why, and how?*
- Remember to use fewer words than the original has.
- Don't forget to use your own words when you summarize.

Here's an example.

> Making healthful choices reduces your risk of getting some diseases. Reduce your risk of heart disease and lung cancer by not using tobacco. Exercise regularly and eat healthful, low-fat foods to help prevent heart disease.

Main Idea

Detail

Here's what you could record in your graphic organizer.

| Main Idea: Healthful choices reduce your risk of disease. | + | Details: Exercise regularly, eat low-fat foods, and don't smoke. | = | Summary: Make healthful choices to live a longer life. |

382

Skills in Context

SUMMARIZE: Wish You Were Here To summarize, you tell briefly the main idea and important details of a passage. Revisit Chapter 12, and write a postcard about an idea for working toward a healthful community.

What You Need

- Writing paper
- Writing and drawing tools
- Index cards

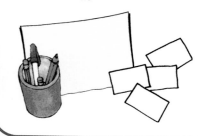

What To Do

1. Identify a topic in Chapter 12 about improving the healthfulness of the community that you wish to share with a classmate. Then identify the main idea of the passage and the important details.

2. On one side of an index card, write a message in your own words about an idea for improving the healthfulness of the community. Be sure to include the main idea and the details.

3. On the other side of the index card, draw a picture that summarizes the passage.

4. "Mail" your postcard to the classmate.

More About Summarizing

Sometimes a paragraph includes information that would not be included in a summary. For example, suppose the paragraph on page 382 included a sentence about the number of people who die of lung cancer each year. The graphic organizer would remain the same, because that detail is not important to understanding the paragraph's main idea.

Main Idea:		Details:		Summary:
Healthful choices reduce your risk of disease.	+	Exercise regularly, eat low-fat foods, and don't smoke.	=	Make healthful choices to live a longer life.

Sometimes the main idea of a paragraph is not in the first sentence. In the following paragraph, two important details are underlined. What is the main idea?

Did you ever wonder how you "catch" an illness from someone else? <u>Infectious diseases are caused by pathogens.</u> Pathogens cause infection when they grow and multiply. <u>They spread disease when they are passed from one person to another.</u>

Skill Practice

Read the following paragraph. Use the Tips for Summarizing to answer the questions.

One important task of a local health department is to inspect restaurants. Restaurants must be clean. The foods must be handled properly and kept at proper temperatures. If the health department finds too many problems, it can close down a restaurant until the problems are corrected.

1. If a friend asked you what this paragraph is about, what information would you include? What would you leave out?
2. What is the main idea of the paragraph?
3. What two details would you include in a summary?

383

Meeting Individual Needs
Leveled Activities

BELOW-LEVEL Have students summarize an event that took place in their neighborhood. Tell them to include the main thing that happened and the three most important details.

ON-LEVEL Have groups identify a passage from Chapter 7 or 12. Set a timer for one minute. Have each member of the group summarize the paragraph in one complete sentence. Ask them to read the summaries aloud for accuracy and then count the words. The student whose summary uses the fewest words may choose the next passage to summarize.

CHALLENGE Have students suppose they are television news reporters who are reporting on a disease they learned about in Chapter 7. They should write news bulletins about a cure for a particular disease. Tell them to use their own words to retell the main idea and details.

2. PRACTICE

More About Summarizing

Remind students that a summary includes only the most important details of a passage. Direct student's attention to the graphic organizer. Discuss why the additional information given would not be included in the summary.

Often, the main idea of a paragraph is in the first sentence of the paragraph. However, it can be elsewhere in the paragraph. Read the paragraph aloud. Read the underlined information, and discuss what makes each sentence a detail. Have students find the main idea of the paragraph. Encourage them to use their own words to write a summary.

3. APPLY

Skill Practice

Have students use the Tips for Summarizing to answer the questions.

1. I would tell a friend that local health departments inspect restaurants to be sure they are clean and the food is safe to eat. I would not include the detail that bacteria grows on food that is not kept at the proper temperature.
2. Local health departments inspect restaurants.
3. Restaurants must be clean; the health department can close a restaurant when problems exist.

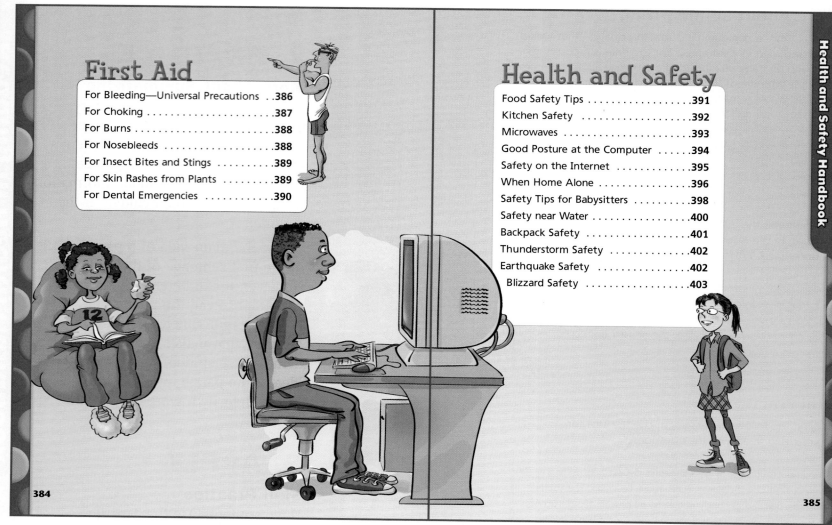

First Aid

Health and Safety

384

385

These pages are available in reproducible format in the *Teaching Resources* book.

USING THE HEALTH AND SAFETY HANDBOOK

This section of the Student Edition provides information that addresses important health concerns of children, such as nutrition, physical fitness, safety, and first aid. It is intended to supplement and extend the content of the Student Edition. **Copying masters of these pages are available in the *Teaching Resources* book.**

In the Classroom

You can use these pages as stand-alone lessons. Discussion questions, activities, and additional background information are provided for you.

You may wish to make copies of these pages for children to refer to as you teach core lessons from the chapters in the Student Edition.

At Home

You may wish to send copies home so that children can discuss the topics with their families. These pages can also serve as a reference if children are completing health projects at home.

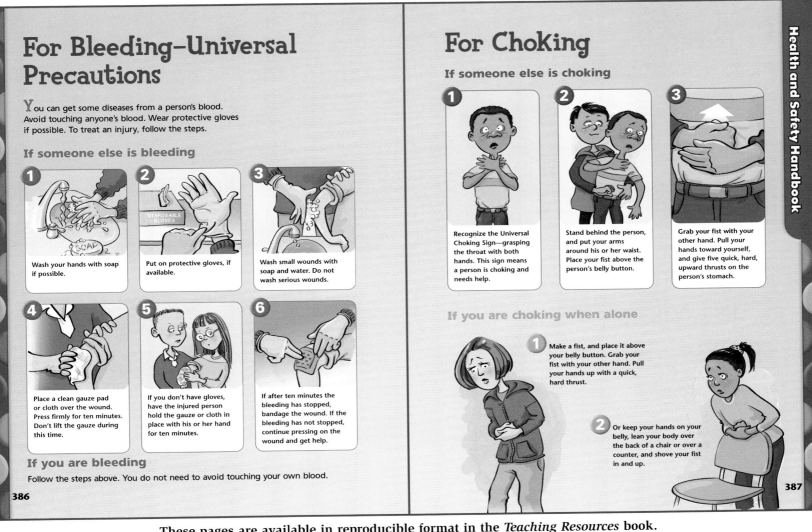

For Bleeding–Universal Precautions

You can get some diseases from a person's blood. Avoid touching anyone's blood. Wear protective gloves if possible. To treat an injury, follow the steps.

If someone else is bleeding

1 Wash your hands with soap if possible.

2 Put on protective gloves, if available.

3 Wash small wounds with soap and water. Do not wash serious wounds.

4 Place a clean gauze pad or cloth over the wound. Press firmly for ten minutes. Don't lift the gauze during this time.

5 If you don't have gloves, have the injured person hold the gauze or cloth in place with his or her hand for ten minutes.

6 If after ten minutes the bleeding has stopped, bandage the wound. If the bleeding has not stopped, continue pressing on the wound and get help.

If you are bleeding

Follow the steps above. You do not need to avoid touching your own blood.

386

For Choking

If someone else is choking

1 Recognize the Universal Choking Sign—grasping the throat with both hands. This sign means a person is choking and needs help.

2 Stand behind the person, and put your arms around his or her waist. Place your fist above the person's belly button.

3 Grab your fist with your other hand. Pull your hands toward yourself, and give five quick, hard, upward thrusts on the person's stomach.

If you are choking when alone

1 Make a fist, and place it above your belly button. Grab your fist with your other hand. Pull your hands up with a quick, hard thrust.

2 Or keep your hands on your belly, lean your body over the back of a chair or over a counter, and shove your fist in and up.

387

These pages are available in reproducible format in the *Teaching Resources* book.

HEALTH BACKGROUND

First-Aid Risks HIV, the virus that causes AIDS, and hepatitis B are life-threatening diseases that can be spread through contact with an infected person's blood. If the person giving first aid has a small cut, even a hangnail, blood from the patient's wound might enter the cut and transmit one of these diseases. Emphasize that wearing disposable gloves or using the patient's own hand to apply pressure to a wound lessens the caregiver's risk of contracting infection. It also reduces the risk of spreading disease-bearing germs from the caregiver's hands to the patient.

Discussion

How can you learn more about first aid? Possible responses: take a first-aid course; ask a person trained to administer first aid to demonstrate techniques

Why is it important to know first aid? So you can help yourself or someone else who is injured; knowing first aid you might help save someone's life. So you can demonstrate how to respond to deliberate or accidental injuries.

ACTIVITIES

Science
Pulse Spots Have students find out the points on the body where it is easy to detect a pulse. Have the school nurse or a health care professional demonstrate how to take the pulse of an adult and a baby.

Drama
Rescue Play Have students work together to write and perform a play that incorporates the first-aid techniques learned, including treatment for choking and bleeding.

For Burns

- Minor burns are called first-degree burns and involve only the top layer of skin. The skin is red and dry, and the burn is painful.
- Second-degree burns cause deeper damage. The burns cause blisters, redness, swelling, and pain.
- Third-degree burns are the most serious because they damage all layers of the skin. The skin is usually white or charred black. The area may feel numb because the nerve endings have been destroyed.

All burns need immediate first aid.

Minor Burns
- Run cool water over the burn, or soak it for at least five minutes.
- Cover the burn with a clean, dry bandage.
- Do not put lotion or ointment on the burn.

More Serious Burns
- Cover the burn with a cool, wet bandage or clean cloth. Do not break any blisters.
- Do not put lotion or ointment on the burn.
- Get help from an adult right away.

For Nosebleeds

- Sit down, and tilt your head forward. Pinch your nostrils together for at least ten minutes.
- You can also put a cloth-covered cold pack on the bridge of your nose.
- If your nose continues to bleed, get help from an adult.

388

For Insect Bites and Stings

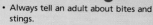

- Always tell an adult about bites and stings.
- Scrape out the stinger with your fingernail.
- Wash the area with soap and water.
- A wrapped ice cube or cold pack will usually take away the pain from insect bites. A paste made from baking soda and water also helps.
- If the bite or sting is more serious and is on an arm or leg, keep the leg or arm dangling down. Apply a cold, wet cloth. Get help immediately.
- If you find a tick on your skin, remove it. Protect your fingers with a tissue or cloth to prevent contact with infectious tick fluids. If you must touch the tick with your bare hands, wash your hands right away.
- If the tick has already bitten you, ask an adult to remove it. Using tweezers, an adult should grab the tick as close to your skin as possible and pull the tick out in one steady motion. Do not use petroleum jelly or oil of any kind because it may cause the tick to struggle, releasing its infectious fluids. Thoroughly wash the area of the bite.

For Skin Rashes from Plants

Many poisonous plants have three leaves. Remember, "Leaves of three, let them be." If you touch a poisonous plant, wash the area and your hands. Change clothes, and wash the ones the plant touched. If a rash develops, follow these tips.

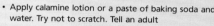
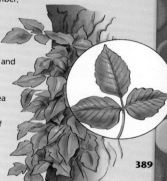

- Apply calamine lotion or a paste of baking soda and water. Try not to scratch. Tell an adult
- If you get blisters, do not pop them. If they burst, keep the area clean and dry. Cover the area with a bandage.
- If your rash does not go away in two weeks or if the rash is on your face or in your eyes, see your doctor.

389

These pages are available in reproducible format in the *Teaching Resources* book.

HEALTH BACKGROUND

Painful Contact At some point in time, everyone may experience the discomfort that comes with having a nosebleed, a burn, a bite or sting from an insect, or an irritating skin rash. Although these problems are usually minor, some people have strong and potentially deadly allergic reactions to poison ivy or insect stings. It pays to learn how to avoid these hazards.

Discussion

What are three types of burns? How do they differ?

First degree, second degree, and third degree. First degree burns, like sunburn, cause redness and temporary discomfort; second degree burns cause some skin damage, are painful, heal in a few weeks, and may leave scars; third degree burns deeply char the skin, require extensive medical attention, and are very painful.

How can wearing proper clothing protect your skin?

by protecting you from the sun and from contact with plants or insects

ACTIVITIES

Science

Skin Deep Demonstrate the absorbency of the skin using a simple model. Have students drip water mixed with food coloring onto an absorbent paper towel. Tell students to describe what happens to the surface of the paper towel. Ask students to explain how this is similar to the skin's reaction to insect bites or stings.

Language Arts

Table It Have students make a table to summarize and organize the information on these pages. Columns should include Injury, Symptoms, and Treatment.

For Dental Emergencies

Dental emergencies occur less often than other health emergencies, but it is wise to know how to handle them.

Broken Tooth

- Rinse your mouth with warm water. Wrap a cloth around a cold pack, and place it on the injured area. Save any parts of the broken tooth. Call your dentist immediately.

Bitten Tongue or Lip

- Apply direct pressure to the bleeding area with a cloth. Use a wrapped cold pack to stop swelling. If the bleeding doesn't stop within fifteen minutes, go to a hospital emergency room.

Knocked-Out Permanent Tooth

- Find the tooth, and clean it gently and carefully. Handle it by the top (crown), not the root. Put it back into the socket if you can. Hold it in place by biting on a piece of clean cloth. If the tooth cannot be put back in, place it in a cup with milk or water. See a dentist immediately because time is very important in saving the tooth.

Food or Object Caught Between Teeth

- Use dental floss to gently take out the food or object. Never use anything sharp to remove what is stuck between your teeth. If it cannot be removed, call your dentist.

Remember that many dental injuries can be prevented if you

- wear a mouth guard while playing sports.
- wear a safety belt while riding in a car.
- inspect your home and get rid of hazards that might cause falls and injuries.
- see your dentist regularly for preventive care.

390

Food Safety Tips

Tips for Preparing Food

- Wash your hands thoroughly before preparing food. Also wash your hands after preparing each dish.
- Defrost meat in a microwave or the refrigerator. Do NOT defrost meat on the kitchen counter.
- Keep raw meat, poultry, and fish and their juices away from other foods.
- Wash cutting boards, knives, and countertops immediately after cutting up meat, poultry, or fish. Never use the same cutting board for meats and vegetables without thoroughly washing the board first.

Tips for Cooking

- Cook all food thoroughly, especially meat. This will kill bacteria that can make you ill.
- Red meats should be cooked to a temperature of 160°F. Poultry should be cooked to 180°F. When fish is safely cooked, it flakes easily with a fork.
- Eggs should be cooked until the yolks are firm. Never eat foods or drink anything containing raw eggs. Never eat uncooked cookie dough made with raw eggs.

Tips for Cleaning Up the Kitchen

- Wash all dishes, utensils, and countertops with hot, soapy water.
- Store leftovers in small containers that will cool quickly in the refrigerator. Don't leave leftovers on the counter to cool.
- Your refrigerator should be 40°F or colder.
- Write the date on leftovers. Don't store them for more than five days.

391

These pages are available in reproducible format in the *Teaching Resources* book.

HEALTH BACKGROUND

Salmonella These are bacteria found most often in raw or undercooked poultry, eggs, meat, or fish, or in unpasteurized milk. Salmonella are killed by cooking.

Staphylococcus aureus (staph) These bacteria are spread to food by people. They can be carried on the skin and in the nose and the throat. Cooking kills the bacteria but leaves behind the toxins that cause disease symptoms. So cleanliness is vital.

Escherichia coli (E. coli) These bacteria are found in the digestive tract. They are spread to food by people with unclean hands. Sometimes ground meats, such as hamburger, are contaminated by bacteria from the digestive tracts of cattle.

Discussion

Why do you think it can be difficult to find the source of food poisoning? Symptoms don't occur right away, and people eat many different foods during a normal day.

Can both primary and permanent teeth be reimplanted? No. A primary (baby) tooth is not re-implanted as it is usually rejected during the healing process. A permanent tooth can be reimplanted if it is handled carefully after being knocked out and if a dentist is seen immediately.

ACTIVITIES

Science

Bacteria and Viruses Have students find out how bacteria and viruses reproduce and how they spread. Students can give an oral report or make a model to share their findings.

Language Arts

Mouth guards A mouth protector can limit the risk of injuries to your teeth as well as to protect the soft tissues of your tongue, lips and cheek lining. Divide students into three teams and have each team research one of the three different types of mouth guards. A team leader can report the results to the rest of the class.

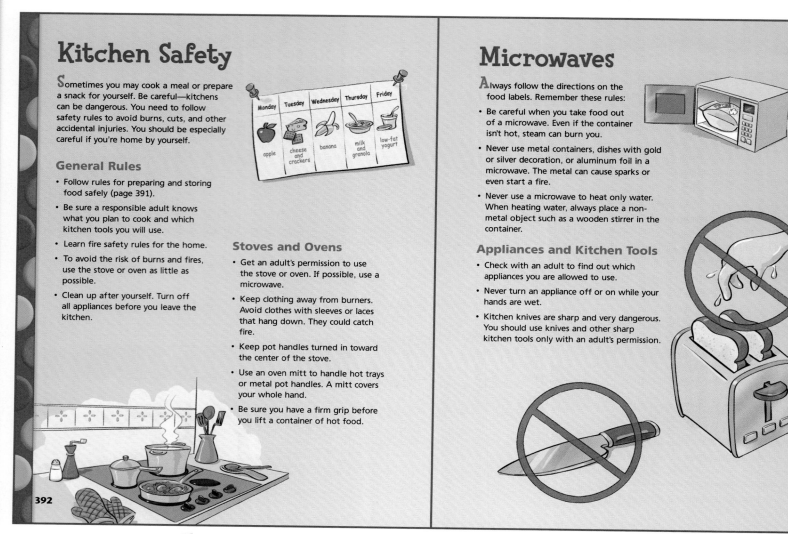

Kitchen Safety

Sometimes you may cook a meal or prepare a snack for yourself. Be careful—kitchens can be dangerous. You need to follow safety rules to avoid burns, cuts, and other accidental injuries. You should be especially careful if you're home by yourself.

General Rules

- Follow rules for preparing and storing food safely (page 391).
- Be sure a responsible adult knows what you plan to cook and which kitchen tools you will use.
- Learn fire safety rules for the home.
- To avoid the risk of burns and fires, use the stove or oven as little as possible.
- Clean up after yourself. Turn off all appliances before you leave the kitchen.

Stoves and Ovens

- Get an adult's permission to use the stove or oven. If possible, use a microwave.
- Keep clothing away from burners. Avoid clothes with sleeves or laces that hang down. They could catch fire.
- Keep pot handles turned in toward the center of the stove.
- Use an oven mitt to handle hot trays or metal pot handles. A mitt covers your whole hand.
- Be sure you have a firm grip before you lift a container of hot food.

392

Microwaves

Always follow the directions on the food labels. Remember these rules:

- Be careful when you take food out of a microwave. Even if the container isn't hot, steam can burn you.
- Never use metal containers, dishes with gold or silver decoration, or aluminum foil in a microwave. The metal can cause sparks or even start a fire.
- Never use a microwave to heat only water. When heating water, always place a non-metal object such as a wooden stirrer in the container.

Appliances and Kitchen Tools

- Check with an adult to find out which appliances you are allowed to use.
- Never turn an appliance off or on while your hands are wet.
- Kitchen knives are sharp and very dangerous. You should use knives and other sharp kitchen tools only with an adult's permission.

393

These pages are available in reproducible format in the *Teaching Resources* book.

HEALTH BACKGROUND

Burn Safety According to the CDC, preschool children (age 5 and under) and older adults (age 65 and older) have the highest fire death rates in U.S. home fires. The most common burns are caused by scalds, building fires, and flammable liquids and gases. The American Burn Association reports that each year in the United States, 1.1 million burn injuries require medical attention. And each year, approximately 4,500 of these people die. Up to 10,000 people die every year of burn-related infections with pneumonia being the most common complication of burns.

Discussion

How important is it to understand and follow rules for kitchen safety when you are preparing and cooking meals? Answers may vary, but should indicate that rules help prevent accidents related to tools, such as knives, and appliances, such as stoves and ovens, that produce heat or open flame.

Why should you have an adult help for some cooking? Answers will vary, but should indicate the importance of having adult help available in case of an accident, injury, or fire.

ACTIVITIES

Language Arts
Safety Guides Have students show an understanding of kitchen safety by writing how-to guides for food preparation involving various tools and appliances. Have students share their guide with the class. Suggest that students take the guides home to share with their families.

Art
Rules Without Words Have students illustrate the safety guides that they developed above. Suggest that they use symbols and warning signs to emphasize important safety issues.

Good Posture at the Computer

Good posture is very important when using the computer. To help prevent eyestrain, muscle fatigue, and injuries, follow the posture tips shown below. Remember to grasp your mouse lightly, keep your back straight, avoid facing your monitor toward a window, and take frequent breaks for stretching.

shoulders in line with ears and hips

top of screen at or just below eye level

neck and shoulders relaxed

arms at sides bent as shown

wrists straight

feet flat on floor

394

Safety on the Internet

The Internet is a remarkable tool. You can use it for fun, education, research, and more. However, like anything else, it has some downsides. Some people compare the Internet to a city—not all the people there are people you want to meet, and not all the places you can go are places you want to be. On the Internet, as in a real city, you have to use common sense and follow safety guidelines to protect yourself. Below are some easy rules you can follow to stay safe online.

Rules for Online Safety

- Talk with an adult family member to set up rules for going online. Decide when you can go online, how long you can be online, and what kinds of places you can visit. Do not break the rules you agree to follow.
- Don't give out personal information such as your name, address, and telephone number or information about your family. Don't give the name or location of your school.
- If you find anything online that makes you uncomfortable, tell an adult family member right away.
- Never agree to meet with anyone in person. If you want to get together with someone you have met online, check with an adult family member first. If a meeting is approved, arrange to meet in a public place, and bring an adult with you.
- Don't send your picture or anything else to a person you meet online without first checking with an adult.
- Don't respond to any messages that are mean or make you uncomfortable. If you receive a message like that, tell an adult right away.

395

These pages are available in reproducible format in the *Teaching Resources* book.

HEALTH BACKGROUND

Wise Computer Use Computer use has grown exponentially in the past three decades. In the United States, 30-50 million children use computers regularly. This regular use of computers may contribute to eyestrain, muscle fatigue, and other injuries. Many of these injuries are preventable if children follow simple guidelines for good posture and safe computing.

Discussion

How can your posture while using the computer affect your work? Practicing good posture can help you avoid muscle fatigue and eyestrain. As a result, it will help you focus on your work.

Why is it wise to follow rules for on-line safety? Answers will vary, but should include the need to protect one's privacy and avoiding unwanted exposure to unhealthful messages or computer viruses.

ACTIVITIES

Language Arts
Keyboarding skills Help students improve their keyboarding skills. Write on the board a list of words that they can use to learn the positions of the letters on the computer keyboard. Then ask students to type sentences using the words. To further the activity or to challenge students, suggest they do the following math activity.

Math
Keystrokes Galore Give students a chance to practice multiplication. Have students measure typing speed in words per minute. Have a student retype a 20-word paragraph as many times as possible in 5 minutes. Then count the paragraphs, multiply by 20, and divide by 5 to get typing speed. Use the typing speed to find the total number of keystrokes the person would make in 7 hours. (7 hours $\times$ 60 minutes/hour $\times$ 50 words/minute $\times$ 5 keystrokes/word = 105, 000 keystrokes)

Health and Safety Handbook

When Home Alone

Everyone stays home alone sometimes. When you stay home alone, it's important to know how to take care of yourself. Here are some easy rules to follow that will help keep you safe when you are home by yourself.

Do These Things

- Lock all the doors and windows. Be sure you know how to lock and unlock all the locks.

- If someone who is nasty or mean calls, say nothing and hang up immediately. Tell an adult about the call when he or she gets home. Your parents may not want you to answer the phone at all.

- If you have an emergency, call 911. Be prepared to describe the problem and to give your full name, address, and telephone number. Follow all instructions given to you. Do not hang up the phone until you are told to do so.

- If you see anyone hanging around outside your home, call a neighbor or the police.

- If you see or smell smoke, go outside right away. If you live in an apartment, do not take the elevator. Go to a neighbor's house, and call 911 immediately.

- Entertain yourself. Time will pass more quickly if you are not bored. Work on a hobby, read a book or magazine, do your homework, or clean your room. Before you know it, an adult will be home.

396

Do NOT Do These Things

- Do NOT use the stove, microwave, or oven unless an adult family member has given you permission and you know how to use these appliances.

- Do NOT open the door to anyone you don't know or to anyone who is not supposed to be in your home.

- Do NOT talk to strangers on the telephone. Do not tell anyone that you are home alone. If the call is for an adult family member, say that he or she can't come to the phone right now and take a message.

- Do NOT have friends over unless an adult family member has given you permission to do so.

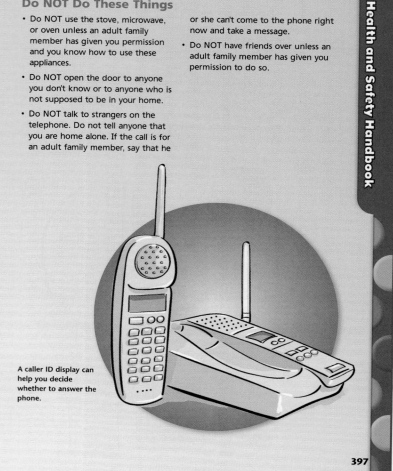

A caller ID display can help you decide whether to answer the phone.

397

These pages are available in reproducible format in the *Teaching Resources* book.

HEALTH BACKGROUND

Latchkey Children The term "latchkey children" originated in the 1800's when children who were responsible for their own care wore their house keys on strings around their necks. Today, this term is used to refer to the estimated 40 percent of school-age children who are at home alone after school each day. When parents or other family members cannot be home, these children must know and follow rules to ensure their health and safety.

Discussion

Why is it important to have house rules for children who are home alone? Answers will vary.

What should you do if there is an emergency when you are at home by yourself? Call 911, describe the problem, give your full name, address, and phone number, and follow the instructions given to you. Do not hang up until the operator tells you to.

ACTIVITIES

Social Studies
Somewhere Else Have students find out about the rules and responsibilities of children in other countries. Ask them to look for examples of latchkey children in other countries.

Drama
Role Play Divide the class into two groups. Have students role-play situations and circumstances that may arise when they are home alone. Instruct one group to act the part of children at home, and have the other group play the role of people or strangers who might call or stop by. Review appropriate, safe responses with students.

Safety Tips for Babysitters

Being a babysitter is a very important job. As a sitter you are responsible for the safety of the children in your care. Adults depend on you to make good decisions. Here are some tips to help you be a successful and safe babysitter.

When you accept a job as a babysitter, ask

- what time you should arrive.
- how long the adults will be away.
- what your responsibilities will be.
- the amount of pay you will receive.
- what arrangements will be made for your transportation to and from the home.

When you arrive to start a job, you should

- arrive several minutes early so that the adults have time to give you information about caring for the child.
- write down the name and phone number of the place the adults are going and what time they will be home.
- find out where emergency phone numbers are listed. The list should have numbers for the police, the fire department, and the children's doctor.
- find out where first-aid supplies are kept. You should be prepared to give first aid in an emergency.
- ask what and when the children should eat.
- ask what activities the children may do.
- ask when the children should go to bed and what their bedtime routine is.

398

While you are caring for children, you should

- never leave a baby alone on a changing table, sofa, or bed.
- never leave a child alone, even for a short time.
- check children often when they are sleeping.
- never leave a child alone near a pool or in the bathtub.
- never let a child play with a plastic bag.
- keep dangerous items out of a child's reach.
- know where all the doors are, and keep them locked. Do not let anyone in without permission from the adults.
- take a message if the phone rings. Do not tell the caller that you are the babysitter or that the adults are out.
- call the adults if there is an injury or illness. If you can't reach them, call the emergency numbers on the list.

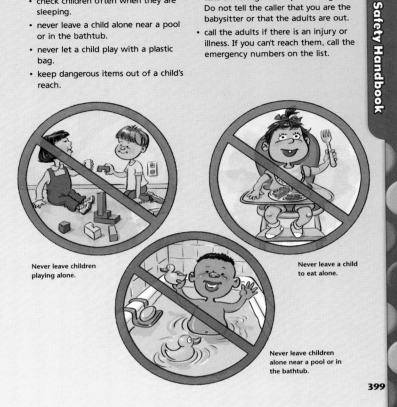

Never leave children playing alone.

Never leave a child to eat alone.

Never leave children alone near a pool or in the bathtub.

399

These pages are available in reproducible format in the *Teaching Resources* book.

HEALTH BACKGROUND

Being Responsible Good babysitters are safety-conscious individuals who take extra precautions to ensure the safety of the children in their care. A good babysitter successfully combines knowledge and the social skills associated with leadership, safety, safe play, basic care, and first aid. A well prepared babysitter is greatly appreciated by parents and will be in great demand.

Discussion

Why is it important to know first aid and basic child care if you are a babysitter? Answers will vary, but should indicate that babysitters must be prepared for the possibility of accident or injury. They also need to be able to handle other situations and behavioral challenges that may occur.

Why should someone be concerned about the abilities of a prospective babysitter? The babysitter will be responsible for the care and safety of a child.

ACTIVITIES

Art
Babysitter Poster Have students make posters to illustrate Safety Tips for Babysitters. Allow volunteers to display and explain their posters.

Language Arts
Babysitter Fact Sheet Have students design and information sheet for parents to give a babysitter. Students should be sure to include blank spaces for recording important information, such as emergency phone numbers and medication instructions.

Safety near Water

Water can be dangerous—a person can drown in five minutes or less. The best way to be safe near water is to learn how to swim. You should also follow these rules:

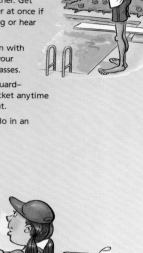

- Never swim without a lifeguard or a responsible adult present.
- If you can't swim, stay in shallow water. Don't rely on an inflatable raft.
- Know the rules for the beach or pool, and obey them. Don't run or play roughly near water.
- Do not dive in head-first until you know the water is deep enough. Jump in feet-first the first time.

- Watch the weather. Get out of the water at once if you see lightning or hear thunder.
- Protect your skin with sunscreen and your eyes with sunglasses.
- Wear a Coast Guard–approved life jacket anytime you are in a boat.
- Know what to do in an emergency.

400

Backpack Safety

Carrying a backpack that is too heavy can injure your back. Carrying one incorrectly also can hurt you.

Safe Use

- Choose a backpack with wide, padded shoulder straps and a padded back.
- Lighten your load. Leave unnecessary items at home.
- Pack heavier items so that they will be closest to your back.
- Always use both shoulder straps to carry the backpack.
- Never wear a backpack while riding a bicycle. The weight makes it harder to stay balanced. Use the bicycle's basket or saddlebags instead.

This is the right way to carry a backpack.

This is the wrong way to carry a backpack.

Safe Weight

A full backpack should weigh no more than 10 to 15 percent of your body weight. Less is better. To find 10 percent, divide your body weight by 10. Here are some examples:

Your Weight (pounds)	Maximum Backpack Weight (pounds)
70	7
80	8
90	9

401

These pages are available in reproducible format in the *Teaching Resources* book.

HEALTH BACKGROUND

Water Safety Four thousand people drown in the United States each year. Of those, more than 300 are children under 5 years of age. Children should always be supervised when they are playing, swimming, or bathing. Everyone should use and understand proper water safety equipment and flotation devices. The number of drowning fatalities can be reduced through swimming instruction and the observance of water safety rules.

Discussion

What can you do to be safer around water? Learn how to swim, use flotation devices, know how to administer rescue breathing and other kinds of first aid.

How can your backpack be a safety problem? Improper use or overloading of a backpack can cause unnecessary strain and pain in your shoulders, neck, and back. It can also make riding a bike more hazardous.

ACTIVITIES

Science
Rescue Breathing Have students find out how to administer rescue breathing. Arrange for the school nurse or first-aid instructor to demonstrate rescue breathing on an instructional dummy. Ask students to find out how they can become certified in CPR and rescue breathing.

Math
Proper Limits Have students calculate a safe weight for their backpacks based on their own weight. Then provide students with a bathroom scale to weigh loaded backpacks. Discuss options for reducing the weight that they usually carry in their backpacks.

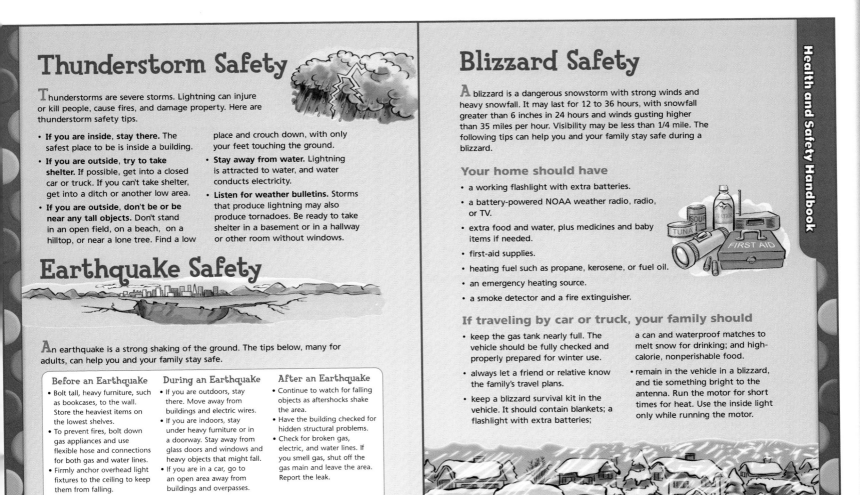

Thunderstorm Safety

Thunderstorms are severe storms. Lightning can injure or kill people, cause fires, and damage property. Here are thunderstorm safety tips.

- **If you are inside, stay there.** The safest place to be is inside a building.
- **If you are outside, try to take shelter.** If possible, get into a closed car or truck. If you can't take shelter, get into a ditch or another low area.
- **If you are outside, don't be or be near any tall objects.** Don't stand in an open field, on a beach, on a hilltop, or near a lone tree. Find a low

place and crouch down, with only your feet touching the ground.
- **Stay away from water.** Lightning is attracted to water, and water conducts electricity.
- **Listen for weather bulletins.** Storms that produce lightning may also produce tornadoes. Be ready to take shelter in a basement or in a hallway or other room without windows.

Earthquake Safety

An earthquake is a strong shaking of the ground. The tips below, many for adults, can help you and your family stay safe.

Before an Earthquake	During an Earthquake	After an Earthquake
• Bolt tall, heavy furniture, such as bookcases, to the wall. Store the heaviest items on the lowest shelves. • To prevent fires, bolt down gas appliances and use flexible hose and connections for both gas and water lines. • Firmly anchor overhead light fixtures to the ceiling to keep them from falling.	• If you are outdoors, stay there. Move away from buildings and electric wires. • If you are indoors, stay under heavy furniture or in a doorway. Stay away from glass doors and windows and heavy objects that might fall. • If you are in a car, go to an open area away from buildings and overpasses.	• Continue to watch for falling objects as aftershocks shake the area. • Have the building checked for hidden structural problems. • Check for broken gas, electric, and water lines. If you smell gas, shut off the gas main and leave the area. Report the leak.

402

Blizzard Safety

A blizzard is a dangerous snowstorm with strong winds and heavy snowfall. It may last for 12 to 36 hours, with snowfall greater than 6 inches in 24 hours and winds gusting higher than 35 miles per hour. Visibility may be less than 1/4 mile. The following tips can help you and your family stay safe during a blizzard.

Your home should have

- a working flashlight with extra batteries.
- a battery-powered NOAA weather radio, radio, or TV.
- extra food and water, plus medicines and baby items if needed.
- first-aid supplies.
- heating fuel such as propane, kerosene, or fuel oil.
- an emergency heating source.
- a smoke detector and a fire extinguisher.

If traveling by car or truck, your family should

- keep the gas tank nearly full. The vehicle should be fully checked and properly prepared for winter use.
- always let a friend or relative know the family's travel plans.
- keep a blizzard survival kit in the vehicle. It should contain blankets; a flashlight with extra batteries;
- a can and waterproof matches to melt snow for drinking; and high-calorie, nonperishable food.
- remain in the vehicle in a blizzard, and tie something bright to the antenna. Run the motor for short times for heat. Use the inside light only while running the motor.

403

These pages are available in reproducible format in the *Teaching Resources* book.

HEALTH BACKGROUND

Earthquake Aftershocks Aftershocks are earthquakes that follow the largest shock of an earthquake sequence. They are smaller than the first one and some distance away. Aftershocks can continue over a period of weeks, months, or years. Generally, the larger the mainshock, the larger and more numerous the aftershocks, and the longer they will continue.

Hypothermia Hypothermia is caused by extended exposure to cold temperatures, and is a life-threatening condition in which the body loses its ability to generate heat. This serious condition requires immediate first aid. However, people suffering from hypothermia often become confused and may not recognize that they need help.

Discussion

How do I know when a situation is an emergency? Although there is no way of knowing for sure, a general rule of thumb is that it usually looks and feels like one! Any time you think that an emergency looks or appears life-threatening, tell an adult or call 911.

Where do earthquakes occur? Earthquakes can occur nearly everywhere although some areas experience more than others. For example, each year the southern California area has about 10,000 earthquakes, most of

which are too small to be felt. Florida and North Dakota have the smallest number in the United States. Alaska is the most earthquake-prone state.

ACTIVITIES

Social Studies

Making Decisions During Disasters The study of geography can include the effects of natural disasters and responses to such emergencies. Suggest students discuss decisions made by their families and their communities during natural disasters, such as thunderstorms, earthquakes, or blizzards.

Science

For Kids Only Have students visit the United States Geological Survey website. This informative government website's *For Kids Only* page contains science activities on earthquakes. Have children work in groups to gather information on a topic of their choosing that they can share with the rest of the class.

Glossary

Numbers in parentheses indicate the pages
on which the words are defined in context.

PRONUNCIATION RESPELLING KEY

Sound	As in	Phonetic Respelling	Sound	As in	Phonetic Respelling	Sound	As in	Phonetic Respelling
a	bat	(BAT)	eye	idea	(eye•DEE•uh)	th	thin	(THIN)
ah	lock	(LAHK)	i	bit	(BIT)	u	pull	(PUL)
air	rare	(RAIR)	ing	going	(GOH•ing)	uh	medal	(MED•uhl)
ar	argue	(AR•gyoo)	k	card	(KARD)		talent	(TAL•uhnt)
aw	law	(LAW)		kite	(KYT)		pencil	(PEN•suhl)
ay	face	(FAYS)	ngk	bank	(BANGK)		onion	(UHN•yuhn)
ch	chapel	(CHAP•uhl)	oh	over	(OH•ver)		playful	(PLAY•fuhl)
e	test	(TEST)	oo	pool	(POOL)		dull	(DUHL)
	metric	(MEH•trik)	ow	out	(OWT)	y	yes	(YES)
ee	eat	(EET)	oy	foil	(FOYL)		ripe	(RYP)
	feet	(FEET)	s	cell	(SEL)	z	bags	(BAGZ)
	ski	(SKEE)		sit	(SIT)	zh	treasure	(TREZH•er)
er	paper	(PAY•per)	sh	sheep	(SHEEP)			
	fern	(FERN)	th	that	(THAT)			

abstinence (AB•stuh•nuhns): Avoiding behavior that puts your health at risk (197)

abstract thinking (ab•STRAKT THING•king): A complex kind of thinking that involves imagining different solutions to problems (27)

acute (uh•KYOOT): Describes the kind of illness that doesn't last for a long time (212)

addiction (uh•DIK•shuhn): A constant need for and use of a substance even though the user knows it is harmful (236)

additives (AD•uh•tivz): Things that food manufacturers add to foods; some are nutrients, such as vitamins or minerals, and some simply improve taste (97)

adolescence (ad•uh•LES•uhnts): A period of rapid growth and development from age ten to age nineteen (22)

aerobic exercise (air•OH•bik EK•ser•syz): Exercise that strengthens the heart and lungs and helps build cardiovascular fitness (121)

aggressive (uh•GREH•siv): Describes forceful behavior that could harm someone physically or emotionally (301)

alcoholism (AL•kuh•hawl•iz•uhm): Addiction to alcohol (270)

alveoli (al•VEE•uh•ly): The lungs' air sacs, in which oxygen and carbon dioxide are exchanged (7)

anabolic steroids (a•nuh•BAH•lik STIR•oydz): Prescription medicines that treat health problems but are abused by people who want to increase the size of their muscles (237)

anaerobic exercise (an•er•OH•bik EK•ser•syz): Brief, intense activity that helps build muscle strength (121)

anorexia (an•uh•REKS•ee•uh): An eating disorder in which a person diets too much or even starves himself or herself (85)

antibiotic (an•ty•by•AHT•ik): A medicine that kills certain bacteria, fungi, or protozoa (203)

antibodies (AN•tih•bahd•eez): Substances made by white blood cells to help fight disease (202)

antiseptic (an•tuh•SEP•tik): A medicine that helps keep a wound from becoming infected (142)

astigmatism (uh•STIG•muh•tiz•uhm): A condition in which the lens of the eye is curved unevenly and everything looks blurry (53)

attitude (A•tuh•tood): The way you feel about something (292)

bacteria (bak•TIR•ee•uh): One-celled pathogens that can, but do not always, cause disease by producing harmful wastes (196)

blood alcohol level (or BAL) (BLUHD AL•kuh•hawl LEH•vuhl): The amount of alcohol in a person's blood (266)

body image (BAH•dee IM•ij): The way you think your body looks (23)

body language (BAH•dee LANG•gwij): The way you use your body to express your feelings (306)

bully (BUL•ee): Someone who hurts or frightens others (177)

calories (KAL•uh•reez): The units used for measuring the amount of energy in a food (86)

capillaries (KAP•uh•lair•eez): Very small blood vessels that connect arteries with veins (6)

carbohydrates (kar•boh•HY•drayts): The starches and sugars that supply most of the body's energy (74)

carbon monoxide (KAR•buhn muh•NAHK•syd): A poisonous gas in tobacco smoke; takes the place of oxygen in the blood (*261*)

carcinogens (kar•SIN•uh•juhnz): Substances that cause cancer (*261*)

cardiovascular fitness (kar•dee•oh•VAS•kyoo•ler FIT•nuhs): Good health of the circulatory system, including a strong heart (*121*)

cartilage (KAR•tuhl•ij): Soft, rubbery material that forms part of the skeleton (*18*)

cell (SEL): The basic unit of structure of all living things (*4*)

chronic (KRAHN•ik): Describes the kind of illness or condition that affects a person for a long time (*212*)

cilia (SIL•ee•uh): Tiny, hairlike structures that line many of the breathing passages (*201*)

clique (KLIK): A group that keeps other people out (*304*)

communicable disease (kuh•MYOO•nih•kuh•buhl dih•ZEEZ): A disease that can be spread from person to person (*190*)

communicate (kuh•MYOO•nih•kayt): To share views, thoughts, and feelings with others and to listen to them (*328*)

concrete thinking (KAHN•kreet THING•king): Solving problems involving real objects that you can see and touch (*27*)

concussion (kuhn•KUHSH•uhn): A brain injury caused by a strong blow to the head (*143*)

conflicts (KAHN•flikts): Struggles over different needs and wants (*312*)

conserve (kuhn•SERV): To save something or use it carefully so it will last (*361*)

decibels (DES•uh•buhlz): The units used for measuring the loudness of sounds (*57*)

dietary supplements (DY•uh•tair•ee SUH•pluh•muhnts): Nutrients in concentrated forms that are taken in addition to food (*80*)

digested: broken down (*8*)

dosage (DOH•sij): The correct amount of medicine to take (*235*)

drug (DRUHG): A substance, other than food, that affects the way the body or mind works (*228*)

emergency (ee•MER•juhn•see): A situation that calls for quick action (*140*)

empathy (EM•puh•thee): Understanding of other people's needs and feelings (*324*)

environment (en•VY•ruhn•muhnt): All the things that surround you every day (*14*)

environmental tobacco smoke (or ETS) (en•vy•ruhn•MEN•tuhl tuh•BA•koh SMOHK): Tobacco smoke in the air; can harm nonsmokers (*263*)

enzyme (EN•zym): A chemical, found in saliva, that helps change food into a form the body can use (*73*)

esophagus: long tube that leads to the stomach (*8*)

evacuation (ee•vak•yoo•AY•shuhn): The removal of people from their homes to a safer place because of a disaster (*355*)

expiration date (ek•spuh•RAY•shuhn DAYT): The date after which a medicine should not be used (*235*)

exploitation (eks•ploy•TAY•shuhn): Taking advantage of someone (*332*)

farsighted (FAR•syt•uhd): Able to see faraway objects clearly, while nearby objects look blurry (*53*)

fats (FATS): The nutrients that contain the most energy (*74*)

first aid (FERST AYD): Immediate care given to an injured person (*142*)

flammable (FLAM•uh•buhl): Relating to materials that will burn if exposed to enough heat (*158*)

flexibility (flek•suh•BIL•uh•tee): The ability to bend and twist your body comfortably (*128*)

food allergy (FOOD AL•er•jee): A bad reaction to a food that most other people can eat without becoming ill (*93*)

Food Guide Pyramid (FOOD GYD PIR•uh•mid): A diagram that helps people choose a balanced diet (*82*)

food poisoning (FOOD POY•zuhn•ing): An illness caused by eating or drinking something that contains harmful germs (*102*)

fungi (FUHN•jy): Small, simple living things such as yeasts and molds; they can invade the skin or respiratory system as pathogens (*196*)

gang (GANG): A group that uses violence; members commit crimes, use and sell drugs, and carry weapons (*178*)

gingivitis (jin•juh•VYT•is): A gum disease that occurs when plaque hardens on the teeth and irritates the gums (*50*)

glands (GLANDZ): Groups of specialized cells that produce hormones (*16*)

goal setting (GOHL SEH•ting): The process of choosing a goal and working toward it (*297*)

growth spurt (GROHTH SPERT): A period of rapid growth (*19*)

habit (HA•buht): Something you do again and again until you do it without thinking about it (*292*)

hair follicle (HAIR FAHL•ih•kuhl): A pitlike structure, in the skin, from which hair grows (*44*)

hazard (HA•zerd): Something in the environment or something a person does that can cause harm or injury (*138*)

health consumer (HELTH kuhn•SOOM•er): A person who buys and uses health products or services (*60*)

health maintenance (HELTH MAYNT•uhn•uhns): Describes a plan that involves laying out steps that need to be taken to reach health goals (*340*)

heredity (huh•RED•ih•tee): The passing of traits from parents to children (*14*)

hormones (HAWR•mohnz): Chemicals, produced by glands, that regulate many body functions (*16*)

hygiene (HY•jeen): Cleanliness (*34*)

illegal drugs (ih•LEE•guhl DRUHGZ): Drugs that are not medicines and that are against the law to sell, buy, have, or use (*238*)

immunity (ih•MYOON•uh•tee): The body's ability to "remember" how to make antibodies to a disease (*202*)

immunization (im•yoo•nuh•ZAY•shuhn): Giving a vaccine to people to make them immune to a disease (*208*)

infection (in•FEK•shuhn): The rapid growth of pathogens in the body (*195*)

ingredients (in•GREE•dee•uhnts): Substances that are in a product (*62, 96*)

inhalants (in•HAYL•uhnts): Substances that people abuse by breathing in their fumes (*244*)

insulin (IN•suh•lin): A chemical that helps body cells take in sugar from the blood (*215*)

intoxicated (in•TAHK•sih•kay•tuhd): Strongly affected by a drug (*267*)

joint (JOYNT): A place where two or more bones fit together (*10*)

ligaments (LIG•uh•muhnts): Tissues that attach bones together at joints and give flexibility for bending and stretching (*10*)

medicine (MED•uh•suhn): A drug used to treat illness or disease (*228*)

medicine abuse (MED•uh•suhn uh•BYOOS): The taking of medicine to do something other than treat an illness (*236*)

medicine misuse (MED•uh•suhn mis•YOOS): The taking of medicine without following directions exactly (*236*)

minerals (MIN•uhr•uhlz): Nutrients that help your body grow and work (*76*)

mucus (MYOO•kuhs): A thick, sticky substance that traps pathogens and keeps them from getting any farther into your body (*200*)

muscular endurance (MUHS•kyuh•ler in•DUR•uhnts): The ability to use your muscles for a long time without getting tired (*129*)

muscular strength (MUHS•kyuh•ler STRENGTH): The ability to use your muscles to lift, push, or pull heavy objects (*128*)

myth (MITH): An idea that is thought to be true by some people, but is actually false (*60*)

natural disasters (NACH•er•uhl dih•ZAS•terz): Events in nature so powerful that they often result in the destruction of buildings and other structures; they include earthquakes, tornadoes, hurricanes, floods, and volcanic eruptions (*164*)

natural resources (NACH•er•uhl REE•sawrs•uhz): Materials from the environment that people use (*360*)

nearsighted (NIR•syt•uhd): Able to see nearby objects clearly, while faraway objects look blurry (*53*)

neglect (nih•GLEKT): Failure to take care of a person's basic needs, such as food and clothing (*333*)

408

409

negotiate (nih•GOH•shee•ayt): To discuss and resolve conflicts with another person (324)

nephrons (NEF•rahnz): Filters, in the kidneys, that remove waste and extract water from the blood (9)

neurons (NOOR•ahnz): Nerve cells; they receive signals from and send signals to other neurons (12)

nicotine (NIK•uh•teen): A drug, found in tobacco, that makes the heart work harder (261)

noncommunicable disease (nahn•kuh•MYOO•nih•kuh•buhl dih•ZEEZ): A disease that does not spread from person to person (190)

nutrients (NOO•tree•uhnts): Substances in food that provide the body with energy and building materials (72)

nutritionist (noo•TRISH•uhn•ist): A scientist who studies ways to prepare healthful diets (79)

oil gland (OYL GLAND): A gland that releases oil which coats the hair and spreads over the skin (44)

organ (AWR•guhn): A group of tissues that work together to perform a particular job (5)

orthodontia (awr•thuh•DAHN•shuh): The correction of crooked teeth (51)

overdose (OH•ver•dohs): A dangerously large drug dose that can cause illness or death (239)

over-the-counter medicines (or OTC medicines) (OH•ver•thuh•KOWN•ter MED•uh•suhnz): Medicines that can be bought without a prescription (231)

pathogens (PATH•uh•juhnz): Organisms or viruses that cause communicable diseases (195)

pedestrians (pih•DES•tree•uhnz): People who are walking (154)

peer pressure (PIR PRESH•er): The influence a group has over your actions and decisions (302)

physical activity (FIZ•ih•kuhl ak•TIV•uh•tee): Any movement of muscles that uses energy (112)

plaque (PLAK): A sticky substance formed on the teeth by bacteria (50)

portion control (PAWR•shuhn kuhn•TROHL): A limit on the number and sizes of the servings you eat (84)

prejudice (PREH•juh•duhs): An unfair negative attitude toward a whole group (315)

prenatal (pree•NAYT•uhl): Before birth (19)

prescription medicines (pree•SKRIP•shuhn MED•uh•suhnz): Medicines that can be bought only with an order from a doctor (230)

preservatives (pree•ZERV•uh•tivz): Chemicals added to foods to keep them from spoiling (97)

proteins (PROH•teenz): The building blocks of the body (75)

protozoa (proh•tuh•ZOH•uh): One-celled organisms that are larger than bacteria and often cause serious diseases (196)

puberty (PYOO•ber•tee): The physical changing that a person experiences during adolescence (22)

public health (PUH•blik HELTH): The health of all the people in a community (346)

recycle (ree•SY•kuhl): To make something old into something new (360)

reduce (ree•DOOS): To use less (360)

reflex action (REE•fleks AK•shuhn): An automatic response in which information from the senses is received and acted on by the spinal cord without first traveling to the brain (13)

refuse (rih•FYOOZ): To say *no* to something (246)

resistance (rih•ZIS•tuhns): Your body's natural ability to fight off diseases on its own (204)

reuse (ree•YOOZ): To use again (360)

sanitary landfills (SAN•uh•tair•ee LAND•filz): Large holes dug in the ground and lined with clay or plastic to contain trash and to keep wastes from seeping into the soil (353)

sanitation (sa•nuh•TAY•shuhn): The disposal of human wastes (349)

seizure (SEE•zher): A sudden attack of unconsciousness or uncontrolled body movement (218)

self-concept (self•KAHN•sept): The way you see yourself most of the time (292)

self-medication (self•med•ih•KAY•shuhn): The process of deciding on your own what medicine to take (236)

410

411

septic tank (SEP•tik TANGK): A concrete or steel tank buried in the ground outside a house to handle wastewater (*352*)

serving (SER•ving): The measured amount of food that is recommended for a meal or a snack (*79*)

sewage (SOO•ij): The mixture of wastewater and human waste that leaves homes and businesses (*352*)

side effects (SYD ih•FEKTS): Unwanted reactions to medicines (*232*)

SPF (Sun Protection Factor): A sunscreen rating that indicates about how much longer the sunscreen enables you to be in the sun without getting a sunburn, compared with no protection at all (*42*)

stereotype (STAIR•ee•uh•typ): A belief based on the idea that everyone in a certain group is the same (*314*)

stress (STRES): A feeling of tension in your body, your mind, or both (*308*)

symptoms (SIMP•tuhmz): Signs and feelings of a disease (*194*)

system (SIS•tuhm): A group of organs that work together to do a job (*5*)

tar (TAR): In tobacco a sticky, dark paste that builds up in the lungs and makes breathing difficult (*261*)

tendons (TEN•duhnz): Strong, flexible bands of tissue that attach muscles to bones, near the joints (*11*)

terrorism (TAIR•er•iz•uhm): The use of force or violence against people or property for a political or social goal (*173*)

tissue (TISH•oo): A group of cells of the same kind that work together (*4*)

ultraviolet rays (uhl•truh•VY•uh•lit RAYZ): The invisible light waves given off by the sun that cause sunburn and tanning (*41*)

vaccine (vak•SEEN): A medicine that can give immunity to a disease (*203*)

violence (VY•uh•luhns): Any act that harms or injures someone (*172*)

viruses (VY•ruh•suhz): The pathogens that are the smallest and cause the most disease (*196*)

vitamins (VYT•uh•minz): Nutrients that help the body do certain things (*76*)

volunteers (vahl•uhn•TIRZ): People who work without pay (*347*)

weapon (WEH•puhn): Anything that can be used to harm someone (*176*)

wellness (WEL•nuhs): A state of good health (*296*)

withdrawal (with•DRAW•uhl): The painful reaction that occurs when an addicted person suddenly stops using a drug (*239*)

zero-tolerance policy (ZIR•oh TAHL•er•uhns PAHL•uh•see): A plan in which no violence, weapons, or threats of any kind are allowed in a school and students who don't follow the plan are punished (*183*)

412

413

Index

Glossary and Index

Read-Aloud Anthology

Read-Aloud Anthology
CONTENTS

Stand Up and be a Winner

Excerpt from Current Health 1®

USING THE SELECTION

Read the selection to students. Then have students take turns standing with their backs to a wall. See if four of their body parts touch the wall easily-the head, upper back, buttocks, and heels. All four body parts should touch.

The WOW Effect

Posture is the way you carry yourself. It includes all of your body movements: standing, sitting, walking.

A person with good posture walks and stands tall and looks alert and comfortable. Good posture helps your self-confidence too. It's like saying, "Wow, I'm worth a million dollars."

Aches Ahead

People can get aches and pains when they sit or stand incorrectly for a period of time. Some weigh themselves down with book bags, backpacks, or heavy purses. The body is designed to line up in a specific way to provide support for internal organs and muscles. Poor posture or heavy loads put a strain on body areas not designed to take it.

Slouching, or leaning forward, puts a lot of pressure on the lower back. Poor posture also allows less room for internal organs to grow and function. It squeezes blood vessels and limits the amount of blood the body's cells receive. Slouching prevents the diaphragm (DIE-uh-fram) from working properly. As a result, your body doesn't get a good supply of oxygen because you aren't breathing deeply enough.

Mirrors Tell All

How do you know if you have good or bad posture? Stand in front of a full-length mirror. Ask yourself these questions:
- Is my head level or does it tilt up or down?
- Are my shoulders level, or is one higher than the other?
- Are my shoulders slumped or rounded?
- Let your arms hang naturally at your sides. Is one arm farther forward than the other?
- Are my hips level?
- Do my knees face forward, or does one or both turn in or out?

No Slouching

Here are some guidelines for you to follow:
- *Stand straight.* Look in the mirror and balance on the balls of your feet. Keep your backbone straight and hold the shoulders back. Pull in your stomach and buttocks, and tuck in the chin. Your head, upper body, and lower body will line up correctly.
- *Sit correctly.* Sit up straight when seated. Balance your head and shoulders directly over your hips. Keep your feet flat on the floor and your back straight against the chair. Sit in chairs with straight backs or with low back support. The seat should be high enough so that your thighs rest totally on the seat.
- *Walk tall.* Walk with your body balanced over the balls of your feet. Hold your shoulders back. Tuck in your stomach.

Here are some other suggestions that will help you improve your posture.
- *Wear shoes with low or flat heels.* High heels throw posture off.
- *Lighten up.* Don't carry heavy book bags, backpacks, or purses.
- *Exercise.* Any kind of exercise is good for you.
- *Practice.* Learning to walk, sit, and stand like a millionaire may take a little time. But with practice, good posture will become natural for you.

The Weekly Reader Corporation, January 2002

Health and Beauty—Then and Now

By Philip E. Bishop, Ph.D.

USING THE SELECTION

Read the selection to introduce beauty and hygiene products. Explain that products such as deodorants may affect health because they are applied to the skin, where they may be absorbed into the body.

The Deadly Mask—Makeup in the Ancient World

The ancient Egyptians and Greeks were probably the first to paint their faces white—that is, to use cosmetics to lighten the color of skin and cover wrinkles. Unfortunately, the ancients didn't know the effects of their cosmetics. The facial covers they used contained lead. Lead-based cosmetics probably caused many illnesses and early deaths in the ancient world.

Rouges and lipsticks were even more harmful than facial covers. Greek society women and men often applied rouge to their cheeks and lips. The rouge was colored with cinnabar, a compound containing mercury, a chemical with highly poisonous vapors. In the process of trying to increase their beauty, the Greeks unknowingly poisoned themselves.

In the 1700s in Europe, a pale complexion was considered a sign of beauty. French aristocrats—both men and women—painted their faces with a deadly lead-based white powder. By this time, lip color was made using the juice of black grapes.

Beauty in a Mark

One harmless cosmetic was the beauty mark, or patch, devised by Europeans who had suffered from smallpox. Smallpox left scars on the face and upper body. The wealthy distracted attention from the scars by placing beauty marks near the eyes or mouth. The stick-on marks, often in the shape of crescents or stars, developed into a sort of code. A mark on a woman's right cheek signaled that she was married. A path near the mouth indicated a willingness to flirt.

Overcoming Odor—From Perfumes to Antiperspirants

Human body odor is always with us. The problem is human sweat, concentrated under the arms. Actually, sweat does not have much of an odor, but it does promote the growth of bacteria that live in the moist armpit. Body odor is really the smell of decaying bacteria.

The ancient Egyptians figured out a simple and effective remedy for the odor—bathing the underarms and scenting the body with citrus and cinnamon perfumes. Bathing was a popular event for the ancient Romans, who visited the public baths several times a week. The Romans probably smelled better than French king Louis XIV, who followed the seventeenth-century custom of bathing once a month. In Louis' time, the wealthy tried to mask their body odor with heavy perfumes.

The first true underarm deodorant was introduced in 1888. It was a zinc cream that temporarily stopped the armpit from sweating. No sweat, no odor—at least for a few hours. No deodorant, including today's products, can suppress underarm glands for very long.

Searching for Healthful Beauty

The search for youthful skin has often led to scams. Most of the products advertised today are no more useful than ancient beauty treatments.

The ancients did create one beauty product that worked: cold cream. Used to remove makeup, it was made of white wax melted in olive oil and blended with water and rose buds. Today's cold creams are made in much the same way.

Another key to youthful skin is sunscreen. Sunscreen not only prevents wrinkles, but also protects us from skin cancer. However, the use of sun lotions dates only to World War II, when American soldiers stationed in the Pacific needed protection from the sun. They were given a reddish petroleum jelly to apply to their skin. Today's sunscreens are much more convenient to use than the greasy red jelly issued to soldiers.

Beauty—More Art than Science

The search for beauty has often lead people to buy useless or even harmful products. We now know that the best recipe for skin care and personal hygiene is simple cleanliness and a healthful lifestyle. However, people will most likely continue to fall for the false promises of beauty merchants.

Beware of the Vegetables!

by Mary Kay Morel

USING THE SELECTION

Draw an imaginary vegetable on the board and ask students to imagine that the space shuttle has brought this new plant back from space. Ask students to speculate about how they would use the plant, if they think it is useful for decoration or food, and how they would go about finding out whether or not the plant is safe to eat.

Do you like tomatoes? Years ago, people grew tomatoes because they thought they were pretty. They did not know that tomatoes were good to eat. Listen to learn more about tomatoes and other common foods people once considered dangerous, silly, or not fit to eat.

Poisonous Potatoes

Today, billions of potatoes are consumed every day. But until Spanish explorers brought them to Europe from South America in the 1530s, few people had ever heard of them. As a result, cooks didn't know what to do with the tubers, and usually cooked the poisonous leaves and stems instead of the vegetable itself.

It's no wonder that so many people thought potatoes were deadly. The government of Burgundy, France, even went so far as to ban this "poisonous and mischievous root" in 1619. Doctors believed that the potato caused leprosy!

When people figured out it was the roots that were supposed to be eaten, the potato's popularity took off. Eventually people accepted the potato as a healthy, tasty vegetable.

Toxic Tomatoes

The tomato was another food find brought to Europe during the 1500s. Italians christened the exotic plant "apple of gold."

Soon red and yellow tomatoes sprouted in fashionable gardens all over Europe, but no one thought to eat the fruit of the tomato plant. People assumed that the little "apples of gold" were poisonous. Another two hundred years would pass before tomatoes became an accepted ingredient in cooking.

Comical Corn

No one ever thought corn was poisonous. It <u>was</u> thought to be food fit only for the pig population. When Columbus returned from the New World with this giant of a plant in tow, Europeans shuddered at the sight. Compared to their beloved wheat, corn looked like a leafy monster. In 1616, one European writer noted, "It nourisheth but little, and is evill of digestion . . . a more convenient food for swine than man."

The American colonies gave corn a much-needed popularity boost. In the New World corn grew where wheat would not, and it saved the early colonists from starvation. Eventually the lowly corn became one of the most important foods throughout the world.

printed in *Highlights for Children*, March, 1997

Get Ready, Get Fit, Go!

Excerpt from Current Health 1®

USING THE SELECTION

After reading the selection, suggest students check out the following Fit4Life Web sites: www.bam.gov/fit4life/fitt.htm, www.bam.gov/fit4life/cards.asp. Then have students create an exercise schedule using all parts of the "FITT" plan.

Getting Started

If you aren't exercising regularly now, you will need to start slowly. Make it your goal to exercise three times a week. Try exercising for 10 minutes or so at first. As you feel stronger, you can work out for a little longer each time. Give your muscles a break between workouts. You may choose to do a different activity on the days you are not working on a specific sport. If you are trying to ride your bike farther three days a week, on the other days, choose something that will strengthen your arms or other muscle groups.

There is more to being fit than just working out for a longer period of time. In order to be truly fit, you need to work on these four areas:

- **endurance** (how long you can exercise)
- **muscle strength** (the ability of a muscle to exert force for a short time)
- **aerobic conditioning** (how well your heart and lungs can take oxygen to your cells)
- **flexibility** (how well your joints and muscles can move)

When you make a plan for exercising, try to include all of these areas of fitness into your plan.

Benefits of Fitness

There are many reasons to get regular exercise. Did you know that your attitude will change? Your body will change? And even your thinking will change? It's true! Regular exercise will improve your attitude and your self-image. You will feel better about yourself. You're less likely to feel stressed. Exercise will help you to release tension and anxiety. Studies have shown that exercise can relieve depression and increase feelings of confidence.

Exercise can help you keep your weight under control. It helps maintain a healthy blood cholesterol level and builds strong bones. It even improves the quality of your sleep. Regular exercise can lower your risk of certain cancers, diabetes, high blood pressure, heart attack, and stroke as you get older.

Exercise, you see, can be a wonderful thing—good for you now and for the rest of your life!

The Weekly Reader Corporation, February 2003

Protecting Life—A Brief History of Safety Equipment

by Philip E. Bishop, Ph.D.

USING THE SELECTION

Have students make a list of safety equipment they have used. Encourage the class to name other kinds of safety equipment that protect people who participate in various sports. Then read aloud the selection.

Throughout time, humans have found ways to protect the body's fragile parts from being injured by collisions. From ancient armor to today's auto safety belt, humans have used helmets, shields, and restraints of all sorts. But safety is not just a question of technology. Technology needs to be supported by laws and education if we're going to protect the fragile human body.

Helmets and Masks: The Earliest Safety Technology

In nearly every ancient civilization, including Greece and Egypt, the first kinds of protective equipment included metal helmets, chest armor, and shields used in military combat. In the Middle Ages, iron and leather were combined to make protective clothing. But the heavy suits of armor that you see in museums were not widely used in actual battles. The metal body casings were so stiff that the wearer could hardly move. The helmet visor did protect the face from injuries but made it almost impossible for the wearer to see.

Some of today's most advanced protective gear is worn in the sports of football and hockey, rather than on the battlefield. The first football helmets were padded leather caps that looked a lot like the helmets of Greek warriors. Hard-shelled football helmets first appeared in the 1950s and were soon outfitted with face masks. Some people complain that the modern helmet, with its padding and suspension, protects the head too well, allowing players to use the hard helmet as a battering ram. This can lead to severe neck injuries for the wearer.

Sporting Safety All Around

In nearly every sport there is a need for some type of safety gear. In soccer, shin pads are necessary. In skateboarding and in-line skating, knee pads, elbow pads, and a helmet greatly reduce the risk of being injured. In football, players need pads covering their shoulders, chest, hips, and thighs, not just their heads.

The Belt of Life

Modern transportation has made travel almost as hazardous as ancient combat. Automobiles traveling at highway speeds can mangle the body's fragile tissue as terribly as an ancient sword or club could. The technology of shields and restraints is responsible for saving thousands of lives.

The modern safety belt was designed soon after the appearance of the first automobiles. Though safety belts were widely used in airplanes and racing cars, they were not available in passenger cars until the 1950s. The Swedish car maker Volvo later perfected the three-point shoulder and lap belt that has become standard equipment.

Auto safety made a huge leap forward with the introduction of air bags. Mounted in a steering wheel or dashboard, the bags inflate in an accident to cushion the front-seat occupants. Manufacturers are also beginning to include side-mounted air bags in automobiles. This comes after studies of side-impact crashes and the recommendation that side-air bags would greatly increase safety in such a crash. When used in combination with safety belts, air bags greatly reduce injury in head-on and side-impact collisions. Although they were invented in 1953, air bags were not available in passenger cars until 1981, when Mercedes-Benz offered the bag as an option.

Safety—Should It Be the Law?

Modern safety technologies have raised an important question: Should safety be optional? There is no doubt that helmets, safety belts and air bags work. The question is whether people should be required by law to use them. Many people feel that whether or not they wear safety belts should be their choice. They figure that they are the only one who will be hurt by not wearing a safety belt. While this is true as far as personal injury goes, the overall medical costs are what can be reduced by use of safety belts. Traffic injuries cost taxpayers and businesses billions of dollars a year. Automobile insurance costs to drivers would also be kept down with greater safety belt usage.

Where governments have said that safety measures should be required by law, the results have been dramatic. Safety belt laws passed in 1980 in most states have increased safety belt use from about 20 percent to nearly 74 percent. Motorcycle injury rates are much lower in states that require all riders to wear helmets. Safety laws do work. The question is: Will modern drivers, riders, and skaters be wise enough to use this technology?

Defusing Difficult Situations

Excerpt from Current Health 1®

USING THE SELECTION

Read the selection to students. Then have them brainstorm ways to resolve conflicts. Suggest they look for more information on conflict resolution on the Internet such as the "Out On A Limb" Web site at www.urbanext.uiuc.edu/conflict

It Happens to Everyone

Everyone gets into conflicts. The reason for this is that "we all see things differently," say experts at the University of Illinois.

There is always at least one loser when people deal with conflict by fighting, yelling, ignoring, or running away. It is wise to run away if someone threatens or tries to hurt you, but most problems are best solved when both parties cooperate.

Coping With Conflict

How would you deal with these conflicts? Choose the answer that best describes what you would actually do.

1. Your brother loses your favorite CD. You
   a. scream at him.
   b. break his CD player.
   c. calmly tell him you are angry and ask him to replace the CD.
2. Your best friend ignores you at lunchtime. You
   a. tell her she's mean and hateful.
   b. tell everyone at school she's mean and hateful.
   c. tell her that you feel hurt when she ignores you and ask her why she did it.
3. Your dad calls you a slob when you spill milk on the floor. You
   a. tell him he's a bigger slob.
   b. tell him you're sorry you're a slob.
   c. explain that his remark makes you feel worthless and stupid, say that spilling the milk was an accident, and offer to clean up the mess.

Answers: If you chose a and b answers, you are not really solving these conflicts. If you chose c answers, you are doing a great job of getting along in difficult situations.

Help Yourself, Help the World

Experts at the Teachers College at Columbia University in New York use three words to sum up the best way to resolve conflicts: *firm, fair,* and *friendly.* Be firm about the need to solve the problem. Be sure the solution is fair to both people. And be friendly rather than hostile.

Once you're skilled at solving conflicts, you are likely to see your self-esteem improve. You will feel better about yourself because you are not letting people push you around. When you feel better about yourself, your family, friends, and community benefit since you become a more pleasant person.

The Weekly Reader Corporation, January 2003

Vaccines—Then and Now

by Philip E. Bishop, Ph.D.

USING THE SELECTION

Write the names of these diseases on the board: smallpox, polio, diphtheria, measles, mumps, whooping cough, and German measles. Then take a poll to see which diseases students have heard of, which diseases their parents or grandparents have mentioned having, and which diseases they have had.

Vaccinations provide you with immunity against many diseases. Once a vaccine is developed against a certain disease, epidemics rarely occur and the disease is eventually wiped out.

The World's First Successful Vaccine

Two hundred years ago, smallpox was a common and dangerous disease in England. Many people died. Those who survived had terrible scars. Some were left blind. A person became infected with smallpox by breathing in droplets expelled from the mouth or nose of an infected person. Within two weeks the person developed aches and a high fever. A horrible rash of pimples then appeared all over the face and body. The pimples filled with pus and eventually scabs formed. When the scabs fell off, a permanent scar was left.

In 1776 Dr. Edward Jenner had noticed that people who had suffered from cowpox, a similar but less dangerous disease, did not catch smallpox. He thought that perhaps cowpox protected them in some way. To test his theory, he took some matter from a cowpox sore, scratched the arm of a healthy boy, and rubbed the matter into the sore. The boy got cowpox, as expected, but recovered within days. Eight weeks later, when Jenner exposed the boy to smallpox matter, the child did not get sick. Having cowpox microbes in his system protected the boy from smallpox. Jenner had created the first successful vaccine.

Scientists now understand how the vaccine worked. When the boy became ill with cowpox, his white blood cells created antibodies to destroy the virus. Those antibodies remained in his system. Since the smallpox virus is much like the cowpox virus, when smallpox was introduced into the boy's system, the cowpox antibodies attacked and destroyed the smallpox virus at once.

The vaccine against smallpox has eliminated that disease from the world. Since Jenner's discovery, scientists have created vaccines for many diseases.

A Modern-Day Epidemic

Polio was once a feared disease. Egyptian engravings show that polio has been around for at least 3,500 years. In 1954 alone, polio infected 35,000–50,000 Americans. It was once called infantile paralysis because it affected mostly children and caused temporary or permanent paralysis.

The polio virus can enter the body through the mouth or nose. Once in the body, it travels to the nervous system and rapidly multiplies, causing the nerve cells to be damaged or to die.

Polio symptoms—fever, headache, and sore throat—resemble those of other illnesses. In severe polio cases the symptoms do not disappear and are followed by muscle stiffness and pain. Paralysis may make it impossible to stand, walk, or breathe. Patients may survive the disease but be left with permanent side effects.

Polio treatments varied. Physical therapy helped loosen tightened muscles. Leg braces and crutches were used to help patients walk and stand. If the muscles of the ribs and abdomen had been paralyzed, breathing became difficult. In these cases, a mechanical breathing device called the iron lung was used. This device saved many lives during the polio epidemics of the 1940s and 1950s.

Another Successful Vaccine

In 1953 Dr. Jonas Salk announced that he had created a vaccine against polio. He first tested the vaccine on himself and his family. The next year it was tested on two million schoolchildren. In 1955 the vaccine was declared safe and effective and began to be widely used.

Dr. Albert Sabin developed another successful vaccine against polio, which was approved for use in 1961. Sabin's vaccine was easier to administer, as it was taken by mouth. The Salk vaccine has to be injected. The Sabin vaccine is no longer used.

Through both the Salk and the Sabin vaccines, polio has been nearly wiped out.

Genetic Vaccines—The New Millennium

Scientists today are experimenting with new types of vaccines. These vaccines don't use small amounts of live or dead versions of the virus they are fighting, like traditional vaccines. These new vaccines could be used for many diseases and disorders for which no vaccines are yet available, such as malaria, AIDS, herpes, and hepatitis C. And even though cancer is not an infectious disease, these vaccines might also be used to fight it by stimulating the body's immune system.

Perhaps in your lifetime, scientists will develop vaccines for these serious diseases. Perhaps you will be one of the scientists who invents one of these lifesaving vaccines.

Learn How to Refuse

Excerpt from Current Health 1®

USING THE SELECTION

After reading the selection to students, ask them to brainstorm other ways to refuse drugs that are offered them. For example, using humor can often be a tension breaker in an unpleasant situation. Have students list other creative ways.

"Go ahead, try it. It won't hurt you."

"Come on, let's get high."

"Let's just take a little sip. No one will know."

Have you heard these before? Maybe you have been a little tempted to try drugs. But no matter what anyone says, drugs can hurt you. Using illegal drugs, misusing legal ones, or inhaling fumes from household chemicals such as paint thinner or glues is extremely harmful—even deadly.

Knowing how to refuse drugs will help you make the right decision in choosing to stay away from harmful drugs.

How to Refuse

Drugs, alcohol, and cigarettes can do serious damage to your body and mind. Most kids keep away from them. But some have a tough time saying no when they are offered harmful substances. Here are some ways to refuse.

- Ignore the question. Then change the topic.
- Think of an alternative. If offered drugs at a party, for example, say, "What I'd really like is another slice of pizza (can of pop, etc.). Want some?" Then move toward the food.
- Give "nondiscussible" reasons. Say, "Cigarettes make me throw up," or "I have asthma. If I smoked, we'd have to call 9-1-1."
- Blame someone else. Say, "My coach would kick me off the team," or "My little sister looks up to me. I don't want to let her down."
- Walk away. Don't explain. Don't discuss. Don't argue.
- Stay away from a possible problem. If you are invited to a party where you know kids will be using drugs, do something else instead.
- Choose friends wisely. Make friends with kids who don't use drugs.
- Do some critical thinking. A friend is someone you like and who likes you too. Why would someone who liked you want to harm your health or get you in trouble?

The Weekly Reader Corporation, September 2002

Tobacco

by Gerald Hausman

USING THE SELECTION

Ask students to imagine a world without tobacco and tobacco products. Ask how life would be better if tobacco did not exist. Explain that before the time of Christopher Columbus and other European explorers, Europeans knew nothing about smoking tobacco. Tell students that, for Americans, tobacco is truly a "home-grown" product. GERALD HAUSMAN has been a teacher, an editor, and a poet. Even when he is writing prose, Hausman feels the influence of poetry. Hausman has written a variety of books for children and adults, ranging from poetry to how-to books.

Americans can be proud of many accomplishments. But one accomplishment many people would rather not take credit for is the worldwide use of tobacco products. This essay on tobacco reports early explorers' observations of the uses of tobacco by peoples in the Americas.

One of the sacred herbs of Turtle Island was tobacco. Used to make offerings to the deities, to treat disease, and to seal agreements, tobacco was also smoked for enjoyment. The word came originally from the Guarani, taboca, and it was allegedly first seen by Christopher Columbus on October 14, 1492. According to journal entries, an Indian man was observed traveling from Santa Maria to Fernandina—the second and third Bahama islands—with a canoe full of dry tobacco leaves. Messengers sent by Columbus stated that on the island of Cuba men took smoke "inside with the breath, by which they became benumbed and almost drunk, and so it is said they do not feel fatigue."

Between 1541 and 1546, the explorer Benzoni encountered Ethiopian slaves who had been brought to the West Indies by the Spanish. According to his report, the slaves took a leaf of maize and a leaf of another plant that "grows in these new countries" and rolled them tightly together. Benzoni said that after the recipients took the smoke, they would "fall down as if they were dead, and remain the greater part of the day or night stupefied." Others who smoked the same herb, he continued, "are content with imbibing only enough of this smoke to make them giddy, and no more."

In 1574, Nicolas Monardes called the plant he found on the islands tobacco. The word stuck. And the mysterious plant was credited with wonderful properties, curing not only disease but also open wounds. Extolled as an intoxicant, a preventative of hunger and thirst, it was even said to ward off disease.

What of the uses of tobacco on Turtle Island at this time? Archaeologists have found votive offerings of sacred cigarettes in cave shrines that date back hundreds of years. It is doubtful that the plant was not being used in the places where it grew naturally, and it is probable that tobacco came into the Southwest [of what is now the United States] through trade channels originating in the jungles of the Yucatán. Parrot feathers came into the desert that way, and even, so the Pueblo Indians say, fresh shrimp, wrapped in moss and carried by runners from the Texas coast.

The ceremonial mixing of tobacco and ganga (marijuana) is a custom shared by Afro-Jamaican people and the Native Americans of Turtle Island . . . I was traveling on the island of Jamaica, where I witnessed a Rastafarian ceremony. Before the chanting, there was a ritual of rolling a corn-husk cigarette and filling it with sensemilla [a variety of marijuana]. This mixing of the two sacred plants of the Americas interested me. I was told by an herbsman there that he had learned the custom from his grandfather, who had learned it from his—all the way back to the Arawak, who showed it to the first slave who had traveled the Middle Passage. "These things," he said, "are our heritage. We believe them."

It is interesting to note that the "American heritage" of tobacco has also taken a kind of legendary turn. The toll of lung cancer from the obsessive smoking of cigarettes is one of the worst diseases in the United States. Of course, this very thing was predicted long ago by the shaman of the Plains. "Leave the white man be," they said, "for he will surely die of his own natural causes." This, I am sure, meant "by his own excesses." The overindulgence of tobacco in this country is as old as its inception. If one looks back to the colonies, the record is bleak even at the start. The cultivation of tobacco to the exclusion of other vegetal products brought the colonies of Virginia and Maryland to the verge of starvation more than once.

excerpt from **Turtle Island Alphabet: A Lexicon of Native American Symbols and Culture**
by Gerald Hausman
St. Martin's Press, 1992

Dealing with Diversity

Excerpt from Current Health 1®

USING THE SELECTION

Read the selection to students. Encourage a discussion about the variety of people who make up the student body in their school. Suggest students talk to someone new at school at least once a month in an effort to learn more about them and to appreciate their differences.

Land of Diversity

Diversity is a fact of daily life in the United States. The people who live here come from a wide variety of backgrounds. This fact shapes many aspects of our lives. Understanding and appreciating diversity is important for all of us.

Appreciating diversity increases harmony and decreases conflict among people. People understand each other better as they gain knowledge about other ethnic groups, languages, customs, music, art, religion, traditions, and so on.

Whoa!

We all tend to label people—he's blond, she's tall—to categorize ourselves and others. But labeling someone based on prejudice (judging someone without knowing anything about him or her) is hurtful. It keeps people from knowing and understanding one another.

If you're tempted to label someone, take a few minutes to think about what you are doing. Here are some things to try:

- Ask yourself if you're using someone's appearance to judge his or her character.
- Feel empathy for the person. You've probably been judged unfairly at some time. Try to remember how it felt. Chances are it didn't feel good.
- Get to know the person, at least a little. You'll probably find you have some common interests or experiences.
- Talk to the person with respect. Treat him or her with respect. Isn't that how you want to be treated?

Getting Along

Appreciating diversity involves keeping an open mind and respecting other people. Acknowledge other people's beliefs and ways of life while taking pride in your own culture. Here are some things you can do to get along better with people who are not just like you.

- Work with kids from different backgrounds on group projects.
- If you're in a group, involve everyone in making rules and decisions.
- Learn about other cultures. Find out about celebrations, holidays, customs, and foods. Look into the differences and similarities in people's home traditions and rituals. These may be birthday celebrations, meal routines, or even relationships with relatives and friends.
- Ask people respectfully about their differences. Carefully listen to the response. You could say, "Tell me why you do this (or say that). Maybe you could help me to understand."
- Don't be silent if people say or do things that show their prejudice. Speak up and say how you feel about their words or actions.

Be open to new opportunities and experiences. It will help you to meet and interact with all kinds of people. And that can lead to friendships and different ways of looking at life. You'll become a more interesting person yourself.

The Weekly Reader Corporation, April/May 2003

Family Ties to Your Health

Excerpt from Current Health 1®

USING THE SELECTION

Modern families are busy. The kids go to school and many parents work. Read the selection to students. Then suggest they brainstorm at least two family activities for categories such as chores, meals, and exercise.

Gotta Move!

Parents and other family members are role models for many things. Their words and actions tell kids what is important. For instance, some parents play tennis, jog, or work out. Their kids learn to value exercise.

But active parents don't automatically produce active kids. The key is fun. Kids need to like what they do, and parents can help by planning fun activities. These might include relay races, soccer, bowling, or planting a garden. Neighborhood kids can join in too.

Happy Mealtime

Experts say family meals lead to happier, healthier kids. Dinner talk also helps families connect. And kids quickly catch on to *etiquette* (ET-uh-kit; good manners).

Good Cheer

Family members influence each other's emotional health. Do you talk problems over with a family member?

Kids with a healthy self-image usually come from cooperative families. Family members cheer each other up. They do this with hugs, advice, sincere praise, and their ability to listen.

Connections

No matter whether the family is large or small, everyone needs close connections with it. People need to trust and take pride in each other. And one-on-one time with parents, grandparents, or a favorite uncle or aunt can make those connections stronger.

Getting Along with Granny

Grandparents play important roles—roles that have gotten harder. More divorces mean more blended families. More grandparents spend extra time with both their grandkids and their step grandkids.

How Healthy Is Your Tree?

Your family also influences the diseases you may get. Your lifestyle influences your health too. Your family history will help you map out a personal prevention plan.

Safe at Home

It's easy to tell which families have safety smarts. They use seatbelts every time they ride in a car. They wear special helmets and pads for sports. They know the basics of fire safety. They are prepared for emergencies and have plans that every family member knows about. They are aware of safety in a wide range of areas, from food handling to first aid.

Game's Over

Most kids learn that their families influence them a lot. But the top winners are kids who do two things. They look over their family influences. Then they keep the good things and trade in the not-so-good ones. You can do the same. It's a smart way to improve your health!

The Weekly Reader Corporation, December 2002

Litterology
by Pat Moon

USING THE SELECTION

Explain that archeologists and historians get much of their information about the past from studying artifacts or objects that people of the past used in their everyday lives. Invite students to imagine that they are archeologists at work in the year 3000. Invite them to list artifacts from our era that they could expect to find.

Litterology

by Pat Moon

When they dig beneath the city
In 2864
And historians look for evidence
Of how men lived before,
Will the life-style and culture
Of twentieth century man
Be represented by the presence
Of the empty ring-pull can?
Will they be enthusiastic
About remains of so much plastic?
Will they carefully be mapping
The position of each wrapping?
Will museums be displaying
Ancient cans once used for spraying
Or building re-constructions
Of hamburger-fry productions,
Or showing the restoring
Of graffiti artists' drawings?
When they dig beneath the city
In 2864
What conclusions will they make about
The men who lived before?

from **Earth Lines Poems for the Green Age**
by Pat Moon
Greenwillow Books, 1991

Teacher Reference Section

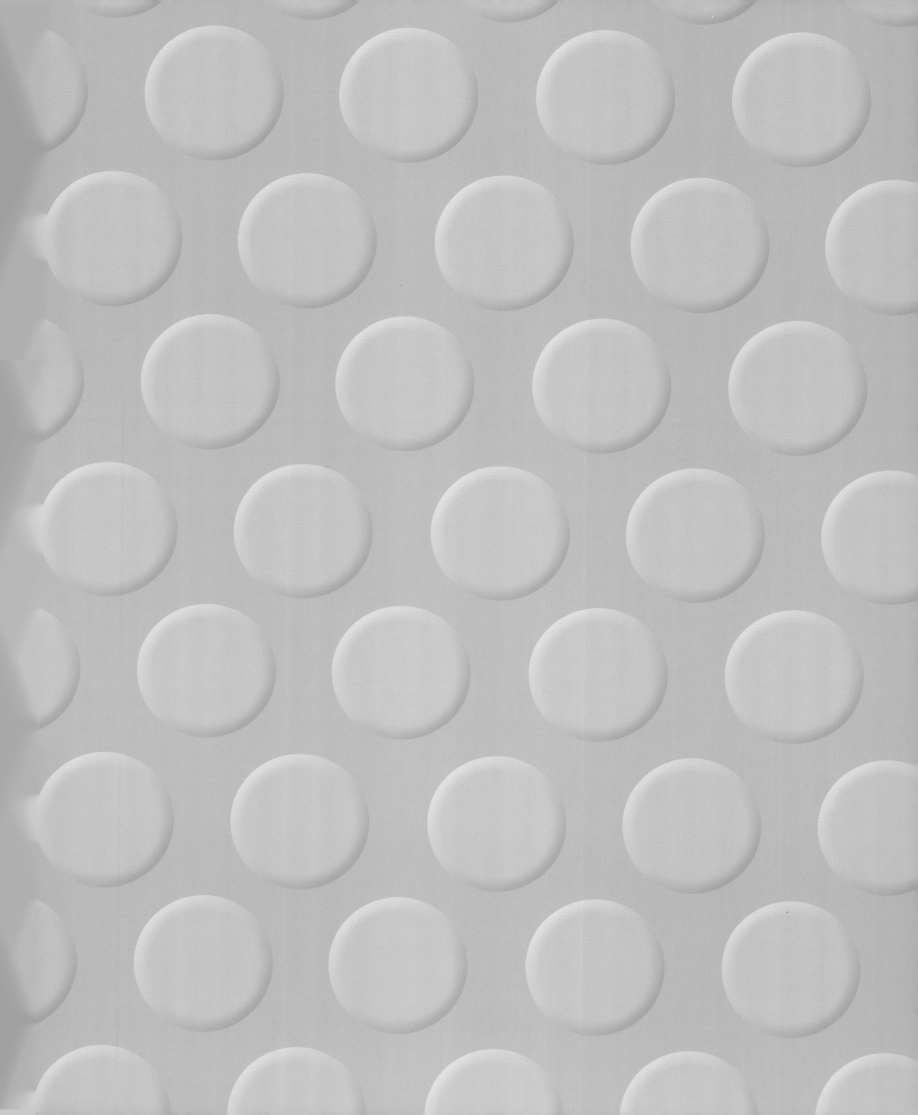

Teacher Reference

RESOURCES FOR DAILY PHYSICAL ACTIVITY

 Be Active!
Music for Daily Physical Activity

Health professionals and health and physical educators recommend that all people add activity to their daily routines. The selections on this CD are designed for classroom and physical educators to use in helping students to be active. The music is high-energy in engaging styles. Timed musical changes can be used to alternate intervals of aerobic activities with intervals of activities to build strength and flexibility. Tracks can be repeated or combined for longer workouts.

Be Active! Music Descriptions

1. **Saucy Salsa** Fun music with a Latin flavor (:30 on, :15 off)

2. **Get on Board** A familiar American railroad tune (continuous music)

3. **Late for Supper** A traditional Appalachian folk tune (continuous music)

4. **Jam and Jive** Music that swings (1:00 on, :15 off)

5. **Flexercise** Familiar Top 40 sounds (varying timing)

6. **Muscle Mambo** Caribbean dance style (:30 on, :15 off)

7. **Movin' and Groovin'** Rhythm is king. (varying tempos, moods)

8. **Jumping and Pumping** High-energy club dance (:30 fast, :30 slow)

9. **Hop to It** A familiar children's song (continuous music)

10. **Super Stress Buster** Mellow, melodic music (continuous music)

11. **Funky Flex** A strong bass beat for moving and stretching (continuous music)

12. **Broadway Bound** A famous Gershwin tune (continuous music)

Instant Activity Cards

Instant Activity Cards are graphic cues to guide physical activity. The cards illustrate exercises. Sets of four cards are preselected for use with each chapter. Display the cards one at a time to lead students through a simple routine. You are also free to select any other cards you like from those provided. You can build a longer routine for daily use and teach it to your students.

Using Instant Activity Cards

Modifying Activities for the Classroom Specific modifications are given for individual cards. Obviously, hoops and jump ropes cannot be used inside a small classroom. Students can pantomime these exercises, for example, by rocking their hips for plastic hoop movements. Some stretches can be done while standing with support from a desk or chair. Some strength exercises can be done while seated.

Activity Routines Each routine should follow the same, basic structure: warm up, work out, and cool down. Begin with low-intensity aerobic exercise followed by stretching. Then move to higher intensity aerobic exercise or a mix of aerobic, strength, and flexibility exercises. End with a cool down of low-intensity aerobic activity and stretching.

CHAPTER 1

Suggested Music: Be Active! Music for Daily Physical Activity, Track 1, Saucy Salsa

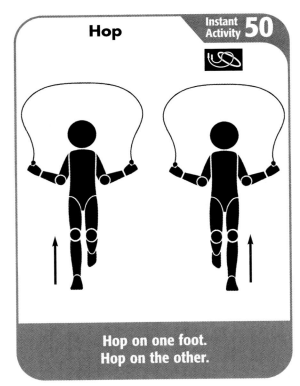

Hop Students can pantomime jump rope movements for this skill. Signal students when to change hopping feet.

Side Stretch

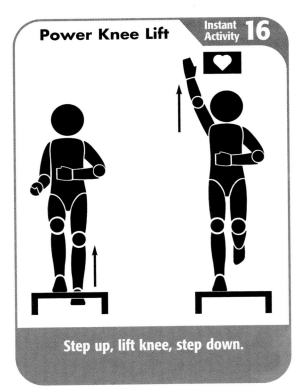

Power Knee Lift Any low, stable object can be used as a step.

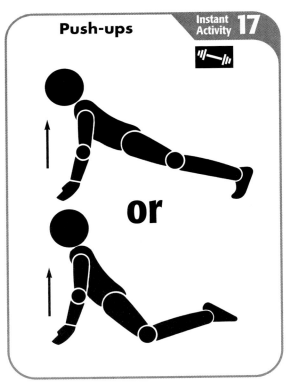

Push-up To avoid floor dirt, students can place their hands on a book or use a chair or shelf that is immobile.

Harcourt

Cardio Combo	Instant Activity 10 ♥

Jog   8
March 8
Jump   8

Cardio Combo

Reach for the Clouds — Instant Activity 37

Reach for the Clouds

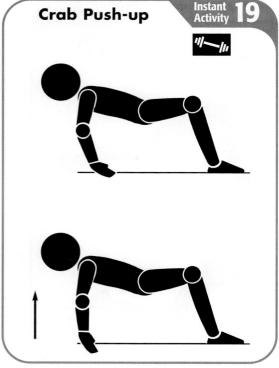

Crab Push-up — Instant Activity 19

Crab Push-up Students can do a similar exercise while seated by lifting themselves off their chairs.

Straddle — Instant Activity 52

Spread your legs on one jump. Bring them together on the next.

Straddle Students can pantomime jump rope movements for this skill. Be sure students have enough lateral space to move their legs.

Harcourt

Hop Instant Activity **1**

Hop Students can hold a desk or chair back for balance while they hop. Signal students when to change feet.

Criss-Cross Stretch Instant Activity **44**

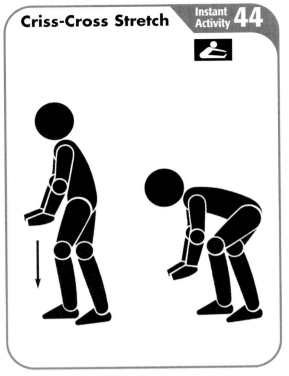

Criss-Cross Stretch Be sure that students do not lock their knees.

Overhead Press Instant Activity **21**

Overhead Press For increased benefit, students can hold and lift any object, such as a textbook.

Skier Instant Activity **53**

Jump side to side.

Skier Students can pantomime jump rope movements for this skill. Be sure that students have enough lateral space to move safely.

Harcourt

CHAPTER 4

Suggested Music: Be Active! Music for Daily Physical Activity, Track 4, Jam and Jive

Run | Instant Activity **7**

Run Have students run in place.

Runner's Stretch | Instant Activity **45**

Runner's Stretch If floor dirt is a concern, students need not touch the floor for an effective stretch.

Biceps Curl | Instant Activity **22**

Biceps Curl To add challenge, students can hold objects of similar weight in each hand, for example notebooks or textbooks.

Criss-cross Jump | Instant Activity **56**

Cross arms and hug.

Criss-Cross Jump Students can pantomime jump rope movements for this skill. It is also known as a matador or matador cross.

Harcourt

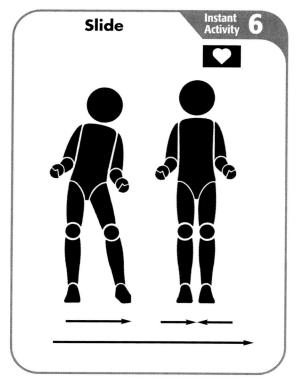

Slide Have students move back and forth rather than continuously in one direction.

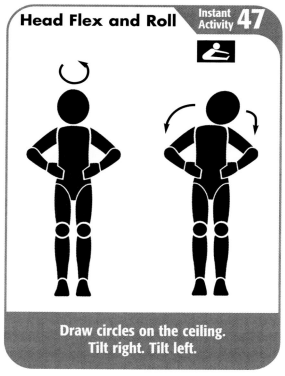

Draw circles on the ceiling.
Tilt right. Tilt left.

Head Flex

Arm Circle Be sure students have enough room to avoid hitting desks, chairs, and other students.

Hip Hoop Students can pantomime the plastic hoop movements for this skill. For the most benefit, encourage students to make large hip motions.

Harcourt

Dance to Music — Instant Activity 8

Dance to Music Students are free to follow the music. Encourage them to use all the space around them by bending low and reaching high.

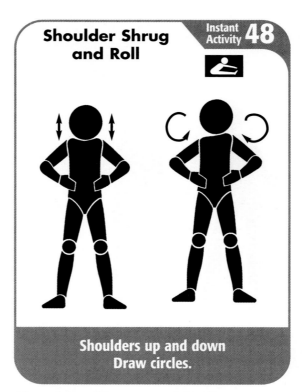

Shoulder Shrug and Roll — Instant Activity 48

Shoulders up and down
Draw circles.

Shoulder Shrug and Roll

Lunge — Instant Activity 23

Lunge

Knee Hoop — Instant Activity 59

Knee Hoop Students can pantomime plastic hoop movements for this skill. Be sure that students use vigorous knee movements.

Harcourt

Grapevine Jog | Instant Activity **9**

Left behind, right, left front, right
Right behind, left, right front, left

Grapevine Jog Students can grapevine back and forth rather than continuously in one direction.

Hamstring Stretch | Instant Activity **41**

Hamstring Stretch This exercise can be done while seated.

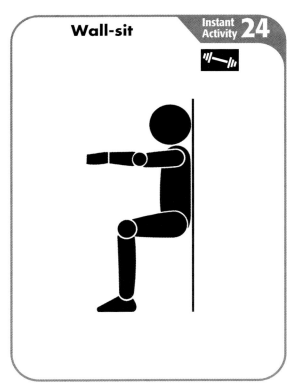

Wall-sit | Instant Activity **24**

Wall-Sit Students can use any stable object for support. Students can do this activity in pairs.

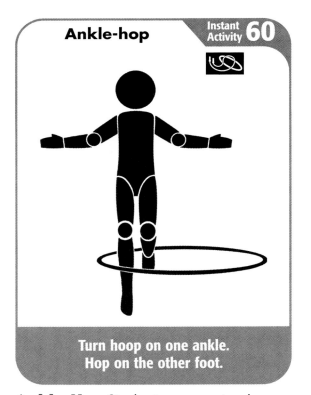

Ankle-hop | Instant Activity **60**

Turn hoop on one ankle.
Hop on the other foot.

Ankle-Hop Students can pantomime plastic hoop movements for this skill.

CHAPTER 8

Suggested Music: Be Active! Music for Daily Physical Activity, Track 8, Jumping and Pumping

Jumping Jack — Instant Activity **11**

Jumping Jack

Quadriceps Stretch — Instant Activity **40**

Quadriceps Stretch Students can do this stretch while standing. They can hold a chair back or desk for balance.

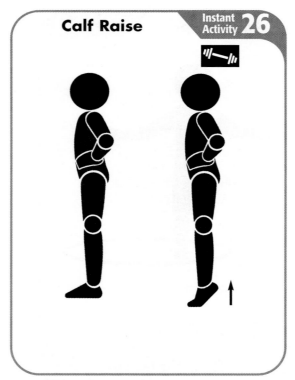

Calf Raise — Instant Activity **26**

Calf Raise Younger students may have problems with balance. They can hold a chair back or desk for balance.

Cardio Combo — Instant Activity **10**

Jog   8

March   8

Jump   8

Cardio Combo

Harcourt

CHAPTER 9
Suggested Music: Be Active! Music for Daily Physical Activity, Track 9, Hop to It

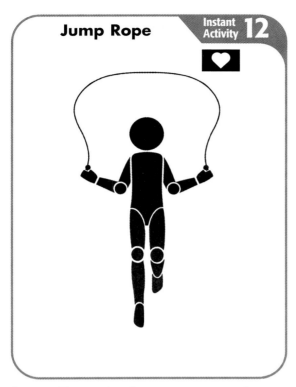

Jump Rope   Instant Activity **12**

Jump Rope Students can pantomime jump rope movements for this skill.

Calf Stretch   Instant Activity **43**

Calf Stretch Students need not touch the floor; they can do the stretch standing and use any stable object for support.

Bear Walk   Instant Activity **32**

Bear Walk Students can move forward and backward in rhythm rather than walking continuously in one direction.

Double Bounce   Instant Activity **49**

Jump twice for each rope turn.

Double Bounce Students can pantomime jump rope movements for this skill.

Harcourt

CHAPTER 10

Suggested Music: Be Active! Music for Daily Physical Activity, Track 10, Super Stress Buster

Bell Jump Instant Activity **13**

Imagine a line.
Jump across. Jump back.

Bell Jump

Stretch Like a Cat Instant Activity **38**

Stretch Like a Cat

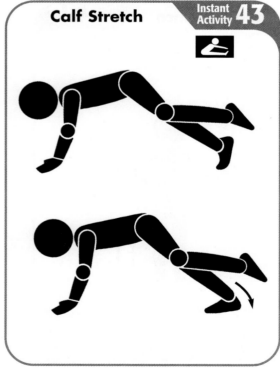

Calf Stretch Instant Activity **43**

Calf Stretch Students need not touch the floor; they can use any stable object for support.

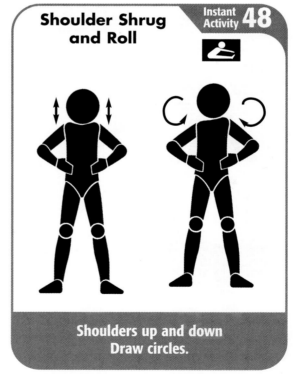

Shoulder Shrug and Roll Instant Activity **48**

Shoulders up and down
Draw circles.

Shoulder Shrug and Roll

Suggested Music: Be Active! Music for Daily Physical Activity, Track 11, Funky Flex

Punch and Kick

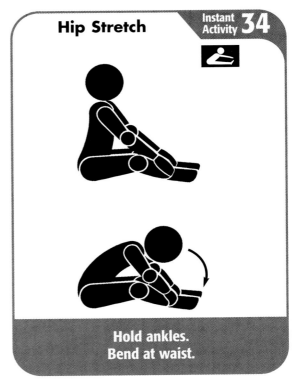

Hip Stretch This stretch can be done while seated by crossing one ankle on the opposite thigh and bending at the waist.

Martial Arts Kick Be sure that students have adequate space for safety. Younger students can hold onto a desk or chair back for balance.

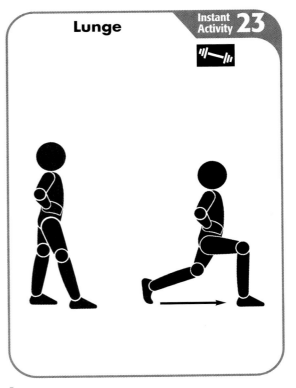

Lunge

Harcourt

CHAPTER 12
Suggested Music: Be Active! Music for Daily Physical Activity, Track 12, Broadway Bound

Four-square Hop Students can hop around the four sides of a book, desk, or chair.

Runner's Stretch

Leg Extension Students can also do this exercise while seated.

Bicycle Students can also do this exercise while seated. Have them sit back in their chairs and hold the chair edges for support.

Harcourt

EXTRA ACTIVITY CARDS

Handwalk — Instant Activity **18**

Feet stay. Hands walk.

Handwalk

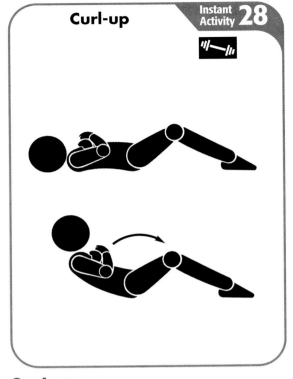

Curl-up — Instant Activity **28**

Curl-up

Twist and Crunch — Instant Activity **29**

Twist and Crunch

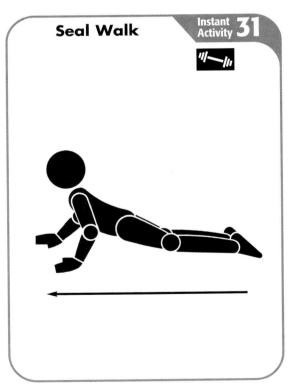

Seal Walk — Instant Activity **31**

Seal Walk

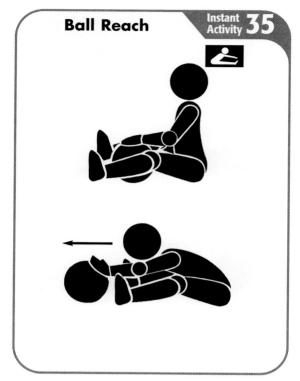

Ball Reach

Push and Pull

Leg Stretch

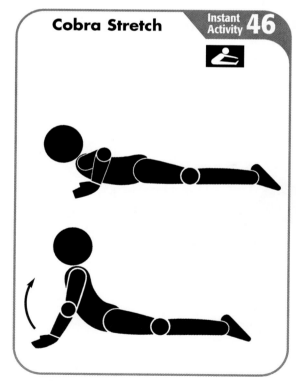

Cobra Stretch

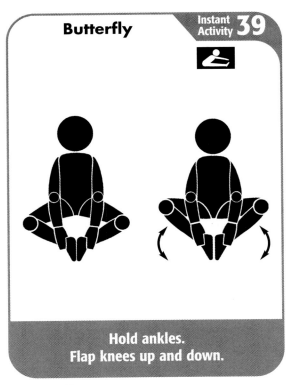

Butterfly — Instant Activity 39

Hold ankles.
Flap knees up and down.

Butterfly

Arms — Instant Activity 61

Turn the hoop on one arm.
Switch to the other.

Arms

Elevator — Instant Activity 62

Move the hoop up and down.

Elevator

360° Spin — Instant Activity 64

Spin your body
all the way around.

360° Spin

Harcourt

HELPING STUDENTS SUCCEED THROUGH COORDINATED SCHOOL HEALTH

by Thomas M. Fleming, Ph.D.

Most of us, whether we are teachers or parents, want the same things for our children. We want them to be successful. We want them to develop intellectually, do well in school, and make good grades. We want our children to be able to express their emotions constructively and to cope successfully with the demands of daily life. We want them to have healthy social lives by developing quality relationships with friends, family, and teachers. We want our children to be happy, and we want this for *all* children, not just our own.

If this positive growth and development is to happen for all children, then the historical role and mission of schools must change—and change is coming. It was once believed that the home, with help and support from community agencies and religious organizations, could prepare the child for the adult world. As adolescent health issues and societal problems in general have escalated during the past twenty years and as dropout rates have increased, school policymakers have begun to rethink the mission of a school. Effective schools see the link between health status and student success and have begun to play a more prominent role in addressing the health needs of their students. If we expect all children to succeed, schools must help them overcome the problems that interfere with learning, such as unsafe environments, drug abuse, family problems, and untreated health problems.

What Is the Mission of a School?

For many people, the following statement describes a school's mission:

> The mission of a school is to promote academic achievement and the intellectual development of students.

This statement, while correct, is incomplete. It is incomplete because to accomplish the mission of helping children develop intellectually, education must occur in an environment that is conducive to learning—in a place where children feel safe, secure, and cared for. Why is a safe, secure, and healthful environment so important for learning to take place? It is important because research indicates that young people do better in school and are less involved in risky behavior when the school atmosphere is caring.

When adolescents feel cared for by people at their school and feel like a part of the school, they are less likely to

use substances, engage in violence, or initiate sexual activity at an earlier age." (National Longitudinal Study of Adolescent Health; *Journal of School Health,* April 2002)

Less risky behavior means better health and more successful students. And, as stated by the Centers for Disease Control and Prevention (CDC) in Atlanta, Georgia "Healthy kids make better students. Better students make healthy communities."

So, a revised statement describing the mission of a school would be the following:

> The mission of a school is to educate students and assist in their intellectual, emotional, physical, and social development by providing a safe, secure, and caring school environment within which learning and student success can best occur.

What Are the Goals of Coordinated School Health?

There is little doubt that a well-supported approach to coordinated school health (CSH) can be instrumental in helping a school fulfill its mission. One of the more obvious goals of a CSH program is to improve the health status of school-age children. But this should not be the only goal. Quality CSH can certainly improve specific health behaviors and outcomes—such as improved dietary and physical activity patterns—but it can also include the goals of helping young people experience academic, emotional, and social success.

In terms of academic success, children who are chronically ill, abused, hungry, depressed, or troubled will have a difficult time functioning well in the classroom, no matter how good the school. These health problems are barriers to learning and will persist unless an intervention is introduced through the school or community. In an era of high-stakes testing and accountability, the academic expectations are the same for all students, regardless of health considerations. A good school health program that reduces barriers to learning will help level the playing field in the arena of high-stakes testing.

What Are the Components of Coordinated School Health?

The Division of Adolescent and School Health (DASH) within the CDC has promoted an eight-component model since the early 1980s. But CSH can be effective with fewer components. For example, Texas has recently mandated a four-component model that all elementary schools in the ate are to implement. Regardless of the number of mponents, the CSH model is a framework that enables mmunities to collaborate with schools in such a way that e physical, mental, and social well-being of students is hanced. Many individuals, from both the school and e community, are involved in a coordinated model by orking together to improve the school environment and, so doing, to provide students with opportunities to iprove their health status and their chances for success. The CDC Coordinated School Health Model has eight mponents:

The Texas model has four components:
► Health Education
► Physical Education
► Nutrition/Cafeteria Services
► Family/Community Involvement

Few school districts in this country currently have quality CSH model in place. One reason is that nplementing such a model means developing alliances nd collaborative associations within communities. That ot only takes work but also runs counter to the role of chools in the minds of many school policymakers. Iowever, the concept of coordinating program components vithin schools and communities has gained public support nd momentum in recent years. Momentum grows as the ublic becomes more aware of the staggering health-care osts of preventable illnesses. Tobacco-related health roblems and the current obesity epidemic alone should erve as indicators of the need for CSH.

In most school districts in this country, for many different reasons, school health has been limited to curricular interventions that have been, at best, fragmented. A few select individuals have delivered the health promotion message to students, regardless of the health topic. These individuals include the classroom teacher, the physical education teacher, or the school nurse. There has been little concentrated effort to coordinate school health services, health education, nutrition/cafeteria services, physical education, and family/community initiatives so that they resemble a coordinated model.

What Does Coordinated School Health Look Like?

A good way to understand coordinated school health is to depict school health programs that are uncoordinated. The January 1999 issue of *Phi Delta Kappan* featured a report on CSH programs. The following examples of an uncoordinated approach to student health are taken from that article:

In the uncoordinated school health program, while teachers are busy explaining the food pyramid to students, the cafeteria manager may be planning a lunch of pizza and french fries, and the school business manager may be counting the proceeds from the soft drink and candy machines. Nobody asks the custodian or the secretary, both of whom probably know more about what the troubled kids are up to than anyone else in the building, to share their observations about kids.

The health education curriculum presents information about the dangers of smoking, but school policy allows students to smoke on the school grounds. A depressed, pregnant, drug-using teenager in Maryland saw three counselors each week—a suicide prevention counselor, a parenting counselor, and a drug abuse counselor—and none of them talked to the others. All the while, the student missed so many classes that she flunked the semester and dropped out when her baby was born.

To begin to dismantle these unproductive approaches to school health programming, communities and schools need to understand the importance of school health promotion— not only to assist in preventing disease but to enhance the school climate and further ensuring the opportunities for student success. All of us who are interested in schools and children must understand the central theme of CSH. That is, the problems associated with adolescent health are more effectively overcome from multiple directions rather than by singular components working in isolation from each other.

How Can You Get Started with Coordinated School Health?

As a classroom teacher, you can help promote a coordinated approach to school health on your campus. Here are some things you can do:

► Become a CSH "champion," or advocate, in your school, district, or community.

► Determine if your district has a school health advisory council in place—a representative school/community group that provides input to the local school board regarding school health issues. Such a representative group can recommend school health strategies that are consistent with local needs and values, including CSH.

► Seek the support of the principal and other interested stakeholders, such as the school nurse, physical education teachers, classroom teachers, nutrition services personnel, and community organizations.

► Obtain material about how to establish CSH, such as the School Health Starter Kit from the CDC.

► Consider a commercial product with a reduced number of program components as a first step. Excellent commercial programs, such as the Coordinated Approach to Children's Health (CATCH) or The Great Body Shop, can provide training and materials.

CSH is a vehicle for bringing families, communities, and schools together to work toward the common goal of enriching the lives of schoolchildren. CSH is not just about student health. It's also about making schools safer and more caring. It's about making schools better places to learn. CSH is not just about kids. It's about all of us. ♥

HOW *HARCOURT HEALTH AND FITNESS* SUPPORTS COORDINATED SCHOOL HEALTH

The development of knowledge and skills alone is not enough to ensure that children achieve health literacy. A collaborative approach that coordinates the efforts of the families, schools, and the community is the most effective way to promote health literacy for all children.

A Coordinated School Health Program involves eight components that work together to develop and reinforce health knowledge, skills, attitudes, and behaviors. Each of these eight components is vital to the overall goal of promoting health literacy. The components are most effective when they are planned and implemented in a consistent and supportive manner.

- The program provides a comprehensive approach to teaching health, with content that addresses all the major strands of health.
- Where appropriate, the program suggests resources that teachers and other school personnel may consult for making the links to all components of CSH. See the Resources page for each chapter in the Teacher Editions. See also the References for Coordinated School Health in the *Teaching Resources* book.
- The content and teaching strategies address the physical, emotional, and social needs of children.
- *Harcourt Health and Fitness* goes beyond the teaching of health content by focusing on healthful skills and behaviors. For example, the Life Skills and Building Good Character features teach life-enhancing behaviors that will contribute to a lifetime of good health.

- Together with *Be Active! Resources for Physical Education*, the program provides a comprehensive and coordinated approach to teaching physical education.
- Specific features of the *Harcourt Health and Fitness Teacher Editions* that support CSH include the following:

 School-Home Connection

 Daily Physical Activity

 Daily Fitness Tip

 Activities for Home and Community

 Health Background: Webliography

INJURY PREVENTION IS A PARTNERSHIP

Jan Marie Ozias, Ph.D., R.N.

Why are injury prevention and control of concern to schools?

► Injuries are the leading killer of children and youth in the United States and a major cause of hospital care and long-term disability. Of the 22 million injuries to children that occur yearly in the United States, it is estimated that 10 to 25 percent occur in and around schools and school events.

► Schools are not only where students learn about safety practices but also where students spend many hours daily. The community expects schools to teach students knowledge and skills for safe, responsible lifestyles. Parents want to trust that school buildings, the ways to and from schools, and school activities are safe—all the time.

► Schools are work sites for many adults in every community. The people who staff schools need protection from unnecessary risks and need to take responsibility for injury prevention practices.

Why don't we use the term *accidents* anymore?

The U.S. Centers for Disease Control and Prevention analyzed "accidents" using the concept of epidemiology (the study of diseases that affect people) and determined that most accidents are not random occurrences. They are predictable and preventable.

Let us examine a fatal car collision caused by a teenage driver who was drinking, showing off, and driving on a rain-slick road without using a safety belt. None of these factors is a random occurrence, that is, a true accident.

The event and the injuries that resulted follow a predictable pattern. Epidemiology examines the relationship among three elements:

► **Host**—a person who could become ill or injured due to his or her own resistance, skills, or state of mind

► **Agent**—a direct cause of illness, such as a virus, or of harm, such as a car

► **Environment**—such as rules, weather conditions, and cleanliness

If we can alter any one of the three epidemiological elements, we can break the chain of events that lead to a high risk of illness or harm. For example, immunizing a child breaks the chain of events leading to disease if the child is later exposed to a virus. Here is a home safety example:

Host: Curious 5-year-old child
Agent: Cigarette lighter
Environment: unsupervised garage with flammable materials

Changing any of the three elements breaks the link between the host and the agent. If you teach young students the skill of self-discipline and the risks of fire, add adult supervision to the environment, or keep lighters out of reach, no fire!

In order to help students and staff identify what can and cannot be controlled, we use *unintended injury* to refer to burns, crashes, and falls. (These were previously called *accidents*.) We distinguish unintended injuries from deliberate or intended injuries, injuries caused by violence, assault, and self-harm.

Do children think injuries are preventable?

Children can tell us about injury prevention—they know it's not just about "accidents" or "kids being kids." In a study of 12 elementary schools, students were asked about their playground injuries. Almost a third of the injured students thought they could have prevented their injuries. When they were asked how, the most common replies were not going so fast, watching, being more careful, not fighting, and avoiding the situation. About half the same injured students thought someone else or something in the environment had influenced the injury. The most frequent reasons were *actions of another student* or *an object*, such as a rock or playground equipment. Developmentally, students can learn to use their senses to recognize hazards like these, connect them to unsafe situations, and then act to prevent injuries.

What do we know about students' injuries?

Detailed reports about student injuries come from the National Pediatric Trauma Registry study of school-age children (5- to 18-year-olds) seen in 74 emergency rooms over an eight year period. Here are some results from that study:

► More injuries (49 percent) occurred in recreational areas than in any other school area.

► Falls were the most common cause of injury (46 percent), followed by sports activities (30 percent).

► Assaults or intended inj   caused 10 percent of the injuries

► Students with disabilities were more likely to be hurt; 17 percent of the injured students already had a disability or chronic illness.

► Forty-six percent of the injuries occurred among 10- to 14-year-olds.

► Almost 40 percent of the cases involved head injuries.

schools handle injuries properly?

The same hospital emergency room study also found
␣at 16 percent of the children received no or inadequate
␣st aid; they were sent home rather than sent to receive
␣re. How prepared is your school to handle injuries? Does
␣have a registered nurse and staff trained in first aid? Who
␣s in for the nurse if he or she is unavailable?

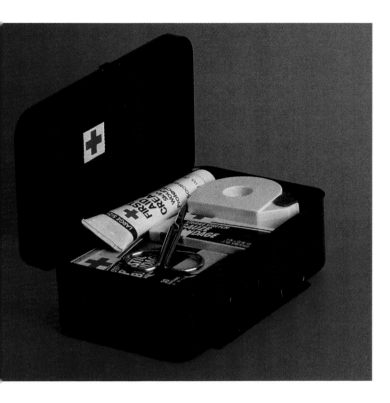

here do violence and abuse fit in injury prevention?

Assault injuries to students seen in emergency rooms
␣luded beatings (more than 50 percent of the assaults),
␣bbings (14 percent), gunshot wounds (10 percent), or
␣ng deliberately hit by an object. Although violence
␣eives much more media attention and causes staff to
␣rry, most of the students injured at school—in a ratio of
␣o 1—are injured unintentionally. Regardless, conflict res-
␣tion as a life skill can reduce aggression and intended
␣uries, especially when it is taught in elementary school
␣d applied in the home, community, and workplace.
␣Student violence prevention in elementary schools
␣gins with recognizing and stopping bullying. Programs
␣ust include prevention but also intervene with students
␣o bully and, separately, the victims and parents. Adults
␣ust create a caring social climate that does not ignore or
␣erate bullying. Two evaluated programs are: *Bullying*
␣*vention Program: Blueprints for violence prevention*
␣ulder, CO) and *Bully-proofing your elementary school*
␣ngmont, CO: Sopris West).
␣"Stranger danger" addresses community concerns for
␣ldren when they are unsupervised. Many children also

may be at risk in the presence of a neighbor, a family
acquaintance, on the Internet, or even a relative. Teachers
should work with approved school resources to include
opportunities for students to learn how to handle uncomfortable situations involving touch, secrets, or pressure by
an older person to do something that children feel is wrong
or unsafe.

Are school buses safe?

While much attention is being given to installing safety
belts in school buses—primarily to reinforce the habit of
using them in cars and to prevent disruptive behavior—
school buses are quite safe. Considering the number of
passenger miles they travel, school buses are 37 times safer
than cars. Even so, an average of seven children die annually in school transportation-related crashes. Another 19
students die getting on or off a bus, or are hit by a bus or a
passing vehicle. Half of these pedestrians are children
between the ages of five and seven!

What needs to happen in schools?

In addition to quality student instruction, the Centers for
Disease Control and Prevention (2001) recommends that
schools

► establish a safety council that includes parents and
   students as part of a school health program advisory
   committee. The safety council would identify and correct
   safety hazards and establish safety policies.
► develop reporting methods so that school staff can
   analyze unintended and intended injuries and target the
   most common or most serious situations and develop
   better prevention strategies.
► develop and implement emergency plans to properly
   assess, manage and refer injured students.

What are safety education priorities for elementary grades?

Among elementary-school children, common unintended
injuries are related to the following:

► traffic   ► playgrounds
► bicycles   ► fire
► water   ► personal trauma (falls, cuts)

Appropriate education goals for elementary grades are to
develop in students **habits** of safety that will guide **behaviors** and prepare students for the risk-taking years of middle school. We must convey more than just knowledge of
safety risks and rules, we must focus on habits and behaviors (what to do) and skills (how to perform the *behaviors*). *Positive* role models at school and at home, guided
practice, and social reinforcement of emerging skills are
appropriate strategies to build these habits and behaviors.♥

NUTRITION BEHAVIORS FOR CHILDREN

Carl A. Stockton, Ph.D.

As I think about promoting positive dietary behaviors in children, I have to look at my fourth-grade daughter's current eating habits. Her eating practices are being molded at this early stage in her life. Children learn at a young age what kinds of food adults around them eat. In trying to teach her about positive nutritional choices, I find myself selecting healthful foods for her, such as green beans, apples, oranges, and other fruits and vegetables, that are part of my own diet. Nutritional eating practices are learned behaviors, and it is important that we start molding these behaviors early in a child's life.

Poor Health Habits

Our society has been extremely negligent in promoting positive eating behaviors in our children. Many studies have shown that poor diets and lack of physical activity together account for more than 300,000 premature deaths among adults each year. These poor health habits begin in our children. According to the U.S. Centers for Disease Control and Prevention, the percentage of children who are overweight has more than doubled in the past 20 years, and more than 9 million children (15 percent) are seriously overweight. Studies have shown that obese children are more likely to become obese adults. As adults, they are at increased risk for many premature diseases.

Eating habits of children and young people in the United States are poor. Children make poor nutritional choices that put them at risk for health problems. Contrary to common misconceptions, children do not instinctively select the nutrients that they need for proper growth and development. If I allowed my daughter to select food instinctively, she would have a diet of candy, soda, and cookies—hardly a healthful diet.

Another common misconception is that children can handle a poor diet when they are young because they will burn off the Calories; this is a dangerous misconception. Although it is true that children are able to metabolize the extra Calories because of increased activity, the poor eating habits they develop in childhood will continue into adulthood and can be detrimental. Establishing good nutritional habits during childhood is critical because changing poor eating behaviors in adulthood is difficult. Think about your own nutritional habits. I challenge you to choose one nutritional habit that you would like to change and to spend one week trying to change that habit. You can probably guess that trying to change the habit would be difficult. Now consider that if you had developed a more positive eating pattern as a child, you would most likely not need to make this behavior change as an adult.

Poor Diets

Children would get the proper amount of nutrients if they could only learn proper eating habits. Contrary to common beliefs, children do not need vitamin and mineral supplements. Unless there is a medical reason for vitamin and mineral supplements, children receive all the nutrients they need through a balanced diet. Taking vitamin pills only seems to be an easy solution for making up the nutrients missed in a child's dietary intake.

On another note, did you know that pound per pound children need to consume more water than do adults? Children lose a greater percent of water through evaporation than adults. Therefore, children need to consume more water per pound of body weight than adults need to consume.

Even though adults have shown some improvement in their dietary patterns, our children's eating habits remain poor. According to the U.S. Department of Health and Human Services, more than 84 percent of children eat too much fat. Children on average consume about 40 percent of their calories from fat. Children are not consuming enough fruits and vegetables in their diet. The National Cancer Institute recommends that children consume five servings of fruits and vegetables per day. Only 20 percent of our children actually meet this recommendation. Did you know that 51 percent of our children eat less than one serving of fruit a day? Furthermore, fried potatoes account for a large proportion of the vegetables eaten by children.

Did you know that one in five students skips breakfast on a regular basis? Several research studies have found that not eating breakfast can affect children's intellectual performance in school. Even moderate malnutrition can have a long-term effect on how well a child performs in school. Several studies have reported that undernourished children become sick, miss school, and score lower on tests than do children who receive the proper amount of nourishment. Therefore, it is important for children to eat properly and not skip meals.

Promoting Good Nutrition

What can we do as teachers to encourage our students to become better eaters? The opportunity to promote better eating habits is in front of us. We have a captive audience

opportunities to practice math problems. The same holds true for developing positive eating practices. Practice, practice, practice!

Practicing Good Nutrition

What types of activities can teachers do to promote positive nutritional practices in children? First of all, request healthful snacks for class parties. This will create a positive atmosphere for eating these kinds of foods. Give students many chances to taste foods low in fat, sodium, and added sugar and foods high in vitamins, minerals, and fiber. Also teach children how to make healthful choices in the school cafeteria or when packing their lunches. This promotes positive behaviors and keeps children involved in learning about nutrition. Emphasize the positive aspects of healthful eating rather than the harmful effects of unhealthful eating.

Finally, make nutrition education activities fun. Be creative with your activities, and try to show your students that learning can be fun. Nutrition education curricula resources exist and are readily available, often for free. Many nutrition-based materials can be obtained from volunteer agencies and governmental offices. Use them!

I would be remiss if I failed to mention the use of computers and technology in the classroom. If you are fortunate enough to have computers in your classroom, integrate the use of these learning tools with nutrition education. Surf the nutrition information highway, search CD-ROMs, and experience nutrition multimedia along with your students. Who knows, even your own nutritional habits may improve! ♥

whom to promote good nutrition and also positive alth behaviors. We as teachers need to develop a mprehensive scope and sequence for nutrition education. is important to keep reinforcing positive eating behaviors every grade level. Nutrition education involves more an just educating students about healthful eating. We ed to help children learn skills, not just facts about trition. The USDA's *Nutrition and Your Health: Dietary idelines For Americans, 2000* is a good source for irning diet and lifestyle skills. In this document, you can d healthful activities and practices that students can tually put into practice.

Give children repeated opportunities to practice healthful ting. Practicing a positive health behavior enough times ll usually make that behavior the norm for children, t the exception. Teaching children about nutrition is no fferent from teaching children math skills. If we want our ildren to excel in mathematics, we give them multiple

BECOMING PHYSICALLY ACTIVE

Charlie Gibbons, Ed.D.

Children have always enjoyed the opportunity to play outdoors and rarely refuse to take advantage of an opportunity to run and have fun. However, in recent years not as many children are outdoors playing. Some studies have shown that children are less active and that childhood obesity is on the rise. How true is this? Are children in the United States becoming less active and more overweight? If they are, what are the influencing factors?

Physical activity and fitness have become such a national health concern that several national documents from the U.S. Department of Health and Human Services have emphasized the importance of physical activity and fitness. *Healthy People 2010* has established objectives aimed at increasing the proportion of adolescents who spend at least 50 percent of school physical education class time being physically active. *Physical Activity and Health: A Report of the Surgeon General* emphasizes that regular participation in moderate physical activity is an essential component of a healthy lifestyle.

How physically active are children and adolescents?

Numerous national studies (First and Second National Children and Youth Fitness Study, The President's Council on Physical Fitness and Sports School Population Fitness Study, Youth Fitness Behavior Surveillance System, and *Healthy People 2010*) have been conducted to determine the physical activity levels of children and adolescents in the United States. The general finding is that children and youth in the United States are less active and physically fit than is recommended for optimal protection against future chronic diseases.

In addition to studies conducted on fitness levels of children and adolescents, a number of studies have been conducted to determine the prevalence of childhood obesity in the United States. The general finding is that children and youth are getting more overweight.

Why are children and adolescents less physically active and fit?

If children and adolescents are less active and are becoming more overweight, there must be some influencing factors. Researchers have emphasized the influencing role of television watching on sedentary (inactive) behavior and obesity. Television watching is a popular childhood leisure activity. The majority of children spend more time watching television than they spend in school. During television watching, physical activity ceases and metabolism slows down. As television watching increases among children and adolescents, physical activity decreases. As physical activity decreases among children and adolescents, obesity increases. According to the U.S. Centers for Disease Control and Prevention (CDC), the percentage of young people who are overweight has more than doubled in the past 30 years, and the number of deaths due to inactivity and poor diet is at least 300,000 a year for all ages.

In recent years there also has been an explosion in the use of computers, computer games, and video games by children and adolescents. These advances in technology also may help to promote sedentary behavior among children and adolescents and to increase the likelihood of obesity and the development of chronic diseases.

Television is a very powerful medium that has a pervasive influence on the health knowledge, attitudes, and behavior of children, adolescents, and adults. Researchers have suggested another avenue in which television watching influences obesity. Television watching may influence obesity among children and adolescents by increasing the number of nutritional messages to which they are exposed. Much too often foods in commercials and the foods shown in television programs are high in Calories and low in nutritional value.

What health problems are associated with inactivity?

Researchers have found obesity in childhood and adolescence to be associated with developmental risk factors for cardiovascular diseases, hypertension, high blood cholesterol, and diabetes. These problems become more pronounced in adulthood. Obese children are at an increased risk of obesity as adults. Recent studies have shown that the problems of obesity and physical inactivity among young adults are increasing at alarming rates. As the prevalence of adult obesity increases, morbidity and mortality increase.

At the same time, children and adolescents today are being bombarded with societal messages that emphasize thinness. These social pressures for thinness increase the health risk for overweight youth suffering from eating disorders.

What are the benefits of regular physical activity?

According to the *Report of the Surgeon General*, regular physical activity that is performed on an almost daily basis reduces the risk of developing or dying from some of the leading causes of illness and death in the United States.

Children should learn the importance of warm-up activities, which prepare the body for physical activity and prevent injuries, and of cool-down activities, which allow for continual blood return from the lower extremities of the body to prevent blood from pooling in the legs.

How can teachers help?

It is important to remember that children and adolescents are less likely to engage in physical activity and will choose inactivity if they are not enjoying the physical activity. A healthy level of physical activity requires regular participation in activities that increase energy expenditure above resting levels. An active child participates in physical education classes, plays sports, performs regular household chores, spends recreational time outdoors, and regularly travels by foot, bicycle, or roller blades. Opportunities for physical activity should be fun, increase confidence in participation in physical activity, and involve friends and peers. Positive role models for physical activity include parents and teachers.

If children and adolescents are supposed to be able to carry out only everyday tasks with vigor and alertness and without undue fatigue, then for too many of them there is no need for physical activity because their everyday tasks do not require much energy. With the increase in television watching, computer use, and playing computer and video games, more and more children and adolescents are engaging in more sedentary practices. The lack of participation in physical activity by the youth of the United States is a national concern. It is imperative that this concern be addressed by the families, schools, and communities in the United States.

As a teacher, you can help alleviate this problem with your students by modeling a physically active lifestyle, helping them understand the importance of being physically active, and encouraging them to participate every day in physical activity that they enjoy. ♥

Regular physical activity improves health in the following ways:

It reduces the risk of dying prematurely from heart disease.

It reduces the risk of developing high blood pressure.

It reduces feelings of depression and anxiety.

It helps control weight.

It reduces the risk of developing diabetes.

It helps build and maintain healthy bones, muscles, and joints.

It promotes psychological well-being.

It helps alleviate stress.

What is physical activity and fitness?

Have you ever gone for a walk? Have you ever done any gardening? If your answer is yes for these activities, or for any activities of this energy level or higher, you have been involved in physical activity. And if you have engaged in these types of activities for at least 30 minutes per day, you have been improving your fitness. You have been engaging in physical activity that will help ensure Calories are expended and health benefits will be conferred.

Children and adolescents should engage in

aerobic activities that will help improve and maintain the cardio-respiratory system,

physically challenging activities that will improve and maintain the muscular system, and

stretching activities that will improve and maintain flexibility and help prevent injuries.

THE NEW FACE OF PHYSICAL EDUCATION

by Lisa Bunting, M.Ed.

Do you remember push-ups and pull-ups, running endless laps to "get in shape," or standing in rows to do military-style calisthenics? How about waiting your turn to run a relay race to see who was the fastest in the class? Perhaps you experienced the stress of watching your peers pick teams to play a competitive game. Your class may have played elimination games like dodge ball. Or you may have participated in athletic games such as basketball, flag football, and softball, designed to parallel college sports. Most of us remember these activities because they represented our school experience in physical education.

The old-style traditional P.E. class focused on competition, winning and losing, and keeping score. This approach to P.E. often featured military-style exercises and drills and tests that were supposedly designed to prepare students to become better athletes. Typically, the instruction showcased a few students who were athletic and already fit, while others sat around and cheered for them. The emphasis in the "old P.E." was on athletic proficiency, sports development, and athletic fitness. Few pieces of equipment were available to students. Sometimes students were punished for mistakes and misconduct in class by being made to run or perform push-ups. Often there were no individual student learning goals based on interest and ability levels, just group goals based on athletics.

By the mid 1990s, studies found that an alarming number of children and adults were overweight and inactive. Research such as that referred to in the 1996 *Surgeon General's Report on Physical Activity and Health* supported the health benefits of regular exercise and physical activity. Educational reformers suggested that new standards and objectives should be written for physical education. The goal of physical education changed from developing athletes and athletic fitness to helping young people become active, now and for the rest of their lives. "New P.E." was born.

The new approach to physical education represents a new philosophy of teaching, as well as a revised curriculum. It is a rethinking of major goals and objectives and signals a shift in focus from physical fitness outcomes toward physical activity goals. New P.E. is centered on standards and objectives, and it features a variety of activities in which all young people are active and successful. Activities are designed to be developmentally appropriate, and instruction meets the needs of all students, especially those who are not athletically gifted. There is an emphasis on competency in many movement forms and proficiency in a few. There is a focus on health-related fitness, rather than athletic fitness, and on the acquisition of knowledge and skills for a lifetime of physical activity.

A P.E. class in a contemporary gym looks vastly different from the classes in gyms of twenty years ago. There is a flurry of activity as students work individually, with partners, and in small groups. Many pieces of equipment are used during the same lesson. For example, during a volleying lesson, students may choose to use foam balls, balloons, beach balls or volleyballs. The variety of equipment and activity choices leads to success in a fun-filled environment. Students remain engaged and active during most of the class time. The teacher facilitates the lesson by integrating warm-up activities, fitness, skills, and social objectives, as well as a cool-down.

Traditional concepts such as the teaching of gross motor skills will always be a part of physical education. But the addition of instruction in health-related activities and a focus on staying active now and in the future reflect a more contemporary model. This new model of physical activity instruction provides students with knowledge and skills to live a healthy, active life now and is essential in meeting the challenges of the national obesity epidemic. ♥

Be Active! Resources for Physical Education provides instructional strategies, games, and activities and a variety of resources designed to meet the needs of contemporary physical education. This program can also be used with Harcourt Health and Fitness. The chart shows a correlation of the two programs.

Harcourt Health and Fitness Correlated to Be Active! Resources for Physical Education

Harcourt Health and Fitness Chapters	Be Active! Resources for Physical Education Lessons
1 A Growing and Changing Body	55, 59, 61, 67, 69
2 Being a Wise Health Consumer	58, 63
3 Foods for Good Nutrition	57, 62, 68
4 Keeping Fit and Active	1–53, 56, 59–61, 63–66, 72–76, 84–87
5 Planning for Safety	73–74, 77–83
6 Preventing Violence	74, 79–81, 90
7 Learning About Disease	53–60, 62–65, 68–71
8 Legal and Illegal Drugs	71
9 About Alcohol and Tobacco	70–71
10 Dealing with Feelings	72–76, 82–83, 88–90
11 Supporting Your Family	88–90
12 Working Toward a Healthful Community	54, 76, 79, 81

STRATEGIES FOR TEACHING ABOUT CHILD ABUSE, INCLUDING SEXUAL EXPLOITATION

All children have a right to be raised in a safe, nurturing, and loving environment. They should understand that saying *no* to abuse of any sort is their personal right and an appropriate response. Children should know that a support network of trusted adults is present to help them understand, confront, and deal with abusive situations. Most importantly, children should be made aware that it is never too late to ask for help.

In some families it can be difficult to discuss sexual abuse and exploitation—the subject is still considered too private to acknowledge or discuss. Fortunately, more communities and schools, with the help of news and entertainment media, are confronting and dealing with incidences of sexual abuse. The consistent message is that it is never acceptable for an adult to use a child for sexual purposes. Learning communication skills and refusal skills empowers more children to recognize sexual abuse, to resist it when possible, and to ask for help—even if they have to ask more than one person.

The lessons on the following pages can be used to help children learn to identify, report, and resist abuse or sexual exploitation. They can also help children explain the impact of neglect and abuse. Be sure to consult your school administration and/or guidance services if you need support or additional resources to discuss these topics with children.

Background

Child abuse and neglect is defined as any act or failure to act on the part of a parent or caregiver that results in death, serious physical or emotional harm, or sexual abuse or exploitation or that presents an imminent risk of serious harm. Child abuse and neglect are defined in both federal and state legislation. The **Federal Child Abuse Prevention and Treatment Act,** as amended in 1996 (CAPTA P. L. 104-235) provides the foundation upon which state definitions are based. For example, the California Child Abuse Reporting Law, like laws in other states, provides the legal basis for action to protect children and allow intervention by public agencies if a child is maltreated. The state of Texas mandates that anyone "having cause to believe that a child's physical or mental health or welfare has been or may be adversely affected by abuse or neglect" *must* report the case immediately to a state or local law enforcement agency or to the Texas Department of Protective and Regulatory Services. Reporting suspected child abuse to any other person or agency will *not* satisfy the reporter's obligation under this law.

The Federal Child Abuse Prevention and Treatment Act identifies four major types of maltreatment: physical abuse, child neglect, sexual abuse, and emotional abuse.

► **Physical abuse** is infliction of physical injury as the result of punching, beating, kicking, biting, burning, shaking, or otherwise harming a child.

► **Child neglect** is failure to provide for a child's basic needs. Neglect can be physical, educational, or emotional. It includes withholding of medically indicated treatment.

► **Sexual abuse** is fondling a child's genitals, intercourse, incest, rape, sodomy, exhibitionism, and commercial exploitation through prostitution or the production of pornographic materials. *Child* is defined as a person under the age of 18. **Sexual abuse is a serious criminal offense and must be handled within state guidelines.**

► **Emotional abuse** (psychological/verbal abuse, mental injury) is an act or failure to act on the part of parents or other caregivers that has caused or could cause serious behavioral, cognitive, emotional, or mental disorders.

People who *must* report child abuse are referred to as mandated reporters. Although these people vary from state to state, they usually include physicians, dentists, police, school counselors, and teachers. Those persons legally mandated to report suspected child abuse have immunity from criminal or civil liability for reporting as required. Mandated reporters should always keep in mind that their responsibility is only to report suspected abuse, not investigate it.

It is, however, the moral responsibility of *every* adult to ensure children's safety, prevent problems before they occur, and resolve problems that do happen before they become crises. If a child becomes a victim, the physical or emotional scars can last a lifetime if not treated.

What Are the Signs of Possible Abuse?

► Nervousness around adults
► Aggression toward adults or other children
► Inability to stay awake or to concentrate for extended periods
► Sudden dramatic changes in personality or activities
► Unnatural interest in sex
► Frequent or unexplained bruises or injuries
► Inconsistent explanations of injury
► Low self-esteem
► Poor hygiene

When Should I Report What I've Observed?

If you suspect that a child has been abused, you can ask the child an open-ended question, such as "How did you get

rt?" to elicit more information. Asking the parent or
ardian open-ended questions may also aid your decision.
u should also listen to what children say as they speak
ectly to you or to a friend and to what they may say
directly through play, schoolwork, or their reaction to
oks they read. However, reporters should always be aware
at children's disclosures are rarely direct and complete.
ten they are tentative and only "hint" at what's going on,
ch as, "I don't want to go home" or "I don't like my
pdad any more." Many times the child will use this
proach to "test the waters" to see how the non-offending
nily member or adult will react to the disclosure.
The bottom line, however, is that if you seriously suspect
use or neglect because of the presence of two or more
dicators and the absence of an adequate explanation, you
ve an obligation to report it.

here Should I Report Suspected Abuse?

If you suspect that a child is victimized, follow any
hool/district procedures and policies. If you believe that
e child is in immediate and serious danger and policies
r reporting abuse are not apparent or a response is not
ident, contact the police or your county department of
man services. The **Childhelp National Child Abuse
otline at 1-800-A-CHILD** will also provide assistance and
lp you determine whether abuse has indeed occurred.
The following agencies provide detailed and specific
formation for dealing with child abuse. To locate each
e online, use an Internet search engine to search for
e agency's name or visit the **National Clearinghouse
1 Child Abuse and Neglect Information,** a national
source for those seeking information on the prevention,
entification, and treatment of child abuse and neglect.

ational Agencies/Organizations

merican Professional Society on the Abuse of Children
Provides professional education, publications, and
legislative updates to ensure that everyone affected by
child maltreatment receives the best possible
professional response.

DC—National Center for Injury Prevention and Control
Defines child maltreatment; cites occurrence and
consequences, groups at risk, risk factors, and
references.

hild Abuse Prevention Network
Provides tools for professionals to identify, investigate,
treat, and prevent all forms of child abuse and neglect.

**Jnited States Department of Health and Human
ervices: Center for Mental Health Services Knowledge
:xchange Network**
Provides access to searchable databases on child welfare.

State Agencies/Departments

**California Institute on Human Services: Child Abuse
Training & Technical Assistance Centers**
Explains the California Child Abuse Reporting Law, the
reporting mandate, responsibilities and protection, and
ways to identify evidence of child abuse.

**Georgia Department of Human Resources: Child Care
and Parent Services Section**
The child abuse and neglect statutes for the state of
Georgia require mandated reporters to report injuries
"inflicted by non-accidental means."

**Indiana Family & Social Services Administration:
Division of Family & Children Bureau of Child
Development**
Indiana state statutes define child abuse "acts or
omissions" as the standard for reporting child abuse and
neglect. The state maintains a hotline for reporting
abuse in the state: 800-800-5556.

Minnesota Department of Human Services
Provides information on child abuse and neglect as
defined by Minnesota law. To report suspected child
abuse or neglect, contact your county social service
agency or the police.

Missouri Department of Social Services
The local Division of Family Services office is available
to discuss concerns and can advise on whether or not to
call the hotline. The DFS maintains a 24-hour hotline at
800-392-3738.

**Ohio Department of Job and Family Services: Bureau of
Child Care Services**
Ohio state statutes define mandatory reporters as those
professionals in health care, mental health, social work,
and education/child care.

**Pennsylvania Department of Public Welfare: Office of
Children, Youth, and Families**
The Pennsylvania state statutes on child abuse require
mandated reporters to report suspected child abuse and
neglect as a "recent act or failure to act." The state
maintains a hotline for reporting abuse: 877-4PA-KIDS.

**South Carolina Department of Health and Human
Services: Child Care and Development Services**
State statutes define maltreatment as physical or sexual
abuse or exploitation, neglect, emotional/mental injury,
and abandonment.

Texas Department of Protective and Regulatory Services
Provides information on child protective services and on
all aspects of child abuse and neglect as defined by
Texas law.

Lesson 1   Defining Sexual Abuse

Objectives: to identify the characteristics of sexual abuse; to have students explain the impact of abuse

Any contact with a child could be considered sexual. It is the intent of the person making the contact that defines the act. The victim knows or can "feel" the difference between hugging and fondling or tender and passionate kissing.

"Good touching," "bad touching," and "secret touching" are three examples that help clarify what is or is not against the law. Any kind of secret touching is against the law.

Good touching is when a child does something he or she is suppose to, like helping a grandparent, and the grandparent then hugs the child. Bad touching is when siblings fight and one child gets injured. Secret touching is any time anyone (man, boy, woman, or girl) wants to touch a child, or wants the child to touch him or her, anywhere that does not seem right to the child or that would be covered with the underclothes or swimming suit of the person being touched.

Lead students in a discussion about good touches, bad touches, and secret touches. Reinforce the idea that the areas covered by the underclothes or bathing suit are the areas that are inappropriate for other people to touch or photograph except in some clinical situations.

Sexual abuse may also include any unwanted conversation or action that is designed to stimulate the abuser. Point out that if someone starts to talk about things that make children uncomfortable or starts to make suggestions that do not seem right, children should leave the place and inform a trusted adult about what happened. If children do not get help from one source, they should continue to seek help until they get it.

You may wish to tell children that if they know or think that they have been sexually abused at any time in their life, they need to tell a trusted adult. Sexual abuse can leave someone with confused and hurtful feelings. The abuse can have a long-lasting negative impact on a person's life. It can also cause suffering among family members. It is important to seek help. Emphasize the three steps toward avoiding sexual abuse: identifying the support network, using refusal skills, and avoiding unsafe situations. These are developed in the following lessons.

Lesson 2   Identifying Your Support Network

Objective: to identify ways to seek assistance from a trusted adult if concerned, abused, or threatened, including how to overcome fear of telling

Discuss the term *trusted adult* with children. Explain that sometimes their parents or guardians may not be nearby when they need help. Such "trusted adults" should be individuals well known to the child and *may* include grandparents, teachers, counselors, nurses, doctors, firefighters, police officers, and neighbors.

Suggest that children think about people who might be able to help them in difficult situations. Have them create a chart with two columns. The first column should have the heading "Family Members, Friends, and Others I Know and Can Trust." The second column should have the heading "Community Members I Can Trust." Instruct children to fill in the first section by writing the names of family members, teachers, and other trusted adults. (Younger children can draw their responses.)

Ask children to work as a group to fill in the second column. Encourage them to name aloud the people they put on the list. After children have listed the members of the support network, ask:

► **What is a support network?** a group of trusted adults who can help you in difficult situations

► **Why is it important to have a support network?** to know that there is someone you can go to if you have a problem; for security

► **What should you do if you go to a member of your support network but don't get help?** Children may have a variety of answers, but emphasize that they should not give up. If children do not say this themselves, tell them, "If one support person can't or won't help, keep asking people until someone does help." You may want to emphasize that feeling safe is a basic right of every person.

Lesson 3   Using Refusal Skills

Objectives: to identify ways to seek assistance if worried, abused, or threatened; to develop and use communication skills to tell others when touching is unwanted

Refusal skills are an important part of staying safe. Discuss the fact that the commnunication skills children can use to say *no* to tobacco, alcohol, and drugs can also be used to combat sexual abuse. Acknowledge that it is more difficult for children to say *no* to an adult or authority figure than to a peer. When refusal skills are directed at adults, not only should the refusal be forceful, but children should remove themselves from the situation as quickly as possible. They should report the situation to a person within their support network as soon as they can. Remind children of these important points to remember:

You are a special person. You have the right to feel safe.

No adult, not even a family member, has the right to touch you in ways that make you feel uncomfortable.

When any person asks you to do anything that makes you feel unsafe or uncomfortable, you can say "No!" or "Stop!" loudly and firmly. You do not have to be polite. Get help from a trusted adult.

Then refer children back to the lessons in the student edition on refusal skills and communication skills. Reread the text, and discuss any of the skills that may be unclear to children. Have them role-play situations in which they are approached by a stranger and asked to go somewhere with him or her. Remind children to refuse the stranger in a firm manner. Then have them make up their own refusal situations to share with the class.

Lesson 4   Avoiding Unsafe Situations

Objective: to recognize and avoid situations that can increase the risk of abuse

Children may think that most child sexual abuse is by strangers. However, relatives and other people who children know well are responsible for more than 80 percent of all abuse that occurs.

To address this misconception, emphasize that no one, including close friends and people in children's families, has the right to touch or relate to children in ways that make them feel uncomfortable. If children find themselves in such a situation, they should leave and tell someone they trust what happened. Stress that there are signs that suggest something is wrong, such as a person's use of threats, bribery, or secrecy.

Reinforce the rules for personal safety by organizing children into groups and holding a "safety bee." Before the safety bee, write on index cards different situations that involve risk. Read each situation to the groups. Ask them to identify the risk and the steps they could take to be safer. Encourage the groups to think about the situation and to check the safety lists they created in Lesson 2 before answering. After two or three rounds, ask them to make up similar situations and write them on index cards. Suggest possible scenarios such as these:

► **When you are alone with your uncle, he talks about things that make you feel uncomfortable.**

► **A family member wants you to go somewhere alone with him or her and insists that you not tell anyone about it.**

Program Organization

Content Areas	Pre-Kindergarten	Kindergarten	Grade 1	Grade 2
Human Body; Growth and Development	**1** Good Health **2** My Body	**1** Growing Inside and Out	**1** You Are Growing	**1** Your Growing Body
Consumer/ Personal Health	**3** Caring for My Skin **4** Staying Clean **5** Caring for My Teeth	**2** Staying Healthy **3** Caring For Your Teeth	**2** Taking Care of Your Body **3** Your Teeth	**2** Caring for Your Body **3** Caring for Your Teeth
Nutrition	**6** Food for Energy **7** Choosing Foods	**4** Food for Health	**4** Wonderful Food	**4** Food for Fitness
Physical Activity and Fitness	**8** Exercise **9** Rest	**5** Being Active	**5** Keeping Active	**5** Keeping Fit and Active
Injury Prevention	**10** Safety at Home **11** Fire Safety **12** Safety Away from Home **13** Safety with Strangers	**6** Home and Travel Safety **7** Safety While Playing	**6** Being Safe **7** Avoiding Danger	**6** Avoiding Danger **7** Staying Safe
Disease Prevention and Control	**14** Staying Well	**8** Staying Well	**8** Staying Well	**8** Staying Well
Drug Use Prevention	**15** Taking Medicine **16** Say No to Drugs	**9** Medicines Help— Drugs Hurt	**9** About Medicines and Drugs	**9** Medicines and Drugs
Emotional, Intellectual, and Social Health	**17** My Feelings **18** Friends	**10** All About Feelings	**10** You Have Feelings	**10** Your Feelings
Family Life	**19** My Family and Me	**11** Family Life	**11** Your Family	**11** Your Family
Community and Environmental Health	**20** My Community	**12** A Healthy Community	**12** A Healthful Neighborhood	**12** Caring for Your Neighborhood

Grade 3	Grade 4	Grade 5	Grade 6
1 Your Amazing Body	**1** Body Systems at Work	**1** A Growing and Changing Body	**1** Growth and Development
2 Taking Care of Yourself	**2** Personal Health	**2** Being a Wise Health Consumer	**2** Personal and Consumer Health
3 Food for a Healthy Body	**3** Food and Your Health	**3** Foods for Good Nutrition	**3** Preparing Healthful Foods
4 Activity for a Healthy Body	**4** Fitness and Activity	**4** Keeping Fit and Active	**4** Keeping Active
5 Keeping Safe	**5** Safe at Home	**5** Planning for Safety	**5** Staying Safe Every Day
6 Emergency Safety	**6** Safe Away from Home	**6** Preventing Violence	**6** Emergencies and First Aid
7 Preventing Disease	**7** Guarding Against Disease	**7** Learning About Disease	**7** Controlling Disease
8 Medicines and Other Drugs	**8** Medicines, Drugs, and Your Health	**8** Legal and Illegal Drugs	**8** Drugs and Health
9 Avoiding Tobacco and Alcohol	**9** Harmful Effects of Tobacco and Alcohol	**9** About Tobacco and Alcohol	**9** Tobacco and Alcohol
10 About Yourself and Others	**10** Your Needs and Feelings	**10** Dealing with Feelings	**10** Setting Goals
11 Your Family and You	**11** Families Together	**11** Supporting Your Family	**11** Family and Responsibility
12 Health in the Community	**12** Living in a Healthful Community	**12** Working Toward a Healthful Community	**12** Community Health

Human Body, Growth, and Development

Grade 3	Grade 4	Grade 5	Grade 6
• Identify the parts and functions of the skeletal, muscular, and nervous systems. (1-1)	• Explain how inherited and acquired traits make an individual unique. (1-1)	• Identify the basic structure of the human body. (1-1)	• Describe the different parts and functions of body systems. (1-1)
• List ways to keep these systems healthy. (1-1)	• Describe how the body is organized from cells to body systems. (1-1)	• Explain the functions of the body transport organs and systems. (1-1)	• Analyze the relationships among body systems. (1-1)
• Explain the interrelationships of body systems. (1-1)	• Compare growth from infancy to adulthood. (1-1)	• Recognize how personal habits affect the health of body systems. (1-1)	• Identify healthful behaviors to care for body systems. (1-1)
• Describe the parts and functions of the respiratory and digestive systems. (1-2)	• Identify steps to manage stress.	• Identify the three body systems that coordinate body movements. (1-2)	• Describe major events in human development from fertilization to birth. (1-2)
• Identify health behaviors related to keeping these systems healthy. (1-2)	• Use stress management skills to deal with stress in a healthful way. (1-LS)	• Explain ways to keep body coordination systems healthy. (1-2)	• Explain how growth occurs. (1-2)
• Explain the interrelationships of body systems. (1-2)	• Explain the functions of the brain and nervous system. (1-2)	• Learn about heredity and environmental influences on growth. (1-3)	• Describe how traits are inherited. (1-2)
• List and explain the stages of growth and development. (1-3)	• Describe behaviors that keep the nervous system healthy. (1-2)	• Identify major hormones of the endocrine system. (1-3)	• Demonstrate ways to show respect and consideration to people who are different from you. (1-BGC)
• Describe physical and mental changes that occur during the stages of growth. (1-3)	• Identify ways to show respect for others by accepting individual differences. (1-BGC)	• Examine some functions of hormones. (1-3)	• Describe changes in male and female anatomy and physiology during puberty. (1-3)
• Identify ways to show respect for adults. (1-BGC)	• Identify the parts and functions of the digestive system. (1-3)	• Describe how growth occurs. (1-3)	• Analyze the role of hormones as they relate to growth and development. (1-3)
• Describe how the body changes as one grows. (1-4)	• Describe behaviors that keep the digestive system healthy. (1-3)	• Describe the growth stages form the prenatal stage to older adulthood. (1-4)	• Identify the varying emotions that adolescents experience and ways to deal with them. (1-4)
• Understand that individuals grow at different rates. (1-4)	• Identify the parts and functions of the respiratory and circulatory systems. (1-4)	• Learn about changes that occur during puberty. (1-4)	• Describe how relationships change during adolescence and healthy ways to communicate with family, friends, and others. (1-4)
• Identify steps for communicating. (1-LS)	• Describe healthful behaviors to take care of the respiratory and circulatory systems. (1-4)	• Identify ways to build a good reputation by showing trustworthiness. (1-BGC)	• Identify effective communication skills. (1-LS)
• Use communication skills to express concerns. (1-LS)	• Explain the functions of the skeletal and muscular systems. (1-5)	• Learn about the physical, mental, and emotional changes accompanying the growth spurt during puberty. (1-5)	• Use communication skills to express feelings. (1-LS)
• Identify healthful habits. (1-5)	• Describe behaviors that keep the skeletal and muscular systems healthy. (1-5)	• Compare and contrast concrete thinking and abstract thinking. (1-5)	• Analyze healthful and unhealthful behaviors during adolescence. (1-5)
• Identify ways to seek assistance if touched in a manner that hurts or feels uncomfortable. (1-5)		• Explain problem-solving choices to handle problems of adolescence. (1-5)	• Explain the importance of regular physical activity. (1-
		• Identify the steps for conflict resolution. (1-LS)	
		• Use the steps to resolve a conflict. (1-LS)	
		• Explain how exercise and good nutrition help growing bodies. (1-6)	
		• Describe how sleep, rest, and hygiene affect growth. (1-6)	

Consumer/Personal Health

Grade 3	Grade 4	Grade 5	Grade 6
• Explain how and why to keep skin clean. (2-1)	• Describe the function and structure of skin. Explain how to take care of skin, including the use of sunscreen. (2-1)	• Explain why it's important to keep your skin, hair, and nails healthy. (2-1)	• Describe the structure of the skin. (2-1)
• Explain how and why to protect skin and eyes from the sun. (2-1)	• Demonstrate the ability to identify personal health needs. (2-1)	• Explain how changes in hormone levels can affect personal health habits. (2-1)	• Explain how to take good care of skin, hair, and nails. (2-1)
• Explain how plaque can lead to cavities and loss of teeth. (2-2)	• Describe tooth and gum problems and explain how to prevent them. (2-2)	• Identify ways to develop self-confidence. (2-BGC)	• Describe the importance of protection from the sun. (2-1)
• Describe and demonstrate how to brush and floss correctly. (2-2)	• Describe and demonstrate how to brush and floss correctly. (2-2)	• Identify the structure and function of teeth. (2-2)	• Identify the importance of making wise choices for hair and skin products. (2-2)
• Explain how to protect teeth from injury. (2-2)	• Identify and explain the causes of common vision and hearing problems. (2-3)	• Explain how to keep teeth and gums healthy. (2-2)	• Describe and demonstrate how to use labels to make wise product decisions. (2-2)
• Identify ways to show self-respect and respect for others through good grooming. (2-BGC)	• Describe and demonstrate how to take good care of eyes and ears. (2-3)	• Identify dental problems. (2-2)	• Identify steps for making decisions. (2-LS)
• Describe problems that can affect the ears. (2-3)	• Identify communication skills. (2-LS)	• Identify parts of the eye and the ear and explain how the parts of each function. (2-3)	• Use the decision-making steps to make choices about health-care products. (2-LS)
• Describe how to protect and care for the ears, eyes, and nose. (2-3)	• Use communication skills to make one's health needs known. (2-LS)	• Describe how to take good care of your eyes and ears. (2-3)	• Identify the importance of caring for teeth and gums. (2-3)
• Identify the importance of information on a health-care product label. (2-4)	• Describe how advertisements can be analyzed to choose products that best meet your needs. (2-4)	• Identify steps to communicate. (2-LS)	• Describe and demonstrate ways to prevent tooth decay and gum disease. (2-3)
• Explain how to choose a health-care product wisely. (2-4)	• Explain how the usefulness and value of health products and services can be determined by comparison. (2-4)	• Use the communicating steps to solve problems. (2-LS)	• Describe the structure and function of the eyes and ears. (2-4)
• Identify the steps for goal setting. (2-LS)	• Explain the importance of refusal skills that are helpful in resisting negative peer pressure and media influences. (2-4)	• Explain the importance of choosing health-care products wisely. (2-4)	• Explain how and why to take good care of the eyes and ears. (2-4)
Use the goal-setting steps to make a healthful choice when buying a health-care product. (2-LS)	• Recognize the importance of trustworthiness and truthfulness with family members about personal care. (2-BGC)	• Identify and evaluate sources of health information. (2-4)	• Recognize the importance of fairness by not taking advantage of others. (2-BGC)
Identify the ways ads get your attention and persuade you to buy products. (2-5)	• Identify factual sources, including media and technology, for obtaining health information. (2-5)	• Demonstrate how to use labels to make wise product choices. (2-4)	• Describe the importance of correct body position for computer use. (2-5)
Explain where to get good information about health-care products. (2-5)	• Describe a variety of ways to convey accurate health information and ideas. (2-5)		• Identify ways to avoid injuries when using technology products. (2-5)
			• Identify sources of reliable health information. (2-6)
			• Determine criteria for evaluating health websites. (2-6)

Scope and Sequence

Nutrition

Grade 3	Grade 4	Grade 5	Grade 6

<table>
<tr><td>

- Identify food sources. (3-1)
- Identify food sources of nutrients. (3-1)
- Identify types of nutrients. (3-1)
- Explain how food choices affect health. (3-1)
- Explain strategies for making a personal health plan as a commitment to a healthful diet. (3-2)
- Describe food combinations in a balanced diet, such as that set out in the USDA Food Guide Pyramid. (3-2)
- Learn how to make decisions affecting health by choosing healthful foods and snacks guided by the USDA Food Guide Pyramid. (3-3)
- Identify ways to show responsibility in making health decisions about lunch. (3-BGC)
- Learn how to make wise choices when shopping for food. (3-4)
- Gather data to make informed health choices. (3-4)
- Identify and practice steps to make responsible decisions about healthful food choices. (3-LS)
- Learn how to handle and store foods to keep them safe to eat. (3-5)

</td><td>

- Identify the six major nutrients, their sources, and their functions in the body. (3-1)
- Explain why mealtimes are important. (3-1)
- Identify ways to show self-respect and respect for others during meals. (3-BGC)
- Identify the food groups and explain why they are important. (3-2)
- Explain what a balanced diet is and why it is important. (3-2)
- Use nutrition information from a food guide pyramid to make healthful food choices. (3-3)
- Demonstrate healthful eating practices by making healthful food choices. (3-3)
- Identify the steps for decision-making. (3-LS)
- Use the decision-making steps to make healthful food choices. (3-LS)
- Learn how to make wise choices when shopping for food. (3-4)
- Gather data to make informed health choices. (3-4)
- Learn how to read and compare food labels. (3-4)
- Describe how food poisoning occurs. (3-5)
- Explain how to handle food safely to prevent food poisoning. (3-5)

</td><td>

- Identify the six basic nutrients. (3-1)
- Describe how the basic nutrients give the body energy. (3-1)
- Explain how to use the USDA Food Guide Pyramid to help plan a balanced diet. (3-2)
- Identify the food groups used in the USDA Food Guide Pyramid. (3-2)
- Understand the size of a serving. (3-2)
- Understand the importance of portion control when deciding on the number and size of servings. (3-3)
- Describe the importance between calories and energy balance. (3-3)
- Explain how family, friends, and culture affect food choices. (3-4)
- Explain how health, the seasons, emotions, and knowledge about foods may affect food choices. (3-4)
- Learn how practicing self-control helps you choose healthful foods. (3-BGC)
- Explain how to use food labels to evaluate the nutrition of foods. (3-5)
- Describe the influences of advertising on food choices. (3-5)
- Identify decision-making steps. (3-LS)
- Use decision-making steps to make healthful food choices. (3-LS)
- Explain how germs get into food and what they do to it. (3-6)
- Describe how to store and prepare food safely. (3-6)

</td><td>

- Identify six types of nutrients important to health. (3-1)
- Describe the role of each type of nutrient in the body. (3-1)
- Explain how the Food Guide Pyramid helps people obtain a balanced diet. (3-2)
- Describe a healthful vegetarian diet. (3-2)
- Identify healthful foods from Mexico, Asia, and the Mediterranean. (3-3)
- Explain how foods from different parts of the world can provide a healthful and balanced diet. (3-3)
- Recognize that good health depends on making food choices that satisfy nutritional needs. (3-4)
- Identify the steps for making responsible food choices. (3-BGC)
- Explain the importance of making healthful food choices. (3-5)
- Explain how to select healthful foods in supermarkets and restaurants. (3-5)
- Identify steps for decision making.
- Use the decision-making steps to make healthful food choices. (3-LS)
- Describe how to store and prepare foods safely. (3-6)
- Identify spices used to enhance food flavors. (3-6)

</td></tr>
</table>

Physical Activity and Fitness

Grade 3	Grade 4	Grade 5	Grade 6
• Understand how to improve fitness. (4-1)	• Describe how good posture can improve wellness and self-image. (4-1)	• List three reasons sleep, food choices, and physical activity are important to a healthful lifestyle. (4-1)	• Examine the components of physical fitness. (4-1)
• Understand how exercise increases strength, flexibility, and endurance. (4-1)	• Demonstrate good posture while sitting, standing, and moving. (4-1)	• Define *physical activity*, and give examples of its benefits and barriers. (4-1)	• Comprehend concepts related to health promotion and disease prevention. (4-1)
• Understand the importance of fitness for overall wellness. (4-1)	• Recognize the importance of fairness by being a good listener. (4-BGC)	• Identify ways to demonstrate fairness during a competitive game. (4-BGC)	• Learn how to use the Activity Pyramid to improve physical fitness. (4-1)
• Identify ways to show fairness to others during sports and games. (4-BGC)	• Explain the benefits of regular physical activity. (4-2)	• List three ways exercise helps the respiratory and circulatory systems. (4-2)	• Understand the importance of good posture. (4-1)
• Describe how to take personal responsibility for preventing injury. (4-2)	• Describe the differences between aerobic and anaerobic exercise. (4-2)	• Apply the Activity Pyramid when planning physical activities. (4-2)	• Identify goal-setting steps. (4-LS)
• Explain the need for obeying safety rules at home, school, work, and play. (4-2)	• Describe the importance of sleep and rest to overall fitness and a proper balance of sleep, rest, and activity. (4-2)	• Identify the four steps in goal setting. (4-LS)	• Practice goal setting for fitness. (4-LS)
• Identify the steps for decision-making. (4-LS)	• Identify goal-setting steps. (4-LS)	• Apply the goal-setting model to set up plans for a healthful lifestyle. (4-LS)	• Describe the importance of different types of exercise. (4-2)
• Use the decision-making steps to make safe choices. (4-LS)	• Practice goal setting for fitness. (4-LS)	• List the three issues that should be addressed to exercise safely. (4-3)	• Develop a personal exercise and fitness program. (4-2)
• Describe the importance of taking personal responsibility for preventing accidental injuries. (4-LS)	• Describe how to use the Activity Pyramid to improve physical fitness. (4-3)	• List three kinds of exercise and give an example of each. (4-3)	• Recognize the importance of respect by being a good sport. (4-BGC)
• Explain individual needs for relaxation and sleep. (4-3)	• Describe the importance of developing a personal health plan for fitness. (4-3)		• Describe safety rules and how to play and exercise safely. (4-3)
• Demonstrate the ability to set a personal health goal. (4-3)	• Identify safety gear necessary for injury prevention. (4-3)		• Identify safety equipment necessary for injury prevention. (4-3)

Injury Prevention

Grade 3	Grade 4	Grade 5	Grade 6
• Explain why obeying safety rules at school and around vehicles is important. (5-1)	• Recognize an emergency and know how to respond. (5-1)	• Recognize and reduce the hazards that lead to unexpected injuries. (5-1)	• Describe the potential hazards in and around the home and how to prevent injury from them. (5-1)
• Describe the importance of taking personal responsibility for reducing hazards and avoiding unsafe situations. (5-1)	• Explain how to develop a family emergency plan. (5-1)	• Explain how to respond to emergency situations. (5-1)	• Identify safety concerns in the kitchen. (5-1)
• Recognize the importance of responsibility for one's own safety at school. (5-BGC)	• Describe ways to demonstrate good citizenship during an emergency or practice drill. (5-BGC)	• Practice first aid for injuries. (5-1)	• Identify common household hazards. (5-2)
• Describe how to stay safe around strangers, bullies, and weapons. (5-2)	• Identify strategies for preventing injuries in the home. (5-2)	• Identify steps for making responsible decisions. (5-LS)	• Explain safe baby-sitting practices. (5-2)
• Explain how to ask for help from a trusted adult when needed. (5-2)	• Develop a fire safety plan. (5-2)	• Use the decision-making steps to make healthful decisions about safety. (5-LS)	• Recognize the importance of fairness by playing by the rules. (5-BGC)
• Identify steps to resolve conflicts. (5-LS)	• Identify the steps for decision-making. (5-LS)	• Practice safety at play and in motor vehicles. (5-2)	• Explain swimming and boating safety rules. (5-3)
• Use negotiation to handle conflicts with friends. (5-LS)	• Use the decision-making steps to staying safe. (5-LS)	• Analyze safety equipment. (5-2)	• Describe how to respond to a water emergency. (5-3)
• Explain how to prevent injuries when participating in activities such as bicycling, skating, skateboarding, or scootering. (5-3)	• Identify safety rules for swimming, diving, and boating. (5-3)	• Identify ways to show compassion for injured persons. (5-BGC)	• Identify steps for conflict resolution. (5-LS)
• Describe how to be safe around vehicles. (5-3)	• Describe how to respond to a water emergency. (5-3)	• Explain how to prevent home fires. (5-3)	• Use conflict resolution to resolve conflicts that could lead to violence. (5-LS)
• Make a home fire escape plan. (6-1)	• Identify strategies for avoiding injuries when camping and hiking, and during cold and hot weather. (6-1)	• Recognize fire hazards in the home. (5-3)	• Describe the danger of gangs and how to avoid conflicts with them. (5-4)
• List safety rules for preventing poisoning. (6-1)	• Describe appropriate responses during weather emergencies. (6-1)	• Describe how to survive a home fire. (5-3)	• Identify ways to stay safe in violent situations. (5-4)
• Explain the need for obeying safety rules. (6-BGC)	• Describe ways to show responsibility during outdoor activities by being a positive role model. (6-BGC)	• Identify acts of violence. (6-1)	• Explain how the media affect violent behavior. (5-4)
• List safety rules for using electricity and household products. (6-2)	• Identify personal behaviors to prevent injuries when skating, skateboarding, biking, and riding in a motor vehicle. (6-2)	• Describe ways to avoid violence. (6-1)	• Explain how to prepare for emergency situations. (6-1)
• Identify kitchen safety rules. (6-2)	• Discuss the use of safety gear and equipment to avoid injuries when traveling. (6-2)	• Describe effective listening skills used in being fair. (6-BGC)	• Describe how to respond to emergency situations in order to reduce risks. (6-1)
• Describe first aid for cuts, insect stings, and choking. (6-2)	• Identify steps for resolving conflicts. (6-LS)	• Explain strategies for avoiding violence, gangs, and weapons. (6-2)	• Identify steps for effective communication. (6-LS)
• Use communication skills to get help in an emergency. (6-LS)	• Apply conflict-resolution skills to handle conflicts with friends. (6-LS)	• Identify alternatives to joining a gang. (6-2)	• Practice communication skills for handling emergencies. (6-LS)
• Identify safety rules in case of disasters. (6-3)	• Identify strategies for avoiding deliberate injuries. (6-3)	• Identify skills used to resolve conflicts. (6-LS)	• Describe first-aid treatment for common injuries. (6-2)
• Recognize emergencies and practice appropriate behaviors. (6-3)	• Develop and use skills to avoid, resolve, and cope with conflicts. (6-3)	• Apply skills to resolve conflicts before conflicts become violent. (6-LS)	• Identify ways to show responsibility when responding to an emergency situation. (6-BGC)
		• Demonstrate strategies for avoiding violence on the street and at school. (6-3)	• Identify life-threatening injuries. (6-3)
		• Describe safe ways to respond to a terrorist attack. (6-3)	• Describe first aid for medical emergencies. (6-3)

Disease Prevention and Control

Grade 3

- Recognize symptoms of common illnesses. (7-1)
- Identify health behaviors that prevent the spread of disease. (7-1)
- Explain what a disability is and discuss how to treat a person with a disability. (7-1)
- Identify some pathogens that cause some communicable diseases. (7-2)
- Identify health behaviors that prevent the spread of disease and behaviors that cause the transmission of disease. (7-2)
- Explain some of the body's defense systems in preventing and fighting disease. (7-3)
- Identify health behaviors that prevent the spread of disease. (7-3)
- Communicate with parents about health problems. (7-3)
- Identify and share feelings in appropriate ways. (7-LS)
- Practice ways to reduce stress. (7-LS)
- Demonstrate the ability to locate health information from parents and family members, the school, and the community. (7-4)
- Explain actions to take when illness occurs, such as informing parents or other trusted adults. (7-4)
- Apply concepts to show concern for people who are hurt or ill. (7-BGC)
- Identify healthful food choices. (7-5)
- Explore activities that promote fitness and health. (7-5)
- Describe the harmful effects of tobacco on health and explain why people should abstain. (7-5)

Grade 4

- Understand what disease is, and how it affects the body. (7-1)
- Distinguish between communicable and noncommunicable diseases. (7-1)
- Learn to be more caring by identifying ways to help those who are ill. (7-BGC)
- Understand that diseases are caused by pathogens. (7-2)
- Distinguish among viruses, bacteria, and fungi as different types of pathogens. (7-2)
- Identify ways that pathogens can be spread. (7-2)
- Describe the immune system's function as a defense against pathogens. (7-3)
- Identify ways of helping the body defend itself against disease. (7-3)
- Learn to identify situations that are stressful. (7-LS)
- Use the steps to manage stress to help lead a more healthful life. (7-LS)
- Identify noncommunicable diseases and their symptoms. (7-4)
- Understand how noncommunicable diseases can be managed. (7-4)
- Identify healthful lifestyle choices that help prevent illness. (7-5)
- Understand how resistance, managing stress, and abstinence from tobacco help prevent disease. (7-5)

Grade 5

- Identify the two types of disease. (7-1)
- Explain how lifestyle choices affect the risk of contracting some diseases. (7-1)
- Develop respect for people with disabilities. (7-1)
- Identify four kinds of pathogens that can cause communicable diseases. (7-2)
- Learn how to protect yourself form these pathogens. (7-2)
- Understand how the body defends itself form disease by blocking and destroying pathogens. (7-3)
- Understand how vaccines and antibiotics can fight disease. (7-3)
- Understand the importance of seeking treatment from health-care professionals. (7-4)
- Learn the role and importance of immunizations. (7-4)
- Identify steps to manage stress. (7-LS)
- Practice steps to manage stress to keep your body healthy. (7-LS)
- Identify the causes and symptoms of noncommunicable diseases. (7-5)
- Understand the difference between chronic and acute diseases. (7-5)
- Learn how to take responsibility for your own health. (7-BGC)
- Learn how to make healthful choices to reduce your risk of disease. (7-6)
- Understand the importance of eating well, exercising, and avoiding tobbaco. (7-6)

Grade 6

- Describe three types of health risk factors. (7-1)
- Give examples of behaviors that promote health and prevent disease. (7-1)
- Demonstrate ways to communicate with and have consideration for others. (7-1)
- List steps for managing stress. (7-LS)
- Apply steps for managing stress to promote health and prevent disease. (7-LS)
- Distinguish among bacteria, viruses, fungi, and protozoa. (7-2)
- Describe various modes of disease transmission. (7-2)
- Explain the benefits of abstinence in sexual activity to prevent STDs. (7-2)
- Identify the body's defenses against disease. (7-3)
- Explain how you can develop immunity to a disease. (7-3)
- Assess the role of antibiotics in fighting disease. (7-3)
- Classify diseases as communicable or noncommunicable. (7-4)
- Compare healthy cell growth to cell growth in the disease process. (7-4)
- List noncommunicable diseases and prevention and treatment techniques. (7-4)
- Demonstrate care and concern toward ill persons in the family, the school, and the community. (7-BGC)
- Describe how to prevent the spread of communicable disease. (7-5)
- Explain how practicing positive health behaviors can reduce the risk of disease. (7-5)
- Describe the impact of tobacco use on personal health. (7-5)

Program Organization

Scope and Sequence

Drug Use Prevention

Grade 3	Grade 4	Grade 5	Grade 6
• Explain what drugs are. (8-1)	• Recognize that medicines are drugs that help the body. (8-1)	• Recognize the warning signs of drug use. (8-1)	• Explain that medicines are drugs that can help you stay healthy when used safely and properly. (8-1)
• Distinguish between drugs that help the body and drugs that harm the body. (8-1)	• Distinguish between prescription and over-the-counter medicines. (8-1)	• Identify people and organizations that can help with drug recovery. (8-1)	• Distinguish between prescription and over-the-counter medicines. (8-1)
• Distinguish between over-the-counter and prescription medicines. (8-1)	• Recognize that medicines are drugs that help the body. (8-2)	• Discuss how to use medicines safely. (8-2)	• Analyze the choices and consequences related to the abuse of drugs. (8-2)
• Explain what caffeine is and what it does to the body. (8-1)	• Distinguish between prescription and over-the-counter medicines. (8-2)	• Interpret a medicine label. (8-2)	• Describe drug dependency and addiction, and relate the impact of these on a person's ability to achieve goals. (8-2)
• Understand that medicines can be helpful only when used correctly. (8-2)	• Identify skills needed to refuse OTC medicines. (8-LS)	• Distinguish between medicine misuse and medicine abuse. (8-2)	• Describe the impact of risky behaviors on personal and family health. (8-2)
• Know rules for using medicines safely. (8-2)	• Use refusal skills to say *no* to over-the-counter medicines. (8-LS)	• Explain how the use of illegal drugs can harm the body. (8-3)	• Recognize that following laws about drug use is central to good citizenship. (8-BGC)
• Recognize the importance of trustworthiness when reporting dangerous situations. (8-BGC)	• Recognize the dangerous effects of marijuana and cocaine. (8-3)	• Describe crack and cocaine and analyze their short-term and long-term effects on the body. (8-3)	• Analyze the use and abuse of prescription and nonprescription drugs. (8-3)
• List the dangerous physical effects of using inhalants, marijuana, or cocaine, and tell why these drugs should be avoided. (8-3)	• Recognize that cocaine use can lead to immediate addiction. (8-3)	• Describe marijuana and inhalants and analyze their short-term and long-term effects on the body. (8-3)	• Identify the choices and consequences related to the abuse of stimulants and depressants. (8-3)
• Describe how to avoid breathing inhalants. (8-3)	• Demonstrate responsibility by recognizing the importance of practicing self-control. (8-BGC)	• Identify ways to be trustworthy about not using drugs. (8-BGC)	• Describe the harmful effects of steroid use. (8-3)
• Identify refusal skills. (8-LS)	• Explain why saying *no* to drugs is a healthful decision. (8-4)	• Describe the negative consequences of illegal drug use. (8-4)	• Describe the dangers of using marijuana, illegal narcotics, inhalants, cocaine, crack, and hallucinogens. (8-4)
• Use refusal skills to say *no* to drug use. (8-LS)	• Demonstrate how to say *no* to illegal drugs. (8-4)	• Analyze how illegal drug use can interfere with activities and goals. (8-4)	• Identify steps for refusing. (8-LS)
• Emphasize the importance of saying *no* to drugs. (8-4)	• Recognize the warning signs of drug use. (8-5)	• Explain strategies for saying *no* to illegal drug use. (8-4)	• Use refusal steps to say *no* to drug use. (8-LS)
• Learn various ways to say *no* to drugs. (8-4)	• Identify people and organizations that can help with drug recovery. (8-5)	• Identify refusal skills. (8-LS)	• Describe the immediate and long-term effects of using drugs. (8-5)
• Identify people who can help you refuse drugs. (8-4)	• Describe tobacco products and the harm they cause to the body. (9-1)	• Use refusal skills to stay drug-free. (8-LS)	• Identify strategies you can use for avoiding drugs. (8-5)
• Identify the effects of tobacco on the body. (9-1)	• Explain why some young people begin smoking and why stopping is difficult. (9-1)	• Recognize when someone needs help refusing or getting off drugs. (8-5)	• Name three harmful substances in tobacco smoke. (9-1)
• Describe the hazards of environmental tobacco smoke. (9-1)	• Describe alcohol and the harm it causes to body systems and behavior. (9-2)	• Describe methods for getting help about illegal drug use. (8-5)	• Identify parts of the body that are affected by tobacco use. (9-1)
• Identify ways to be trustworthy in situations concerning tobacco and alcohol. (9-BGC)	• Identify some effects of problem drinking. (9-2)	• Name three harmful substances in tobacco smoke. (9-1)	
• Describe some effects of alcohol on the body and on behavior. (9-2)		• Describe the harmful effects of tobacco use on parts of the body. (9-1)	
• Identify safety risks associated with alcohol use. (9-2)			

Drug Use Prevention (continued)

Grade 3

- Identify skills needed to refuse. (9-LS)
- Use refusal skills to say *no* to alcohol and tobacco. (9-LS)
- Explain reasons for refusing alcohol and tobacco and demonstrate ways to refuse alcohol and tobacco. (9-3)
- Describe laws regarding the use and packaging of alcohol and tobacco products. (9-3)

Grade 4

- Demonstrate strategies for refusing the use of alcohol and tobacco. (9-3)
- Discuss ways to resist peer pressure to use alcohol and tobacco. (9-3)
- Identify ways to say *no*. (9-LS)
- Practice ways to refuse alcohol and tobacco. (9-LS)
- List warning signs of alcohol and tobacco use. (9-4)
- Name sources of help for alcohol or tobacco users. (9-4)
- Identify ways to show trustworthiness by reporting dangerous situations. (9-BGC)

Grade 5

- Identify reasons people use tobacco. (9-1)
- Explain what blood alcohol level is and what it measures. (9-2)
- Describe how alcohol affects health, abilities, and body functions. (9-2)
- Explain what alcoholism is and who might suffer from it. (9-2)
- Identify ways to be a good citizen by showing respect for authority. (9-BGC)
- List reasons for choosing not to use alcohol or tobacco. (9-3)
- Develop strategies for dealing with peer pressure. (9-3)
- Analyze advertisements for alcohol and tobacco products. (9-3)
- Identify ways to say *no*. (9-LS)
- Use refusal skills to say *no* to alcohol and tobacco. (9-LS)
- Identify the warning signs of a problem with alcohol. (9-4)
- Explain why people who are addicted to alcohol or tobacco need help to stop using these drugs. (9-4)
- Identify sources of support available to people who want to stop using alcohol or tobacco. (9-4)

Grade 6

- Describe the effects of tobacco use on parts of the body. (9-1)
- Define environmental tobacco smoke (ETS).
- List three dangers of using smokeless tobacco. (9-2)
- Explain why it is difficult for an addicted person to stop using tobacco. (9-2)
- Identify ways to be trustworthy when talking about problems. (9-BGC)
- Describe the effects of alcohol on a person who drinks it. (9-3)
- Explain blood alcohol level (BAL) and its relation to the amount of alcohol a person drinks. (9-3)
- List four ways that drinking alcohol can affect a person's safety. (9-3)
- Describe the effects of peer pressure. (9-4)
- Analyze advertisements for tobacco and alcohol products. (9-4)
- Practice strategies for refusing offers of alcohol or tobacco products. (9-4)
- Identify ways of refusing. (9-LS)
- Apply refusal strategies to situations in which alcohol or tobacco are offered. (9-LS)
- Identify places where a person with alcoholism can get help. (9-5)
- Identify people who could help a young person with an alcohol problem. (9-5)
- Describe three kinds of recovery programs. (9-5)

Program Organization

Emotional, Intellectual, and Social Health

Grade 3	Grade 4	Grade 5	Grade 6
• Understand that each person is unique and worthwhile. (10-1)	• Identify personality traits, and differentiate between those that can and cannot be changed. (10-1)	• Recognize that each person shapes his or her own self-concept. (10-1)	• Identify elements that contribute to a strong self-concept. (10-1)
• Recognize the importance of respecting and taking care of oneself. (10-1)	• Describe how a good attitude and a positive self-concept contribute to self-confidence and high self-esteem. (10-1)	• Realize that a positive self-concept helps a person make healthful decisions. (10-1)	• Explain the importance of being aware of personal strengths and weaknesses. (10-1)
• Learn ways to control uncomfortable feelings and express them in healthy, responsible ways. (10-1)	• Identify the four basic physical needs. (10-2)	• Distinguish between needs and wants. (10-2)	• Explain the differences between long-term goals and short-term goals. (10-2)
• Identify effective strategies for coping with fear, stress, anger, and grief. (10-2)	• Identify examples of basic emotional, mental, and social needs. (10-2)	• Identify practical strategies for setting and achieving short-term and long-term goals. (10-2)	• Identify steps for setting goals. (10-2)
• Know when to seek help with these emotions from a parent or other trusted adult. (10-2)	• Recognize how setting goals helps people meet their needs. (10-2)	• Identify sources of help in setting and working toward goals. (10-2)	• Explain how having goals can help you make wise decisions. (10-2)
• Identify ways to manage stress. (10-LS)	• Recognize the importance of expressing feelings in safe ways. (10-3)	• Identify strategies for making and keeping friends. (10-3)	• Explain the meaning and importance of self-control. (10-3)
• Apply stress-management skills to situations at school. (10-LS)	• Learn to identify feelings such as grief, stress, and anger. (10-3)	• Explain how to deal with peer pressure. (10-3)	• Describe strategies for coping with anger, stress, and grief. (10-3)
• Describe ways to have healthful relationships with family members and friends. (10-3)	• List and apply effective steps for anger management. (10-3)	• Practice communication skills. (10-3)	• Know when to ask for help in dealing with unpleasant feelings. (10-3)
• Understand the difference between positive and negative peer pressure and know how to stand up to peer pressure that is not helpful or positive. (10-3)	• Describe self-control strategies for expressing feelings. (10-3)	• Distinguish between healthy and unhealthy relationships. (10-3)	• Identify ways to manage stress. (10-LS)
	• Recognize shared interests, goals, and values as factors in friendship. (10-4)	• Recognize the importance of respecting individual differences, including speech problems. (10-BGC)	• Apply stress management skills to situations at school. (10-LS)
	• Identify and practice effective strategies for resolving conflicts by using negotiation and compromise. (10-4)	• Identify three ways in which people communicate their feelings. (10-4)	• Recognize that lasting friendships depend on shared interests and values. (10-4)
	• Describe characteristics needed to be a responsible friend and family member. (10-4)	• Explain and practice effective strategies for stress management. (10-4)	• Understand the positive and negative aspects of peer pressure. (10-4)

Emotional, Intellectual, and Social Health (continued)

Grade 3	Grade 4	Grade 5	Grade 6
• Know how to resolve conflicts in a way that everyone involved can accept. (10-3) • Recognize how to be a good friend by caring. (10-BGC) • Understand that effective communication includes both speaking and listening. (10-4) • Recognizing the importance of being kind, apologizing, and forgiving others for their mistakes. (10-4)	• Identify skills to resolve conflicts. (10-LS) • Apply conflict resolution skills to conflicts at school. (10-LS) • Explain the steps in conflict resolution. (10-LS) • Explain the importance of respecting differences in people. (10-5) • Describe how people can work together to help others. (10-5) • Learn ways to make a difference as a role model. (10-5) • Recognize the importance of caring by being a good friend. (10-BGC) • Describe the qualities of a good friend. (10-BGC) • Describe how peer pressure works and how you can effectively respond to it. (10-6) • Explain how a strong self-concept can help you avoid the influences of negative peer pressure. (10-6) • Demonstrate refusal and negotiation skills to enhance health. (10-6)	• Identify steps to cope with and manage stress. (10-LS) • Use the stress management skills to deal with stress. (10-LS) • Learn effective strategies for resolving conflicts. (10-5) • Explain the importance of respecting differences. (10-5) • Analyze respectful ways of communicating with others. (10-5) • Define boredom, anger, loneliness, grief, and shyness, and identify possible sources of these feelings. (10-6) • Learn effective strategies for coping with uncomfortable feelings. (10-6)	• Recognize the importance of trustworthiness by being a dependable friend. (10-BGC) • Describe skills that people can use to work collaboratively. (10-5) • Analyze ways students can make a difference in their communities. (10-5) • Emphasize the role of brainstorming in mediation and conflict resolution. (10-6) • Summarize how to resolve a conflict in a way that all parties can accept. (10-6)

Program Organization

Family Life

Grade 3	Grade 4	Grade 5	Grade 6
• Describe different kinds of families and the basic needs that families have and try to meet. (11-1)	• Describe the different types of families children live in. (11-1)	• Identify some kinds of changes that families experience. (11-1)	• Identify the skills of a responsible family member. (11-1)
• Describe ways family members can work and play together. (11-1)	• Identify the roles of family members. (11-1)	• Describe how children's responsibilities change as they mature. (11-1)	• Identify the skill of self-discipline. (11-1)
• Describe respectful communication among family members. (11-1)	• Explain how and why family members' roles change. (11-1)	• Recognize the importance of caring by supporting and forgiving family members. (11-BGC)	• Identify and practice caring behaviors with family members. (11-BGC)
• Recognize the importance of fairness by not taking advantage of others. (11-BGC)	• Define and describe extended families. (11-1)	• Describe ways to communicate effectively with family members. (11-2)	• Recognize the importance of communication, cooperation, and compromise in a family. (11-2)
• Describe some major changes that can affect family members. (11-2)	• Recognize the importance of fairness in the family and in life. (11-BGC)	• Identify causes of conflicts in the family and ways to resolve them. (11-2)	• Identify strategies for resolving conflicts. (11-2)
• Describe strategies for coping with changes in the family. (11-2)	• Explain why family members get along well when they communicate. (11-2)	• Explain what to do if something bad happens in the family. (11-2)	• Identify and practice strategies for resolving conflicts. (11-LS)
• Use "I" messages to communicate feelings. (11-LS)	• Describe the many different ways to communicate with family members. (11-2)	• Identify the steps used to communicate effectively. (11-LS)	• Identify some changes that affect families. (11-3)
• Use listening and negotiating skills to help resolve conflicts. (11-LS)	• Explain how communicating with your family helps you resist peer pressure. (11-2)	• Use communication to solve problems. (11-LS)	• Describe ways in which family members might respond to changes. (11-3)
• Identify strategies for resolving conflicts. (11-LS)	• Identify steps for good communication. (11-LS)	• Explain why the family should be the focal point for seeking health advice and promoting good health. (11-3)	• Identify times a family may need help form someone. (11-3)
• Define roles and responsibilities in the context of a family. (11-3)	• Practice solving communication problems. (11-LS)	• Recognize the importance of developing a family health plan. (11-3)	
• Name ways family members can help each other when changes occur. (11-3)	• Identify the values learned from the family and how they are taught. (11-3)		
	• Explain why cooperation is important in families. (11-3)		
	• Describe some family rules, and explain why they are important. (11-3)		

Community and Environmental Health

Grade 3	Grade 4	Grade 5	Grade 6
• Identify the various places and people one can go to for health care. (12-1)	• Identify clean air, land, and water as parts of a healthful environment. (12-1)	• Identify programs that promote community health. (12-1)	• Describe natural disasters and their effects. (12-1)
• Distinguish between different healthcare facilities. (12-1)	• Analyze factors that influence individual, family, and community health. (12-1)	• Identify private groups as sources of health information. (12-1)	• Identify groups and agencies that respond to natural disasters. (12-1)
• Define and identify pollution, noise pollution, and air pollution. (12-2)	• Describe healthful recreational activities. (12-1)	• Find our about roles of the World Health Organization and local health agencies in disease prevention. (12-1)	• Describe response procedures to natural disasters. (12-1)
• Describe how to protect yourself and the environment from pollution. (12-2)	• Identify ways in which community workers promote healthful environments. (12-2)	• Explain the role of health agencies involved in community health. (12-2)	• Identify ways to prepare for emergencies such as earthquakes and severe weather. (12-2)
• Identify ways to build citizenship by taking pride in your school. (12-BGC)	• Identify a variety of community workers and their roles in promoting a healthful community. (12-2)	• Identify sources of assistance in the event of an emergency. (12-3)	• Learn how to prepare a disaster kit. (12-2)
• Identify sources of water pollution. (12-3)	• Describe the jobs of emergency medical technicians and dispatchers. (12-2)	• List some causes of forest fires and explosions. (12-3)	• Identify agencies that are responsible for food safety. (12-3)
• Describe the steps in the treatment of sewage. (12-3)	• Learn to be part of a community. (12-BGC)	• Demonstrate ways to help support positive family interactions. (12-3)	• Understand the procedures that ensure water quality. (12-3)
• Identify ways that individuals can prevent water pollution. (12-3)	• Keep your environment clean and safe. (12-BGC)	• Participate in community efforts to address local issues. (12-BGC)	• Understand how solid wastes are disposed of and can be used to enhance a community. (12-3)
• Identify ways to improve the community environment. (12-LS)	• Define and identify natural resources as renewable or nonrenewable. (12-3)	• Identify environmental factor that affect community health. (12-4)	• Identify and describe energy resources. (12-4)
• Use the steps for setting goals to successfully complete a community improvement project. (12-LS)	• Identify ways that people use natural resources. (12-3)	• Analyze how environmental and personal health are related. (12-4)	• Identify water resources and their uses. (12-4)
• Describe how littering affects the environment and the community. (12-4)	• Explain how fossil fuels are used. (12-3)	• Identify environmental protection programs that promote community health, such as recycling and waste disposal. (12-4)	• Understand how to conserve energy and water resources and why conservation is important. (12-4)
• Explain how to protect the environment by reducing, reusing, and recycling. (12-4)	• Identify sources of air, water, and land pollution, and explain how these types of pollution affect human health. (12-4)	• Describe how a safe school leads to a healthful community. (12-LS)	• Identify ways to maintain or improve a healthful school environment. (12-BGC)
	• Identify several ways to prevent air, water, and land pollution. (12-4)	• Identify ways in which communication skills enhance goal achievement. (12-LS)	• Describe the effects of air pollution on human health. (12-5)
	• Identify strategies to set goals. (12-LS)	• Identify methods of accessing valid health information. (12-5)	• Identify the effects of acid rain, water pollution, and toxic wastes. (12-5)
	• Practice setting goals to conserve resources. (12-LS)	• Cite ways of knowing if health information, products, and services are valid and reliable. (12-5)	• Use strategies for setting goals to solve environmental problems. (12-LS)
	• Define conservation. (12-5)	• Identify programs that promote community health through consumer protection. (12-5)	• Identify and give example of the Three R's. (12-6)
	• Describe ways to conserve water, air, land, and other resources. (12-5)		• Identify the causes of noise pollution. (12-6)
			• Understand what you can do to protect the environment. (12-6)

Harcourt Health and Fitness Chapter	Reading Skill	
	Collections, Grade 5 (A Harcourt Reading Program)	**Trophies, Grade 5** (A Harcourt Reading Program)
1 A Growing and Changing Body	**Sequencing**	
	Iditarod Dream: T342–T 343, T348, T349, T352, T360–T361, *Woodsong*: 387, *Island of the Blue Dolphins*: 425, *Off and Running*: T965	*The Case of the Flying-Saucer People*: 365D, *Dear Mr. Henshaw*: 563D
2 Being a Wise Health Consumer	**Draw Conclusions**	
	We'll Never Forget You, Roberto Clemente: T260–T261, T264, T266, T268, T269, T280–T281, T290, *The Boonsville Bombers*: T305, *Island of the Blue Dolphin*: T429, *Hattie's Birthday Box*: T739	*We'll Never Forget You, Roberto Clemente*: 138I, 142, 144, 146, 156, 160–161, *Folk Tales from Asia*: 183D, *Iditarod Dream*: 184I, 188, 190, 192, 194, 200–201, *The Fun They Had*: 582I, 586, 588, 590, 596–597
3 Foods for Good Nutrition	**Compare/ Contrast**	
	Sees Behind Trees: T80, *The Boonsville Bombers*: T300–T301, T306, T311, T312, T322–T323, *Earthquake Terror*: T498, *Oceans*: T582, *Seeing Earth from Space*: T672, *Little by Little*: T1018	*Off and Running*: 490I, 494, 498, 504, 510–511, *Little by Little*: 533B, *Dear Mr. Henshaw*: 534I, 538, 542, 544, 548, 562–563
4 Keeping Fit and Active	**Main Idea and Details**	
	Black Frontiers: T1288, T1289, T1292, T1294, T1298, T1306–T1307, *Cowboys of the Wild West*: T1337, T1379	*Oceans*: 296I, 300, 304, 306, 311, 318–319, *Seeing Earth from Space*: 347D, *The Case of the Flying-Saucer People*: 348I, 352, 354, 358, 364–365, *Evelyn Cisneros: Prima Ballerina*: 464I, 468, 472, 476, 481, 486–487
5 Planning for Safety	**Sequencing**	
	Iditarod Dream: T342–T343, T348, T349, T352, T360–T361, *Woodsong*: 387, *Island of the Blue Dolphins*: 425, *Off and Running*: T965	*The Case of the Flying-Saucer People*: 365D, *Dear Mr. Henshaw*: 563D
6 Preventing Violence	**Cause and Effect**	
	The Hot and Cold Summer: T32, *Sees Behind Trees*: T70, *Mick Harte Was Here*: T202, *We'll Never Forget You, Roberto Clemente*: T272, *Iditarod Dream*: T348, *Earthquake Terror*: T488–T489, T494, T500, T502, T512–T513, T523	*Name This American*: 624I, 628, 630, 632, 634, 636, 646–647, *What's the Big Idea, Ben Franklin?*: 675B, *Lewis and Clark*: 676I, 680, 682, 684, 686, 688, 696–697
7 Learning About Disease	**Summarize**	
	Yang the Third and Her Impossible Family: T114, T116, *Dear Mrs. Parks*: T156, *We'll Never Forget You, Roberto Clemente*: T270, *Iditarod Dream*: T350, *Summer of Fire*: T540, T548, *Oceans*: T584, T588, *Pandora's Box*: T784, *Evelyn Cisneros*: T898, T904, *Little by Little*: T1006, *Dear Mr. Henshaw*: T1056, *Across the Wide Dark Sea*: T1202, T1208, *Cowboys of the Wild West*: T1344, *Name This American*: T1390	*Folk Tales from Asia*: 162I, 166, 168, 170, 176, 182–183, *Iditarod Dream*: 201D, *Woodsong*: 202I, 206, 208, 212, 222–223, *Island of the Blue Dolphins*: 224J, 229, 233, *Evelyn Cisneros: Prima Ballerina*: 464J, 469, 477, *The Fun They Had*: 582J, 587, 591, *Black Frontiers*: 698I, 702, 706, 708, 714–715

Harcourt Health and Fitness Chapter	Reading Skill	
	Collections, Grade 5 (A Harcourt Reading Program)	**Trophies**, Grade 5 (A Harcourt Reading Program)
8 Legal and Illegal Drugs	**Cause and Effect**	
	The Hot and Cold Summer: T32, *Sees Behind Trees:* T70, *Mick Harte Was Here:* T202, *We'll Never Forget You, Roberto Clemente:* T272, *Iditarod Dream:* T348, *Earthquake Terror:* T488–T489, T494, T500, T502, T512–T513, T523	*Name This American:* 624I, 628, 630, 632, 634, 636, 646–647, *What's the Big Idea, Ben Franklin?:* 675B, *Lewis and Clark:* 676I, 680, 682, 684, 686, 688, 696–697
9 About Tobacco and Alcohol	**Draw Conclusions**	
	We'll Never Forget You, Roberto Clemente: T260–T261, T264, T266, T268, T269, T280–T281, T290, *The Boonsville Bombers:* T305, *Island of the Blue Dolphin:* T429, *Hattie's Birthday Box:* T739	*We'll Never Forget You, Roberto Clemente:* 138I, 142, 144, 146, 156, 160–161, *Folk Tales from Asia:* 183D, *Iditarod Dream:* 184I, 188, 190, 192, 194, 200–201, *The Fun They Had:* 582I, 586, 588, 590, 596–597
10 Dealing with Feelings	**Compare/Contrast**	
	Sees Behind Trees: T80, *The Boonsville Bombers:* T300–T301, T306, T311, T312, T322–T323, *Earthquake Terror:* T498, *Oceans:* T582, *Seeing Earth from Space:* T672, *Little by Little:* T1018	*Off and Running:* 490I, 494, 498, 504, 510–511, *Little by Little:* 533B, *Dear Mr. Henshaw:* 534I, 538, 542, 544, 548, 562–563
11 Supporting Your Family	**Main Idea and Details**	
	Black Frontiers: T1288, T1289, T1292, T1294, T1298, T1306–T1307, *Cowboys of the Wild West:* T1337, T1379	*Oceans:* 296I, 300, 304, 306, 311, 318–319, *Seeing Earth from Space:* 347D, *The Case of the Flying-Saucer People:* 348I, 352, 354, 358, 364–365, *Evelyn Cisneros: Prima Ballerina:* 464I, 468, 472, 476, 481, 486–487
12 Working Toward a Healthful Community	**Summarize**	
	Yang the Third and Her Impossible Family: T114, T116, *Dear Mrs. Parks:* T156, *We'll Never Forget You, Roberto Clemente:* T270, *Iditarod Dream:* T350, *Summer of Fire:* T540, T548, *Oceans:* T584, T588, *Pandora's Box:* T784, *Evelyn Cisneros:* T898, T904, *Little by Little:* T1006, *Dear Mr. Henshaw:* T1056, *Across the Wide Dark Sea:* T1202, T1208, *Cowboys of the Wild West:* T1344, *Name This American:* T1390	*Folk Tales from Asia:* 162I, 166, 168, 170, 176, 182–183, *Iditarod Dream:* 201D, *Woodsong:* 202I, 206, 208, 212, 222–223, *Island of the Blue Dolphins:* 224J, 229, 233, *Evelyn Cisneros: Prima Ballerina:* 464J, 469, 477, *The Fun They Had:* 582J, 587, 591, *Black Frontiers:* 698I, 702, 706, 708, 714–715

National Health Education Standards

HEALTH EDUCATION STANDARD 1:
Students will comprehend concepts related to health promotion and disease prevention.

Rationale Basic to health education is a foundation of knowledge about the interrelationship of behavior and health, interactions within the human body, and the prevention of diseases and other health problems. Experiencing physical, mental, emotional and social changes as one grows and develops provides a self-contained "learning laboratory." Comprehension of health-promotion strategies and disease prevention concepts enables students to become health-literate, self-directed learners which establishes a foundation for leading healthy and productive lives.

PERFORMANCE INDICATORS:
As a result of health instruction in Grades K–4, students will:

1	describe relationships between personal health behaviors and individual well being.	**Grade K:** 12, 14, 22–29, 48–55, 74–85, 92–103, 164–169
		Grade 1: 26–29, 43–59, 102–127, 130–141, 164–181, 205
		Grade 2: 9, 15, 16, 17, 25–28, 32–33, 34–35, 42–43, 64–85, 88–103
		Grade 3: 30–55, 86–102, 126–140, 164–166, 216–231
		Grade 4: 32–57, 92–110, 136–152, 248–276, 282–298
2	identify indicators of mental, emotional, social and physical health during childhood.	**Grade K:** 14, 15, 23, 24, 25, 29, 75, 76, 77, 79, 81, 82, 83, 84, 85, 92, 93, 94, 95, 96, 97, 99, 100, 101, 157
		Grade 1: 28, 29, 31, 35, 37, 49, 52–53, 55, 74–75, 87, 90, 92–93, 96, 99, 103, 109, 112, 116, 134–135, 147, 150–151, 155, 178–179, 192–193, 211, 213, 214–215, 230–231
		Grade 2: 27, 36–37, 42, 56–57, 94–95, 131–133, 139, 218–229
		Grade 3: 22–23, 116–117, 156–157, 206–207, 231, 233–236, 250–251, 272–273
		Grade 4: 10–11, 33, 39, 40, 46–47, 49, 53, 76–77, 104–105, 123, 126–127, 129, 137, 139, 146–147, 149, 150, 172–173, 198, 199, 234–235, 250, 253, 257, 261, 266–267, 271, 275, 284, 289, 290, 292–293, 296, 297, 322–333
3	describe the basic structure and functions of the human body systems.	**Grade K:** 2, 8, 10, 11, 22, 23, 24, 25, 27, 36, 39, 64, 65, 111
		Grade 1: 10–17
		Grade 2: 6–17
		Grade 3: 4–13
		Grade 4: 2–27
4	describe how the family influences personal health.	**Grade K:** 75, 85, 117, 152–157
		Grade 1: 167–168
		Grade 2: 36–37, 45, 58–59, 103, 129, 132–133, 139–141, 148–151, 161, 212–213, 215–216, 230–231, 232–233, 234–235, 245
		Grade 3: 242–254
		Grade 4: 107, 116, 118–125, 141, 282–298
5	describe how physical, social and emotional environments influence personal health.	**Grade K:** 74–85, 95–103, 110–117, 152–157
		Grade 1: 42–59, 130–141, 282–298
		Grade 2: 25–26, 27–31, 188–207
		Grade 3: 86–102, 164–165, 216–236
		Grade 4: 32–57, 158–182, 248–276, 282–298
6	identify common health problems of children.	**Grade K:** 110–117
		Grade 1: 42–59, 146–149
		Grade 2: 28–31, 34–35, 146–163
		Grade 3: 34–39, 78–80, 146–166
		Grade 4: 32–57, 158–182

PERFORMANCE INDICATORS:

As a result of health instruction in Grades K–4, students will:

7 identify health problems that should be detected and treated early.

Grade K: 110–117
Grade 1: 42–59, 146–159
Grade 2: 28–31, 146–163
Grade 3: 34–39, 146–166
Grade 4: 158–182

8 explain how childhood injuries and illnesses can be prevented or treated.

Grade K: 10, 12, 14, 22–29, 48–55, 74–85, 95–103, 110–117, 124–127
Grade 1: 26–29, 130–141, 146–159
Grade 2: 9, 17, 25–26, 28–31, 33, 124–143, 146–153
Grade 3: 34–39, 106–119, 126–140, 146–166
Grade 4: 114–133, 136–152, 158–182

As a result of health instruction in Grades 5–8, students will:

1 explain the relationship between positive health behaviors and the prevention of injury, illness, disease and premature death.

Grade 5: 38–67, 72–106, 110–121, 138–166, 188–222, 228–237, 289–316, 324–331, 345–368
Grade 6: 4–36, 41–74, 118–140, 144–172, 176–200, 204–241, 246–251, 294–295, 332–333, 334–349

2 describe the interrelationship of mental, emotional, social and physical health during adolescence.

Grade 5: 2–34, 38–51, 73, 92–94
Grade 6: 20–36, 41–74

3 explain how health is influenced by the interaction of body systems.

Grade 5: 2–34, 38–51, 73, 118–121
Grade 6: 4–11, 20–25, 204–241

4 describe how family and peers influence the health of adolescents.

Grade 5: 30–31, 58–59, 124–125, 160–161, 230–231, 292–293, 298–303, 321–340, 354–358
Grade 6: 32–33, 135, 178–181, 294–295, 328–333

5 analyze how environment and personal health are interrelated.

Grade 5: 90, 323, 345–368, 376–397
Grade 6: 41, 46–47, 376–397

describe ways to reduce risks related to adolescent health problems.

Grade 5: 38–43, 58–59, 92–94, 110–132, 138–166, 188–222, 306–311
Grade 6: 126–127, 138–166, 214–216, 345–368

explain how appropriate health care can prevent premature death and disability.

Grade 5: 126–127, 138–166, 214–216, 345–368
Grade 6: 118–140, 144–172, 176–200, 298–301, 386–397

describe how lifestyle, pathogens, family history and other risk factors are related to the cause or prevention of disease and other health problems.

Grade 5: 41, 46, 50, 53, 54, 56, 58–59, 93–94, 188–222, 259–284, 306–311, 345–368
Grade 6: 41, 46–47, 144–172, 204–241, 278–303, 322–327, 354–358

HEALTH EDUCATION STANDARD 2:

Students will demonstrate the ability to access valid health information and health-promoting products and services.

Rationale Accessing valid health information and health-promoting products and services is important in the prevention, early detection, and treatment of most health problems. Critical thinking involves the ability to identify valid health information and to analyze, select, and access health-promoting services and products. Applying skills of information analysis, organization, comparison, synthesis and evaluation to health issues provides a foundation for individuals to move toward becoming health literate and responsible, productive citizens.

PERFORMANCE INDICATORS:

As a result of health instruction in Grades K–4, students will:

1	identify characteristics of valid health information and health-promoting products and services.	**Grade K:** 124–131 **Grade 1:** 25, 30–35, 164–169 **Grade 2:** 38–41 **Grade 3:** 46–49, 50–54, 72–75 **Grade 4:** 8, 108
2	demonstrate the ability to locate resources from home, school and community that provide valid health information.	**Grade K:** 37, 74–85, 124–131, 164–169 **Grade 1:** 25, 30–35 **Grade 2:** 38–41, 228–245 **Grade 3:** 46–49, 50–54, 64–75, 95, 97, 242–254, 260–263 **Grade 4:** 8, 114–133, 190–192
3	explain how media influences the selection of health information, products and services.	**Grade K:** No correlation **Grade 1:** 25, 30–35 **Grade 2:** 38–41 **Grade 3:** 46–49, 50–55, 108 **Grade 4:** 48–50, 52–55
4	demonstrate the ability to locate school and community health helpers.	**Grade K:** 74–85, 117, 124–131, 164–169 **Grade 1:** 34, 56–57 **Grade 2:** 150–151, 155–156, 228–245 **Grade 3:** 150, 153, 223, 260–263 **Grade 4:** 48–55, 114–133

As a result of health instruction in Grades 5–8, students will:

1	analyze the validity of health information, products, and services.	**Grade 5:** 11, 33, 38–67, 91, 96–99, 230–231, 234–235, 282–284, 345–368 **Grade 6:** 48–59, 70–74, 226–227, 246–251, 296–297
2	demonstrate the ability to utilize resources from home, school, and community that provide valid health information.	**Grade 5:** 33, 38–67, 91, 230–231, 234–235, 282–284, 321–340, 345–368 **Grade 6:** 70–74, 174–200, 222–226, 246–251, 385
3	analyze how media influences the selection of health information and products.	**Grade 5:** 11, 38–67, 91, 96–99, 278–279, 296–297 **Grade 6:** 2, 25, 48–53, 62, 70, 74, 136, 139, 250, 294, 296, 304, 333
4	demonstrate the ability to locate health products and services.	**Grade 5:** 33, 38–67, 91, 96–99, 234–235, 282–284, 345–368 **Grade 6:** 48–59, 70–74, 222–226, 246–251, 304–306
5	compare the costs and validity of health products.	**Grade 5:** 33, 38–67, 91, 96–99, 234–235, 282–284, 345–368 **Grade 6:** 48–59, 70–74, 222–226, 246–251, 304–306

As a result of health instruction in Grades 5–8, students will:	
6 describe situations requiring professional health services.	**Grade 5:** 41, 50–51, 53, 56, 188–222 **Grade 6:** 176–200, 210–211, 302–303, 334–335

HEALTH EDUCATION STANDARD 3:

Students will demonstrate the ability to practice health-enhancing behaviors and reduce health risks.

Rationale Research confirms that many diseases and injuries can be prevented by reducing harmful and risk taking behaviors. More importantly, recognizing and practicing health enhancing behaviors can contribute to a positive quality of life. Strategies used to maintain and improve positive health behaviors will utilize knowledge and skills that help students become critical thinkers and problem solvers. By accepting responsibility for personal health, students will have a foundation for living a healthy, productive life.

PERFORMANCE INDICATORS:

As a result of health instruction in Grades K–4, students will:

1	identify responsible health behaviors.	**Grade K:** 10, 12, 14, 22–29, 48–55, 74–85, 95–103, 110–117, 124–127 **Grade 1:** 24, 32, 37, 42, 47, 84, 87, 104, 123, 125, 135, 137, 141, 149, 153, 157, 159, 196–197, 204, 212, 215, 235 **Grade 2:** 2, 15, 16, 17, 25–26, 27–31, 33–35, 41, 42–63, 64–85, 88–103, 126–127, 128–129, 130–131, 134–137, 138–191, 230–231 **Grade 3:** 24–25, 30–57, 60–81, 86–102, 164–165, 282–298 **Grade 4:** 32–57, 92–110, 114–133, 135–152, 198–199, 248–276
2	identify personal health needs.	**Grade K:** 22–29, 48–55, 124–127 **Grade 1:** 26–29, 42–59, 130–141 **Grade 2:** 15, 16, 25–27, 33, 42–43, 48–63, 64–85, 88–103 **Grade 3:** 24–25, 30–57, 60–81, 86–102, 106–119, 164–165 **Grade 4:** 32–59, 92–110, 248–276
3	compare behaviors that are safe to those that are risky or harmful.	**Grade K:** 10, 12, 14, 22–29, 36–39, 48–55, 95–103, 128–131, 152–157 **Grade 1:** 26–29, 42–59, 104–127, 130–141, 164–181 **Grade 2:** 9, 17, 25–27, 28–31, 48–63, 124–143, 166–185 **Grade 3:** 33, 39, 106–119, 126–140, 196–270 **Grade 4:** 32–57, 114–133, 136–152, 194–197, 188–215, 218–242
	demonstrate strategies to improve or maintain personal health.	**Grade K:** 10, 12, 14, 22–29, 36–39, 48–55, 95–103, 124–127 **Grade 1:** 26–29, 42–59, 104–127, 130–141, 188–202 **Grade 2:** 15, 16, 25–27, 28–31, 33, 41, 42–43, 48–63, 64–85, 88–103 **Grade 3:** 30–57, 86–102, 106–119, 164–166 **Grade 4:** 32–57, 92–110, 248–276
	develop injury prevention and management strategies for personal health.	**Grade K:** 10, 12, 14, 36–39, 74–85, 95–103, 104–127, 130–141 **Grade 1:** 42–59 **Grade 2:** 9, 17, 25–27, 33, 124–143 **Grade 3:** 106–119, 126–140 **Grade 4:** 92–110, 114–133, 136–152
	demonstrate ways to avoid and reduce threatening situations.	**Grade K:** 10, 12, 14, 22–29, 36–39, 48–55, 74–85, 94–103, 128–131, 152–157 **Grade 1:** 26–29, 42–59, 104–127, 130–141, 164–181 **Grade 2:** 9, 17, 25–27, 28–31, 48–63, 124–143, 166–185 **Grade 3:** 33, 39, 106–119, 126–140, 196–270 **Grade 4:** 32–57, 114–133, 136–152, 194–215, 218–242

PERFORMANCE INDICATORS:

As a result of health instruction in Grades K–4, students will:

7 | **apply skills to manage stress.** | **Grade K:** 28–29, 152–157
Grade 1: 90–93, 122–123, 192–193
Grade 2: 92, 132, 172, 198, 217, 223
Grade 3: 112–113, 116–117, 222–227
Grade 4: 146–147

As a result of health instruction in Grades 5–8, students will:

1 | **explain the importance of assuming responsibility for personal health behaviors.** | **Grade 5:** 22, 30–31, 72–106, 110–132, 219, 274–277, 327–331, 334–340
Grade 6: 4–36, 41–74, 118–140, 176–200, 346, 349, 374

2 | **analyze a personal health assessment to determine health strengths and risks.** | **Grade 5:** 234–244, 332–333, 345–368
Grade 6: 41, 46–47, 118–140

3 | **distinguish between safe and risky or harmful behaviors in relationships.** | **Grade 5:** 84–85, 91–92, 102, 170–184, 259–284, 332–333, 345–368
Grade 6: 41, 46–47, 250–252, 350–355

4 | **demonstrate strategies to improve or maintain personal and family health.** | **Grade 5:** 28, 100–101, 124–125, 294–296, 354–365
Grade 6: 41–74, 118–140, 311–319

5 | **develop injury prevention and management strategies for personal and family health.** | **Grade 5:** 126–127, 259–284
Grade 6: 118–140, 144–172, 176–200, 246–251, 386–397

6 | **demonstrate ways to avoid and reduce threatening situations.** | **Grade 5:** 170–184, 332–333
Grade 6: 166–172

7 | **demonstrate strategies to manage stress.** | **Grade 5:** 92, 170–184, 210–211, 304–311, 332–333
Grade 6: 166–172, 212–213, 238–239, 322–327, 354–358

HEALTH EDUCATION STANDARD 4:

Students will analyze the influence of culture, media, technology and other factors on health.

Rationale Health is influenced by a variety of factors that co-exist within society. These include the cultural context as well as media and technology. A critical thinker and problem solver is able to analyze, evaluate and interpret the influence of these factors on health. The health literate, responsible and productive citizen draws upon the contributions of culture, media, technology and other factors to strengthen individual, family and community health.

PERFORMANCE INDICATORS:
As a result of health instruction in Grades K–4, students will:

1 describe how culture influences personal health behaviors.

Grade K: 49, 63
Grade 1: 20, 96, 117
Grade 2: 70, 102, 135, 178, 193, 215
Grade 3: 39
Grade 4: 16, 34, 268–269

2 explain how media influences thoughts, feelings, and health behaviors.

Grade K: 124–131
Grade 1: 25, 30–35, 164–169
Grade 2: 38–41
Grade 3: 46–49, 50–54, 72–75
Grade 4: 8, 108

3 describe ways technology can influence personal health.

Grade K: No correlation
Grade 1: 5, 28, 33, 45, 90, 139, 148, 154, 208
Grade 2: 58–59, 240–243
Grade 3: 27, 55, 81, 103, 121, 141, 167, 211, 237, 255, 279
Grade 4: 27, 55, 87, 95, 111, 131, 153, 183, 213, 243, 277, 299, 327

4 explain how information from school and family influences health.

Grade K: 37, 117, 164–169
Grade 1: 164–181, 204–217
Grade 2: 98, 188–203
Grade 3: 46–49, 222–223, 228–229, 242–254
Grade 4: 8, 114–133, 282–298

s a result of health instruction in Grades 5–8, students will:

describe the influence of cultural beliefs on health behaviors and the use of health services.

Grade 5: 20, 21, 51, 88–91, 272
Grade 6: 19

analyze how messages from media and other sources influence health behaviors.

Grade 5: 11, 38–67, 91, 96–99, 278–279, 296–297
Grade 6: 2, 25, 48–53, 62, 70, 74, 136, 139, 250, 294, 296, 304, 333

analyze the influence of technology on personal and family health.

Grade 5: 6, 35, 65, 97, 107, 133, 162, 167, 185, 223, 255, 285, 317, 341
Grade 6: 66–69, 113

analyze how information from peers influences health.

Grade 5: 175, 178, 181, 292–293, 298–305, 312–313
Grade 6: 19, 65, 159, 252–254, 328–333

HEALTH EDUCATION STANDARD 5:

Students will demonstrate the ability to use interpersonal communication skills to enhance health.

Rationale Personal, family, and community health are enhanced through effective communication. A responsible individual will use verbal and non-verbal skills in developing and maintaining healthy personal relationships. Ability to organize and to convey information, beliefs, opinions, and feelings are skills which strengthen interactions and can reduce or avoid conflict. When communicating, individuals who are health literate, demonstrate care, consideration, and respect of self and others.

PERFORMANCE INDICATORS:
As a result of health instruction in Grades K–4, students will:

1 distinguish between verbal and non-verbal communication.

Grade K: 75, 111, 141, 155

Grade 1: 7, 11, 15, 17, 33, 40, 51, 57, 58, 60, 61, 65, 73, 77, 79, 80, 87, 91, 97, 99, 101, 103, 116, 133, 137, 139, 142, 149, 155, 157, 159, 163, 169, 171, 173, 175, 177, 180, 183, 187, 195, 199, 200, 207, 209, 213, 219, 225, 229, 233, 234, 237

Grade 2: 29, 31, 35, 41, 42, 50, 55, 59, 63, 93, 99, 101, 102, 105, 120, 127, 131, 137, 141, 145, 149, 155, 159, 161, 162, 165, 217, 224, 227, 231, 235, 247

Grade 3: 29, 31, 35, 41, 42, 55, 59, 63, 93, 99, 101, 102, 105, 127, 131, 137, 141, 145, 149, 155, 159, 161, 162, 165, 217, 219, 224, 227, 231, 235, 247

Grade 4: 9, 14, 19, 23, 29, 35, 41, 45, 50, 54, 57, 64, 71, 75, 83, 86, 89, 96, 110, 113, 120, 125, 130, 133, 140, 145, 152, 155, 160, 165, 171, 179, 182, 185, 193, 197, 204, 209, 215, 223, 229, 233, 238, 242, 245, 251, 255, 259, 265, 272, 276, 279, 286, 291, 298, 307, 310, 315, 321, 326, 329

2 describe characteristics needed to be a responsible friend and family member.

Grade K: 29, 62–63, 74–77, 82–85, 94–95, 96–103, 117, 152–157

Grade 1: 24, 32, 37, 42, 47, 84, 87, 104, 123, 125, 135, 137, 141, 149, 153, 157, 159, 196–197, 204, 212, 215, 235

Grade 2: 98, 188–203, 210–225

Grade 3: 17, 51, 222–223, 228–229, 242–254

Grade 4: 46–47, 141, 205, 260–265, 273, 282–298

3 demonstrate healthy ways to express needs, wants, and feelings.

Grade K: 9, 11, 12, 13, 15, 23, 24, 25, 26, 27, 28, 29, 36, 37, 38, 39, 40, 41, 49, 51, 52, 53, 55, 62, 63, 64, 66, 67, 74, 75, 76, 77, 83, 84, 85, 94, 97, 98, 101, 103, 110, 113, 115, 117, 124, 125, 126, 128, 129, 130, 131, 152, 153, 154, 155, 156, 157, 164, 165, 166, 167, 168, 169

Grade 1: 7, 9, 11, 13, 17, 20, 23, 29, 33, 35, 38, 41, 47, 51, 55, 57, 58, 59, 61, 64, 65, 68, 69, 72, 73, 75, 77, 79, 80, 83, 87, 91, 92, 93, 97, 99, 100, 101, 103, 105, 107, 109, 111, 112, 116, 119, 121, 122, 123, 125, 133, 135, 137, 139, 140, 141, 145, 151, 153, 157, 159, 160, 163, 169, 171, 173, 175, 177, 179, 180, 181, 183, 187, 188, 191, 193, 195, 199, 200, 201, 203, 207, 209, 211, 213, 215, 217, 223, 225, 227, 229, 231, 233, 234, 235, 237

Grade 2: 98, 188–203

Grade 3: 22–23, 116–117, 156–157, 206–207, 231, 233–236, 250–251, 272–273

Grade 4: 8, 15, 18, 21, 22, 34, 40, 44, 49, 51, 53, 146–148, 198–199, 205, 260–265, 282–298

4 demonstrate ways to communicate care, consideration, and respect of self and others.

Grade K: 29, 62–63, 74–77, 82–85, 94–95, 96–103, 117, 152–157

Grade 1: 24, 32, 37, 42, 47, 84, 87, 104, 123, 125, 135, 137, 141, 149, 153, 157, 159, 196–197, 204, 212, 215, 235

Grade 2: 29, 39, 61, 103, 132–133, 150–151, 188–203, 214–217

Grade 3: 22–23, 116–117, 156–157, 206–207, 231, 233–236, 250–251, 272–273

Grade 4: 141, 146–148, 260–265, 282–298

PERFORMANCE INDICATORS:

As a result of health instruction in Grades K–4, students will:

5 **demonstrate attentive listening skills to build and maintain healthy relationships.**

Grade K: 14, 15, 23, 24, 25, 29, 75, 76, 77, 79, 81, 82, 83, 84, 85, 92, 93, 94, 95, 96, 97, 99, 100, 101, 157

Grade 1: 28, 29, 31, 35, 37, 49, 52–53, 55, 74–75, 87, 90, 92–93, 96, 99, 103, 109, 112, 116, 134–135, 147, 150–151, 155, 178–179, 192–193, 211, 213, 214–215, 230–231

Grade 2: 36–37, 42, 56–57, 94–95, 131–133, 139, 218–219

Grade 3: 22–23, 116–117, 156–157, 206–207, 231, 233–236, 250–251, 272–273

Grade 4: 10–11, 33, 39, 40, 46–47, 49, 53, 76–77, 104–105, 123, 126–127, 129, 137, 139, 146–147, 149, 150, 172–173, 198, 199, 234–235, 250, 253, 257, 261, 266–267, 271, 275, 284, 289, 290, 292–293, 296, 297, 322–333

6 **demonstrate refusal skills to enhance health.**

Grade K: 74–85, 94–95, 128–131

Grade 1: 35, 122–125, 130–141, 164–165, 172–179

Grade 2: 129, 166–185

Grade 3: 128, 206–210

Grade 4: 141, 149–150, 198–199, 206–209, 234–235, 276

7 **differentiate between negative and positive behaviors used in conflict situations.**

Grade K: 14, 15, 23, 24, 25, 29, 75, 76, 77, 79, 81, 82, 83, 84, 85, 92, 93, 94, 95, 96, 97, 99, 100, 101, 157

Grade 1: 28, 29, 31, 35, 37, 49, 52–53, 55, 74–75, 87, 90, 92–93, 96, 99, 103, 109, 112, 116, 134–135, 147, 150–151, 155, 178–179, 192–193, 211, 213, 214–215, 230–231

Grade 2: 27, 36–37, 42, 56–57, 94–95, 131–133, 139, 218–229

Grade 3: 22–23, 116–117, 156–157, 206–207, 231, 233–236, 250–251, 272–273

Grade 4: 10–11, 33, 39, 40, 46–47, 49, 53, 76–77, 104–105, 123, 126–127, 129, 137, 139, 146–147, 149, 150, 172–173, 198, 199, 234–235, 250, 253, 257, 261, 266–267, 271, 275, 284, 289, 290, 292–293, 296, 297, 322–333

8 **demonstrate non-violent strategies to resolve conflicts.**

Grade K: 14, 15, 23, 24, 25, 29, 75, 76, 77, 79, 81, 82, 83, 84, 85, 92, 93, 94, 95, 96, 97, 99, 100, 101, 157

Grade 1: 28, 29, 31, 35, 37, 49, 52–53, 55, 74–75, 87, 90, 92–93, 96, 99, 103, 109, 112, 116, 134–135, 147, 150–151, 155, 178–179, 192–193, 211, 213, 214–215, 230–231

Grade 2: 27, 36–37, 42, 56–57, 94–95, 131–133, 139, 218–229

Grade 3: 22–23, 116–117, 156–157, 206–207, 231, 233–236, 250–251, 272–273

Grade 4: 10–11, 33, 39, 40, 46–47, 49, 53, 76–77, 104–105, 123, 126–127, 129, 137, 139, 146–147, 149, 150, 172–173, 198, 199, 234–235, 250, 253, 257, 261, 266–267, 271, 275, 284, 289, 290, 292–293, 296, 297, 322–333

As a result of health instruction in Grades 5–8, students will:

demonstrate effective verbal and non-verbal communication skills to enhance health.

Grade 5: 11, 21, 27, 44, 88, 92, 95, 96, 98, 145, 205, 233, 252–255, 272, 307

Grade 6: 19, 27, 36, 47, 53, 59, 69, 74, 125, 134, 140, 151, 158, 165, 172, 183, 192, 200, 256, 272, 283, 293, 299, 306, 315, 325, 338, 351, 358

describe how the behavior of family and peers affects interpersonal communication.

Grade 5: 30–31, 58–59, 175, 180–182, 230, 252–253, 273, 321–340

Grade 6: 30–31, 52, 54–55, 65, 135, 159, 176–200, 294–295, 334–349

demonstrate healthy ways to express needs, wants and feelings.

Grade 5: 30–31, 58–59, 206–207, 230, 328–331

Grade 6: 28–33, 159, 176–200, 320–327

demonstrate ways to communicate care, consideration, and respect of self and others.

Grade 5: 30–31, 58–59, 175, 230, 252–254, 273, 328–331

Grade 6: 19, 65, 135, 159, 184–185, 273–274, 332–333, 352–353

5	demonstrate communication skills to build and maintain healthy relationships.	**Grade 5:** 30–31, 58–59, 175, 206–207, 230, 273, 328–331 **Grade 6:** 19, 32–33, 65, 273–274, 304–306, 332–333, 352–353
6	demonstrate refusal and negotiation skills to enhance health.	**Grade 5:** 176–177, 246–251, 274–277, 332–333 **Grade 6:** 165–172, 252–256, 268–272
7	analyze the possible causes of conflict among youth in schools and communities.	**Grade 5:** 30–31, 178–179, 332–333 **Grade 6:** 166–172, 350–353
8	demonstrate strategies to manage conflict in healthy ways.	**Grade 5:** 30–31, 176–177, 332–333 **Grade 6:** 166–172, 350–353

HEALTH EDUCATION STANDARD 6:

Students will demonstrate the ability to use goal-setting and decision-making skills to enhance health.

Rationale Decision making and goal setting are essential lifelong skills needed in order to implement and sustain health-enhancing behaviors. These skills make it possible for individuals to transfer health knowledge into healthy lifestyles. When applied to health issues, decision-making and goal-setting skills will enable individuals to collaborate with others to improve the quality of life in their families, schools and communities.

PERFORMANCE INDICATORS:

As a result of health instruction in Grades K–4, students will:

1	demonstrate the ability to apply a decision-making process to health issues and problems.	**Grade K:** 10, 12, 14, 92 **Grade 1:** 42–59, 107, 124, 146–159, 164–181 **Grade 2:** 18–19, 25, 41–43, 53, 56–57, 73, 92 **Grade 3:** 23, 41, 50, 51, 91, 109, 117, 123, 251, 253 **Grade 4:** 104–105, 114–133, 141, 248–276
2	explain when to ask for assistance in making health-related decisions and setting health goals.	**Grade K:** 26–27, 37, 74–85, 117, 124–127 **Grade 1:** 7, 23, 38, 41, 59, 73, 83, 93, 100, 109, 125, 137, 145, 151, 163, 171, 183, 193, 209, 211, 223, 231, 237 **Grade 2:** 59, 61, 169–170 **Grade 3:** 27, 243, 249, 254 **Grade 4:** 141
3	predict outcomes of positive health decisions.	**Grade K:** 10, 12, 14, 22–29, 48–55, 74–85, 95–103, 110–117, 124–127 **Grade 1:** 24, 32, 37, 42, 47, 84, 87, 104, 123, 125, 135, 137, 141, 149, 153, 157, 159, 196–197, 204, 212, 215, 235 **Grade 2:** 2, 15, 16, 17, 25–26, 27–31, 33–35, 41, 42–63, 64–85, 88–103, 126–127, 128–129, 130–131, 134–137, 138–191, 230–231 **Grade 3:** 24–25, 30–57, 60–81, 86–102, 164–165, 282–298 **Grade 4:** 32–57, 92–110, 114–133, 135–152, 198–199, 248–276
4	set a personal health goal and track progress toward its achievement.	**Grade K:** 10, 12, 14, 92 **Grade 1:** 42–59, 107, 124, 146–159, 164–181 **Grade 2:** 18–19, 25, 41–43, 53, 56–57, 73, 92 **Grade 3:** 23, 41, 50, 51, 91, 109, 117, 123, 251, 253 **Grade 4:** 104–105, 114–133, 141, 248–276

As a result of health instruction in Grades 5–8, students will:		
1	demonstrate the ability to apply a decision-making process to health issues and problems individually and collaboratively.	**Grade 5:** 30–31, 38–67, 188–222, 321–340, 345–368 **Grade 6:** 204–241, 273–274, 287, 302–303, 307, 334–335, 352–358, 386–397
2	analyze how health-related decisions are influenced by individuals, family, and community values.	**Grade 5:** 30–31, 38–67, 188–222, 321–340, 345–368 **Grade 6:** 204–241, 273–274, 287, 302–303, 307, 334–335, 352–358, 386–397
3	predict how decisions regarding health behaviors have consequences for self and others.	**Grade 5:** 30–31, 38–67, 188–222, 321–340, 345–368 **Grade 6:** 204–241, 273–274, 287, 302–303, 307, 334–335, 352–358, 386–397
4	apply strategies and skills needed to attain personal health goals.	**Grade 5:** 28, 100–101, 124–125, 294–296, 354–365 **Grade 6:** 41–74, 118–140, 311–319
5	describe how personal health goals are influenced by changing information, abilities, priorities, and responsibilities.	**Grade 5:** 28, 100–101, 124–125, 294–296, 354–365 **Grade 6:** 41–74, 118–140, 311–319
6	develop a plan that addresses personal strengths, needs, and health risks.	**Grade 5:** 28, 100–101, 124–125, 294–296, 354–365 **Grade 6:** 41–74, 118–140, 311–319

HEALTH EDUCATION STANDARD 7:

Students will demonstrate the ability to advocate for personal, family and community health.

Rationale Quality of life is dependent on an environment that protects and promotes the health of individuals, families, and communities. Responsible citizens, who are health literate, are characterized by advocating and communicating for positive health in their communities. A variety of health advocacy skills are critical to these activities.

PERFORMANCE INDICATORS:

As a result of health instruction in Grades K–4, students will:

	describe a variety of methods to convey accurate health information and ideas.	**Grade K:** 8, 12, 14, 22, 26, 40, 48, 50, 62, 64, 65, 66, 76, 78, 80, 82, 84, 92, 94, 96, 98, 100, 102, 110, 112, 114, 116, 124, 126, 128, 130, 152, 154, 156, 164, 166, 168 **Grade 1:** 7, 9, 11, 13, 17, 20, 23, 29, 33, 35, 38, 41, 47, 51, 55, 57, 58, 59, 61, 64, 65, 68, 69, 72, 73, 75, 77, 79, 80, 83, 87, 91, 92, 93, 97, 99, 100, 101, 103, 105, 107, 109, 111, 112, 116, 119, 121, 122, 123, 125, 133, 135, 137, 139, 140, 141, 145, 151, 153, 157, 159, 160, 163, 169, 171, 173, 175, 177, 179, 180, 181, 183, 187, 188, 191, 193, 195, 199, 200, 201, 203, 207, 209, 211, 213, 215, 217, 223, 225, 227, 229, 231, 233, 234, 235, 237 **Grade 2:** 9, 98, 180–203, 228–245 **Grade 3:** 22–23, 116–117, 156–157, 206–207, 231, 233–236, 250–251, 272–273 **Grade 4:** 8, 15, 18, 21, 22, 34, 40, 44, 49, 51, 53, 146–148, 198–199, 205, 260–265, 282–298

As a result of health instruction in Grades K–4, students will:

2 | **express information and opinions about health issues.**

Grade K: 79, 83, 85, 153, 157

Grade 1: 164–181, 184–201, 204–218

Grade 2: 35, 42, 44, 55, 59, 60, 63, 93, 99, 101, 105, 127, 129, 131, 137, 141, 145, 149, 155, 159, 161, 165, 213, 217, 223, 227, 231, 237, 243, 247

Grade 3: 5, 7, 13, 16, 18, 21, 26, 33, 35, 37, 39, 40, 42, 45, 46, 49, 53, 54, 61, 63, 67, 70, 74, 75, 90, 95, 97, 102, 110, 114, 115, 120, 128, 133, 138, 140, 147, 151, 155, 162, 166, 199, 200, 205, 210, 221, 223, 225, 232, 236, 242, 244, 247, 249, 254, 263, 271, 276, 277, 278

Grade 4: 9, 14, 19, 23, 26, 35, 41, 45, 50, 54, 64, 67, 75, 83, 84, 86, 94, 96, 103, 125, 130, 140, 145, 152, 160, 165, 171, 179, 182, 189, 193, 195, 197, 201, 204, 207, 209, 210, 212, 223, 229, 233, 236, 238, 242, 251, 253, 255, 259, 265, 272, 276, 283, 286, 291, 297, 298, 307, 308, 310, 315, 321, 326

3 | **identify community agencies that advocate for healthy individuals, families, and communities.**

Grade K: 39, 74–85, 164–169, 222–236

Grade 1: 114, 119, 126, 131, 220–235

Grade 2: 232–235

Grade 3: 64–67, 137–138, 210–211, 260–263, 279

Grade 4: 52–55, 117–118, 131, 144, 153, 271, 277, 304–327

4 | **demonstrate the ability to influence and support others in making positive health choices.**

Grade K: 14, 15, 23, 24, 25, 29, 75, 76, 77, 79, 81, 82, 83, 84, 85, 92, 93, 94, 95, 96, 97, 99, 100, 101, 152–157, 164–169, 220–235

Grade 1: 28, 29, 31, 35, 37, 42–59, 74–75, 87, 90, 92–93, 96, 99, 103, 104–127, 134–135, 147, 150–151, 155, 178–179, 192–193, 211, 213, 214–215, 230–231

Grade 2: 9, 10, 15, 17, 25, 27, 36–37, 41, 42, 56–57, 94–95, 131–133, 139, 188–203, 218–245

Grade 3: 22–23, 89–91, 95, 116–117, 156–157, 163, 206–207, 231, 233–236, 250–251, 260–279

Grade 4: 10–11, 33, 39, 40, 46–47, 49, 53, 76–77, 97, 104–105, 123, 126–127, 129, 137, 139, 141, 146–147, 149, 150, 172–173, 198, 199, 234–235, 250, 253, 257, 261, 266–267, 271, 275, 284, 289, 290, 292–293, 296, 297, 322–333

As a result of health instruction in Grades 5–8, students will:

1 | **analyze various communication methods to accurately express health information and ideas.**

Grade 5: 11, 38–67, 91, 96–99, 296–297

Grade 6: 2, 25, 48–53, 62, 70, 74, 136, 139, 250, 294, 296, 304, 333

2 | **express information and opinions about health issues.**

Grade 5: 29, 33, 39, 42, 46, 48, 51, 57, 61, 66, 83, 96, 111, 116, 130, 133, 153, 195, 218, 240

Grade 6: 32–33, 294–295, 302–303, 334–335, 386–397

3 | **identify barriers to effective communication of information, ideas, feelings, and opinions about health issues.**

Grade 5: 15, 25, 27, 30–31, 58–59, 100–101, 114, 124–125, 140–143, 147, 158–159, 160–163, 171–175, 176–179, 180–181, 183, 210–211, 240, 248, 250, 251, 264, 276, 277, 281, 307, 308, 309, 311, 314–316, 334–335, 348, 357, 361, 362–363, 364–365

Grade 6: 8, 10, 16, 32–33, 45, 46, 49, 54–55, 67, 73, 126–127, 149, 150, 153, 155, 166–167, 170, 179, 181, 184–185, 189, 191, 210, 213, 230, 237, 268–269, 295, 300–301, 326–327, 336–337, 345, 352–353, 355, 366, 368, 372, 378, 382, 393

4 | **demonstrate the ability to influence and support others in making positive health choices.**

Grade 5: 265, 273, 275, 280–281, 324–326, 332–333

Grade 6: 32–33, 302–306, 352–353

5 | **demonstrate the ability to work cooperatively when advocating for healthy individuals, families, and schools.**

Grade 5: 90, 323, 345–368, 376–397

Grade 6: 41, 46–47, 376–397